Contents

W9-BGQ-080

The Meaning of Sociology

EIGHTH EDITION

The Meaning of Sociology

A READER

Joel M. Charon
Professor Emeritus
Minnesota State University Moorhead

PEARSON

Prentice
Hall

Upper Saddle River, New Jersey 07458

Library of Congress Cataloging-in-Publication Data
The meaning of sociology : a reader / Joel M. Charon.—8th ed.
    p. cm.
  Includes bibliographical references.
  ISBN 0-13-185080-6 (pbk.)
  1. Sociology. I. Charon, Joel M.

HM585.M43 2004
301—dc22   2004012425

Publisher: Nancy Roberts
Executive Editor: Chris DeJohn
Managing Editor (Editorial): Sharon Chambliss
Editorial Assistant: Lee Peterson
Full Service Production Liaison: Joanne Hakim
Senior Marketing Manager: Marissa Feliberty
Marketing Assistant: Adam Laitman
Assistant Manufacturing Manager: Mary Ann Gloriande
Cover Art Director: Jayne Conte
Cover Design: Bruce Kenselaar
Manager, Cover Visual Research & Permissions: Karen Sanatar
Cover Illustration/Photo: Doree Loschiavo, "Arrivals and Departures"
Composition/Full-Service Project Management: Michael Bohrer-Clancy/ICC

Credits and acknowledgments borrowed from other sources and reproduced, with
permission, in this textbook appear on appropriate page within text.

Pearson Education LTD., London
Pearson Education Singapore, Pte. Ltd
Pearson Education, Canada, Ltd
Pearson Education–Japan
Pearson Education Australia PTY, Limited

Pearson Education North Asia Ltd
Pearson Educación de Mexico, S.A. de C.V.
Pearson Education Malaysia, Pte. Ltd
Pearson Education, Upper Saddle River, New Jersey

10 9 8 7 6 5 4 3 2

ISBN 0-13-185080-6

PART VIII Social Institutions: Economic and Political 223

PART IX Social Institutions: Familial, Religious, Educational 265

PART X Social Change 315

Preface

Sociology is an academic discipline, with a history going back to at least the eighteenth century. It became recognized in the nineteenth century, and its accumulated body of knowledge has arisen from ongoing debate, analysis, and critical evaluation. Sociologists are social scientists, and therefore they attempt to understand society in a highly disciplined manner, developing ideas that arise from evidence gathered in a large number of studies. The purpose of sociology is to understand society in an objective manner, creatively doing scientific research that tries to uncover solutions to the difficult puzzle of human society.

Part I of this Reader—as well as selections presented throughout—attempts to introduce the kind of analysis and studies that inspire those who are part of the discipline.

Sociology is also a perspective. It is a unique, interesting, critical, and useful way of approaching an understanding of the human being. The reason that I have chosen these particular selections is to give examples of the power of this perspective, and to inspire readers to see the benefits of using this perspective in understanding their own lives. Each selection had to interest me to be included; it had to be clear, sociological, and useful. Diversity and balance have been my aim. Some selections were written by professional sociologists, others by writers who simply think like sociologists. Some are very recent, whereas some happen to be older. Some are considered classic, and included in almost every sociological reader; others are not widely known, but have contributed greatly to my own understanding. Some are fairly simple and can be grasped immediately; others are more complex and must be studied more thoroughly by the student.

This is the eighth edition of this Reader. It is always difficult to determine which selections should be kept from the previous edition and which should be replaced. In making my decisions for this edition, I relied heavily on a poll of a number of users of the seventh edition. Although I did not always take their suggestions, they caused me to question my choices, and they gave me good leads.

After careful analysis, I added 17 new selections and kept 38 from the previous edition. Because my editor and I wanted to keep down the cost to the student as much as possible, I included 55 selections rather than 65, and this edition is shorter than the previous edition by about 100 pages.

I really like what this book has become. It represents well what I believe is the "meaning of sociology." If you read it carefully, you will be rewarded; it will contribute to your understanding of human beings, society, and your own personal life.

I welcome feedback. If something is especially interesting or enlightening, let me know. If some selections are either not interesting or bothersome to you in some way, let me know. Please contact me at charonj@mnstate.edu.

I would like to thank Sharon Chambliss for her encouragement and guidance. Both she and Nancy Roberts have been editors that I have very much enjoyed working with. They are important for what this book has become. I would also like to thank professor Audra Kallimanis, Mount Olive College, who has reviewed the text and made suggestions for this edition.

I dedicate this book to my wife Susan and to my sons Andrew and Daniel. They are models to me; they give me inspiration and confidence; they give me meaning.

Joel M. Charon

The Meaning
of Sociology

Part I

THE DISCIPLINE
OF SOCIOLOGY

The first two selections in Part I are classic statements about the discipline of sociology. Peter Berger calls sociology a "passion," a "demon" that captures those interested in understanding the human condition. C. Wright Mills calls it a very special "imagination," a creative and important way of understanding the human being and his or her relationship with the larger society. Both statements reveal an excitement that many of us feel about sociology, and both also reveal the ultimate purpose of sociology: to understand the human being in a social context, carefully and systematically.

The third selection is a brief description of the philosophy of Max Weber, who represents, for many of us, a model for what a science of social life should be. It is from an excellent book by Ronald Fernandez that describes the lives and work of the great social thinkers in the history of sociology.

Joel Best introduces us to another aspect of the principles that sociologists try to follow: to be critical of what we discover. The science of sociology must use statistics (as do all sciences), but statistics must never drive us: instead, statistics must be a tool, and we must recognize the need to intelligently question all statistics in order to determine which are objective and careful—and thus useful for understanding—and which are sloppy, careless, or used for self-serving propaganda. Indeed, it is not only statistics that need careful understanding, but every part of the scientific enterprise—from theoretical conclusions to every aspect of the research endeavor—that must be carefully and objectively questioned by the reader. Being intelligently critical of our own work and the work of others is essential.

My own selection concerns generalizing, stereotyping, and why social science is necessary for understanding human life. Everyone generalizes; many people stereotype; the purpose of social science is to generalize without stereotyping.

The last selection is an introduction to an actual study. The author—Nancy Tatom Ammerman—describes in detail the way she attempted to study a fundamentalist church. I use this, not because it is the best of all studies or because it represents what we all do, but because it is a good example of many of the important issues that are necessary to face if one is going to do or to understand social research. It exhibits a variety of research methods, each having both strengths and limitations. It is a careful statement by the researcher as to how exactly the work has been done. Ammerman's detailed description exhibits honesty in my opinion, and it highlights characteristics that each researcher must try to achieve: objectivity, good sampling, accurate conclusions, and careful generalization.

◆ 1 ◆

Sociology as a Passion to Understand

Peter L. Berger

The sociological perspective is more like a demon that possesses one, that drives one compellingly, again and again, to the questions that are its own.

This first reading is Chapter 1 from the excellent book by Peter L. Berger, *Invitation to Sociology*. There, the chapter is entitled "Sociology as an Individual Pastime," but Berger's point is that it is much more than that—it is an exciting passion, a perspective that truly helps us understand our social world. In this selection, Berger shows us the many misunderstandings about sociology, emphasizing always that it is a scientific attempt to understand. "The sociologist," he says, "is someone concerned with understanding society in a disciplined way." It "will be satisfying, in the long run, only to those who can think of nothing more entrancing than to watch men and to understand things human." It might be helpful to divide Berger's selection into three parts:

1. What are the misconceptions people have about sociology? Why are they misconceptions?
2. What is sociology? What do sociologists do?
3. Why do sociologists do what they do? What drives them?

(By the way, you might notice that Berger uses the term *he*, not *he or she*. Things have changed a great deal in society and in sociology since 1963, when this article was written. Today, few people would attempt to publish a work in sociology that makes it appear that only men contribute to the world. This problem reappears in many other selections in this book. It is very difficult for me to change other people's work in this book for the purposes of inclusion—sometimes, it is impossible. Please do not let this detract from your enjoyment or learning.)

If one asks undergraduate students why they are taking sociology as a major, one often gets the reply, "because I like to work with people." If one then goes on to ask such students about their occupational future, as they envisage it, one

From *An Invitation to Sociology*, by Peter L. Berger. Copyright © 1963 by Peter L. Berger. Used by permission of Doubleday, a division of Random House, Inc.

often hears that they intend to go into social work. Of this, more in a moment. Other answers are more vague and general, but all indicate that the student in question would rather deal with people than with things. Occupations mentioned in this connection include personnel work, human relations in industry, public relations, advertising, community planning, or religious work of the unordained variety. The common assumption is that in all these lines of endeavor, one might "do something for people," "help people," "do work that is useful for the community." The image of the sociologist involved here could be described as a secularized version of the liberal Protestant ministry, with the YMCA secretary perhaps furnishing the connecting link between sacred and profane benevolence. Sociology is seen as an up-to-date variation on the classic American theme of "uplift." The sociologist is understood as someone professionally concerned with edifying activities on behalf of individuals and of the community at large. . . .

It is, of course, true that some Boy Scout types have become sociologists. It is also true that a benevolent interest in people could be the biographical starting point for sociological studies. But it is important to point out that a malevolent and misanthropic outlook could serve just as well. Sociological insights are valuable to anyone concerned with action in society. But this action need not be particularly humanitarian. Some American sociologists today are employed by governmental agencies seeking to plan more livable communities for the nation. Other American sociologists are employed by governmental agencies concerned with wiping communities of hostile nations off the map, if and when the necessity should arise. Whatever the moral implications of these respective activities may be, there is no reason why interesting sociological studies could not be carried on in both. Similarly, criminology, as a special field within sociology, has uncovered valuable information about processes of crime in modern society. This information is as valuable for those seeking to fight crime as it would be for those interested in promoting it. The fact that more criminologists have been employed by the police than by gangsters can be ascribed to the ethical bias of the criminologists themselves, the public relations of the police, and perhaps the lack of scientific sophistication of the gangsters. It has nothing to do with the character of the information itself. In sum, "working with people" can mean getting them out of slums or getting them into jail, selling them propaganda or robbing them of their money (be it legally or illegally), making them produce better automobiles or making them better bomber pilots. As an image of the sociologist, then, the phrase leaves something to

be desired, even though it may serve to describe at least the initial impulse as a result of which some people turn to the study of sociology. . . .

Social work, whatever its theoretical rationalization, is a certain *practice* in society. Sociology is not a practice, but an *attempt to understand*. Certainly, this understanding may have use for the practitioner. For that matter, we would contend that a more profound grasp of sociology would be of great use to the social worker, and that such a grasp would obviate the necessity of his descending into the mythological depths of the "subconscious" to explain matters that are typically quite conscious, much more simple, and indeed social in nature. But there is nothing inherent in the sociological enterprise of trying to understand society that necessarily leads to this practice or to any other. Sociological understanding can be recommended to social workers, but also to salesmen, nurses, evangelists, and politicians—in fact, to anyone whose goals involve the manipulation of men, for whatever purpose and with whatever moral justification.

This conception of the sociological enterprise is implied in the classic statement by Max Weber, one of the most important figures in the development of the field, to the effect that sociology is "value-free." Since it will be necessary to return to this a number of times later, it may be well to explicate it a little further at this point. Certainly the statement does not mean that the sociologist has or should have no values. In any case, it is just about impossible for a human being to exist without any values at all, although, of course, there can be tremendous variation in the values one may hold. The sociologist will normally have many values as a citizen, a private person, a member of a religious group, or as an adherent of some other association of people. But within the limits of his activities as a sociologist, there is one fundamental value only—that of scientific integrity. Even there, of course, the sociologist, being human, will have to reckon with his convictions, emotions, and prejudices. But it is part of his intellectual training that he tries to understand and control these as *biases* that ought to be eliminated, as far as possible, from his work. It goes without saying that this is not always easy to do, but it is not impossible. The sociologist tries to see what is there. He may have hopes or fears concerning what he may find. But he will try to see, regardless of his hopes or fears. It is thus an act of pure perception, as pure as humanly limited means allow, toward which sociology strives. . . .

We would stress strongly that saying this does not imply that the sociologist has no responsibility to ask about the goals of his employers or the use to which they will put his work. But this asking is not sociological asking. It is asking the same questions that any man ought to ask himself about his actions in society. Again, in the same way, biological knowledge can be employed to heal or to kill. This does not mean that the biologist is free of responsibility as to which use he serves. But when he asks himself about this responsibility, he is not asking a biological question.

Another image of the sociologist, related to the two already discussed, is that of social reformer. . . .

It is gratifying from certain value positions (including some of this writer's) that sociological insights have served in a number of instances to improve the lot of groups of human beings by uncovering morally shocking conditions, or by clearing away collective illusions, or by showing that socially desired results could be obtained in a more humane fashion. One might point, for example, to some applications of sociological knowledge in the penological practice of Western countries. Or one might cite the use made of sociological studies in the Supreme Court decision of 1954 on racial segregation in the public schools. Or one could look at the applications of other sociological studies to the humane planning of urban redevelopment. Certainly, the sociologist who is morally and politically sensitive will derive gratification from such instances. But, once more, it will be well to keep in mind that what is at issue here is not sociological understanding as such but certain applications of this understanding. It is not difficult to see how the same understanding could be applied with opposite intentions. Thus the sociological understanding of the dynamics of racial prejudice can be applied effectively by those promoting intragroup hatred as well as by those wanting to spread tolerance. And the sociological understanding of the nature of human solidarity can be employed in the service of both totalitarian and democratic regimes. It is

sobering to realize that the same processes that generate consensus can be manipulated by a social group worker in a summer camp in the Adirondacks and by a communist brainwasher in a prisoner camp in China. One may readily grant that the sociologist can sometimes be called upon to give advice when it comes to changing certain social conditions deemed undesirable. But the image of the sociologist as social reformer suffers from the same confusion as the image of him as social worker.

If these images of the sociologist all have an element of "cultural lag" about them, we can now turn to some other images that are of more recent date and that refer themselves to more recent developments in the discipline. One such image is that of the sociologist as a gatherer of statistics about human behavior. The sociologist is here seen essentially as an aide-de-camp to an IBM machine. He goes out with a questionnaire, interviews people selected at random, then goes home, enters his tabulations onto innumerable punch cards, which are then fed into a machine. In all of this, of course, he is supported by a large staff and a very large budget. Included in this image is the implication that the results of all this effort are picayune, a pedantic restatement of what everybody knows anyway. As one observer remarked pithily, a sociologist is a fellow who spends $100,000 to find his way to a house of ill repute.

This image of the sociologist has been strengthened in the public mind by the activities of many agencies that might well be called parasociological—mainly agencies concerned with public opinion and market trends. The pollster has become a well-known figure in American life, importuning people about their views from foreign policy to toilet paper. Because the methods used in the pollster business bear close resemblance to sociological research, the growth of this image of the sociologist is understandable. The Kinsey studies of American sexual behavior have probably greatly augmented the impact of this image. The fundamental sociological question, whether concerned with premarital petting or with Republican votes or with the incidence of gang knifings, is always presumed to be "how often?" or "how many?" (Incidentally, the very few jokes current about sociologists usually relate to this statistical image . . . which jokes had better be left to the imagination of the reader.)

Statistical data by themselves do not make sociology. They become sociology only when they are sociologically interpreted, put within a theoretical frame of reference that is sociological. Simple counting, or even correlating different items that one counts, is not sociology. There is almost no sociology in the Kinsey reports. This does not mean that the data in these studies are not true or that they cannot be relevant to sociological understanding. They are, taken by themselves, raw materials that can be used in sociological interpretation. The interpretation, however, must be broader than the data themselves. So the sociologist cannot arrest himself at the frequency tables of premarital petting or extramarital pederasty. These enumerations are meaningful to him only in terms of their much broader implications for an understanding of institutions and values in our society. To arrive at such understanding, the sociologist will often have to apply statistical techniques, especially when he is dealing with the mass phenomena of modern social life. But sociology consists of statistics as little as philology consists of conjugating irregular verbs or chemistry of making nasty smells in test tubes. . . .

How, then, are we to conceive of the sociologist? In discussing the various images of him that abound in the popular mind, we have already brought out certain elements that would have to go into our conception. We can now put them together. In doing so, we shall construct what sociologists themselves call an "ideal type." This means that what we delineate will not be found in reality in its pure form. Instead, one will find approximations to it and deviations from it, in varying degrees. Nor is it to be understood as an empirical average. We would not even claim that all individuals who now call themselves sociologists will recognize themselves without reservations in our conception, nor would we dispute the right of those who do not so recognize themselves to use the appellation. Our business is not excommunication. We would, however, contend that our "ideal type" corresponds to the self-conception of most sociologists in the mainstream of the discipline, both historically (at least in this century) and today.

The sociologist, then, is someone concerned with understanding society in a disciplined way. The nature of this discipline is scientific. This means that what the sociologist finds and says about the social phenomena he studies occurs with a certain rather strictly defined frame of reference. One of the main characteristics of this scientific frame of reference is that operations are bound by certain rules of evidence. As a scientist, the sociologist tries to be objective, to control his personal preferences and prejudices, to perceive clearly rather than to judge normatively. This restraint, of course, does not embrace the totality of the sociologist's existence as a human being but is limited to his operations as sociologist. Nor does the sociologist claim that his frame of reference is the only one within which society can be looked at. For that matter, very few scientists in any field would claim today that one should look at the world only scientifically. The botanist looking at a daffodil has no reason to dispute the right of the poet to look at the same object in a very different manner. There are many ways of playing. . . .

The game of the sociologist, then, uses scientific rules. As a result, the sociologist must be clear in his own mind as to the meaning of these rules.

. . . [T]he interest of the sociologist is primarily theoretical. That is, he is interested in understanding for its own sake. He may be aware of or even concerned with the practical applicability and consequences of his findings—but at that point, he leaves the sociological frame of reference as such and moves into realms of values, beliefs, and ideas that he shares with other men who are not sociologists. . . .

The sociologist . . . is a person intensively, endlessly, shamelessly interested in the doings of men. His natural habitat is all the human gathering places of the world, wherever men come together. The sociologist may be interested in many other things. But his consuming interest remains in the world of men, their institutions, their history, their passions. And because he is interested in men, nothing that men do can be altogether tedious for him. He will naturally be interested in the events that engage men's ultimate beliefs, their moments of tragedy and grandeur and ecstasy. But he will also be fascinated by the commonplace, the everyday. He will know reverence, but this reverence will not prevent him from wanting to see and to understand. He may sometimes feel revulsion or contempt, but this also will not deter him from wanting to have his questions answered. The sociologist, in his quest for understanding, moves through the world of men without respect for the usual lines of demarcation. Nobility and degradation, power and obscurity, intelligence and folly—these are equally interesting to him, however unequal they may be in his personal values or tastes. Thus his questions may lead him to all possible levels of society, the best and least known places, the most respected and the most despised. And, if he is a good sociologist, he will find himself in all these places because his own questions have so taken possession of him that he has little choice but to seek for answers.

It would be possible to say the same things in a lower key. We could say that the sociologist, but for the grace of his academic title, is the man who must listen to gossip despite himself, who is tempted to look through keyholes, to read other people's mail, to open closed cabinets. Before some otherwise unoccupied psychologist sets out now to construct an aptitude test for sociologists on the basis of sublimated voyeurism, let us quickly say that we are speaking merely by way of analogy. Perhaps some little boys consumed with curiosity to watch their maiden aunts in the bathroom later become inveterate sociologists. This is quite uninteresting. What interests us is the curiosity that grips any sociologist in front of a closed door behind which there are human voices. If he is a good sociologist, he will want to open that door, to understand these voices. Behind each closed door he will anticipate some new facet of human life not yet perceived and understood.

The sociologist will occupy himself with matters that others regard as too sacred or as too distasteful for dispassionate investigation. He will find rewarding the company of priests or of prostitutes, depending not on his personal preferences but on the questions he happens to be asking at the moment. He will also concern himself with matters that others may find much too boring. He will be interested in the human interaction that goes with warfare or with great intellectual discoveries, but also be interested in the relations between people employed in a restaurant or between a group of little girls playing with their dolls. His main focus of attention is not the ultimate significance of what men do, but the action in itself, as another example of the infinite richness of human conduct. So much for the image of our playmate.

In these journeys through the world of men, the sociologist will inevitably encounter other professional Peeping Toms. Sometimes, these will resent his presence, feeling that he is poaching on their preserves. In some places, the sociologist will meet up with the economist; in others, with the political scientist; in yet others, with the psychologist or the ethnologist. Yet chances are that the questions that have brought him to these same places are different from the ones that propelled his fellow trespassers. The sociologist's questions always remain essentially the same: "What are people doing with each other here?" "What are their relationships to each other?" "How are these relationships organized in institutions?" "What are the collective ideas that move men and institutions?" In trying to answer these questions in specific instances, the sociologist will, of course, have to deal with economic or political matters, but he will do so in a way rather different from that of the economist or the political scientist. . . .

The fascination of sociology lies in the fact that its perspective makes us see in a new light the very world in which we have lived all our lives. This also constitutes a transformation of consciousness. Moreover, this transformation is more relevant existentially than that of many other intellectual disciplines because it is more difficult to segregate in some special compartment of the mind. The astronomer does not live in the remote galaxies, and the nuclear physicist can, outside his laboratory, eat and laugh and marry and vote without thinking about the insides of the atom. The geologist looks at rocks only at appropriate times, and the linguist speaks English with his wife. The sociologist lives in society, on the job and off it. His own life, inevitably, is part of his subject matter. Men being what they are, sociologists manage to segregate their professional insights from their everyday affairs. But it is a rather difficult feat to perform in good faith.

The sociologist moves in the common world of men, close to what most of them would call *real*. The categories he employs in his analyses are only refinements of the categories by which other men live: power, class, status, race, ethnicity. As a result, there is a deceptive simplicity and obviousness about some sociological investigations. One reads them, nods at the familiar scene, remarks that one has heard all this before and don't people have better things to do than to waste their time on truisms—until one is suddenly brought up against an insight that radically questions everything one had previously assumed about this familiar scene. This is the point at which one begins to sense the excitement of sociology.

Let us take a specific example. Imagine a sociology class in a southern college at which almost all the students are white southerners. Imagine a lecture on the subject of the racial system of the South. The lecturer is talking here of matters that have been familiar to his students from the time of their infancy. Indeed, it may be that they are much more familiar with the minutiae of this system than he is. They are quite bored as a result. It seems to them that he is only using more pretentious words to describe what they already know. Thus he may use the term "caste," one commonly used now by American sociologists to describe the southern racial system. But in explaining the term, he shifts to traditional Hindu society, to make it clearer. He then goes on to analyze the magical beliefs inherent in caste taboos, the social dynamics of commensalism and connubium, the economic interests concealed within the system, the way in which religious beliefs relate to the taboos, the effects of the caste system on the industrial development of the society and vice versa—all in India. Suddenly, India is not very far away at all. The lecture then goes back to its southern theme. The familiar now seems not quite so familiar any more. Questions are raised that are new, perhaps raised angrily, but raised all the same. And at least some of the students have begun to understand that there are functions involved in this business of race that they have not read about in the newspapers (at least not those in their hometowns) and that

their parents have not told them—partly, at least, because neither the newspapers nor the parents knew about them.

It can be said that the first wisdom of sociology is this: Things are not what they seem. This, too, is a deceptively simple statement. It ceases to be simple after a while. Social reality turns out to have many layers of meaning. The discovery of each new layer changes the perception of the whole. . . .

People who like to avoid shocking discoveries, who prefer to believe that society is just what they were taught in Sunday School, who like the safety of the rules and the maxims of what Alfred Schuetz has called the "world-taken-for-granted," should stay away from sociology. People who feel no temptation before closed doors, who have no curiosity about human beings, who are content to admire scenery without wondering about the people who live in those houses on the other side of that river, should probably also stay away from sociology. They will find it unpleasant or, at any rate, unrewarding. People who are interested in human beings only if they can change, convert, or reform them should also be warned, for they will find sociology much less useful than they hoped. And people whose interest is mainly in their own conceptual constructions will do just as well to turn to the study of little white mice. Sociology will be satisfying, in the long run, only to those who can think of nothing more entrancing than to watch men and to understand things human.

It may now be clear that we have, albeit deliberately, understated the case in the title of this chapter. To be sure, sociology is an individual pastime in the sense that it interests some men and bores others. Some like to observe human beings, others like to experiment with mice. The world is big enough to hold all kinds, and there is no logical priority for one interest as against another. But the word *pastime* is weak in describing what we mean. Sociology is more like a passion. The sociological perspective is more like a demon that possesses one, that drives one compellingly, again and again, to the questions that are its own. An introduction to sociology is, therefore, an invitation to a very special kind of passion. . . .

◆ 2 ◆

The Sociological Imagination

C. Wright Mills

The individual can . . . know his own chances in life only by becoming aware
of those of all individuals in his circumstances.

C. Wright Mills, who died in 1962 at the age of 46, published two classic sociological works: *The Power Elite* and *The Sociological Imagination*. The first of these proved to be extremely important for studying the power structure in the United States. It inspired many sociologists to do research on power and inequality. It is also to Mills's credit that he saw that sociology, in its attempt to be scientific, was losing a spirit that had to be recovered. He called this spirit the "sociological imagination." In his book by that name, he criticized those of us who have lost that imagination, and he called for a renewed effort to help people deal with human problems through sharing the sociological perspective. The section that follows is most of Chapter 1 from *The Sociological Imagination*, entitled "The Promise." Here Mills, like Berger, shows us the possibilities that sociology holds for those who come to understand it. What people need, Mills contends, "is a quality of mind that will help them use information and to develop reason" to better understand the world and "what may be happening within themselves." This quality is "the sociological imagination."

Here is Mills's organization. It might help you to keep it in mind as you read:

1. "Ordinary men" have problems looking beyond their immediate situation at history and society.
2. The sociological imagination includes three questions that can be applied to a number of human situations.
3. The sociological imagination is the linking of personal problems to public issues.

(Mills, too, used the language of his time; again, you might notice the use of *he*, *him*, and *his*. Mills gives one the impression that only men can have the sociological imagination, but I am positive that he did not intend this.)

Nowadays, men often feel that their private lives are a series of traps. They sense that within their

From *Sociological Imagination*, by C. Wright Mills. Copyright © 1959, 2000 by Oxford University Press, Inc. Used by permission of Oxford University Press, Inc.

everyday worlds, they cannot overcome their troubles, and in this feeling, they are often quite correct: What ordinary men are directly aware of and what they try to do are bounded by the private orbits in which they live. Their visions and their powers are limited to the close-up scenes of job, family, neighborhood. In other milieux, they move vicariously and remain spectators. And the more aware they become, however vaguely, of ambitions and of threats that transcend their immediate locales, the more trapped they seem to feel.

Underlying this sense of being trapped are seemingly impersonal changes in the very structure of continent-wide societies. The facts of contemporary history are also facts about the success and the failure of individual men and women. When a society is industrialized, a peasant becomes a worker; a feudal lord is liquidated or becomes a businessman. When classes rise or fall, a man is employed or unemployed; when the rate of investment goes up or down, a man takes new heart or goes broke. When wars happen, an insurance salesman becomes a rocket launcher; a store clerk, a radar man; a wife lives alone; a child grows up without a father. Neither the life of an individual nor the history of a society can be understood without understanding both.

Yet men do not usually define the troubles they endure in terms of historical change and institutional contradiction. The well-being they enjoy, they do not usually impute to the big ups and downs of the societies in which they live. Seldom aware of the intricate connection between the patterns of their own lives and the course of world history, ordinary men do not usually know what this connection means for the kinds of men they are becoming and for the kinds of history-making in which they might take part. They do not possess the quality of mind essential to grasp the interplay of man and society, of biography and history, of self and world. They cannot cope with their personal troubles in such ways as to control the structural transformations that usually lie behind them.

Surely it is no wonder. In what period have so many men been so totally exposed at so fast a pace to such earthquakes of change? That Americans have not known such catastrophic changes as have the men and women of other societies is caused by historical facts that are now quickly becoming "merely history." The history that now affects every man is world history. Within this scene and this period, in the course of a single generation, one-sixth of mankind is transformed from all that is feudal and backward into all that is modern, advanced, and fearful. Political

colonies are freed, new and less visible forms of imperialism are installed. Revolutions occur; men feel the intimate grip of new kinds of authority. Totalitarian societies rise and are smashed to bits—or succeed fabulously. After two centuries of ascendancy, capitalism is shown up as only one way to make society into an industrial apparatus. After two centuries of hope, even formal democracy is restricted to a quite small portion of mankind. Everywhere in the underdeveloped world, ancient ways of life are broken up and vague expectations become urgent demands. Everywhere in the overdeveloped world, the means of authority and of violence become total in scope and bureaucratic in form. Humanity itself now lies before us, the supernation at either pole concentrating its most coordinated and massive efforts on the preparation of World War III.

The very shaping of history now outpaces the ability of men to orient themselves in accordance with cherished values. And which values? Even when they do not panic, men often sense that older ways of feeling and thinking have collapsed and that newer beginnings are ambiguous to the point of moral stasis. Is it any wonder that ordinary men feel they cannot cope with the larger worlds with which they are so suddenly confronted? That they cannot understand the meaning of their epoch for their own lives? That—in defense of selfhood—they become morally insensible, trying to remain altogether private men? Is it any wonder that they come to be possessed by a sense of the trap?

It is not only information that they need. In this Age of Fact, information often dominates their attention and overwhelms their capacities to assimilate it. It is not only the skills of reason that they need—although their struggles to acquire these often exhaust their limited moral energy.

What they need, and what they feel they need, is a quality of mind that will help them to use information and to develop reason in order to achieve lucid summations of what is going on in the world and of what may be happening within themselves. It is this quality, I am going to contend, that journalists and scholars, artists and publics, scientists and editors are coming to expect of what may be called the *sociological imagination*.

The sociological imagination enables its possessor to understand the larger historical scene in terms of its meaning for the inner life and the external career of a variety of individuals. It enables him to take into account how individuals, in the welter of their daily experience, often become falsely conscious of their social positions. Within that welter, the framework of modern society is sought; within that framework, the psychologies of a variety of men and women are formulated. By such means the personal uneasiness of individuals is focused on explicit troubles, and the indifference of publics is transformed into involvement with public issues.

The first fruit of this imagination—and the first lesson of the social science that embodies it—is the idea that the individual can understand his own experience and gauge his own fate only by locating himself within his period, that he can know his own chances in life only by becoming aware of those of all individuals in his circumstances. In many ways, it is a terrible lesson; in many ways, a magnificent one. We do not know the limits of man's capacities for supreme effort or willing degradation, for agony or glee, for pleasurable brutality or the sweetness of reason. But in our time, we have come to know that the limits of "human nature" are frighteningly broad. We have come to know that every individual lives, from one generation to the next, in some society; that he lives out a biography, and that he lives it out within some historical sequence. By the fact of his living, he contributes—however minutely—to the shaping of this society and to the course of its history, even as he is made by society and by its historical push and shove.

The sociological imagination enables us to grasp history and biography and the relations between the two within society. That is its task and its promise. To recognize this task and this promise is the mark of the classic social analyst. It is characteristic of Herbert Spencer—turgid, polysyllabic, comprehensive; of E. A. Ross—graceful, muckraking, upright; of Auguste Comte and Emile Durkheim; of the intricate and subtle Karl Mannheim. It is the quality of all that is intellectually excellent in Karl Marx; it is the clue to Thorstein Veblen's brilliant and ironic insight, to Joseph Schumpeter's many-sided constructions of reality; it is the basis of the psychological sweep of W. E. H. Lecky no less than of the profundity and clarity of Max Weber. And it is the signal of what is best in contemporary studies of man and society.

No social study that does not come back to the problems of biography, of history, and of their intersections within a society has completed its intellectual journey. Whatever the specific problems of the classic social analysts, however limited or however broad the features of social reality they have examined, those who have been imaginatively aware of the promise of their work have consistently asked three sorts of questions:

1. What is the structure of this particular society as a whole? What are its essential components, and how are they related to one another? How does it differ from other varieties of social order? Within it, what is the meaning of any particular feature for its continuance and for its change?
2. Where does this society stand in human history? What are the mechanics by which it is changing? What is its place within and its meaning for the development of humanity as a whole? How does any particular feature we are examining affect—and how is it affected by—the historical period in which it moves? And this period—what are its essential features? How does it differ from other periods? What are its characteristic ways of history making?
3. What varieties of men and women now prevail in this society and in this period? And what varieties are coming to prevail? In what ways are they selected and formed, liberated and repressed, made sensitive and blunted? What kinds of "human nature" are revealed in the conduct and character we observe in this society in this period? And what is the meaning for "human nature" of each and every feature of the society we are examining?

Whether the point of interest is a great power state or a minor literary mood, a family, a prison, a creed—these are the kinds of questions the best social analysts have asked. They are the intellectual pivots of classic studies of man in society—and they are the questions inevitably raised by any mind possessing the sociological imagination. For that imagination is the capacity to shift from one perspective to another—from the political to the psychological; from the examination of a single family to the comparative assessment of the national budgets of the world; from the theological school to the military establishment; from considerations of an oil industry to studies of contemporary poetry. It is the capacity to range from the most impersonal and remote transformations to the most intimate features of the human self—and to see the relations between the two. Back of its use there is always the urge to know the social and historical meaning of the individual in the society and in the period in which he has his quality and his being.

That, in brief, is why it is by means of the sociological imagination that men now hope to grasp what is going on in the world, and to understand what is happening in themselves as minute points of the intersections of biography and history within society. In large part, contemporary man's self-conscious view of himself as at least an outsider, if not a permanent stranger, rests on an absorbed realization of social relativity and of the transformative power of history. The sociological imagination is the most fruitful form of this self-consciousness. By its use, men whose mentalities have swept only a series of limited orbits often come to feel as if suddenly awakened in a house with which they had only supposed themselves to be familiar. Correctly or incorrectly, they often come to feel that they can now provide themselves with adequate summations, cohesive assessments, comprehensive orientations. Older decisions that once appeared sound now seem to them products of a mind unaccountably dense. Their capacity for astonishment is made lively again. They acquire a new way of thinking, they experience a transvaluation of values. In a word, by their reflection and by their sensibility, they realize the cultural meaning of the social sciences.

Perhaps the most fruitful distinction with which the sociological imagination works is between "the personal troubles of milieu" and "the public issues of social structure." This distinction is an essential tool of the sociological imagination and a feature of all classic work in social science.

Troubles occur within the character of the individual and within the range of his immediate relations with others; they have to do with his self and with those limited areas of social life of which he is directly and personally aware. Accordingly, the statement and the resolution of troubles properly lie within the individual as a biographical entity and within the scope of his immediate milieu—the social setting that is directly open to his personal experience and, to some extent, his willful activity. A trouble is a private matter: values cherished by an individual are felt by him to be threatened.

Issues have to do with matters that transcend these local environments of the individual and the range of his inner life. They have to do with the organization of many such milieux into the institutions of an historical society as a whole, with the ways in which various milieux overlap and interpenetrate to form the larger structure of social and historical life. An issue is a public matter: some value cherished by publics is felt to be threatened. Often, there is a debate about what that value really is and about what it is that really threatens it. This debate is often without focus if only because it is the very nature of an issue, unlike even widespread trouble, that it cannot be very well defined in terms of the immediate and everyday environments of ordinary men. An issue, in fact, often involves a crisis in institutional arrangements; often, it also involves what Marxists call "contradictions" or "antagonisms."

In these terms, consider unemployment. When, in a city of 100,000, only one man is unemployed, that is his personal trouble. For its relief, we properly look to the character of the man, his skills, and his immediate opportunities. But when in a nation of 50 million employees, 15 million are unemployed, that is an issue, and we may not hope to find its solution within the range of opportunities open to any one individual. The very structure of opportunities has collapsed. Both the correct statement of the problem and the range of possible solutions require us to consider the economic and political institutions of the society, not merely the personal situation and character of a scatter of individuals.

Consider war. The personal problem of war, when it occurs, may be how to survive it or how to die in it with honor; how to make money out of it; how to climb into the higher safety of the military apparatus; or how to contribute to the war's termination. In short, according to one's values, to find a set of milieux and within it to survive the war or make one's death in it meaningful. But the structural issues of war have to do with its causes; with what types of men it throws up into command; with its effects on economic, political, family, and religious institutions; with the unorganized irresponsibility of a world of nation-states.

Consider marriage. Inside a marriage, a man and a woman may experience personal troubles, but when the divorce rate during the first four years of marriage is 250 out of every 1,000 attempts, this is an indication of a structural issue having to do with the institutions of marriage and family and other institutions that bear upon them.

Or consider the metropolis—the horrible, beautiful, ugly, magnificent sprawl of the great city. For many upper-class people, the personal solution to "the problem of the city" is to have an apartment with a private garage under it in the heart of the city, and forty miles out, a house by Henry Hill, garden by Garrett Eckbo, on a hundred acres of private land. In these two controlled environments—with a small staff at each end and a private helicopter connection—most people could solve many of the problems of personal milieux caused by the facts of the city. But all this, however splendid, does not solve the public issues that the structural fact of the city poses. What should be done with this wonderful monstrosity? Break it all up into scattered units, combining residence and work? Refurbish it as it stands? Or, after evacuation, dynamite it and build new cities according to new plans in new places? What should those plans be? And who is to decide and to accomplish whatever choice is made? These are structural issues; to confront them and to solve them requires us to consider political and economic issues that affect innumerable milieux.

Insofar as an economy is so arranged that slumps occur, the problem of unemployment becomes incapable of personal solution. Insofar as war is inherent in the nation-state system and in the uneven industrialization of the world, the ordinary individual in his restricted milieu will be powerless—with or without psychiatric aid—to solve the troubles this system (or lack of system) imposes on him. Insofar as the family as an institution turns women into darling little slaves and men into their chief providers and unweaned dependents, the problem of a satisfactory marriage remains incapable of purely private solution. Insofar as the overdeveloped megalopolis and the overdeveloped automobile are built-in features of the overdeveloped society, the issues of urban living will not be solved by personal ingenuity and private wealth.

What we experience in various and specific milieux, I have noted, is often caused by structural changes. Accordingly, to understand the changes of many personal milieux, we are required to look beyond them. And the number and variety of such structural changes increase as the institutions within which we live become more embracing and more intricately connected with one another. To be aware of the idea of social structure and to use it with sensibility is to be capable of tracing such linkages among a great variety of milieux. To be able to do that is to possess the sociological imagination. . . .

Max Weber, Social Science, and Sociology

Ronald Fernandez

[Weber believed that] the sociologists' job is to use "technical means and calculations" to achieve greater knowledge of how the world actually works, knowing all the while that this knowledge is so hard to get, their work will inevitably be surpassed by those who pick up a calculator after their death.

For many sociologists Max Weber is one of the most outstanding founders of sociology. He believed in sociology as a scientific understanding of human social action. This is difficult to do well, but helps assure honesty and self discipline in the search for truth. This short selection by Ronald Fernandez captures both the ideas that Weber teaches and the spirit he brings to his theoretical and empirical work.

In 1918 Weber spoke to a group of students at Munich University. By this time he was a professor of international distinction, so the students (it is hoped) listened with both respect and interest. The professor began by spotlighting a passion. Anyone who wanted to be a scientist needed to know that "nothing is worthy of man as man unless he can pursue it with passionate devotion." You must be lovingly wedded to your work, but never assume that passion alone gives birth to great and new ideas. Granted, ideas often occurred at the strangest times, when a person walked or, sat with friends, smoking a Cuban cigar. An amateur might assume that the idea came from nowhere; a scientist knew that, as much as two plus two equals four, no idea would

ever "come to mind had we not brooded at our desks and searched for answers with passionate devotion."[1]

Scientists also embraced a peculiar sense of satisfaction, the knowledge that successors inevitably improved or surpassed even the best work of the best scientists. This was the "very meaning of scientific work," the certainty that "every scientific fulfillment raises new questions; it asks to be surpassed and outdated." In principle, this progress lasted forever, so "why does one engage in doing something that in reality never comes, and never can come, to an end?"[2]

What a great question. Were scientists just a bunch of masochists? Why work with passion, devotion, and tenacity, knowing all the while that in ten, twenty, or (if you were very lucky) fifty years, you would be thrown on the scrap heap, replaced by the latest formulations and theories?

This is Weber's answer: "Scientific progress is a fraction, the most important fraction of the

From Ronald Fernandez, *Mappers of Society: The Lives, Times and Legacies of the Great Sociologists.* Copyright © 2003 by Ronald Fernandez. Reproduced with permission of Greenwood Publishing Group, Inc. Westport, CT.

process of intellectualization which we have been undergoing for thousands of years." Think of a Native American. He knows "incomparably more about his tools" than we know about many vital aspects of our civilization. How does a plane fly or a computer process its information with such incredible speed? Most of us are ignorant of the workings of the tools we use everyday yet the beauty of science—its significance for everyone—is "the knowledge or belief that if one wished one *could* learn it at any time. Hence it [science] means that in principle there are no mysterious, incalculable forces that come into play, but rather that one can, in principle, master all things by calculation."[3]

Weber now introduces one of the principal themes of his work: the world is disenchanted. The gods are gone and we are here, with no need to resort to mysterious forces or prayers, to the spirits that supposedly inhabit the universe. Science replaces faith with reason; the sociologists' job is to use "technical means and calculations" to achieve greater knowledge of how the world actually works, knowing all the while that this knowledge is so hard to get, their work will inevitably be surpassed by those who pick up a calculator after their death.

But what about someone like Tolstoy, the masterful Russian novelist? Tolstoy writes that "science is meaningless because it gives no answer to our question, the only question important for us: 'What shall we do and how shall we live?'"[4] Weber confronts this conundrum with a blunt instrument: the truth. Science can never answer Tolstoy's question. Go to a church, synagogue, or mosque if you seek those answers. But if you accept that science provides knowledge that is "worth knowing," then it—and especially sociology—can provide a good measure of assistance, even with the questions posed by Tolstoy. . . .

Clarity has a special meaning for Weber, a meaning that is arguably as relevant today as it was in 1918. Clarity signifies that if we are "competent" in our work, "we can force the individual, or at least we can help him, to give himself an *account of the ultimate meaning of his own conduct*" (emphasis added). By offering a series of inconvenient facts—for example, about the crucial, continuing role of tradition in shaping military beliefs and practices—teachers demand that students rethink their inherited and learned assumptions. In deliberately challenging the traditional wisdom about the way the world works, the sociologist "stands in the service of 'moral' forces; he fulfills the duty of bringing about self-clarification and a sense of responsibility." Equally important, any sociologist will produce the greatest successes "the more conscientiously he avoids the desire personally to impose upon or suggest to his audience his own stand."[5]

Stay in the background. Guard the combination to the value judgments locked away in your mind. But never forget to be ruthlessly honest. "The fate of our times is characterized by rationalization and intellectualization, and, above all, by the disenchantment of the world." If not dead, God was dying, yet Weber had more respect for someone who retreated to the churches than for an "academic prophet" who forgot "that in the lecture-rooms of the university no other virtue holds but plain intellectual integrity."[6] Facts worth knowing were the sociologist's only stock in trade. And yes, it was very difficult to live at a time when science undermined the legitimacy of the religious truths that provided the answers sought by a writer like Tolstoy. But that was the "fate of the times," and the sociologist still performed an invaluable role by offering the inconvenient facts that "forced" people to ask the ultimate questions that no sociologist—as a sociologist—could ever answer.

NOTES

1. Max Weber, "Science as a Vocation," in *From Max Weber*, ed. Hans Gerth and C. Wright Mills (New York: Oxford University Press, 1958), 135–36.
2. Ibid., 138.
3. Ibid., 139.
4. Ibid., 143.
5. Paul Honigsheim, *On Max Weber* (New York: Free Press, 1968), 152.
6. Ibid., 145–47.

◆ 4 ◆

Critical Thinking About Statistics

Joel Best

Statistics are not magical. Nor are they always true—or always false. Nor need they
be incomprehensible. . . . Being Critical requires more thought, but failing to adopt
a Critical mind-set makes us powerless to evaluate what others tell us. When
we fail to think critically, the statistics we hear might just as well be magical.

Joel Best's book *Damned Lies and Statistics* should be required reading for all social
scientists (and critics of social scientists), for it attempts to explain the importance of
statistics for making and understanding conclusions and making complexities useful. However, statistics are created by human beings. They involve counting and analyzing information that always involves human definitions and distinctions. There
are good statistics and there are bad ones. We can be fooled or we can learn a great
deal about what we are observing. We can lie with statistics, be sloppy, be misleading, exaggerate, or we can use statistics carefully and thoughtfully. Best describes
three ways of approaching statistics from the point of view of the reader: the naive,
the cynical, and the critical. He makes the argument that we lose a great deal by
being naive or cynical, but we can gain much by critically evaluating the statistics
that we encounter in our search for understanding.

There are cultures in which people believe that
some objects have magical powers; anthropolo-
gists call these objects fetishes. In our society, statistics are a sort of fetish. We tend to regard statistics as though they are magical, as though they
are more than mere numbers. We treat them as
powerful representations of the truth; we act as
though they distill the complexity and confusion
of reality into simple facts. We use statistics to
convert complicated social problems into more
easily understood estimates, percentages, and
rates. Statistics direct our concern; they show us

what we ought to worry about and how much we
ought to worry. In a sense, the social problem becomes the statistic and, because we treat statistics
as true and incontrovertible, they achieve a kind
of fetishlike, magical control over how we view
social problems. We think of statistics as facts that
we discover, not as numbers we create.

But, of course, statistics do not exist independently; people have to create them. Reality is complicated, and every statistic is someone's summary,
a simplification of that complexity. Every statistic
must be created, and the process of creation
always involves choices that affect the resulting
number and therefore affect what we understand
after the figures summarize and simplify the
problem. People who create statistics must
choose definitions—they must define what it is

From Joel Best, *Damned Lies and Statistics: Untangling Num-*
bers from the Media, Politicians, and Activists, pp. 160–170.
Copyright © 2001. Permission granted by the Regents of the
University of California and the University of California Press.

15

they want to count—and they must choose their methods—the ways they will go about their counting. Those choices shape every good statistic, and every bad one. Bad statistics simplify reality in ways that distort our understanding, while good statistics minimize that distortion. No statistic is perfect, but some are less imperfect than others. Good or bad, every statistic reflects its creators' choices. . . .

In order to interpret statistics, we need more than a checklist of common errors. We need a general approach, an orientation, a mind-set that we can use to think about new statistics that we encounter. We ought to approach statistics thoughtfully. This can be hard to do, precisely because so many people in our society treat statistics as fetishes. We might call this the mind-set of the Awestruck—the people who don't think critically, who act as though statistics have magical powers. The Awestruck know they don't always understand the statistics they hear, but this doesn't bother them. After all, who can expect to understand magical numbers? The reverential fatalism of the Awestruck is not thoughtful—it is a way of avoiding thought. We need a different approach. Three come to mind; they are the mind-sets of the Naive, the Cynical, and the Critical.

THE NAIVE

The Naive are slightly more sophisticated than the Awestruck. Many people believe they understand a bit about statistics—they know something about percentages, rates, and the like—but their approach is basically accepting. They presume that statistics are generally accurate, that they mean what they seem to mean. The Naive are often at least somewhat innumerate; they occasionally may be confused by basic mathematical ideas ("A million, a billion—what's the difference? They're all big numbers."). And, as the name suggests, the Naive tend to be innocent and trusting; they don't question numbers or wonder how those numbers might be shaped by interests of the people behind them. The Naive are sincere, and they assume that the people who present statistics are equally sincere, and that their numbers are valid.

The Naive are not just consumers of others' numbers; they also can create and disseminate statistics. When activists offer estimates for the scope of some social problem, their attitude is often one of naïveté ("It's a big problem, and this is a big number—it must be about right."). And, once a number is in circulation, Naive reporters may be willing to repeat it and pass it along ("This is the only number out there, so it must be pretty accurate."). When they are innumerate, the Naive often generate mutant statistics; when they try to repeat figures they don't completely understand, it is easy for them to produce new, mangled numbers.

In addition to creating, spreading, and mangling statistics, the Naive (and their slightly less critical cousins, the Awestruck) probably account for the vast majority of the audience that hears these numbers. The Naive are unlikely to question numbers—not even the most implausible exaggerations; after all, the Naive usually don't suspect statistics might be bad, and even if they do, they have no good ways of detecting bad statistics. They are unlikely to wonder about definitions or measurements, or to spot inappropriate comparisons, and they find debates over statistics completely bewildering. The Naive form a wonderfully receptive audience ("They say 150,000 young women die from anorexia each year! That's terrible!"), easily influenced and not at all critical. At the same time, the Naive assign no special value to statistics; they may be equally influenced by a disturbing example, an acquaintance's opinion, a rumor, or other sources of information. The Naive not only fail to suspect that bad statistics have flaws, but they often do not recognize when statistics are pretty good. The great majority of the audience for social statistics is, at least to some degree, Naive.

THE CYNICAL

Fewer people can be described as Cynical, but they are extremely important. The Cynical are suspicious of statistics; they are convinced that numbers are probably flawed, and that those flaws are probably intentional. They view statistics as efforts to manipulate—they are worse than "damned lies." They don't trust numbers ("You can prove anything with statistics.").

The Cynical are most important as originators of statistics. People who create statistics often have an agenda—to promote their industry, their cause, their ideology, their group—and they view statistics as a means of furthering that end. The Cynical design research that will produce the results they want: they word questions so as to encourage particular responses; they choose samples likely to respond the way they want; they massage the data until the results take the form they desire; in extreme instances, they simply lie and make up whatever numbers suit their purposes. The Cynical count on their audience being mostly Naive; the Naive will accept whatever numbers they're given, so why not give them whatever numbers will influence them to think or do whatever the Cynical want?

The distinction between the Cynical and the Naive is not as sharp as it first seems. Many people who promote statistics want to persuade; they have interests and agendas to promote, and they see statistics as a tool toward that end. These qualities might seem to place them among the Cynical. Yet, at the same time, these people often have an imperfect understanding of the limitations of the numbers they are promoting—the Cynical are not immune to innumeracy. This means that they also are, in a sense, Naive, and may believe whatever their own figures seem to show.

Another role the Cynical play is as members of the audience for statistics. Here they suspect there must be something wrong with whatever numbers they hear. Because the Cynical suspect that "you can prove anything with statistics," they can justify ignoring all numbers—particularly those that challenge their beliefs. This sort of cynicism is most obvious in debates over contentious social issues, such as abortion or gun control. The Cynical allied with one side on an issue are quick to discount any statistics offered by the other side. They may be surprisingly sophisticated when pointing out the flaws in numbers they don't like, although they rarely examine their own side's figures with the same critical eye. And, of course, their cynical discounting of statistics and the people who use them further confuses the Naive.

It is important to be clear: this book is not intended to swell the ranks of the Cynical; I do not want to encourage you to discount every statistic as worthless. We need not choose between remaining among the Naive or joining the Cynical. There is a third, far superior option.

THE CRITICAL

This third choice is to approach statistics critically. Being critical does not mean being negative or hostile—it is not cynicism. The Critical approach statistics thoughtfully; they avoid the extremes of both naive acceptance and cynical rejection of the numbers they encounter. Instead, the Critical attempt to evaluate numbers, to distinguish between good statistics and bad statistics.

The Critical understand that, while some social statistics may be pretty good, they are never perfect. Every statistic is a way of summarizing complex information into relatively simple numbers. Inevitably, some information, some of the complexity, is lost whenever we use statistics. The Critical recognize that this is an inevitable limitation of statistics. Moreover, they realize that every statistic is the product of choices—the choice between defining a category broadly or narrowly, the choice of one measurement over another, the choice of a sample. People choose definitions, measurements, and samples for all sorts of reasons: perhaps they want to emphasize some aspect of a problem; perhaps it is easier or cheaper to gather data in a particular way—many considerations can come into play. Every statistic is a compromise among choices. This means that every definition—and every measurement and every sample—probably has limitations and can be criticized.

Being Critical means more than simply pointing to the flaws in a statistic. Again, every statistic has flaws. The issue is whether a particular statistic's flaws are severe enough to damage its usefulness. Is the definition so broad that it encompasses too many false positives (or so narrow that it excludes too many false negatives)? How would changing the definition alter the statistic? Similarly, how do the choices of measurements and samples affect the statistic? What would happen if different measures or samples were chosen? And how is the statistic used? Is it being interpreted appropriately, or has its meaning been mangled to create a mutant statistic? Are the comparisons that are being made appropriate, or are apples being confused with oranges? How do different choices produce the conflicting numbers found in stat wars? These are the sorts of questions the Critical ask.

CONFRONTING THE INEVITABLE

As a practical matter, it is virtually impossible for citizens in contemporary society to avoid statistics about social problems. Statistics arise in all sorts of ways, and in almost every case the people promoting statistics want to persuade us. Activists use statistics to convince us that social problems are serious and deserve our attention and concern. Charities use statistics to encourage donations. Politicians use statistics to persuade us that they understand society's problems and that they deserve our support. The media use statistics to make their reporting more dramatic, more convincing, more compelling. Corporations use statistics to promote their products and improve their profits. Researchers use statistics to document their findings and support their conclusions. Those with whom we agree use statistics to reassure us that we're on the right side, while our opponents use statistics to try and convince us that we are wrong. Statistics are one of the standard types of evidence used by people in our society.

It is not possible simply to ignore statistics, to pretend they don't exist. That sort of head-in-the-sand approach would be too costly. Without statistics, we limit our ability to think thoughtfully about our society; without statistics, we have no accurate ways of judging how big a problem may be, whether it is getting worse, or how well the policies designed to address that problem actually work. And Awestruck or Naive attitudes toward statistics are no better than ignoring statistics; statistics have no magical properties, and it is foolish to assume that all statistics are equally valid. Nor is a Cynical approach the answer; statistics are too widespread and too useful to be automatically discounted.

It would be nice to have a checklist, a set of items we could consider in evaluating any statistic.

One could think of the topics discussed in this book as an outline for such a checklist: the list might detail potential problems with definitions, measurements, sampling, mutation, and so on. These are in fact common sorts of flaws found in many statistics, but they should not be considered a formal, complete checklist. It is probably impossible to produce a complete list of statistical flaws—no matter how long the list, there will be other possible problems that could affect statistics.

The goal is not to memorize a list, but to develop a thoughtful approach. Becoming Critical about statistics requires being prepared to ask questions about numbers. When encountering a new statistic in, say, a news report, the Critical try to assess it. What might be the sources for this number? How could one go about producing the figure? Who produced the number, and what interests might they have? What are the different ways key terms might have been defined, and which definitions have been chosen? How might the phenomena be measured, and which measurement choices have been made? What sort of sample was gathered, and how might that sample affect the result? Is the statistic being properly interpreted? Are comparisons being made, and if so, are the comparisons appropriate? Are there competing statistics? If so, what stakes do the opponents have in the issue, and how are those stakes likely to affect their use of statistics? And is it possible to figure out why the statistics seem to disagree, what the differences are in the ways the competing sides are using figures?

At first, this list of questions may seem overwhelming. How can an ordinary person—someone who reads a statistic in a magazine article or hears it on a news broadcast—determine the answers to such questions? Certainly news reports rarely give detailed information on the processes by which statistics are created. And few of us have time to drop everything and investigate the background of some new number we encounter. Being Critical, it seems, involves an impossible amount of work.

In practice, however, the Critical need not investigate the origin of every statistic. Rather, being Critical means appreciating the inevitable limitations that affect all statistics, rather than being Awestruck in the presence of numbers. It means not being too credulous, not accepting every statistic at face value (as the Naive do). But it also means appreciating that statistics, while always imperfect, can be useful. Instead of automatically discounting every statistic (in the fashion of the Cynical), the Critical reserve judgment. When confronted with an interesting number, they may try to learn more, to evaluate, to weigh the figure's strengths and weaknesses.

Of course, this Critical approach need not—and should not—be limited to statistics. It ought to apply to all the evidence we encounter when we scan a news report, or listen to a speech, whenever we learn about social problems. Claims about social problems often feature dramatic, compelling examples; the Critical might ask whether an example is likely to be a typical case or an extreme, exceptional instance. Claims about social problems often include quotations from different sources, and the Critical might wonder why those sources have spoken and why

they have been quoted: Do they have particular expertise? Do they stand to benefit if they influence others? Claims about social problems usually involve arguments about the problem's causes and potential solutions. The Critical might ask whether these arguments are convincing. Are they logical? Does the proposed solution seem feasible and appropriate? And so on. Being Critical—adopting a skeptical, analytical stance when confronted with claims—is an approach that goes far beyond simply dealing with statistics.

Statistics are not magical. Nor are they always true—or always false. Nor need they be incomprehensible. Adopting a Critical approach offers an effective way of responding to the numbers we are sure to encounter. Being Critical requires more thought, but failing to adopt a Critical mind-set makes us powerless to evaluate what others tell us. When we fail to think critically, the statistics we hear might just as well be magical.

◆ 5 ◆

Generalizing, Stereotyping, and Social Science

Joel M. Charon

Social science is a highly disciplined process of investigation whose purpose is to question many of our uncritically accepted stereotypes and generalizations. . . . The whole thrust and spirit of social science is to control personal bias, to uncover unfounded assumptions about people, and to understand as objectively as possible.

We all generalize. Generalization is basic to all human understanding. Most of us stereotype. We do not have to, and it hurts understanding. Charon's point is that the purpose of social science is to generalize without stereotyping.

From *Ten Questions: A Sociological Perspective*, 5th edition, by Joel Charon © 2004. Reprinted with permission of Wadsworth, a division of Thomson Learning: www.thomsonrights.com. Fax 800-730-2215.

CATEGORIES AND GENERALIZATIONS

The Importance of Categories and Generalizations to Human Beings

Sociology is a social science, and therefore it makes generalizations about people and their social life. "The top positions in the economic and political structures are far more likely to be filled by men than by women." "The wealthier the individual, the more likely he or she will vote Republican." "In the United States the likelihood of living in poverty is greater among the African-American population than among whites." "American society is segregated." "Like other industrial societies, American society has a class system in which more than three-fourths of the population end up in approximately the same social class as they were at birth."

But such generalizations often give me a lot of trouble. I know that the sociologist must learn about people and generalize about them, but I ask myself: "Are such generalizations worthwhile? Shouldn't we simply study and treat people as individuals?" An English professor at my university was noted for explaining to his class that "you should not generalize about people—that's the same as stereotyping and everyone knows that educated people are not supposed to stereotype. Everyone is an individual." (Ironically, this is *itself* a generalization about people.)

However, the more I examine the situation, the more I realize that all human beings categorize and generalize. They do it every day in almost every situation they enter, and they almost always do it when it comes to other people. In fact, we have no choice in the matter. "Glass breaks and can be dangerous." We have learned what "glass" is, what "danger" means, and what "breaking" is. These are all categories we apply to the situations we enter so that we can understand how to act. We generalize from our past. "Human beings who have a cold are contagious, and, unless we want to catch a cold, we should not get close to them." We are here generalizing about "those with colds," "how people catch colds," and "how we should act around those with colds." In fact, every noun and verb we use is a generaliza-tion that acts as a guide for us. The reality is that we are unable to escape generalizing about our environment. That is one aspect of our essence as human beings. This is what language does to us. Sometimes our generalizations are fairly accurate; sometimes they are unfounded. However, we do in fact generalize: all of us, almost all the time! The question that introduces this chapter is a foolish one. *Should we generalize about people?* This is not a useful question simply because we have no choice. A much better question is:

How Can We Develop Accurate Generalizations About People?

The whole purpose of social science is to achieve accurate categorizations and generalizations about human beings. Indeed, the purpose of almost all academic pursuits involves learning, understanding, and developing accurate categories and generalizations.

For a moment let us consider other animals. Most are prepared by instinct or simple conditioning to respond in a certain way to a certain stimulus in their environment. So, for example, when a minnow swims in the presence of a hungry fish, then that particular minnow is immediately responded to and eaten. The fish is able to distinguish that type of stimulus from other stimuli, and so whenever something identical to it or close to it appears, the fish responds. The minnow is a concrete object that can be immediately sensed (seen, smelled, heard, touched), so within a certain range the fish is able to easily include objects that look like minnows and to exclude those that do not. Of course, occasionally a lure with a hook is purposely used to fool the fish, and a slight mistake in perception ends the fish's life.

Human beings are different from the fish and other animals because we have *words for objects and events* in the environment, and this allows us to *understand* that environment and not just respond to it. With words we are able to make many more distinctions, and we are able to apply knowledge from one situation to the next far more easily. We are far less dependent on immediate physical stimuli. So, for example, we come to learn what fish, turtles, and whales are, as well as what minnows, worms, lures, and boats are. We read and learn what qualities all fish have, how fish differ from whales, and what differences fish have from one another. We learn how to catch fish, and we are able to apply what we learn to some fish but not other fish. We begin to understand the actions of all fish—walleyes, big walleyes, big female walleyes. Some of us decide to study pain, and we try to determine if all fish feel pain, if some do, or if all do not. Humans do not then simply respond to the environment, but they label that environment, study and understand that environment, develop categories and subcategories for objects in that environment, and constantly try to generalize from what they learn in specific situations about those categories. Through understanding a category we are able to see important and subtle similarities and distinctions that are not available to animals who do not categorize and generalize with words.

Generalizing allows us to walk into situations and apply knowledge learned elsewhere to understanding objects there. When we enter a classroom we know what a teacher is, and we label the person at the front of the room as a teacher. We know from past experience that teachers give grades, usually know more than we do about things we are about to learn in that classroom, have more formal education than we do, and usually resort to testing us to see if we learned something they regard as important. We might have also learned that teachers are usually kind (or mean), sensitive (or not sensitive), authoritarian (or democratic); or we might have had so many diverse experiences with teachers that whether a specific teacher is any of these things will depend on that specific individual. If we do finally decide that a given teacher is, in fact, authoritarian, then we will now see an "authoritarian teacher," and we will now apply what we know about such teachers from our past.

This is a remarkable ability. We are able to figure out how to act in situations we enter because we understand many of the objects we encounter there by applying relevant knowledge about them that we learned in the past. This allows us to act intelligently in a wide diversity of situations, some of which are not even close to what we have already

experienced. If we are open-minded and reflective, we can even evaluate how good or how poor our generalizations are, and we can alter what we know as we move from situation to situation.

The problem for almost all of us, however, is that many of our generalizations are not carefully arrived at or accurate, and it is sometimes difficult for us to recognize this and change them. Too often our generalizations actually stand in the way of our understanding, especially when we generalize about human beings.

To better understand what human beings do and how that sometimes gets us into trouble, let us look more closely at what "categories" and "generalizations" are.

THE MEANING OF CATEGORIZATION

Human beings categorize their environment; that is, *we isolate a chunk out of our environment, distinguish that chunk from all other parts of the environment, give it a name, and associate certain ideas with it.* Our chunks—or categories—arise in interaction; they are socially created. We discuss our environment, and we categorize it with the words we take on in our social life: "living things," "animals," "reptiles," "snakes," "poisonous snakes," "rattlers." A category is created, and once we understand it, we are able to compare objects in situations we encounter to that category. The number of distinctions we are able to make in our environment increases manyfold. It is not only nouns that represent categories (men, boys) but also verbs (run, walk, fall), adverbs (slow, fast), and adjectives (weak, strong, intelligent, married). Much of our learning is simply aimed at understanding what various categories mean, and this involves understanding the qualities that make up those categories and the ideas associated with them.

Through learning about people (a category) we come to recognize that "all people" possess certain qualities, some of which they share with other animals (cells, brains, reproductive organs), and some of which seem unique to them (language, stereoscopic vision, conscience). We understand that people can be divided into young and old, white and black, men and women, single and married. Most of us have a pretty good idea of what a male is and a female. If asked, we could explain who belongs to the categories of homosexual and heterosexual. We do not simply recognize objects that do or do not belong; we *understand* the category by being able to describe the qualities we believe belong to objects that fit and objects that do not. We might say that a male has a penis, an old person is anyone older than 60, a teacher is someone who transmits knowledge, a human being is an animal who has a soul.

We argue over these definitions, and the more we understand, the more complex these definitions become. But categories and definitions are a necessary part of all of our lives. Armed with these, we go out and are able to cut up our environment in complex and sophisticated ways. We see an object and determine what it is (that is, what category it belongs in), and because we know something about that category, we are able to apply what we already know to that object. This allows us to act appropriately in many different situations. Simply think of all the people we meet in a given day, most of whom we know nothing about except for whatever we gather from a quick glance. We may note age, gender, dress, hairstyle, demeanor, or just a smile, and we quickly determine how to act. We are forced to place individuals into categories so we know what to do in a multitude of social situations.

It is necessary for all human beings to categorize, define, and understand their environment. (This statement is itself a generalization about all human beings.) If we are honest with ourselves, we should recognize that each of us has created or learned thousands—even tens of thousands—of categories that we use as we look at what happens around us. The purpose of a biology class is to create useful categories of living things so that we can better understand what these things are—how they are similar, how they differ from nonliving things, and how they differ from one another. Musicians, artists, baseball players, political leaders, students, parents, scientists, con artists, and police—all of us live our lives assuming certain things about our environment based on the categories we have learned in interaction with others. . . .

THE MEANING OF GENERALIZATION

A *category is an isolated part of our environment that we notice.* We generalize about that category by observing specific instances of objects included in it and by isolating common qualities that seem to characterize those included in that category, including other yet unobserved members we might observe in the future. We watch birds build a nest, and we assume that all birds build nests out of sticks (including birds other than the robins and sparrows we observed). We continue to observe and note instances where birds use materials other than sticks, and then we learn that some birds do not build nests but dig them out. More often, our generalizations are a mixture of observation and learning from others: We learn that wealthy people often drive Mercedes and that police officers usually carry guns. On the basis of generalizing about a category, we are able to predict future events where that category comes into play. When we see a wealthy person, we expect to see a Mercedes (or something that we learn is comparable); and when we see a police officer, we expect to see a gun. That is what a generalization is.

A *generalization describes the category. It is a statement that characterizes objects within the category and defines similarities and differences with other categories.* "This is what an educated person is!" (in contrast to an uneducated person). "This is what wealthy people do to help ensure that privilege is passed down to their children." "This is what U.S. presidents have in common." "This is what Catholic people believe in."

As we shall see shortly, a generalization sometimes goes beyond just describing the category. It also explains why a particular quality develops. *That is, a generalization about a category will often be a statement of cause.* "Jewish people are liberal on social issues because of their minority position in Western societies." "U.S. presidents are male because . . ." "Wealthy people send their children to private schools because . . ."

Human beings, therefore, categorize their environment by using words. On the basis of observation and learning, they come to develop ideas concerning what qualities are associated with those categories. They also develop ideas as to why those qualities develop. *Ideas that describe the qualities that belong to a category and ideas that explain why those qualities exist are what we mean by generalizations.*

THE STEREOTYPE

When it comes to people, generalization is difficult to do well. The principal reason for this is that we are judgmental, and too often it is much easier for us to generalize for the purpose of evaluating (condemning or praising) others than for the purpose of understanding them. When we do this we fall into the practice of *stereotyping*.

A *stereotype is a certain kind of categorization.* It is a category and a set of generalizations characterized by the following qualities:

1. A *stereotype is judgmental.* It is not characterized by an attempt to understand, but by *an attempt to condemn or praise* the category. It makes a value judgment, and it has a strong emotional flavor. Instead of simple description of differences, there is a *moral evaluation* of those differences. People are judged good or bad because of the category. Examples: "The poor are lazy and no-good." "Students are a bunch of cheaters nowadays." "Stupid people," "crazies," "heathens," and "pigs" are some names we give to people we would have a very difficult time understanding, given the emotional names we attribute.

2. A *stereotype tends to be an absolute category.* That is, there is a *sharp distinction made between those inside and those outside the category.* There is little recognition that the category is merely a guide to understanding and that, in reality, there will be many individuals—even a majority—within a category who are exceptions to any generalization. Examples: "Men are oppressive." "Women are compassionate." "Politicians are all dishonest." "All moral people are Christian." "African Americans are poor."

3. *The stereotype tends to be a category that overshadows all others in the mind of the observer.* All other categories to which the individual belongs tend to be ignored. A stereotype treats the human being as simple and unidimensional, belonging to only one category of consequence. In fact, we are all part of a large number of categories. There is an assumption that if someone belongs to that particular category, *that is all one needs to know about the person.* A stereotype creates the human being as *simple and unidimensional.* Examples: "He is a homosexual. Therefore he lives a gay lifestyle." "She is a woman. Therefore, she must be attracted to that man." "He is a churchgoer. Therefore, he can't be guilty of theft." No matter how accurate one category is, it is very important to remember that all of us are complex mixtures of many categories. Who, after all, is the African-American divorced intelligent poet, who never finished his freshman year of college, who is a Baptist, bisexual, a father of three, and grandfather of four? Which category matters? When we stereotype, it is the category that emotionally matters to us, but not necessarily the actor.

4. A *stereotype does not change with new evidence.* When one accepts a stereotype, the category and the ideas associated with it are *rigidly accepted,* and the individual who holds it is *unwilling to alter it.* The stereotype, once accepted, becomes a filter through which evidence is accepted or rejected. Examples: "Students don't care about college anymore—I really don't care what your study shows." "I believe that people who pray together stay together. Don't confuse me with evidence that people who play together stay together too."

5. *The stereotype is not created carefully in the first place.* It is either learned culturally and simply accepted by the individual or created through *uncritical acceptance of a few concrete personal experiences.* Examples: "Politicians are bureaucrats who only care about keeping their job," "Obese people simply have no will power. My sister was obese and she just couldn't stop eating."

6. *The stereotype does not encourage a search for understanding why human beings are different from one another.* Instead of seeking to understand the cause as to why a certain quality is more in evidence in a particular category of people, a stereotype aims at exaggerating and judging differences. There is often an underlying assumption that *this is the way these people are,* it is part of their *essence,* and there seems to be little reason to try to understand the cause of differences any further than this. Examples: "Jewish people are just that way." "Poor people are just lazy." "Women don't know how to drive. That's the way they are."

Stereotypes are *highly oversimplified, exaggerated views of reality. They are especially attractive to people who are judgmental of others and who are quick to condemn people who are different from themselves.* They have been used to justify ethnic discrimination, war, and systematic murder of whole categories of people. Far from arising out of careful and systematic analysis, stereotypes *arise out of limited experience, hearsay, and culture,* and instead of aiding our understanding of the human being, *they always stand in the way of accurate understanding.*

It is not always easy to distinguish a stereotype from an accurate category. It is probably best to consider stereotypes and their opposites as extremes on a continuum. In actual fact, most categories will be neither perfectly accurate nor perfect examples of stereotypes. There are, therefore, *degrees of stereotyping* that we should recognize (see below).

One final point. Stereotypes, we have emphasized, are judgmental. They are meant to simplify people so that we know which categories of people are good and which are to be avoided or condemned. This is the link between stereotypes and prejudice. Prejudice is an attitude toward a category of people that leads the actor to discriminate against individuals who are placed in that category. Always the category is a stereotype (judgmental, absolute, central, rigid, cultural, and uninterested in cause). When a prejudiced actor identifies an individual in the category, a lot is assumed to be true and disliked about that individual, and a negative response results. And once he or she acts in a negative way toward that individual, there is a ready-made justification: the stereotype ("I discriminate *because* this is the way they are!"). Stereotypes are oversimplifications of reality, and they act as both necessary elements of prejudice and rationalizations of it. Unfortunately, the stereotype also acts as a set of role expectations for those in the category, and too often people who are judged negatively are influenced to judge themselves accordingly.

SOCIAL SCIENCE: A REACTION TO STEREOTYPES

. . . *Social science is a highly disciplined process of investigation whose purpose is to question many of our uncritically accepted stereotypes and generalizations.* Social science does not always succeed. There are many instances of inaccuracies and even stereotyping that have resulted from poor science or from scientists simply not being sensitive to their own biases. It is important, however, to recognize that even though scientists make mistakes in their attempts to describe reality accurately, the whole thrust and spirit of social science is to control personal bias, to uncover unfounded assumptions about people, and to understand reality as objectively as possible. Here are some of the ways that social science (as it is supposed to work) aims at creating accurate categories and generalizations about human beings:

1. *Social science tries hard not to be judgmental about categories of people.* We recognize that generalizations and categories must not condemn or praise but must simply be guides to understanding. . . .
2. *Categories in social science are not assumed to be all-important for understanding the individual.* A stereotype is itself an assumption that a certain category necessarily dominates an individual's life. We might meet a young African-American single male artist. The role of each of these categories may or may not be important to the individual. For some individuals, being male or single or an artist will be most influential; for others it will be being African American. For those of us who stereotype by race, it will almost always be African American. . . .
3. *Social science tries to create categories and generalizations through carefully gathered evidence.* Stereotypes tend to be cultural; that is, they are taught by people around us who have generalized based on what they have simply accepted from others or what

Stereotype	Accurate Categorization
Judgmental	Descriptive
No exceptions	Exceptions
All-powerful category	One of many
Rejects new evidence	Changes with evidence
Not carefully created	Carefully created
Not interested in cause	Interested in cause

they have learned through personal experience (which is usually extremely limited in scope, unsystematic, subject to personal and social biases, and uncritically observed). . . .

4. *Generalizations in social science are tentative and subject to change because new evidence is constantly being examined.* Stereotypes, on the other hand, are unconditionally held. Once accepted, a stereotype causes the individual to select only that evidence that reaffirms that stereotype. A stereotype resists change. . . .

5. *Scientists do not categorize as an end in itself.* Instead, scientists categorize because they seek a certain kind of generalization: They seek to understand cause. In social science that means we seek to know *why* a category of people tends to have a certain quality. We generalize about categories of people *to better understand what causes* the existence of qualities that belong to a given category. . . .

Those of us who are *victims* of stereotyping know full well the dangers of sloppy generalization. It is one thing to stereotype plants or rocks or stars; it is quite another to stereotype people. When we stereotype people, our carelessness normally has a negative effect on individuals who are part of that particular category. We unfairly place them at a disadvantage, not giving them a chance as individuals, making judgments about them based on inaccuracies and on our own unwillingness to evaluate our generalization critically.

Even those of us who are not victims will occasionally cry out, "I am an individual! Do not categorize me." We *are* individuals. *No one is exactly like us.* Yet, if we are honest, we must also recognize that those who do not know us will be forced to categorize us, and those who honestly want to understand humans better will have to. It is not a problem for us if the category is carefully created; and it is not a problem for us if the category is a positive one. If we apply for a job, we want the employer to categorize us as dependable, hard-working, knowledgeable, intelligent, and so on. Actually, we will even try to control how we present ourselves in situations so that we are able to influence others to place us in favorable categories: I'm cool, intelligent, sensitive, athletically talented, educated. When I write a letter of recommendation for students, I place the individual into several categories so that the reader will be able to apply what he or she knows about that category to the individual. The doctor may tell people "I am a physician" so that they will think highly of him or her as an individual. The person who announces himself as a boxer is telling us that he is tough; the rock musician is telling us that she is talented; the minister that he or she is caring—in many such cases it does not seem so bad if we are being categorized. For almost all of us, however, it is the *negative* categorization that we wish to avoid. And this makes good sense: No one wants to be put into a category and negatively judged without having a chance to prove him- or herself as an individual. . . .

But no matter how we might feel about others categorizing us and applying what they know to understanding us as a member of that category, the fact is that, except for those we know well, human beings can only be understood if we categorize and generalize. If we do this carefully, we can understand much about them, but if we are sloppy, we sacrifice understanding and end up making irrationally based value judgments about people before we have an opportunity to know them as individuals. . . .

Social science—and sociology as a social science—is an attempt to categorize and generalize about human beings and society, but always in a careful manner. Its purpose is to reject stereotyping. It is a recognition that generalizing about people is necessary and inevitable, but stereotyping is not.

If we have to generalize, let's try to be careful. Stereotyping does not serve our own interests well because it blocks understanding; nor does it help those we stereotype.

◆ **6** ◆

Religious Fundamentalism: A Sociological Study

Nancy Tatom Ammerman

My attempt throughout the study was to take seriously the world in which these people live, their noncognitive symbols as well as their rational structures and doctrines, the meaning of their experience as well as its form. I began with the premise that an interacting group of people comes to common understandings (often unstated) about who they are and what the social world is like. What people do and say is built on the assumption that others will understand what they mean by those actions and words.

I decided to introduce a book-length study done by Nancy Tatom Ammerman called *Bible Believers*, because I like the way she introduces us to her research. I believe it is good research—not perfect, but careful, intelligent, and done with honesty and self-criticism. For one year she studied a fundamentalist Christian congregation, participating, observing, and interviewing. In this introductory chapter she lays out how and why she studied the congregation, as well as what she saw as the strengths and weaknesses of her approach. Those of us who read the way she tries to approach her work as well as studying some of her data and conclusions are then able to critically evaluate her science and determine how valid we believe her study to be. If we wish to build on it, or if we wish to show that her conclusions are not valid, we too can complete a study, hopefully one that adds to whatever she presents. There are many studies on religion, fundamentalism, American society, family, and sex roles in sociology; together we are able to critically accumulate more and more information and understanding concerning these and other topics.

This selection is only the first chapter. It describes her methods. You are the reader: What do you think of her approach? Is there something important that can be understood through her study? (By the way—selection 46 in this reader contains what she observed concerning the family life of the congregants.) How would you have improved on what she tried to do?

This study is an effort to introduce the lives of ordinary Fundamentalists into the larger discussion

From Ammerman, Nancy Tatom, *Bible Believers: Fundamentalists in the Modern World*, copyright © 1987, by Rutgers, The State University. Reprinted by permission of Rutgers University Press.

of Fundamentalism's place in American society. Fundamentalism is examined here not as a cultural or political phenomenon but as a way of life. The primary units of analysis are individuals and the groups to which they most immediately belong. We will learn why Fundamentalism exists by listening to the stories of people who have chosen it. We will listen to how one group of Fundamentalists defines itself and how it gives order to the world. And in so doing we will hope to gain a detailed understanding with which to return to the public issues raised by Fundamentalism.

Understanding the everyday world of Fundamentalism requires much more than a demographic profile. It requires the kind of personal encounter that is possible only when researcher and subjects meet each other and spend a part of their lives together. The view of Fundamentalism presented here comes through the lens of such shared experience. For the year that stretched between June 1979 and May 1980, I became a participant in the congregation I will call Southside Gospel Church.[1] Members knew I was a researcher, but they also accepted me as "one of us." I attended almost every time the church doors were open, sang in the choir, helped in Sunday School and Junior Church, and even helped paint their Academy building. I celebrated their births and mourned their deaths. I listened to them describe and explain the world and tried to hear with the ears of an insider while watching with the eyes of a trained observer. In short, my effort was to get as close as possible to the way Fundamentalism is experienced in everyday life.

I chose participant observation as a method despite possible difficulties in gaining access to a Fundamentalist congregation. For most researchers, doing any sociological study of Fundamentalism is difficult and often nearly impossible. Fundamentalists often distrust secular researchers so much that they will not even complete questionnaires; gaining access for participant observation is even less likely. Part of the problem is that we sociologists are seen as chief among the "secular humanists" who have corrupted traditional ways of thinking. We use secular categories to explain everything, ignoring the actions of Almighty God. Likewise, in the Fundamentalist view, most sociologists are unrepentant sinners who live worldly lives that are unwelcome in a Fundamentalist congregation. Believers simply do not expect anyone who is not saved to be able to understand or empathize with their beliefs (cf. Robbins et al. 1973).

Nevertheless, after visiting a Sunday morning service at Southside, I approached the pastor about studying his church. For all the reasons I have just described, it is not surprising that his first question was "Are you born again?" Because my religious history is Evangelical, I could honestly answer "yes." The religious experiences of my childhood had prepared me for the language and expectations of a group like this, and those experiences opened doors that might have been closed to other researchers. Although I am not a Fundamentalist (and I disclaimed that identity whenever it was explicitly bestowed on me), I am committed to the Christian faith; and I knew that I could translate much of my experience into terms this group would recognize and accept (cf. Ammerman 1982). I could speak the language of an insider, and I was willing to live by an insider's rules. Where they had norms about drinking, dancing, and how to dress, I conformed. When they sang, I sang too; when they prayed, so did I; and when they read the Bible, I followed along in a King James Version. Because I was identified as saved and spoke the language of a saved person, I was accepted by most of the congregation and granted access that a complete outsider might never have gained.

I promised in return that I would present an inside view of Fundamentalism that was fair and accurate. Where I describe their ideas and experiences, I hope the people I studied find it so. Where I analyze what I saw, using the categories of secular sociology, I do not expect that they will accept my explanations. Although I would never wish to argue that sociological views of reality are any more true than religious ones (cf. Berger 1969:179ff.), accepting multiple explanations is not a comfortable position for the people of Southside.

While Southside's members may not find my sociological analysis agreeable, other information from this study may be of practical value. I prepared especially for them material on the demographics and organizational structure of the congregation—material that they subsequently used to develop new programs. While the research was in progress, I was careful to avoid disturbing the natural processes of the church; but after I left the field, it seemed only right to give back something of what I had taken.

My attempt throughout the study was to take seriously the world in which these people live, their noncognitive symbols as well as their rational structures and doctrines, the meaning of their experience as well as its form (cf. Bellah 1970, Geertz 1966). I began with the premise that an interacting group of people comes to common understandings (often unstated) about who they are and what the social world is like. What people do and say is built on the assumption that others will understand what they mean by those actions and words. Mead (1934) would say that people understand each other because meaning has been negotiated in a "conversation of gestures." Berger and Luckmann (1966), similarly, would say that a group's reality is "socially constructed." That construction process involves not only explicit ideas and values but the "strategies of action" that make most sense in a given corner of the social world (see Swidler 1986). My aim as an observer, then, was to understand the group's shared meanings and to uncover the subtle assumptions about reality that support and are supported by their everyday lives (cf. Blasi and Weigert 1976, Glaser and Strauss 1967, Truzzi 1974).

Although participant observation offers the best possibility for understanding a group's meanings and assumptions, we can never be quite sure how the observer has changed the world she is observing. Sometimes events seem to flow along undisturbed, while at other times the observer's presence brings an abrupt halt to the action. In this case, the disturbances seemed to be rare. Although I never sought to hide my research role, neither did I go out of my way to advertise it. Even after seven or eight months, people were sometimes surprised to find out that I was not just an ordinary participant. When they found out what I was doing, they treated me with a mixture of curiosity and acceptance—as long as they were sure the pastor approved of me. Most people were never quite sure what a sociologist would be studying, especially in their church and especially since I did not seem to be doing anything unusual. I was always there and often did things to help. I took notes during the pastor's sermons, but then so did a lot of other people. In the public context of church activities, I was more often treated as a participant than as an observer.

My role as observer involved much more than what my subjects saw of course. Besides taking notes while the pastor was preaching and

teaching, I recorded other observations as soon as it was possible—often into a tape recorder as I was making the trip home. All these notes were typed, filed, and cross-filed into categories that began to reflect the dominant themes and concerns of the congregation. Out of this body of data specific areas were identified for further exploration in interviews. After about four months in the field, I began selecting a sample and contacting people to be interviewed.

Obtaining this sample was among the most difficult parts of the research process. Not surprisingly, the church did not have an accurate, up-to-date listing of its members, and the church clerk balked at turning over the list she did have. My list, then, was compiled with the aid of the church secretary and the pastor from the mailing list, their membership lists, and a recent pictorial directory. We arrived at an available population of 167 households in which there was at least one member. I used a table of random numbers to select fifty-nine of those households as my sample. Of that number, nine families could not be contacted because they had apparently moved out of the area; and nine others refused to be interviewed. To these were added samples from the 1,000+ mailing list and from the list of people converted in recent months. The final result was completed interviews with sixty-two adult members, twelve adult nonmembers, and four children.

My role as an interviewer often placed an initial distance between me and my subjects that was not present in my role as a participant observer. Those who had been selected to be interviewed received an introductory letter from me and from the pastor and a phone call to arrange a time to meet. But despite our efforts to preempt worries, a good many people approached the interview full of apprehension about what it would be like to be interviewed by someone who was getting a Ph.D. from Yale. After they had cleaned their houses, prepared special food, and even bought new clothes, some still worried about whether they would know the "right" answers and why I had chosen them instead of someone who was a stronger Christian or had been in the church longer or had a more interesting testimony.

Once we began to talk, however, people almost always became more comfortable. They told me how they had been saved and what they do at church. We talked about what it means to them to be a Christian and the things they like most to do. We discussed families, jobs, neighbors, politics, and the state of the world. I guided the conversation and asked enough questions to make sure that certain topics were covered, but much of our talk was not different from what it might have been if they had simply invited a new church member home for dinner. Sometimes they stopped halfway through the interview to ask when the "real" questions would begin. By the time we parted, they often commented about how much easier it had been than they had thought it would be. They felt that we had become friends.

This study reflects both the strengths and the weaknesses of such personal involvement. Its strength is understanding and richness of detail, in Geertz's (1973) words "thick description." Its weakness is the absence of comparative data and quantitative testing, which would place these findings in their proper context. Everyday life in one congregation does not represent that in all of American Fundamentalism. Such congregations pride themselves on their independence, which results in hundreds of major and minor variations in faith and practice. Almost anything one church does may be done differently in another Fundamentalist church somewhere else. Yet, despite their independence, Fundamentalist churches exhibit a remarkable uniformity. The common ground they share makes it possible for them to cooperate with each other in various evangelistic efforts, for members to move from one church to another, for churches to participate in common organizational networks and mutually to claim the name *Fundamentalist*.

Southside Gospel Church advertises itself as "Independent, Fundamental, Premillennial, and Baptistic." Its self-identification (along with its convenient location) initially justified its selection for this study. That selection was justified further by the extent to which this congregation is integrated into the network of Fundamentalist institutions throughout the country. Nearly every major Fundamentalist publication is read; there are ties to many Fundamentalist colleges; and most of the nationally known revivalists have

supporters in the church. In addition, the ideas presented from Southside's pulpit never deviated in significant detail from the ideas described by historians, theologians, and sociologists who have studied Fundamentalism. Although not technically representative, Southside can safely be assumed to be fairly typical. Although not randomly selected, its identity and way of life place it squarely in the midst of the larger Fundamentalist movement. . . .

NOTE

1. As is customary, the names of people and places have been changed to protect the anonymity of those who so graciously allowed me to share in their lives. For further details on my role in the congregation, see Ammerman (1982).

REFERENCES

Ammerman, N. T. 1982. "Dilemmas in establishing a research identity." *The New England Sociologist* 4:21–27.

Bellah, R. N. 1970. "Christianity and symbolic realism." *Journal for the Scientific Study of Religion* 9:89–96.

Berger, P. L. 1969. *The Sacred Canopy*. Garden City, N.Y.: Doubleday, Anchor Books.

Berger, P. L., and T. Luckmann. 1966. *The Social Construction of Reality*. Garden City, N.Y.: Doubleday, Anchor Books.

Blasi, A. J., and A. J. Weigert. 1976. "Towards a sociology of religion: An interpretive sociology approach." *Sociological Analysis* 37:189–204.

Geertz, C. 1966. "Religion as a cultural system." Pp. 1–46 in M. Banton (ed.), *Anthropologial Approaches to the Study of Religion*. New York: Praeger.

———. 1973. *The Interpretation of Cultures*. New York: Basic Books.

Glaser, B. G., and A. L. Strauss. 1967. *The Discovery of Grounded Theory: Strategies for Qualitative Research*. Hawthorne, New York: Aldine.

Mead, G. H. 1934. *Mind, Self and Society*. Chicago: University of Chicago Press.

Robbins, T., D. Anthony, and T. E. Curtis. 1973. "The limits of symbolic realism: Problems of empathetic field observation in a sectarian context." *Journal for the Scientific Study of Religion* 12:259–272.

Swidler, A. 1986. "Culture in action: Symbols and strategies." *American Sociological Review* 51:273–286.

Truzzi, M., ed. 1974. *Verstehen: Subjective Understanding in the Social Sciences*. Reading, Mass.: Addison-Wesley.

Part II

THE PERSPECTIVE
OF SOCIOLOGY: HUMANS
AS SOCIAL BEINGS

What is the essence of the human being? That is, what are we, naturally, biologically, universally?

To the sociologist, human beings cannot be understood apart from society. We are, by our very nature, social beings. It is impossible to conceive of human beings living in the natural world who are not also ultimately social beings.

Part II is an attempt to introduce many of the ways that humans are essentially social. Charles Cooley's brief statement gets at the heart of the matter. He challenges the reader to conceive what we might be without socialization. Peter Berger and Thomas Luckmann more systematically introduce us to the power of socialization, the process by which the individual comes to internalize society and ultimately control himself or herself according to society's rules. Society, that which exists "out there," becomes a part of the individual "inside."

Erving Goffman describes human social interaction, and many of the processes that take place as we act around one another. Other people matter to us as we act, one way or another. Richard Jenkins highlights one of the most important ways social interaction matters to us: it creates our identities. Identity is socially created, socially sustained, and sometimes socially lost.

Dexter Dunphy introduces the importance of primary groups, and Kai Erikson shows us the importance of community to our lives. Charles Lindholm describes an example of how society or community sometimes becomes even more important than our own individual lives. Part II ends with an excellent selection from Peter Berger's *Invitation to Sociology*, describing in some detail many of the ways in which we are surrounded by society, and how society exercises a mixture of controls over every aspect of our lives.

Together, these selections are meant to introduce the student to the "perspective" of sociology, a perpsective whose major focus is "humans as social beings."

◆ 7 ◆

Human Nature

Charles Cooley

Human functions are so numerous and intricate that no fixed mechanism could provide for them. They are also subject to radical change, not only in the life of the individual but from one generation to another.

Human beings are characterized by flexibility, plasticity, and teachability. Our nature is not commanded by what we inherit in our genes, but by our social life. Charles Cooley's description still represents well the sociological view of human nature.

. . . Thus the plastic, indeterminate character of human heredity involves a long and helpless infancy; and this, in turn, is the basis of the human family, because the primary and essential function of the family is the care of children. Those species of animals in which the young are adequately prepared for life by definite heredity have no family at all, while those which more or less resemble man as regards plastic heredity, resemble him also in having some rudiments, at least, of a family. Kittens, for instance, are cared for by the mother for several months and profit in some measure by her example and instruction.

More generally, this difference as regards plasticity means that the life-activities of the animal are comparatively uniform and fixed, while those of man are varied and changing. Human functions are so numerous and intricate that no fixed mechanism could provide for them. They are also subject to radical change, not only in the life of the individual but from one generation to

another. The only possible hereditary basis for them is an outfit of indeterminate capacities that can be developed and guided by experience as the needs of life require.

I see a flycatcher sitting on a dead branch, where there are no leaves to interrupt his view. Presently, he darts toward a passing insect, hovers about him a few seconds, catches him, or fails to do so, and returns to his perch. That is his way of getting a living: He has done it all his life and will go on doing it to the end. Millions of other flycatchers on millions of other dead branches are doing precisely the same thing. And this has been the life of the species for unknown thousands of years. They have, through the germ-plasm, a definite capacity for this—the keen eye, the swift, fluttering movement to follow the insect, the quick, sure action of the neck and bill to seize him—all effective with no instruction and very little practice.

Man has a natural hunger, like the flycatcher, and a natural mechanism of tasting, chewing, swallowing, and digestion; but his way of getting the food varies widely at different times of his life, is not the same with different individuals, and often changes completely from one generation to another. The great majority of us gain our food,

From *Human Nature and Social Order*, by Charles Horton Cooley, 1922, pp. 20–22, 31–34, Schocken Books, Inc. Originally published by Scribner and Sons.

after we have left the parental nest, through what we call a job, and a job is any activity whatever that a complex and shifting society esteems sufficiently to pay us for. It is very likely, nowadays, to last only part of our lives and to be something our ancestors never heard of. Thus whatever is most distinctively human—our adaptability, our power of growth, our arts and sciences, our social institutions and progress—is bound up with the indeterminate character of human heredity.

Of course, there is no sharp line, in this matter of teachability, between man and the other animals. The activities of the latter are not wholly predetermined, and in so far as they are not, there is a learning process based on plastic heredity. The higher animals—horses, dogs, and elephants, for example—are notably teachable, and may even participate in the changes of human society, as when dogs learn to draw carts, trail fugitives, guide the lost, or perform in a circus. And, on the other side, those activities of man that do not require much adaptation, such as the breathing, sucking, and crying of infants, and even walking (which is learned without instruction when the legs become strong enough), are provided for by definite heredity. . . .

◆ 8 ◆

Socialization: The Internalization of Society

Peter L. Berger and Thomas Luckmann

Primary socialization accomplishes what (in hindsight, of course) may be seen as the most important confidence trick that society plays on the individual—to make appear as necessity what is in fact a bundle of contingencies, and thus to make meaningful the accident of his birth.

From beginning to end, the human being is socialized. Socialization brings the external world inside the individual. Both "primary socialization" and "secondary socialization" cooperate to do this, but, as Peter Berger and Thomas Luckmann emphasize, "primary socialization is really the most important one for the individual." This selection examines primary socialization, and it is organized as follows:

1. Significant others are representatives of society and social class.
2. Significant others form the individual's identity.
3. Eventually, a generalized other is created that represents a coherent society.

. . . Only when he has achieved this degree of internalization is an individual a member of society. The ontogenetic process by which this is brought about is socialization, which may thus be defined as the comprehensive and consistent induction of an individual into the objective world of a society or a sector of it. Primary socialization is the first socialization an individual undergoes in childhood through which he becomes a member of society. Secondary socialization is any subsequent process that inducts an already socialized individual into new sectors of the objective world of his society. . . .

It is at once evident that primary socialization is usually the most important one for an individual, and that the basic structure of all secondary socialization has to resemble that of primary socialization. Every individual is born into an objective social structure within which he encounters the significant others who are in charge of his socialization.[1] These significant others are imposed on him. Their definitions of his situation are posited for him as objective reality. He is thus born into not only an objective social structure but also an objective social world. The significant others who mediate this world to him modify it in the course of mediating it. They select aspects of it in accordance with their own location in the social structure, and also by virtue of their individual, biographically rooted idiosyncrasies. The social world is "filtered" to the individual through this double selectivity. Thus the lower-class child not only absorbs a lower-class perspective on the social world, he absorbs it in the idiosyncratic coloration given it by his parents (or whatever other individuals are in charge of his primary socialization). The same lower-class perspective may induce a mood of contentment, resignation, bitter resentment, or seething rebelliousness. Consequently, the lower-class child will not only come to inhabit a world greatly different from that of an upper-class child, but may do so in a manner quite different from the lower-class child next door.[2]

It should hardly be necessary to add that primary socialization involves more than purely cognitive learning. It takes place under circumstances that are highly charged emotionally. Indeed, there is good reason to believe that without such emotional attachment to significant others, the learning process would be difficult if not impossible.[3] The child identifies with the significant others in a variety of emotional ways. Whatever they may be, internalization occurs only as identification occurs. The child takes on the significant others' roles and attitudes, that is, internalizes them and makes them his own. And by this identification with significant others, the child becomes capable of identifying himself, of acquiring a subjectively coherent and plausible identity. In other words, the self is a reflected entity, reflecting the attitudes first taken by significant others toward it;[4] the individual becomes what he is addressed as by his significant others. This is not a one-sided, mechanistic process. It entails a dialectic between identification by others and self-identification, between objectively assigned and subjectively appropriated identity. . . .

What is most important for our considerations here is the fact that the individual not only takes on the roles and attitudes of others, but in the same process takes on their world. Indeed, identity is objectively defined as location in a certain world and can be subjectively appropriated only *along with* that world. Put differently, all identifications take place within horizons that imply a specific social world. The child learns that he is what he is called. Every name implies a nomenclature, which in turn implies a designated social location.[5] To be given an identity involves being assigned a specific place in the world. Because this identity is subjectively appropriated by the child ("I *am* John Smith"), so is the world to which this identity points. Subjective appropriation of identity and subjective appropriation of the social world are merely different aspects of the *same* process of internalization, mediated by the *same* significant others.

Primary socialization creates in the child's consciousness a progressive abstraction from the roles and attitudes of specific others to roles and attitudes *in general*. For example, in the internalization of norms, there is a progression from "Mummy is angry with me now" to "Mummy is angry with me *whenever* I spill the soup." As additional significant others (father, grandmother, older sister, and so on) support the mother's negative attitude toward soup-spilling, the generality of the norm is subjectively extended. The decisive step comes when the child recognizes that *everybody* is against soup-spilling, and the norm is generalized to "one does not spill soup"—"one" being himself as part of a generality that includes, in principle, *all* of society insofar as it is significant to the child. This abstraction from the roles and attitudes of concrete significant others is called the *generalized other.*[6] Its formation within consciousness means that the individual now identifies not only with concrete others but with a generality of others, that is, with a society. Only by virtue of this generalized identification does his own self-identification attain stability and continuity. He now has not only an identity vis-à-vis this or that significant other, but an identity *in general*, which is subjectively apprehended as remaining the same no matter what others, significant or not, are encountered. This newly coherent identity incorporates within itself all the various internalized roles and attitudes—including, among many other things, the self-identification as a non-spiller of soups.

The formation within consciousness of the generalized other marks a decisive phase in socialization. It implies the internalization of society as such and of the objective reality established therein, and, at the same time, the subjective establishment of a coherent and continuous identity. Society, identity, *and* reality are subjectively crystallized in the same process of internalization. This crystallization is concurrent with the internalization of language. Indeed, for reasons evident from the foregoing observations on language, language constitutes both the most important content and the most important instrument of socialization.

When the generalized other has been crystallized in consciousness, a symmetrical relationship is established between objective and subjective reality. What is real "outside" corresponds to what is real "within." Objective reality can readily be "translated" into subjective reality, and vice versa. Language, of course, is the principal vehicle of this ongoing translating process in both directions. It should, however, be stressed that the symmetry between objective and subjective reality cannot be complete. The two realities correspond to each other, but they are not co-extensive. There is always more objective reality "available" than is actually internalized in any

individual consciousness, simply because the contents of socialization are determined by the social distribution of knowledge. No individual internalizes the totality of what is objectivated as reality in his society, not even if the society and its world are relatively simple ones. On the other hand, there are always elements of subjective reality that have not originated in socialization, such as the awareness of one's own body prior to and apart from any socially learned apprehension of it. Subjective biography is not fully social. The individual apprehends himself as being both inside *and* outside society.[7] This implies that the symmetry between objective and subjective reality is never a static, once-for-all state of affairs. It must always be produced and reproduced *in actu*. In other words, the relationship between the individual and the objective social world is like an ongoing balancing act. . . .

In primary socialization, there is no *problem* of identification. There is no choice of significant others. Society presents the candidate for socialization with a predefined set of significant others, whom he must accept as such with no possibility of opting for another arrangement. *Hic Rhodus, hic salta.* One must make do with the parents fate has regaled one with. This unfair disadvantage inherent in the situation of being a child has the obvious consequence that, although the child is not simply passive in the process of his socialization, it is the adults who set the rules of the game. The child can play the game with enthusiasm or with sullen resistance. But, alas, there is no other game around. This has an important corollary. Because the child has no choice in the selection of his significant others, his identification with them is quasi-automatic. For the same reason, his internalization of their particular reality is quasi-inevitable. The child does not internalize the world of his significant others as one of many possible worlds. He internalizes it as *the* world, the only existent and only conceivable world, the world *tout court*. It is for this reason that the world internalized in primary socialization is so much more firmly entrenched in consciousness than worlds internalized in secondary socializations. However much the original sense of inevitability may be weakened in subsequent disenchantments, the recollection of a never-to-be-repeated certainty—the certainty of the first dawn of reality—still adheres to the first world of childhood. Primary socialization thus accomplishes what (in hindsight, of course) may be seen as the most important confidence trick that society plays on the individual—to make appear as necessity what is in fact a bundle of contingencies, and thus to make meaningful the accident of his birth.

The specific contents that are internalized in primary socialization vary, of course, from society to society. Some are found everywhere. It is language that must be internalized above all. With language, and by means of it, various motivational and interpretative schemes are internalized as institutionally defined—wanting to act like a brave little boy, for instance, and assuming that little boys are naturally divided into the brave and the cowardly. These schemes provide the child with institutionalized programs for everyday life, some immediately applicable to him, others anticipating conduct socially defined for later biographical stages—the bravery that will allow him to get through a day beset with tests of will from one's peers and from all sorts of others, and also the bravery that will be required of one later—when one is initiated as a warrior, say, or when one might be called by the god. These programs, both the immediately applicable and the anticipatory, differentiate one's identity from that of others—such as girls, slave boys, or boys from another clan. Finally, there is internalization of at least the rudiments of the legitimating apparatus; the child learns "why" the programs are what they are. One must be brave because one wants to become a real man; one must perform the rituals because otherwise the gods will be angry; one must be loyal to the chief because only if one does will the gods support one in times of danger; and so on.

In primary socialization, then, the individual's first world is constructed. Its peculiar quality of firmness is to be accounted for, at least in part, by the inevitability of the individual's relationship to his very first significant others. . . .

Primary socialization ends when the concept of the generalized other (and all that goes with it) has been established in the consciousness of the individual. At this point, he is an effective member of society and in subjective possession of a self and a world. But this internalization of society, identity, and reality is not a matter of once and for all. Socialization is never total and never finished.

NOTES

1. Our description here, of course, leans heavily on the Meadian theory of socialization.
2. The concept of "mediation" is derived from Sartre, who lacks, however, an adequate theory of socialization.
3. The affective dimension of early learning has been especially emphasized by Freudian child psychology, although there are various findings of behavioristic learning theory that would tend to confirm this. We do not imply acceptance of the theoretical presuppositions of either psychological school in our argument here.
4. Our conception of the reflected character of the self is derived from both Cooley and Mead. Its roots may be found in the analysis of the "social self" by William James (*Principles of Psychology*).
5. On nomenclature, *cf.* Claude Lévi-Strauss, *La pensée sauvage*, pp. 253 *ff.*
6. The concept of the "generalized other" is used here in a fully Meadian sense.
7. Compare Georg Simmel on the self-apprehension of man as both inside and outside society. Plessner's concept of "eccentricity" is again relevant here (*Die des Organischen und der Mensch*, 1928 and 1965).

Presentation of Self in Everyday Life

Erving Goffman

When an individual appears in the presence of others, there will usually be some reason for him to mobilize his activity so that it will convey an impression to others that is in his interests to convey.

Erving Goffman approaches the human being as an actor performing on a stage. His descriptions of interaction are classic. This insightful selection is one of his most famous.

What happens when we enter the presence of others? Use this as a guide to your reading:

1. Others seek to know who we are. We control our actions to give off the picture we want to give off.
2. Others will also seek to act to control the definition of the situation.
3. A working consensus is created.
4. Ongoing interaction may question the initial picture.
5. Preventive tactics help preserve the interaction and keep actors from embarrassment.

Here, Goffman brilliantly describes something that occurs in all of our lives, every day. He gives us insight into something familiar.

When an individual enters the presence of others, they commonly seek to acquire information about him or to bring into play information about him already possessed. They will be interested in his general socio-economic status, his conception of self, his attitude toward them, his competence, his trustworthiness, and so on. Although some of this information seems to be sought almost as an end in itself, there are usually quite practical rea-

sons for acquiring it. Information about the individual helps to define the situation, enabling others to know in advance what he will expect of them and what they may expect of him. Informed in these ways, the others will know how best to act in order to call forth a desired response from him.

For those present, many sources of information become accessible and many carriers (or "sign-vehicles") become available for conveying this information. If unacquainted with the individual, observers can glean clues from his conduct and appearance that allow them to apply their previous experience with individuals roughly similar to the one in front of them or, more important, to apply untested stereotypes to him. They can also assume from past experience that only individuals of a particular kind are likely to be found in a given social setting. They can rely on what the individual says about himself or on documentary evidence he provides as to who and what he is. If they know, or know of, the individual by virtue of experience prior to the interaction, they can rely on assumptions as to the persistence and generality of psychological traits as a way of predicting his present and future behavior.

However, during the period in which the individual is in the immediate presence of the others, few events may occur that directly provide the others with the conclusive information they will need if they are to direct wisely their own activity. Many crucial facts lie beyond the time and place of interaction or lie concealed within it. For example, the "true" or "real" attitudes, beliefs, and emotions of the individual can be ascertained only indirectly, through his avowals or through what appears to be involuntary expressive behavior. Similarly, if the individual offers the others a product or service, they will often find that, during the interaction, there will be no time and place immediately available for eating the pudding that the proof can be found in. They will be forced to accept some events as conventional or natural signs of something not directly available to the senses. In Ichheiser's terms,[1] the individual will have to act so that he intentionally or unintentionally *expresses* himself, and the others will in turn have to be *impressed* in some way by him.

The expressiveness of the individual (and therefore his capacity to give impressions) appears to involve two radically different kinds of sign activity: the expression that he *gives*, and the expression that he *gives off*. The first involves verbal symbols or their substitutes that he uses admittedly and solely to convey the information he and the others are known to attach to these symbols. This is communication in the traditional and narrow sense. The second involves a wide range of action that others can treat as symptomatic of the actor, the expectation being that the action was performed for reasons other than the information conveyed in this way. As we shall have to see, this distinction has an only initial validity. The individual does, of course, intention-

ally convey misinformation by means of both of these types of communication, the first involving deceit, the second feigning. . . .

He may wish [others] to think highly of him, or to think that he thinks highly of them, or to perceive how in fact he feels toward them, or to obtain no clear-cut impression; he may wish to ensure sufficient harmony so that the interaction can be sustained, or to defraud, get rid of, confuse, mislead, antagonize, or insult them. Regardless of the particular objective the individual has in mind and of his motive for having this objective, it will be in his interest to control the conduct of the others, especially their responsive treatment of him.[2] This control is achieved largely by influencing the definition of the situation the others come to formulate, and he can influence this definition by expressing himself in such a way as to give them the kind of impression that will lead them to act voluntarily in accordance with his own plan. Thus, when an individual appears in the presence of others, there will usually be some reason for him to mobilize his activity so that it will convey an impression to others that is in his interest to convey. Because a girl's dormitory mates will glean evidence of her popularity from the calls she receives on the phone, we can suspect that some girls will arrange for calls to be made, and Willard Waller's finding can be anticipated:

> It has been reported by many observers that a girl who is called to the telephone in the dormitories will often allow herself to be called several times, in order to give all the other girls ample opportunity to hear her paged. . . .[3]

I have said that when an individual appears before others, his actions will influence the definition of the situation they come to have. Sometimes, the individual will act in a thoroughly calculating manner, expressing himself in a given way solely to give the kind of impression to others that is likely to evoke from them a specific response he is concerned to obtain. Sometimes, the individual will be calculating in his activity but be relatively unaware that this is the case. Sometimes, he will intentionally and consciously express himself in a particular way, but chiefly because the tradition of his group or social status require this kind of expression and not because of any particular response (other than vague acceptance or approval) that is likely to be evoked from those impressed by the expression. Sometimes, the traditions of an individual's role will lead him to give a well-designed impression of a particular kind, and yet he may be neither consciously nor unconsciously disposed to create such an impression. The others, in their turn, may be suitably impressed by the individual's efforts to convey something, or may misunderstand the situation and come to conclusions that are warranted neither by the individual's intent nor by the facts. In any case, in so far as the others act *as if* the individual had conveyed a particular impression, we may take a functional or pragmatic view and say that the individual has "effectively" projected a given definition of the situation and "effectively" fostered the understanding that a given state of affairs obtains. . . .

When we allow that the individual projects a definition of the situation when he appears before others, we must also see that the others, however passive their role may seem to be, will themselves effectively project a definition of the situation by virtue of their response to the individual and by virtue of any lines of action they initiate to him. Ordinarily, the definitions of the situation projected by the several different participants are sufficiently attuned to one another so that open contradiction will not occur. I do not mean that there will be the kind of consensus that arises when each individual present candidly expresses what he really feels and honestly agrees with the expressed feelings of the others present. This kind of harmony is an optimistic ideal, and in any case is not necessary for the smooth working of society. Rather, each participant is expected to suppress his immediate heartfelt feelings, conveying a view of the situation he feels the others will be able to find at least temporarily acceptable. The maintenance of this surface of agreement, this veneer of consensus, is facilitated by each participant concealing his own wants behind statements that assert values to which everyone present feels obliged to give lip service. Further, there is usually a kind of division of definitional labor. Each participant is allowed to establish the tentative official ruling regarding matters that are vital to him but not immediately important to others, for example, the rationalizations and justifications by

which he accounts for his past activity. In exchange for this courtesy, he remains silent or noncommittal on matters important to others but not immediately important to him. We have then a kind of interactional *modus vivendi*. Together, the participants contribute to a single overall definition of the situation that involves not so much a real agreement as to what exists but rather a real agreement as to whose claims concerning what issues will be temporarily honored. Real agreement will also exist concerning the desirability of avoiding an open conflict of definitions of the situation.[4] I will refer to this level of agreement as a "working consensus." It is to be understood that the working consensus established in one interaction setting will be quite different in content from the working consensus established in a different type of setting. Thus, between two friends at lunch, a reciprocal show of affection, respect, and concern for the other is maintained. In service occupations, on the other hand, the specialist often maintains an image of disinterested involvement in the problem of the client, while the client responds with a show of respect for the competence and integrity of the specialist. Regardless of such differences in content, however, the general form of these working arrangements is the same.

In noting the tendency for a participant to accept the definitional claims made by the others present, we can appreciate the crucial importance of the information the individual *initially* possesses or acquires concerning his fellow participants, for it is on the basis of this initial information that the individual starts to define the situation and starts to build up lines of responsive action. The individual's initial projection commits him to what he is proposing to be and requires him to drop all pretenses of being other things. As the interaction among the participants progresses, additions and modifications in this initial informational state will of course occur, but it is essential that these later developments be related without contradiction to, and even built up from, the initial positions taken by the several participants. It would seem that an individual can more easily make a choice as to what line of treatment to demand from and extend to the others present at the beginning of an encounter than he can alter the line of treatment being pursued once the interaction is underway. . . .

Given the fact that the individual effectively projects a definition of the situation when he enters the presence of others, we can assume that events may occur within the interaction that contradict, discredit, or otherwise throw doubt on this projection. When these disruptive events occur, the interaction itself may come to a confused and embarrassed halt. Some of the assumptions on which the responses of the participants had been predicated become untenable, and the participants find themselves lodged in an interaction for which the situation has been wrongly defined and is now no longer defined. At such moments, the individual whose presentation has been discredited may feel ashamed while the others present may feel hostile, and all the participants may come to feel ill at ease, nonplussed, out of countenance, embarrassed, experiencing the kind of anomie generated when the minute social system of face-to-face interaction breaks down.

In stressing the fact that the initial definition of the situation projected by an individual tends to provide a plan for the cooperative activity that follows—in stressing this action point of view—we must not overlook the crucial fact that any projected definition of the situation also has a distinctive moral character. It is this moral character of projections that will chiefly concern us in this report. Society is organized on the principle that any individual who possesses certain social characteristics has a moral right to expect that others will value and treat him in an appropriate way. Connected with this principle is a second, namely that an individual who implicitly or explicitly signifies that he has certain social characteristics ought, in fact, to be what he claims he is. In consequence, when an individual projects a definition of the situation and thereby makes an implicit or explicit claim to be a person of a particular kind, he automatically exerts a moral demand on the others, obliging them to value and treat him in the manner that persons of his kind have a right to expect. He also implicitly forgoes all claims to be things he does not appear to be[5] and hence forgoes the treatment that would be appropriate for such individuals. The others find, then, that the individual has informed them as to what *is*, and as to what they *ought* to see as the "is."

One cannot judge the importance of definitional disruptions by the frequency with which they occur, for apparently they would occur more frequently were not constant precautions taken. We find that preventive practices are constantly employed to avoid these embarrassments, and that corrective practices are constantly employed to compensate for discrediting occurrences that have not been successfully avoided. When the individual employs these strategies and tactics to protect his own projections, we may refer to them as "defensive practices"; when a participant employs them to save the definition of the situation projected by another, we speak of "protective practices" or "tact." Together, defensive and protective practices comprise the techniques employed to safeguard the impression fostered by an individual during his presence before others. It should be added that although we may be ready to see that no fostered impression would survive if defensive practices were not employed, we are less ready perhaps to see that few impressions could survive if those who received the impression did not exert tact in their reception of it.

In addition to the fact that precautions are taken to prevent disruption of projected definitions, we may also note that an intense interest in these disruptions comes to play a significant role in the social life of the group. Practical jokes and social games are played in which embarrassments that are to be taken unseriously are purposely engineered.[6] Fantasies are created in which devastating exposures occur. Anecdotes from the past—real, embroidered, or fictitious—are told and retold, detailing disruptions that occurred, almost occurred, or occurred and were admirably resolved. There seems to be no grouping that does not have a ready supply of these games, reveries, and cautionary tales to be used as a source of humor, a catharsis for anxieties, and a sanction for inducing individuals to be modest in their claims and reasonable in their projected expectations. The individual may tell himself through dreams of getting into impossible positions. Families tell of the time a guest got his dates mixed and arrived when neither the house nor anyone in it was ready for him. Journalists tell of times when an all-too-meaningful misprint occurred, and the paper's assumption of objectivity or decorum was humorously discredited. Public servants tell of times a client ridiculously misunderstood form instructions, giving answers that implied an unanticipated and bizarre definition of the situation.[7] Seamen, whose home away from home is rigorously he-man, tell stories of coming back home and inadvertently asking mother to "pass the fucking butter."[8] Diplomats tell of the time a near-sighted queen asked a republican ambassador about the health of his king.[9]

To summarize, then, I assume that when an individual appears before others, he will have many motives for trying to control the impression they receive of the situation. This report is concerned with some of the common techniques that persons employ to sustain such impressions and with some of the common contingencies associated with the employment of these techniques. The specific content of any activity presented by the individual participant, or the role it plays in the interdependent activities of an ongoing social system, will not be at issue; I shall be concerned only with the participant's dramaturgical problems of presenting the activity before others. The issues dealt with by stagecraft and stage management are sometimes trivial, but they are quite general; they seem to occur everywhere in social life, providing a clear-cut dimension for formal sociological analysis.

NOTES

1. Gustav Ichheiser, "Misunderstandings in Human Relations," Supplement to *The American Journal of Sociology*, LV (September, 1949), pp. 6–7.
2. Here I owe much to an unpublished paper by Tom Burns of the University of Edinburgh. He presents the argument that in all interaction a basic underlying theme is the desire of each participant to guide and control the responses made by the others present. A similar argument has been advanced by Jay Haley in a recent unpublished paper, but in regard to a special kind of control, that having to do with defining the nature of the relationship of those involved in the interaction.
3. Willard Waller, "The Rating and Date Complex," *American Sociological Review*, II, p. 730.
4. An interaction can be purposely set up as a time and place for voicing differences in opinion, but in such cases, participants must be careful to agree not to disagree on the proper tone of voice, vocabulary, and degree of seriousness in which all arguments are to be phrased, and on the mutual respect that disagreeing participants must carefully continue to express toward one another. The debaters' or an academic definition of the situation may also be invoked suddenly and judiciously as a way of translating a serious conflict of views into one that can be handled within a framework acceptable to all present.
5. This role of the witness in limiting what it is the individual can be has been stressed by Existentialists, who see it as a basic threat to individual freedom. See Jean Paul Sartre, *Being and Nothingness*, trans. by Hazel E. Barnes (New York: Philosophical Library, 1956), pp. 365 *ff.*
6. E. Goffman, "Communication Conduct in an Island Community," (unpublished Ph.D. dissertation, Department of Sociology, University of Chicago, 1953).
7. Peter Blau, "Dynamics of Bureaucracy" (Ph.D. dissertation, Department of Sociology, Columbia University, forthcoming, University of Chicago Press), pp. 127–129.
8. Walter M. Beattie, Jr., "The Merchant Seaman" (unpublished M.A. report, Department of Sociology, University of Chicago, 1950), p. 35.
9. Sir Frederick Ponsonby, *Recollections of Three Reigns* (New York: Dutton, 1952), p. 46.

◆ 10 ◆

Social Identity

Richard Jenkins

All human identities are in some sense—and usually a stronger rather than a weaker sense—social identities. It cannot be otherwise. . . .

The title Jenkins gives this chapter in his book is "Knowing Who We Are." How do we know who we are? How do we know who other people are? Why is it important? It all relates to our everyday social interaction, the negotiation of who we are as we relate to one another in our social life.

It is a cold Friday night, and windy. You are dressed for dancing, not the weather. Finally, you reach the head of the queue outside the night club. The bouncer—although nowadays they prefer to be called doormen—raises his arm and lets your friend in. He takes one look at you and demands proof of your age. All you have in your pockets is money. That isn't enough.

You telephone the order line of a clothing catalog to buy a new jacket. The young man who answers asks for your name, address, credit card number and expiration date, your customer reference number if you have one; all in order to establish your status as someone to whom, in the absence of a face-to-face encounter, goods can be dispatched in confidence. And also, of course, to make sure that you're on the mailing list.

The immigration official asks you for your passport. She looks at your nationality, at where you were born. Your name. She checks your visa. These indicate your legitimacy as a traveler, your desirability as an entrant. She looks at the photograph, she looks at you. She asks you the purpose of your visit. She stamps the passport and wishes you a pleasant stay. Already she is looking over your shoulder at the person behind you.

On a train, the stranger in the opposite seat excuses herself. She has noticed you reading last week's newspaper from a small town several hundred miles to the east. You explain that your mother posts it to you so that you can keep up with the news from home. She recognized the newspaper because her husband is from your home town. You, it turns out, were at school with her brother-in-law. Before leaving the train she gives you her telephone number.

In everyday situations such as these, one's identity is called into question and established (or not). But the presentation or negotiation of identity is not always so ordinary or trivial: It can shake the foundations of our lives. Imagine, for example, the morning of your sixty-fifth birthday. With it, as well as birthday cards, will come retirement, a pension, a concessionary public transport pass, special rates every Tuesday at the hairdresser. Beyond that again, in the promise of free medical prescriptions and the beckoning Day Centre, hover the shades of infirmity, of dependence, of disability. Although it will be the same face you see in the bathroom mirror, you

From Chapter 1 of *Social Identity*, by Richard Jenkins. London: Routledge, 1996.

will no longer be quite the person you were yesterday. Nor can you ever be again.

Sometimes, a changed or strange situation makes the difference. An unfamiliar neighborhood, an ethnically divided city: a casual encounter can transform one's taken-for-granted identity into a dangerous liability. Something as simple as the "wrong" accent or an "ethnic" surname on your driving license can become a warrant for violence, even murder. Whether the ethnic identification is "correct" or not—in your eyes—may make no difference. Identity is often in the eye of the beholder.

Or take a different time scale, and another kind of transformation. What changes and negotiations are required by "coming out," to assume a public identification as a gay man or a lesbian? What kind of response from others is the "right" response? Which others matter? And what does such a process represent? The construction of a new identity, or the revelation of an authentic and primordial self?

Social identity is also important on a wider stage than the encounters or thresholds of individual lives. Imagine a contested border region. It might be anywhere in the world. There are different ways to settle the issue: warfare, a referendum, international arbitration. Whatever the means adopted, the outcome has implications for the identities of people on both sides. And it may not be accepted by those who find their new national identity uncongenial. Similarly, the referenda about the European Union in the early 1990s in Scandinavia were as much about the preservation and transformation of identity as anything else.

To return to gay and lesbian identity, mass public occasions such as Gay Pride in London or the Sydney Mardi Gras are affirmations that being gay or being lesbian are collective identifications. For individual participants, these occasions may (or, indeed, may not) affirm their own particular sexual identities, but these gatherings are collective rituals of identification and political mobilization before they are anything else.

These scenarios, different as they are, exemplify social identity in everyday life. It is the most mundane of things, and it can be the most extraordinary. But what does it mean to say that these situations all involve social identity? What do they have in common? How do we know who

we are, and how do others identify us? How does our sense of ourselves as unique individuals square with the realization that, always and everywhere, we share aspects of our identity with many others? To what extent is it possible to become someone, or something, other than what we now are? Is it possible to "just be myself?". . .

What is identity, and what is social identity? Social identity is a characteristic or property of humans as social beings. The word *identity*, however, embraces a universe of creatures, things, and substances that is wider than the limited category of humanity. As such, its general meanings are worthy of brief attention, to provide a base line from which to begin our consideration of specifically social identity.

Consulting the Oxford English Dictionary yields a Latin root (*identitas*, from *idem*, "the same") and two basic meanings. The first is a concept of absolute sameness: "this is identical to that." The second is a concept of distinctiveness that presumes consistency or continuity over time. Approaching the idea of sameness from two different angles, the notion of identity simultaneously establishes two possible relations of comparison between persons or things: *similarity* on the one hand, and *difference* on the other.

Exploring the matter further, the verb *to identify* is a necessary accompaniment of identity: There is something active about the word that cannot be ignored. Identity is not "just there," it must always be established. This adds two further meanings to our catalog: to classify things or persons, and to associate oneself *with* something or someone else (for example, a friend, a hero, a party, or a philosophy). Each locates identity within the ebb and flow of practice and process; they are both things people do. The latter, in the context of social relations, also implies a degree of reflexivity.

We are now firmly in the realm of social identity. . . . All human identities are in some sense—and usually a stronger rather than a weaker sense—*social* identities. It cannot be otherwise, if only because identity is about meaning, and meaning is not an essential property of words and things. Meanings are always the outcome of agreement or disagreement, always a matter of convention and innovation, always to some extent shared, always to some extent negotiable.

Some contemporary writers about identity treat it as a basic datum that simply "is." This pays insufficient attention to how identity "works" or "is worked," to process and reflexivity, to the social construction of identity in interaction and institutionally. Understanding these processes is central to understanding what social identity is. Identity can in fact only be understood *as* process. As "being" or "becoming." One's social identity—indeed, one's social identities, for who we are is always singular and plural—is never a final or settled matter. Not even death can freeze the picture: There is always the possibility of a *post mortem* revision of identity (and some identities, that of a martyr, for example, can only be achieved beyond the grave).

So, how to define "social identity"? Minimally, the expression refers to the ways in which individuals and collectivities are distinguished in their social relations with other individuals and collectivities. It is the systematic establishment and signification, between individuals, between collectivities, and between individuals and collectivities, of relationships of similarity and difference. Taken—as they can only be—together, similarity and difference are the dynamic principles of identity, the heart of social life:

> ...The practical significance of men for one another... is determined by both similarities and differences among them. Similarity as fact or tendency is no less important than difference. In the most varied forms, both are the great principles of all internal and external development. In fact, the cultural history of mankind can be conceived as the history of the struggles and conciliatory attempts between the two.
>
> (Simmel 1950: 30)

Social identity is a game of "playing the *vis-à-vis*" (Boon 1982: 26). Social identity is our understanding of who we are and of who other people are, and, reciprocally, other people's understanding of themselves and of others (which includes us). Social identity, is, therefore, no more essential than meaning; it too is the product of agreement and disagreement, it too is negotiable.

Human social life is unimaginable without some means of knowing who others are and some sense of who we are. Because we cannot rely on our sense of smell or our animal non-verbals (although these are not insignificant in the negotiation of identity during encounters), one of the first things we do on meeting a stranger is attempt to locate them on our social maps, to identify them. And not always successfully: "Mistaken identity" is a common motif of interaction. Someone we thought was Ms. A in fact turns out to be Mrs. Q, or we take someone for French when they are Belgian.

All kinds of people other than social scientists have cause to reflect on social identity during their everyday lives. A common theme in everyday discourse, for example, is lost or confused identity, about people not knowing "who they are," about a "crisis of identity." Sometimes people talk about "social identity"; sometimes they simply talk about "identity." More often than not, however, men and women going about the business of their daily lives are concerned with *specific* social identities. We talk, for example, about whether people are born gay or become gay as a result of the way in which they were brought up. About what it means to be "grown up." About what the difference is between Canadians and Americans. We observe the family who has just moved in around the corner and shake our heads: What can you expect? They come from the wrong part of town. We watch the television news and jump to all kinds of conclusions about current events on the basis of identifications such as "Muslim," "fundamentalist Christian," or whatever.

Social change is often accompanied by rhetoric about "identity under threat." Take, for example, the public debate in the United Kingdom about the European Union. While the regulations governing sausage manufacture are presented as a threat to the "British way of life," the prospect of monetary union in Europe conjures up centuries of strife with our continental neighbors and is interpreted as another attempt to undermine British national identity. Recent debates within the Scandinavian countries about the European Union have thrown a similar barrage of concerns, albeit triggered by different issues.

Whether in the abstract or the concrete, with reference to ourselves or to others, in personal depth or during superficial casual chat, with reference to individuality, nationality, social class, gender or age (etcetera...), it seems that we cannot do without some concepts with which to think about social identity, with which to query and confirm who we are and who others are. This is probably true no matter the language or culture; it has probably always been true. Without frameworks for delineating social identity and identities, I would be the same as you and neither of us could relate to the other meaningfully or consistently. Without social identity, there is, in fact, no society.

REFERENCES

Boon, J. A. 1982. *Other Tribes, Other Scribes: Symbolic Anthropology in the Comparative Study of Cultures, Histories, Religions and Texts.* Cambridge: Cambridge University Press.

Simmel, G. 1950. *The Sociology of Georg Simmel*, ed. K. H. Wolff. New York: Free Press.

◆ 11 ◆

The Importance of Primary Groups

Dexter C. Dunphy

Ideology had only an indirect effect on fighting effectiveness in both the U.S. and the German armies. The crucial variable was the degree of preservation of the cohesive primary unit.

Humans exist in a host of groups. One type of group is called the primary group, originally described by Charles Cooley. This article describes the meaning and importance of primary groups. It examines one example: the military unit.

Over our lifetime, we spend much of our time in small groups. We are born into a family. As we grow older, we venture out from our family into the play groups of childhood and later into the cliques and crowds of adolescence. We marry and establish a new family group of our own and participate in the work groups and leisure groups of adulthood. Out of the associations formed in these groups, we fashion and have fashioned in us a changing and developing conception of self; we learn ways of behaving appropriate to varied social situations, and we acquire a set of social values and attitudes that allow us to respond to the structure and pressures of the larger society about us. . . .

For reasons that we will examine here, social scientists have devoted relatively little effort to a close and detailed study of such groups, even though these groups play a vital part in creating human personality and maintaining the integration of the secondary structures of society. We use the term *primary group* to describe groups of this kind. The term was first introduced into social science by Charles Horton Cooley in 1909.

At that time, Cooley wrote in his book *Social Organization:*

> By primary groups, I mean those characterized by intimate face-to-face association and cooperation. They are primary in several senses, but chiefly in that they are fundamental in forming the social nature and ideas of the individual. The result of intimate association, psychologically, is a certain fusion of individualities in a common whole, so that one's very self, for many purposes at least, is the common life and purpose of the group. Perhaps the simplest way of describing this wholeness is by saying that it is a "we," it involves the sort of sympathy and mutual identification for which "we" is the natural expression.[1]

In Cooley's definition, the word *primary* is used mainly in reference to the fundamental effect such groups have on the formation of the individual personalities of their members. Cooley makes this even clearer when he goes on to state: "The view here maintained is that human nature is not something existing separately in the individual, but a *group-nature* or *primary phase of society*, a relatively simple and general condition of the social mind."[2] Thus the term *primary* refers to the fact that such groups are the earliest kind of human association experienced by the maturing individual and also that the primary, or basic, human qualities are learned in them. Cooley's definition also makes it clear that the effect of such groups on the personalities of members derives from the internalization by them of a psychological representation or image of the group, and that such an identification is indicated by a strong emotional involvement with the group and its members.

In *Introductory Sociology*, written with Angell and Carr, Cooley specified five basic characteristics of primary groups:

- Face-to-face association
- The unspecialized character of the association
- Relative permanence
- The small number of persons involved
- The relative intimacy prevailing among the participants[3]

Cooley himself did not designate larger, more formally organized groups as *secondary groups* but the latter term is now widely used and the two kinds of groups are frequently contrasted.

Later writers dealing specifically with the concept have attempted to modify it in various ways. For instance, Shils gave explicit and thoughtful attention to Cooley's criteria in his important work on the effects of primary group membership in the army in World War II[4] and in his more recent review of primary group research.[5] Shils argues that the existence of an implicit set of group norms is another necessary aspect of the primary group:

> By "primary group" we mean a group characterized by a high degree of solidarity, informality in the code of rules that regulate the behavior of its members, and autonomy in the creation of these rules.[6]

THE STUDY OF PRIMARY GROUPS

Thus, although the primary group is a "small group" in the sense in which that term is used in the social sciences, it is a particular kind of small group. Small groups vary all the way from *ad hoc* collections of students assembled for a single experimental hour to long-term emotionally involving, highly institutionalized groups such as families. It is the latter rather than the former kind of small group to which the term *primary group* refers.

However, the concept of a primary group is better thought of as a variable than as categorical. A group is primary insofar as it is based on and sustains spontaneous participation, particularly emotional involvement and expression. It also provides intrinsic personal satisfaction, that is, personal relationships in the primary group are considered valuable in themselves and not only as means to other ends. This element of intrinsic value is often lacking in formal secondary relations that are explicitly designed to be instrumental.

We define a primary group therefore as *a small group that persists long enough to develop strong emotional attachments between members, at least a set of rudimentary, functionally differentiated roles, and a subculture of its own that includes both an image of the group as an entity and an informal normative system that controls group-relevant action of members.* For Cooley, the important general categories of such groups in our society were "groups of the family, the playground, and the neighborhood."[7] We feel it is necessary to include other kinds of groups that meet our definition but that Cooley did not recognize. As we see it, the following general classes of groups are properly referred to as primary groups:

- Families.
- Free association peer groups of childhood, adolescence, and adulthood. This category would include delinquent gangs and some small, cohesive political elites ("cabals").
- Informal groups existing in organizational settings such as classroom groups, factory work groups, small military units, and "house churches."
- Resocialization groups such as therapy groups, rehabilitation groups, and self-analytic groups. . . .

AN EXAMPLE: PRIMARY GROUPS IN MILITARY ORGANIZATION

There is a . . . tradition of organizational analysis that has centered about the problem of maintaining the morale and combat effectiveness of military personnel in armies. Morale has always been a central issue in military organizations, and military organizations have often been organized in small units. However, it was not until World War II that the crucial role of primary groups in maintaining military morale and effectiveness was seriously studied.

A number of excellent studies,[8] appearing since World War II, present information on the role of primary groups in military organizations in both the allied and German armies. However, we shall focus on Shils and Janowitz's study[9] of the Wehrmacht because their conclusions are most succinctly stated and are representative of those found in other studies.

Shils and Janowitz set out to explain the reasons why German army units continued fighting even after central command disintegrated, supplies ceased, and it was obvious that German capitulation was inevitable. During this time, there was remarkably little desertion or active surrender by individuals or groups. It had been suggested that the morale and resistance of the German forces could be attributed to the effectiveness of the Nazi propaganda machine. Shils and Janowitz reviewed the extensive studies made by the Intelligence Section of the Psychological Warfare Division of SHAEF and came to conclusions that challenge this assumption.

They stated their basic hypotheses, which are confirmed by their analysis, as follows:

1. It appears that a soldier's ability to resist is a function of the capacity of his immediate primary group (his squad or section) to avoid social disintegration. When the individual's immediate group, and its supporting formations, met his basic organic needs, offered him affection and esteem from both officers and comrades, supplied him with a sense of power, and adequately regulated his relations with authority, the element of self-concern in battle, which would lead to disruption of the effective functioning of his primary group, was minimized.
2. The capacity of the primary group to resist disintegration was dependent on the acceptance of political, ideological, and cultural symbols (all secondary symbols) only to the extent that these secondary symbols became directly associated with primary gratifications.
3. Once disruption of primary group life resulted through separation, breaks in communications, loss of leadership, depletion of personnel, or major and prolonged breaks in the supply of food and medical care, such an ascendancy of preoccupation with physical survival developed that there was very little "last ditch" resistance.
4. Finally, as long as the primary group structure of the component units of the Wehrmacht persisted, attempts by the Allies to cause disaffection by the invocation of secondary and political symbols (e.g., about the ethical wrongness of the Nationalist Socialist system) were mainly unsuccessful. By contrast, where Allied propaganda dealt with primary and personal values, particularly physical survival, it was more likely to be effective.[10]

From the point of view of the conscripted soldier, this had the following meaning:

For the ordinary German soldier, the decisive fact was that he was a member of a squad or section that maintained its structural integrity and that coincided roughly with the *social* unit that satisfied some of his major primary needs. He was likely to go on fighting, provided he had the necessary weapons, as long as the group possessed leadership with which he could identify himself, and as long as he gave affection to and received affection from the other members of his squad and platoon. In other words, as long as he felt himself to be a member of his primary group and therefore bound by the expectations and demands of its other members, his soldierly achievement was likely to be good.[11]

The authors pointed out that the German general staff instituted a replacement system that maintained the integrity of the primary groups in the army. Units that had undergone a victory were maintained as units as far as possible and when replacements were necessary, the entire personnel of a division would be withdrawn from the front as a unit. Replacements were made while the unit was out of the front line so that a unit was given time to assimilate new members before going into battle again.

Janowitz and Little also suggest[12] that the existence of cohesive primary groups does not necessarily contribute to the goals of the military organization. If this is to happen, the primary group must actively espouse the goals of the larger organization of which it is a part. Essentially the same conclusion was reached by Speien. He noted that studies of U.S. soldiers during World War II showed that they had little knowledge of and little verbalized commitment to the war.[13] He then raised the question: Why, if this were true, did they fight so well? He concluded, on reviewing the evidence available, that this was because primary group relations sustained morale and supported a generalized commitment to the military and its goals. Janowitz and Little illustrate this with the case of segregated Negro units in World War II, which were very cohesive but developed "defensive norms" that broke with the general commitment because these groups interpreted military authority as depreciating their personal dignity. Shils has also argued along the same lines, stating that "primary group solidarity functions in the corporate body to strengthen the motivation for the fulfillment of substantive prescriptions or sense of obligation. . . . It cannot be said that goals are set by membership in the primary group but only that efforts to achieve the legitimate, formally prescribed goals may be strengthened by such membership."[14]

A key position in terms of the integration of primary group goals and organizational goals is that of the formal leader of the unit, for example, the platoon leader. The leader occupies the classical position of middle man similar to the role of foreman of a work team in industry. He must be close enough to the men for them to identify with him and yet, at the same time, he must also represent the demands of higher authority. Shils

has stressed the enlisted man's desire for a protective personal relationship with an authority figure in this kind of position, and emphasized the effectiveness of "an exemplary and protective leader" in raising morale in U.S. military units.[15]

Shils and Janowitz give evidence that indicates that the primary group in the army acts as a family surrogate, and that a man's real family loyalties were one of the most substantial threats to the solidarity of the army unit.[16] The captured German soldiers themselves identified with the family-like nature of their units with statements like: "We were a big happy family." In addition, it became clear that soldiers were most likely to desert while on furlough, or after receiving distressing news from their families. Similarly, the members of units were most likely to discuss surrendering among themselves after concretely recalling family experiences. Because of these factors, families of soldiers were instructed to avoid mentioning family deprivations in letters to the front and, as Allied bombing of the civilian population became more severe, personal messages to the front were censored to prevent distressing family news reaching the men. Thus the soldier was able to transfer his primary loyalties to his unit while physically with the unit, providing that he felt secure about his family. While actually with his family, his loyalties to them tended to be reactivated at the expense of those to his military unit. Interestingly enough, it was those men who had the most normal identification pattern in the family who were able to identify most firmly with the military unit. This same point is also supported by evidence presented by Grinker and Spiegal.[17] It is the person with a faulty family identification pattern who is most likely to be a deviant member of a military unit and a deserter to the other side in a stress situation.

A limiting variable influencing the cohesiveness in military organizations, as in factories, is the technology with which the military unit is working. Different weapons systems require different kinds of team relationships. A submarine, for example, demands continued close contact among the crew over lengthy periods of time and virtually cuts off outside social contact. An airplane is similar but returns more quickly to base and so allows more frequent contact with non-crew members. By contrast, the members of a rifle squad in battle may readily lose contact with one another and so experience a sense of isolation from the expectations and support of other group members.

Evidence to clinch the importance of primary group cohesion as a basis for morale and effectiveness comes from those German units whose integrity was not established or adequately maintained. As the war progressed, it became increasingly difficult to maintain the integrity of primary groups. The survivors of groups suffering severe casualties were regrouped and new units of recruits were thrust directly into battle without the opportunity of solidifying primary group ties. It was in units of these kinds that desertions and active surrender occurred. In these situations, the individual seemed to readily remove his emotional ties and identifications from the group and refocus them on himself. The individual regressed to a narcissistic state and became concerned with saving his own skin — marked contrast to situations in which men in intact primary groups would fight to the bitter end.

Shils has argued that the primary group reduces a soldier's fear of death and injury by counterposing against such fear a need for approval by his comrades.[18] As evidence, he quoted the fact that replacements to U.S. combat units were more likely to say "prayer helps a lot" whereas veterans looked to concrete support from their comrades.

Thus ideology had only an indirect effect on fighting effectiveness in both the U.S. and the German armies. The crucial variable was the degree of preservation of the cohesive primary unit. The soldier fights to protect the primary group and to live up to the expectations of his fellow group members. The army in battle is the prototype of the organization under stress, and military studies illustrate most vividly the crucial role of the primary group in preserving organizational cohesiveness and goal directedness. . . .

NOTES

1. Cooley, Charles H. 1909. *Social Organization: A Study of the Larger Mind.* New York: Scribners, p. 23.
2. Ibid., p. 29.
3. Cooley, Charles H., Robert C. Angell, and Lowell J. Carr. 1933. *Introductory Sociology.* New York: Scribners, p. 53.
4. Shils, Edward. 1950. "Primary Groups in the American Army" in Robert K. Merton and Paul F. Lazarsfeld, Eds., *Continuities in Social Research.* Glencoe, IL: Free Press, pp. 16–25.
5. Shils, Edward. 1952. "The Study of the Primary Group" in Daniel Lerner and Harold Lasswell, *The Policy Sciences.* Stanford, CA: Stanford University Press, pp. 44–69.
6. Ibid., p. 44.
7. Cooley, Charles H. *Introductory Sociology*, p. 32.
8. Shils, Edward S. and Morris Janowitz, "Cohesion and Disintegration in the Wehrmacht in World War II," *Public Opinion Quarterly,* Vol. 12 (Summer 1948), (reprinted by permission of Elsevier Science Publishing Co., Inc. Copyright © 1948 by the Trustees of Columbia University). Samuel A. Stouffer. et al., eds., *The American Soldier,* vols. 1 and 2 (Princeton, NJ: Princeton University Press, 1949); Morris Janowitz and Roger Little, *Sociology and the Military Establishment,* rev. ed. (New York: Russell Sage Foundation, 1965), particularly Chap. 4, "Primary Groups and Military Effectiveness," pp. 77–99; Robert K. Merton and Paul L. Lazarsfeld, eds., *Continuities in Social Research: Studies in the Scope and Method of the American Soldier* (Glencoe, IL: Free Press, 1950); Roy R. Grinker and John P. Spiegal, *Men Under Stress* (Philadelphia: Blakiston, 1945).
9. Shils and Janowitz. "Cohesion and Disintegration in the Wehrmacht," pp. 280–315.
10. Ibid., pp. 281–2.
11. Ibid., p. 284.
12. Janowitz and Little, *Sociology and the Military Establishment,* p. 78.
13. Speien in *Continuities in Social Research.*
14. Shils in *Continuities in Social Research,* op. cit., p. 22.
15. Ibid.
16. Shils and Janowitz, "Cohesion and Disintegration in the Wehrmacht."
17. Grinker and Spiegal, *Men Under Stress,* Chap. 2.
18. Shils in *Continuities in Social Research.*

◆ 12 ◆

Collective Trauma at Buffalo Creek

Kai Erikson

Most of the traumatic symptoms experienced by the Buffalo Creek survivors are a reaction to the loss of communality as well as a reaction to the disaster itself: The fear, apathy, and demoralization one encounters along the entire length of the hollow are derived from the shock of being ripped out of a meaningful community setting as well as the shock of meeting that cruel black water. The line between the two phenomena is difficult to draw. But it seems clear that much of the agony experienced on Buffalo Creek is related to the fact that the hollow is quiet, devastated, without much in the way of a nourishing community life.

Humans are social beings. Their lives are embedded in social organization. They live their lives in groups, communities, and societies. Organization is something we take for granted. Really, how important is it? Sometimes it is easiest to understand something when it is no longer there for us. Here is a tragic episode in the history of West Virginia, in which several communities were wiped out by a disastrous flood. Kai Erikson studied the people along Buffalo Creek, and described the effects of this tragedy on their lives in his book *Everything in Its Path*, N.Y.: Simon and Schuster, 1976. (The article reprinted here highlights a section from the book.) In the process, Erikson tried to understand what the end to community meant to these people, creating a loss that nothing could correct. How important was their community? Read this and imagine yourself in their place.

History stopped on the day of the flood.

[Editor's Note: The disastrous Buffalo Creek, West Virginia, flood occurred on February 26, 1972. The sudden collapse of the Pittston Company's (the local coal company and absentee landlord's) massive refuse pile dam unleashed 132 million gallons of water and coal waste materials on the unsuspecting residents of Buffalo Creek. The rampaging wave of water and sludge traveled down the creek in waves of between twenty and thirty feet and at speeds sometimes approaching thirty miles per hour. Buffalo Creek's sixteen small towns were devastated by the deluge, over 125 people were killed, and over four thousand survivors were left homeless.]

Some 615 survivors of the Buffalo Creek flood were examined by psychiatrists one and one-half years after the event, and 570 of them, a grim 93 percent, were found to be suffering from an identifiable emotional disturbance. A skeptical neighbor from another of the behavioral sciences may want to make allowance for the fact that psychiatrists looking for mental disorder are more than apt to find it; but even so, the sheer volume of pathology is horrifying.

The medical names for the conditions observed are depression, anxiety, phobia, emotional liability, hypochondria, apathy; and the broader syndrome into which these various symptoms naturally fall is post-traumatic neurosis, or, in a few cases, post-traumatic psychosis. But the nearest expressions in everyday English would be something like confusion, despair, and hopelessness.

Most of the survivors responded to the disaster with a deep sense of loss—a nameless feeling that something had gone grotesquely awry in the order of things, that their minds and spirits had been bruised beyond repair, that they would never again be able to find coherence, that the world as they knew it had come to an end. Now these feelings, of course, were experienced as a generalized, pervading sense of gloom, and the men and women of the hollow did not try to catalog the various strains that contributed to it. But there are recognizable themes in the stories they tell that give us some idea of what the sources of their pain might be.

ON BEING NUMBED

Almost everybody who survived the disaster did so by the thinnest of margins; and the closeness of their escapes, combined with the relentless savagery of the water, left them feeling numbed and depleted—almost as if the mad rush to safety had consumed most of their energy and the ferocity of the waves passing below them had somehow drawn off what reserves were left.

No sooner had they escaped, however, then people began to feel that they were unable to move, caught in a sluggish bank of fog, held back—as in a dream—by forces that slackened the muscles and paralyzed the will. A number of people remember having gone limp or having lost control of their limbs. Quite a few others compared their reactions to a dream state. And some simply went blank in mind as well as limp in body, as if yielding to the enormity of what was happening.

This process of retreating into a limp slump has been noted again and again in disaster research. But on Buffalo Creek, the process appears to have been somewhat exaggerated by the extraordinary power of the flood and by the helpless state in which it left its victims. To be drained of energy, to be emptied of motive and self, is to be on the verge of death itself—and that is how many of the survivors viewed their own condition later.

FACES OF DEATH

Virtually everyone on Buffalo Creek had a very close encounter with death, either because they felt doomed themselves or because they lost relatives and friends or because they came into contact with dead bodies. The upper half of the valley, where most of the serious destruction took place, was strewn with the signs of a terrible tragedy. But people who lived downstream were not spared the agony of this scene either, for the current carried it to them. So death seemed to be everywhere, overhead, underfoot, crouched in every pile of wreckage, waiting to be recognized. . . .

SURVIVAL AND GUILT

Where one finds death on so large a scale, one also finds guilt. It is one of the ironies of human life that individuals are likely to regret their own survival when others around them are killed in what seems like a meaningless and capricious way, in part because they cannot understand by what logic they came to be spared. People who sense the hand of God in it have many hard questions to ponder, and none of them are very comforting. . . .

THE FURNITURE OF SELF

. . . It is important to remember that the people of the creek had invested a great deal of time and money and pride in the process of converting the old company shacks into comfortable new dwellings. The flood cleaned out some ragged housing as it made its way down the hollow—more than the residents like to remember—but the average home had been renovated in a hundred ways. A refurbished house on Buffalo Creek served as the emblem of one's rise out of poverty. It was a measure of security, an extension of self, a source of identity. It was not only the outer shell in which one lived out one's life, but a major feature of that life.

Moreover, people lost possessions of considerable meaning to them—not only trucks and cars and appliances with an established trade-in value but mementos of no measurable worth that were highly cherished. Objects such as family Bibles or photographs, a father's favorite gun or a mother's proudest embroidery, had a place in the household almost like holy relics, and their loss was deeply mourned. They were a link with the past, and they were a link with the future.

LOSS OF FAITH IN ORDER

The disaster on Buffalo Creek had the effect of reducing people's already brittle confidence in the natural and especially in the social order. . . .

The Buffalo Creek survivors, without saying so directly, have quite clearly lost much of their confidence in the workings of nature. They are troubled about the condition of the mountains, now scraped out inside and slashed with strip mine benches; they are troubled about the water poised over their heads in other dams both real and imaginary; they are troubled about tornadoes and avalanches, floods and rock slides, earthquakes and explosions; and they are troubled about the natural capacity of their bodies and spirits to handle all the emergencies of life.

Moreover, the people of Buffalo Creek have lost their confidence in the coal company responsible for the dam. This point may be difficult to explain, because most readers will have no difficulty at all understanding why they might resent the company. But it was part of the life of the creek. It employed hundreds of people and was represented locally by officials who lived in the area, were known by first names, and were merged into the community as individual persons. The residents knew that the company was a giant corporation with headquarters in New York, but they continued to visualize it as a kind of manorial presence at the head of the hollow that

was implicated somehow in the affairs of the community. It was a proprietor, a patron—and it had obligations to fulfill.

The company violated those obligations, first by building an unworthy dam, and second by reacting to the disaster in the manner of a remote bureaucracy with holdings to protect rather than in the manner of a concerned patron with constituents to care for. The heart of the company turned out to be located a thousand miles away, and its first reflex was to treat the survivors—many of them employees with decades of loyal service—as potential adversaries in a court action.

The people who speak for the company would not come out into the light, would not take the risk of establishing eye contact, would not expose themselves even for the purposes of finding out how the residents of the hollow were faring; and if this situation provoked a gentle annoyance in some survivors, it provoked a deep indignation in others. So the prevailing feeling is one of bitterness, a bitterness so sharp that it seems to speak of betrayal as well as of personal injury.

UNIQUENESS OF BUFFALO CREEK

So these were some of the effects of the individual trauma—that first numbing moment of pain and shock and helplessness. A few paragraphs of description can scarcely begin to convey what the tragedy must have felt like to the survivors or how it has influenced their lives, but the themes noted here correspond closely to ones noted in reports of other disasters; to that extent at least, what happened on Buffalo Creek is similar to all those other floods and bombings and hurricanes and earthquakes that interrupt the flow of human life so often.

But there are differences, too. Two years after the flood, Buffalo Creek was almost as desolate as it had been the day following—the grief as intense, the fear as strong, the anxiety as sharp, the despair as dark. People still looked out at the world with vacant eyes and drifted from one place to another with dulled and tentative movements. They rarely smiled and rarely played. They were not sure how to relate to one another. They were unsettled and deeply hurt.

Under normal circumstances, one would expect the survivors of such a disaster to convalesce gradually as the passage of time acted to dim old memories and generate new hopes. It is a standard article of psychiatric wisdom that the symptoms of trauma ought to disappear over time, and when they do not—as was generally the case on Buffalo Creek—a peculiar strain of logic is likely to follow. If one has not recovered from the effects of trauma within a reasonable span of time, or so the theory goes, it follows that the symptoms themselves must have been the result of a mental disorder predating the event itself.

Unless we are ready to entertain the possibility that virtually all the people on Buffalo Creek suffered from a palpable emotional disorder on the morning of February 26, 1972, we will have to look elsewhere for a way to explain their distress; and my argument is that a second trauma, a *collective trauma*, followed closely on the first, immobilizing recovery efforts and bringing a number of other problems into focus.

LOSS OF COMMUNALITY

The people of Buffalo Creek were wrenched out of their communities and torn away from the very human surround in which they had been so deeply enmeshed. Much of the drama is drained away when we begin to talk of such things, partly because the loss of communality seems a step removed from the vivid terror of the disaster itself and partly because the people of the hollow, so richly articulate when describing the flood and their reaction to it, do not really know how to express what their separation from the familiar tissues of home has meant to them. The closeness of communal ties is experienced on Buffalo Creek as a part of the natural order of things, and residents are no more aware of that presence than fish are aware of the water they swim in. It is simply there, the envelope in which they live, and it is taken entirely for granted.

Communality on Buffalo Creek can best be described as a state of mind shared among a particular gathering of people; and this state of mind, by definition, does not lend itself to sociological abstraction. It does not have a name or a cluster of distinguishing properties. It is a quiet set of understandings that become absorbed into the atmosphere and are thus a part of the natural order. And the key to that network of understanding is a constant readiness to look after one's neighbors—or rather, to know without being asked what needs to be done.

The difficulty is that people invest so much of themselves in that kind of social arrangement that they become absorbed by it, almost captive to it, and the larger collectivity around you becomes an extension of your own personality, an extension of your own flesh. This pattern not only means that you are diminished as a person when that surrounding tissue is stripped away, but that you are no longer able to reclaim as your own the emotional resources invested in it. To "be neighborly" is not a quality you can carry with you into a new situation like negotiable emotional currency: The old community was your niche in the classical ecological sense, and your ability to relate to that niche meaningfully is not a skill easily transferred to another setting. This situation is true whether you move into another community, or whether a new set of neighbors moves in around your old home. . . .

In places like Buffalo Creek, the community in general can be described as the locus for activities that are normally regarded as the exclusive property of individuals. It is the *community* that cushions pain, the *community* that provides a context for intimacy, the *community* that represents morality and serves as the repository for old traditions.

Most of the traumatic symptoms experienced by the Buffalo Creek survivors are a reaction to the loss of communality as well as a reaction to the disaster itself: The fear, apathy, and demoralization one encounters along the entire length of the hollow are derived from the shock of being ripped out of a meaningful community setting as well as the shock of meeting that cruel black water. The line between the two phenomena is difficult to draw. But it seems clear that much of the agony experienced on Buffalo Creek is related to the fact that the hollow is quiet, devastated, without much in the way of a nourishing community life.

MORALE AND MORALITY

The Buffalo Creek survivors must face the post-disaster world in a state of severe demoralization, both in the sense that they have lost much of their individual morale and in the sense that they have lost (or fear they have lost) many of their moral anchors. The lack of morale is reflected in a weary apathy, a feeling that the world has more or less come to an end and that there are no longer any compelling reasons for doing anything. People are drained of energy and conviction in part because the activities that once sustained them on an everyday basis—working, caring, playing—seem to have lost their direction and purpose in the absence of a larger communal setting. They feel that the ground has gone out from under them.

The clinical name for this state of mind, of course, is *depression*; and one can hardly escape the impression that it is, at least in part, a reaction to the ambiguities of post-disaster life in the hollow. Most of the survivors never realized the extent to which they relied on the rest of the community to reflect back a sense of meaning to them, never understood the extent to which they depended on others to supply them with a point of reference. When survivors say they feel "adrift," "displaced," "uprooted," "lost," they mean that they do not seem to belong to anything and that there are no longer any familiar social landmarks to help them fix their position in time and space. They are depressed, yes, but it is a depression born of the feeling that they are suspended pointlessly in the middle of nowhere.

This failure of personal morale is accompanied by a deep suspicion that moral standards are beginning to collapse all over the hollow; and in some ways, at least, it would appear that they are. As so frequently happens in human life, the forms of misbehavior people find cropping up in their midst are exactly those about which they are most sensitive. The use of alcohol, always problematic in mountain society, has evidently increased, and there are rumors spreading throughout the trailer camps that drugs have found their way to the creek. The theft rate has risen too, and this rise has always been viewed in Appalachia as a sure index of social disorganization.

The cruelest cut of all, however, is that once close and devoted families are having trouble staying within the pale they formerly observed so carefully. Adolescent boys and girls appear to be slipping away from parental control and are becoming involved in nameless delinquencies, and there are reports from several of the trailer camps that younger wives and husbands are meeting one another in circumstances that violate all the local codes. A home is a moral sphere as well as a physical dwelling, of course, and it would seem that the boundaries of moral space began to splinter as the walls of physical space were washed down the creek.

Yet the seeming collapse of morality on Buffalo Creek differs in several important respects from the kinds of anomie sociologists think they see elsewhere in modern America. For one thing, those persons who seem to be deviating most emphatically from prevailing community norms are usually the first to judge their own behavior as unacceptable and even obnoxious. Adolescents are eager to admit that they sometimes get into trouble, and those of their elders who drink more than the rules of the hollow normally permit are likely to call themselves "alcoholics" under circumstances that seem remarkably premature to jaded strangers from the urban North. To that extent, the consensus has held: local standards as to what qualifies as deviation remain largely intact, even though a number of people see themselves as drifting away from that norm.

Moreover, there is an interesting incongruity in the reports of immorality one hears throughout the hollow. It would seem that virtually everyone in the trailer camps is now living next to persons of lower moral stature than was the case formerly, and this situation, of and by itself, is a logistical marvel. Where did all those sordid people come from? How could a community of decent souls suddenly generate so much iniquity?

It probably makes sense to suppose that quite a few of the survivors are acting more coarsely now than they did before the disaster. But something else may be going on here, too. The relative strangers who move next door and bring their old life-styles with them may be acting improperly by some objective measure or they may not, but they are always acting in an unfamiliar way—and the fact of the matter may very well be that strangers, even if they come from the same general community, are almost by definition less "moral" than neighbors. They do not fall within the pale of local clemency and so do not qualify for the allowances neighbors make for one another on the grounds that they know the motives involved.

The old community had niches for some forms of deviation, like the role of the town drunk, and ways to absorb others into the larger tissue of communal life. But the disaster washed away the packing around those niches, leaving the occupants exposed to the frowning glances of new neighbors. So the problem has two dimensions. On the one hand, people who had not engaged in any kind of misbehavior before are now, by their own admission, doing so. On the other hand, the unfamiliar manners of a stranger seem to hint darkly of sin all by themselves, and personal habits that once passed as mild eccentricities in the old neighborhood now begin to look like brazen vices in the harsher light of the new. . . .

LOSS OF CONNECTION

It would be stretching a point to imply that the communities strung out along Buffalo Creek were secure nests in which people had found a full measure of satisfaction and warmth, but it is wholly reasonable to insist that they were like the air people breathed—sometimes harsh, sometimes chilly, but always a basic fact of life. For better or worse, the people of the hollow were deeply enmeshed in the fabric of their community; they drew their very being from it. And when the fabric was torn away by the disaster, people found themselves exposed and alone, suddenly dependent on their own personal resources.

And the cruel fact of the matter is that many survivors, when left on their own mettle, proved to have but few resources—not because they lacked the heart or the competence, certainly, but because they had always put their abilities in the service of the larger society and did not know how to recall them for their own purposes. A good part of their personal strength turned out to be the reflected strength of the collectivity—on loan, as it were, from the communal store—and they discovered to their great discomfort that they were not good at making decisions, not good at getting along with others, not good at maintaining themselves as separate persons in the absence of a supportive surround.

Many survivors fear that they are beginning to suffer the kind of stunned disorientation and even madness that can result from prolonged stretches of isolation. One result of this fear is that people tend to draw further and further into themselves and to become even more isolated. This behavior is that of wounded animals who crawl off somewhere to nurse their hurts. It is also the behavior of people who string rough coils of barbed wire around their lonely outposts because they feel they have nothing to offer those who draw near.

So the lonesomeness increases and is reinforced. People have heavy loads of grief to deal with, strong feelings of inadequacy to overcome, blighted lives to restore—and they must do all these things without much in the way of personal resources or self-confidence. Solving problems and making decisions—those are the hard part.

The inability of people to come to terms with their own isolated selves is counterpointed by an inability to relate to others on an interpersonal, one-to-one basis. Human relations along Buffalo Creek took their shape from the expectations pressing in on them from all sides like a firm but invisible mold: They were governed by the customs of the neighborhood, the traditions of the family, the ways of the community. And when the mold was stripped away by the disaster, something began to happen to those relationships. This situation was true of everyday acquaintances, but it was doubly true of marriages. . . .

In places like Buffalo Creek, where attachments between people are seen as a part of the natural scheme of things—inherited by birth or acquired by proximity—the idea of "forming" friendships or "building" relationships seems a little odd. These attachments are not engineered; they simply happen when the communal tone is right. So people are not sure what to do.

One result of these problems is that what remains of the community seems to have lost its most significant quality—the power it generated in people to care for each other in times of need, to console each other in times of distress, to protect each other in times of danger. Looking back, then, it does seem that the general community was stronger than the sum of its parts. When the people of the hollow were sheltered together in the embrace of a secure community, they were capable of extraordinary acts of generosity; but when they tried to relate to one another as individuals, as separate entities, they found that they could no longer mobilize whatever resources are required for caring and nurturing.

Behind this inability to care is a wholly new emotional tone on the creek—a deep distrust even of old neighbors, a fear, in fact, of those very persons on whom one once staked one's life. A disaster like the one that hammered Buffalo Creek makes everything in the world seem unreliable, even other survivors, and that base is a very fragile one on which to build a new community.

NOTE

The conclusions expressed in this article are based on personal interviews with the flood's survivors, legal depositions, psychiatric evaluations, letters from survivors to their attorneys, and answers to mail questionnaires developed and administered by the author. The excerpts have been presented without supporting documentation in the interests of space.

◆ 13 ◆

Jim Jones and the Peoples Temple

Charles Lindholm

Organized as a cooperative community, with Jim Jones as the orienting element, the Peoples Temple offered an alternative to lives of desperation, isolation, and humiliation; a new vision was not only talked about, it was lived. Middle-class whites, as well as impoverished blacks, found in the experience of the Temple something of absolute value. They chose to live in this community, and many of them chose to die rather than forgo it. That this was so is not a testament to the insanity of the Peoples Temple as much as it is an indictment of the ordinary world. . . .

It is easy to forget that in 1978 in a community called Jonestown in Guyana hundreds of people decided to kill themselves because of their strong ties to a community that seemed threatened from the outside world.

There are many explanations given for this, but Charles Lindholm presents an insightful one highly consistent with a sociological view. His explanation is the combination of a people seeking meaning in community and a charismatic leader who understood and manipulated their yearning.

Jim Jones and his followers offer an instructive example of a charismatic movement that begins from very different premises and appealed to a different constituency than the Manson Family, but

From *Charisma*, by Charles Lindholm, B. Blackwell Press, 1990. By permission of the author.

aroused in its membership the same ecstatic communal selflessness, stimulated the same paranoid intensity in the leader, and ended in a similar catastrophic bloodbath—though in the Temple the members killed themselves as well as others. It remains the most enigmatic modern cult movement, since the mass suicides at Jonestown that shocked the world in 1978 were and remain difficult to conceptualize except by postulating insanity or else the use of force.

The evidence, however, does not indicate either insanity or force to be the case. The armed guards who surrounded Jonestown drank the poison that killed their friends when they could easily have escaped, and the only shots that were fired took the lives of Jones himself and Anne Moore, one of his closest disciples, in an apparent double suicide.[1] Some converts who, through happenstance, were not at Jonestown killed themselves later, and others who remained alive expressed regret: "I wanted to die with my friends. I wanted to do whatever they wanted to do" (a survivor quoted in Gallagher 1979). Nor were the members of the commune "insane" in any clinical sense. In fact, as one commentator writes, "the frightening thing about most of Jones's followers is that they were amazingly normal" (Richardson 1982: 21), and even hostile witnesses testified that the Jonestown populace were "far from the robots I first expected" (Reston 1981: 229).

THE PEOPLES TEMPLE

To understand the tragedy of Jonestown, we first need to look at what it offered to those who participated. Unlike the Manson Family, the Peoples Temple (it was always written without an apostrophe) was not based on an antinomian belief system that repudiated the reality of the world. Instead, the Temple combined Pentecostal faith-healing with left-wing political activism. It opposed the divisions of modern society, and the invidious distinctions of racism, and favored instead a new communal ideology in which everyone would be treated equally and share in the common good, welded together in a loving community of healing and mutual caring under the leadership of Jim Jones.

The group itself was a much more complex and powerful organization than any of the other communes that thrived in the California atmosphere, involving about 5,000 followers at its largest. In attempting to implement his political program, Jones could mobilize his supporters in letter-writing campaigns and picket lines, giving the impression that his support base was even wider than it really was; he therefore was courted by a number of politicians, and was appointed to a city commissioner's job in San Francisco. The Temple in its prime was not a group that withdrew from the world; it was active, visible, and powerful; operating within the system to change the system.

Much of the early success of the Peoples Temple came because of the tremendous appeal Jones had for the black community, and this also differentiates the Temple sharply from most countercultural organizations, whose membership consisted of young, white, middle-class ex-students. While Jones did draw in a middle-class base of ex-political radicals and activists, as well as a cadre of white fundamentalist believers from his early evangelizing in the midwest, he was most successful at proselytizing impoverished and culturally oppressed blacks, who were impressed by the fact that the Temple was an encompassing, interracial community where people worked and lived together in harmony, without fear of hunger, loneliness, prejudice, or poverty.

Of the membership in the fully formed Peoples Temple, 80 percent were black, two-thirds of them women, many elderly, many from extremely impoverished backgrounds, many ex-drug addicts or ex-criminals. Even in his early days in Indianapolis, when his church was mostly white, Jones had had a special capacity to appeal to the outsiders and the stigmatized. As one of his followers from that era says, Jones attracted "the kind of people most folks don't want to have nothing to do with. Fat, ugly old ladies who didn't have nobody in the world. He'd pass around hugs and kisses like he really did love them, and you could see it on their faces what he meant to them" (quoted in Feinsod 1981: 17). Within the Temple the deprived, the downtrodden, the unloved found a better world, working together and united by Jim Jones's love and caring, which apparently went beyond all social boundaries. He loved them all, he would take care of them all, he would struggle tirelessly for them, he would sacrifice himself for them without any concern for material rewards. "Here's a man who says as long as I have a home, you have a home. Here's a man with only one pair of shoes and no car, one suit of clothing—I think the suit he's got on tonight was borrowed. Here's a man who works over twenty hours a day. Here's JIM JONES" (Jones's introduction at a revival meeting, quoted in Reiterman and Jacobs 1982: 307).

Indeed, this portrait was a true one as far as it went. Even though the Temple took in enormous sums of donations, and had a bankroll of about twenty million dollars in its final days, Jones, as a true charismatic in the Weberian mold, had little interest in wealth. According to one convert, "It [the money] became almost a joke with Jim. . . . We used to wonder what to do with it all. But we never spent it on much" (quoted in Kilduff and Javers 1979: 82). And Jones did devote himself completely to the church, and to his congregation, working almost around the clock to achieve his dream of an interracial socialist community.

Another appeal of the Temple, aside from its mixture of classes and races, and the loving commitment of the leader, was the fact that many whole families participated, including, in some cases, three generations. This again is very unlike other cultic groups, which generally appealed to a narrow age range of converts. In the Temple, on the other hand, one did not have to give up attachments to one's closest relatives.

Being in the Peoples Temple was therefore a far cry from membership in an isolated, powerless group living on fantasies. It was a large community with a strong socialistic ideology of sharing and activism. It had achieved real successes and had real power. Many members testified that they had faith in Jones and in his vision precisely because, as one ex-temple member recalls, it seemed that "Jim has the knowledge and ability to make this world a better place. This is the only place I've seen true integration practiced" (Mills 1979: 137). Organized as a cooperative community, with Jim Jones as the orienting element, the Peoples Temple offered an alternative to lives of desperation, isolation and humiliation; a new vision was not only talked about, it was lived. Middle-class whites, as well as impoverished blacks, found in the experience of the Temple something of absolute value. They chose to live in this community, and many of them chose to die rather than forgo it. That this was so is not a testament to the insanity of the Peoples Temple as much as it is an indictment of the ordinary world. . . .

Consequently, as in the Hitler cult, the elite cadre not only promoted, but also actually believed strongly in their leader's charisma. They had faith that Jones did have a magical power to heal, but that using this power exhausted him unduly, so that fakery was necessary to keep him alive. They believed in his Godlike qualities, and "were convinced that Jones could foresee the future, that he had information that no one else was aware of. These members also believed that the Temple was the only antidote to all the ills of the world" (Yee and Layton 1981: 165).

This process of destabilization of the individual personality and recombination into the charismatic group was accomplished incrementally through a number of methods we have already noted: constant confrontations and public confessions, which revealed each person's weaknesses and sexual inadequacies, as well as the untrustworthiness of friends and family; the denial of all emotional bonds between individuals and a focusing of affect on Jones; obligatory participation in group rituals of emotional intensification; propaganda that played upon the corruption and evil of the outer world; forced, self-incriminating confessions of homosexuality, and so on.

Their shared deceptions about Jones's ability to heal, about his sexuality, about his omnipotence, which were originally engaged in for the sake of group solidarity, also increased commitment among the elite by eroding their own ability to distinguish between truth and falsehood. Lies constantly repeated have a transforming effect, redefining reality not only for the listener, but for the speaker as well, who sees that the delusions become reality, and that assertions of transcendent power are associated with the actual inner experience of transcendence.

Commitment was further solidified by the requirements Jones made of his disciples. All worldly goods had to be invested in the Temple; children had to be given up into the Temple. Jones continually demanded that his followers cut their ties with the past completely and move from place to place, first from Indiana to California, then to the even greater isolation of Guyana. There solidarity reached its maximum, stimulated by Jones's absolute control of information, by the near continuous group meetings, by the fatigue and hunger of the members, by the blaring of loudspeakers bringing Jones's message to the people at any hour of the day, and by the atmosphere of paranoia that Jones emanated and cultivated.[2]

This process of amalgamation into the group took place within a typically charismatic command structure in which rules were strict, rigid, and highly elaborated, as the community reflected the leader's struggle to construct a world that would contain and channel his rage and fear. At the same time, the rules could change instantaneously, according to the leader's whim. As a result, "well-intentioned people, trying to obey the rules and regulations, often committed . . . crimes without realizing it" (Mills 1979: 288). The followers had to learn to live in a total universe where complete arbitrariness was combined paradoxically with obsessional regimentation. The anxieties aroused by this situation pressed the disciples to greater identification with Jones as the sole point of orientation and guidance.

Jones's charisma was also maintained by the distance he kept from actual policy implementation. The community was run on a daily basis by an administrative core of eight to ten young white women.[3] They stood above the PC and were Jones's closest and most loyal associates and confidants. They served to deflect any hostility felt by the rank and file for the direction of the commune. When things went wrong, they were to blame, not Jones; like Hitler, he kept his pronouncements on a transcendental plane.

The identity-challenging techniques, the community structure, and the willingness of the group to participate thus all combined to create a powerful communal experience centered around the volatile personality of Jim Jones. Those who gave themselves up to the experience found themselves within a total community that they had helped to construct. And once it was built, most of them did not wish to escape it. When Jones asked them to destroy others, and then themselves, they did so. . . .

"SPIRITUAL ENERGY": JIM JONES'S CHARISMATIC APPEAL

. . . As with other charismatics, this reconfiguration of personality gave Jim Jones a fantastic quality; he was the man able to walk the tightrope above nothingness, to play with the deepest human fears of death and dissolution, to express the most vivid feelings, to intuit and meet the inner desires of others, to shift and change at will, while still maintaining his control. Jim Jones became a man who could make others feel as they had never felt before, an emphatic mirror for their sufferings and desires, so that even those who later left the Temple testify that Jones seemed to have paranormal abilities to intuit their thoughts and feelings.

It was from this matrix that Jones convinced his followers of his ability to heal, to forestall death, to foretell the future, to read people's thoughts, to merge into their minds: "Twice while I was at work, I had actually felt as if Jim Jones were in my head and I was looking out at the world through his eyes" (Mills 1979: 126).

The major way Jones revealed his spiritual power was in his sermons; they were carefully constructed to heighten his immediate emotional appeal by a dramatic setting and choreography. Jones, the evangelical showman, knew how important theatricality was for creating the proper mood for achieving charismatic transference. In his earlier performances he stressed his ordinariness and his similarity to the audience in order to gain their trust, but as the congregation increased in size, as his reputation grew, and as his personal magic no longer could be applied in one-on-one confrontations, he relied more and more on trappings and effects that set him conspicuously apart from the community. The congregation encouraged him in this. They now knew him as God, and they wanted their God to be elevated.

So, in his Californian church, infectious gospel music, often proclaiming Jim Jones as the Messiah, preceded his arrival on stage and provided an atmosphere of excitement and anticipation. He dressed in a scintillating red satin robe and sunglasses; surrounding him were his multiracial, red-shirted, black-tied aides, who merged into an indistinguishable enthusiastic chorus that echoed his sermon. Jones sat in a high chair above them all, in a setting that combined spiritual and national symbols: an American flag on one side, a framed Declaration of Independence on the other, a magnificent stained-glass window in the background. . . .

REVOLUTIONARY SUICIDE

His techniques, coupled with the intensity of his charismatic personality and the desires of the followers for community, did indeed increase members' ties to the Temple. It was, as we have seen, a highly successful enterprise, both economically and politically. But there was a time bomb within it, since the communal dynamic demanded continued expansion; yet as the group grew, it reached its outer limits. Jones could no longer interact with everyone and fuel them with his fire; the necessities of bureaucratic planning and group maintenance meant that work was harder and less rewarding; the expansion of the group became more difficult. But most threatening were defections. In fact, withdrawal from the group paradoxically reflected the Temple's very success at giving its members improved senses of self-worth and empowerment. Some of them now felt they could deal with the world on their own terms.

But Jones and the Temple could not accept anyone growing beyond them. For Jones and the committed members, the community was everything; it provided the structure that kept them from falling into the void. Jones had spent his entire life creating relations of dependency, warding off emptiness by placing himself in the center of the worlds of others, absorbing them into his expansive fantasy. He, who had not had love, would give love completely; he, who never trusted, would command absolute trust; he, who was torn by ambivalence, would be a rock; he, who had a damaged family, would manufacture the perfect family—but it was a family no one could ever leave; it had to be eternal, and it had to engulf the world.

The community was caught in a downward spiral as Jones's paranoia and desire to maintain control created tensions that led some members to reconsider their ties to the Temple. The last straw for Jones was the effort by one apostate couple to gain custody of their child, whom Jones claimed as his heir. In response, Jones sent many of his followers to Guyana to build a refuge in the jungle which would form a nexus for a new, millennial society, and provide as well a safe place where his enemies could no longer threaten him. Of course, the demons could not be warded off; they were too deep in Jones's soul.

Furthermore, the truly heroic struggle by the emigrants to build Jonestown undercut community solidarity. Productive work in common gave many who participated an increased belief in themselves, a feeling that they were active and creative individuals. As Eric Hoffer writes, "the taste of continuous successful action is fatal to the spirit of the collectivity" (1951: 120). Jones could not countenance this challenge to the group and to his dominance. Therefore, when he arrived in Jonestown he immediately acted to erode the achievements of the pioneers who had preceded him and who had almost unbelievably managed to construct a viable enterprise in the middle of the jungle. He began to implement increasingly irrational procedures and focused on ideological indoctrination instead of farm production. And he soon talked of abandoning the commune in favor of migration to the Soviet Union. This led to resentment, to further defections, and more paranoia, in a fateful movement toward the eventual mass suicide.

The thrust toward death had long been part of Jones's character and the ideology of the Temple. Like Hitler, his fascination with death was revealed as he frightened and coerced his associates by saying he might soon give up the life he hated. He was, he said, already dead at heart, and it was only his compassion for others who depended on him that kept him alive. . . .

When Congressman William Ryan's investigating team arrived in Jonestown from the United States to see if members were being held against their wills, Jones felt his paranoid vision was coming true. At first, he managed to keep himself under control, and even provided hospitality and entertainment for his guests. The breaking point came when a few Temple members asked to leave Jonestown with the congressional party. This meant that even in Guyana, betrayal and disintegration were possible. The social world of the Temple no longer was solid; it was being torn apart by the blandishments of Satan.

For some weeks Jones had been preparing for this moment, claiming that CIA troops were already in the jungle, and manufacturing fake attacks on the compound—just as he had manufactured attacks on his early church in Indiana. This time, however, there was no place to run. Jones burned his bridges by having the congressional party attacked. He thus took revenge on America and on those who had betrayed him. Then he told his followers that instead of succumbing to the inexorable power of the state, the Peoples Temple would destroy itself in an act of defiance.

Suicide was proclaimed a revolutionary victory, an escape from inevitable corruption, an entrance into history, and a claim for the power of the love of Jim Jones, a love that would carry the followers to their ultimate merger with him in the unity of death, which Jones typically sexualized as "the orgasm of the grave" (Jim Jones quoted in Reston 1981: 265). Jones could see this as a triumph because it matched his grandiose vision and permitted him the positive expression of his self-hatred. The fates of his individual followers were of no concern to Jones; they were nothing more than extensions of himself, poor weak beings whom he could not leave behind on his journey to death: "I did not bring you to this point to leave you without a future, without someone who loves you, who will plan and care for you" (Jim Jones quoted in Reiterman and Jacobs 1982: 451).

The only thing that could save him would be if he could have faith in something outside himself: "If I had a leader—oh, how I would love to have a leader. . . . If I had a God—and oh how I wish I had a God like you . . . because I'm the only one there is as far as I could see. And I have searched all over heaven and earth and I certainly looked through the belly of hell" (Jim Jones quoted in Reiterman and Jacobs 1982: 226).

But Jim Jones found no escape, no matter where he looked, neither in the world, where he saw himself rejected and persecuted, nor in his heart, where the love of the Temple could no longer ward off rage and fear. Meanwhile, the community had been practicing for mass suicide for some time. The notion of death had lost its terror for them. Like their leader, they believed themselves besieged by a hostile world; the defections of their fellows solidified them all the more, and they were ready to share the ultimate emptiness with the man who had brought them

together for eternity. It was not Jim Jones, but the world, that was driving them to self-destruction:

> Jim was the most honest, loving, caring concerned person whom I ever met and knew. . . . He knew how mean the world was and he took any and every stray animal and took care of each one. His love for humans was insurmountable. . . . Jim Jones showed us all this—that we could live together with our differences, that we are all the same human beings. . . . We died because you would not let us live in peace. (Anne Moore's last testament quoted in Moore 1986: 285–6.)

Because Jim Jones had brought them together, because they had lost themselves and been reborn in the Temple, because they could not imagine any alternative to their unity, because they believed themselves to be under attack, the members were ready and willing to give up their lives rather than lose their community or the leader who crystallized it. As one of them said, "any life outside of this collective is shit. . . . All I want is to die a revolutionary death" (quoted in Reston 1981: 265–6). And so they killed themselves just as they killed Congressman Ryan and his party; quite willingly, and without compunction. Far from being inhuman, the suicide was a quintessentially human act; one derived from the power of the group, and the dream of transcendence.

NOTES

1. Although tape recordings make most of the sequence of the mass suicide clear, the final act remains equivocal. Jones sent some of his closest followers out of Jonestown with large sums of money before the carnage, leading some to think he may have intended to decamp, but was killed before he could escape. However, his own words seem to indicate a man very tired of living.
2. In fact, Judith Weightman (1983) has estimated that of the 26 different possible commitment mechanisms outlined by Rosabeth Kanter (1972), Jonestown used 24. It is worth mentioning here that Jones, like Hitler and many other charismatic actors, had actually studied crowd psychology and the sociology of groups, and used information in this literature to initiate new indoctrination procedures.
3. All of these women were rivals for his attention, and he was well aware how jealousy could be used to maintain their loyalty. "I tell them all I love them most," Jones said. "Actually, I love only the Cause" (Jim Jones quoted in Mills 1979: 256).

REFERENCES

Feinsod, Ethan. 1981. *Awake in a Nightmare*. New York: Norton.

Gallagher, Nora. 1979. "Jonestown: The Survivors Story." *New York Times Magazine*, 18 November, 124–36.

Hoffer, Eric. 1951. *The True Believer*. New York: Harper and Row.

Kanter, Rosabeth Moss. 1972. *Commitment and Community: Communes and Utopias in Sociological Perspective*. Cambridge, MA: Harvard University Press.

Kilduff, Marshall and Javers, Ron. 1979. *The Suicide Cult*. New York: Bantam.

Mills, Jeannie. 1979. *Six Years with God: Life Inside Rev. Jim Jones's Peoples Temple*. New York: A & W Publishers.

Moore, Rebecca. 1986. *The Jonestown Letters: Correspondence of the Moore Family 1970–1985*. Lewiston, MN: Edwin Mellen Press.

Reiterman, Tim with Jacobs, John. 1982. *Raven: The Untold Story of the Rev. Jim Jones and his People*. New York: Dutton.

Reston, James Jr. 1981. *Our Father Who Art in Hell*. New York: Times Books.

Richardson, James T. 1982: "A Comparison Between Jonestown and Other Cults." In Ken Levi (ed.), *Violence and Religious Commitment: Implications of Jim Jones's People's Temple Movement*. University Park, PA: Pennsylvania State.

Weightman, Judith Mary. 1983. *Making Sense of the Jonestown Suicides: A Sociological History of the People's Temple*. New York: Edwin Mellen Press.

Yee, Min S. and Layton, Thomas. 1981. *In My Father's House*. New York: Holt, Rinehart and Winston.

◆ 14 ◆

Society, Social Control, and the Individual

Peter L. Berger

No society can exist without social control. Even a small group of people meeting but occasionally will have to develop their mechanisms of control if the group is not to dissolve in a very short time.

Social control is the "mechanism" used to "eliminate undesirable personnel and . . . 'to encourage the others.' " It is the "means used by a society to bring its recalcitrant members back into line. . . . It is the negative sanctions or punishments that await those who attempt to stray from the fold." Peter Berger does two things in this article: (1) He describes the various kinds of controls, from violence to economic pressure to "ridicule, gossip, and opprobrium" (rejection). (2) He describes the many "systems" that exercise such controls, including the political system, employers, colleagues, various "social involvements," and finally "the circle of one's family and personal friends."

This is a fascinating description, but it is also a nightmare of sorts. "The individual who, thinking consecutively of all the people he is in a position to have to please, from the collector of the Internal Revenue Service to his mother-in-law, gets the idea that all of society sits right on top of him." But Berger tells us only half of the social control story. There is also a whole host of rewards that operate to encourage conformity, from getting an "A" on an exam to a promotion on the job. These things also constitute social controls.

Social control is one of the most generally used concepts in sociology. It refers to the various means used by a society to bring its recalcitrant members back into line. No society can exist without social control. Even a small group of people meeting but occasionally will have to develop their mechanisms of control if the group is not to dissolve in a very short time. It goes without saying that the instrumentalities of social control vary greatly from one social situation to another. Opposition to the line in a business organization may mean what personnel directors call a *terminal interview* and what those in a criminal syndicate call a *terminal automobile ride*. Methods of control vary with the purpose and character of the group in question. In either case, control mechanisms function to eliminate undesirable personnel and (as it was put classically by King Christopher of Haiti when he had every tenth man in his forced-labor battalion executed) "to encourage the others."

The ultimate and, no doubt, the oldest means of social control is physical violence. In the savage society of children, it is still the major one. But even in the politely operated societies of modern democracies, the ultimate argument is violence. No state can exist without a police force or its equivalent in armed might. This ultimate violence may not be used frequently. There may be innumerable steps before its application, in the way of warnings and reprimands. But if all the warnings are disregarded, even in so slight a matter as paying a traffic ticket, the last thing that will happen is that a couple of cops show up at the door with handcuffs and a Black Maria. Even the moderately courteous cop who hands out the initial traffic ticket is likely to wear a gun — just in case. And even in England, where he does not in

the normal course of events, he will be issued one if the need arises. . . .

In any functioning society, violence is used economically and as a last resort, with the mere threat of this ultimate violence sufficing for the day-to-day exercise of social control. For our purposes in this argument, the most important matter to underline is that nearly all men live in social situations in which, if all other means of coercion fail, violence may be officially and legally used against them. . . .

Next in line after the political and legal controls, one should probably place economic pressure. Few means of coercion are as effective as those that threaten one's livelihood or profit. Both management and labor effectively use this threat as an instrument of control in our society. But economic means of control are just as effective outside the institutions properly called the economy. Universities or churches use economic sanctions just as effectively in restraining their personnel from engaging in deviant behavior deemed by the respective authorities to go beyond the limits of the acceptable. It may not be actually illegal for a minister to seduce his organist, but the threat of being barred forever from the exercise of his profession will be a much more effective control over this temptation than the possible threat of going to jail. It is undoubtedly not illegal for a minister to speak his mind on issues that the ecclesiastical bureaucracy would rather have buried in silence, but the chance of spending the rest of his life in minimally paid rural parishes is a very powerful argument indeed. Naturally such arguments are employed more openly in economic institutions proper, but the administration of economic sanctions in churches or universities is not very different in its end results from that used in the business world.

Where human beings live or work in compact groups, in which they are personally known and to which they are tied by feelings of personal loyalty (the kind that sociologists call *primary groups*), very potent and simultaneously very subtle mechanisms of control are constantly brought to bear on the actual or potential deviant. These are the mechanisms of persuasion, ridicule, gossip, and opprobrium. It has been discovered that in group discussions going on over a period of time, individuals modify their originally held opinions to conform to the group norm, which corresponds to a kind of arithmetic mean of all the opinions represented in the group. Where this norm lies obviously depends on the constituency of the group. For example, if you have a group of twenty cannibals arguing over cannibalism with one noncannibal, the chances are that in the end he will come to see their point and, with just a few face-saving reservations (concerning, say, the consumption of close relatives), will go over completely to the majority's point of view. But if you have a group discussion between ten cannibals who regard human flesh aged over sixty years as too tough for a cultivated palate and ten other cannibals who fastidiously draw the line at fifty, the chances are that the group will eventually agree on fifty-five as the age that divides the *déjeuner* from the *débris* when it comes to sorting out prisoners. Such are the wonders of group dynamics. What lies at the bottom of this apparently inevitable pressure toward consensus is probably a profound human desire to be accepted, presumably by whatever group is around to do the accepting. This desire can be manipulated most effectively—as is well known by group therapists, demagogues, and other specialists in the field of consensus engineering.

Ridicule and gossip are potent instruments of social control in primary groups of all sorts. Many societies use ridicule as one of the main controls over children—the child conforms not for fear of punishment but in order not to be laughed at. Within our own larger culture, "kidding" in this way has been an important disciplinary measure among southern Negroes. But most men have experienced the freezing fear of making oneself ridiculous in some social situation. Gossip, as hardly needs elaboration, is especially effective in small communities, where most people live their lives in a high degree of social visibility and inspectability by their neighbors. In such communities, gossip is one of the principal channels of communication, essential for the maintenance of the social fabric. Both ridicule and gossip can be manipulated deliberately by any intelligent person with access to their lines of transmission.

Finally, one of the most devastating means of punishment at the disposal of a human community is to subject one of its members to systematic opprobrium and ostracism. It is somewhat ironic to reflect that this is a favorite control mechanism with groups opposed on principle to the use of violence. An example of this would be "shunning" among the Amish and Mennonites. An individual who breaks one of the principal taboos of the group (for example, by getting sexually involved with an outsider) is "shunned." This means that, while permitted to continue to work and live in the community, not a single person will speak to him—ever. It is hard to imagine a more cruel punishment. But such are the wonders of pacifism. . . .

It is possible, then, to perceive oneself as standing at the center (that is, at the point of maximum pressure) of a set of concentric circles, each representing a system of social control. The outer ring might well represent the legal and political system under which one is obligated to live. This is the system that, quite against one's will, will tax one, draft one into the military, make one obey its innumerable rules and regulations, if need be put one in prison, and in the last resort will kill one. One does not have to be a right-wing Republican to be perturbed by the ever-increasing expansion of this system's power into every conceivable aspect of one's life. A salutary exercise would be to note down for the span of a single week all the occasions, including fiscal ones, in which one came up against the demands of the politico-legal system. The exercise can be concluded by adding up the sum total of fines and/or terms of imprisonment that disobedience to the system might lead to. The consolation, incidentally, with which one might recover from this exercise would consist of the recollection that law-enforcement agencies are normally corrupt and of only limited efficiency.

Another system of social control that exerts its pressures towards the solitary figure in the center is that of morality, custom, and manners. Only the most urgent-seeming (to the authorities, that is) aspects of this system are endowed with legal sanctions. This does not mean, however, that one can safely be immoral, eccentric, or unmannered. At this point, all the other instrumentalities of social control go into action. Immorality is punished by loss of one's job, eccentricity by the loss of one's chances of finding a new one, bad manners by remaining uninvited and uninvitable in the groups that respect what they consider good manners. Unemployment and loneliness may be minor penalties compared to being dragged away by the cops, but they may not actually appear so to the individuals thus punished. Extreme defiance against the mores of our particular society, which is quite sophisticated in its control apparatus, may lead to yet another consequence—that of being defined, by common consent, as "sick."

Enlightened bureaucratic management (such as, for example, the ecclesiastical authorities of some Protestant denominations) no longer throws its deviant employees out on the street, but instead compels them to undergo treatment by its consulting psychiatrists. In this way, the deviant individual (that is, the one who does not meet the criteria of normality set up by management or by his bishop) is still threatened with unemployment and with the loss of his social ties, but in addition, he is also stigmatized as one who might very well fall outside the pale of responsible men altogether, unless he can give evidence of remorse ("insight") and resignation ("response to treatment"). Thus, the innumerable "counseling," "guidance," and "therapy" programs developed in many sectors of contemporary institutional life greatly strengthen the control apparatus of the society as a whole and especially those parts of it where the sanctions of the politico-legal system cannot be invoked.

But in addition to those broad coercive systems that every individual shares with vast numbers of fellow controllees, there are other and less extensive circles of control to which he is subjected. His choice of an occupation (or, often more accurately, the occupation in which he happens to end up) inevitably subordinates the individual to a variety of controls, often stringent ones. These are the formal controls of licensing boards, professional organizations, and trade unions—in addition, of course, to the formal requirements set by his particular employers. Equally important are the informal controls imposed by colleagues and coworkers. Again, it is hardly necessary to elaborate overly on this point. The reader can construct his own examples—the physician who participates in a prepaid comprehensive health insurance program, the undertaker who advertises inexpensive funerals, the engineer in industry who does not allow for planned obsolescence in his calculations, the minister who says that he is not interested in the size of the membership of his church (or rather, the one who acts accordingly—they nearly all say so), the government bureaucrat who consistently spends less than his allotted budget, the assembly-line worker who exceeds the norms regarded as acceptable by his colleagues, and so on. Economic sanctions are, of course, the most frequent and effective ones in these instances—the physician finds himself barred from all available hospitals, the undertaker may be expelled from his professional organization for "unethical conduct," the engineer may have to volunteer for the Peace Corps, as may the minister and the bureaucrat (in, say, New Guinea, where there is as yet no planned obsolescence, where Christians are few and far between, and where the governmental machinery is small enough to be relatively rational), and the assembly-line worker may find that all the defective parts of machinery in the entire plant have a way of congregating on his workbench. But the sanctions of social exclusion, contempt, and ridicule may be almost as hard to bear. Each occupational role in society, even in very humble jobs, carries with it a code of conduct that is very hard indeed to defy. Adherence to this code is normally just as essential for one's career in the occupation as technical competence or training.

The social control of one's occupational system is so important because the job decides what one may do in most of the rest of one's life—which voluntary associations one will be allowed to join, who will be one's friends, where one will be able to live. However, quite apart from the pressures of one's occupation, one's other social involvements also entail control systems, many of them less unbending than the occupational one, but some even more so. The codes governing admission to and continued membership in many clubs and fraternal organizations are just as stringent as those that decide who can become an executive at IBM (sometimes, luckily for the harassed candidate, the requirements may actually be the same). In less exclusive associations, the rules may be more lax and one may only rarely get thrown out, but life can be so thoroughly unpleasant for the persistent nonconformist to the local folkways that continued participation becomes humanly impossible. The items covered by such unwritten codes will, naturally, vary greatly. They may include ways of dressing, language, aesthetic taste, political or religious convictions, or simply table manners. In all these cases, however, they constitute control circles that effectively circumscribe the range of the individual's possible actions in the particular situation.

Finally, the human group in which one's so-called private life occurs, that is the circle of one's family and personal friends, also constitutes a control system. It would be a grave error to assume that this is necessarily the weakest of them all just because it does not possess the formal means of coercion of some of the other control systems. It is in this circle that an individual normally has his most important social ties. Disapproval, loss of prestige, ridicule, or contempt in this intimate group has far more serious psychological weight than the same reactions encountered elsewhere. It may be economically disastrous if one's boss finally concludes that one is a worthless nobody, but the psychological effect of such a judgment is incomparably more devastating if one discovers that one's wife has arrived at the same conclusion. What is more, the pressures of this most intimate control system can be applied at those times when one is least prepared for them. At one's job, one is usually in a better position to brace oneself, to be on one's guard, and to pretend than one is at

home. Contemporary American "familism," a set of values that strongly emphasizes the home as a place of refuge from the tensions of the world and of personal fulfillment, contributes effectively to this control system. The man who is at least relatively prepared psychologically to give battle in his office is willing to do almost anything to preserve the precarious harmony of his family life. Last but not least, the social control of what German sociologists have called the "sphere of the intimate" is particularly powerful because of the very factors that have gone into its construction in the individual's biography. A man chooses a wife and a good friend in acts of essential self-definition. His most intimate relationships are those he must count on to sustain the most important elements of his self-image. To risk, therefore, the disintegration of these relationships means to risk losing himself in a total way. It is no wonder then that many an office despot promptly obeys his wife and cringes before the raised eyebrows of his friends.

If we return once more to the picture of an individual located at the center of a set of concentric circles, each one representing a system of social control, we can understand a little better that location in society means to locate oneself with regard to many forces that constrain and coerce one. The individual who, thinking consecutively of all the people he is in a position to have to please, from the Collector of Internal Revenue to his mother-in-law, gets the idea that all of society sits right on top of him—and had better not dismiss that idea as a momentary neurotic derangement. The sociologist, at any rate, is likely to strengthen him in this conception, no matter [how much] other counselors may tell him to snap out of it. . . .

Part III

SOCIAL STRUCTURE

Over time, social interaction creates social organization: groups, formal organizations, communities, and societies.

All organized life develops *social structure*, the network of statuses or positions that people come to occupy in relation to one another. Student and professor are positions in a classroom; husband, wife, and child are positions in many families; upper class, middle class, and working class are positions in society. Our position in each social structure influences much of what we do, what we think, and who we are. Our position also ranks us in relation to other positions in the organization.

When sociologists try to understand social organization, social structure often is the most important concept we use. Organization needs structure, and human beings are influenced very much by the structures they exist within, and the positions they hold in the structures. Part III introduces social structure. Parts IV, V, and VI continue to develop the idea of structure by describing class as structure, racial and ethnic groups as part of a structure, and gender as structure.

Philip Zimbardo's selection is an excellent example of the power of structure. It is an experiment that took "mature, emotionally stable, normal, intelligent college students" and transformed them by placing them into dehumanizing positions in a structure. Philip Meyer's selection describes a set of experiments by Stanley Milgram in which people agreed to inflict pain on others because they were told to in the positions they were placed in.

Almost all social structures are unequal, and all of the selections in Part III contain elements of social power. Where positions are formal, they become "authority," and people who fill these positions claim the "legitimate right to command" some and the "obligation to obey" others. In the third selection, Herbert Kelman and V. Lee Hamilton remind us of the atrocities carried out in times of war, when people act as they claim they were ordered to by others who had legitimate authority within social structure.

Part III closes with an excellent summary of social structure by William Dugger, who very systematically describes four modes of structural inequality: class, gender, race, and nation.

Pathology of Imprisonment

Philip E. Zimbardo

*At the end of only six days, we had to close down our mock prison because
what we saw was frightening.*

This article needs little introduction because it truly speaks for itself. It represents
the very best example of the power of social structure; how situations place people
in roles, and how people subsequently become transformed, doing things they
would never think of doing outside those roles.

In an attempt to understand just what it means
psychologically to be a prisoner or prison guard,
Craig Haney, Curt Banks, Dave Jaffe, and I created our own prison. We carefully screened over
70 volunteers who answered an ad in a Palo Alto
city newspaper and ended up with about two
dozen young men who were selected to be part of
this study. They were mature, emotionally stable,
normal, intelligent college students from middle-
class homes throughout the United States and
Canada. They appeared to represent the cream
of the crop of this generation. None had any
criminal record and all were relatively homogeneous on many dimensions initially.

Half were arbitrarily designated as prisoners
by a flip of a coin, the others as guards. These
were the roles they were to play in our simulated
prison. The guards were made aware of the potential seriousness and danger of the situation
and their own vulnerability. They made up their
own formal rules for maintaining law, order, and
respect, and were generally free to improvise new

ones during their eight-hour, three-man shifts.
The prisoners were unexpectedly picked up at
their homes by a city policeman in a squad car,
searched, handcuffed, fingerprinted, booked at
the Palo Alto station house, and taken blind-
folded to our jail. There they were stripped, de-
loused, put into a uniform, given a number, and
put into a cell with two other prisoners where
they expected to live for the next two weeks. The
pay was good ($15 a day) and their motivation
was to make money.

We observed and recorded on videotape the
events that occurred in the prison, and we interviewed and tested the prisoners and guards at various points throughout the study. Some of the
videotapes of the actual encounters between the
prisoners and guards were seen on the NBC News
feature "Chronolog" on November 26, 1971.

At the end of only six days, we had to close
down our mock prison because what we saw was
frightening. It was no longer apparent to most
of the subjects (or to us) where reality ended
and their roles began. The majority had indeed
become prisoners or guards, no longer able to
clearly differentiate between role playing and
self. There were dramatic changes in virtually
every aspect of their behavior, thinking, and

From "Pathology of Imprisonment," by Philip E. Zimbardo,
in *Society*, Vol. 9, No. 6. Copyright © 1972 by Transaction
Publishers; all rights reserved. Reprinted by permission of
Transaction Publishers.

feeling. In less than a week, the experience of imprisonment undid (temporarily) a life-time of learning; human values were suspended, self-concepts were challenged, and the ugliest, most base, pathological side of human nature surfaced. We were horrified because we saw some boys (guards) treat others as if they were despicable animals, taking pleasure in cruelty, while other boys (prisoners) became servile, dehumanized robots who thought only of escape, of their own individual survival, and of their mounting hatred for the guards.

We had to release three prisoners in the first four days because they had such acute situational traumatic reactions as hysterical crying, confusion in thinking, and severe depression. Others begged to be paroled, and all but three were willing to forfeit all the money they had earned if they could be paroled. By then (the fifth day), they had been so programmed to think of themselves as prisoners that when their request for parole was denied, they returned docilely to their cells. Now, had they been thinking as college students acting in an oppressive experiment, they would have quit once they no longer wanted the $15 a day we used as our only incentive. However, the reality was not quitting an experiment but "being paroled by the parole board from the Stanford County Jail." By the last days, the earlier solidarity among the prisoners (systematically broken by the guards) dissolved into "each man for himself." Finally, when one of their fellows was put in solitary confinement (a small closet) for refusing to eat, the prisoners were given a choice by one of the guards: give up their blankets and the incorrigible prisoner would be let out, or keep their blankets and he would be kept in all night. They voted to keep their blankets and to abandon their brother.

About a third of the guards became tyrannical in their arbitrary use of power, in enjoying their control over other people. They were corrupted by the power of their roles and became quite inventive in their techniques of breaking the spirit of the prisoners and making them feel they were worthless. Some of the guards merely did their jobs as tough but fair correctional officers, and several were good guards from the prisoners' point of view because they did them small favors and were friendly. However, no good guard ever interfered with a command by any of the bad guards; they never intervened on the side of the prisoners, they never told the others to ease off because it was only an experiment, and they never even came to me as prison superintendent or experimenter in charge to complain. In part, they were good because the others were bad; they needed the others to help establish their own egos in a positive light. In a sense, the good guards perpetuated the prison more than the other guards because their own needs to be liked prevented them from disobeying or violating the implicit guards' code. At the same time, the act of befriending the prisoners created a social reality that made the prisoners less likely to rebel.

By the end of the week, the experiment had become a reality, as if it were a Pirandello play directed by Kafka that just keeps going after the audience has left. The consultant for our prison, Carlo Prescott, an exconvict with 16 years of imprisonment in California's jails, would get so depressed and furious each time he visited our prison, because of its psychological similarity to his experiences, that he would have to leave. A Catholic priest who was a former prison chaplain in Washington, D.C., talked to our prisoners after four days and said they were just like the other first-timers he had seen.

But in the end, I called off the experiment, not because of the horror I saw out there in the prison yard, but because of the horror of realizing that *I* could have easily traded places with the most brutal guard or become the weakest prisoner full of hatred at being so powerless that I could not eat, sleep, or go to the toilet without permission of the authorities. *I* could have become Calley at My Lai, George Jackson at San Quentin, one of the men at Attica.

Individual behavior is largely under the control of social forces and environmental contingencies rather than personality traits, character, will power, or other empirically unvalidated constructs. Thus we create an illusion of freedom by attributing more internal control to ourselves, to the individual, than actually exists. We thus underestimate the power and pervasiveness of situational controls over behavior because (a) they are often nonobvious and subtle, (b) we can often avoid entering situations in which we might be so controlled, and (c) we label as "weak" or "deviant" people in those situations who do behave differently from how we believe we would.

Each of us carries around in our heads a favorable self-image in which we are essentially just, fair, humane, and understanding. For example, we could not imagine inflicting pain on others without much provocation or hurting people who had done nothing to us, who in fact were even liked by us. However, there is a growing body of social psychological research which underscores the conclusion derived from this prison study. Many people, perhaps the majority, can be made to do almost anything when put into psychologically compelling situations—regardless of their morals, ethics, values, attitudes, beliefs, or personal convictions. My colleague, Stanley Milgram, has shown that more than 60 percent of the population will deliver what they think is a series of painful electric shocks to another person even after the victim cries for mercy, begs them to stop, and then apparently passes out. The subjects complained that they did not want to inflict more pain but blindly obeyed the command of the authority figure (the experimenter) who said that they must go on. In my own research on violence, I have seen mild-mannered coeds repeatedly give shocks (which they thought were causing pain) to another girl, a stranger whom they had rated very favorably, simply by being made to feel anonymous and put in a situation in which they were expected to engage in this activity.

Observers of these and similar experimental situations never predict their outcomes and estimate that it is unlikely that they themselves would behave similarly. They can be so confident only when they are outside the situation. However, because the majority of people in these studies do act in nonrational, nonobvious ways, it follows that the majority of observers would also succumb to the social psychological forces in the situation.

With regard to prisons, we can state that the mere act of assigning labels to people and putting them into a situation in which those labels acquire validity and meaning is sufficient to elicit pathological behavior. This pathology is not predictable from any available diagnostic indicators we have in the social sciences, and it is extreme enough to modify in very significant ways fundamental attitudes and behavior. The prison situation, as presently arranged, is guaranteed to generate severe enough pathological reactions in both guards and prisoners as to debase their humanity, lower their feelings of self-worth, and make it difficult for them to be part of a society outside their prison.

◆ 16 ◆

If Hitler Asked You to Electrocute a Stranger, Would You? Probably

Philip Meyer

They are somehow engaged in something from which they cannot liberate themselves. They are locked into a structure, and they do not have the skills or inner resources to disengage themselves.

No systematic study of positions and power is as clearly to the point as were the Milgram experiments done at Yale University in the 1960s. Here is an article written about Milgram's findings. The importance of social structure is made clear: In the position of experimental subject, the individual is transformed, willing to take orders from the scientist, an authority seen as having a legitimate right to command. It is easy to react to this by claiming "I would never do it," but maybe a more objective response would be, "Why do people do things like this? Why might I do something like this?" What forces are at work in social situations that lead the individual to do things he or she might not normally do?

In the beginning, Stanley Milgram was worried about the Nazi problem. He doesn't worry much about the Nazis anymore. He worries about you and me, and, perhaps, himself a little bit, too.

Stanley Milgram is a social psychologist, and when he began his career at Yale University in 1960, he had a plan to prove, scientifically, that Germans are different. The Germans-are-different hypothesis had been used by historians, such as William L. Shirer, to explain the systematic destruction of the Jews by the Third Reich. One madman could decide to destroy the Jews and even create a master plan for getting it done. But to implement it on the scale that Hitler did

meant that thousands of other people had to go along with the scheme and help to do the work. The Shirer thesis, which Milgram set out to test, is that Germans have a basic character flaw that explains the whole thing, and this flaw is a readiness to obey authority without question, no matter what outrageous acts the authority commands.

The appealing thing about this theory is that it makes those of us who are not Germans feel better about the whole business. Obviously, you and I are not Hitler, and it seems equally obvious that we would never do Hitler's dirty work for him. But now, because of Stanley Milgram, we are compelled to wonder. Milgram developed a laboratory experiment that provided a systematic way to measure obedience. His plan was to try it out in New Haven on Americans and then go to

Germany and try it out on Germans. He was strongly motivated by scientific curiosity, but there was also some moral content in his decision to pursue this line of research, which was in turn colored by his own Jewish background. If he could show that Germans are more obedient than Americans, he could then vary the conditions of the experiment and try to find out just what it is that makes some people more obedient than others. With this understanding, the world might, conceivably, be just a little bit better.

But he never took his experiment to Germany. He never took it any farther than Bridgeport. The first finding, also the most unexpected and disturbing finding, was that we Americans are an obedient people: not blindly obedient, and not blissfully obedient, just obedient. "I found so much obedience," says Milgram softly, a little sadly, "I hardly saw the need for taking the experiment to Germany."

There is something of the theater director in Milgram, and his technique, which he learned from one of the old masters in experimental psychology, Solomon Asch, is to stage a play with every line rehearsed, every prop carefully selected, and everybody an actor except one person. That one person is the subject of the experiment. The subject, of course, does not know he is in a play. He thinks he is in real life. The value of this technique is that the experimenter, as though he were God, can change a prop here, vary a line there, and see how the subject responds. Milgram eventually had to change a lot of the script just to get people to stop obeying. They were obeying so much that the experiment wasn't working—it was like trying to measure oven temperature with a freezer thermometer.

The experiment worked like this: If you were an innocent subject in Milgram's melodrama, you read an ad in the newspaper or received one in the mail asking for volunteers for an educational experiment. The job would take about an hour and pay $4.50. So you make an appointment and go to an old Romanesque stone structure on High Street with the imposing name of The Yale Interaction Laboratory. It looks something like a broadcasting studio. Inside, you meet a young, crew-cut man in a laboratory coat who says he is Jack Williams, the experimenter. There is another citizen, fiftyish, Irish face, an accountant, a little

overweight, and very mild and harmless looking. This other citizen seems nervous and plays with his hat while the two of you sit in chairs side by side and are told that the $4.50 checks are yours no matter what happens. Then you listen to Jack Williams explain the experiment.

It is about learning, says Jack Williams in a quiet, knowledgeable way. Science does not know much about the conditions under which people learn, and this experiment is to find out about negative reinforcement. Negative reinforcement is getting punished when you do something wrong, as opposed to positive reinforcement, which is getting rewarded when you do something right. The negative reinforcement in this case is electric shock. You notice a book on the table, titled, *The Teaching-Learning Process*, and you assume that this has something to do with the experiment.

Then Jack Williams takes two pieces of paper, puts them in a hat, and shakes them up. One piece of paper is supposed to say, "Teacher" and the other, "Learner." Draw one and you will see which you will be. The mild-looking accountant draws one, holds it close to his vest like a poker player, looks at it, and says, "Learner." You look at yours. It says, "Teacher." You do not know that the drawing is rigged, and both slips say "Teacher." The experimenter beckons to the mild-mannered "learner."

"Want to step right in here and have a seat, please?" he says. "You can leave your coat on the back of that chair . . . roll up your right sleeve, please. Now, what I want to do is strap down your arms to avoid excessive movement on your part during the experiment. This electrode is connected to the shock generator in the next room.

"And this electrode paste," he says, squeezing some stuff out of a plastic bottle and putting it on the man's arm, "is to provide a good contact and to avoid a blister or burn. Are there any questions now before we go into the next room?"

You don't have any, but the strapped-in "learner" does.

"I do think I should say this," says the learner. "About two years ago, I was in the veterans' hospital . . . they detected a heart condition. Nothing serious, but as long as I'm having these shocks, how strong are they—how dangerous are they?"

Williams, the experimenter, shakes his head casually. "Oh, no," he says. "Although they may be painful, they're not dangerous. Anything else?"

Nothing else. And so you play the game. The game is for you to read a series of word pairs: for example, *blue-girl, nice-day, fat-neck*. When you finish the list, you read just the first word in each pair and then a multiple-choice list of four other words, including the second word of the pair. The learner, from his remote, strapped-in position, pushes one of four switches to indicate which of the four answers he thinks is the right one. If he gets it right, nothing happens and you go on to the next one. If he gets it wrong, you push a switch that buzzes and gives him an electric shock. And then you go on to the next word. You start with 15 volts and increase the number of volts by 15 for each wrong answer. The control board goes from 15 volts on one end to 450 volts on the other. So that you know what you are doing, you get a test shock yourself, at 45 volts. It hurts. To further keep you aware of what you are doing to that man in there, the board has verbal descriptions of the shock levels, ranging from "Slight Shock" at the left-hand side, through "Intense Shock" in the middle, to "Danger: Severe Shock" toward the far right. Finally, at the very end, under the 435-volt and 450-volt switches, there are three ambiguous Xs. If, at any point, you hesitate, Mr. Williams calmly tells you to go on. If you still hesitate, he tells you again.

Except for some terrifying details, which will be explained in a moment, this is the experiment. The object is to find the shock level at which you disobey the experimenter and refuse to push the switch.

When Stanley Milgram first wrote this script, he took it to 14 Yale psychology majors and asked them what they thought would happen. He put it this way: Out of one hundred persons in the teacher's predicament, how would their break-off points be distributed along the 15-volt to 450-volt scale? They thought a few would break off very early, most would quit someplace in the middle, and a few would go all the way to the end. The highest estimate of the number out of 100 who would go all the way to the end was three. Milgram then informally polled some of his fellow scholars in the psychology department. They agreed that very few would go to the end. Milgram thought so, too.

"I'll tell you quite frankly," he says, "before I began this experiment, before any shock generator was built, I thought that most people would break off at 'Strong Shock' or 'Very Strong Shock.' You would get only a very, very small proportion of people going out to the end of the shock generator, and they would constitute a pathological fringe."

In his pilot experiments, Milgram used Yale students as subjects. Each of them pushed the shock switches, one by one, all the way to the end of the board.

So he rewrote the script to include some protests from the learner. At first, they were mild, gentlemanly, Yalie protests, but "it didn't seem to have as much effect as I thought it would or should," Milgram recalls. "So we had more violent protestation on the part of the person getting the shock. All the time, of course, what we were trying to do was not to create a macabre situation, but simply to generate disobedience. And that was one of the first findings. This was not only a technical deficiency of the experiment, that we didn't get disobedience. It really was the first finding: that obedience would be much greater than we had assumed it would be and that disobedience would be much more difficult than we had assumed."

As it turned out, the situation did become rather macabre. The only meaningful way to generate disobedience was to have the victim protest with great anguish, noise, and vehemence. The protests were tape-recorded so that all the teachers ordinarily would hear the same sounds and nuances, and they started with a grunt at 75 volts, proceeded through a "Hey, that really hurts," at 125 volts, got desperate with, "I can't stand the pain, don't do that," at 180 volts, reached complaints of heart trouble at 195, an agonized scream at 285, a refusal to answer at 315, and only heart-rending, ominous silence after that.

Still, 65 percent of the subjects, 20-to-50-year-old American males, everyday, ordinary people, like you and me, obediently kept pushing those levers in the belief that they were shocking the mild-mannered learner, whose name was Mr. Wallace, and who was chosen for the role because of his innocent appearance, all the way up to 450 volts.

Milgram was now getting enough disobedience so that he had something he could measure. The next step was to vary the circumstances to see what would encourage or discourage obedience. There seemed very little left in the way of discouragement. The victim was already screaming at the top of his lungs and feigning a heart attack. So whatever new impediment to obedience reached the brain of the subject had to travel by some route other than the ear. Milgram thought of one.

He put the learner in the same room with the teacher. He stopped strapping the learner's hand down. He rewrote the script so that, at 150 volts, the learner took his hand off the shock plate and declared that he wanted out of the experiment. He rewrote the script some more so that the experimenter then told the teacher to grasp the learner's hand and physically force it down on the plate to give Mr. Wallace his unwanted electric shock.

"I had the feeling that very few people would go on at that point, if any," Milgram says. "I thought that would be the limit of obedience that you would find in the laboratory."

It wasn't.

Although seven years have now gone by, Milgram still remembers the first person to walk into the laboratory in the newly rewritten script. He was a construction worker, a very short man. "He was so small," says Milgram, "that when he sat on the chair in front of the shock generator, his feet didn't reach the floor. When the experimenter told him to push the victim's hand down and give the shock, he turned to the experimenter, and he turned to the victim, his elbow went up, he fell down on the hand of the victim, his feet kind of tugged to one side, and he said, 'Like this, boss?' Zzumph!"

The experiment was played out to its bitter end. Milgram tried it with 40 different subjects. And 30 percent of them obeyed the experimenter and kept on obeying.

"The protests of the victim were strong and vehement, he was screaming his guts out, he refused to participate, and you had to physically struggle with him in order to get his hand down on the shock generator," Milgram remembers. But 12 out of 40 did it.

Milgram took his experiment out of New Haven. Not to Germany, just 20 miles down the road to Bridgeport. Maybe, he reasoned, the people obeyed because of the prestigious setting of Yale University. If they couldn't trust a learning

center that had been there for two centuries, whom could they trust? So he moved the experiment to an untrustworthy setting.

The new setting was a suite of three rooms in a run-down office building in Bridgeport. The only identification was a sign with a fictitious name: "Research Associates of Bridgeport." Questions about professional connections got only vague answers about "research for industry."

Obedience was less in Bridgeport. Forty-eight percent of the subjects stayed for the maximum shock, compared to 65 percent at Yale. But this was enough to prove that far more than Yale's prestige was behind the obedient behavior.

For more than seven years now, Stanley Milgram has been trying to figure out what makes ordinary American citizens so obedient. The most obvious answer—that people are mean, nasty, brutish, and sadistic—won't do. The subjects who gave the shocks to Mr. Wallace to the end of the board did not enjoy it. They groaned, protested, fidgeted, argued, and in some cases, were seized by fits of nervous, agitated giggling.

"They even try to get out of it," says Milgram, "but they are somehow engaged in something from which they cannot liberate themselves. They are locked into a structure, and they do not have the skills or inner resources to disengage themselves. . . ."

"The results, as seen and felt in the laboratory," he has written, "are disturbing. They raise the possibility that human nature, or more specifically the kind of character produced in American democratic society, cannot be counted on to insulate its citizens from brutality and inhumane treatment at the direction of malevolent authority. A substantial proportion of people do what they are told to do, irrespective of the content of the act and without limitation of conscience, so long as they perceive that the command comes from a legitimate authority. If, in this study, an anonymous experimenter can successfully command adults to subdue a 50-year-old man and force on him painful electric shocks against his protest, one can only wonder what government, with its vastly greater authority and prestige, can command of its subjects. . . ."

Stanley Milgram has his problems, too. He believes that in the laboratory situation, he would not have shocked Mr. Wallace. His professional critics reply that in his real-life situation, he has done the equivalent. He has placed innocent and naive subjects under great emotional strain and pressure in selfish obedience to his quest for knowledge. When you raise this issue with Milgram, he has an answer ready. There is, he explains patiently, a critical difference between his naive subjects and the man in the electric chair. The man in the electric chair (in the mind of the naive subject) is helpless, strapped in. But the naive subject is free to go at any time.

Immediately after he offers this distinction, Milgram anticipates the objection.

"It's quite true," he says, "that this is almost a philosophic position, because we have learned that some people are psychologically incapable of disengaging themselves. But that doesn't relieve them of the moral responsibility."

The parallel is exquisite. "The tension problem was unexpected," says Milgram in his defense. But he went on anyway. The naive subjects didn't expect the screaming protests from the strapped-in learner. But they went on.

"I had to make a judgment," says Milgram. "I had to ask myself, was this harming the person or not? My judgment is that it was not. Even in the extreme cases, I wouldn't say that permanent damage results."

Sound familiar? "The shocks may be painful," the experimenter kept saying, "but they're not dangerous."

After the series of experiments was completed, Milgram sent a report of the results to his subjects and a questionnaire, asking whether they were glad or sorry to have been in the experiment. Eighty-three and seven-tenths percent said they were glad and only 1.3 percent were sorry; 15 percent were neither sorry nor glad. However, Milgram could not be sure at the time of the experiment that only 1.3 percent would be sorry.

Kurt Vonnegut, Jr., put one paragraph in the preface to *Mother Night*, in 1966, which pretty much says it for the people with their fingers on the shock-generator switches, for you and me, and maybe even for Milgram. "If I'd been born in Germany," Vonnegut said, "I suppose I would have *been* a Nazi, bopping Jews and gypsies and Poles around, leaving boots sticking out of snow-banks, warming myself with my sweetly virtuous insides. So it goes."

Just so. One thing that happened to Milgram back in New Haven during the days of the experiment was that he kept running into people he'd watched from behind the one-way glass. It gave him a funny feeling, seeing those people going about their everyday business in New Haven and knowing what they would do to Mr. Wallace if ordered to. Now that his research results are in and you've thought about it, you can get this funny feeling too. You don't need one-way glass. A glance in your own mirror may serve just as well.

17

The My Lai Massacre: A Military Crime of Obedience

Herbert C. Kelman and V. Lee Hamilton

The slaughter at My Lai is an instance of a class of violent acts that can be described as sanctioned massacres. . . . The occurrence of sanctioned massacres cannot be adequately explained by the existence of psychological forces. . . . Instead, the major instigators for this class of violence derive from the policy process. . . . Thus it is more instructive to look not at the motives for violence but at the conditions under which the usual moral inhibitions against violence become weakened.

This selection is part of Chapter 1 in the book, *Crimes of Obedience*. The My Lai massacre is one example of a crime in which individuals claimed that they were simply following the orders of someone who had a right to command them.

The My Lai massacre took place in the midst of war. The soldier is supposed to obey—yet obedience is supposed to be tempered by "ordinary sense and understanding," by moral convictions that make disobedience an obligation and obedience a crime. How is one supposed to know? Crimes committed in the midst of authority structures are all too common, not because people are simply mean or violent, but because the nature of the structure itself makes obedience seem morally acceptable.

In their conclusion to the chapter, the authors identify three processes that encourage people to surrender moral standards to commit sanctioned massacres: authorization, routinization, and dehumanization. There is a warning here: Each of us may be moral in most situations, but we may sometimes find ourselves in positions within social structures in which we are told to do something we know is wrong. What will we do?

March 16, 1968, was a busy day in U.S. history. Stateside, Robert F. Kennedy announced his

Excerpted from *Crimes of Obedience*, by Herbert C. Kelman and V. Lee Hamilton, pp. 1–22. Copyright © 1989, by Yale University. All rights reserved. Reprinted by permission of Yale University Press.

presidential candidacy, challenging a sitting president from his own party—in part out of opposition to an undeclared and disastrous war. In Vietnam, the war continued. In many ways, March 16 may have been a typical day in that war. We will probably never know. But we do know that on that day, a typical company went on a mission—which may or may not have been typical—to a village called Son (or Song) My. Most of what is remembered from that mission occurred in the subhamlet known to Americans as My Lai 4.

The My Lai massacre was investigated, and charges were brought in 1969 and 1970. Trials and disciplinary actions lasted into 1971. Entire books have been written about the army's year-long cover-up of the massacre (for example, Hersh 1972), and the cover-up was a major focus of the army's own investigation of the incident. Our central concern here is the massacre itself—a crime of obedience—and public reactions to such crimes, rather than the lengths to which many went to deny the event. Therefore this account concentrates on one day: March 16, 1968.[1]

Many verbal testimonials to the horrors that occurred at My Lai were available. More unusual was the fact that an army photographer, Ronald Haeberle, was assigned the task of documenting the anticipated military engagement at My Lai—he documented a massacre instead. Later, as the story of the massacre emerged, his photographs were widely distributed and seared the public conscience. What might have been dismissed as unreal or exaggerated was depicted in photographs of demonstrable authenticity. The dominant image appeared on the cover of *Life*: Piles of bodies jumbled together in a ditch along a trail—the dead all apparently unarmed. All were Oriental, and all appeared to be children, women, or old men. Clearly there had been a mass execution, one whose image would not quickly fade.

So many bodies (over twenty in the cover photo alone) are hard to imagine as the handiwork of one killer. These were not. They were the product of what we call a *crime of obedience*. Crimes of obedience begin with orders. But orders are often vague and rarely survive with any clarity the transition from one authority down a chain of subordinates to the ultimate actors. The operation at Son My was no exception.

"Charlie" Company, Company C, under Lt. Col. Frank Barker's command, arrived in Vietnam in December 1967. As the army's investigative unit, directed by Lt. Gen. William R. Peers, characterized the personnel, they "contained no significant deviation from the average" for the time. Seymour S. Hersh (1970) described

the "average" more explicitly: "Most of the men in Charlie Company had volunteered for the draft, only a few had gone to college for even one year. Nearly half were black, with a few Mexican-Americans. Most were eighteen to twenty-two years old. The favorite reading matter of Charlie Company, like that of other line infantry units in Vietnam, was comic books" (p. 18). The action at My Lai, like that throughout Vietnam, was fought by a cross-section of those Americans who either believed in the war or lacked the social resources to avoid participating in it. Charlie Company was indeed average for that time, that place, and that war.

Two key figures in Charlie Company were more unusual. The company's commander, Capt. Ernest Medina, was an upwardly mobile Mexican-American who wanted to make the army his career, although he feared that he might never advance beyond captain because of his lack of formal education. His eagerness had earned him a nickname among his men: "Mad Dog Medina." One of his admirers was the platoon leader, Second Lt. William L. Calley, Jr., an undistinguished, five-foot-three-inch junior-college dropout who had failed four of the seven courses in which he had enrolled his first year. Many viewed him as one of those "instant officers" made possible only by the army's then-desperate need for manpower. Whatever the cause, he was an insecure leader whose frequent claim was "I'm the boss." His nickname among some of the troops was "Surfside 5 1/2," a reference to the swashbuckling heroes of a popular television show, "Surfside 6."

The Son My operation was planned by Lieutenant Colonel Barker and his staff as a search-and-destroy mission with the objective of rooting out the Forty-Eighth Viet Cong Battalion from their base area of Son My village. Apparently, no written orders were ever issued. Barker's superior, Col. Oran Henderson, arrived at the staging point the day before. Among the issues he reviewed with the assembled officers were some of the weaknesses of prior operations by their units, including their failure to be appropriately aggressive in pursuit of the enemy. Later briefings by Lieutenant Colonel Barker and his staff asserted that no one except Viet Cong was expected to be in the village after 7 A.M. on the following day.

The "innocent" would all be at the market. Those present at the briefings gave conflicting accounts of Barker's exact orders, but he conveyed at least a strong suggestion that the Son My area was to be obliterated. As the army's inquiry reported: "While there is some conflict in the testimony as to whether LTC Barker ordered the destruction of houses, dwellings, livestock, and other foodstuffs in the Song My area, the preponderance of the evidence indicates that such destruction was implied, if not specifically directed, by his orders of 15 March" (Peers Report, in Goldstein et al. 1976, p. 94).

Evidence that Barker ordered the killing of civilians is even more murky. What does seem clear, however, is that—having asserted that civilians would be away at the market—he did not specify what was to be done with any who might nevertheless be found on the scene. The Peers Report therefore considered it "reasonable to conclude that LTC Barker's minimal or nonexistent instructions concerning the handling of noncombatants created the potential for grave misunderstandings as to his intentions and for interpretation of his orders as authority to fire, without restriction, on all persons found in target area" (Goldstein et al. 1976, p. 95). Because Barker was killed in action in June 1968, his own formal version of the truth was never available.

Charlie Company's Captain Medina was briefed for the operation by Barker and his staff. He then transmitted the already vague orders to his own men. Charlie Company was spoiling for a fight, having been totally frustrated during its months in Vietnam—first by waiting for battles that never came, then by incompetent forays led by inexperienced commanders, and finally by mines and booby traps. In fact, the emotion-laden funeral of a sergeant killed by a booby trap was held on March 15, the day before My Lai. Captain Medina gave the orders for the next day's action at the close of that funeral. Many were in a mood for revenge.

It is again unclear what was ordered. Although all participants were still alive by the time of the trials for the massacre, they were either on trial or probably felt under threat of trial. Memories are often flawed and self-serving at such times. It is apparent that Medina relayed to the men at least some of Barker's general message—to expect Viet

Cong resistance, to burn, and to kill livestock. It is not clear that he ordered the slaughter of the inhabitants, but some of the men who heard him thought he had. One of those who claimed to have heard such orders was Lt. William Calley.

As March 16 dawned, much was expected of the operation by those who had set it into motion. Therefore a full complement of "brass" was present in helicopters overhead, including Barker, Colonel Henderson, and their superior, Major General Koster (who went on to become commandant of West Point before the story of My Lai broke). On the ground, the troops were to carry with them one reporter and one photographer to immortalize the anticipated battle.

The action for Company C began at 7:30 as their first wave of helicopters touched down near the subhamlet of My Lai 4. By 7:47, all of Company C was present and set to fight. But instead of the Viet Cong Forty-Eighth Battalion, My Lai was filled with the old men, women, and children who were supposed to have gone to market. By this time, in their version of the war, and with whatever orders they thought they had heard, the men from Company C were nevertheless ready to find Viet Cong everywhere. By nightfall, the official tally was 128 VC killed and three weapons captured, although later unofficial body counts ran as high as 500. The operation at Son My was over. And by nightfall, as Hersh reported: "the Viet Cong were back in My Lai 4, helping the survivors bury the dead. It took five days. Most of the funeral speeches were made by the Communist guerrillas. Nguyen Bat was not a Communist at the time of the massacre, but the incident changed his mind. 'After the shooting,' he said, 'all the villagers became Communists'" (1970, p. 74). To this day, the memory of the massacre is kept alive by markers and plaques designating the spots where groups of villagers were killed, by a large statue, and by the My Lai Museum, established in 1975 (Williams 1985).

But what could have happened to leave American troops reporting a victory over Viet Cong when in fact they had killed hundreds of noncombatants? It is not hard to explain the report of victory; that is the essence of a cover-up. It is harder to understand how the killings came to be committed in the first place, making a cover-up necessary.

MASS EXECUTIONS AND THE DEFENSE OF SUPERIOR ORDERS

Some of the atrocities on March 16, 1968, were evidently unofficial, spontaneous acts: rapes, tortures, killings. For example, Hersh (1970) describes Charlie Company's Second Platoon as entering "My Lai 4 with guns blazing" (p. 50); more graphically, Lieutenant "Brooks and his men in the second platoon to the north had begun to systematically ransack the hamlet and slaughter the people, kill the livestock, and destroy the crops. Men poured rifle and machine-gun fire into huts without knowing—or seemingly caring—who was inside" (pp. 49—50).

Some atrocities toward the end of the action were part of an almost casual "mopping-up," much of which was the responsibility of Lieutenant LaCross's Third Platoon of Charlie Company. The Peers Report states: "The entire 3rd Platoon then began moving into the western edge of My Lai (4), for the mop-up operation. . . . The squad . . . began to burn the houses in the southwestern portion of the hamlet" (Goldstein et al. 1976, p. 133). They became mingled with other platoons during a series of rapes and killings of survivors for which it was impossible to fix responsibility. Certainly, to a Vietnamese, all GIs would by this point look alike: "Nineteen-year-old Nguyen Thi Ngoc Tuyet watched a baby trying to open her slain mother's blouse to nurse. A soldier shot the infant while it was struggling with the blouse, and then slashed it with his bayonet." Tuyet also said she saw another baby hacked to death by GIs wielding their bayonets. "Le Tong, a twenty-eight-year-old rice farmer, reported seeing one woman raped after GIs killed her children. Nguyen Khoa, a thirty-seven-year-old peasant, told of a thirteen-year-old girl who was raped before being killed. GIs then attacked Khoa's wife, tearing off her clothes. Before they could rape her, however, Khoa said, their six-year-old son, riddled with bullets, fell and saturated her with blood. The GIs left her alone" (Hersh 1970, p. 72). All of Company C was implicated in a pattern of death and destruction throughout the hamlet, much of which seemingly lacked rhyme or reason.

But a substantial amount of the killing was *organized* and traceable to one authority: the First Platoon's Lt. William Calley. Calley was originally charged with 109 killings, almost all of them mass executions at the trail and other locations. He stood trial for 102 of these killings, was convicted of 22 in 1971, and at first received a life sentence. Although others—both superior and subordinate to Calley—were brought to trial, he was the only one convicted for the My Lai crimes. Thus, the only actions of My Lai for which *anyone* was ever convicted were mass executions, ordered and committed. We suspect that there are commonsense reasons why this one type of killing was singled out. In the midst of rapidly moving events with people running about, an execution of stationary targets is literally a still life that stands out and whose participants are clearly visible. It can be proven that specific people committed specific deeds. An execution, in contrast to the shooting of someone on the run, is also more likely to meet the legal definition of an act resulting from intent—with malice aforethought. Moreover, American military law specifically forbids the killing of unarmed civilians or military prisoners, as does the Geneva Convention between nations. Thus common sense, legal standards, and explicit doctrine all made such actions the likeliest target for prosecution. . . .

The day's quiet beginning has already been noted. Troops landed and swept unopposed into the village. The three weapons eventually reported as the haul from the operation were picked up from three apparent Viet Cong who fled the village when the troops arrived and were pursued and killed by helicopter gunships. Obviously, the Viet Cong did frequent the area. But it appears that by about 8:00 A.M., no one who met the troops was aggressive, and no one was armed. By the laws of war, Charlie Company had no argument with such people.

As they moved into the village, the soldiers began to gather its inhabitants together. Shortly after 8:00 A.M., Lieutenant Calley told Pfc. Paul Meadlo that "you know what to do with" a group of villagers Meadlo was guarding. Estimates of the numbers in the group ranged as high as eighty women, children, and old men, and Meadlo's own estimate under oath was thirty to fifty people. As Meadlo later testified, Calley returned after ten or fifteen minutes: "He [Calley] said, 'How come they're not dead?' I said, 'I didn't know we were supposed to kill them.' He said, 'I want them dead.' He backed off twenty or thirty feet and started shooting into the people—the Viet Cong—shooting automatic. He was beside me. He burned four or five magazines. I burned off a few, about three. I helped shoot 'em" (Hammer 1971, p. 155). Meadlo himself and others testified that Meadlo cried as he fired; others reported him later to be sobbing and "all broke up." It would appear that to Lieutenant Calley's subordinates, something was unusual and stressful in these orders.

At the trial, the first specification in the murder charge against Calley was for this incident; he was accused of the premeditated murder of "an unknown number, not less than thirty, Oriental human beings, males and females of various ages, whose names are unknown, occupants of the village of My Lai 4, by means of shooting them with a rifle" (Goldstein et al. 1976, p. 497).

Among the helicopters flying reconnaissance above Son My was that of CWO Hugh Thompson. By 9:00 or soon after, Thompson had noticed some horrifying events from his perch. As he spotted wounded civilians, he sent down smoke markers so that soldiers on the ground could treat them. They killed them instead. He reported to headquarters, trying to persuade someone to stop what was going on. Barker, hearing the message, called down to Captain Medina. Medina, in turn, later claimed to have told Calley that it was "enough for today." But it was not yet enough.

At Calley's orders, his men began gathering the remaining villagers—roughly seventy-five individuals, mostly women and children—and herding them toward a drainage ditch. Accompanied by three or four enlisted men, Lieutenant Calley executed several batches of civilians who had been gathered into ditches. Some of the details of the process were entered into testimony in such accounts as Pfc. Dennis Conti's: "A lot of them, the people, were trying to get up and mostly they was just screaming and pretty bad shot up. . . . I seen a woman tried to get up. I seen Lieutenant Calley fire. He hit the side of her head and blew it off" (Hammer 1971, p. 125).

Testimony by other soldiers presented the shooting's aftermath. Specialist Four Charles

Hall, asked by Prosecutor Aubrey Daniel how he knew the people in the ditch were dead, said: "There was blood coming from them. They were just scattered all over the ground in the ditch, some in piles and some scattered out 20, 25 meters perhaps up the ditch. . . . They were very old people, very young children, and mothers. . . . There was blood all over them" (Goldstein et al. 1976, pp. 501–02). And Pfc. Gregory Olsen corroborated the general picture of the victims: "They were—the majority were women and children, some babies. I distinctly remember one middle-aged Vietnamese male dressed in white right at my feet as I crossed. None of the bodies were mangled in any way. There was blood. Some appeared to be dead, others followed me with their eyes as I walked across the ditch" (Goldstein et al. 1976, p. 502).

The second specification in the murder charge stated that Calley did "with premeditation, murder an unknown number of Oriental human beings, not less than seventy, males and females of various ages, whose names were unknown, occupants of the village of My Lai 4, by means of shooting them with a rifle" (Goldstein et al. 1976, p. 497). Calley was also charged with and tried for shootings of individuals (an old man and a child); these charges were clearly supplemental to the main issue at trial—the mass killings and how they came about.

It is noteworthy that, during these executions, more than one enlisted man avoided carrying out Calley's orders, and more than one, by sworn oath, directly refused to obey them. For example, Pfc. James Joseph Dursi testified, when asked if he fired when Lieutenant Calley ordered him to: "No. I just stood there. Meadlo turned to me after a couple of minutes and said 'Shoot! Why don't you shoot! Why don't you fire!' He was crying and yelling. I said, 'I can't! I won't!' And the people were screaming and crying and yelling. They kept firing for a couple of minutes, mostly automatic and semi-automatic" (Hammer 1971, p. 143). . . .

Disobedience of Lieutenant Calley's own orders to kill represented a serious legal and moral threat to a defense *based* on superior orders, such as Calley was attempting. This defense had to assert that the orders seemed reasonable enough to carry out, that they appeared to be legal orders.

Even if the orders in question were not legal, the defense had to assert that an ordinary individual could not and should not be expected to see the distinction. In short, if what happened was "business as usual," even though it might be bad business, then the defendant stood a chance of acquittal. But under direct command from "Surfside 5 1/2," some ordinary enlisted men managed to refuse, to avoid, or at least to stop doing what they were ordered to do. As "reasonable men" of "ordinary sense and understanding," they had apparently found something awry that morning; and it would have been hard for an officer to plead successfully that he was more ordinary than his men in his capacity to evaluate the reasonableness of orders.

Even those who obeyed Calley's orders showed great stress. For example, Meadlo eventually began to argue and cry directly in front of Calley. Pfc. Herbert Carter shot himself in the foot, possibly because he could no longer take what he was doing. We were not destined to hear a sworn version of the incident because neither side at the Calley trial called him to testify.

The most unusual instance of resistance to authority came from the skies. CWO Hugh Thompson, who had protested the apparent carnage of civilians, was Calley's inferior in rank but was not in his line of command. He was also watching the ditch from his helicopter and noticed some people moving after the first round of slaughter—chiefly children who had been shielded by their mothers' bodies. Landing to rescue the wounded, he also found some villagers hiding in a nearby bunker. Protecting the Vietnamese with his own body, Thompson ordered his men to train their guns on the Americans and to open fire if the Americans fired on the Vietnamese. He then radioed for additional rescue helicopters and stood between the Vietnamese and the Americans under Calley's command until the Vietnamese could be evacuated. He later returned to the ditch to unearth a child buried, unharmed, beneath layers of bodies. In October 1969, Thompson was awarded the Distinguished Flying Cross for heroism at My Lai, specifically (albeit inaccurately) for the rescue of children hiding in a bunker "between Viet Cong forces and advancing friendly forces" and for the rescue of a wounded child "caught in

the intense crossfire" (Hersh 1970, p. 119). Four months earlier, at the Pentagon, Thompson had identified Calley as having been at the ditch.

By about 10:00 A.M., the massacre was winding down. The remaining actions consisted largely of isolated rapes and killings, "clean-up" shootings of the wounded, and the destruction of the village by fire. We have already seen some examples of these more indiscriminate and possibly less premeditated acts. By the 11:00 A.M. lunch break, when the exhausted men of Company C were relaxing, two young girls wandered back from a hiding place only to be invited to share lunch. This surrealist touch illustrates the extent to which the soldiers' action had become dissociated from its meaning. An hour earlier, some of these men were making sure that not even a child would escape the executioner's bullet. But now, the job was done and it was time for lunch—and in this new context, it seemed only natural to ask the children who had managed to escape execution to join them. The massacre had ended. It remained only for the Viet Cong to reap the political rewards among the survivors in hiding.

The army command in the area knew that something had gone wrong. Direct commanders, including Lieutenant Colonel Barker, had firsthand reports, such as Thompson's plaints. Others had such odd bits of evidence as the claim of 128 Viet Cong dead with a booty of only three weapons. But the cover-up of My Lai began at once. The operation was reported as a victory over a stronghold of the Viet Cong Forty-Eighth. . . .

William Calley was not the only man tried for the events at My Lai. The actions of over thirty soldiers and civilians were scrutinized by investigators; over half of these had to face charges or disciplinary action of some sort. Targets of investigation included Captain Medina, who was tried, and various higher-ups, including General Koster. But Lieutenant Calley was the only person convicted, the only person to serve time.

The core of Lieutenant Calley's defense was superior orders. What this meant to him—in contrast to what it meant to the judge and jury—can be gleaned from his responses to a series of questions from his defense attorney, George Latimer, in which Calley sketched out his understanding of the laws of war and the actions that constitute doing one's duty within those laws:

Latimer: Did you receive any training . . . which had to do with the obedience to orders?

Calley: Yes, sir.

Latimer: . . .what were you informed [were] the principles involved in that field?

Calley: That all orders were to be assumed legal, that the soldier's job was to carry out any order given him to the best of his ability.

Latimer: . . .what might occur if you disobeyed an order by a senior officer?

Calley: You could be court-martialed for refusing an order and refusing an order in the face of the enemy, you could be sent to death, sir.

Latimer: [I am asking] whether you were required in any way, shape, or form to make a determination of the legality or illegality of an order?

Calley: No, sir. I was never told that I had the choice, sir.

Latimer: If you had a doubt about the order, what were you supposed to do?

Calley: . . .I was supposed to carry the order out and then come back and make my complaint (Hammer 1971, pp. 240–41).

Lieutenant Calley steadfastly maintained that his actions within My Lai had constituted, in his mind, carrying out orders from Captain Medina. Both his own actions and the orders he gave to others (such as the instruction to Meadlo to "waste 'em") were entirely in response to superior orders. He denied any intent to kill individuals and any but the most passing awareness of distinctions among the individuals: "I was ordered to go in there and destroy the enemy. That was my job on that day. That was the mission I was given. I did not sit down and think in terms of men, women, and children. They were all classified the same, and that was the classification that we dealt with, just as enemy soldiers." When Latimer asked if in his own opinion Calley had acted "rightly and according to your understanding of

your directions and orders," Calley replied, "I felt then and I still do that I acted as I was directed, and I carried out the orders that I was given, and I do not feel wrong in doing so, sir" (Hammer 1971, p. 257).

His court-martial did not accept Calley's defense of superior orders and clearly did not share his interpretation of his duty. The jury evidently reasoned that, even if there had been orders to destroy everything in sight and to "waste the Vietnamese," any reasonable person would have realized that such orders were illegal and should have refused to carry them out. The defense of superior orders under such conditions is inadmissible under international and military law. The U.S. Army's *Law of Land Warfare* (Dept. of the Army, 1956), for example, states that "the fact that the law of war has been violated pursuant to an order of a superior authority, whether military or civil, does not deprive the act in question of its character of a war crime, nor does it constitute a defense in the trial of an accused individual, unless he did not know and could not reasonably have been expected to know that that act was unlawful" and that "members of the armed forces are bound to obey only lawful orders" (Falk et al. 1971, pp. 71–72).

The disagreement between Calley and the court-martial seems to have revolved around the definition of the responsibilities of a subordinate to obey, on the one hand, and to evaluate, on the other. . . . For now, it can best be captured via the charge to the jury in the Calley court-martial, made by the trial judge, Col. Reid Kennedy. The forty-one pages of the charge include the following:

> Both combatants captured by and noncombatants detained by the opposing force . . . have the right to be treated as prisoners . . . . Summary execution of detainees or prisoners is forbidden by law. . . . I therefore instruct you . . . that if unresisting human beings were killed at My Lai (4) while within the effective custody and control of our military forces, their deaths cannot be considered justified. . . . Thus if you find that Lieutenant Calley received an order directing him to kill unresisting Vietnamese within his control or within the control of his troops, *that order would be an illegal order.*

A determination that an order is illegal does not, of itself, assign criminal responsibility to the person following the order for acts done in compliance with it. Soldiers are taught to follow orders, and special attention is given to obedience of orders on the battlefield. Military effectiveness depends on obedience of orders. On the other hand, the obedience of a soldier is not the obedience of an automaton. A soldier is a reasoning agent, obliged to respond, not as a machine, but as a person. The law takes these factors into account in assessing criminal responsibility for acts done in compliance with illegal orders.

The acts of a subordinate done in compliance with an unlawful order given him by his superior are excused and impose no criminal liability upon him unless the superior's order is one which a man of *ordinary sense and understanding* would, under the circumstances, know to be unlawful, or if the order in question is actually known to the accused to be unlawful (Goldstein et al. 1976, pp. 525–526; emphasis added).

By this definition, subordinates take part in a balancing act, one tipped toward obedience but tempered by "ordinary sense and understanding."

A jury of combat veterans proceeded to convict William Calley of the premeditated murder of no less than twenty-two human beings. (The army, realizing some unfortunate connotations in referring to the victims as "Oriental human beings," eventually referred to them as "human beings.") Regarding the first specification in the murder charge, the bodies on the trail, he was convicted of premeditated murder of not less than one person. (Medical testimony had been able to pinpoint only one person whose wounds as revealed in Haeberle's photos were sure to be immediately fatal.) Regarding the second specification, the bodies in the ditch, Calley was convicted of the premeditated murder of not less than twenty human beings. Regarding additional specifications that he had killed an old man and a child, Calley was convicted of premeditated murder in the first case and of assault with intent to commit murder in the second.

Lieutenant Calley was initially sentenced to life imprisonment. That sentence was reduced: first to twenty years, eventually to ten (the latter

by Secretary of Defense Callaway in 1974). Calley served three years before being released on bond. The time was spent under house arrest in his apartment, where he was able to receive visits from his girlfriend. He was granted parole on September 10, 1975.

SANCTIONED MASSACRES

The slaughter at My Lai is an instance of a class of violent acts that can be described as sanctioned massacres (Kelman 1973): acts of indiscriminate, ruthless, and often systematic mass violence, carried out by military or paramilitary personnel while engaged in officially sanctioned campaigns, the victims of which are defenseless and unresisting civilians, including old men, women, and children. Sanctioned massacres have occurred throughout history. Within American history, My Lai had its precursors in the Philippine war around the turn of the century (Schirmer 1971) and in the massacres of American Indians. Elsewhere in the world, one recalls the Nazis' "final solution" for European Jews, the massacres and deportations of Armenians by Turks, the liquidation of the kulaks and the great purges in the Soviet Union, and more recently the massacres in Indonesia and Bangladesh, in Biafra and Burundi, in South Africa and Mozambique, in Cambodia and Afghanistan, in Syria and Lebanon. . . .

The occurrence of sanctioned massacres cannot be adequately explained by the existence of psychological forces—whether these be characterological dispositions to engage in murderous violence, or profound hostility against the target—so powerful that they must find expression in violent acts unhampered by moral restraints. Instead, the major instigators for this class of violence derive from the policy process. The question that really calls for psychological analysis is why so many people are willing to formulate, participate in, and condone policies that call for the mass killings of defenseless civilians. Thus it is more instructive to look not at the motives for violence but at the conditions under which the usual moral inhibitions against violence become weakened. Three social processes that tend to create such conditions can be identified: authorization, routinization, and dehumanization. Through *authorization*, the situation becomes so defined that the individual is absolved of the responsibility to make personal moral choices. Through *routinization*, the action becomes so organized that there is no opportunity for raising moral questions. Through *dehumanization*, the actors' attitudes toward the target and toward themselves become so structured that it is neither necessary nor possible for them to view the relationship in moral terms.

Authorization

Sanctioned massacres by definition occur in the context of an authority situation, a situation in which, at least for many of the participants, the moral principles that generally govern human relationships do not apply. Thus, when acts of violence are explicitly ordered, implicitly encouraged, tacitly approved, or at least permitted by legitimate authorities, people's readiness to commit or condone them is enhanced. That such acts are authorized seems to carry automatic justification for them. Behaviorally, authorization obviates the necessity of making judgments or choices. Not only do normal moral principles become inoperative, but—particularly when the actions are explicitly ordered—a different kind of morality, linked to the duty to obey superior orders, tends to take over.

In an authority situation, individuals characteristically feel obligated to obey the orders of the authorities, whether or not these orders correspond with their personal preferences. They see themselves as having no choice as long as they accept the legitimacy of the orders and of the authorities who give them. Individuals differ considerably in the degree to which—and the conditions under which—they are prepared to challenge the legitimacy of an order on the grounds that the order itself is illegal, or that those giving it have overstepped their authority, or that it stems from a policy that violates fundamental societal values. Regardless of such individual differences, however, the basic structure of a situation of legitimate authority requires subordinates to respond in terms of their role obligations rather than their personal preferences; they can openly disobey only by challenging the legitimacy of the authority. Often, people obey without question even though the behavior they engage in may entail great personal sacrifice or great harm to others.

An important corollary of the basic structure of the authority situation is that actors often do not see themselves as personally responsible for the consequences of their actions. Again, there are individual differences, depending on actors' capacity and readiness to evaluate the legitimacy of orders received. Insofar as they see themselves as having had no choice in their actions, however, they do not feel personally responsible for them. They were not personal agents, but merely extensions of the authority. Thus, when their actions cause harm to others, they can feel relatively free of guilt. A similar mechanism operates when a person engages in antisocial behavior that was not ordered by the authorities but was tacitly encouraged and approved by them—even if only by making it clear that such behavior will not be punished. In this situation, behavior that was formerly illegitimate is legitimized by the authorities' acquiescence.

In the My Lai massacre, it is likely that the structure of the authority situation contributed to the massive violence in both ways—that is, by conveying the message that acts of violence against Vietnamese villagers were *required*, as well as the message that such acts, even if not ordered, were *permitted* by the authorities in charge. The actions at My Lai represented, at least in some respects, responses to explicit or implicit orders. Lieutenant Calley indicated, by orders and by example, that he wanted large numbers of villagers killed. Whether Calley himself had been ordered by his superiors to "waste" the whole area, as he claimed, remains a matter of controversy. Even if we assume, however, that he was not explicitly ordered to wipe out the village, he had reason to believe that such actions were expected by his superior officers. Indeed, the very nature of the war conveyed this expectation. The principal measure of military success was the "body count"—the number of enemy soldiers killed—and any Vietnamese killed by the U.S. military was commonly defined as a "Viet Cong." Thus, it was not totally bizarre for Calley to believe that what he was doing at My Lai was to increase his body count, as any good officer was expected to do.

Even to the extent that the actions at My Lai occurred spontaneously, without reference to superior orders, those committing them had reason to assume that such actions might be tacitly approved of by the military authorities. Not only had they failed to punish such acts in most cases, but the very strategies and tactics that the authorities consistently devised were based on the proposition that the civilian population of South Vietnam—whether "hostile" or "friendly"—was expendable. Such policies as search-and-destroy missions, the establishment of free-shooting zones, the use of antipersonnel weapons, the bombing of entire villages if they were suspected of harboring guerrillas, the forced migration of masses of the rural population, and the defoliation of vast forest areas helped legitimize acts of massive violence of the kind occurring at My Lai.

Some of the actions at My Lai suggest an orientation to authority based on unquestioning obedience to superior orders, no matter how destructive the actions these orders call for. Such obedience is specifically fostered in the course of military training and reinforced by the structure of the military authority situation. It also reflects, however, an ideological orientation that may be more widespread in the general population, as some of the data presented in this volume will demonstrate.

Routinization

Authorization processes create a situation in which people become involved in an action without considering its implications and without really making a decision. Once they have taken the initial step, they are in a new psychological and social situation in which the pressures to continue are powerful. As Lewin (1947) has pointed out, many forces that might originally have kept people out of a situation reverse direction once they have made a commitment (once they have gone through the "gate region") and now serve to keep them in the situation. For example, concern about the criminal nature of an action, which might originally have inhibited a person from becoming involved, may now lead to deeper involvement in efforts to justify the action and to avoid negative consequences.

Despite these forces, however, given the nature of the actions involved in sanctioned massacres, one might still expect moral scruples to intervene; but the likelihood of moral resistance is greatly reduced by transforming the action into routine, mechanical, highly programmed operations. Routinization fulfills two functions. First, it reduces the necessity of making decisions, thus minimizing the occasions in which moral questions may arise. Second, it makes it easier to avoid the implications of the action because the actor focuses on the details of the job rather than on its meaning. The latter effect is more readily achieved among those who participate in sanctioned massacres from a distance—from their desks or even from the cockpits of their bombers.

Routinization operates both at the level of the individual actor and at the organizational level. Individual job performance is broken down into a series of discrete steps, most of them carried out in automatic, regularized fashion. It becomes easy to forget the nature of the product that emerges from this process. When Lieutenant Calley said of My Lai that it was "no great deal," he probably implied that it was all in a day's work. Organizationally, the task is divided among different offices, each of which has responsibility for a small portion of it. This arrangement diffuses responsibility and limits the amount and scope of decision making that is necessary. There is no expectation that the moral implications will be considered at any of these points, nor is there any opportunity to do so. The organizational processes also help further legitimize the actions of each participant. By proceeding in routine fashion—processing papers, exchanging memos, diligently carrying out their assigned tasks—the different units mutually reinforce each other in the view that what is going on must be perfectly normal, correct, and legitimate. The shared illusion that they are engaged in a legitimate enterprise helps the participants assimilate their activities to other purposes, such as the efficiency of their performance, the productivity of their unit, or the cohesiveness of their group (Janis 1972).

Normalization of atrocities is more difficult to the extent that there are constant reminders of the true meaning of the enterprise. Bureaucratic inventiveness in the use of language helps to cover up such meaning. For example, the SS had a set of *Sprachregelungen*, or "language rules," to govern descriptions of their extermination program. As Arendt (1964) points out, the term *language rule* in itself was "a code name; it meant what in ordinary language would be called a *lie*" (p. 85). The code names for killing and liquidation were "final solution," "evacuation," and "special treatment." The war in Indochina produced its own set of euphemisms, such as "protective reaction," "pacification," and "forced-draft urbanization and modernization." The use of euphemisms allows participants in sanctioned massacres to differentiate their actions from ordinary killing and destruction and thus to avoid confronting their true meaning.

Dehumanization

Authorization processes override standard moral considerations; routinization processes reduce the likelihood that such considerations will arise. Still, the inhibitions against murdering one's fellow human beings are generally so strong that the victims must also be stripped of their human status if they are to be subjected to systematic killing. Insofar as they are dehumanized, the usual principles of morality no longer apply to them.

Sanctioned massacres become possible to the extent that the victims are deprived in the perpetrators' eyes of the two qualities essential to being perceived as fully human and included in the moral compact that governs human relationships: *identity* (standing as independent, distinctive individuals, capable of making choices and entitled to live their own lives) and *community* (fellow membership in an interconnected network of individuals who care for each other and respect each other's individuality and rights) (Kelman 1973; see also Bakan 1966 for a related distinction between "agency" and "communion"). Thus, when a group of people is defined entirely in terms of a category to which they belong, and when this category is excluded from the human family, moral restraints against killing them are more readily overcome.

Dehumanization of the enemy is a common phenomenon in any war situation. Sanctioned massacres, however, presuppose a more extreme degree of dehumanization, insofar as the killing is not in direct response to the target's threats or provocations. It is not what they have done that marks such victims for death but who they are — the category to which they happen to belong. They are the victims of policies that regard their systematic destruction as a desirable end or an acceptable means. Such extreme dehumanization becomes possible when the target group can readily be identified as a separate category of people who have historically been stigmatized and excluded by the victimizers. Often, the victims belong to a distinct racial, religious, ethnic, or political group regarded as inferior or sinister. The traditions, the habits, the images, and the vocabularies for dehumanizing such groups are already well established and can be drawn on when the groups are selected for massacre. Labels help deprive the victims of identity and community, as in the epithet "gooks" that was commonly used to refer to Vietnamese and other Indochinese peoples.

The dynamics of the massacre process itself further increase the participants' tendency to dehumanize their victims. Those who participate as part of the bureaucratic apparatus increasingly come to see their victims as bodies to be counted and entered into their reports, as faceless figures that will determine their productivity rates and promotions. Those who participate in the massacre directly — in the field, as it were — are reinforced in their perception of the victims as less than human by observing their very victimization. The only way they can justify what is being done to these people — both by others and by themselves — and the only way they can extract some degree of meaning out of the absurd events in which they find themselves participating (see Lifton 1971, 1973) is by coming to believe that the victims are subhuman and deserve to be rooted out. And thus the process of dehumanization feeds on itself.

NOTE

1. In reconstructing the events of that day, we consulted Hammer (1970), in addition to the sources cited in the text. Schell (1968) provided information on the region around My Lai. Concerning Vietnam and peasant rebellions, we consulted FitzGerald (1972), Paige (1975), Popkin (1979), and Wolf (1969).

REFERENCES

Arendt, H. 1964. *Eichmann in Jerusalem: A Report on the Banality of Evil.* New York: Viking Press.

Bakan, D. 1966. *The Duality of Human Existence.* Chicago: Rand McNally.

Department of the Army. 1956. *The Law of Land Warfare* (Field Manual, No. 27–10). Washington, DC: U.S. Government Printing Office.

Falk, R. A., G. Kolko, & R. J. Lifton (Eds.). 1971. *Crimes of War.* New York: Vintage Books.

FitzGerald, F. 1972. *Fire in the Lake: The Vietnamese and the Americans in Vietnam.* Boston: Atlantic-Little, Brown.

Goldstein, J., B. Marshall, & J. Schwartz (Eds.). 1976. *The My Lai Massacre and Its Cover-Up: Beyond the Reach of Law?* (The Peers report with a supplement and introductory essay on the limits of law). New York: Free Press.

Hammer, R. 1970. *One Morning in the War.* New York: Coward-McCann.

————. 1971. The *Court-Martial of Lt. Calley.* New York: Coward, McCann, & Geoghegan.

Hersh, S. 1970. *My Lai 4: A Report on the Massacre and Its Aftermath.* New York: Vintage Books.

————. 1972. *Cover-Up.* New York: Random House.

Janis, I. L. 1972. *Victims of Groupthink: A Psychological Study of Foreign-Policy Decisions and Fiascoes.* Boston: Houghton Mifflin.

Kelman, H. C. 1973. "Violence without Moral Restraint: Reflections on the Dehumanization of Victims and Victimizers." *Journal of Social Issues,* 29(4), 25–61.

Lewin, K. 1947. "Group Decision and Social Change." In T. M. Newcomb & E. L. Hartley (Eds.), *Readings in Social Psychology.* New York: Holt.

Lifton, R. J. 1971. "Existential Evil." In N. Sanford, C. Comstock, & Associates, *Sanctions for Evil: Sources of Social Destructiveness.* San Francisco: Jossey-Bass.

————. 1973. *Home from the War—Vietnam Veterans: Neither Victims nor Executioners.* New York: Simon & Schuster.

Paige, J. 1975. *Agrarian Revolution: Social Movements and Export Agriculture in the Underdeveloped World.* New York: Free Press.

Popkin, S. L. 1979. *The Rational Peasant: The Political Economy of Rural Society in Vietnam.* Berkeley: University of California Press.

Schell, J. 1968. *The Military Half.* New York: Vintage Books.

Schirmer, D. B. 1971, April 24. *My Lai Was Not the First Time.* New Republic, pp. 18–21.

Williams, B. 1985, April 14–15. " 'I Will Never Forgive,' Says My Lai Survivor." *Jordan Times* (Amman), p. 4.

Wolf, E. 1969. *Peasant Wars of the Twentieth Century.* New York: Harper & Row.

18

Four Modes of Inequality

William M. Dugger

*Gender inequality is the domination of one gender by another. . . . Race inequality
is practiced by one race discriminating against another. . . . Class inequality in
capitalism is practiced through the exploitation of the workers by the capitalists. . . .
Nation inequality is practiced through the predation of powerful nations on weak
nations. . . . The groups are separate and unequal. Individuals do not choose to
join one group or the other, but rather are assigned to a particular group by the
operation of law, tradition, and myth. Culture and coercion, not
individual preference and choice, are the operative factors.*

William M. Dugger describes the meaning of structure related to gender, race,
class, and nation. Structure is inequality, and inequality is practiced through domination, discrimination, exploitation, and predation. Dugger describes the myths
that support inequality, and shows us how myths and practices are mutually supportive. He also criticizes the myths.

THE INEQUALITY TABLEAU

A mode of inequality is a social process whereby a
powerful group of humans (top dogs) reaps benefits for itself at the expense of a less powerful
group (underdogs). The process involves an institutionalized struggle over power, status, and
wealth. Four modes of inequality will be discussed: (1) gender, (2) race, (3) class, and (4) nation. These do not include all of the ways in
which humans take advantage of each other, but
they do cover much of the ground. Moreover, the
four modes overlap and reinforce each other.

Corresponding to each mode is a set of practices whereby the top dogs take advantage of the
underdogs. These practices ensure that the top
dogs win. Corresponding to each mode of inequality is also a set of enabling myths that culturally enforce the practices and "make the
game seem fair" to both the top dogs and the
underdogs. A focal point also exists for each
mode of inequality. The focal point is a particular institution where the inequality resides—
where the myths justifying it are learned and the
practices realizing it actually take place. These
focal points frequently change as the particular
mode of inequality evolves. Moreover, corresponding to each mode is an antidote—a set of
values, meanings, and beliefs—that can debunk
the enabling myths. Inequality, then, is a whole
complex of modes, practices, enabling myths,

focal points, and antidotes. This complex does not reach a balance of forces. It is not an equilibrium system, but an interacting process of cumulative causation in which inequality either gets worse or better. Seldom, if ever, does it stay the same.

Values are central to inequality. They either rationalize it by making it seem fair and true, or they debunk it by pointing out its injustice and falsehood. We can pretend to be value neutral about inequality, but we never are.

Four Modes of Inequality Defined

Gender inequality is the domination of one gender by another. In our time and place (the twentieth century in the Western Hemisphere), men dominate women through a whole series of gendered practices. These practices are supported and justified by myths about female inferiority and male superiority. These myths are the substance of sexism. Sexist myths enable men to dominate women without feeling guilty and also enable women to be dominated without mass rebellion or suicide. The antidote to gender inequality is feminism.

Race inequality is practiced by one race discriminating against another. In our time and place, the most significant form is the discrimination of white Europeans against black Africans or other people of color. It is justified by myths about African, Asian, and Latin American inferiority and about European superiority. These myths are the substance of today's racism. Racist myths enable white Europeans to discriminate against non-European people of color without feeling guilty and also enable those people of color to adjust to their unfair treatment without fully realizing that it is unfair. The antidote to discrimination is civil rights.

Class inequality in capitalism is practiced through the exploitation of the workers by the capitalists. In Soviet communism, the workers were exploited by the nomenklatura. Class exploitation is supported by its own myths. In the West, the myths are about market efficiency, while in the East, the myths were formerly about the dictatorship of the proletariate. Class myths enable a powerful class to exploit a powerless

TABLE 1 The Inequality Tableau

Modes	Practices	Myths	Antidotes
Gender	Domination	Sexism	Feminism
Race	Discrimination	Racism	Civil Rights
Class	Exploitation	Classism	Economic Democracy
Nation	Predation	Jingoism	Internationalism

class and are comparable to racist and sexist myths in terms of effect, if not in terms of content. The antidote to exploitation is economic democracy (see Dugger 1984).

Nation inequality is practiced through the predation of powerful nations on weak nations and is supported by jingoistic myths about national honor and foreign treachery. Jingoistic myths allow the members of powerful nations to take pride in the killing of the members of weak nations rather than feel shame. The antidote to national predation is internationalism. Table 1 summarizes all the modes, practices, myths, and antidotes.

FOUR MODES OF INEQUALITY EXPLAINED INSTITUTIONALLY

Mode of inequality refers to the way in which people are grouped for giving offense and for receiving it. The groups are separate and unequal. Individuals do not choose to join one group or the other, but rather are assigned to a particular group by the operation of law, tradition, and myth. Culture and coercion, not individual preference and choice, are the operative factors.

Grouping (1): The Class Mode of Inequality

When individuals are grouped into classes, the boundaries are based mainly on how they appropriate their incomes, but also on how large the incomes are. The upper class is composed of capitalists and people who have managed to appropriate large incomes for themselves. An exact number cannot be placed on just how large that income has to be, but the inexact nature of its boundary does not mean an upper class does not exist. It exists because its members have acquired and used differential economic advantages and have kept the lower strata from doing the same. The appropriation of large incomes can be done through the control of wealth or important services. Those who own or control industrial and financial capital—wealthy families, corporate executives, investment bankers, and the like—can use their capitalist position to enlarge their income. Such capitalists are the most powerful members of the upper class; they set its ideological tone and make it essentially a capitalist class. Those who control the delivery of financially important services—corporate lawyers, lobbyists, politicians, and the like—can also appropriate large incomes. The middle class is composed of the "wannabe" groups—those who want to appropriate large incomes but lack the differential advantage needed to do so. They are contenders but were born to the wrong parents; they were sent to the wrong schools, had access to the wrong social connections, or were steered into the wrong professions. Members of the lower class are not in contention, whether they themselves realize it or not. Enough class overlap and circulation between classes exists to allow a limited role for individual choice, merit, and luck. Nonetheless, membership in a particular class is determined primarily by what class a person is born into rather than that individual person's rise or fall (see Osberg 1984).

Although class is an economic category, it is also strongly influenced by cultural factors. The kind of school attended and the kind of learning that takes place there vary by class, as do family structures, religions, beliefs, values, and meanings. (For a conservative view of cultural factors and class, see Berger and Berger 1983. For a liberal view, see Jencks et al., 1972, 1979. For a radical view, see Green 1981; Harrington 1983.) All the basic institutions teach the youth of each class the values, beliefs, and meanings appropriate to their economic station in life. When the class role has been learned and accepted, the person will be well adjusted, perhaps even happy. When the class role is rejected, unhappiness and maladjustment result, and either a change in class will be attempted or a rebel will be made. (For further discussion see Moore 1978.)

Grouping (2): The Race Mode of Inequality

When individuals are grouped into races, the boundary between discriminating and discriminated groups is based on race, but race itself is as much a cultural heritage as it is a biological endowment. The particular form that the race mode of inequality takes in the United States will illustrate the point. (The classic work is Myrdal 1962.) "African American" is as much a cultural as a biological grouping. It does not necessarily include all people whose skin is black. Many people from India, Melanesia, and Sri Lanka are black, as are Native Australians. Many have their own problems and face their own injustices, but they are not in the racially discriminated group of African Americans. Even though the group of African Americans excludes many people whose skin is black, it also includes some people whose skin is white. People with white skins are African Americans if their ancestors were seized for slaves in Africa and forcibly transported to the Americas, where miscegenation and a whole myriad of laws, traditions, and myths forced generation after generation of, not only the dark-skinned, but also the fair-skinned, members of the group into an inferior position relative to "white" Europeans. Cultural learning, not genetics, was the principal factor operating throughout the period.

Grouping (3): The Gender Mode of Inequality

Females (those with ovaries) are assigned to the group called women and males (those with testicles) are assigned to the group called men. However, gender, like race, is as much cultural as it is biological. Female humans are taught to be women by their culture; male humans are taught to be men by their culture as well. What the assignees learn to become is determined by what the culture teaches them, not by their gonads. Humans with ovaries are expected to learn to be women. Humans with testicles are expected to learn to be men. That is, they learn how they are expected to behave in their assigned roles. Their genitals do not teach them; their culture does. (The classic is Mead 1949.) The males of today are expected to be superior to the females, and the females are expected to be inferior to the males.

Grouping (4): The Nation Mode of Inequality

When people are grouped into nations, arbitrary geopolitical boundaries separate the groups into the chosen people and the foreigners. Such groupings are also based on ethnic differences within individual nations, and can produce a considerable degree of inequality. However, when ethnic differences are combined with the power of the nation-state, an even more effective mode of inequality is formed. (Religion plays a role as well but will not be discussed in this chapter.) A nation is an area controlled by one state, where allegiance is to that state rather than another. Cultural and language differences may further differentiate the people in one state from those in another. Moreover, the controlling states may accentuate the differences through state education, state religion, and other forms of propaganda. The individuals who happen to find themselves identified as French, German, Italian, or Russian are not so by nature. They must be taught these identities. Since the nation mode of grouping people is particularly arbitrary, it relies very heavily on the teaching of alleged group differences. People must be taught that foreigners are untrustworthy, ignorant, brutal, and inferior. Only then can national leaders use their jingoism for supporting attacks against other nations or for mounting a defense against (imagined) attacks. Those members of the underlying population who do not accept their assigned roles in these jingoistic activities are exiled, ridiculed, imprisoned, or executed. A complex system of passports and identification papers keeps track of people and makes sure they are assigned to the "correct" national group—whether they want to be or not. Formidable security agencies are created by each nation to implement the groupings. Security agencies such as the former Soviet State Security Committee (KGB) and the U.S. Central Intelligence Agency (CIA) and Federal Bureau of Investigation (FBI) become focal points of nationalism.

FOUR PRACTICES OF INEQUALITY

The practices of inequality are interrelated forms of parasitic collective action. They cannot be reduced down to just one abstract practice without doing great damage to the multifaceted reality of inequality. The domination of women by men is really not the same as the exploitation of workers by capitalists, nor is the discrimination against African Americans by European Americans the same as the German invasion of Poland. Consequently, each practice will be discussed separately.

Practice (1): Domination

The domination of women by men has an institutionalized focal point in patriarchal societies—the family. An institution—and the family is no exception—is made up of people performing activities according to a set of rules that are justified by a set of values, beliefs, and meanings. As people perform their activities according to the rules, they internalize the values, beliefs, and meanings that justify the rules. Domination within the patriarchal family involves the male parent telling the female parent and her offspring (if any) how to conduct family activities. The patriarch exercises power over the other family members, assigning them most of the burdens and appropriating for himself most of the benefits of the family's activities. The patriarch enjoys liberties, and the other family members suffer exposure to the liberties. The patriarch appropriates most of the family status, wealth, and power. In full-blown patriarchy, the family becomes the extension of the patriarch's will. The other family members cannot own property or appropriate income in their own names; they cannot display status on their own behalves, nor exercise power to serve their own authentic wills.

Following the path of least resistance, as most of us do, the members of the family accept the rules that support the male parent's practices because they accept the values, beliefs, and meanings that support them. Male parents come to believe that they are the best judges of what is best for the other members of the family and that resistance to their will is not just inconvenient to them, but harmful for the family and immoral as well. Female parents come to believe that *family* means the patriarchal family only, and that no other types of families or meanings are possible. The female parent also learns to value her subservient role in patriarchy and to feel a real loss if deprived of it.

The values, beliefs, and meanings that support male domination within the family also spread to other social institutions. The acceptance of the subservient wife/mother role generalizes to the acceptance of a subservient worker role—including the acceptance of low-paid occupations or of lower pay for the same kind of work that males do. In the twentieth century, domination originating in the family has been picked up by a new and rising social control mechanism—bureaucracy. As women have moved into paid work outside the home, they have partially escaped the practices of domination within the home only to become enmeshed in the practices of domination within the modern bureaucracy, which now controls the workplace in both capitalist enterprises and government agencies. Access to the highest-paying jobs is controlled by a web of rules and traditions favoring males over females; so, too, is access to status and power within the workplace. Furthermore, if women turn from the family to the welfare agency instead of the workplace, the story is largely the same. State and federal welfare agencies control access to the welfare system through a web of rules and regulations formulated by males and based on the traditional roles of the patriarchal family.

Practice (2): Discrimination

I will focus on discrimination against African Americans. While the focal point for patriarchy begins with the family and the process of procreation, the focal point for discrimination began with slavery and the process of production. Although slavery varied from state to state and even from region to region within the same state, it always was supported by a racist culture in which Europeans were considered to be the superiors and Africans, the inferiors. The racist culture dehumanized Africans, turning them into property that could be bought and sold at will. Although the brutality of slavery varied, it always was coercive. Although the frequency of selling slaves varied, the owner's right to sell a human being as a commodity always was retained.

Agitation by whites for reform and resistance from slaves generally hardened the attitudes of slave owners and increased their coercive hold over their slaves. Neither the slaves' resistance nor the abolitionists' moral outrage led to reform. Slavery was an either/or institution. It could not be reformed; it could only be abolished. It was not amenable to institutional adjustment. In this lies a lesson: incremental institutional adjustment, though desirable on its own merits, can lead to a hardening of inequality. Incremental institutional adjustment can act more like a vaccine against progress toward equality than a means of actually attaining equality. The Civil War finally ended slavery. (For further discussion, see Fogel and Engerman 1974; Genovese 1965, 1969; Hirshson 1962; Mellon 1988; Oates 1975; Stampp 1956; Low and Clift 1981, 756–96.)

Racism did not end with slavery; it has continued for 130 years. After reconstruction in the South, Jim Crow laws and sharecropping replaced slave codes and slavery itself. Now, however, instead of supporting slavery or sharecropping, racism supports a whole series of discriminatory practices diffused throughout the economy, society, and polity. In developments similar to those that are moving male domination over females out of the old focal point in the family and into the larger arena of the modern bureaucracy, the focal point for discrimination has moved, first out of slavery into sharecropping, and now out of sharecropping into bureaucracy. Now, educational bureaucracies control access to good education and training, while corporate and government bureaucracies control access to good jobs. Zoning laws, public housing bureaucracies, lending agent bureaucracies, and municipalities all control access to good housing. The bureaucratic rules and regulations are stacked against the African American in favor of the European American. The practice of discrimination has become institutionalized in the bureaucratic life of modern society. It has moved out of the production processes of the old agrarian South into the whole of society, where it is joined by male domination over females, upper class exploitation of the lower class, and the predation of the chosen people on foreigners.

Practice (3): Exploitation

The practice of class inequality is exploitation. Its focal point in capitalism is the hierarchical workplace, where owners hire workers and use them for producing commodities for a profit. The owners try to enlarge the flow of income that goes to them after all contractual costs are paid and after all costs that can be avoided are avoided (externalities). As in gender and race inequality, the practice of class inequality has become bureaucratized, and far more so than in the other modes of inequality. The production and sale of commodities for a profit is now organized by corporate bureaucracies. The income appropriated by the wage workers, middle managers, engineers, equity owners, and debt owners (rentier capital) is now the subject of bureaucratic rules, state regulations, court decisions, and continual struggle between different organizations and different hierarchical levels within organizations. The struggle is to obtain a differential economic advantage that will allow the appropriation of more income at the expense of those who have no such advantages. Such advantages are usually obtained through property ownership, but physicians, hospital administrators, lawyers, lobbyists, politicians, and even celebrities are also involved in the acquisition and use of differential economic advantages. The practices of exploitation are quite varied. Owners enlarge their incomes by pushing down wages and pushing up the prices of their products and by paying out higher dividends, interest, and rent to themselves. Chief executive officers of corporations enlarge their incomes by downsizing their companies and upsizing their own compensation packages. Physicians and hospital administrators charge exorbitant fees, perform unneeded services, and reap their rewards. Celebrities in the sports and entertainment fields push up their fees and salaries, endorsements, and such. We pay the higher ticket prices and wish that we could raise our "rates" as well. Lobbyists and politicians work out agreements between conflicting factions and pass new legislation that affects us all. Then they collect their fees for service rendered or leave public service for more lucrative private service, hoping the rest of us will not come to see whom they really serve.

Practice (4): Predation

The nation state is the focal point for predation, which is practiced through war and diplomacy. Favorable treatment is sought for the nation's elite groups of capitalist corporations and state bureaucracies (military or civilian). Successful predator nations build empires by forming shifting alliances with other predators, occupying opposing nations, subjecting opposing nations to unfavorable trade relations, or setting up puppet regimes within opposing nations.

Predation also allows the predatory apparatus of each state to extract status, power, and wealth from the underlying population of that state. The underlying population is induced to grant the state's predatory apparatus exceptional power in the name of defending the homeland. The liberties of citizens are reduced in the name of national security, and their exposure to arbitrary action by security officials is increased. Dissent becomes treason. Power is concentrated in the internal security apparatus and the external predatory apparatus. The status of the nation's predatory apparatus is increased by instilling in the underlying population the great importance of defending the homeland and of honoring those who do. Numerous medals and awards are granted to the national heroes as they fill up the cemeteries, hospitals, and prisons. The wealth of the nation's predatory apparatus is increased by inducing the underlying population to grant it exemplary taxing authority. (For further discussion see Melman 1983; Dumas 1986.)

Opposing predatory nations are busy doing the same thing. The activities of the one predatory apparatus gives the other predators stronger motivation to step up their own war preparations to a more feverish pitch. Each nation's predatory apparatus comes to serve as the reason for each other nation's predatory apparatus to expand itself. They are as much allies in their predation of their underlying populations as they are adversaries in their struggle against each other.

ENABLING MYTHS: THE CULTURAL SUPPORT OF INEQUALITY

Enabling myths are composed primarily of the stereotypes men believe about women, European Americans believe about African Americans, the upper class believes about the lower class, and the chosen people believe about foreigners. However, enabling myths are more than the stereotypes believed by the beneficiaries of inequality. Inequality must be justified, in the minds of both its victims and its beneficiaries. To avoid unrest among the victims, they must be taught that their treatment is not really unfair. To avoid guilty consciences among the beneficiaries—which is not nearly as important nor as difficult as avoiding unrest among the victims—the beneficiaries must be taught that their advantages are due them. Such learning is not resisted. It is easy to be convinced that one deserves all the good things that come one's way. Teaching acceptance to the victims is much harder and more important than teaching it to the beneficiaries, so it is the primary function of enabling myths. It is not easy to be convinced that one deserves all the bad things that come one's way.

Enabling myths also create "otherness" and this involves more than just instilling superiority in the top dogs and inferiority in the underdogs but also centrality and marginality For one to be superior, an "other" must be inferior. For one to be the center of things, an "other" must be on the margin. The enabling myths of sexism, for example, put males at the center of humanity and females on the margin. Simone de Beauvoir explained;

> Thus humanity is male and man defines woman not in herself but as relative to him; she is not regarded as an autonomous being. . . . She is defined and differentiated with respect to man and not he with reference to her; she is the incidental, the inessential as opposed to the essential. He is the Subject, he is the Absolute—she is the Other. (Beauvoir [1952] 1989, xxii–xxiii)

(1) Sexism: The Myths Supporting Gender Inequality

Sexist myths begin with the category of "otherness." Males are the ones; they are the center. Females are the others; they are the margin. Thus, when categorizing the human species we say "mankind" or "man." However, when we say "womankind" or "woman," we do not mean the human species. We mean women, the margin. Men are the categorically human; women are other. The justification for males dominating females begins here. Then it ranges far and wide. Public activities—those that yield wealth, status, and power—are the realm of men. Private activities—those that do not yield wealth, status, and power—are the realm of women. Men can speak better than women in public. Men are more intelligent and articulate. Men make better bosses. They are less emotional than women, more straightforward and honest in the pursuit of goals. Women are too emotional and intuitive, less straightforward. Their place is in the home. Man's place is in the world. Women who internalize these myths find it easier to accept their narrowed role in life. Men who internalize these myths find it easier to keep women in their narrowed role, to exclude them with no regrets. Well-adjusted men and women may even succeed in putting the confined role of women on a pedestal, and idealizing it as the embodiment of feminine truth and beauty.

This feminine mystique is a myth about the proper role of woman (Friedan [1963] 1983). It contains positive inducements to reward women for accepting it—they are put on a pedestal, and raised to the height of feminine truth and beauty. The myth also contains negative sanctions (taboos) to punish women for violating it—they are put in the pit, and accused of being untrue to their femininity and ugly to boot. (Just three centuries ago, we burned such women as witches.)

(2) Racism: The Myths Supporting Race Discrimination

Like sexist myths, racist myths also begin with "otherness." In the United States, literature refers to the writings of white Europeans; art means the works of white Europeans; culture, in short, means Greco-Roman culture. African writings are other; African art is other. Some exceptions exist: blues and jazz in music, and Pablo Picasso's adaptations of African art in painting and sculpture are notable. Nonetheless, in the United States, the African American is still *the other*, and the European is still *the one*.

From the foundation of otherness, the myths of racism spring forth. Racist beliefs, like the other enabling myths, are opportunistic. They serve a purpose, even though their propagation and acceptance need not be consciously opportunistic. Racial myths are resistant to evidence contradicting them. They exist in the realm of magic and superstition, not that of fact and experience (Myrdal 1962, 100). They are related directly to the otherness of the African American in the mind of the European American. Racial myths are rational in the sense that they serve the purpose of enabling "whites" to take advantage of "blacks." However, racial myths are also profoundly irrational in the sense that they are psychologically grounded in magic and in superstitious dread of the unknown, of the other.

(3) Classism: The Myths Supporting Class Exploitation

Classist myths are the most sophisticated of all, as they are layered. The first layer of class myths supports the denial of class exploitation, while the second layer of myths supports the belief that the capitalist/Western world is a free market system. The third layer supports the belief that a free market system is neutral with respect to class, and that it involves no class exploitation, but only individual competition, which results in benefits for all.

We are constantly aware of class and of our own class standing relative to others. However, while we constantly think in terms of class, we do not think in terms of class exploitation. One of the most profound discoveries of Thorstein Veblen was that Americans in the lower strata seldom think of the upper strata in the bitter terms of exploitation. Rather than feel resentment, those in the lower strata feel envy. They do not want to overthrow their exploiters. They want to move up into the higher strata themselves (Veblen [1899] 1975). Americans do not think straight when it comes to class because they do not think of it in terms of exploitation. (For further discussion, see DeMott 1991.)

The denial of class exploitation is supported by the belief that ours is a free market system. Beneficial market competition, not differential economic advantage, is believed to be the way in which our economy distributes income. Milton Friedman's two works for the general reader, *Capitalism and Freedom* (1962) and *Free to Choose* (with Rose Friedman; 1980), are the most popular representations of the myth of the market system. In the mythical world of these two popular books, free markets are those that are unfettered by government interference. In such markets, monopolies cannot exist for long, and so the freedom of the market becomes the foundation for the freedom of the polity and the society. Furthermore, in these free markets, individuals are "free to choose," not only what they will buy and what they will sell, but also how prosperous they will become. If they are thrifty, innovative, willing to take risks, and hard working, they can rise very far. No barriers hold them back, unless government interferes with their efforts or unions either keep them out of lucrative employment or take away their profits with exorbitant wages.

The Friedmans do qualify their market utopia. They add in a central bank that provides a framework of monetary stability by following a growth rate rule for the money stock, if we could just agree how to measure the money stock. They also add in a negative income tax to help the poor and maybe also an educational voucher, allegedly to help poor children. They even recognize the need for a limited court system—one that enforces the rules and makes sure that contracts are performed. Nonetheless, the market utopia they describe will benefit us all, provided we keep government interference at a minimum.

There is no class exploitation in the Friedmans' world; no gender domination, racial discrimination, or national predation—unless it is instigated by government interference. The Friedmans' utopia sounds very much like the utopia of Adam Smith, with his system of natural liberty. However, a major difference destroys the similarity. Smith's utopia was used to attack the tyranny of the monarchy's mercantilism. It was used by the underdogs of the time to push their way through the barriers erected by the top dogs of the time. It was used by the upstart merchants and mechanics to rise up against the resistance of the landed aristocracy and against the power of the great, royally-chartered, monopoly-granted, trading companies (Smith 1937; Dugger 1990). While Smith's utopia was used to defend the efforts of the upstarts, the Friedmans' utopia is used to attack the efforts of the upstarts. The upstarts of Smith's time were the merchants and mechanics, but they have grown rich and become established. They are no longer the underdogs but rather the top dogs. The upstarts of the Friedmans' time now must push against the former merchants and mechanics, who have become great retailing corporations, giant industrial conglomerates, and entrenched managerial and professional groups.

The upstarts of the Friedmans' time are women dominated by men, African Americans discriminated against by European Americans, workers and communities exploited by corporate capital, and foreign devils preyed upon by the predatory apparatus of powerful nations. Moreover, the way they push up against the top dogs is to call upon the state, particularly the welfare state, to aid them in their struggle. However, the Friedmans insist that the underdogs should not call for help, or try to improve their position through state aid. Instead, they should simply aid themselves by working harder, being smarter, and saving more. If they do not thrive, it is their own fault. They were not talented enough or did not work hard enough. If the victims of domination, discrimination, exploitation, and predation actually believe that, the top dogs are safe.

What a powerful enabling myth this is. It not only enables class inequality, it enables all the other forms of inequality as well. The wretched of the earth have only themselves to blame for their wretchedness. Here is another important intersection of the different modes of inequality. They are all enabled by the market utopian myth. In fact, the market utopian myth is so powerful that its pull became irresistible to even the former Soviet nomenklatura, who abandoned the myth of the dictatorship of the proletariat for the myth of the utopian market. No longer able to keep the former Soviet masses in their subservient places with the old myth, the nomenklatura adopted a new myth. The new propaganda is for free markets, while the reality involves reconstructed centers of differential economic advantage hidden by a new cover of darkness.

(4) Jingoism: The Myths Supporting National Predation

Jingoism supports national predation. In the United States, jingoism means that "Americans" are "the one" and foreigners, "the other." We are the ones with the manifest destiny. This belief has been with us for a very long time and needs little further discussion here (see Baritz 1985; Slotkin, 1985). Jingoism also involves denial and projection, which form an effective mechanism to justify attack and this requires further elaboration.

When the predatory apparatus of the United States attacks another nation, the attack is accompanied by a denial of our own hostile intentions and by projection of hostile intentions onto the nation being attacked. The best recent example of the denial-projection mechanism involved stories circulated in the United States about Libyan hit squads infiltrating the country with instructions to assasinate important U.S. leaders. We subsequently learned that the stories and other alleged hostilities were not true, but they did provide us with the opportunity to justify an air raid against Libya by projecting our own hostile intentions onto the Libyans (see Woodward 1987).

The denial and projection mechanism also allowed us to take a number of hostile actions against the Sandinista government in Nicaragua. It is the foundation of our great fear of international terrorism. We see Saddam Hussein of Iraq as being at the center of a vast network of terrorists who are poised for a myriad of attacks against the United States, both at home and abroad. (For further discussion of the "terrorism terror" see Perdue 1989; Herman and O'Sullivan 1990.)

Jingoism differs from the other enabling myths in a very important and tragic way. In gender, class, and race inequality the enabling myths of sexism, classism, and racism can be inculcated in their negative forms in the underdog groups. However, this is far less possible in nation inequality. Leaders of one nation are hard-pressed to convince the people of the opposing nation that they are inferior foreign devils, which makes the nation mode of inequality a particularly unstable and violent form. With the underdog groups harder to fool, inequality between nations requires more violence to enforce. Husbands have killed their wayward wives in patriarchal societies. European Americans have killed disrespectful African Americans, and capitalists have killed revolting workers. However, such killing does not occur on the same vast scale as it does in nation inequality. Indeed, "chosen peoples" (nations) have killed tens of millions of foreigners in the last century alone. It seems easier to kill foreigners than to pacify them with myths.

Enabling myths do four related things simultaneously: (1) they provide an opportunistic rationalization of privilege, (2) they create a superstitious dread of the unknown in the minds of the top dogs, (3) they create the otherness of the victim, and (4) they make it possible to deny that injustice occurs by encouraging the underdogs to blame themselves.

THE ANTIDOTES FOR INEQUALITY

Means of debunking myths are readily available. However, debunking specific myths is not enough because as long as the practices of inequality persist, innovative minds will create new myths to support them. The practices of inequality must be changed, and doing so will take more than just a change of heart. It takes collective action to change social practices. The adage that "you cannot legislate morality" is exactly wrong. In fact, you cannot change morality unless you legislate change in practices. Change the practices and the morals will follow. What people come to believe derives, in large part, from what they do (see Veblen 1919, 1–31, 32–55). Then, however, they use some of their beliefs to justify what they do. In the first instance, their beliefs come from their habits of life; beliefs are largely habitual constructs. Thus, to change the beliefs, the myths that support inequality, the practices of inequality must also be changed.

Inequality, then, must be attacked from two directions simultaneously. First, the irrational myths that support inequality must be debunked. This is the responsibility of the churches, the schools, the sciences, the arts, and the social movements. Second, the actual practices of inequality must be transformed through collective action. This is the responsibility of the unions, the professional associations, the corporate boards, the courts, the legislatures, and, again, the social

movements. The following remarks deal with debunking the myths rather than changing the practices.

Debunking the Myths

Unfortunately, rumors of evil foreign intentions spring up eternally, so they must continually be investigated and the truth or falsehood of them exposed on a case-by-case basis. The only way to deal with them as they arise is to have faith and insist upon an open society, an aggressive press, and an informed citizenry. Racist, sexist, and classist myths already have been debunked at length by numerous researchers. For my purposes here, only a brief discussion of the highlights of these debunking efforts is necessary.

With social Darwinism, enabling myths became "scientific." Biological differences between the races and sexes were measured and listed by researchers of high standing in scientific circles. One of the most infamous "scientific" myths supporting racism and sexism had to do with the allegedly biologically determined mental superiority of men over women and of the "white" race over the "black" race. The biological determinists were avid bone collectors and skull measurers— rigorously mathematical and objective. They created the "science" of craniometry. The craniometricians "proved" that the white race was mentally superior to the black race and that men were mentally superior to women because the craniums of men were larger than those of women and the craniums of whites were larger than those of blacks. Of course, many of their measurements were inaccurate and their samples biased. Nevertheless, their findings were accepted in wide university and scientific circles. However, when cranium size was finally related to body size, the results took a dramatic turn. Women were found to have larger craniums relative to their body size than men! Thus, the craniometricians lost heart, and face. How could they admit that women were actually more mentally advanced than men? Of course, the craniometricians were men, and white ones at that. Moreover (needless to say), no evidence of any kind exists that can link mental ability to the size of the cranium of a healthy human of any color or sex (see Gould 1981;

Montagu 1974; Ayres [1927] 1973). These first biological determinists, who were supporters of racism and sexism, were eventually debunked by other, better scientists. However, a new crop of biological determinists has stepped into the cultural vacuum to conjure up deceptive bell curves in place of cranium sizes.

Although the keepers of the sacred truths of classism behave much like the biological determinists before them, the myths of classism have a very different origin. The market myth goes back to Adam Smith, in whose hands it was not an enabling myth. It did not justify the inequality of the status quo; instead, it attacked that inequality. The market myth now defends inequality, but it did not start out that way. The market myth's origin is noble, not base, so debunking it is much harder.

THE DYNAMICS OF INEQUALITY: CIRCULAR PROCESS

Inequality is not an equilibrium state but a circular process. Inequality either gets worse or better, but it does not reach an equilibrium. The continued practice of inequality strengthens the myths that support it, and the stronger myths then lend even greater support to the practice. The resulting circular process is not characterized by offsetting forces that reach a balance but by cumulative causation that continues to move an inegalitarian society toward more inequality or continues to move an egalitarian society toward more equality. The inequality process is a vicious circle, but the equality process is a virtuous circle. Both processes are cumulative, not offsetting.

The Vicious Circle

Collective action of the top dogs against the underdogs establishes the practices of inequality. White Europeans established the great Atlantic slave trade. Males established patriarchy; state leaders established the system of nation-states; and property holders established capitalism. They all did so through collective action. Then, the myths of each form of inequality strengthened the practices of inequality. White Europeans came to

believe themselves racially superior to black Africans. Black Africans, who were trapped in slavery, were taught that they must adjust to it or perish. The practice of patriarchy strengthened sexist myths, and the sexist myths then strengthened the sexist practices. State leaders established nation-states. We learned that we were English or French or German and that the foreigners were plotting against us. This strengthened the hands of the state leaders as they extracted more income, status, and power from the underlying populations. They used their gains in foreign plots, teaching us the truth in jingoism. Feudal property holders pushed us off the commons and taught us to value their private property. We believed them and worked ever harder for them, hoping that we could save enough to get some property for ourselves. In each mode of inequality, parasitic practices are established through collective action, and then enabling myths make the practices seem legitimate. The practices then become more entrenched because of the myths, and the myths begin to seem like truths because of the practices. The process is circular.

The Virtuous Circle

If the vicious circle were all there is to the story, we humans would probably have destroyed ourselves long ago. However, there is more. Just as there is a vicious circle of inequality, there is a virtuous circle of equality. Collective action of the underdogs against the top dogs can put an end to the practices of inequality, albeit perhaps only to establish another set of parasitic practices whereby the old underdogs attack the old top dogs. The first become last and the last become first; the meek inherit the earth. Perhaps however, the practices of inequality can be replaced with the practices of equality. The possibility of a virtuous circle replacing the vicious circle is not that remote. The religious leaders of the American civil rights movement did not seek to replace white racism with black racism. Malcolm X became an enlightened antiracist, an egalitarian. Setting the example for the rest of us to follow, African-American collective action took the high road. African Americans took collective action against inequality and made considerable progress in eliminating racist practices and myths. Of course, much more needs to be done. Nevertheless, as racist practices were resisted by collective action and as racist myths were debunked, it became harder for white people to believe the myths and continue the practices. Thus, a virtuous circle was begun. Then, however, racial progress was interrupted, and then reversed by the Ronald Reagan administration and retrenchment. The vicious circle has replaced the virtuous, once again.

CONCLUDING REMARKS

This chapter supplied a simple vocabulary for describing inequality and suggested a dynamic framework of circular and cumulative causation for showing how the forces of inequality move in a reinforcing, rather than offsetting, fashion. The vocabulary includes the modes, practices, myths, focal points, and antidotes for inequality. A few examples and a bit of institutional context were provided to illustrate the concepts. The overall purpose was to help elucidate inequality and the different forms it takes, and to put the forms in an appropriate context. The treatment was introductory and exploratory, not exhaustive or definitive.

REFERENCES

Ayres, Clarence E. [1927] 1973. *Science: The False Messiah*. Clifton, NJ: Augustus M. Kelley.

Baritz, Loren. 1985. *Backfire*. New York: William Morrow.

Beauvoir, Simone de. [1952] 1989. *The Second Sex*. Translated and edited by H. M. Parshley. New York: Random House.

Becker, Gary S. 1971. *The Economics of Discrimination*. 2d ed. Chicago: University of Chicago Press.

_____. 1981. *A Treatise on the Family*. Cambridge: Harvard University Press.

Berger, Brigitte, and Peter L. Berger. 1983. *The War over the Family*. Garden City, NY: Anchor Press/Doubleday.

Braverman, Harry. 1974. *Labor and Monopoly Capital*. New York: Monthly Review Press.

Coleman, Richard P., and Lee Rainwater, with Kent A. McClelland. 1978. *Social Standing in America*. New York: Basic Books.

DeMott, Benjamin. 1991. *The Imperial Middle*. New York: William Morrow.

Dugger, William M. 1984. "The Nature of Capital Accumulation and Technological Progress in the Modern Economy." *Journal of Economic Issues*, 18 (Sept.): 799–823.

_____. 1989a. *Corporate Hegemony*. Westport, CT: Greenwood Press.

_____. 1989b. "Instituted Process and Enabling Myth: The Two Faces of the Market." *Journal of Economic Issues*, 23 (June): 606–15.

_____. ed. 1989c. *Radical Institutionalism*. Westport, CT: Greenwood Press.

_____. 1990. "From Utopian Capitalism to the Dismal Science: The Effect of the French Revolution on Classical Economics." In Warren J. Samuels, ed., *Research in the History of Economic Thought and Methodology*. Vol. 8. Greenwich, CT.: JAI Press, pp. 153–73.

Dumas, Lloyd Jeffry. 1986. *The Overburdened Economy*. Berkeley: University of California Press.

Fogel, Robert William, and Stanley L. Engerman. 1974. *Time on the Cross*. Boston: Little, Brown and Company.

Friedan, Betty. [1963] 1983. *The Feminine Mystique*. New York: Dell Publishing.

Friedman, Milton. 1962. *Capitalism and Freedom*. Chicago: University of Chicago Press.

Friedman, Milton, and Rose Friedman, 1980. *Free to Choose*. New York: Avon Books.

Genovese, Eugene D. 1965. *The Political Economy of Slavery*. New York: Pantheon.

_____. 1969. *The World the Slaveholders Made*. New York: Vintage Books.

Gould, Stephen Jay. 1981. *The Mismeasure of Man*. New York: W. W. Norton.

Green, Philip, 1981. *The Pursuit of Inequality*. New York: Pantheon.

Hacker, Andrew. 1995. *Two Nations*. New York: Ballantine Books.

Harrington, Michael. 1983. *The Politics at God's Funeral*. New York: Holt, Rinehart and Winston.

Herman, Edward S., and Gerry O'Sullivan. 1990. *The "Terrorism" Network*. New York: Pantheon.

Hirshon, Stanley P. 1962. *Farewell to the Bloody Shirt*. Chicago: Quadrangle Books.

Jencks, Christopher, and Marshall Smith, Henry Acland, Mary Jo Bane, David Cohen, Herbert Gintis, Barbara Heyns, Stephan Michelson. 1972. *Inequality*. New York: Basic Books.

Jencks, Christopher, and Susan Bartlett, Mary Corcoran, James Crouse, David Eaglesfield, Gregory Jackson, Kent McClelland, Peter Mueser, Michael Olneck, Joseph Schwartz, Sherry Ward, Jill Williams. 1979. *Who Gets Ahead?* New York: Basic Books.

Low, W. Augustus, and Virgil A. Clift. 1981. *Encyclopedia of Black America*. New York: Da Capo Press.

Mead, Margaret. 1949. *Male and Female*. New York: Dell Publishing.

Mellon, James, ed. 1988. *Bullwhip Days*. New York: Avon Books.

Melman, Seymour. 1983. *Profits without Production.* New York: Alfred A. Knopf.

Montagu, Ashley. 1974. *The Natural Superiority of Women.* Rev. ed. New York: Macmillan Publishing Company.

Moore, Barrington, Jr. 1978. *Injustice: The Social Bases of Obedience and Revolt.* White Plains, NY: M. E. Sharpe.

Myrdal, Gunnar. 1962. *An American Dilemma.* New York: Harper and Row.

Oates, Stephen B. 1975. *The Fires of Jubilee.* New York: Harper and Row.

Osberg, Lars. 1984. *Economic Inequality in the United States.* Armonk, NY: M. E. Sharpe.

Perdue, William D. 1989. *Terrorism and the State.* New York: Praeger.

Slotkin, Richard. 1985. *The Fatal Environment.* New York: Atheneum.

Smith, Adam. 1937. *The Wealth of Nations.* Edited by Edwin Canaan. New York: Modern Library.

Stampp, Kenneth M. 1956. *The Peculiar Institution.* New York: Vintage Books.

Stanfield, J. Ron. 1982. "Toward a New Value Standard in Economics." *Economic Forum,* 13 (Fall): 67–85.

Veblen, Thorstein. [1899] 1975. *The Theory of the Leisure Class.* New York: Augustus M. Kelley.

———. 1919. *The Place of Science in Modern Civilization and Other Essays.* New York: B. W. Huebsch.

Woodward, Bob. 1987. *Veil.* New York: Simon and Schuster.

Part IV

SOCIAL STRUCTURE: CLASS

Social class is probably the most obvious way people are structured in society. Increasingly Americans have come to realize that some people are born into poverty and find it very difficult to escape, while others are born into luxury with almost no chance to become poor. Many people change their class to some extent, but the amount of change is usually small. No matter how we might try to deny its importance, class remains an important part of all of our lives. If affects our "life chances" (our opportunities in life), and our "lifestyle" (how we live our lives) in very direct and indirect ways. The thoughtful person living in a democratic society must somehow confront a class system that excludes large numbers of people from participating, and that seems to be getting more extreme and less mobile.

Sociologists tend to see class as an economic rank in society that makes a big difference in everyone's life. It ranks people in privilege, prestige, and power. It influences socialization, healthcare, opportunities in education, and it creates ranks that have real consequences for self-concept and expectations.

The five selections in Part IV introduce many of the issues that sociologists care about concerning class. You will also notice that there are many other selections scattered throughout this Reader that also involve class as a core concept.

Robert Perrucci and Earl Wysong have influenced my own view of class in the United States and the trends that seem to be dominating. Our class structure is not a diamond and not a pyramid, they contend, but more like a double diamond, weakest in the middle. Robert Coles describes the socialization of children of affluence, their views of their place in society, their expectations, their lives of luxury. Herbert Gans describes the many ways that poverty functions in society; his point is that it is very difficult to rid society of poverty; for most of us it is too costly. Bernard Rosen describes the blue-collar working class, both its decline in and anger toward recent economic developments. Robert Bellah ends Part IV with an essay on the increasing gulf between the rich and poor in the world and in our society, and why it is important to care—and to do something—before the gulf tears apart the society and the world.

19

The New American Class Structure

Robert Purrucci and Earl Wysong

> *... although there may be 130 million Americans involved in occupations and jobs*
> *for which they are compensated, their amount of compensation varies widely*
> *according to how they are related to the production process. . . . The groups*
> *are distinguished as (1) those who own capital and business, (2) those who*
> *control corporations and the workers in those corporations, (3) those who*
> *possess credentialed knowledge, which provides a protected place in the labor*
> *market, (4) the self-employed, small-business owners who operate as solo*
> *entrepreneurs with limited capital, and (5) those with varying skills*
> *who have little to offer in the labor market but their capacity to work.*

Here is an interesting and insightful analysis of class structure in America today. There are many ways to divide people into classes, but Perrucci and Wysong focus our attention on people's relationships to one another in the economic order rather than simply on income or wealth. They arrive at what they call a double-diamond diagram of class structure rather than the usual pyramid or single diamond. This emphasizes two major classes: a privileged class and a new working class.

In our society, the occupational structure as embedded in organizations is the key to understanding the class structure, and a person's occupation is one aspect of class position. But how do the hundreds of different occupations combine to create a structure of distinct classes with different amounts of economic, political, and social power? What aspects of occupations determine their position in the class structure?

People often speak of their occupation or their job as what they do for a living. An occupation or job describes how a person is related to the economy in a society or what one does in the process

of the production of goods and services. An occupation or job provides people with the means to sustain life ("to make a living"); and the sum total of the work done by people in their occupations or jobs is the wealth generated by the economic system. In one sense there is a parallel or symmetric relation between the availability of jobs and the amount of wealth that is generated. The more people in a society are working at making a living, the better the economic health of the total society. But there is also a sense in which there is an asymmetric relationship between the well-being of working people ("how much of a living they make") and the total wealth that is generated. Some people contribute more to the total wealth than they receive for their work, as in the case of some workers whose wages are a

From Robert Perrucci and Earl Wysong, *The New Class Society*, Rowman & Littlefield Publishers, Inc., 1999. By permission.

fraction of the value of their products when they are sold. And some people may receive ten or twenty times more in income for their work than that received by others. So although there may be 130 million Americans involved in occupations and jobs for which they are compensated, their amount of compensation varies widely according to how they are related to the production process. There are a variety of ways in which people are related to the production process in today's economy.

The Privileged Class

The activity of some people in the system of production is focused on their role as owners of investment capital. Such a person may be referred to colloquially as the "boss" or, in more respectful circles, as a "captain of industry," an "entrepreneur," or a "creator of wealth," but in the language of class analysis they are all owner-employers. The owner may actually be the sole proprietor of the XYZ Corporation and be involved in the day-to-day decisions of running that corporation. But ownership may also consist in the possession of a large number of shares of stock in one or several corporations in which many other persons may also own stock. However, the ownership of stock is only socially and economically meaningful when (1) the value of shares owned is sufficient to constitute "making a living," or (2) the percentage of shares of stock owned relative to all shares is large enough to permit the owner of said shares to have some say in how the company is run. Members of this group (along with the managers and professionals) control most of the wealth in America. The point of this discussion is to distinguish owners of investment capital from the millions of Americans who own shares of stock in companies, who own mutual funds, or whose pension funds are invested in the stock market. The typical American stock owner does not make a living from that ownership and has nothing to say about the activities of the companies he or she "owns."

On the lower rungs of the owner-employer group are the proprietors of small but growing high-tech firms that bring together venture capital and specialized knowledge in areas involving biomedical products or services and computer software firms. These are "small" businesses only in Department of Commerce classifications (less than $500,000 in sales), for they bear no resemblance to the Korean grocer, the Mexican restaurant owner, or the African American hair salon found in many American cities. They are more typically spin-off firms created by technical specialists who have accumulated some capital from years of employment in an industrial lab or a university and have obtained other investment capital from friends, family, or private investors.

A second activity in the system of production is that of manager, the person who makes the day-to-day decisions involved in running a corporation, a firm, a division of a corporation, or a section within a company. Increasingly, managers have educational credentials and degrees in business, management, economics, or finance. Managers make decisions about how to use the millions of dollars of investment capital made available to them by the owners of investment capital.

The upper levels of the managerial group include the top management of the largest manufacturing, financial, and commercial firms in the United States. These managers receive substantial salaries and bonuses, along with additional opportunities to accumulate wealth. Table 1 presents a typical pattern of "modest" compensation for the officers of a large firm. We refer to this compensation as "modest" because it is far below the multimillion-dollar packages of compensation for CEOs at IBM, AT&T, Disney, and Coca-Cola (which range from $20 million to $50 million). But such distinctions are probably pointless, because we are describing executives whose wealth is enormous in comparison with others not in their class. For example, the top CEO in the listing above also owns 102,772 shares of stock in the corporation he heads. The value of these shares is $8,220,000. The executive vice president owns 166,488 shares, and the other VPs own "only" 25,000 to 75,000 shares.

Lower levels of the managerial group carry out the important function of supervising the work done by millions of workers who produce goods and services in the economy. The success of these managers, and their level of rewards, is determined by their ability to get workers to be

TABLE 1 Compensation for Corporate Executives

Position	Annual Compensation	Bonus	Stock Options
President and chief executive officer	$608,846	$325,000	$2,159,916
Executive vice pres. and financial officer	376,769	142,000	732,493
Senior vice president	267,861	146,000	390,663
Vice president	292,577	86,000	488,324
Vice president	262,500	67,000	488,329

Source: Based on data from the Annual Report and Proxy Statements, Great Lakes Chemical Corporation, 1997, West Lafayette, IN.

more productive, which means to produce more at a lower cost.

Professionals carry out a third activity in the economic system. This group's power is based on the possession of credentialed knowledge or skill, such as an engineering degree, a teaching degree, or a degree in public relations. Some may work as "free professionals," providing service for a fee, such as doctors, dentists, or lawyers. But most professionals work for corporations, providing their specialized knowledge to enhance the profit-making potential of their firm or of firms that buy their services. The professional group is made up of university graduates with degrees in the professional schools of medicine, law, business, and engineering and in a variety of newly emerging fields (e.g., computer sciences) that serve the corporate sector. The possession of credentialed knowledge unifies an otherwise diverse group, which includes doctors who may earn $500,000 a year and computer specialists who earn $50,000 a year.

The potential to accumulate wealth is very great among certain segments of professionals. Median net salary in 1995 for all doctors was $160,000, ranging from a high median salary of $240,000 in radiology to $125,000 in family practice. Unfortunately, these averages hide the salaries of graduates from elite medical schools and those affiliated with the most prestigious hospitals. Also absent is information about doctor's entrepreneurial activities such as ownership of nursing homes or pharmaceutical firms.

Similar opportunities for high income exist among lawyers, where partners at the nation's elite law firms average $335,000 and associates average $80,000 (1988). Even law professors at prestigious law schools have a chance to amass a small fortune while teaching and practicing law or consulting. A recent *New York Times* story reported that a professor at Harvard Law School gave the school a bequest of $5 million.[1] The *Times* reported that the professor is "not one of the school's prominent moonlighters" and is "unlike Prof. Alan M. Dershowitz, the courtroom deity who has defended Leona Helmsley and Mike Tyson and is on the O.J. Simpson defense team." So how did the professor do it? By "writing and consulting."

Professors at elite universities who are in selected fields like law, medicine, business, biomedical engineering, or electrical engineering have opportunities to start high-tech firms and to consult for industry in ways that can significantly enhance income. Even "modest" activities, like becoming an outside director for a bank or industrial firm, can be very rewarding. A colleague in a business school at a Big Ten university who is a professor of management has been on the board of directors of a chemical corporation for twenty years. His annual retainer is $26,000. He gets an additional $1,000 a day for attending meetings of the board or committee meetings and $500 a day for participating in telephone conference meetings (the board meets six times a year, and committees from one to six times a year). Each nonemployee director gets a $50,000 term life insurance policy and a $200,000 accidental death and dismemberment insurance policy. After serving on the board for a minimum of five years, directors are eligible for retirement benefits equal to the amount of the annual retainer at the time of retirement. Retirement benefits begin at the time of the director's retirement from the board and continue for life.

Why does the president of this university, or its Board of Trustees, allow a professor to engage in such lucrative "outside activities"? Maybe it's because the president, whose annual salary is $200,000, holds four director positions that give him more than $100,000 a year in additional income.

Professionals in elite settings not only make six-figure salaries, but they have enough "discretionary time" to pursue a second line of activity that may double or triple their basic salaries. Not a bad deal for the professional class.

Not everyone with a credentialed skill is in the privileged professional class. We exclude from this group workers like teachers, social workers, nurses, and most university professors at nonelite schools. They are excluded because of where they obtained their degrees, where they are employed, and the market for their skills. Each of these factors limits job security and provides very modest levels of income (i.e., consumption capital) and little investment capital. Thus, we distinguish between elite and marginal professional groups, with only the former being in the privileged class.

The New Working Class

Finally, there is the large majority of Americans: employees who sell their capacity to work to an employer in return for wages. This group typically carries out its daily work activities under the supervision of the managerial group. They have limited skills and limited job security. Such workers can see their jobs terminated with virtually no notice. The exception to this rule is the approximately 14 percent of workers who are unionized; but even union members are vulnerable to having their jobs eliminated by new technology, restructuring and downsizing, or the movement of production to overseas firms.

This working group also consists of the many thousands of very small businesses that include self-employed persons and family stores based on little more than "sweat equity." Many of these people have been "driven" to try self-employment

as a protection against limited opportunities in the general labor market. But many are attracted to the idea of owning their own business, an idea that has a special place in the American value system: it means freedom from the insecurity and subservience of being an employee. For the wage worker, the opportunities for starting a business are severely limited by the absence of capital. Aspirations may be directed at a family business in a neighborhood where one has lived, such as a dry-cleaning store, a beauty shop, a gas station, or a convenience store. Prospects for such businesses may depend upon an ethnic "niche" where the service, the customer, and the entrepreneur are tied together in a common cultural system relating to food or some personal service. The failure rate of these small businesses is very high, making self-employment a vulnerable, high-risk activity.

Another sizable segment of wage earners, perhaps 10–15 percent, has very weak links to the labor market. For these workers, working for wages takes place between long stretches of unemployment, when there may be shifts to welfare benefits or unemployment compensation. This latter group typically falls well below official poverty levels and should not be considered as part of the "working poor." The working poor consists of persons who are working full-time at low wages, with earnings of about $12,000 a year—what you get for working full-time at $6.00 an hour.

Table 2 provides a summary of these major segments of Americans with different standing in the current economy. The groups are distinguished as (1) those who own capital and business, (2) those who control corporations and the workers in those corporations, (3) those who possess credentialed knowledge, which provides a protected place in the labor market, (4) the self-employed, small-business owners who operate as solo entrepreneurs with limited capital, and (5) those with varying skills who have little to offer in the labor market but their capacity to work.

These segments of the class structure are defined by their access to essential life-sustaining resources and the stability of those resources over time. As discussed earlier, these resources include consumption capital, investment capital, skill capital, and social capital. The class segments differ in their access to stable resources

TABLE 2   Class Structure in America

Class Position	Class Characteristics	Percentage of Population
PRIVILEGED CLASS (20%)		
Superclass	Owners and employers. Make a living from investments or business ownership; incomes at six- to seven-figure level, yielding sizable consumption and investment capital.	1–2%
Credentialed Class		
Managers	Mid- and upper-level managers and CEOs of corporations and public organizations. Incomes for upper-level CEOs in seven-figure range, others, six-figures.	13–15%
Professionals	Possess credentialed skill in form of college and professional degrees. Use of social capital and organizational ties to advance interests. Wide range of incomes, from $75K to upper-six figures.	4–5%
NEW WORKING CLASS (80%)		
Comfort Class	Nurses, teachers, civil servants, very-small-business owners, and skilled and union carpenters machinists, or electricians. Incomes in the $35–50K range but little investment capital.	10%
Contingent Class		
Wage earners	Work for wages in clerical and sales jobs, personal services, and transportation and as skilled craft workers, machine operators, and assemblers. Members of this group are often college graduates. Incomes at $30K and lower.	50%
Self-employed	Usually self-employed with no employees, or family workers. Very modest incomes, with high potential for failure.	3–4%
Excluded class	In and out of the labor force in a variety of unskilled, temporary jobs.	10–15%

over time, and they represent what is, for all practical purposes, a two-class structure, represented by a double diamond (see figure 1). The top diamond represents the privileged class, composed of those who have stable and secure resources that they can expect will be available to them over time. This privileged class can be subdivided into the superclass of owners, employers, and CEOs, who directly or indirectly control enormous economic resources, and the credentialed class of managers and professionals with the knowledge and expertise that is essential to major industrial, financial, commercial, and media corporations and key agencies of government. The bottom diamond is the new working class, composed of those who have unstable and insecure resources over time. One segment of this class has a level of consumption capital that provides income sufficient for home ownership

and for consumption patterns that suggest they are "comfortable." Thus, we label this segment the comfort class, represented by school teachers, civil servants, social workers, nurses, some small-business owners, and skilled unionized carpenters, machinists, or electricians. Despite their relatively "high" incomes ($35,000–$50,000), the comfort class is vulnerable to major economic downturns or unforeseen crises (e.g., health problems) and has limited investment capital to buffer such crises.

The largest segment of the new working class is composed of the wage earners with modest skills and unpredictable job security. This group includes the machine operators in a manufacturing plant, bank clerks, and the supervisors who could be displaced by new production technology, computerized information systems, or other "smart" machines. Their job insecurity is

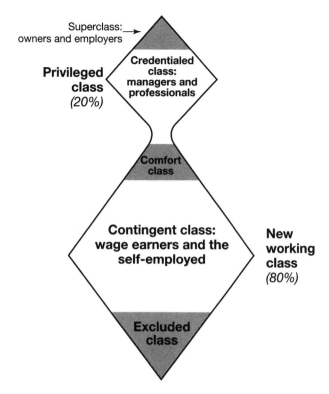

FIGURE 1. Double-diamond Diagram of Class Structure and Class Segments

similar to that of the growing segment of temporary and part-time workers, thereby making them the contingent class.

At the bottom of the new working class are those without marketable skills who move in and out of the labor force in temporary jobs or in seasonal employment. They are the excluded class, who either are treated as "waste," because they are no longer needed as either cheap labor or as consumers, or fill the most undesirable jobs in restaurant kitchens or as nighttime cleaners of downtown buildings.

It is important to keep in mind that a person's location in the double-diamond class structure is related to his or her occupation but not determined by that occupation (as is the case in the production and functionalist models of class, discussed earlier in this chapter). Some lawyers are in the top diamond, and some in the bottom. Some engineers, scientists, and professors are in the privileged class, and some in the new working class. It is not occupation that determines

class position but access to generative capital—stable, secure resources over time.

THE NEW AMERICAN CLASS STRUCTURE DEFINED

Figure 1 provides a picture of the new American class structure as a "double diamond," divided between the privileged and those lacking the privileges that come with money, elite credentials, and social connections. This two-class structure is composed of approximately 20 percent privileged Americans and 80 percent nonprivileged Americans. Members of the employer, managerial, and professional classes have a stable income flow, employment stability, savings, pensions, and insurance. Their positions in the economy enable them to use their resources to accumulate more resources and to insure their stability over time. The new working class has little in the way of secure resources. Their jobs are unstable, as they can be eliminated by labor-replacing technology or corporate moves to off-shore production. Only marginal professionals and craft workers possess some skills that provide short-term security, but even their skills are being eroded by new technology, the reorganization of work, and the decline of union power.[2]

This image of class structure in American society is based on three important principles that define the new American class structure and how it works in practice.

Class Structure Is Intergenerationally Permanent

One of the most significant aspects of class structures is their persistence over time. The inequality that a person experiences today provides the conditions that determine the future. This aspect of class structure is rarely discussed by the media or even by scholars devoted to the layer-cake image of inequality. In fact, most discussion of class structure views that structure, and one's place in it, as temporary and ever changing. The belief in equality of opportunity states that regardless of where a person starts out in life it is possible to move up through hard work, motivation, and education. Similarly, the overall structure is viewed as changing, as revealed in statistics on the median income, the expanding middle class, or the declining percentage of the population living below the poverty line. In short, the popular image of class differences is that they are temporary and constantly changing. But in fact, nothing could be further from the truth when it comes to the new class system in the United States.

The "rules of the game" that shape the class structure are designed to reproduce that structure. Let's consider a few of those "rules" and how they work.

First, our legal system gives corporations the right to close down a plant and move the operation overseas, but it does not give workers a right to their jobs. Owners and employers have property rights that permit wide latitude in making decisions that impact on workers and communities. But workers' jobs are not viewed as a property right in the law. The protected right to a secure job would provide workers with a stable

resource over time and modify their vulnerable situation in the class system.

Second, people in privileged classes have unrestricted opportunities to accumulate wealth (i.e., extensive consumption capital and investment capital). The accumulation process is based on tax laws that favor the rich, a variety of loopholes to avoid taxes, and an investment climate that enables the rich to get richer. The share of net worth and financial wealth going to the top 20 percent of the population is staggering (see figure 1). One out of five Americans owns almost everything, while the other four are on the outside looking in.[3]

This extraordinary disparity in wealth not only provides a clear picture of the polarized two-class structure, it also provides the basis for persistence of that structure. Because inheritance and estate laws make it possible to do so, wealth is transmitted across generations, and privilege is thereby transmitted to each succeeding generation.

Another feature of the American class structure that contributes to its permanence is the sheer size of the privileged class. It consists of approximately twenty million households, or between forty million and fifty million people. A class of this numerical size, with its associated wealth, is able to fill all the top positions across the institutional spectrum. Moreover, it is able to fill vacant positions or newly created positions from among its own members. Thus, recruitment of talented women and men from the non-privileged class will become increasingly rare.

Third, the so-called equality of opportunity in America is supposed to be provided by its system of public education. Yet anyone who has looked at the quality of education at the primary and secondary levels knows that it is linked to the class position of parents. Spending-per-pupil in public schools is tied to property taxes, and therefore the incomes of people in school districts. Schools in poor districts have the poorest physical facilities, libraries, laboratories, academic programs, and teachers.[4] Some of the children who survive this class-based public education are able to think about some sort of post-secondary education. But even here the game is stacked against them.

Going to college is based on the ability to pay the costs of tuition and, unless the student lives at home, room and board. Even at low-cost city colleges and state universities the expenses exceed what many working-class families can afford. On the other hand, even if college attendance were not tied to the ability to pay, it is not likely that many youngsters from low-income families would think of college as a realistic goal, given the low quality of their educational experience in primary and secondary grades.

Thus, the "rules of the game" that are the foundation for the class structure are designed primarily to transmit advantage and disadvantage across generations. This persistence of structure exists even when there are instances of upward social mobility—the sons and daughters of working-class families who move into the professional classes. This upward mobility occurs in a very selective way and without changing the rules of the game. For example, when the birthrates among the privileged class fail to produce enough children to fill all the jobs for doctors, lawyers, engineers, computer specialists, and managers, it is necessary to recruit the most talented young men and women from the working class. The most talented are identified through special testing programs and curriculum tracking and are encouraged to consider advanced education. "Elite" colleges and universities develop special financial and academic programs for talented working-class students, and a variety of fellowship programs support those with financial need. Upward mobility is made possible not by changing the rules of the game but by "creaming" the most talented members of the working class. The "creaming" process has the dual effect of siphoning off potential leaders from the working class and supporting the belief in equality of opportunity and upward mobility.

There Is No Middle Class

Most views of class structure, as noted earlier, present a "layer-cake" image of class differences. There are six or eight classes made up of groups of occupations that differ in prestige, education level, or income. These differences between classes are not sharp and discontinuous but gradual shadings of difference between one class and another. The layer-cake image encourages a belief in a "center" or a "middle class" that is large and stands between the upper and lower classes. The different groups in the middle may think of

themselves as being "better off" than those below them and may see opportunities to move up the "ladder" by improving education, job skills, or income.

This image of class structure is stabilizing, in that it encourages the acceptance of enormous material inequality in American society because of the belief that anyone can improve his or her situation and become one of the "rich and famous." It also encourages greater attention to the small differences between groups and tends to ignore the large differences. For example, many Americans are hardworking men and women who often work two jobs to make ends meet but are limited by these low-wage and no-benefit jobs. These people are often most hostile to the welfare benefits provided for people who are just below them in income. A working poor person gets $12,000 a year for full-time work, whereas a welfare family may get the same amount in total benefits without working. However, these same working poor rarely have their hostility shaped and directed toward the rich, who may be more responsible for the low wages, limited benefits, and inadequate pensions of the working poor.

The belief in a middle class also allows politicians to proclaim their support for tax breaks for what they call the middle class while debating whether the middle class includes those with incomes up to $150,000 a year or only those earning up to $100,000.

In our conception of class structure, there can be no middle class. Either you have stable, secure resources over time, or you do not. Either you have a stable job and income, or you do not. Either you have secure health insurance and pensions that provide adequate income, or you do not.

Classes Have Conflicting Interests

In the layer-cake theory of class structure, each class is viewed as having more or less of some valued quality or commodity such as education, occupational skill, or income. Members of each class may aspire to become members of classes above them, and they may harbor negative opinions and prejudices of those in classes below them. But classes, in this theory, are not fundamentally opposed to one another. Of course, there is often discussion of why members of certain classes might support or oppose particular political candidates because of their social or economic policies. But these alliances or oppositional views are seen as linked to shifting issues and are not tied to class interests.

In our view, the two large classes of privileged and working-class Americans have fundamentally different and opposed objective interests, so that when one class improves its situation the other class loses. The advantages of the privileged class, expressed in its consumption capital, investment capital, skill capital, and social capital, are enjoyed at the expense of the working class. Any action to make the resources of the working class more stable, by improving job security or increasing wages and pensions, for example, would result in some loss of capital or advantage for the privileged.

Consider the most extreme test of the existence of oppositional interests between the privileged and exploited classes. One might expect that the highest unifying symbol of the country—the presidency—might be above the taint of class interests. However, a recent unauthorized disclosure of a transcript of President Bill Clinton's meeting with President Boris Yeltsin of Russia sounds like two "petty professionals" trying to make the best deal for their services. "Collusion was recently exposed in a classified transcript of the Presidents' private meeting at the anti-terrorism summit in February [1996]. According to the leaked memorandum, Clinton promised Yeltsin support for his reelection bid with 'positive' U.S. policies toward Russia. In exchange, Clinton asked Yeltsin to lift trade barriers on imports of U.S. chicken parts (40 percent of which come from Arkansas—specifically, a large portion from Tyson Foods, a heavy contributor to Clinton's campaign)."[5] "Pimping" for chicken parts! If this is what goes on at the level of presidential discourse, what might be discussed at meetings of corporate executives, doctors, lawyers, and other credentialed elites? How do the sons, daughters, nephews, nieces, and probably even cousins of the elites get their jobs in the media, foundations, and other plush appointments in the nation's institutions? Slim chance that some bright graduate of a regional college (one with a direction in its name) who submits a resumé believing that the potential employer wants "the best person for the job" will ever be considered.

Given the existence of oppositional interests, it is expected that members of the privileged class will work to advance their interests. As employers they will seek to minimize worker wages and benefits and to fight efforts by workers to organize. As media owners, filmmakers, and writers they will produce cultural products and information that undermine efforts by the working class to organize and advance their interests. Think, for example, about how the media and opinion makers are quick to cry "class warfare" whenever someone points to the wealth of the privileged. Think also about how the opinion makers reacted to the role of Nation of Islam leader Louis Farrakhan in the Million-Man March on the Capitol mall in October of 1995. Every effort was made to discredit Farrakhan and to separate him from the march. The integrationist ideology of the slain civil rights leader Martin Luther King Jr. was resurrected over and over again, as if to say that the privileged class supports the legitimate aspirations of African Americans but not their efforts to develop their own social and economic communities and to ignore white society while doing so.

These three principles—Class structure has intergenerational permanence, There is no middle class, and Classes have conflicting interests—provide a basis for understanding the central defining features of the American class structure. We have, in effect, tried to answer the question, What is class inequality? In the next chapter we address the question, How does class inequality work?

NOTES

1. David Herzenhorn, "The Story Behind a Generous Gift to Harvard Law School," *New York Times*, April 7, 1995.
2. Harley Shaiken, *Work Transformed: Automation and Labor in the Computer Age* (New York: Holt, Rinehart and Winston, 1985); David F. Noble, *Forces of Production: A Social History of Industrial Automation* (New York: Knopf, 1984).
3. Edward N. Wolff, *Top Heavy* (New York: Twentieth Century Fund, 1996).
4. Jonathan Kozol, *Savage Inequalities: Children in America's Schools* (New York: Harper, 1991).
5. "Chicken on Chechnya?" *Nation*, April 29, 1996, 3.

◆ 20 ◆

The Children of Affluence

Robert Coles

There is, I think, a message that virtually all quite well-off American families
transmit to their children—an emotional expression of those familiar,
classbound prerogatives—money and power. I use the word
entitlement *to describe that message.*

Robert Coles has done a number of studies concerning class in the United States, focusing especially on the ideas and lives of children of poverty. This article is about the children of the affluent—those whom Coles describes as possessing a state of mind called *entitlement*, which claims as rights that which others regard as luxuries. This analysis goes far in showing how one's class influences what one expects from life, how those expectations are claimed as a matter of right, and how they influence what the child actually "chooses" to do in life.

Dramatic and secluded; old, historic, and architecturally interesting; large and with good grounds; private and palatial; beautifully restored; big, interesting, high up, and with an uninterrupted view; so the real-estate descriptions go. In the cities, it is a town house or luxury apartment on Nob Hill, Beacon Hill, the Near North Side, the Garden District. Outside the major cities, the house is in a town, township, village, station, even crossing. Anything to make it clear that one does not live simply "in the suburbs," that one is outside or away—well outside or well away, as it is so often put. The houses vary: imitation English castles; French provincial; nineteenth-century American; contemporary one-levels in the tradition of Gropius or Neutra. Sometimes the setting is formal, sometimes it is a farm—animals, rail fences, pastureland, a barn,

maybe a shed or two, a flower garden, and more recently, a few rows of vegetables. Sometimes there is a swimming pool, a tennis court, a greenhouse. Sometimes the house stands on a hill, affords a view for miles around. Sometimes trees stand close guard; and beyond them, thick brush and more trees, a jumble of them: no view, but complete privacy. Sometimes there is a paved road leading from a street up to the house's entrance. Sometimes the road is a dusty path or a trail—the casual countrified scene, prized and jealously guarded.

The trees matter; so do the grass and the shrubbery. These are not houses in a row, with patches of new grass, fledgling trees, and a bush or two. These are homes surrounded by spacious lawns and announced by tall, sturdy trees. Hedges are common, carefully arranged. And often there is a brook running through the land.

In Texas or in New Mexico, the architecture of the houses changes, as do to a degree the flora and fauna. Now the homes are ranches, big

From *The Atlantic Monthly*, September 1977. By permission of Robert Coles.

sprawling ones, many rooms in many wings. Acres and acres of land are given over to horse trails, gardens, large swimming pools, even airplane strips for private planes. In New Mexico, the large adobe houses boast nearby cacti, corrals, and so often, stunning views: across a valley, over toward mountains miles and miles away.

In such settings are a small group of America's children raised. I have for years visited the homes of boys and girls whose parents are well-to-do indeed, and sometimes quite wealthy. They are parents whose decisions have affected, in one way or another, the working-class and poor families I have worked with—growers, mine owners, other prominent businessmen, lawyers, and bankers, or real estate operators. I have wanted to know how their children grew up, how their children see themselves—and how they see their much more humble age-mates, with whom they share American citizenship, if nothing else. Put differently, I have wanted to know how the extremes of class, poverty, and wealth variously affect the psychological and moral development of a particular nation's particular century's children.

"Comfortable, comfortable places" was the way one girl described her three homes: an enormous duplex apartment in Chicago, a ski lodge in Aspen, and a lovely old New England clapboard home by the ocean toward the end of Cape Cod. She was not bragging; she knew a pleasurable, cozy, even luxurious life when she saw one (had one), and was at ease describing its many, consistent comforts. She happened to be sitting on a large sofa as she offered her observation. She touched a nearby pillow, also rather large, then moved it a bit closer to herself. In a rather uncharacteristic burst of proprietary assertiveness, the girl said: "I'd like to keep this pillow for my own house, when I'm grown up."

Children like her have a lot to look after and, sometimes, feel attached to. At the same time, they may often be overwhelmed with toys, gadgets, presents. These are children who have to contend with, as well as to enjoy, enormous couches, pillows virtually as big as chairs, rugs that were meant to be in the palaces of the Middle East, dining room tables bigger than the rooms many American children share with brothers or sisters. Always they are aware of the importance and fragility of objects: a vase, a dish,

a tray, a painting or lithograph or pencil sketch, a lamp. How much of that world can the child even comprehend? Sometimes, in a brave attempt to bring everything under control, a young child will enumerate (for the benefit of a teacher or a friend) all that is his or hers, the background against which a life is carried on.

Finally, the child may grow weary, abandon the spoken catalog and think of one part of his or her life that means *everything*: a snake that can reliably be seen in a certain stretch of mixed grass and shrubbery along the driveway; a pair of pheasants who come every morning to the lawn and appear remarkably relaxed as they find food; a dog or a cat or a pony or a pet bird; a friend who lives near a summer home, or the son or daughter of a Caribbean cook or maid; a visit to an amusement park—a visit which, for the child, meant more than dozens of toys, some virtually untouched since they arrived; or a country remembered above all others—Ireland or England, France or Switzerland.

These are children who learn to live with *choices*: more clothes, a wider range of food, a greater number of games, toys, hobbies, than other boys and girls may ever be able to imagine for themselves. They learn also to assume instruction—not only at school, but at home—for tennis, swimming, dancing, horseback riding. And they learn, often enough, to feel competent at those sports, in control of themselves while playing them, and not least, able to move smoothly from one to the other rather than driven to excel. It is as if the various outdoor sports are like suits of clothing, to be put on, enjoyed, then casually slipped off.

Something else many of these children learn: The newspapers, the radio, the television offer news not merely about "others" but about neighbors, friends, acquaintances of one's parents—or about issues one's parents take seriously, talk about, sometimes get quite involved in. These are children who have discovered that the "news" may well be affected, if not crucially molded, by their parents as individuals or as members of a particular segment of society. Similarly, parental authority wielded in the world is matched by parental authority exerted at home. Servants are called in, are given instructions or, indeed, even replaced summarily. In a way, those servants—by whatever name or names they are called—are for these American children a microcosm of the larger world, as they will experience it. They are the people who provide convenience and comfort. They are the people who, by and large, aim to please. Not all of them "live in"; there are cleaning women, delivery people, caretakers, town inspectors, plumbers and carpenters and electricians, carriers of telegrams, of flowers, of special delivery letters. Far more than their parents, the children observe the coming and going, the back-door bustle, the front-door activity of the "staff."

It is a complicated world, a world that others watch with envy and with curiosity, with awe, anger, bitterness, resentment. It is a world, rather often, of action, of talk believed by the talkers to have meaning and importance, of schedules or timetables. It is a world in motion—yet, at times, one utterly still: a child in a garden, surrounded by the silence that acres of lawn or woods can provide. It is a world of excitement and achievement. It is an intensely private world that can suddenly become vulnerable to the notice of others. It is, obviously, a world of money and power—a twentieth-century American version of both. It is also a world in which children grow up, come to terms with their ample surroundings, take to them gladly, deal with them anxiously, and show themselves boys and girls who have their own special circumstances to master—a particular way of life to understand and become a part of.

ENTITLED

It won't do to talk of *the* affluent in America. It won't do to say that in our upper-middle-class suburbs, or among our wealthy, one observes clear-cut, consistent psychological or cultural characteristics. Even in relatively homogeneous places, there are substantial differences in home-life, in values taught, hobbies encouraged, beliefs advocated or sometimes virtually instilled.

But it is the obligation of a psychological observer like me, who wants to know how children make sense of a certain kind of life, to document as faithfully as possible the way a common heritage of money and power affects the assumptions of particular boys and girls. Each child, of course, is also influenced by certain social, racial, cultural, or

religious traditions, or thoroughly idiosyncratic ones—a given family's tastes, sentiments, ideals. And yet, the sheer fact of class affiliation has enormous power over a child's inner life. . . .

Wealth does not corrupt nor does it ennoble. But wealth does govern the minds of privileged children, gives them a peculiar kind of identity that they never lose, whether they grow up to be stockbrokers or communards, and whether they lead healthy or unstable lives. There is, I think, a message that virtually all quite well-off American families transmit to their children—an emotional expression of those familiar, classbound prerogatives, money and power. I use the word *entitlement* to describe that message.

The word was given to me by the rather rich parents of a child I began to talk with almost two decades ago, in 1959. I have watched those parents become grandparents, and have seen what they described as "the responsibilities of entitlement" handed down to a new generation. When the father, a lawyer and stockbroker from a prominent and quietly influential family, referred to the "entitlement" his children were growing up to know, he had in mind a social rather than a psychological phenomenon: the various juries or committees that select the Mardi Gras participants in New Orleans's annual parade and celebration. He knew that his daughter was "entitled" to be invited.

He wanted, however, to go beyond that social fact. He talked about what he had received from his parents and what he would give to his children, "automatically, without any thought," and what they too would pass on. The father was careful to distinguish between the social entitlement and "something else," a "something else" he couldn't quite define but knew he had to try to evoke if he was to be psychologically candid:

> Our children have a good life ahead of them; and I think they know it now. I think they did when they were three or four, too. It's *entitlement*, that's what I call it. My wife didn't know what I was talking about when I first used the word. She thought it had something to do with our ancestry. Maybe it does. I don't mean to be snide. I just think our children grow up taking a lot for granted, and it can be good that they do, and it can be bad. It's like anything else; it all depends. I mean, you can have spoiled brats for children, or you can have kids who want to share what they have. I don't mean give

away all their money. I mean be responsible, and try to live up to their ideals, and not just sit around wondering which island in the Caribbean to visit this year, and where to go next summer to get away from the heat and humidity here in New Orleans.

At the time, he said no more; at the time, I wasn't especially interested in pursuing the subject. But as months became years, I came back to that word *entitlement*. There is, as it happens, a psychiatric term that closely connects with it. *Narcissistic entitlement* is the phrase, when referring to a particular kind of "disturbed" child. The term could be used in place of the more conventional, blunter ones: a smug, self-satisfied child; or a child who thinks he owns the world, or will one day. It is an affliction that strikes particularly the wealthy child. . . .

If narcissism is something a migrant child or a ghetto child has to contend with, it will take on one flavor (narcissistic despair, for instance), whereas for a child of wealth, narcissistic entitlement is the likely possibility. The child has much, but wants and expects more, all assumed to be his or hers by right—at once a psychological and material inheritance that the world will provide. One's parents will oblige, will be intermediaries, will go back and forth—bringing from stores or banks or wherever those various offerings that serve to gratify the mind's sense of its own importance, its own *due*.

This syndrome is one that wealthy parents recognize instinctively, often wordlessly—and fear. When their children are four, five, and six, parents able to offer them virtually anything sometimes begin to pull back, in concern if not in outright horror. Not only has a son become increasingly demanding or petulant; even when he is quiet, he seems to be sitting on a throne of sorts—expecting things to happen, wondering with annoyance why they don't, reassuring himself and others that they will or, if they don't, shrugging his shoulders and waiting for the next splendid moment.

It was just such an impasse—not dramatic, but quite definite and worrisome—that prompted the New Orleans father quoted earlier to use the word *entitlement*. He had himself been born to wealth, as will be the case for generations of his family to come, unless the American economic system changes drastically in the future. But he

was worried about what a lot of money can do to a personality. When his young daughter, during a Mardi Gras season, kept *assuming* she would one day receive this honor and that honor—indeed, become a Mardi Gras queen—he realized that his notion of "entitlement" was not quite hers. *Noblesse oblige* requires a gesture toward others.

He was not the only parent to express such a concern to me in the course of my work. In homes where mothers and fathers profess no explicit reformist persuasions, they nevertheless worry about what happens to children who grow up surrounded by just about everything they want, virtually on demand. "When they're like that, they've gone from spoiled to spoiled rotten—and beyond, to some state I don't know how to describe."

Obviously, it is possible for parents to have a lot of money yet avoid bringing up their children in such a way that they feel like members of a royal family. But even parents determined not to spoil their children often recognize what might be called the existential (as opposed to strictly psychological) aspects of their situation. A father may begin rather early on lecturing his children about the meaning of money; a mother may do her share by saying *no*, even when *yes* is so easy to say. Such a child, by the age of five or six, has very definite notions of what is possible, even if it is not always permitted. That child, in conversation, and without embarrassment or the kind of reticence and secretiveness that come later, may reveal a substantial knowledge of economic affairs. A six-year-old girl I spoke to knew that she would, at twenty-one, inherit half a million dollars. She also knew that her father "only" gave her twenty-five cents a week, whereas some friends of hers received as much as a dollar. She was vexed; she asked her parents why they were so "strict." One friend had even used the word "stingy" for the parents. The father, in a matter-of-fact way, pointed out to the daughter that she did, after all, get "anything she really wants." Why, then, the need for an extravagant allowance? The girl was won over. But admonitions don't always modify the quite realistic appraisal children make of what they are heir to; and they don't diminish their sense of entitlement—a state of mind that pervades their view of the world. . . .

◆ 21 ◆

The Uses of Poverty: The Poor Pay All

Herbert J. Gans

Many of the functions served by the poor could be replaced if poverty were eliminated, but almost always at higher costs to others, particularly more affluent others.

This article examines the poor in America and shows how they are used in society and how they function for the rest of us. Herbert J. Gans is saying: Let's face it, you and I benefit from having the poor. Do not think that Gans is saying there must be a class of poor; instead he is arguing that, in capitalism, the poor are exploited in a number of ways. Eliminating the poor will be costly to the affluent. Poverty is then tied to the structure of society: People are kept in low positions in large part for the benefit of those in high positions. Those in high positions, because they benefit, refuse to make real changes that deal with ending poverty.

Associating poverty with positive functions seems at first glance to be unimaginable. Of course, the slumlord and the loan shark are commonly known to profit from the existence of poverty, but they are viewed as evil men, so their activities are classified among the dysfunctions of poverty. However, what is less often recognized, at least by the conventional wisdom, is that poverty also makes possible the existence or expansion of respectable professions and occupations, for example, penology, criminology, social work, and public health. More recently, the poor have provided jobs for professional and paraprofessional "poverty warriors," and for journalists and social scientists, this author included, who have

supplied the information demanded by the revival of public interest in poverty.

Clearly, then, poverty and the poor may well satisfy a number of positive functions for many nonpoor groups in American society. I shall describe thirteen such functions—economic, social, and political—that seem to me most significant.

THE FUNCTIONS OF POVERTY

First, the existence of poverty ensures that society's "dirty work" will be done. Every society has such work: physically dirty or dangerous, temporary, dead-end and underpaid, undignified and menial jobs. Society can fill these jobs by paying higher wages than for "clean" work, or it can force people who have no other choice to do the dirty work—and at low wages. For America, poverty functions to provide a low-wage labor pool that is willing—or, rather, unable to be un-willing—to perform dirty work at low cost. In-deed, this function of the poor is so important that in some southern states, welfare payments have been cut off during the summer months when the poor are needed to work in the fields. Moreover, much of the debate about the negative income tax and the family assistance plan has concerned their impact on the work incentive, by which is actually meant the incentive of the poor to do the needed dirty work if the wages there-from are no larger than the income grant. Many economic activities that involve dirty work de-pend on the poor for their existence: restaurants, hospitals, parts of the garment industry, and "truck farming," among others, could not persist in their present form without the poor.

Second, because the poor are required to work at low wages, they subsidize a variety of economic activities that benefit the affluent. For example, domestics subsidize the upper-middle and upper classes, making life easier for their employers and freeing affluent women for a variety of profes-sional, cultural, civic, and partying activities. Similarly, because the poor pay a higher propor-tion of their income in property and sales taxes, among others, they subsidize many state and local governmental services that benefit more af-fluent groups. In addition, the poor support inno-vation in medical practice as patients in teaching and research hospitals and as guinea pigs in med-ical experiments.

Third, poverty creates jobs for a number of oc-cupations and professions that serve or "service" the poor, or protect the rest of society from them. As already noted, penology would be minuscule without the poor, as would the need for police. Other activities and groups that flourish because of the existence of poverty are the numbers game, the sale of heroin and cheap wines and liquors, Pente-costal ministers, faith healers, prostitutes, pawn shops, and the peacetime army, which recruits its enlisted men mainly from among the poor.

Fourth, the poor buy goods others do not want and thus prolong the economic usefulness of such goods—day-old bread, fruit and vegetables that would otherwise have to be thrown out, sec-ondhand clothes, and deteriorating automobiles and buildings. They also provide incomes for doctors, lawyers, teachers, and others who are too old, poorly trained, or incompetent to attract more affluent clients.

In addition to economic functions, the poor perform a number of social functions.

Fifth, the poor can be identified and punished as alleged or real deviants in order to uphold the legitimacy of conventional norms. To justify the desirability of hard work, thrift, honesty, and monogamy, for example, the defenders of these norms must be able to find people who can be accused of being lazy, spendthrift, dishonest, and promiscuous. Although there is some evidence that the poor are about as moral and law-abiding as anyone else, they are more likely than middle-class transgressors to be caught and punished when they participate in deviant acts. Moreover, they lack the political and cultural power to cor-rect the stereotypes that other people hold of them and thus continue to be thought of as lazy, spendthrift, and so on, by those who need living proof that moral deviance does not pay.

Sixth, and conversely, the poor offer vicarious participation to the rest of the population in the uninhibited sexual, alcoholic, and narcotic be-havior in which they are alleged to participate and which, being freed from the constraints of af-fluence, they are often thought to enjoy more than the middle classes. Thus many people, some social scientists included, believe that the poor not only are more given to uninhibited be-havior (which may be true, although it is often motivated by despair more than by lack of inhibi-tion) but derive more pleasure from it than afflu-ent people (a finding that research by Lee Rainwater, Walter Miller, and others shows to be patently untrue). However, whether the poor ac-tually have more sex and enjoy it more is irrele-vant; as long as middle-class people believe this to be true, they can participate in it vicariously when instances are reported in factual or fic-tional form.

Seventh, the poor also serve a direct cultural function when culture created by or for them is adopted by the more affluent. The rich often collect artifacts from extinct folk cultures of poor people; and almost all Americans listen to the blues, Negro spirituals, and country music, which originated among the southern poor. Re-cently, they have enjoyed the rock styles that were born, like the Beatles, in the slums, and in the last year, poetry written by ghetto children has become popular in literary circles. The poor also serve as culture heroes, particularly, of course, to the left; but the hobo, the cowboy, the hipster, and the mythical prostitute with a heart of gold have performed this function for a variety of groups.

Eighth, poverty helps guarantee the status of those who are not poor. In every hierarchical society, someone has to be at the bottom; but in American society, in which social mobility is an important goal for many and people need to know where they stand, the poor function as a reliable and relatively permanent measuring rod for status comparisons. This is particularly true for the working class, whose politics is influenced by the need to maintain status distinctions between themselves and the poor, much as the aristocracy must find ways of distinguishing itself from the *nouveaux riches*.

Ninth, the poor also aid the upward mobility of groups just above them in the class hierarchy. Thus a goodly number of Americans have entered the middle class through the profits earned from the provision of goods and services in the slums, including illegal or nonrespectable ones that upper-class and upper-middle-class businessmen shun because of their low prestige. As a result, members of almost every immigrant group have financed their upward mobility by providing slum housing, entertainment, gambling, narcotics, and the like to later arrivals—most recently to blacks and Puerto Ricans.

Tenth, the poor help to keep the aristocracy busy, thus justifying its continued existence. "Society" uses the poor as clients of settlement houses and beneficiaries of charity affairs; indeed, the aristocracy must have the poor to demonstrate its superiority over other elites who devote themselves to earning money.

Eleventh, the poor, being powerless, can be made to absorb the costs of change and growth in American society. During the nineteenth century, they did the backbreaking work that built the cities; today, they are pushed out of their neighborhoods to make room for "progress." Urban renewal projects to hold middle-class taxpayers in the city and expressways to enable suburbanites to commute downtown have typically been located in poor neighborhoods because no other group will allow itself to be displaced. For the same reason, universities, hospitals, and civic centers also expand into land occupied by the poor. The major costs of the industrialization of agriculture have been borne by the poor, who are pushed off the land without recompense; and they have paid a large share of the human cost of the growth of American power overseas, for they have provided many of the foot soldiers for Vietnam and other wars.

Twelfth, the poor facilitate and stabilize the American political process. Because they vote and participate in politics less than other groups, the political system is often free to ignore them. Moreover, because they can rarely support Republicans, they often provide the Democrats with a captive constituency that has no other place to go. As a result, the Democrats can count on their votes, and be more responsive to voters—for example, the white working class—who might otherwise switch to the Republicans.

Thirteenth, the role of the poor in upholding conventional norms (see the fifth point, earlier) also has a significant political function. An economy based on the ideology of *laissez faire* requires a deprived population that is allegedly unwilling to work or that can be considered inferior because it must accept charity or welfare in order to survive. Not only does the alleged moral deviancy of the poor reduce the moral pressure on the present political economy to eliminate poverty, but socialist alternatives can be made to look quite unattractive if those who will benefit most from them can be described as lazy, spendthrift, dishonest, and promiscuous.

THE ALTERNATIVES

I have described thirteen of the more important functions poverty and the poor satisfy in American society, enough to support the functionalist thesis that poverty, like any other social phenomenon, survives in part because it is useful to society or some of its parts. This analysis is not intended to suggest that because it is often functional, poverty *should* exist, or that it *must* exist. For one thing, poverty has many more dysfunctions than functions; for another, it is possible to suggest functional alternatives.

For example, society's dirty work could be done without poverty, either by automation or by paying "dirty workers" decent wages. Nor is it necessary for the poor to subsidize the many activities they support through their low-wage jobs. This would, however, drive up the costs of these activities, which would result in higher prices to their customers and clients. Similarly, many of the professionals who flourish because of the poor could be given other roles. Social workers could provide counseling to the affluent, as they prefer to do anyway; and the police could devote themselves to traffic and organized crime. Other roles would have to be found for badly trained or incompetent professionals now relegated to serving the poor, and someone else would have to pay their salaries. Fewer penologists would be employable, however. And Pentecostal religion could probably not survive without the poor—nor would parts of the second-hand and third-hand goods market. And in many cities, "used" housing that no one else wants would have to be torn down at public expense.

Alternatives for the cultural functions of the poor could be found more easily and cheaply. Indeed, entertainers, hippies, and adolescents are already serving as the deviants needed to uphold traditional morality and as devotees of orgies to "staff" the fantasies of vicarious participation.

The status functions of the poor are another matter. In a hierarchical society, some people must be defined as inferior to everyone else with respect to a variety of attributes, but they need not be poor in the absolute sense. One could conceive of a society in which the "lower class," though last in the pecking order, received 75 percent of the median income, rather than 15 to 40 percent, as is now the case. Needless to say, this would require considerable income redistribution.

The contribution the poor make to the upward mobility of the groups that provide them with goods and services could also be maintained without the poor's having such low incomes. However, it is true that if the poor were more affluent, they would have access to enough capital to take over the provider role, thus competing with, and perhaps rejecting, the "outsiders." (Indeed, owing in part to antipoverty programs, this is already happening in a number of ghettos, where white storeowners are being replaced by blacks.) Similarly, if the poor were more affluent, they would make less willing clients for upper-class philanthropy, although some would still use settlement houses to achieve upward mobility, as they do now. Thus "society" could continue to run its philanthropic activities.

The political functions of the poor would be more difficult to replace. With increased affluence, the poor would probably obtain more political power and be more active politically. With higher incomes and more political power, the poor would be likely to resist paying the costs of growth and change. Of course, it is possible to imagine urban renewal and highway projects that properly reimbursed the displaced people, but such projects would then become considerably more expensive, and many might never be built. This, in turn, would reduce the comfort and convenience of those who now benefit from urban renewal and expressways. Finally, hippies could serve also as more deviants to justify the existing political economy—as they already do. Presumably, however, if poverty were eliminated, there would be fewer attacks on that economy.

In sum, then, many of the functions served by the poor could be replaced if poverty were eliminated, but almost always at higher costs to others, particularly more affluent others. Consequently, a functional analysis must conclude that poverty persists not only because it fulfills a number of positive functions but also because many of the functional alternatives to poverty would be quite dysfunctional for the affluent members of society. A functional analysis thus ultimately arrives at much the same conclusion as radical sociology, except that radical thinkers treat as manifest what I describe as latent: That social phenomena that are functional for affluent or powerful groups and dysfunctional for poor or powerless ones persist; that when the elimination of such phenomena through functional alternatives would generate dysfunctions for the affluent or powerful, they will continue to persist; and that phenomena like poverty can be eliminated only when they become dysfunctional for the affluent or powerful, or when the powerless can obtain enough power to change society.

Blue Collar Blues

Bernard Carl Rosen

*[The working class] have suffered the cruelest fate that can befall a social class: they
have lost a social revolution. Through no fault of their own they have been
grievously hurt by the techno-service system's triumph over manufacturing.
They have become losers, and losing is hard to take. What is even sadder,
they still do not fully understand what is going on.*

Bernard Rosen examines how the economy has changed dramatically in the past
twenty years and with it the increasing decline of importance and power of the blue-
collar worker. He describes a "new elite" surfacing in the American economy,
which ignores and even is hostile toward the working class, causing the latter to lose
the security and self confidence they once had before the "information revolution."

No group feels more badly treated than the working class. No group feels more keenly that its interests are being neglected, that its status is in freefall, that its economic security is in jeopardy. And perhaps no group feels more worried and angry. To sympathetic observers the reason for the workers' discontent seems obvious enough: the techno-service society has treated them shabbily. How can anyone doubt this? Haven't their wages been slashed, their claim to a job ignored, perhaps the job itself eliminated? Is not their condition dire? Haven't they, as one newsmagazine put it, been shafted?[1] And isn't this the cause of their disgruntled mood?

It is not that simple. Economic factors alone do not explain working-class discontent. It is true that many factory workers feel pinched. Some

have lost their jobs; others have taken pay cuts; most find pay increases harder to come by. This is painful and no doubt contributes to blue-collar anxiety. But it is not the only cause of their discontent, not even the most important one. In fact, on average, objective conditions have not deteriorated to the extent workers think they have. In many cases they have remained the same; in some cases they have improved.

General opinion notwithstanding, it is not only economic deprivation, a state of the pocketbook, from which some workers suffer; it is also relative social deprivation, a state of the mind. What has in truth declined for almost all blue-collar workers is their satisfaction with their social position. When they contrast their position with what they think it should be, they feel a distinct sense of loss. But it is less a loss of dollars than a loss of respect.

Many workers are angry because they believe they have been cheated out of what is rightly theirs: an honored place in society. They feel

From Bernard Carl Rosen, *Winners and Losers of the Information Revolution: Psychosocial Change and Its Discontents.* Copyright © 1998 by Bernard Carl Rosen. Praeger Publishers, an imprint of Greenwood Publishing Group, Inc.

unwelcome and ridiculed, like an old suit, out-of-fashion and shabby, ready for the trash can. The skills and muscles that once assured them an honored place in society have declined in value, and as a result so have they. Their values are being replaced by new values and their needs and those of society no longer mesh harmoniously. A new social order now calls the tune, and blue-collar workers, like musicians in a strange orchestra playing an unfamiliar tune, are now minor performers—off key and getting little applause.

Blue-collar workers feel powerless to protect themselves against forces they don't understand, and vulnerable to the scorn and slander of people they despise and fear. They are becoming deracinated. Their roots are in a world that is rapidly losing influence and, as a result, so are they. The old manufacturing economy in which they played an important role no longer rules the economic roost. Its place has been taken by a new system, the information society produced by the Second Great Transformation—a system to which they are ill-adapted and in which they feel poorly rewarded.

Their place in this world is not the one they expected and feel they rightly deserve. As they see it, their contributions to society are undervalued and taken for granted. Unfortunately society no longer sees it their way, and they are having difficulty accepting this sad fact. In truth, they have suffered the cruelest fate that can befall a social class: they have lost a social revolution. Through no fault of their own they have been grievously hurt by the techno-service system's triumph over manufacturing. They have become losers, and losing is hard to take. What is even sadder, they still do not fully understand what is going on. . . .

Mostly, factory workers produce objects for unknown customers, whose personality needs they need never consider. No one asks the production worker to greet the customer with a smile and an offer to be of service. Nor is the workplace as competitive for blue-collar workers as it is for knowledge creators and information processors. Competition exists, of course, on the factory floor, but it tends to be controlled by company and union rules. Also, the production worker has less opportunity to threaten others or be threatened by them, and thus less reason to adopt the chameleon's disguise.

On those occasions when they try to play the chameleon's game, dealing in intangible images rather than material objects, the factory worker's relative lack of the verbal and interpersonal skills intrinsic to the Chameleon Complex is a distinct liability. The Chameleon Complex may be an asset to middle-class men and women; its absence can be a handicap for blue-collar workers trying to get ahead in situations where impression management counts a lot. Perhaps for all these reasons, chameleonism strikes blue-collar workers as downright dishonest. And they feel awkward and out of place in a society that tacitly accepts chameleonism as the norm.

THE END OF AN ERA

Even though . . . the economy remains strong, it would be foolish to deny that some workers have experienced severe economic loss and that this has contributed to their anxiety. Massive economic change—the Second Great Transformation—is costing some workers their jobs. This has caused pain and it deserves discussion, even though, as I believe, it is only one of several factors contributing to the current mood of discontent among blue-collar workers.

Workers are learning that lean and mean corporations are hard to live with, that job security is something their parents may have known but which is no longer certain for them. They are learning that improved productivity and economic growth do not necessarily create jobs for everyone, and that a continually rising standard of living can no longer be taken for granted. In brief, they are learning an old, if obvious, lesson—that slim wallets depress the spirit and joblessness can lead to despair. Unfortunately, Americans are ill-prepared for the school of economic hard knocks. They have grown accustomed to more work benefits, greater job security, and larger paychecks than workers have ever known before.

The current plight of workers mauled by economic change is particularly excruciating because for a brief period, from the end of World War II to the early 1970s, blue-collar workers enjoyed an astounding improvement in social position and living standard. During that period the economy became significantly more productive, enriching the lives of people in almost every station in life. Never before had the material condition of so many Americans changed so much for the better in so short a time with such far-reaching consequences.

The extraordinary growth of the American economy after 1945 created a wealth of good-paying jobs that was unprecedented anywhere in the world. Skilled workers, and even those with few if any skills, enjoyed incomes never dreamed of by previous generations. Real earnings of the typical worker were twice as high around 1972 than they had been in the late 1940s.[2] Automatically, almost magically, the children of the working class, many of them factory workers like their parents, stepped on the escalator that is the American Dream, moved into well-paying jobs, bought houses in the suburbs, and took on the title and accoutrements of the middle class. Ambitious war veterans from every social stratum equipped themselves with college degrees bought with money provided by the GI Bill, and buoyed by a burgeoning economy became managers, entrepreneurs, and professionals, joining the ranks of the upper-middle class.

But this period of exuberant economic growth and fabulous social mobility did not last. In mid-1973, the bright days of seemingly endless and effortless growth came to an end. The economy, which had been growing at a brisk average rate of 3.9 percent during the period 1950 to 1970, slowed to a modest growth rate of 1 or 2 percent. Jobs became scarcer and real wages increased slowly; the upward movement of average family income slowed to a crawl.[3]

Among the first to feel the pinch of the slowdown were factory workers doing routine, repetitive work. Many of them began to live in fear of the ax. Across the nation, workers who once felt secure started to churn with anxiety about their future in companies for which they had worked for many years and to which they had given, as the saying goes, the best years of their lives. Looking about them or following the news in the media, they discovered that workers were losing their jobs. Many companies began reacting to grim economic news: they were losing money. Profit margins had slipped disastrously. Pretax profits, which had averaged 16.9 percent in the

1950s, fell to 10.7 percent in the 1970s and to 8.7 percent in the 1980s. Companies had to respond to this progressive decline or go under. Some in fact became bankrupt, others were taken over by competitors, but many survived.

Stung by foreign competition, desperate to survive in a fiercely competitive global market, eager to fend off angry stockholders and keep their own jobs, corporate managers undertook a number of draconian measures to return their companies to profitability. For one thing, some of them began moving production abroad to locations where routine work could be quickly learned and efficiently performed, where workers could make things comparable in quality to that obtained from more highly-paid Americans.

Consider these sobering statistics. It costs about $16 an hour to employ a production worker in the United States, as compared with $2.40 in Mexico, $1.50 in Poland, and 50 cents or less in China, India, Malaysia, and Indonesia. Auto manufacturing highlights the extent of international wage differentials. Mexican workers producing 1993 Ford Escorts earned $2.38 an hour; Americans working on the same car earned $17.50 an hour. With wage differentials this large it does not take a rocket scientist to figure out how the *Fortune* 500 firms across America were able to cut their American payroll from 16.2 million in 1990 to 11.8 million in 1993 and still keep production high. Many of them had transferred some of their production to low-cost countries.

Employers in poor countries often force their workers to accept wages Americans would not tolerate. Some workers in Shenzhen, China, earn as little as one yuan (12 American cents) an hour, and work 12 to 13 hour days, seven days a week. In India millions of children, some as young as seven years of age, weave carpets for a pittance. Factory conditions are often Dickensian—dark and dismal and dangerous. Hundreds of workers die needlessly in factory fires, trapped in buildings that lack the simplest precautions against accidental conflagration or provisions for escape once a fire breaks out. Industrial accidents are common; the risk of being accidentally killed in a factory is six times higher in South Korea and fifteen times higher in Pakistan than in the United States. Competition for manufacturing jobs with workers willing to work under such conditions seems hopelessly unfair to many Americans.[4]

Transferring some of their production to low-wage countries was only one of the strategies companies employed to stay afloat in turbulent economic waters. There were others. Where possible manufacturers began employing robots and computers, increasing productivity but also putting people out of work. Like the Luddites (1811–16), who smashed machines in the textile mills of industrializing England in a futile effort to save their jobs, few workers have difficulty comprehending the connection between technology and unemployment. In 1930, John Maynard Keynes saw it too. "We are being afflicted with a new disease . . . technological unemployment," he explained to policy makers worried by a sinking economy that, as time would show, was slowly slipping into the worst depression of modern times.[5] And even more recently, economist Paul Krugman reminded us that machine-driven efficiency inevitably hurts some workers. The gain in long term riches must be paid for in the short run by production workers whose jobs and skills are being swallowed up by technological progress. This is regrettable but unavoidable, he concluded. There is no gain without pain.

In addition to transferring production abroad and introducing advanced technologies, managers began to reduce their workforces. In some industries, appreciable numbers of production workers were laid off or forced into retirement. In one year alone, 1993, the top 100 American electronic companies eliminated 480,000 jobs. For example, Compaq Computer Corporation, the world's biggest maker of computers, laid off 20 percent of its staff. In a different field, Caterpillar, the manufacturer of construction and mining machinery, took an even harsher step: it slashed its work force 31 percent. U.S. West, a Baby Bell telephone company headquartered in Englewood, Colorado, began phasing out 9,000 jobs, about one-seventh of its work force. American Telephone and Telegraph, mother of phone companies, announced in 1996 that it would lay off no less than 40,000 of its employees. Albert J. Dunlap ("Chainsaw Al" to his critics), chairman of the Sunbeam Corporation, announced in 1997 that he would slash Sunbeam's overall workforce in half, having previously lopped off one-third of the workforce at the Scott Paper Company in just 28 months.[6]

Rather than lay off employees, some corporations seek to reduce expenses by simply not filling vacant slots, forcing the remaining employees to carry the workload of their former co-workers. At the General Motors Fisher Body plant in Flint, Michigan, employees gripe that they are being asked to do what used to be several different jobs. "If somebody retires, all they do is take the work and give it to other people," said one worker. That complaint is echoed by others in many industries across the country. Said one employee of Gamma, a large photo lab in Chicago, which had dismissed 16 percent of the staff the year before: "Everyone has to do everyone's job in addition to their own."[7] When the workload becomes too burdensome and the complaints of workers too noisy to be ignored, some companies fill full-time positions with part-time or temporary hired hands, who receive no expensive benefits, health insurance, unemployment payments, and paid vacations, and can be laid off at a moment's notice.

Another tactic is to pile on the overtime. Some companies use overtime to wring the most out of their facilities without having to hire new people or expand the plant. The factory workweek in 1994, a robust year when the economy grew at a 4 percent annual rate, averaged a near record 42 hours, including 4.6 hours of overtime. The big-three auto makers pushed this figure to ten hours a week overtime. "We are the workingest people in the world," says Audrey Freedman, a labor economist.[8] But workers complain of exhaustion. One worker even welcomed a brief strike just to get a few days off. Still, notwithstanding bone-weariness and the loss of precious time with family and friends, overtime pay is welcome to most workers and princely to some. Many autoworkers are earning $65,000 to $70,000 a year, and electricians on plant-maintenance crews working seven-day weeks can push their income to as much as $100,000 annually.[9] Paying overtime is expensive to the company, of course, but it is cheaper than building new plants and hiring new workers.

Some companies sought to increase production without cutting the work force or substantially increasing overtime. The Birmingham

Steel Corporation took this route. As recently as 1987, it had produced 167,000 tons of steel with 184 workers, an average of 912 tons per worker. Six years later, after tightening production procedures and strictly controlling new hiring, it produced 276,000 tons with 207 workers, an average of 1,335 per person, which works out to an 8 percent increase in productivity per year, a remarkable figure by any standard. Many other industries have also become more productive, bringing down costs and boosting production. In the entire country, overall industrial production was 40 percent higher in 1994 and four times higher than in 1950. In effect, more was being made with fewer people. . . .

THE WAR AGAINST THE WORKING CLASS

. . . Whom then do they blame for their unhappy condition? Who are the people who make them feel unappreciated and insecure? The villain is the New Elite, the upwardly-mobile, bright, hardworking, eager for power and wealth, information processors who dominate the techno-service society.

Elitists rub blue-collar workers the wrong way. For one thing, the Elite's wealth and power are too new, too different, too offensive to working-class sensibilities to have won the acceptance given to the inheritors of old money and to the possessors of valued talent and quirky good fortune. For another thing, the masters of the information society make no bones about their own moral and intellectual superiority. With grating hauteur, they have announced to the world that their special mission is to save America and make it atone for its sins. Such pretensions to superiority stick in the worker's craw. Worse yet, as a demonstration of its moral superiority the Elite is pushing affirmative action policies that undermine the workers' sense of security and confidence in themselves. It is this loss of security and self-confidence, this feeling of having lost status respect, at least as much as anything else, that accounts for blue-collar disaffection.

The hostility many workers feel for the New Elite surfaced during the debates about the wisdom of enlarging the free trade pact with Canada to include Mexico. Elitists generally supported the North American Free Trade Agreement. Said one young lawyer, interviewed as she was catching a train bound for a Chicago suburb, "We've got to keep up with the world. It's just smart economic policy." Other lawyers, stockbrokers, and accountants catching the same train also enthusiastically supported the treaty. It was, as one man put it, a "no brainer." As he saw it, the United States has everything to gain and nothing to lose by opening its gates to trade with Mexico.

But to many workers the issue looked entirely different. To Sharon Jones, a 36-year-old union worker who cleans train cars for $8 an hour, the treaty presented a threat to her livelihood. "It's going to take our jobs away," she said. And then she added, in angry tones that revealed the blue-collar suspicion of the credentialed class, "I know the rich people say it won't. But what do they care about working people? The only ones looking to protect people like us is the A.F.L.-C.I.O. And if the union says it's bad, I trust them. Got no reason to trust those other folks." And to another worker, a Chicago truck driver named Dennis McGue, the treaty looked like the work of "fancy-pants elites" who cared nothing for the workers. "I guess when you live up on a hill," he said, "you just don't see the people in the valley."[10]

The "people on the hill" generally know little about the "people in the valley" and care little that the blue-collar class has had to endure a steady deterioration in status. Nor are they impressed when factory workers point to the importance of their work. Quite the reverse. For one thing, many arts and skills are in decline. Ancient crafts have been broken into simple operations, routinized and robbed of intrinsic merit. Old skills, painfully acquired through long years of apprenticeship, have fallen into disuse, replaced by robots and computers. And for another thing, even granted that workers still make things that move on roads and fly through the air, that clothe and house the nation, that arm the military and win wars, these are the products of an old regime, the manufacturing system, now in relative decline. A new system, the information economy, is in ascendance, and its masters take for granted the goods the old system still builds. As the New Elite sees it, building bridges and roads, making cars and airplanes, count for less in the national scheme of things than building pyramids of words. Possessing and processing information are what really matter; manual work can be delegated to lesser breeds.

This attitude baffles and infuriates most blue-collar workers. It is not what they had expected. In the past, society understood their importance and visibly showed its respect. Organized in powerful labor unions, as many of them were, blue-collar workers were people to whom politicians and employers paid heed. They lobbied for legislation to protect their interests; they demanded wage increases that appreciably lifted their pay. And if their demands were not met they tied a company up in strikes that in time would bring it to its knees. Taken all in all, with its voice in the councils of government, its contributions to political parties and the clout that resulted from judiciously placed money, organized labor had won a place at the table of power. It negotiated as equals with employers and politicians over its share of the nation's economic pie. And as labor's influence grew, the worker enjoyed the esteem that power always brings.

Needless to say, much has changed since the glory days of working-class influence. Blue-collar clout has declined as the unions, particularly in manufacturing industries, have lost members. In the 1950s about a quarter of all workers in the private sector belonged to labor unions. Today, only 11 percent are union members, about the same as in the 1930s. And in a marked change with the past, while blue-collar membership declined service sector membership grew: today service workers are the most rapidly growing segment of unionized labor.

As though economic disappointment and declining influence were not trouble enough, workers must also contend with attacks upon their values and personal worth. At times the media portray them, especially the white males, as louts, beer-sodden inebriates, mindless television addicts, coarse boors oblivious to the needs of women, lesbians, and gays, to the sensibilities of the crippled, the old, the fat, the ugly, and other fashionable minorities. Their lives are ridiculed as shallow and crude, wasted years spent in the pursuit of tawdry pleasure, without commitment to ideas, to the joys of self-discovery, and to the advancement of high culture. They feel under attack from all sides. Call this paranoia if you like. Say it will go away when times get better, when factory jobs once again become well paid and secure, when the golden past is somehow recaptured. But remember that working class anxiety persists in these relatively good times, that it hangs on even as the gross national product grows briskly, employment goes up and inflation down. . . .

Perhaps most damaging is the charge that factory workers are dumb. Social researchers, psychometricians, and other elite members of the information society bluntly question the blue-collar worker's ability to cope with the demands of the information age. They assert that the average blue-collar worker lacks the intelligence to cope with the technical requirements of the information system. Blue-collar IQ scores, researchers report, tend to fall on the wrong side of the bell curve, below the median. In the judgment of Richard Herrnstein and Charles Murray, authors of *The Bell Curve*, blue-collar workers tend to be deficient in "cognitive ability," the capacity to handle abstractions and process information.[11] Many of them cannot puzzle out the instructions in work manuals or understand complex job processes, and for these reasons are doomed to stay in the lower reaches of the workforce. Rattled by this low assessment of their intelligence, some workers wonder whether the elite may not be right. Certainly, the jabberwocky jargon of computer technology leaves most of them at sea, adrift and bewildered. Worse than that, they feel diminished.

But it is not the assessment of their IQ that most troubles blue-collar workers. What troubles them even more is the feeling that they no longer fit into the economy in the comfortable, reassuring way they once did, that they no longer mesh neatly with the rest of society—and that no one cares. In this conclusion they are entirely correct. They are, in fact, out-of-synch with the new system. They had been educated to work in harmony with other parts of a complex machine called the manufacturing system. But since this system has been downgraded by the techno-service economy, which needs a different kind of workforce, they sense, quite accurately, that they have been relegated to second place, along with the system they were trained to fit.

In a manufacturing system the factory is the major trainer of workers. The factory is a forceful school: its spirit enters the mind and marrow of the worker. It is in the factory that workers acquire many of the traits that define their character: respect for authority and tradition, a need for order and predictability, an admiration for technical competence. The rhythm of its machines, the constant insistence on efficiency and reliability, these attributes of the factory subtly shape workers in ways that make them suitable for life in an industrial society. Day in and day out, by example and direct instruction, the modern factory teaches him how to function in a formally organized, deeply hierarchical system, characterized by a complex division of labor, an emphasis on specialization and technical skill, a devotion to competence and efficiency. . . .

When workers complain about workforce reductions and plant shutdowns, they are told this drastic action had to be taken, even though it meant throwing people out of work and shattering their lives. The plant had to be closed because it was losing money. People had to be laid off because meticulously conducted studies showed the work force was bloated and the work shoddy. That these actions caused some people pain was regrettable, but it was for the greater good of the company and the country. Workers often find these arguments hard to refute. Sheepishly, they admit the workforce had become too large and the work may have been sloppy. Why else were Americans buying Japanese cars in preference to American ones?

Blue-collar workers cannot hope to beat the Elite at its own game. Elite arguments were fashioned by people who are extremely skilled in the use of language, expert at using words to confuse as well as to enlighten, weaving a web of verbiage to trap the unwary. Words make workers uncomfortable. They are accustomed to making tangible objects and tend to judge the value of things by their obvious utility. They are suspicious of the tools Elitists use to ply their trades: words and images, mysterious devices of dubious value. But without words and the skill to use them, workers lack the right weapons to deal with the Elite. And so, when told that their anger is not justified and must not be expressed, that it must be swallowed, bottled up, reasoned away, and treated with scorn

for the selfish, ugly thing it is, they are dumbstruck, literally at a loss for words.

Though baffled and beaten into silence by abstruse argument and softened by appeals to their better nature, many workers nevertheless remain angry. Occasionally, their anger erupts in bursts of sporadic violence or electoral revolt. The abrupt dismissal of many Democratic party politicians in the 1994 midterm elections was said to have been due to the revolt of blue-collar voters furious at the way elite politicians had been treating them. At other times blue-collar anger has taken the form of nativist outbursts at immigrants, sporadic bombings of government buildings, and attempts to set up sovereign enclaves in isolated areas—for example, an Aryan nation in the Northwest or a separate republic in Texas.

But usually the rage is hidden, buried beneath a mountain of denial, repressed from consciousness. Nonetheless, the anger is still there. It can be denied, but it can't be eliminated by denial. Boiling beneath the surface and unable to find an acceptable outlet, repressed rage takes a terrible revenge on people who will not admit its existence. For rage will be heard from, whether its possessor likes it or not. Repressed anger surfaces in feelings of irrational fear and restlessness and in a sense of drift and alienation. Its effects can be seen in the pervasive anxiety that afflicts blue-collar losers. . . .

NOTES

1. Cover of *U.S. News and World Report,* January 22, 1996.
2. The growth rate in income was part of a long-term process. From 1839 to 1886 real income doubled, and between 1913 and 1950 the Gross Domestic Product grew an average of 1.6 percent annually, which is striking considering that this period included the Great Depression. See Paul Krugman, *Peddling Prosperity* (New York: W. W. Norton, 1994), p. 3; see also *The Economist,* June 5, 1993, p. 22.
3. Steven Ratner, *New York Times Magazine,* September 19, 1993, p. 96. See also Robert J. Samuelson, *The Good Life and Its Discontents* (New York: Times Books, 1995), p. 114.
4. Data on the effects of foreign competition on American workers were taken from "Global Survey," *The Economist,* October 1, 1994, p. 32.
5. Steven Ratner, *New York Times Magazine,* September 19, 1993, p. 96.

6. For data on downsizing, see *The Economist*, July 31, 1993, p. 59; and Jon D. Hull, "The State of the Union," *Time*, January 30, 1995, pp. 53–75. For a description of its often cruel and demoralizing effects, see William Hoffman et al., "Impact of Plant Closings on Automobile Workers and Their Families," *Journal of Contemporary Human Services*, February 1991, pp. 103–107; Barry Bluestone and Bennett Harrison, *The Deindustrialization of America* (New York: Basic Books, 1982), p. 32; and Kevin Kelly, *Business Week* (Industrial Technology Edition), March 9, 1992, p. 33.

7. The quotations on downsizing are taken from George J. Church, "We're No. 1," *Time*, October 24, 1994, pp. 51–56.

8. Quoted in ibid.

9. Ibid.

10. Dirk Johnson, "Chicago on Trade Accord: A Split Along Class Lines," *New York Times*, November 14, 1993. Quotations on the trade accord are taken from this article.

11. Richard J. Herrnstein and Charles Murray, *The Bell Curve* (New York: Free Press, 1994).

◆ 23 ◆

The Polarization of Class in the World

Robert N. Bellah

The problem today is that, with the new technology, most people are no longer needed: not needed in the army, where technological sophistication, not masses of infantry, is the key to success . . . not needed in the factory where computerization and robotization has replaced the assembly line. In short, besides the elite and its immediate subordinates, most people today are just not needed for anything except minimum-wage service jobs. The problem becomes again, as it was in the old agricultural societies, how to control them, not how to include them.

Robert Bellah believes that it is class more than anything else that divides people within and between societies. This division is increasing, and its increase spells some very important problems.

Unlike in the past, capitalism and capitalists have no effective opposition. Unlike during the Cold War, poor nations are no longer courted. The global market is exaggerating class differences; winners are increasingly becoming richer, losers are increasingly becoming poorer. Those who know how to use the new technologies are becoming the new elite class; others are left behind; an impoverished underclass grows. Working for the benefit of others and for the community become less evident.

This is a moral problem to Robert Bellah. It has happened because of the "deindustrialization of our cities." Blue-collar jobs and many white-collar jobs are gone. Public support has declined. Those left behind are increasingly left out of the larger society.

To Robert Bellah class polarization has become the great enemy of people living together cooperatively in community; it encourages the tearing apart of society.

. . . Among the many differences and cleavages that seem to be driving us apart in the world today, the most pernicious are class differences, indeed the massive polarization of social classes in our country and in the world. It is much more common today to focus on racial differences, cultural differences, ethnic differences, and religious differences. Though real enough, all that serves in part as a smokescreen to divert attention from the most profound difference opening up in our world, the difference between the winners and the losers, the rich and the poor.

There is a strange resonance between the last years of the nineteenth century and the last years of our own. In the late nineteenth century capitalist development was in full swing, but it was a development so grossly exploitative, so unequal in its rewards, so patently unfair, that it stimulated the massive opposition of labor unions and socialist parties, which challenged the control of the capitalist class through much of the twentieth century. Now for the first time in one hundred years capitalism has no effective opposition. Not only is Communism dead and socialism discredited but labor unions are everywhere in shambles. Not only is the difference between the rich and the poor growing rapidly in most of the world (nowhere quite so rapidly as in the United States), but the difference between rich nations and poor nations is also growing apace. During the Cold War the poor nations had some leverage: They were courted by both sides in the global struggle for strategic advantage. With the Cold War over they can simply be abandoned. In some ways the situation is even worse today than it was one hundred years ago.

When someone emphasizes class disparities today he will be accused by conservative ideologists of preaching class war, as I have been. There is a class war today, but it is neither being waged by people like me nor by the people suffering most in today's world. Class war today is being waged ruthlessly, largely effectively, and with little resistance, by the rich on the poor both nationally and globally. Let me be more specific.

It is the global market that is literally tearing the world apart. The forces of the global market economy are impinging on all societies in the world with increasing pressure and the capacity of nation-states to protect their own populations from these pressures—one of the primary functions of the nation-state since the nineteenth century—is everywhere weakening. That means that all of us are subject to similar pressures with similar disconcerting results. I take the chief consequence of these pressures to be the growing disparity between winners and losers in the global marketplace. The result is not only income polarization, with the rich growing richer and the poor poorer, but a shrinking middle class increasingly anxious about its future.

Let us consider some of the tendencies these global pressures are creating everywhere, but with particular sharpness in the United States. First is the emergence of a deracinated elite composed of those Robert Reich calls "symbolic analysts," that is, the people who know how to use the new technologies and information systems that are transforming the global economy. Such people are located less securely in communities than in networks that may link them, flexibly and transiently, to others all over the world. Educated in the highly competitive atmosphere of excellent universities and graduate schools, such persons have learned to travel light with regard to family, church, locality, even nation. It is here, though not exclusively here, that we clearly see the cultural profile of individualization that we studied in *Habits of the Heart.*

In this powerful elite the crisis of civic membership is expressed in the loss of civic consciousness, of a sense of obligation to the rest of society, which leads to a secession from society into guarded, gated residential enclaves and ultra-modern offices, research centers and universities. A sense of a social covenant, of the idea that we are all members of the same body, is singularly weak in this new elite.

What is even more disturbing about this knowledge/power elite than its secession from the rest of society is its predatory attitude toward the rest of society, its willingness to pursue its own interests without regard to anyone else. Lester Thurow has spoken of the difference between an establishment and an oligarchy. Japan, he argues, has an establishment, while much of Latin America suffers under an oligarchy. Both are privileged elites; the essential difference is that an establishment seeks its own good by working for the good of the whole society (*noblesse oblige*) whereas an oligarchy looks out for its own interests by exploiting the rest of society. Another way of putting it would be to say that an establishment has a strong sense of civic membership while an oligarchy lacks one. One of the key differences has to do with taxation: an oligarchy taxes itself least; an establishment taxes itself most. In American history we have had establishments—most notably in the founding generation and the period after World War II—but we have also had oligarchies. It is not hard to see what we have today.

Thurow more recently has pointed out the growing disparity in incomes when an oligarchy replaces an establishment: "Never before have a majority of American workers suffered real wage reductions while the per capita domestic product was advancing." The real per capita gross domestic product went up 29 percent between 1973 and 1993. That was a lower rate of increase than in the previous twenty years, but it was still a significant increase. Yet that increase in per capita GDP was not shared equally: 80 percent of workers either lost ground or barely held their own. Among men, the top 20 percent of the labor force has been winning not some, but all of the country's wage increases. This is not a feature of all high-tech economies. Other countries comparable to ours, such as Japan and Germany, shared their increase in GDP across the board. And if we look at the top 20 percent in the United States, we will see inordinate differences. It is the top 5 percent that has gained the most and particularly the top 1 percent.

Together with the growth of this knowledge/power elite there has been the growth of an impoverished underclass. This underclass is to be found in the great urban sprawls that no longer deserve the dignity of being called cities, all over the world from Los Angeles to Calcutta. But it is also to be found in rural areas like Chiapas where peasants have lost their land and lead a precarious existence on the margins of an increasingly industrialized agriculture. The global underclass, as in a distorting mirror, reflects individualizing tendencies evident in the new elite. Here too family, locality, and religious belonging are weakened, not because of successful individual competition, as in the case of the elite, but because of a Hobbesian struggle for existence that is always only one step away from catastrophe.

In many parts of the world—for example Guatemala where 86 percent of the population is below the poverty line—there are only these two classes. Indeed, one of the features of our current situation is not only the polarization within countries but between countries. However in Europe and North America there is still a sizable, if shrinking, middle class, large enough to attract the politicians' rhetoric but not powerful enough to outweigh the influence of the international bond market on government policy. Given the significance of the middle class for modern civic life, the loss of confidence here and the growing cynicism about all institutions, including democratic institutions, is worrisome indeed.

If we wish to place the United States in this global picture there are some respects in which we are better off and some in which we are worse off. With respect to economic polarization, at least in the developed world, the United States leads the way. In 1960 American CEOs made forty times the average factory worker's income; in 1990 it was eighty times the average factory worker's income, and more recently it is estimated at one hundred or two hundred times the average factory worker's income. In 1959 the top 4 percent of our population earned $31 billion in wages and salaries, the same as the bottom 35 percent. In 1989 the top 4 percent earned $452 billion in wages and salaries, the same as the bottom 51 percent. If you look at wealth, not income, we find an even more skewed distribution. The most subsidized American is not the welfare mother but the Western rancher.

In tandem with the growth of this knowledge/power elite, as we have seen, there has been the growth of an impoverished underclass, the people from whom the elite are most eager to secede. Forty years ago people living in urban ghettoes could go to sleep with their doors unlocked. They were poor and they were segregated but relatively few of them were unemployed and relatively few of them had out-of-wed-lock babies. They were not called the underclass, a term invented in 1963 by the Swedish social analyst Gunnar Myrdal to apply to those who suffered most from poverty and segregation. He carefully hyphenated the term and put it in quotes, and it was known only to a few policy specialists. By the late 1970s it had become both a term and a problem widely recognized by the general public and even recognized by ghetto-dwellers themselves. Although originally a neutral term used in social scientific analysis, it became a pejorative term, a way to blame the poor for their poverty. I wish to be clear that I am using the term only in its analytical sense.

As a term, "underclass" had the great advantage of being color-blind in a period when we have become sensitive about racial language. Yet for most Americans the underclass was a term applied primarily to Blacks, indeed to those Blacks who still inhabited the depopulated ghettoes, which now resembled nothing so much as the bombed-out remnants of the thriving communities they had once been. It is worth remembering that five out of six poor people in America are white and that poverty breeds drugs, violence, and unstable families without regard to race.

How could all this have happened and why did we let it happen? Part of the answer is the deindustrialization of our cities. Hundreds of thousands of blue-collar jobs, and many thousands of white-collar jobs too, have left our major cities in the last thirty years. Those African Americans with enough education to enter the professional or subprofessional skilled workforce have been able to leave the old ghetto—not for integrated housing since housing segregation remains unchanged in most areas over the last three decades—but for new black neighborhoods and suburbs with some of the amenities of white neighborhoods of comparable income; thus the depopulation of the old ghettoes, which are now half or a third the population they were in their prime.

Those left behind were then subjected to the systematic withdrawal of institutional support, public and private. Middle-class African Americans took with them when they left many of the churches and clubs they had always initiated. Cities under increasing fiscal pressure closed schools, libraries, and clinics, and even police and fire stations, in ghetto areas. The most vulnerable left behind had to fend for themselves in a Hobbesian world where just making it through the month with enough to eat is often a major problem. Far from breeding dependency, life in the ghetto today requires the most urgent kind of self-reliance. Unlike some sectors of the elite, the underclass has suffered a crisis of civic membership not because its members have opted out, but because they have been pushed out, denied civic membership, by economic and political forces for which they are simply redundant. Other societies, less blinded by cultural individualism, are more sensitive to these matters than we are. In France, for example, the unemployed have come to be called *"les exclus"* (the excluded) and as such have become a central moral concern of the whole society.

This is not a story the elite wants to hear, and some journalists and even some social scientists have obliged them with another story, a story made plausible by our individualist ideology. The underclass is not, according to this alternative story, the result of the systematic withdrawal of economic and political support from the most deprived and segregated portion of our society. Members of the underclass have only themselves to blame. It is their resistance to all efforts to help them that has caused the problem. Or, in another widely believed elaboration on the underclass story, the underclass was actually created by the efforts to help its members, above all by the Great Society welfare programs, which caused self-perpetuating, indeed permanent, welfare dependency. The fact that welfare payments, including AFDC, have systematically declined in real dollars over the last twenty years, and that they have fallen by half during the 1980s alone, is ignored by those who tell this story, as is the fact that over 70 percent of those on welfare stay on it for less than two years, and over 90 percent for less than eight years.

The underclass story, which involves blaming the victims rather than recognizing a catastrophic economic and political failure of American society, serves to soothe the conscience of the affluent, and it even allows them to wax indignant at the cost of welfare in a time of expanding deficits. But more important, the underclass story serves to frighten and to warn all those who are not so affluent, who have seen what they have erode or who have had to battle just to stay even. The underclass gives people something to define themselves against, it tells them what they are not, it tells them what it would be most fearful to become. And it gives them people to blame. In the shrinking middle class, shorn of its postwar job security by the pressure of global competitiveness, it is tempting to look down at those worse off as the source of our national problems. If success and failure are the result of individual effort, who can blame those at the top, unless, of course, they are politicians?

Robert Reich elaborated this three-class typology of our current socioeconomic life when he spoke of our three classes as an "overclass," living in the safety of elite suburbs, an "underclass quarantined in surroundings that are unspeakably bleak, and often violent," and a new "anxious class" trapped in "the frenzy of effort it takes to preserve their standing." More and more families are trying to patch together two and sometimes more paychecks to meet the widening income, health care, and pension gaps that are spurring the "disintegration" of the middle class as it has historically been defined. In the anxious class the crisis of civic membership takes the form of disillusion with politics and a sense of uncertainty about the economic future so pervasive that concern for individual survival threatens to replace social solidarity.

In 1970 after twenty-five years of economic growth in which almost everyone shared, America reached the greatest degree of income equality in its recent history and enjoyed a vigorous civic culture. The challenges of the sixties were deeply unsettling but also stimulating, and a sense of civic membership continued to characterize the society as a whole. In 1995 after twenty-five years in which the profits of economic growth went entirely to the top 20 percent of the population, we have reached the high point of income inequality in our recent history and our civic life is in shambles. We have seen what Michael Lind calls the revolution of the rich and what Herbert Gans calls the war against the poor. A polarized society in which most of the population is treading water,

the bottom is sinking and the top is rising in a society in which a crisis of civic membership is vividly evident at every level. . . .

The problem today is that, with the new technology, most people are no longer needed: not needed in the army, where technological sophistication, not masses of infantry, is the key to success (see the Gulf War); not needed in the factory where computerization and robotization has replaced the assembly line. In short, besides the elite and its immediate subordinates, most people today are just not needed for anything except minimum-wage service jobs. The problem becomes again, as it was in the old agricultural societies, how to control them, not how to include them. And if this is true within the advanced nations, it is equally true between the advanced nations and the nations who are essentially left out of the technological revolution. The daunting task before us, if we are unwilling to return to a world of closed classes and mercilessly exploitative elites, is how to share the enormous productivity of the new economy with those who in the narrow sense are no longer required by it. . . .

Meeting the problems of the underclass and attempting to reincorporate its members into the larger society is the most challenging task of all. The basic problem stems from economic developments that have simply rendered the twenty or thirty million members of the underclass superfluous (and rendered much of the anxious class only marginally relevant, we should not forget). Only a fundamental change in public policy will begin to alter the situation, and in the present atmosphere such a change is hardly to be expected.

But even indispensable changes in public policy cannot alone meet the situation. Where social trust is limited and morale is blasted one of the most urgent needs is a recovery of self-respect and a sense of agency, which can only come from the participation that enables people to belong and contribute to the larger society. Participatory justice asks each individual to give all that is necessary to the common good of society. In turn it obliges society to order its institutions so that all can work to contribute to the commonweal in ways that respect their dignity and renew their freedom. Not by transfer payments alone or the compassion of social workers will the problems of the underclass be solved.

Part V

SOCIAL STRUCTURE: RACE AND ETHNICITY

Society is not only structured by class, but also by race and ethnic-group membership.

To many Americans, diversity is a quality that makes us a unique and great society. To others, diversity is regarded as a basic cause for many of our problems. In either case, diversity has been and remains a way that power, privilege, and prestige is distributed in society. Life chances and lifestyle are influenced. Placement in the class system is influenced by our place in the racial and ethnic social structure.

It is difficult to adequately describe all the various ethnic and racial minorities in the United States, and all aspects of the inequality that exists, so these selections must be treated as only a beginning for understanding. Note that other selections in this Reader also focus on issues related to ethnic and racial inequality.

Two selections focus on African Americans: Stephen Steinberg examines discrimination in occupational opportunities, and Clarence Page describes his experience and perceptions as a middle-class African American.

The third selection by Roberto Suro is an excellent description of Latino lives in the United States, and the fourth selection by Robert G. Lee examines Asian Americans in popular culture.

Everyone seems to have some position on race and ethnic group relations. For the sociologist, it is critical to understand why there is inequality, what forces favor some over others, how both historical and contemporary forces must be understood objectively. For the sociologist, it is structure that must be examined, rather than blaming others for the positions in which they find themselves. Structure matters; for inequality between people to become less of an issue means that structure must somehow change.

Sociologists sometimes describe those at the bottom of the racial and ethnic group structure "minorities." The meaning of this term has to do with power relationships, not numbers. A minority position is lower in society's power structure, and although minorities have this in common, each minority has its own history and its own difficulties. And although this part of the Reader does not examine other minorities besides ethnic and racial minorities, there are others we also need to understand—for example, sexual minorities, children, and the mentally ill.

◆ 24 ◆

Occupational Opportunities and Race

Stephen Steinberg

This job crisis is the single-most important factor behind the familiar tangle of problems that beset black communities. Without jobs, nuclear families become unglued or are never formed. Without jobs, or husbands with jobs, women with young children are forced onto the welfare rolls. Without jobs, many ghetto youth resort to the drug trade or other illicit ways of making money. . . . In short, there is no exit from the racial quagmire unless there is a national commitment to address the job crisis in black America.

The real source of the oppression of African Americans in the United States lies in our occupational structure. In the world of work, we are segregated and we always have been. Where opportunities to correct this have arisen, we have not committed ourselves to correcting this. Stephen Steinberg looks at the history of slavery and immigration and how both have produced and maintained this segregation. Then he examines the "myth of the black middle class" and points out that instead of bringing about true integration of the work force, middle-class occupations have continued to perpetuate a society of occupational segregation. Finally, he examines job discrimination in relation to the black working class and poor. Without solving the problem of work, according to Steinberg, "the legacy of slavery," American racism in all areas of life, will continue.

The essence of racial oppression is not the distorted and malicious stereotypes that whites have of blacks. These constitute the *culture* of oppression, not to be confused with the thing itself. Nor is the essence of racism epitomized by sitting in the back of a bus. In South Africa, this was called "petty apartheid" as opposed to "grand apartheid," the latter referring to political disfranchisement and the banishment of millions of blacks to isolated and impoverished "homelands." In the United States, the essence of racial oppression— *our* grand apartheid—is a racial division of labor, a system of occupational segregation that relegates most blacks to work in the least desirable job sectors or that excludes them from job markets altogether.[1]

The racial division of labor had its origins in slavery when some 650,000 Africans were imported to provide cheap labor for the South's evolving plantation economy. During the

From *Turning Back*, by Stephen Steinberg. Copyright © 1995, 2001 by Stephen Steinberg. Reprinted by permission of Beacon Press, Boston.

century after the abolition of slavery, the nation had the perfect opportunity to integrate blacks into the North's burgeoning industries. It was not Southern racism but its Northern variant that prevented this outcome. This is worth emphasizing because it has become customary—part of America's liberal mythology on race—to place the blame for the nation's racist past wholly on the South. But it was not Southern segregationists and lynch mobs who excluded blacks from participating in the critical early phases of industrialization. Rather, it was an invisible color line across *Northern* industry that barred blacks categorically from employment in the vast manufacturing sector, except for a few menial and low-paying jobs that white workers spurned. Nor can the blame be placed solely on the doorstep of greedy capitalists, those other villains of liberal iconography. Workers themselves and their unions were equally implicated in maintaining a system of occupational apartheid that reserved industrial jobs for whites and that relegated blacks to the preindustrial sector of the national economy. The long-term effects were incalculable because this closed off the only major channel of escape from racial oppression in the South. Indeed, had the industrial revolution not been "for whites only," it might have obviated the need for a civil rights revolution a century later.

The exclusion of blacks from the industrial sector was possible only because the North had access to an inexhaustible supply of immigrant labor. Some 24 million immigrants arrived between 1880 and 1930. A 1910 survey of twenty principal mining and manufacturing industries conducted by the United States Immigration Commission found that 58 percent of workers were foreign born. When the Commission asked whether the new immigration resulted in "racial displacement," it did not have blacks in mind, but rather whites who were native born or from old immigrant stock. Except for a cursory examination of the competition between Italian and black agricultural workers in Louisiana, nothing in the forty-volume report so much as hints at the possibility that mass immigration might have deleterious consequences for blacks, even though black leaders had long complained that immigrants were taking jobs that, they insisted, rightfully belonged to blacks.[2]

If blacks were superfluous so far as Northern industry was concerned, the opposite was true in the South, where black labor was indispensable to the entire regional economy. Furthermore, given the interdependence between the regional economies of the South and the North, occupational apartheid had indirect advantages for the North as well. Remember that the cotton fiber that Irish, Italian, and Jewish immigrants worked with in mills and sweatshops throughout the North was supplied by black workers in the South. In effect, a system of labor deployment had evolved whereby blacks provided the necessary labor for Southern agriculture, and European immigrants provided the necessary labor for Northern industry.

This regional and racial division of labor cast the mold for generations more of racial inequality and conflict. Not until the First World War were blacks given significant access to Northern labor markets. In a single year—1914—the volume of immigration plummeted from 1.2 million immigrant arrivals to only 327,000. The cut-off of immigration in the midst of an economic expansion triggered the Great Migration, as it was called, of Southern blacks to the urban North. Industries not only employed blacks in large numbers but even sent labor agents to the South to recruit black workers. Between 1910 and 1920, there was a net migration of 454,000 Southern blacks to the North, a figure that exceeded the volume of the previous forty years combined. Here is historical proof that blacks were just as willing as Europe's peasants to uproot themselves and migrate to cities that offered the opportunity for industrial employment. To suggest that blacks "were not ready to compete with immigrants," as the author of a recent volume on immigration does, is a flagrant distortion of history.[3] The simple truth is that Northern industry was open to immigrants and closed to blacks. Whatever opprobrium was heaped on these immigrants for their cultural and religious difference, they were still beneficiaries of racial preference.

It is generally assumed that the Second World War provided a similar demand for black labor, but initially this was not the case. Because the war came on the heels of the Depression, there was a surfeit of white labor and no compelling need to hire blacks.[4] Indeed, it was blacks' frustration with their exclusion from wartime industries that prompted A. Philip Randolph and his followers to threaten a march on Washington in 1941 until Roosevelt issued his executive order banning discrimination in federal employment and defense contracts. The opening up of Northern labor markets triggered another mass migration of Southern blacks—1.6 million migrated between 1940 and 1950; by the end of the war, 1.5 million black workers were part of the war-production work force. This represented an unprecedented breach in the nation's system of occupational apartheid—one that set the stage for future change as well.

Still, as recently as 1950, two-thirds of the nation's blacks lived in the South, half of them in rural areas. It was not the Civil War, but the mechanization of agriculture a century later that finally liberated blacks from their historic role as agricultural laborers in the South's feudal economy. By the mid-fifties, even the harvest of cotton became mechanized with the mass production of International Harvester's automatic cotton picking machine. The number of man-hours required to produce a bale of cotton was reduced from 438 in 1940, to 26 in 1960, to only 6 in 1980.[5] Agricultural technology had effectively rendered black labor obsolete, and with it the caste system whose underlying function had been to regulate and exploit black labor.[6] Thus it was that in one century, white planters went all the way to Africa to import black laborers; in the next century, the descendants of Southern planters gave the descendants of African slaves one-way bus tickets to Chicago and New York.

When blacks finally arrived in Northern cities, they encountered a far less favorable structure of opportunity than had existed for immigrants decades earlier.[7] For one thing, these labor markets had been captured by immigrant groups who engaged in a combination of ethnic nepotism and unabashed racism. For another, the occupational structures were themselves changing. Not only were droves of manufacturing jobs being automated out of existence, but a reorganization of the global economy resulted in the export of millions of manufacturing jobs to less developed parts of the world.

Thus the fact that the technological revolution in agriculture lagged nearly a half-century behind the technological revolution in industry had fateful consequences for blacks at both junctures. First, blacks were restricted to the agricultural sector during the most expansive periods of the industrial revolution. Then, they were evicted from rural America and arrived in Northern cities at a time when manufacturing was beginning a steep and irreversible decline. Yet . . . the fact that more blacks were not integrated into Northern labor markets cannot be explained only in terms of the operation of color-blind economic forces. At least as important was the pervasive racism that restricted the access of black workers not only to jobs in declining industries, but also to new jobs in the expanding service sector.

THE IMMIGRATION DILEMMA

The economic fortunes of African-Americans have always been linked to immigration. Suppose that Europe's "huddled masses" had been flocking to the New World in the seventeenth century. Then Southern planters would not have been impelled to go all the way to Africa to find laborers, and the nation would have been spared the ignominy of slavery. Suppose, on the other hand, that the huddled masses of Europe had *not* flocked to America's cities during the century after slavery. Then Northern industrialists would have had to put aside their racist predilections and tapped the pool of black laborers in the South who were desperate to escape the yoke of Southern oppression. Indeed, this is precisely what happened during both World Wars when the cutoff of immigration led to the absorption of blacks into Northern labor markets. The two brief intervals in the twentieth century when immigration was at low ebb marked the two major periods of economic and social advancement for African-Americans.

The post-civil rights era presented yet another opportunity to integrate blacks into the occupational mainstream, especially given the sharp decline of the white birth rate and the improved climate of tolerance toward blacks. But once again, African-Americans have had to cope with an enormous influx of immigrants, this time from Asia, Latin America, and the Caribbean. Ironically, it was the civil rights movement that led to the passage of the 1965 Hart-Celler Act, which abolished the national origins quotas that had restricted immigration outside of Europe. In the two ensuing decades, there have been some 15 million immigrant arrivals, not to mention millions more who are undocumented.[8]

This massive volume of immigration amounts to a double whammy as far as African-Americans are concerned: Not only has there been an erosion of job structures in cities with high concentrations of blacks, but black workers must compete with increasing numbers of immigrants for scarce jobs. William Julius Wilson's whole emphasis is that the United States has been exporting millions of jobs to the Third World. However, the nation is also importing workers from these same countries at an even faster rate. The availability of large numbers of foreign workers allows employers to exercise their racial preferences when it comes to hiring new workers. As the last hired, blacks often find themselves in the hiring queue even behind recent immigrants. . . .

To be sure, immigration may on balance be beneficial for the economy as a whole, as the apostles of immigration contend. There is obvious validity in the claim that immigrants do not just take jobs, they create them as well. This is especially evident when one examines the thriving ethnic economies in "gateway cities" like Los Angeles, New York, San Francisco, and Miami. On the other hand, as Jacqueline Jackson has pointed out, "too often the jobs created are not for domestic minorities but for the next wave of immigrants recruited through ethnic networks."[9] Besides, what is at issue here is not whether immigration is generally beneficial to the American economy, but whether it is specifically detrimental to the interests of African-Americans and other marginal workers. . . .

While demographers, economists, and sociologists debate the effects of immigration, a groundswell of resentment has built up within the black community itself. Public opinion polls indicate that a solid majority of blacks see immigrants as competitors for jobs and would favor lowering the ceiling on immigration.[10] Yet most black leaders have been reluctant to speak out against immigration policy. For one thing, many

blacks sympathize with these struggling minorities, some of whom are also of African descent. For another, black leaders do not want to feed the forces of xenophobia and reaction that are behind the recent upsurge of nativism. Finally, black leaders have been wary about jeopardizing their coalition with Hispanics in Congress and elsewhere, even though public opinion polls indicate that most rank-and-file Hispanics also would support a lower ceiling on immigration.[11] . . .

Here we arrive at the critical question. If the rationale behind immigration has to do with declining fertility rates and an anticipated decline in new labor force entrants, why is policy not directed at addressing the scandalously high rates of black unemployment? Why is there no crash program to provide job training for minority youth whose detachment from the job market has so many deleterious consequences for themselves as well as the rest of the society? Why is there no serious effort to enforce antidiscrimination laws and to tear down racist barriers in major occupational structures, including the so-called "ethnic economy" in which racial discrimination is virtually endemic? Why are there no incentives or mandates to induce employers to hire and train unemployed youths?

It is difficult to escape the conclusion that political and economic leaders have given up on black youth and opted to rely on immigrants to make up for any labor deficits. . . .

The immigration of some 15 million documented immigrants over the past several decades represents another missed opportunity in American history. The nation could have taken advantage of a secular decline in its working-age population to integrate blacks and other marginal groups into the occupational mainstream. More is involved here than achieving parity and justice for blacks. This was the nation's chance to attack the structures of inequality that rend the society, undermining the stability of political institutions and compromising the quality of life.

Why was the opportunity missed? To have acted otherwise would have required a level of commitment to racial equality that was lacking. It would also have required programs and expenditures for which there was no political will. In the final analysis, the nation succumbed once again to its endemic racism and to its collective indifference to the plight of its black citizens. Although immigration has produced a more racially diverse population, paradoxically, this new diversity has reinforced the preexisting structure of occupational apartheid.[12]

THE MYTH OF THE BLACK MIDDLE CLASS

At first blush, the existence of a large black middle class would suggest that racist barriers in occupations are no longer insurmountable—in other words, that occupational apartheid is not the problem it was in times past. To be sure, the existence of this middle class signifies a historic breakthrough. Never before have so many blacks been represented at the higher echelons of the occupational world—in the professions and in corporate management. Never before have so many blacks found employment in core industries, in both the white-collar and blue-collar sectors. Nor can this new black middle class, given its size, be dismissed as "window dressing" or "tokenism." . . .

The sheer existence of a large black middle class means that blacks are no longer a uniformly downtrodden people. On the other hand, it may signify not the *dissolution* so much as an *artful reconfiguration* of caste boundaries in the occupational world. To control the disorder emanating from the ghettos of America, a new class of "Negro jobs" has been created. They are not the dirty, menial, and backbreaking jobs of the past. On the contrary, they are coveted jobs that offer decent wages and job security. Nevertheless, they are jobs that are pegged for blacks and that function within the context of racial hierarchy and division.

Precisely because the new black middle class is largely a product of government policy, its future is subject to the vagaries of politics. Already it is apparent, as two economists have concluded, that "the epoch of rapid black relative economic advance ended sometime in the late 1970s and early 1980s and . . . some of the earlier gains eroded in the 1980s."[13] Court decisions restricting minority set-asides have already had a severe impact on black businesses.[14] The current attack on affirmative action will inevitably lead to a further erosion

of black socioeconomic gains. Finally, just as blacks benefited disproportionately from the growth of government, they will certainly be severely affected by the current movement to cut the size of the government and the scope of government services. Black public-sector workers are especially vulnerable to layoffs because they are disproportionately found in positions that are heavily dependent on federal subsidies.[15]

THE JOB CRISIS IN BLACK AMERICA

If the new black middle class does not signify a fundamental decline in racial inequality, then what are we to conclude about the persistence and growth of the black underclass? In *Poor People's Movements*, written in 1979, Piven and Cloward provided an apt description of the current situation when they wrote: "In effect, the black poor progressed from slave labor to cheap labor to (for many) no labor at all."[16] Indeed, a job crisis of the magnitude that existed in the society at large during the Great Depression afflicts black America today. In the Depression, the crisis was defined as such, and extraordinary programs were developed to overhaul basic economic institutions and to create jobs for the unemployed. In the case of the black job crisis, however, social policy has been predicated on the assumption that black unemployment stems from the deficiencies of black workers, and social policy has rarely advanced beyond some meager job training programs.[17]

A few statistics will suffice to convey the dimensions of this job crisis. In 1994, the unemployment rate was 11.5 percent for blacks and 5.3 percent for whites.[18] According to one estimate, blacks would need 1.6 million jobs to achieve parity with whites. The job deficit for black men over 20 is 736,000 jobs; for black women over 20, it is 150,000 jobs; and for black teenagers it is 500,000 jobs.[19]

As is often pointed out, the government's measure of unemployment is only the tip of the iceberg because it leaves out "discouraged workers" who have given up looking for work, as well as "involuntary part-time workers" who want full-time employment. The National Urban League has developed its own measure of "hidden unemployment" that includes these two groups. In 1992, the League's hidden unemployment rate was 13.3 percent for whites and 25.5 percent for blacks. Thus, one-quarter of the black population, involving roughly 3 million workers, are effectively jobless.[20] Even this figure does not sufficiently reflect the depth of the problem because it leaves out the working poor—those who are employed full time, but whose wages leave them below the poverty line.

This job crisis is the single-most important factor behind the familiar tangle of problems that beset black communities. Without jobs, nuclear families become unglued or are never formed. Without jobs, or husbands with jobs, women with young children are forced onto the welfare rolls. Without jobs, many ghetto youth resort to the drug trade or other illicit ways of making money. Ironically, those who end up in prison do find work—in prison shops that typically pay fifty cents or less an hour—only to find themselves jobless on the outside. Given this fact, the high rate of recidivism should come as no surprise. For different reasons, schools are generally ineffective in teaching children whose parents lack stable jobs and incomes. In short, there is no exit from the racial quagmire unless there is a national commitment to address the job crisis in black America.

Tragically, this nation does not have the political will to confront its legacy of slavery, even if this means nothing more than providing jobs at decent wages for blacks who continue to be relegated to the fringes of the job market. Instead, a mythology has been constructed that, in ways reminiscent of slavery itself, alleges that blacks are inefficient and unproductive workers, deficient in the work habits and moral qualities that delivered other groups from poverty. . . .

We need a renewed national commitment to dealing with the job crisis that afflicts black America. This would begin with vigorous enforcement of antidiscrimination laws. However, the lesson of the post-civil-rights era is that antidiscrimination laws are minimally effective unless they are backed up with compliance checks and other enforcement mechanisms—in short, affirmative action. The significance of affirmative action is that it amounts to a frontal assault on the racial division of labor. Whatever its limitations, affirmative action has produced the most significant departure from the occupational caste system that has existed since slavery. If racial progress is to continue, affirmative action must be extended to wider segments of the work force.

Again, it may seem gratuitous to say this at a time when racism and reaction are feeding on one another, and there is a tidal wave of opposition against affirmative action. However, there is a maddening illogic to the current crusade against welfare, crime, out-of-wedlock births, and the other "pathologies" associated in the popular mind with the ghetto population. Unless jobs and opportunities are targeted for black youth and young adults, punitive legislation and the withdrawal of public assistance will only produce more desperation and even greater disorder. . . .

The job crisis in black America is allowed to fester for one basic reason: Because the power elites of this nation regard these black communities as politically and economically expendable. They can afford to do so as long as they are not under great countervailing pressure, either from a mobilized black protest movement or from spontaneous ghetto uprisings. This is a situation of politics-as-usual so long as poverty and joblessness manifest themselves as "quiet riots"—that is, as crime and violence that can be contained through a criminal justice system that currently has a prison population exceeding one million people.

On the other hand, when these communities do finally erupt in full-scale riots, as South Central Los Angeles did in the aftermath of the Rodney King episode, suddenly race is back on the national agenda. Even the mainstream media resisted the temptation merely to resort to moral platitudes. *Newsweek* proclaimed that "This Was No Riot, It Was a Revolt," and described "the siege of LA" as a "bloody wake-up call" to reverse the neglect of America's inner cities.[21]

NOTES

1. For an excellent analysis of the historical relationship between race and occupational structures, see Harold M. Baron, "The Demand for Black Labor," *Radical America* 5 (March-April 1971); and idem, "The Web of Urban Racism," in *Institutional*

Racism in America, ed. Louis L. Knowles and Kenneth Prewitt (Upper Saddle River, NJ: Prentice Hall, 1969), pp. 134–76.

2. See Lawrence H. Fuchs, "The Reactions of Black Americans to Immigration," in *Immigration Reconsidered*, ed. Virginia Yans-McLaughlin (New York: Oxford University Press, 1990), especially pp. 295–97, and David J. Hellwig, "Patterns of Black Nativism," *American Studies* 23 (Spring 1982).

3. Muller, Thomas. 1993. *Immigrants and the American City*. New York: New York University Press, p. 91.

4. Myrdal, Gunnar. 1994. *An American Dilemma: The Negro Problem and Modern Democracy*. New York: Harper & Row, p. 1005.

5. Government Printing Office. 1975. *Historical Statistics of the United States*. Washington, DC: Government Printing Office, p. 500. Jaynes, Gerald David and Robin M. Williams, Jr. 1989. *A Common Destiny*. Washington, D.C.: National Academy Press, p. 273.

6. Piven, Frances Fox and Richard A. Cloward. 1979. *Poor People's Movements*. New York: Vintage Books, Chapter 4.

7. In a paper written for the National Advisory Commission on Civil Disorders in 1968, Herbert Gans debunked the notion that blacks arriving in Northern cities were following in the footsteps of earlier immigrants and could therefore anticipate the same beneficial outcomes. "Escaping from Poverty: A Comparison of the Immigrant and Black Experience," in *People, Plans, and Policies* (New York: Columbia University Press, 1991), Chapter 18.

8. For a recent demographic analysis of the new immigration, see Reuben C. Rumbaut, "Origins and Destinies: Immigration to the United States Since World War II," *Sociological Forum* 9 (December 1994), pp. 583–621.

9. Jacquelyne Johnson Jackson, "Seeking Common Ground for Blacks and Immigrants," in *U.S. Immigration in the 1980s: Reappraisal and Reform*, ed. David. E Simcox (Boulder: Westview Press, 1988), p. 95.

10. For example, a 1983 national poll found that 69 percent of black respondents agreed that "illegal immigrants are a major harm to U.S. jobless," and 73 percent said that "the U.S. should admit fewer or a lot fewer legal immigrants." Jackson, "Seeking Common Ground for Blacks and Immigrants," p. 96. For a comprehensive review of poll findings on the immigration issue, see Muller, *Immigrants and the American City*, pp. 161–66.

A recent New York Times/CBS News Poll found that the percentage of Americans who favored a decrease in immigration had risen to 61 percent, up from 49 percent when the question was last asked in 1986. Compared to whites, black Americans were nine percentage points more likely to see immigrants taking jobs away, but nine percentage points less likely to prefer a decrease in immigration. Seth Mydans, "Poll Finds Tide of Immigration Brings Hostility," *New York Times*, June 27, 1993.

11. For an informative discussion of the role that black organizations and the Congressional Black Caucus played in the debate over the Simpson-Mazzoli bill in 1983 and 1984, see Muller, *Immigrants and the American City*, pp. 52–67.

12. A note on the politics of immigration. As Otis L. Graham, Jr., suggests, it is a mistake to equate immigration restriction with xenophobia or reaction; "Illegal Immigration and the Left," *Dissent* 29 (Summer 1980). Historically, elements of organized labor, including unions made up largely of immigrants, have favored restrictive immigration policies because they feared that unlimited immigration depressed wages and standards, created a bottom tier of immigrant workers, and prevented changes in the structure of the secondary labor market. For Graham's more recent statements on this issue, see "Immigration and the National Interest," in *U.S. Immigration in the 1980s: Reappraisal and Reform*, ed. David Simcox, pp. 124–36; and "Uses and Misuses of History in the Debate Over Immigration Reform," *The Public Historian*, 8, no. 2 (Spring 1986), pp. 41–64.

Although working-class opposition to immigration often stemmed from xenophobia and racism, other legitimate interests were also involved. This has been acknowledged by John Higham, author of *Strangers in the Land*—the classic history of nativism—in the preface to the book's second edition. In the revised edition of *Send These to Me: Immigrants in Urban America* (Baltimore: Johns Hopkins University Press, 1984), Higham writes sympathetically of the Simpson-Mazzoli bill, which included sanctions on employers who hired undocumented workers. The commission that led to the passage of this legislation was headed by a prominent liberal, Father Theodore Hesburgh.

On the other hand, free-market economists and business interests have championed the cause of expanded immigration. See, for example, M. S. Forbes, Jr., "We Need More People," *Forbes* (February 9, 1987); "The Rekindled Flame," Editorial, *Wall Street Journal*, July 3, 1989; Michael J. Mandel and Christopher Farrell, "The Immigrant: How They're Helping to Revitalize the U.S. Economy," *Business Week* (July 13, 1992); Ben J. Wattenberg and Karl Zinsmeister, "The Case for More Immigration," *Commentary* 89 (April 1990): pp. 19–25, and Julian L. Simon, "The Case for Greatly Increased Migration," *Public Interest* no. 102 (Winter 1991): pp. 89–103.

13. Bound, John and Richard B. Freeman, "Black Economic Progress: Erosion of the Post-1965 Gains in the 1980s," in *The Question of Discrimination*, ed. Steven Shulman and William Darity, Jr. (Middletown, Conn.: Wesleyan University Press, 1989): p. 47.

14. de Courcy Hinds, Michael. "Minority Business Set Back Sharply by Courts' Rulings," *New York Times*, December 23, 1991.

15. For example, when the Reagan administration reduced social spending between 1980 and 1981, 76 percent of the 400 employees laid off in Chicago's Department of Human Services were black, as were 40 percent of the 186 workers laid off in the Department of Health. In contrast, the federal cutbacks barely affected the predominantly white work force in Chicago's Streets and Sanitation Department, which is funded with local revenues. Collins, Sharon M., "The Making of the Black Middle Class," *Social Problems* 30 (April 1983), p. 377.

16. Piven and Cloward, *Poor People's Movements*, p. 184.

17. As Margaret Weir points out with respect to the 1960s: "This decade of intellectual ferment and policy experimentation left a surprisingly meager legacy for employment policy. Labor market policy became subsumed into the poverty program, offering job preparation to those on the fringes on the labor market, and to the black poor in particular." *Politics and Jobs* (Princeton, NJ: Princeton University Press, 1992). For an incisive analysis of the political functions of job training programs, see Gordon Lafer, "Minority Unemployment, Labor Market Segmentation, and the Failure of Job Training Policy in New York City," *Urban Affairs Quarterly* 28 (December 1992).

18. U.S. Department of Labor, Bureau of Labor Statistics. *Employment and Earnings, January 1995.* Washington, DC: Government Printing Office.

19. Swinton, David H. "The Economic Status of African-Americans: 'Permanent' Poverty and Inequality," in *The State of Black America* (Washington, DC: National Urban League, 1991), p. 53. Swinton states that the remainder of the overall shortage is caused by demographic factors.

20. "Quarterly Economic Report on the African-American Worker," National Urban League, Report No. 32 (September 1992). Jim Sleeper writes: ". . . what kinds of hard work and moral discipline may people who envision a democratic and just society demand even of the poorest and most oppressed; what, indeed, would it be condescending and worse not to demand of 'the least among us'?" *The Closest of Strangers* (New York: W. W. Norton, 1990), p. 37. Regarding the scarcity of jobs, see George James, "The Job Is Picking Up Garbage; 100,000 Want It," *New York Times*, September 21, 1990.

21. Hackworth, David H. "This Was No Riot, It Was a Revolt." *Newsweek* (May 11, 1992), p. 30; and ibid. (May 25, 1992), p. 33.

◆ 25 ◆

Race and Middle Class Identity in America

Clarence Page

Today I live a well-integrated life in the suburbs. Black folks still tell me how to be "black" when I stray from the racial party lines, while white folks tell me how to be "color-blind." I still feel as frustrated in my attempts to transcend race as a reluctant lemming must feel while being rushed over the brink by its herd. But I find I have plenty of company in my frustration. Integration has not been a simple task for upwardly mobile African-Americans, especially for those of us who happen also to be parents.

Here is the perspective of a commentator, essayist, journalist, African American, who has become middle class and "integrated." Yet he expresses uneasiness about his identity in American society. Color always was and continues to be an important part of American society, he writes. Although choices abound for black people ("if they can afford them"), we are not a colorblind society, and we need to be honest about that. Change is taking place, but serious questions remain about "who I am" and what kind of society we should become. Page describes the importance of living in a diverse society, but a diverse society should not allow race to matter for purposes of discrimination and oppression of people.

The message in this essay is not an easy one to understand because it shows the complexities of racial and ethnic differences: the desire to claim an identity for oneself, yet the discrimination that others use to exclude those who claim it; the opportunities that exist for many African Americans, yet the continued denial of opportunity for large numbers; the integration that is at the surface, the sharp division underneath.

Race has long had a rude presence in my life. While visiting relatives in Alabama as a child in the 1950s, I first saw water fountains marked "white" and "colored." I vaguely recall being excited. I rushed over to the one marked "colored" and turned it on, only to find, to my deep disappointment, that the water came out clear, just like the water back home in Ohio.

"Segregation," my dad said. I'd never heard the word before. My southern-born parents explained that it was something the white folks "down home" practiced. Some "home." Yet unpleasant experiences in the North already had taught me a more genteel, yet no less limiting, version.

"There are places white people don't want colored to go," my elders told me in their soft southern accents, "and white people make the rules."

We had plenty of segregation like that in the North. We just didn't have the signs, which made it cheaper and easier to deny. We could look out of my schoolhouse window to see a public swimming pool closed to nonwhites. We had to go across town to the separate-but-equal "pool for colored." The steel mill that was our town's biggest employer held separate picnics for colored and white employees, which seemed to be just fine with the employees. Everyone had a good time, separately and unequally. I think the colored folks, who today would be called the "black community," were just happy to have something to call their own.

When I was about six years old, I saw a television commercial for an amusement park near the southern Ohio factory town where I grew up.

I chose to go. I told my parents. They looked at each other sadly and informed me that "little colored kids can't go there." I was crushed.

"I wish I was white," I told my parents.

"No, you don't!" Mom snapped. She gave me a look terrible enough to persuade me instantly that no, I didn't.

"Well, maybe for a few minutes, anyway?" I asked. "Just long enough for me to get past the front gate?" Then I could show them, I thought. I remember I wanted to show them what a terrific kid I was. I felt sorry for the little white children who would be deprived of getting to know me.

Throughout our childhood years, my friendships with white schoolchildren (and with Pancho from the only Latino family in the neighborhood) proceeded without interruption. Except for the occasional tiff over some injudicious use of the N-word or some other slur we had picked up from our elders, we played in each other's backyards as congenially as Spanky, Buckwheat, and the rest of the gang on the old Hal Roach Our Gang comedies we used to watch on television.

Yet it quickly became apparent to me that my white friends were growing up in a different reality from the one to which I was accustomed. I could tell from the way one white friend happily discussed his weekend at LeSourdesville Lake that he did not have a clue of my reality.

"Have you been?" he asked.

"Colored can't go there," I said, somewhat astonished that he had not noticed.

"Oh, that can't be," he said.

For a moment, I perked up, wondering if the park's policy had changed. "Have you seen any colored people there?" I asked.

My white friend thought for a moment, then realized that he had not. He expressed surprise. I was surprised that he was surprised.

By the time I reached high school in the early 1960s, LeSourdesville Lake would relax its racial prohibitions. But the lessons of it stuck with me. It taught me how easily white people could ignore the segregation problem because, from their vantage point, it was not necessarily a problem. It was not necessarily an advantage to them, either, although some undoubtedly thought so. White people of low income, high insecurity, or fragile ego could always say that, no matter how badly off they felt, at least they were not black. Segregation helped them uphold and maintain this illusion of superiority. Even those white people who considered themselves to have a well-developed sense of social conscience could easily rationalize segregation as something that was good for both races. We played unwittingly into this illusion, I thought, when my friends and I began junior high school and, suddenly thrust into the edgy, high hormonal world of adolescence, quickly gravitated into social cliques according to tastes and race.

It became even more apparent to me that my white friends and I were growing up in *parallel realities*, not unlike the parallel universes described in the science fiction novels and comic books I adored—or the "parallel realities" experienced by Serbs, Bosnians, and Croatians as described years later by feminist writer Slavenka Drakulic in *The Balkan Express*. Even as the evil walls of legal segregation were tumbling down, thanks to the hard-fought struggles of the civil rights movement, it occurred to me that my reality might never be quite the same as that experienced by my white friends. We were doomed, I felt, to dwell in our parallel realities. Separated by thick walls of prejudice, we would view each other through windows of stained-glass perceptions, colored by our personal experiences. My parents had taught me well.

"Don't be showin' yo' color," my parents would admonish me in my youth, before we would go out in public, especially among white folks. The phrase had special meaning in Negro conversations. Imbued with many subtle meanings and nuances, the showing of one's "color" could be an expression of chastisement or warning, admonishment or adulation, satire or self-hatred, anger or celebration. It could mean acting out or showing anger in a loud and uncivilized way.

Its cultural origins could be traced to the Africa-rooted tradition of "signifying," a form of witty, deliberately provocative, occasionally combative word play. The thrill of the game comes from taking one's opponent close to the edge of tolerable insult. Few subjects—except perhaps sex itself—could be a more sensitive matter between black people than talk about someone else's "color." The showing of one's "color," then, connoted the display of the very worst stereotypes anyone ever dreamed up about how black people behaved. "White people are not really white," James Baldwin wrote in 1961, "but colored people can sometimes be extremely colored."

Sometimes you can still hear black people say, in the heat of frustration, "I almost showed my color today," which is a way of saying they almost lost their "cool," "dropped the mask," or "went off." Losing one's cool can be a capital offense by black standards, for it shows weakness in a world in which spiritual rigor is one of the few things we can call our own. Those who keep their cool repress their "color." It is cool, in other words, to be colorless.

The title of [the volume from which this chapter is taken], *Showing My Color,* emerged from my fuming discontent with the current fashions of *racial denial,* steadfast repudiations of the difference race continues to make in American life. Old liberals, particularly white liberals who have become new conservatives, charge that racial pride and color consciousness threaten to "Balkanize" American life, as if it ever was a model of unity. Many demand that we "get past race." But denials of a cancer, no matter how vigorous they may be, will not make the malignancy go away.

No less august a voice than the Supreme Court's conservative majority has taken to arguing in the 1990s for a "colorblind" approach to civil rights law, the area of American society in which color and gender consciousness have made the most dramatic improvement in equalizing opportunities.

The words of the Reverend Martin Luther King, Jr., have been perverted to support this view. Most frequently quoted is his oft-stated dream of the day when everyone would "not be judged by the color of their skin but by the content of their character." I would argue that King never intended for us to forget *all* about color. Even in his historic "I Have a Dream" speech, from which this line most often is lifted, he also pressed the less-often quoted but piquantly salient point about "the promissory note" America gave freed slaves, which, when they presented it, was returned to them marked "insufficient funds."

• • •

I would argue that too much has been made of the virtue of "color-blindness." I don't want Americans to be blind to my color as long as color continues to make a profound difference in determining life chances and opportunities. Nor do I wish to see so significant a part of my identity denied. "Ethnic differences are the very essence of cultural diversity and national creativity," black social critic Albert Murray wrote in *The Omni-Americans* (1970). "The problem is not the existence of ethnic differences, as is so often assumed, but the intrusion of such differences into areas where they do not belong."

Where, then, *do* they belong? Diversity is enriching, but race intrudes rudely on the individual's attempts to define his or her own identity. I used to be "colored." Then I was "Negro." Then I became "black." Then I became "African-American." Today I am a "person of color." In three decades, I have been transformed from a "colored person" to a "person of color." Are you keeping up with me?

Changes in what we black people call ourselves are quite annoying to some white people, which is its own reward to some black people. But if white people are confused, so are quite a few black people. There is no one way to be black. We are a diverse people amid a nation of diverse people. Some black people are nationalists who don't want anything to do with white people. Some black people are assimilationists who don't want anything to do with other black people. Some black people are integrationists who move in and out of various groups with remarkable ease. Some of us can be any of the three at any given time, depending on when you happen to run into us.

Growing up as part of a minority can expose the individual to horrible bouts of identity confusion. I used to think of myself as something of a *transracial man,* a figure no less frustrated than a transsexual who feels trapped in the body of something unfamiliar and inappropriate to his or her inner self.

These bouts were most torturous during adolescence, the period of life when, trembling with the shock of nascent independence from the ways of one's elders, the budding individual stitches together the fragile garments of an identity to be worn into adulthood. Stuttering and uncooperative motor skills left me severely challenged in dancing, basket shooting, and various social applications; I felt woefully inadequate to the task of being "popular" in the hot centers of black social activity at my integrated high school and college. "Are you black?" an arbiter of campus militancy demanded one day, when he "caught" me dining too many times with white friends. I had the skin pass, sure enough, but my inclinations fell well short of his standards. But I was not satisfied with the standards of his counterparts in the white world, either. If I was not "black" enough to please some blacks, I would never be "white" enough to please all whites.

Times have changed. Choices abound for black people, if we can afford them. Black people can now go anywhere they choose, as long as they can pay the bill when they get there. If anyone tries to stop them or any other minorities just because of their color, the full weight of the federal government will step in on the side of the minorities. I thank God and the hard-won gains of the civil rights revolution for my ability to have more choices. But the old rules of race have been replaced in many ways by new ones.

• • •

Today, I live a well-integrated life in the suburbs. Black folks still tell me how to be "black" when I stray from the racial party lines, while white folks tell me how to be "color-blind." I still feel as frustrated in my attempts to transcend race

as a reluctant lemming must feel while being rushed over the brink by its herd. But I find I have plenty of company in my frustration. Integration has not been a simple task for upwardly mobile African-Americans, especially for those of us who happen also to be parents.

A few years ago, after talking to black friends who were raising teenage boys, I realized that I was about to face dilemmas not unlike those my parents faced. My son was turning three years old. Everyone was telling me that he was quite cute, and because he was the spitting image of his dad, I was the last to argue.

But it occurred to me that in another decade he would be not three but thirteen. If all goes well, somewhere along the way he is going to turn almost overnight from someone who is perceived as cute and innocent into someone who is perceived as a menace, the most feared creature on America's urban streets today, a *young black male.* Before he, like me when I was barred from a childhood amusement park, would have a chance to let others get to know him, he would be judged not by the content of his character, but by the color of his skin. . . .

• • •

My mom is gone now, after helping set me up with the sort of education that has freed me to make choices. I have chosen to move my father to a nice, predominantly white, antiseptically tidy retirement village near me in Maryland with large golf courses and swimming pools. It is the sort of place he might have scrubbed floors in but certainly not have lived in back in the old days. It has taken him a while to get used to having so many well-off white people behaving so nicely and neighborly to him, but he has made the adjustment well.

Still the ugly specter of racism does not easily vanish. He and the other hundred or so African-American residents decided to form a social club like the other ethnically or religiously based social clubs in the village. One night during their meeting in the main social room, someone scrawled *KKK* on little sheets of paper and slipped them under the windshields of some of their cars in the parking lot. "We think maybe some of the white people wanted the blacks to socialize with the whites, not in a separate group," one lady of the club told me. If so, they showed an unusual method for extending the arms of brotherhood.

I live in a community that worships diversity like a state religion, although individuals sometimes get tripped up by it. The excellent Spanish "immersion" program that one of the county's "magnet" schools installed to encourage middle-class parents to stay put has itself become a cover for "white flight" by disgruntled white parents. Many of them, despite a lack of empirical evidence, perceive the school's regular English program as inferior, simply because it is 90 percent minority and mostly composed of children who come from a less-fortunate socioeconomic background. So the Spanish immersion classes designed to encourage diversity have become almost exclusively white and Asian America, while the English classes have become almost exclusively—irony of ironies—black and Latino, with many of the children learning English as a second language. Statistically, the school is "diverse" and "integrated." In reality, its student body is divided by an indelible wall, separate but supposedly equal. . . .

Despite all these color-conscious efforts to educate the county's children in a color-blind ideal of racial equality, many of our children seem to be catching on to race codes anyway, although with a twist suitable to the hip-hop generation. One local junior high school teacher, when he heard his black students referring to themselves as "bad," had the facts of racial life explained to him like this: They were not talking about the "bad means good" slang popularized by Michael Jackson's *Bad* album. They meant "bad" in the sense of misbehaving and poorly motivated. The black kids are "bad," the students explained, and the white kids are "good." The Asian kids are "like white," and the Latino kids "try to be bad, like the blacks." Anyone who tried to break out of those stereotypes was trying to break the code, meaning that a black or Latino who tried to make good grades was "trying to be white."

It is enough, as Marvin Gaye famously sang, to make you want to holler and throw up both your hands. Yet my neighbors and I hate to complain too loudly because, unlike other critics you may read or hear about, we happen to be a liberal community that not only believes in the dream of integration and true diversity, but actually is trying to live it.

We reside in Montgomery County, Maryland, the most prosperous suburban county per capita in the Washington, D.C., area. Each of the above-mentioned controversies has been reported in the pages of the *Washington Post* and other local media, right under the noses and, in some cases, within the families of some of the nation's top policy makers. . . .

We see icons of black success—Colin Powell, Douglas Wilder, Bill Cosby, Oprah Winfrey, Bryant Gumbel, the two Michaels: Jordan and Jackson—not only accepted but adored by whites in ways far removed from the arm's-length way white America regarded Jackie Robinson, Willie Mays, Lena Horne, and Marian Anderson.

Yet, although the media show happy images of blacks, whites, Asians, and Hispanics getting along, amicably consuming the good life, a fog of false contentment conceals menacing fissures cracking the national racial landscape.

Despite the growth of the black middle class, most blacks and whites live largely separate lives. School integration actually peaked in 1967, according to a Harvard study, and has declined ever since. Economic segregation has proceeded without interruption, distancing poor blacks not only from whites but also from upwardly mobile blacks, making the isolation and misery of poor blacks worse. One out of every two black children lives below the poverty line, compared to one out of every seven white children. Black infants in America die at twice the rate of white infants. A record-setting million inmates crowd the nation's prisons, half of them black. The black out-of-wedlock birth rate has grown from about 25 percent in 1965 to more than 60 percent (more than 90 percent in the South Bronx and other areas of concentrated black poverty) in 1990.

The good news is very good, but the bad news has become steadily worse. Economically, we are still playing catch-up. In 1865, newly freed from slavery, African Americans controlled 3 percent of the wealth in America, United States Civil Rights Commissioner Arthur Fletcher tells me. Today, we still control just 3 percent of the wealth. After all this time, we have become free, more often than not, to make other people wealthier. The decline of industrial America, along with low-skill, high-pay jobs, has left much of black America split in two along lines of class, culture, opportunity and hope. The "prepared" join the new black middle class, which grew rapidly in the 1970s and early 1980s. The unprepared populate a new culture, directly opposed not only to the predominantly white mainstream, but also to any blacks who aspire to practice the values of hard work, good English, and family loyalty that would help them to join the white mainstream. The results of this spiritual decline, along with economic decline, have been devastating. Although more black women go to college than ever before, it has become a commonplace to refer to young black males as an endangered species. New anti-black stereotypes replace the old. Prosperous, well-dressed African Americans still complain of suffering indignities when they try to hail a taxicab. The fact that the taxi that just passed them by was driven by a black cabby, native born or immigrant, makes no difference. . . .

Behind our questions of race lurk larger questions of identity, our sense of who we are, where we belong, and where we are going. Our sense of place and peoplehood within groups is a perpetual challenge in some lives, particularly lives in America, a land where identity bubbles quite often out of nothing more than a weird alchemy of history and choice. "When I discover who I am, I'll be free," Ralph Ellison once wrote.

I reject the melting pot metaphor. People don't melt. Americans prove it on their ethnic holidays, in the ways they dance, in the ways they sing, in the culturally connected ways they worship. Displaced peoples long to celebrate their ethnic roots many generations and intermarriages after their ancestors arrived in their new land. Irish-American celebrations of St. Patrick's Day in Boston, Chicago, and New York City are far more lavish than anything seen on that day in Dublin or Belfast. Mexican-American celebrations of Cinco de Mayo, the Fifth of May, are far more lavish in Los Angeles and San Antonio than anything seen that day in Mexico City. It is as if holidays give us permission to expose our former selves as we imagine them to be. Americans of European descent love to show their ethnic cultural backgrounds. Why do they get nervous only when black people show their love for theirs? Is it that black people on such occasions suddenly remind white people of vulnerabilities black people feel quite routinely as a minority in a majority white society? Is it that white people, by and large, do not like this feeling, that they want nothing more than to cleanse themselves of it and make sure that it does not come bubbling up again? Attempts by Americans to claim some ephemeral, all-inclusive "all-American" identity reminds me of Samuel Johnson's observation: "Sir, a man may be so much of everything, that he is nothing of anything."

Instead of the melting pot metaphor, I prefer the mulligan stew, a concoction my parents tell me they used to fix during the Great Depression, when there was not a lot of food around the house and they "made do" with whatever meats, vegetables, and spices they had on hand. Everything went into the pot and was stirred up, but the pieces didn't melt. Peas were easily distinguished from carrots or potatoes. Each maintained its distinctive character. Yet each loaned its special flavor to the whole, and each absorbed some of the flavor from the others. That flavor, always unique, always changing, is the beauty of America to me, even when the pot occasionally boils over. . . .

African Americans are as diverse as other Americans. Some become nationalistic and ethnocentric. Others become pluralistic or multicultural, fitting their black identity into a comfortable niche among other aspects of themselves and their daily lives. Whichever they choose, a comfortable identity serves to provide not only a sense of belonging and protection for the individual against the abuses of racism, but also, ultimately, a sturdy foundation from which the individual can interact effectively with other people, cultures, and situations beyond the world of blackness.

"Identity would seem to be the garment with which one covers the nakedness of the self," James Baldwin wrote in *The Devil Finds Work* (1976), "in which case, it is best that the garment be loose, a little like the robes of the desert, through which one's nakedness can always be felt, and, sometimes, discerned. This trust in one's nakedness is all that gives one the power to change one's robes."

The cloak of proud black identity has provided a therapeutical warmth for my naked self after the chilly cocoon of inferiority imposed early in my life by a white-exalting society. But it is best worn loosely, lest it become as constricting and isolating for the famished individual soul as the garment it replaced.

The ancestral desire of my ethnic people to be "just American" resonates in me. But I cannot forget how persistently the rudeness of race continues to intrude between me and that dream. I can defy it, but I cannot deny it. . . .

◆ 26 ◆

Latino Lives in a Changing America

Roberto Suro

No other democracy has ever experienced an uninterrupted wave of migration that has lasted as long and that has involved as many people as the recent movement of Spanish-speaking people to the United States. . . . Despite some differences among them, Latinos constitute a distinctive linguistic and cultural group. . . . Latinos are hardly the only immigrants coming to the United States in the 1990s, but they will define this era of immigration, and this country's response to them will shape its response to all immigrants.

With both sensitivity and understanding, Roberto Suro introduces the hopes, problems, and lives of Latinos in the United States. He describes a unique group of immigrants; he describes what it means for people to leave their country of birth and settle here; he describes what it means to American society to try to tackle the problems of a great immigration of people, mostly poor, many illegally arriving, becoming integrated in established Latino communities, and trying to make it in a modern economy that increasingly has less and less opportunity for poor and working-class immigrants.

On Imelda's fifteenth birthday, her parents were celebrating everything they had accomplished by coming north to make a new life in the

From *Strangers Among Us* by Roberto Suro, copyright © 1998 by Roberto Suro. Used by permission of Alfred A. Knopf, a division of Random House, Inc.

United States. Two short people in brand-new clothes, they stood in the driveway of their home in Houston and greeted relatives, friends, and neighbors, among them a few people who had come from the same village in central Mexico and who would surely carry gossip of the party back home. A disc jockey with a portable stereo presided over the backyard as if it were a cabaret instead of a patch of grass behind an overcrowded bungalow where five people shared two bedrooms. A folding table sagged with platters of tacos and fajitas. An aluminum keg of beer sat in a wheelbarrow atop a bed of half-melted ice cubes. For Imelda's parents, the festivities that night served as a triumphant display of everything they had earned by working two jobs each. Like most of the other adults at the party, they had come north to labor in restaurants, factories, warehouses, or construction sites by day and to clean offices at night. They had come to work and to raise children in the United States.

Imelda, who had been smuggled across the Rio Grande as a toddler, wore a frilly dress ordered by catalog from Guadalajara, as befits a proper Mexican celebrating her *quinceañera*, which is the traditional coming-out party for fifteen-year-old Latin girls. Her two younger sisters and a little brother, all U.S. citizens by birth, wore new white shirts from a discount store. Their hair had been combed down with sharp, straight parts and dabs of pomade.

When it came time for Imelda to dance her first dance, her father took her in his arms for one of the old-fashioned polkas that had been his favorite when a band played in the town square back home. By tradition, boys could begin courting her after that dance. Imelda's parents went to bed that night content they had raised their children according to proper Mexican custom.

The next morning at breakfast, Imelda announced that she was pregnant, that she was dropping out of school, and that she was moving in with her boyfriend, a Mexican-American who did not speak Spanish and who did not know his father. That night, she ate a meal purchased with food stamps and cooked on a hot plate by her boyfriend's mother. She remembers the dinner well. "That night, man, I felt like an American. I was free."

This is the promise and the peril of Latino immigration. Imelda's parents had traveled to Texas on a wave of expectations that carried them from the diminishing life of peasant farmers on a dusty *rancho* to quiet contentment as low-wage workers in an American city. These two industrious immigrants had produced a teenage welfare mother, who in turn was to have an American baby. In the

United States, Imelda had learned the language and the ways. In the end, what she learned best was how to be poor in an American inner city.

Latino immigration delivers short-term gains and has long-term costs. For decades now, the United States has engaged in a form of deficit spending that can be measured in human lives. Through their hard work at low wages, Latinos have produced immediate benefits for their families, employers, and consumers, but American society has never defined a permanent place for these immigrants or their children and it has repeatedly put off considering their future. That future, however, is now arriving, and it will produce a reckoning. The United States will need new immigration policies to decide who gets into the country. More importantly, the nation will need new means of assuring political equality and freedom of economic opportunity. Soon Americans will learn once again that in an era of immigration, the newcomers not only demand change; they create change.

When I last met Imelda, she was just a few weeks short of her due date, but she didn't have anything very nice to say about her baby or her boyfriend. Growing up in Houston as the child of Mexican immigrants had filled her with resentment, especially toward her parents, and that was what she wanted to talk about.

"We'd get into a lot of yelling and stuff at home because my parents, they'd say, 'You're Mexican. Speak Spanish. Act like a Mexican girl,' and I'd say, 'I'm here now and I'm going to be like the other kids.' They didn't care."

Imelda is short and plump, with wide brown eyes and badly dyed yellow hair. She wore a denim shirt with the sleeves ripped off, and her expression was a studied pout. Getting pregnant was just one more way of expressing anger and disdain. She is a dimestore Madonna.

Imelda is also a child of the Latino migration. She is a product of that great movement of people from Latin America into the United States that is older than any borders but took on a startling new meaning when it gradually gained momentum after the 1960s and then turned into something huge in the 1980s. Latino immigrants were drawn north when America needed their services, and they built communities known as barrios in every major city. But then in the 1990s, as these newcomers began to define their permanent place here, the ground shifted on them. They and their children—many of them native-born Americans—found themselves struggling with an economy that offered few opportunities to people trying to get off the bottom. They also faced a populace sometimes disconcerted by the growing number of foreigners in its midst. Immigration is a transaction between the newcomers and the hosts. It will be decades before there is a final tally for this great wave of immigration, but the terms of the deal have now become apparent.

Imelda's story does not represent the best or the worst of the Latino migration, but it does suggest some of the challenges posed by the influx. Those challenges are defined first of all by demography. No other democracy has ever experienced an uninterrupted wave of migration that has lasted as long and that has involved as many people as the recent movement of Spanish-speaking people to the United States. Twelve million foreign-born Latinos live here. If immigration and birth rates remain at current levels, the total Hispanic population will grow at least three times faster than the population as a whole for several decades, and Latinos will become the nation's largest minority group, surpassing the size of the black population a few years after the turn of the [twenty-first] century. Despite some differences among them, Latinos constitute a distinctive linguistic and cultural group, and no single group has ever dominated a prolonged wave of immigration the way Latinos have for thirty years. By contrast, Asians, the other large category of immigrants, come from nations as diverse as India and Korea, and although the Latino migration is hardly monolithic, the Asian influx represents a much greater variety of cultures, languages, and economic experiences. Moreover, not since the Irish potato famine migration of the 1840s has any single nationality accounted for such a large share of an immigrant wave as the Mexicans have in recent decades. The 7 million Mexican immigrants living in the United States in 1997 made up 27 percent of the entire foreign-born population, and they outnumbered the entire Asian immigrant population by more than one million people. Latinos are hardly the only immigrants coming to the United States in the 1990s, but they will define this era of immigration, and this country's response to them will shape its response to all immigrants.

Latinos, like most other immigrants, tend to cluster together. Their enclaves are the barrios, a Spanish word for neighborhoods that has become part of English usage because barrios have become such a common part of every American city. Most barrios, however, remain a place apart, where Latinos live separated from others by custom, language, and preference. They are surrounded by a city but are not part of it. Imelda lived in a barrio named Magnolia Park, after the trees that once grew along the banks of the bayou there. Like other barrios, Magnolia is populated primarily by poor and working-class Latinos, and many newly arrived immigrants start out there. Magnolia was first settled nearly a hundred years ago by Mexicans who fled revolution in their homeland and found jobs dredging the ship channel and port that allowed Houston to become a great city. Latinos continued to arrive off and on, especially when Houston was growing. Since the 1980s, when the great wave of new arrivals began pouring into Magnolia, it hasn't mattered whether the oil city was in boom or bust—Latinos always find jobs, even when they lack skills and education. Most of Magnolia is poor, but it is also a neighborhood where people go to work before dawn and work into the night.

Like other barrios, Magnolia serves as an efficient port of entry for Latino immigrants because it is an easy place to find cheap housing, learn about jobs, and keep connected to home. Some newcomers and their children pass through Magnolia and find a way out to more prosperous neighborhoods where they can leave the barrio life behind. But for millions like Imelda who came of age in the 1990s, the barrios have become a dead end of unfulfilled expectations.

"We could never get stuff like pizza at home," Imelda went on, "just Mexican foods. My mother would give me these silly dresses to wear to school. No jeans. No jewelry. No makeup. And they'd always say, 'Stick with the Mexican kids. Don't talk to the Anglos; they'll boss you. Don't run around with the Chicanos [Mexican-Americans]; they take drugs. And just don't go near the *morenos* [blacks] for any reason.'"

Imelda's parents live in a world circumscribed by the barrio. Except for the places where they work, the rest of the city, the rest of America, seems to them as remote as the downtown skyline visible off in the distance on clear days. After more than a dozen years, they speak all the English they need, which isn't much. What they know best is how to find and keep work.

Imelda learned English from the television that was her constant childhood companion. Outside, as Magnolia became a venue for gangs and drug sales, she learned to be streetwise and sassy. Growing up fast in Magnolia, Imelda learned how to want things but not how to get them.

Many families like Imelda's and many barrios like Magnolia are about to become protagonists in America's struggles with race and poverty. Latino immigrants defy basic assumptions about culture and class because they undermine the perspective that divides the nation into white and nonwhite, a perspective that is the oldest and most enduring element of America's social structure. Are Latinos white or nonwhite? There is only one correct answer, though it is often ignored: They are neither one nor the other. This is more than a matter of putting labels on people. Americans either belong to the white majority or to a nonwhite minority group. That status can determine access to social programs and political power. It decides the way people are seen and the way they see the world. White and nonwhite represent two drastically dissimilar outcomes. They constitute different ways of relating to the United States and of developing an American identity. Latinos break the mold, sometimes entering the white middle-class mainstream, often remaining as much a group apart as poor blacks.

Most European immigrants underwent a period of exclusion and poverty but eventually won acceptance to the white majority. This process of incorporation occurred across generations as the immigrants' economic contributions gained recognition and their American-born children grew up without foreign accents. Too many Latinos are poor, illegal, and dark-skinned for that path to serve as a useful model.

African-Americans traveled an even greater distance to achieve levels of material and political success unthinkable fifty years ago, but as a racial group, they remain juxtaposed to the white majority. Blacks have formally become part of

the body politic, but they remain aggrieved plaintiffs. Latino immigrants lack both the historical standing and the just cause to win their place by way of struggle and petition. And these newcomers are not likely to forge an alliance with blacks, but instead, these two groups are already becoming rivals.

Neither the European ethnics nor the African-Americans were free to choose the means by which they became part of American society. Their place in this country is a product of history, and in each case it is a history of conflict. After centuries of slavery and segregation, it took the strife and idealism of the civil rights era to create a new place for African-Americans within the national identity. The Irish, the Italians, and other European ethnics had been coming here for decades but did not win full acceptance until after the Great Depression and World War II reforged and broadened the American identity to include them. Now the Latinos stand at the gate, looking for a place in American society, and the conflict that will inevitably attend their arrival is just beginning to take shape.

Latinos are different from all other immigrants past and present because they come from close by and because many come illegally. No industrialized nation has ever faced such a vast migration across a land border with the virtual certainty that it will continue to challenge the government's ability to control that border for years to come. No immigrant group has carried the stigma of illegality that now attaches itself to many Latinos. Unlike most immigrants, Latinos arrive already deeply connected to the United States. Latinos come as relations, distant relations perhaps, but familiar and connected nonetheless. They seem to know us. We seem to know them, and almost as soon as they are in the house, they become part of our bedroom arguments. They are newcomers, and yet they find their culture imbedded in the landscape of cities that have always had Spanish names, such as Los Angeles and San Antonio, or that have become largely Spanish-speaking, such as Miami and New York. They do not consider themselves strangers here because they arrive to something familiar.

They come from many different nations, many different races, yet once here they are treated like a pack of blood brothers. In the

United States, they live among folk who share their names but have forgotten their language, ethnic kinsmen who are Latinos by ancestry but U.S. citizens by generations of birthright. The newcomers and the natives may share little else, but for the most part they share neighborhoods, the Magnolias, where their fates become intertwined. Mexican-Americans and Puerto Ricans account for most of the native-born Latino population. They are the U.S.-made vessel into which the new immigration flows. They have been Americans long enough to have histories, and these are sad histories of exploitation and segregation abetted by public authorities. As a result, a unique designation was born. "Hispanics" became a minority group. This identity is an inescapable aspect of the Latino immigrant experience because newcomers are automatically counted as members of the group for purposes of public policy and because the discrimination that shaped that identity persists in some segments of the American public. However, it is an awkward fit for several reasons. The historical grievances that led to minority group designation for Latinos are significant, but compared to slavery or Jim Crow segregation they are neither as well known nor as horrible. As a result, many Americans simply do not accept the idea that Latinos have special standing, and not every native Latino embraces this history as an inescapable element of self-concept. Moreover, Latinos do not carry a single immutable marker, like skin color, that reinforces group identity. Minority group status can be an important element of a Latino's identity in the United States, but it is not such a clear and powerful element of American life that it automatically carries over to Latino immigrants.

"Hispanic" has always been a sweeping designation attached to people of diverse cultures and economic conditions, different races and nationalities, and the sweep has vastly increased by the arrival of immigrants who now make up nearly 40 percent of the group. The designation applies equally to a Mexican-American whose family has been in Texas since before the Alamo and a Mexican who just crossed the Rio Grande for the first time. Minority group status was meant to be as expansive as the discrimination it had to confront. But now for the first time, this concept is being stretched to embrace both a large native Latino population with a long undeniable history of discrimination and immigrants who are just starting out here. The same is occurring with some Asian groups, but the Latino phenomenon has a far greater impact because of the numbers involved. Latino immigrants are players in the old and unresolved dilemma of race in America, and because they do not fit any of the available roles, they are a force of change.

Like all other newcomers, Latino immigrants arrive as blank slates on which their future course has yet to be written. They are moving toward that future in many directions at once, not en masse as a single cohesive group. Some remain very Latino; others become very American. Their skin comes in many different colors and shades. Some are black, and some of them can pass very readily as white. Most Latinos arrive poor. Some stay poor, many do not. Latino immigrants challenge the whole structure of social science, politics, and jurisprudence that categorizes people in terms of lifetime membership in racial or ethnic groups. The barrios do not fit into an urban landscape segregated between rich and poor, between the dependent and the taxed.

Latino immigrants come in large numbers. They come from nearby. They join fellow Latinos who are a native minority group. Many arrive poor, illegally, and with little education. Those are the major ingredients of a challenge unlike any other. . . .

More than a third of all Latinos are younger than eighteen years old. This vast generation is growing faster than any other segment of the population. It is also failing faster. While dropout rates among Anglos and African-Americans steadily decline, they continue to rise among Latino immigrants, and mounting evidence suggests that many who arrive in their teens simply never enter American schools at all. A 1996 Rand study of census data found that high school participation rates were similarly high—better than 90 percent—for whites, blacks, and Asians, native and immigrant alike, and for native Latinos, as well. Latino immigrants, especially from Mexico, were the only group lagging far behind, with less than 75 percent of the school-age teens getting any education. Only 62 percent of the Mexican immigrant seventeen-year-olds were in school, and these young people are the fuel of U.S. population growth into the twenty-first century.

Dropout rates are only one symptom. This massive generation of young people is adapting to an America characterized by the interaction of plagues. Their new identities are being shaped by the social epidemics of youth homicides, pregnancy, and drug use, the medical epidemic of AIDS, and a political epidemic of disinvestment in social services. These young Latinos need knowledge to survive in the workforce, but the only education available to them comes from public school systems that are on the brink of collapse. They are learning to become Americans in urban neighborhoods that most Americans see only in their nightmares. Imelda and a vast generation of Latino young people like her are the victims of a vicious bait and switch. The United States offered their parents opportunities. So many of the children get the plagues.

For the parents, movement to the United States almost always brings tangible success. They may be poor by U.S. standards, but they measure their accomplishments in terms of what they have left behind. By coming north, they overcome barriers of race and class that have been insuperable for centuries in Latin America. Meanwhile, the children are left on the wrong side of the barriers of race and class that are becoming ever more insuperable in the United States. With no memory of the *rancho*, they have no reason to be thankful for escaping it. They look at their parents and all they see is toil and poverty. They watch American TV, and all they see is affluence. Immigrant children learning to live in this dark new world face painful challenges but get little help. Now, on top of everything else, they are cursed by people who want to close the nation's doors against them. The effects are visible on their faces. . . .

The latest wave of immigrants has come to the United States only to find the ladder broken. Their arrival has coincided with changes in the structure of the U.S. economy that make the old three-generation formula obsolete. The middle rungs of the ladder, which allowed for a gradual transition into American life, are more precarious because so many jobs disappeared along with the industrial economy of smokestacks and assembly lines. In addition, the wages paid at the bottom of the labor force have declined in value since the early 1980s.

The old blue-collar jobs are not the only rungs of the ladder that are now wobbly. The United States greatly expanded its system of public education in order to prepare the children and the grandchildren of the European immigrants for the workforce, extending it first to high schools and then to universities. Latino immigrants have arrived, only to find this education system dangerously in disrepair. As with the demise of the industrial economy, this reflects a fundamental change in the structure of American society. Government's priorities have shifted in ways that alter the nature of opportunity. The results have quickly become apparent. The State of California now pays better salaries to experienced prison guards than to tenured Cal State professors. The guards are more in demand. Labor unions, big-city political machines, and other institutions that helped the European immigrants are also less vigorous and far less interested in the immigrants' cause than in the early decades of this century. The Roman Catholic church gave vital help to the Europeans in establishing enclaves, gaining education, and developing ethnic solidarity, but it moved to the suburbs with the second and third generations and has played a minor institutional role—primarily as a lobbyist for liberal immigration policies—in helping the new Latinos gain a foothold in the United States.

Starting at the bottom has usually been an immigrant's fate, but this takes on a new meaning in an increasingly immobile and stratified society. Skills and education have come to mark a great divide in the U.S. workforce, and the gap is growing ever broader. The entire population is being divided into a two-tier workforce, with a college education as the price of admission to the upper tier. In the new knowledge-based economy, people with knowledge prosper. People without it remain poor. These divisions have the makings of a new class system because this kind of economic status is virtually hereditary. Very few Latino immigrants arrive with enough education to make it into the upper tier of the workforce. Their children, like the children of all poor people, face the greatest economic pressures to drop out and find work. When they do stay in school, the education they receive is, for the most part, poor. . . .

Latinos are rapidly becoming the nation's largest minority group at a time when that term is quickly losing its meaning. Latino immigration can prompt the creation of a new civil rights framework that distinguishes between two distinct tasks—redressing the effects of past discrimination and providing protection against new forms of bias—and undertakes both tasks aggressively.

Latinos are also rapidly adding to the ranks of the working poor at a time when the nation is redefining the role of its lower classes. The divisions between rich and poor, between the knowledgeable and the unskilled, grow greater even as a broad political consensus favors reducing services and benefits for the poor. Understanding recent Latino immigrants, however, involves appreciating a very distinct kind of poverty. The ambition and optimism of the Latino poor could sour in the future, especially if the second generation gets nowhere, but in the meantime Latino immigration offers this country a chance to revise its attitudes toward the poor. Understanding the poverty of hard work will carry Americans beyond the common misperception that the poor are no more than an unsightly appendage to an affluent society. Instead they will be viewed as an integral part of the larger whole, one that must have opportunities to escape poverty in order for the whole to prosper.

These changes can occur, however, only if Latinos alter some attitudes of their own. Long-term residents of the barrios—natives and immigrants alike—must realize that they, more than anyone else, suffer the ill-effects of illegal immigration and that it is in their self-interest to turn illegals away from their communities. Latinos must also take a new approach to language. Instead of preserving Spanish as a way to redress past grievances with the education system, English-language training should be pursued as a means of securing a successful future in a new land.

Finally, Latino immigration will cause the United States to rethink the connection between the issues of race and poverty. For too long, the two have been linked in an easy but false equation that renders the problems of the poor as the problems of African-Americans and vice versa. This constitutes a form of prejudice and, like all prejudice, it is blinding. The arrival of Latino immigrants tangibly breaks the connection.

Addressing these challenges will require a cohesion and purposefulness that the United States has sorely missed for many years. By their numbers alone, the Latinos will require the country to find a place for them. Along the way, there is a chance that America might find itself again.

In the meantime, they will keep coming.

Yellow Face: Asian Americans in Popular Culture

Robert G. Lee

*Not until 1952, after more than a century of settlement in the United States, were
Asian immigrants finally granted the right to become naturalized citizens.
Even so, long after the legal status of "alien" has been shed, the "common
understanding" that Asians are an alien presence in America, no matter how
long they may have resided in the United States nor how assimilated they
are, is still prevalent in American culture.*

One of my best friends, an English professor born and raised in Singapore, made
me sensitive to the fact that for many people the word "oriental" is derogatory. It de-
notes strangeness, foreign, alien, mysterious, and even noncivilized. It was with surprise that I discovered a book by Robert G. Lee called *Orientals*, and as I read the
book I saw the wisdom of my friend's criticism of the label.

What Lee does in his book is to show the racist stereotypes associated with Asian
Americans, especially the tendency for white Americans to think of Asian Americans
as permanent aliens in America. Lee shows us that in popular culture Asians are
defined as a "foreign racial category" which makes them threats to the "American
national family."

MARKING THE ORIENTAL

In March 1997, the cover of *National Review* featured President William Jefferson Clinton, first
lady Hillary Rodham Clinton, and Vice President Al Gore, all in yellowface. The president,
portrayed as a Chinese houseboy—buck-toothed,
squinty-eyed and pigtailed, wearing a straw
"coolie" hat—serves coffee. The first lady, similarly buck-toothed and squinty-eyed, outfitted as

From *Orientals: Asian Americans in Popular Culture*, by
Robert G. Lee. Reprinted by permission of Temple University
Press. © 1999 by Temple University. All Rights Reserved.

a Maoist Red Guard, brandishes a "Little Red
Book," while the vice president, robed as Bud-
dhist priest, beatifically proffers a begging bowl
already stuffed with money.

In using the yellowface cartoon to illustrate a
story about alleged political corruption, the editors of *National Review* simultaneously emphasized their racial point and revived a tradition of
racial grotesques that had illustrated broadsides,
editorials, and diatribes against Asians in America
since the mid-nineteenth century. The cover
story summarized allegations that the Clinton
administration had solicited campaign donations
from Asian contributors in exchange for policy

153

favors. These allegations virtually ignored the much larger illegal campaign contributions of non-Asians and focused almost exclusively on Asian and Asian American contributors.[1] Like most of the mainstream media, *National Review* was silent on the broader questions: the impact of multinational corporations on American politics and the baleful influence of big money on big politics. *National Review* instead played the race card. Focusing only on the Asian and Asian American campaign contributions, *National Review* made it clear that it was not corporate money, or even foreign money generally, but specifically Asian money that polluted the American political process. In the eyes of the *National Review* editors, the nation's first family (with Al Gore as potential heir) had been so polluted by Asian money that they had literally turned yellow.

Yellowface marks the Asian body as unmistakably Oriental; it sharply defines the Oriental in a racial opposition to whiteness. Yellowface exaggerates "racial" features that have been designated "Oriental," such as "slanted" eyes, overbite, and mustard-yellow skin color. Only the racialized Oriental is yellow; Asians are not. Asia is not a biological fact but a geographic designation. Asians come in the broadest range of skin color and hue.

Because the organizing principle behind the idea of race is "common ancestry," it is concerned with the physical, the biological, and the reproductive. But race is not a category of nature; it is an ideology through which unequal distributions of wealth and power are naturalized—justified in the language of biology and genealogy. Physiognomy is relevant to race only insofar as certain physical characteristics, such as skin color or hue, eye color or shape, shape of the nose, color or texture of the hair, over- or underbite, etc., are *socially defined* as markers of racial difference.

The designation of yellow as the racial color of the Oriental is a prime example of this social constructedness of race. In 1922, the U.S. Supreme Court denied Takao Ozawa, an immigrant from Japan, the right to become a naturalized citizen. In its ruling, the court recognized the fact that some Asians, including Ozawa, were of a paler hue than many European immigrants already accepted into the nation as "white."

Race, the court concluded, was not a matter of actual color but of "blood" or ancestry, and Ozawa, being of Japanese "blood," could not claim to be white, no matter how white his skin.[2]

What does Yellowface signify? Race is a mode of placing cultural meaning on the body. Yellowface marks the Oriental as indelibly alien. Constructed as a race of aliens, Orientals represent a present danger of pollution. An analysis of the Oriental as a racial category must begin with the concept of the alien as a polluting body.

The cultural anthropologist Mary Douglas argues that fears of pollution arise when things are out of place. Soil, she observes, is fertile earth when on the ground with tomatoes growing in it; it is polluting dirt when on the kitchen table. Pollutants are objects, or persons, perceived to be out of place. They create a sense of disorder and anomaly in the symbolic structure of society. Douglas observes that pollution is not a conscious act. Mere presence in the wrong place, the inadvertent crossing of a boundary, may constitute pollution.[3] Aliens, outsiders who are inside, disrupt the internal structure of a cultural formation as it defines itself vis-à-vis the Other; their presence constitutes a boundary crisis. Aliens are always a source of pollution.

Not all foreign objects, however, are aliens—only objects or persons whose presence disrupts the narrative structure of the community. It is useful here to distinguish between the alien and the merely foreign. Although the two terms are sometimes used interchangeably, they carry different connotations. "Foreign" refers to that which is outside or distant, while "alien" describes things that are immediate and present yet have a foreign nature or allegiance. The difference is political. According to the *Oxford English Dictionary*, as early as the sixteenth century "alien" referred to things whose allegiance lay outside the realm in which they resided, as in "alien priories"—monasteries in England whose loyalty was to Rome. This early definition of "alien" emphasized the unalterable nature of the foreign object and its threatening presence.

Only when the foreign is present does it become alien. The alien is always out of place, therefore disturbing and dangerous. The difference between the alien and the merely foreign is exemplified by the difference between the immigrant and the tourist. Outsiders who declare their intention of leaving may be accorded the status of guest, visitor, tourist, traveler, or foreign student. Such foreigners, whose presence is defined as temporary, are seen as innocuous and even desirable. On the other hand, if the arriving outsiders declare no intention to leave (or if such a declared intention is suspect), they are accorded the status of alien, with considerably different and sometimes dire consequences. Only when aliens exit or are "naturalized" (cleansed of their foreignness and remade) can they shed their status as pollutants.

Alienness is both a formal political or legal status and an informal, but by no means less powerful, cultural status. The two states are hardly synonymous or congruent. Alien legal status and the procedures by which it can be shed often depend on the cultural definitions of difference. In 1923, a year after it denied Takao Ozawa the right to naturalize, the Supreme Court stripped Bhagat Singh Thind, an Indian immigrant who was already an American through naturalization, of his U.S. citizenship.[4] In *Ozawa v. United States*, the court had ruled that no matter what the actual color of his skin, nor how much he could prove himself culturally assimilated, Ozawa's Japanese "blood" made him "unamalgamable" by marriage into the American national family. In *United States v. Thind*, despite the ethnological evidence presented by Thind that he, a high-caste Hindu, was a descendent of Aryans and hence white by "blood," the court ruled that he was not, holding that race was not a scientific category but a social one, and upheld the revocation of Thind's citizenship.

In both *Ozawa* and *Thind*, the Supreme Court tacitly recognized race to be a product of popular ideology. In both cases, Chief Justice Sutherland, writing for the court, cited the existence of a "common understanding" of racial difference which color, culture, and science could not surmount. The important thing about race, the Supreme Court held, was not what social or physical scientists at the time may have had to say about it, but rather how it was "popularly" defined.

Not until 1952, after more than a century of settlement in the United States, were Asian immigrants finally granted the right to become naturalized citizens. Even so, long after the legal status of "alien" has been shed, the "common understanding" that Asians are an alien presence in America, no matter how long they may have resided in the United States nor how assimilated they are, is still prevalent in American culture. In 1996, the immediate response of the Democratic National Committee to allegations that it had accepted illegal campaign donations from foreigners was to call Asian American contributors to the party's coffers and demand that they verify their status as citizens or permanent residents. One such donor, Suzanne Ahn, a prominent Houston physician and civic leader, reported to the U.S. Commission on Civil Rights that DNC auditors threatened to turn her name over to the news media as "uncooperative" if she did not release personal financial information to them. Ahn concluded that she had been investigated by the DNC, the FBI, and the news media simply because she had contributed to the DNC and was Asian American. Even public figures do not escape the assumption that Asian Americans are really foreigners in disguise. When Matthew Fong, a fourth-generation Californian, ran as a Republican candidate for Secretary of State in California—a position his mother March Fong Yu had held for the better part of two decades—he was asked by news reporters whether his loyalties were divided between the U.S. and China.[5]

In the run-up to the 1996 presidential elections, a cartoon by syndicated cartoonist Pat Oliphant played on the persistent "common understanding" of Asian Americans as permanent aliens in America. It showed a befuddled poll watcher confronted with a long line of identically short Oriental men with identical black hair, slit eyes behind glasses, and buck teeth, all wearing identical suits and waving ballots. Referring to the Asian American DNC official who was made the poster boy of the fund-raising scandal, the caption reads, "The 3,367th John Huang is now voting." Echoing the public comment of presidential candidate Ross Perot that none of the Asian names brought out in the campaign finance scandal thus far sounded like they belonged to "real" Americans, one of Oliphant's signature nebbishes asks from the margin, "Just how many John Huangs are there? How many you want?"[6] The cartoon plays on the "common understanding" that Orientals are indistinguishable as individuals and thus ultimately fail as "real" Americans. How could Oliphant's poll watcher, the yeoman guardian of the American political process and embodiment of "common understanding," possibly hope to distinguish among all the Orientals flooding into the nation's body politic?

POPULAR CULTURE AND RACE

The Oriental as a racial category is never isolated from struggles over race, ethnicity, sexuality, gender, and national identity. The Supreme Court's "common understanding" is a legal fiction. It gives popular convention, the common sense of "real" Americans, the power to define race. The "common understanding" of the Oriental as racialized alien therefore originates in the realm of popular culture, where struggles over who is or who can become a "real American" take place and where the categories, representations, distinctions, and markers of race are defined. Some studies attribute hostility toward Asian immigrants directly to economic competition and the creation of an ethnically defined segmented labor market. They provide us with an economic framework for understanding the dynamics of class and race and a map of the economic terrain on which anti-Asian hostility has been built. By themselves, however, those studies do not account for the development or functioning of specific racial images of Asians in American culture.[7]

This book takes up popular culture as a process, a set of cultural practices that define American nationality—who "real Americans" are in any given historical moment. American citizenship and American nationality are not synonymous; citizenship carries with it an implicit assumption or promise of equality, at least in political and legal terms, while nationality contains and manages the contradictions of the hierarchies and inequalities of a social formation. Nationality is a constantly shifting and contested terrain that organizes the ideological struggle over hierarchies and inequalities.

The nature of popular culture is the subject of much debate.[8] Popular culture is most often identified as having its roots in the organic culture of the common folk or peasant life, in opposition to court or bourgeois culture. Popular culture, then, is often characterized by politically resistant, if often nostalgic, qualities. Ever since the rise of industrial capitalism in the early nineteenth century, popular culture has been in reality complex, increasingly shaped by the capitalist processes of its production and circulation. Nevertheless, popular culture, albeit sometimes reconstituted as co-opted or deracinated mass culture, continues to be identified with subordinated groups, as opposed to the dominant ruling class.

The mobilization of national identity under the sign "American" has never been a simple matter of imposing elite interests and values on the social formation, but is always a matter of negotiation between the dominant and the dominated. Subordinated groups offer resistance to the hegemony of elite culture; they create subaltern popular cultures and contest for a voice in the dominant public sphere.[9] The saloon vies with the salon, the boardwalk with the cafe, and the minstrel theater with the opera house as an arena for public debate and political ideas.[10]

Although it mobilizes legitimacy, the cultural hegemony of dominant groups is never complete; it can render fundamental social contradictions invisible, explain them away, or ameliorate them, but it cannot resolve them.[11] However deracinated, whether co-opted, utopian, nostalgic, or nihilist, popular culture is always contested terrain. The practices that make up popular culture are negotiations, in the public sphere, between and among dominant and subaltern groups around the questions of national identity: What constitutes America? Who gets to participate and on what grounds? Who are "real Americans"?

Since popular culture is a significant arena in which the struggle over defining American nationality occurs, it also plays a critical role in defining race. Race is a principal signifier of social differences in America. It is deployed in assigning differential political rights and capital and social privilege, it distinguishes between citizens presumed to have equal rights and privileges and inherently unequal, subordinated subjects.[12] Although race is often camouflaged or rendered invisible, once produced as a category of social difference it is present everywhere in the social formation and deeply imbedded in the popular culture. The Oriental as a racial category is produced, not only in popular discourse about race *per se* but also in discourses having to do with class, gender and sexuality, family, and nation. Once produced in those discourses, the Oriental becomes a participant in the production and reproduction of those social identities.[13] . . .

THE SIX FACES OF THE ORIENTAL

Six images—the pollutant, the coolie, the deviant, the yellow peril, the model minority, and the gook—portray the Oriental as an alien body and a threat to the American national family. From each of these racial paradigms emerges a wide array of specific images. Each of these representations was constructed in a specific historical moment, marked by a shift in class relations accompanied by cultural crisis. At such times American nationality—who the "real Americans" are—is redefined in terms of class, gender, race, and sexuality.

The representation of the Asian as pollutant originated in mid-nineteenth-century California. For white settlers from the East, Chinese settlers from the West disrupted the mythic narrative of westward expansion. The Chinese constituted an alien presence and a threat of pollution which earlier fantasies of exotic but distant Asia could not contain. In the popular imagination, California was a free-soil Eden, a place where small producers, artisans, farmers, and craftsmen might have a second chance to build a white republic, unstained by chattel slavery or proletarian labor.[14] In this prelapsarian imagery, the Chinese were both identified with the moral chaos of the Gold Rush and portrayed as the harbingers of industrial wage slavery. As the national debate over slavery, abolition, and statehood came to a boiling point in the late 1860s, the ideal of establishing California as both free and racially pure demanded the removal, or at least the exclusion, of both Chinese and African Americans.

The representation of the Chinese immigrant worker as a coolie came about as the U.S. working class was formed in the 1870s and 1880s. Although they had come to America as free (albeit highly proletarianized) workers, Chinese immigrants found themselves segregated into a racially defined state of subordination as "coolie labor." The Chinese "coolie" was portrayed as unfree and servile, a threat to the white working man's family, which in turn was the principal symbol of an emergent working-class identity that fused class consciousness with gendered national and racial identity. The coolie representation not only allowed the nascent labor movement, dominated by its skilled trades, to exclude Chinese from the working class; it also enabled the skilled trades to ignore the needs of common labor, which it racialized as "coolie labor" or "nigger work."[15] Irish immigrants who were in the process of consolidating their own claim to Americanness and a white racial identity led the popular anti-Chinese movement.

The Oriental as deviant, in the person of the Chinese household servant, is a figure of forbidden desire. The deviant represents the possibility of alternative desire in a period during which middle-class gender roles and sexual behavior were being codified and naturalized into a rigid heterosexual cult of domesticity. In the West, the Chinese immigrant played a central role in the transition from a male-dominated, frontier culture shaped by the rituals of male bonding to a rigidly codified heterosexual Victorian culture. In the 1860s and early 1870s, hundreds of Chinese women were brought to San Francisco and forced into prostitution. By the end of the decade, thousands of Chinese immigrant men were driven out of the mines and off farms and ranches and were hired into middle-class households as domestic servants. Both of these situations opened up possibilities of interracial sex and intimacy. Middle-class whites regarded the Chinese with ambivalence. On the one hand, the Chinese were indispensable as domestic labor; on the other, they represented a threat of racial pollution within the household. A representation of the Oriental as both seductively childlike and threateningly sexual allowed for both sympathy and repulsion. The representation of the Oriental as deviant justified a taboo against intimacy through which racial and class stability could be preserved.

By the turn of the century, Asian immigrants were represented as the yellow peril, a threat to nation, race, and family. The acquisition of territories and colonies brought with it a renewed threat of "Asiatic" immigration, an invasion of "yellow men" and "little brown brothers." At the moment when the United States prepared to pick up "the white man's burden" in the Caribbean and the Pacific, "Asiatic immigration" was said to pose "the greatest threat to Western civilization and the White Race."[16] Domestically, the triumph of corporatism, the homogenization or deskilling of industrial labor, urbanization, and immigration had all contributed to massive changes in both middle-and working-class families. These changes contributed to the construction of a culture of consumption, reflected in new gender roles as well as new sexual attitudes and behavior among men and women of both classes. In the aftermath of the First World War and the Bolshevik Revolution, these domestic social and cultural transformations were accompanied by deep anxieties about racial suicide and class struggle.[17] Through its supposed subversion of the family, the yellow peril threatened to undermine what Lothrop Stoddard, a popular advocate of eugenics and racial geopolitics, called the "inner dikes" of the white race.

The representation of Asian Americans as a model minority, although popularly identified with the late 1960s and 1970s, originated in the racial logic of Cold War liberalism of the 1950s. The image of Asian Americans as a successful case of "ethnic" assimilation helped to contain three spectres that haunted Cold War America: the red menace of communism, the black menace of racial integration, and the white menace of homosexuality. In place of a radical critique calling for structural changes in American political economy, the model minority mythology substituted a narrative of national modernization and ethnic assimilation through heterosexuality, familialism, and consumption. By the late 1960s, an image of "successful" Asian American assimilation could be held up to African Americans and Latinos as a model for nonmilitant, nonpolitical upward mobility.

Since the 1970s, the model minority image has coexisted with and reinforced a representation of the Asian American as the gook. The shift in the U.S. economy from large-scale industrial production to flexible accumulation and the global realignment of capital and labor have brought about new crises of class, race, and national identity. In the context of these contemporary crises, the "intact" and "traditional" Asian American family is promoted as a model of productivity, savings, and mobility, not just for African America or Latino families but now for all American families, including those of the white middle class. Simultaneously, however, in post-Vietnam and post-liberal American popular culture, the Asian American is represented as the invisible enemy and the embodiment of inauthentic racial and national identities—the gook. The Vietnam War is replayed in popular culture as the narrative of American decline in the post-industrial era. The received wisdom of the Vietnam War narrative is that America's defeat in Southeast Asia was brought about by a faceless and invisible Asian enemy, aided and abetted by an American counterculture. The rapid growth of the Asian American population and its apparent success render the model minority, like the now-mythic Viet Cong, everywhere invisible and powerful. In the narrative of American decline, Asian Americans are represented as the agents of foreign or multinational capital. In this narrative of national decline, Asian American success is seen as camouflage for subversion. The model minority is revealed to be a simulacrum, a copy for which no original exists, and thus a false model of the American family. In the dystopic narrative of American national decline, the model minority resembles the replicants in the science fiction book and film *Blade Runner*—a cyborg, perfectly efficient but inauthentically human, the perfect gook.

The cultural crises in American society that give rise to these representations of the Oriental come in the wake of economic change, particularly in what economic historians Gordon and Reich call transformations of the structure of accumulation.[18] The transformation of the social relations of production and the organization of work and segmentation of the labor market have profound effects on the structures, relations, and meaning of families, gender, and race. At each stage of capitalist development, new "emergent" public spheres are constituted and new demands arise for participation in the dominant public sphere.[19] The popular discourse of race in which these constructions of the Oriental were produced and deployed is not a transparent or unmediated reflection of the economy, but rather an expression of social contradictions drawing on images of the present, visions of the future, and memories of the past. . . .

NOTES

1. Non-Asians fined by the Federal Election Commission for illegal contributions to the Clinton-Gore re-election campaign included Simon Fireman, who was fined $6 million (the largest such fine ever levied), and Thomas Kramer, a German national who was fined $323,000. See "Petition of the National Asian Pacific American Legal Consortium et al. to the United States Commission on Civil Rights," September 10, 1997, reprinted at http://www2.ari.net/oca/camp/complain.html.
2. *Takao Ozawa v. United States*, 260 U.S. 178 (1922).
3. Mary Douglas, *Purity and Danger: An Analysis of the Concepts of Pollution and Taboo* (London and New York: Ark Paperbacks, 1966), 54.
4. *Ozawa*, and *United States v. Bhagat Singh Thind*, 261 U.S. 204 (1923). For an analysis of these cases, see Philip Tajitsu Nash in Hyung Chan Kim, ed., *Asian Americans and the Supreme Court* (Hamden, Conn.: Greenwood Press, 1993), and Jeff H. Lesser, "Always Outsiders: Asians, Naturalization and the Supreme Court: 1740–1944," *Amerasia Journal* 12 (1985):83–100.
5. See "Petition of the National Asian Pacific American Legal Consortium et al. to the United States Commission on Civil Rights."
6. For a detailed analysis of the media coverage of the John Huang affair, see Frank Wu and May Nicholson, "Racial Aspects of Media Coverage of the John Huang Matter," *Asian American Policy Review* 7(1997):1–37.
7. An alternative view, which locates the image of the Chinese immigrant in America in the constellation of racial images in nineteenth-century American culture, is Ronald Takaki, *Iron Cages: Race and Culture in Nineteenth-Century America* (Seattle: University of Washington Press, 1979). Takaki's view, like Alexander Saxton's in *The Rise and Fall of the White Republic* (London and New York: Verso, 1990), is a Gramscian class analysis.
8. For a succinct review of these debates, see John Storey, *An Introductory Guide to Cultural Theory and Popular Culture* (Athens, GA.: University of Georgia Press, 1993).
9. Jurgen Habermas argues that the idea of the citizen came into being in the public sphere that emerged in the seventeenth and eighteenth centuries in bourgeois drawing rooms, salons, and cafes. This public sphere was a social space

between the realm of the state and the realm of civil society (composed of the private family sphere and the sphere of commodity exchange and social labor). The public sphere is the realm in which the individual is constituted as public citizen and where he (the bourgeois male, in Habermas's historical account) makes his interests heard by the state. See Jurgen Habermas, *The Structural Transformation of the Public Sphere: An Inquiry into a Category of Bourgeois Society*, translated by Thomas Burger (Cambridge: Massachusetts Institute of Technology Press, 1989). Habermas's focus on a single public sphere defined by the political emancipation of the bourgeois male has been challenged by Nancy Fraser and others, who argue for the existence of multiple public spheres whose participants include the disenfranchised and the marginalized: women, racial minorities, and the working class. See Nancy Fraser, *Power, Discourse, and Gender in Contemporary Social Theory* (Minneapolis: University of Minnesota Press, 1989), and "What's Critical about Critical Theory? The Case of Gender," in *Unruly Practices* (Minneapolis: University of Minnesota Press, 1990); and Craig Calhoun, "Populist Politics, Communications Media, and Large Scale Societal Integration," *Sociological Theory* 6 (no. 2, 1988): 219–241.
10. On the significance of saloon, boardwalks, and popular theater see, respectively, Roy Rosenzweig, *Eight Hours for What We Will: Workers and Leisure in an Industrial City, 1870–1920* (New York: Cambridge University Press, 1983); Kathy Peiss, *Cheap Amusements: Working Women and Leisure in Turn-of-the-Century New York* (Philadelphia: Temple University Press, 1986); and Sean Wilentz, *Chants Democratic: New York City & the Rise of the American Working Class, 1788–1850* (New York: Oxford University Press, 1984).
11. The notion of hegemony comes, of course, from Gramsci. For a critique that emphasizes the incomplete and contested nature of hegemony, see James Scott, *Domination and the Arts of Resistance: Hidden Transcripts* (New Haven: Yale University Press, 1990).
12. The thesis that sovereignty rests in the privatized body is John Locke's. See the chapter "On Property" in *The Second Treatise of Government*, edited by Thomas P. Reardon (Indianapolis: Bobbs-Merrill, 1952), 16–30. On the "abstract citizen," see also Lisa Lowe, *Immigrant Acts: On Asian American Cultural Politics* (Durham, NC: Duke University Press, 1996), 2.
13. Sociologists Michael Omi and Howard Winant argue that race cannot be explained as simply a subcategory or an epiphenomenon of another single social dynamic such as class formation or ethnicity, but instead exists as a separate category of social difference. They argue that the production and reproduction of race is historically contingent, decentered, and contested. Michael Omi and Howard

Winant, *Racial Formation in the United States: From the 1960s to the 1990s*, 2nd ed. (New York and London: Routledge, 1994), 53–76 passim.

14. See David Roediger, *The Wages of Whiteness: Race and the Making of the American Working Class* (London and New York: Verso, 1991).

15. Alexander Saxton, *The Indispensable Enemy: Labor and the Anti-Chinese Movement in California* (Berkeley, University of California Press, 1971).

16. Lothrop Stoddard, *The Rising Tide of Color Against White World-Supremacy* (New York: Charles Scribner's Sons, 1920).

17. See, for example, T. J. Jackson Lears, *No Place of Grace: Antimodernism and the Transformation of American Culture, 1880–1920* (New York: Pantheon Books, 1981).

18. Of the many and varied periodizations of American economic history, the one I have found must useful for this study is the analysis of changes in the labor market and the social structure of accumulation by David M. Gordon, Richard Edwards, and Michael Reich, *Segmented Work, Divided Workers: The Historical Transformation of Labor in the United States* (New York: Cambridge University Press, 1982). They examine the relationship between long cycles of economic activity and the social structure of accumulation. They outline three periods in the development of American capitalism with regard to labor:

- Initial proletarianization, from the 1820s to the 1890s.
- Homogenization, from the 1870s to the onset of World War I, during which the labor markets became more competitive and the dominance of skilled crafts positions was diminished by the large-scale introduction of semiskilled labor.
- Segmentation, from the 1920s to the present, during which political and economic forces have produced qualitative differences in the organization of work and three distinct labor markets: a secondary labor market, plus a primary labor market divided into independent and subordinate sectors.

Gordon et al. link these broad periods to long swings (on the order of twenty-five years) in global economic activity, each associated with a distinct social structure of accumulation, the institutional environment in which capital accumulation takes place. For a periodization shaped by both economy and culture, see Herbert Gutman, *Work, Culture, and Society in Industrializing America: Essays in American Working-Class and Social History* (New York: Knopf, 1976), 1–78.

19. I use "emergent" here in the same counterhegemonic sense that Raymond Williams uses the term in *Culture and Society* (London: Penguin, 1971).

Part VI

SOCIAL STRUCTURE: GENDER

Probably all societies are structured by gender. Men and women are differentiated, categorized, assigned roles and identities, and ranked by power, prestige, and privilege in society. Although a numerical majority in society, women still constitute a minority in the United States in terms of their position in relation to men. History, family life, economic and educational opportunities, sex, cultural values and norms, stereotypical roles, and socialization into structure are the forces we must examine if we are to to understand the relations between men and women in society.

Judith Howard and Jocelyen Hollander begin their selection by carefully defining sex, gender, gender difference, gender role, gender stereotype, gender identity, sexuality, and sexual orientation. Their purpose is to try to distinguish those differences whose origins are biological and those whose are social, and differences that are important and those that are not.

Barbara Risman describes the meaning of social structure, and shows how gender structure makes a difference in all aspects of our lives. She neatly describes how it affects us as individuals, in social interaction, and in our institutions, and she tries to get us to see social inequality at the level of society, rather than at the level of isolated individual desires and choices.

Arlie Russell Hochschild's selection from *The Second Shift* focuses our attention on the "working wife": the role the modern woman plays in both occupation and home. The changes in women's working life outside the home is truly an important revolution, but its promise is accompanied by new and serious problems.

Susan Faludi's selection discusses the American male, controlled by a society's structure. Men are not the source of the problems associated with gender inequality; instead, it is the social structure that ranks and forms us all. Faludi's discussion is a sympathetic one; she gets above blame, and she sees men today needing a way to free themselves from a societal crisis that they too often do not understand, and ignore.

◆ 28 ◆

The Meaning of Gender

Judith A. Howard and Jocelyn A. Hollander

*. . . although gender differences may exist, they are not the same as sex differences.
In other words, just because women and men may appear to behave or
think differently does not mean that they have different innate
characteristics or abilities. Instead, these differences may be (and, we
believe, generally are) constructed through social processes.*

What exactly are the differences between men and women, and are they important?
Judith Howard and Jocelyn Hollander carefully define several words associated with
this issue and try to show that whatever real differences exist—and these tend to be
exaggerated by most people—are gender related, meaning socially constructed.
They conclude that sex differences are exaggerated, and gender differences are important only because society regards them as so.

Over the last 30 years, social psychologists (and
others) have become more and more interested
in gender. But what exactly is "gender"? When
we talk about gender, do we mean the biological
characteristics of females and males, such as
genes or genitals? Do we mean the social roles
that men and women play—mother, father,
breadwinner, caretaker? Or are we talking about
personal characteristics, such as aggressiveness or
nurturance?

Another source of confusion is that the relationship between *gender* and other terms is
poorly defined. Some writers use the term
gender, some discuss *sex*, and some examine *sex
roles* or *gender roles*. Moreover, some authors use
these words interchangeably, whereas others

distinguish carefully between them. Our goal in
the rest of this chapter is to untangle these confu-
sions and spell out exactly what we mean—and
do not mean—by the term gender. In this section, we define gender and compare it with related terms: *sex*, *gender role*, *gender stereotype*,
gender identity, *sexuality*, and *sexual orientation*.
We also define two other terms, *race* and *social
class*, that we use throughout this book. Our discussion will help to illuminate precisely what we
mean by a gender lens.

SEX

What is sex? When we fill out official forms,
whether applying for a job, a driver's license, admission to college, or a credit card, we are usually
asked to declare our sex by checking the box
marked "male" or the box marked "female." How
do we know which box to check?

From Judith A. Howard and Jocelyn A. Hollander, *Gendered
Situations, Gendered Selves: A Gender Lens on Social Psychology*, Sage Publications, 1996. By permission.

The definition of sex seems straightforward: The term is generally used to refer to the biological characteristics that distinguish males and females, such as reproductive organs or chromosomes. Most people in this society think of sex as dichotomous and unchangeable. That is, they assume that there are only two boxes one can check, female and male, and that everyone falls into one (and only one) of these categories. Moreover, they assume that one always falls into the same category: Someone who checks the "female" box at age 20 will have checked the same box at age 10, and will check it at ages 50 and 85 as well.

However, these assumptions are not always correct. *Hermaphrodites*, for example, are people who are not easily classified as male or female: Their reproductive organs and chromosomal structures are ambiguous (Money and Ehrhardt 1972). For example, a child may be born with both male and female genitalia. Which box would this person check on official forms? Specialists estimate that up to 4% of the population may be intersexed in this way. In fact, Fausto-Sterling (1993) suggests that a more logical categorization scheme would actually include five sexes: males, females, and three types of hermaphrodites. *Transsexuals*, on the other hand, are people who have literally changed their sex—they have been surgically and hormonally altered so that they appear to be a sex different from that as which they were born. A well-known example is Jan Morris, a writer who began life as a boy, James, but who now lives as a woman, Jan. (Transsexuals are distinct from *transvestites*, who wear the clothes associated with the other sex.) Because transsexuals have the genetic structure of one sex but the physical appearance of another, they are also not easily classified as one or the other sex.

The belief in two sexes is an example of what Mehan and Wood (1975) have called an "incorrigible proposition": an unquestioned belief that cannot be proven wrong, even in the face of contradictory evidence. In this society, we believe that there are two, and only two, sexes, and when we encounter a situation that challenges this belief, such as a person who doesn't fit neatly into one of these two categories, we adjust the situation to fit our beliefs rather than adjusting our beliefs to fit the situation. In the case of hermaphroditism, for example, we "correct" the ambiguity by surgical or hormonal means and assign the person to one of our two categories rather than admitting the possibility of more than two categories.

How do we determine someone's sex? Most people would answer this question by appealing to biology: Males have penises and XY chromosomes, whereas females have vaginas, more prominently developed breasts, and XX chromosomes. In everyday life, however, we do not normally use these criteria to distinguish between males and females. Yet we rarely have trouble classifying those we meet as male or female:

> When encountering older children or adults for the first time, most of us do not usually examine their genitals to label their sex! Instead, we use their attire, movements, sex-related characteristics such as height or musculature, and their general style of self-presentation as cues to their sex. (Unger and Crawford 1992:17–18)

Thus assigning someone to a sex category is as much a social process as the application of physiological criteria. As we shall see in the next section, the way we ascribe sex is deeply intertwined with gender.

GENDER

Gender is a slippery term. Most scholars would agree with the statement that gender has something to do with the social behaviors and characteristics associated with biological sex; however, there is substantially less agreement on exactly what this statement means.

Social scientists use the term gender in two different ways. Some use gender interchangeably with sex, suggesting that sex and gender are essentially the same thing. (Indeed, some argue that the term gender is meaningless and should be abandoned, because everything, they believe, reduces to sex.) These researchers might assume, for example, that women care for children (and are nurturing in general) because of their biological ability to bear children. This perspective sees gender as somehow essential to males and females; it is believed to be both innate and unchanging. For this reason, this approach is sometimes called the *essentialist perspective* on gender. Biology is believed to determine the social behaviors and characteristics of males and females.

Other scholars distinguish between sex and gender, using sex to refer to biological characteristics as we have described above but using gender to mean the culturally determined behaviors and personality characteristics that are associated with, but not determined by, biological sex. These writers do not assume that the relationship between sex and gender is direct or automatic. Rather, they believe that some mediating process, such as socialization, leads individuals to behave in gendered ways.[1] Thus different cultures may develop distinct notions of gender, which seem natural because they are associated with sex but that are socially, rather than biologically, driven. In contrast with the essentialist perspective described above, this nonessentialist perspective does not see gendered characteristics and behaviors as innate or unchangeable. It is this perspective that we adopt in this book, for reasons we detail below.

What does it mean to say that something is *gendered*? In this book, we use this phrase to mean that ideas about gender—assumptions and beliefs on both individual and societal levels— affect the thoughts, feelings, behaviors, resources, or treatment of women and men. Thus, to the extent that women and men dress, talk, or act differently because of societal expectations, their behavior is gendered. To the extent that an organization assigns some jobs to women and others to men on the basis of their assumed abilities, that organization is gendered. And to the extent that a professor treats a student differently because that student is a man or a woman, their interaction is gendered.

There are a number of variations on the nonessentialist perspective, which we discuss at greater length in Chapter 2. For now, we simply note that essentialist and nonessentialist positions are often at loggerheads. This is true not only in scholarly analyses but in the nonacademic world as well. For example, these perspectives were hotly debated at the United Nations Fourth World Conference on Women in Beijing, China, in 1995. At a preparatory meeting in New York City, former U.S. Representative Bella Abzug read the following statement:

> The current attempt by several Member States to expunge the word "gender" from the Platform for Action and to replace it with the word "sex" is an insulting and demeaning attempt to reverse the gains made by women, to intimidate us and to block further progress. We will not be forced back into the "biology is destiny" concept that seeks to define, confine, and reduce women and girls to their physical sexual characteristics. . . .
>
> The meaning of the word "gender" has evolved as differentiated from the word "sex" to express the reality that women's and men's roles and status are socially constructed and subject to change. In the present context, "gender" recognizes the multiple roles [filled] throughout our life cycles, the diversity of our needs, concerns, abilities, life experiences, and aspirations—as individuals, as members of families and households, and in society as a whole. The concept of "gender" is embedded in contemporary social, political, and legal discourse. . . . The infusion of gender perspectives into all aspects of UN activities is a major commitment approved at past conferences and it must be reaffirmed and strengthened at the Fourth World Conference on Women. (Abzug 1995)

As Abzug notes, the choice of perspective (here symbolized by the choice between the terms sex and gender) can have real consequences for women—and for men as well—when those perspectives are used to guide public policy.

GENDER AS DIFFERENCE

In practice, research on gender—from any perspective—has tended to focus on differences between women and men. This tendency persists despite the fact that research shows very few significant sex differences (e.g., Maccoby and Jacklin 1974; Fausto-Sterling 1985). In fact, the distributions of women and men on most characteristics tend to be overlapping rather than separate. Nonetheless, many researchers continue to focus on differences rather than on the extensive similarities between the sexes or even on the extensive variations within each sex. This pattern of research reinforces the essentialist belief that there are large, stable, innate differences between the sexes and encourages biological explanations for those few differences that are resilient. Thorne, Kramarae, and Henley (1983) write that these studies mistake "description . . . for explanation" (p. 15) and warn that just because studies find differences between males and females does not mean that sex is the *cause* of the differences. For example, one analysis of gender differences in conversational patterns concluded that power, not sex per se, was the source of those differences (Kollock, Blumstein, and Schwartz 1985).

There are a number of reasons why researchers continue to prioritize sex differences. One of these reflects a pattern typical of human cognition. As we noted in [earlier chapters], human beings have a tendency to categorize information wherever possible. As an ostensibly dichotomous characteristic with highly visible social trappings (e.g., hairstyle and apparel), sex is a prime basis for cognitive categorization. The pervasive tendency to focus on sex differences rather than on similarities thus may derive partly from cognitive processes.

The persistent belief in sex difference in the face of contradictory evidence is also tied in part to the human quest for self-identity; we want to know who we are. This quest has a peculiar character, at least in Western culture: Knowing who we are implies knowing who we are not. Gender is one fundamental source of identity. Although there are several contradictory theories of how gender identity is created, most social psychologists concur that children learn at a very young age to adopt gender as a basic organizing principle for themselves and the social worlds they are learning about. In particular, children tend to regard gender as bipolar. "Children regard a broad range of activities as exclusively appropriate for only one sex or the other, and . . . they strongly prefer same-sex playmates . . . and gender-appropriate toys, clothes, and activities" (Bem 1993:111). As studies of gender stereotypes among adults reveal, gender polarization does not wane as children grow older. The cultural centrality of gender, together with the susceptibility of gender to a bipolar model, defines the contemporary social psychological approach to gender.

Perhaps as a result of these tendencies, researchers often expect to find sex differences. Social psychologists are not immune from popular essentialist beliefs about gender. These expectations often act as self-fulfilling prophecies, predisposing the researchers to focus on or even to elicit information that confirms their beliefs. Many studies have shown that experimenters' hypotheses affect research findings. According to Weisstein (1970),

> These studies are enormously important when assessing the validity of psychological studies of women. Since it is beyond doubt that most of us start with notions as to the nature of men and women, the validity of a number of observations of sex differences is questionable, even when these observations have been made under carefully controlled conditions. Second, and more important, [these studies] point quite clearly to the influence of social expectation. In some extremely important ways, people are what you expect them to be or at least they behave as you expect them to behave. (p. 215)

The biases that have plagued social psychology were apparent as early as 1910, when psychologist Helen Thompson Wooley commented, "There is perhaps no field aspiring to be scientific where flagrant personal bias, logic martyred in the cause of supporting a prejudice, unfounded assertions, and even sentimental rot and drivel, have run riot to such an extent as here" (Wooley 1910:340).

Another reason for social psychology's focus on sex differences has to do with the structure of the field itself. Over the past century, psychology and sociology (like other sciences) have become more and more reliant on statistical tests. These tests are designed to identify significant differences between groups and therefore shape a search for differences rather than similarities (Unger and Crawford 1992:12). Moreover, even if a difference is *statistically* significant (i.e., unlikely to have occurred by chance), it may not be *substantively* significant (i.e., meaningful). For example, Eagly and Carli's (1981) review of the literature on social influence found that even though sex differences were often statistically significant, they explained less than 1% of the variance in influenceability and thus contributed very little to understanding influenceability. Reviews of other sex differences have found similar patterns of statistically, but not substantively, significant effects (Deaux 1984).

Researchers may also have a difficult time disseminating the results of studies that find no evidence of sex differences. Findings of similarity are not "newsworthy"; academic journals are much less likely to publish such studies. Newspapers and other media are similarly disposed: Whereas reports of sex differences in math abilities garner headlines and news-magazine cover stories, reports of similarity are relegated to short, unobtrusive articles, if indeed they are reported at all (Eccles and Jacobs 1986). Thus, even if the majority of research projects were to find no significant differences between women and men, *published* research might actually consist of only those few studies that do find differences.

Sex differences research also tends to ignore the fact that *different* often means *unequal*. In other words, such research tends to ignore power relationships. Carrigan and his colleagues write that in the study of gender, "relations have been interpreted as differences. The greater social power of men and the sexual division of labor are interpreted as 'sexual dimorphism' in behavior. With this, the whole question of social structure is spirited away" (Carrigan, Connell, and Lee 1987, pp. 75–76). Even when research considers power differences between genders, it rarely looks at power differences within genders—that is, it ignores very real differences among women and among men, homogenizing each category as though gender is the most important differentiating feature (Fine and Gordon 1989).

Research on gender differences also ignores the fact that behavior is specific to situations, depending on factors such as the structure of the social context or the attitudes and expectations of others in that context. For example, one study found that women's behavior in a simulated job interview depended on the perceived gender stereotypes of the interviewer. When the research participants believed the interviewer to hold traditional views of women, they behaved in a more stereotypically feminine manner (von Baeyer, Sherk, and Zanna 1981). These women altered the femininity of their behavior to best achieve their goals in the interview. Individuals' behavior may change significantly from one situation to the next, and the results of a psychological study may depend on which situation is examined.

Indeed, the experimental laboratory itself affects the expression of gender. Although it purportedly allows scientists to study gender in an objective context, the laboratory is in fact a specific social setting that affects the respondent as do all social contexts. The laboratory is no more neutral than any other situation.

Thus it is important to exercise caution when interpreting research reports of sex difference. Findings of difference may be due not so much to meaningful differences in the abilities or behavior of women and men as to a host of other factors, including the norms of publishing and research and the biases of researchers. On the other hand, just because these reports of sex differences may be misleading does not mean that they should be ignored. The belief that males and females are fundamentally different is widely shared among Americans and, indeed, among most peoples of the world. These beliefs, regardless of their validity, influence our identities, thoughts, and behaviors and may cause men and women to behave differently (gender difference) even if no underlying difference in ability (sex difference) exists. In other words, these beliefs have material consequences regardless of their basis in fact. Thus we contend that sex differences research must be taken seriously—if only to understand how essentialist beliefs shape social psychological research and social life. We suggest that readers keep these issues in mind as they proceed through the next chapters. For now, however, we return to our definitions of key terms.

GENDER ROLE

Another common term in social psychology is gender role, which is often used interchangeably with sex role. Sociologists use the term *role* to refer to "a set of prescriptions and proscriptions for behavior—expectations about what behaviors are appropriate for a person holding a particular position within a particular social context" (Kessler and McKenna 1978:11). The term gender role, then, refers to the characteristics and behaviors believed to be appropriate for men or for women. People expect that others will behave in accord with their gender role, and they punish those who violate these expectations.

The concept of gender role has been strongly criticized, however. For example, some note that these roles are based on the theorist's ideas of what people should be like rather than on what people really are like (Carrigan et al. 1987). Most people's lives, in fact, do not conform to what gender roles prescribe. Moreover, talking about "the male gender role" and "the female gender role" also ignores the very real variation among women and among men, and overlooks the substantial overlap in the characteristics and behaviors of males and females.

Perhaps more important, the concept of gender roles ignores issues of power and inequality. Gender role theory describes the relationship between women and men as one of difference and complementarity: The sexes are "separate but equal," and both roles serve important functions in society. But in fact male and female "roles" are not equally valued and are not necessarily "functional" for everyone. The concept of roles masks, for example, that women have traditionally been legally subservient to men in the family. Until relatively recently in the United States, women could not own property or enter into a contract, and men were (and still are in some states) legally allowed to rape and beat their wives. These are not the hallmarks of an equal relationship, a fact that is hidden by role terminology (Carrigan et al. 1987; Lopata and Thorne 1978). As a result of these critiques, many scholars have discarded the terms sex role and gender role. However, we discuss these terms here because they are still very much a part of both popular and social psychological discourse.

GENDER STEREOTYPE

Stereotypes are "strongly held overgeneralizations about people in some designated social category" (Basow 1992:3). For example, many Americans have stereotypes about athletes, professors, or police officers. These beliefs are "not necessarily based on fact or personal experience, but applied to each role occupant regardless of particular circumstance" (Kessler and McKenna 1978:12). Unlike roles, stereotypes do not imply that individuals should conform to particular expectations for behavior. Nor do they suggest that these beliefs are useful, either for individuals or for societies. Because stereotypes are oversimplifications, they may be inaccurate for a group

as a whole, as well as for any particular member of that group.

Gender stereotypes, then, are beliefs about the characteristics of women and men, including their physical characteristics, typical behaviors, occupational positions, or personality traits. Reflecting the assumption that sex is dichotomous, stereotypes for women and men often involve polar opposites. For example, "Traits related to instrumentality, dominance, and assertiveness . . . are believed more characteristic of men, while such traits as warmth, expressiveness, and concern for other people are thought more characteristic of women" (Deaux and Major 1990:95; see also Rosenkrantz et al. 1968). Such polarizations serve to increase the perception of difference between women and men, and mask the ways in which they are similar.

This does not mean that stereotypes paint all women or all men as the same. Indeed, stereotypes for certain subgroups of men and women, such as businesswomen, homemakers, or bluecollar working men, are common. Stereotypes may also vary by race, ethnicity, or class. . . . However, these variations are accommodated as subtypes subsumed under the more general stereotypes of women and men. The fact that we create subtypes rather than modifying our dichotomous view of gender suggests our deep investment in the idea of gender differences.

GENDER IDENTITY

The term gender identity refers to one's inner sense of oneself as female or male; it is a major part of one's self-concept. Gender identity develops during very early childhood, and once established, it is quite resistant to change (Kessler and McKenna 1978:9). Gender identity tends to be dichotomous—people generally think of themselves as male or female, not something in between. This is probably due to our "incorrigible proposition" that there are two, and only two, sexes. Kate Bornstein (1994), a male-to-female transsexual, writes that

> I know I'm not a man—about that much I'm very clear, and I've come to the conclusion that I'm probably not a woman either, at least not according to a lot of people's rules on this sort of thing. The

trouble is, we're living in a world that insists we be one or the other—a world that doesn't bother to tell us exactly what one or the other is. (p. 8)

Gender identity is a subjective feeling; it cannot be determined without asking a person directly. Gender identity may or may not be congruent with someone's sex or gender, and it is unrelated to sexual orientation. Transsexuals, for example, generally go through sex-change operations because they feel that they do not "fit" their biological sex. Jan Morris (1974) describes her gender identity in this way: "I was born with the wrong body, being feminine by gender but male by sex, and I could achieve completeness only when the one was adjusted to the other" (p. 26). Like many other transsexuals, however, Morris ultimately found that it was easier to change her body than her social identity.

Although everyone has a gender identity, the salience of this identity may vary among people. For example, women are more likely than men to spontaneously mention gender when asked to describe themselves (Deaux and Major 1990:93). The salience of gender identity may also vary between situations: A woman alone in a group of men, for example, is likely to find her gender to be more salient than when she is in a group of other women (Cota and Dion 1986). Indeed, group identity is generally more salient for those in any kind of subordinate position, indicating the relevance of social position and power to identity.

SEXUALITY

Sexuality is a fuzzy term, often used to refer to a group of related concepts, including sexual behavior (what you do), eroticism (what turns you on), sexual orientation (who turns you on), or desire to engage in sexual activity. A discussion of sexuality may seem out of place in a book focusing on gender and social psychology. Nonetheless, sexuality is often associated with gender, although the two are not equivalent. This association probably results from the popular essentialist belief that gender is the natural outgrowth of biological sex. Because sexuality is also believed to be biologically driven, gender and sexuality are often thought to be directly related (Schwartz and Rutter, forthcoming).

As with gender, however, there are other perspectives on sexuality. Like other activities, sexual behavior has a social and symbolic component. Consider the activity of a woman baring her breasts. Now vary the social context: How would this action be interpreted if the woman is in her lover's bedroom, her doctor's consulting room, or a public place? Now take the last location, a public place, and vary the reasons for her action: She is participating in a public demonstration, performing at a strip joint, or breast-feeding her baby. It is the social context, not the activity itself, that leads us to impute meaning to the woman's action as being erotic, clinical, political, exhibitionist, or maternal. The meaning of sexual behaviors varies by situation, and we evaluate behavior on the basis of goals and motivations. Meaning also varies by culture: In some societies, women's breasts are always bare and thus do not elicit the charged interpretations that they do in our own culture. Sexual meanings are thus socially constructed, not inherent in an activity.

Similarly, sexuality is not innate in individuals. For evidence, we can point to the fact that expectations for the sexual behavior of men and women vary historically and cross-culturally. Traditional Western dating scripts, for example, expected men to be more physical and aggressive and women to be more passive and emotional in sexual situations. Although it might appear that these expectations have changed (and they have, to varying extents among different social groups and regions), they have not entirely disappeared. Men, for example, are still expected to take the lead in sexual situations, and women who violate gender expectations by being sexually assertive risk being labeled "pushy," "aggressive," or worse. However, other cultures have very different expectations for women and men. For example, Ford and Beach (1951) report that women are expected to be the sexual aggressors among societies such as the Maoris and the Trobriand Islanders. Sexual behavior is thus guided by social factors as much as by biology.

What, then, is the relationship between sexuality and gender? Expectations for "appropriate" sexual behavior and characteristics differ by gender; sexuality becomes a way of expressing gender. For example, Lillian Rubin's (1976) study of U.S. working-class families found that women were expected to be sexually passive and inexperienced, whereas men were expected to be more dominant, experienced, and adventurous. And as the next section points out, there are also expectations about whom we perform sexual behaviors with. An important point, however, is that this society's construction of sexuality helps maintain the existing gender hierarchy. The definition of men as aggressive and women as passive reinforces men's power over women and women's dependence on men. Popular culture's ideology of love and romance also reinforces gender inequality: For example, Cantor (1987) found that in popular media "women are usually depicted as subordinate to men and passive-dependent. . . . The basic message is that sexual relationships are all-important in women's lives" (1987:190). Thus, when women attempt to meet cultural expectations about heterosexual relationships, they contribute to their own subordination. However, the examples provided by other cultures show us that this pattern is not innate in human beings.

SEXUAL ORIENTATION

Sexual orientation, the match between one's sex and the sex of one's (desired or actual) sexual partners, is one component of sexuality. Like sexuality more generally, sexual orientation is part of gender expectations. For example, the expectations for a "real man" include heterosexuality. Think of male icons such as James Bond, Indiana Jones, or Rocky: Besides being strong and daring, these characters were all attracted and attractive to beautiful women. Thus, in this society, "Mainstream masculinity is heterosexual masculinity" (Carrigan et al. 1987:83; see also Connell 1987, 1995). This version of masculinity is a yardstick against which all men are measured: "The homosexual-heterosexual dichotomy acts as a central symbol in all rankings of masculinity. Any kind of powerlessness, or refusal to compete among men readily becomes involved with the imagery of homosexuality" (Carrigan et al. 1987:86). A similar argument can be made for

women: Mainstream femininity entails heterosexuality, and any deviation from feminine norms risks "accusations" of lesbianism (Rich 1980), a status to which many people attach stigma. Thus sexual orientation is integrally related to gender. Sexual orientation is one of the ways in which gender is performed, while at the same time, gender incorporates and depends on sexual orientation.

Like sex and gender, people tend to think of sexual orientation as dichotomous: One is either heterosexual or homosexual. But sexual orientation is better described as a continuum, with many possible variations between the two poles. Some people (bisexuals) are attracted to people of both sexes. Some people are attracted to people of one sex but maintain relationships with people of another; these people cannot be easily classified. Many people who define themselves as heterosexual, in fact, have had some sort of homosexual experiences (Blumstein and Schwartz 1983:43). It should be noted that sexual orientation is distinct from gender identity. Although some people think that those who prefer same-sex partners must be "confused" . . . about their own gender identity, this is not the case. In fact "most gay men and lesbian women have no confusion about their gender identity; they simply prefer sexual partners of the same sex" (Vander Zanden 1990:358).

What is the source of sexual orientation? Debate rages in the scientific community and the popular press about whether sexual orientation is genetically or environmentally determined; at the moment, there is no consensus on the answer. One thing is certain, however: Like sexuality, the meaning of sexual orientation is socially constructed. Homosexuality is not everywhere as stigmatized as it is in the United States: Many past and present societies of the world, including the ancient Greeks and the modern Sambia of New Guinea, condone and practice both heterosexuality and homosexuality in some forms (Ford and Beach 1951). Moreover, the meanings of homosexuality and heterosexuality vary depending on the social context, even within the United States. Childhood sexual play, for example, is interpreted very differently from adult relationships. Or to give another example, the same man who might never consider engaging in homosexual activity in everyday life might practice it within an all-male prison context. Like the meaning of sexuality more broadly, the meaning of sexual orientation varies depending on context, goals, and motivations. . . .

To conclude this chapter, we return to the metaphor of the *gender lens*. What do we mean by this term? What can we see through the gender lens that we cannot see without it?

Throughout this book, we emphasize two points. First, we argue that social psychology has simultaneously ignored and been deeply influenced by gender. Social psychologists have assumed that situations and behavior are gender neutral; yet they have nonetheless allowed prevailing cultural assumptions about gender to affect the questions they have posed and the answers they have provided. Most obviously, as we discussed earlier, social psychologists have focused on gender differences in personality and behavior and have often assumed that these difference are fixed, stable, and rooted in biological sex.

Our second argument in this book is that although gender differences may exist, they are not the same as sex differences. In other words, just because women and men may appear to behave or think differently does not mean that they have different innate characteristics or abilities. Instead, these differences may be (and, we believe, generally are) constructed through social processes. Thus, in a sense, we are arguing that these differences are not as meaningful as people—both social psychologists and laypeople—believe they are.

This does not mean that we should ignore these differences, however. If that were the case, there would be no reason to write (or read) this book. On the contrary, these ideas about gender deeply affect people's thoughts and behaviors and are central to the ways in which resources, power, and status are distributed in most (if not all) societies. In other words, despite its lack of grounding in sex, gender has real, material consequences for people's lives. For this reason, it is crucial to understand gender and the role it plays in the social world. Only through such an understanding can we hope to address the pervasive and deeply damaging social problems (discrimination, violence, injustice, and so on) that continue to plague our society.

Looking at the world through a gender lens, then, means recognizing and analyzing the central role that gender plays in social life. More concretely, it implies two seemingly contradictory tasks. First, it means unpacking the taken-for-granted assumptions about gender that pervade social psychology and, more generally, social life. We must show how the terms we use to discuss gender (such as gender role) naturalize inequality and perpetuate gender difference. We must question the truth of these assumptions and, where warranted, reveal them as the illusions they are.

At the same time, looking through the gender lens means showing just how central these assumptions about gender continue to be to the perception and interpretation of the world, regardless of their grounding in reality. We must show how our unquestioned ideas about gender affect the world we see, the questions we ask, and the answers we can envision. In other words, we must show how deeply the social world is gendered and how far-reaching the consequences are. Looking at social life through the gender lens means asking where gender is overemphasized and where it is ignored; it means making the invisible visible and questioning the reality of what we see.

NOTE

1. Indeed, some authors also argue that sex itself is a social construction (Kessler and McKenna 1978; Scott 1988). According to this view,

   Society not only shapes personality and behavior, it also shapes the ways in which the body appears. But if the body is itself always seen through social interpretation, then sex is not something that is separate from gender but is, rather, that which is subsumable under it. (Nicholson 1994:79)

REFERENCES

Abzug, Bella. 1995. "A Message from NGO Women to U.N. Member States, the Secretariat, and the Commission on the Status of Women." Speech delivered at the Final Preparatory Meeting for the Fourth World Conference on Women, April 3. (Press release from the Women's Environment and Development Organization [WEDO], 212-759-7982).

Basow, Susan A. 1992. *Gender: Stereotypes and Roles.* Pacific Grove, CA: Brooks/Cole.

Bem, Sandra L. 1993. *The Lenses of Gender: Transforming the Debate on Sexual Inequality.* New Haven, CT: Yale University Press.

Blumstein, Philip and Pepper Schwartz. 1983. *American Couples: Money, Work, and Sex.* New York: Morrow.

Bornstein, Kate. 1994. *Gender Outlaw: On Men, Women, and the Rest of Us.* New York: Vintage.

Cantor, Muriel G. 1987. "Popular Culture and the Portrayal of Women: Content and Control." Pp. 190–214 in *Analyzing Gender,* edited by B. B. Hess and M. M. Ferree. Newbury Park, CA: Sage.

Carrigan, Tim, R. W. Connell, and John Lee. 1985. "Toward a New Sociology of Masculinity." *Theory and Society* 14:551–604.

———. 1987. *Toward a New Sociology of Masculinity.* Boston: Allen & Unwin.

Connell, R. W. 1987. *Gender and Power: Society, the Person, and Sexual Politics.* Stanford, CA: Stanford University Press.

———. 1995. *Masculinities.* Berkeley: University of California Press.

Cota, Albert A. and Kenneth L. Dion. 1986. "Salience of Gender and Sex Composition of Ad Hoc Groups. An Experimental Test of Distinctiveness Theory." *Journal of Personality and Social Psychology* 50:770–76.

Deaux, Kay. 1976. *The Behavior of Women and Men.* Monterey, CA: Brooks/Cole.

———. 1984. "From Individual Differences to Social Categories: Analysis of a Decade's Research on Gender." *American Psychologist* 39:105–16.

Deaux, Kay and Brenda Major. 1990. *A Social-Psychological Model of Gender.* New Haven, CT: Yale University Press.

Eagly, Alice H. and Linda L. Carli. 1981. "Sex of Researchers and Sex-Typed Communications as Determinants of Sex Differences in Influenceability: A Meta-Analysis of Social Influence Studies." *Psychological Bulletin* 90:1–20.

Eccles, Jacquelynne S. and Janis E. Jacobs. 1986. "Social Forces Shape Math Attitudes and Performance." *Signs: Journal of Women in Culture and Society* 11:367–89.

Fausto-Sterling, Anne. 1985. *Myths of Gender: Biological Theories About Women and Men.* New York: Basic Books.

———. "The Five Sexes: Why Male and Female Are Not Enough." *Science,* 32(2):20–5.

Fine, Michelle and Susan M. Gordon. 1989. "Feminist Transformations Of/Despite Psychology." Pp. 147–74 in *Gender and Thought: Psychological Perspectives,* edited by M. Crawford and M. Gentry. New York: Springer-Verlag.

Ford, Clellan S. and Frank A. Beach. 1951. *Patterns of Sexual Behavior.* New York: Harper.

Kessler, Susan J. and Wendy McKenna. 1978. *Gender: An Ethnomethodological Approach.* New York: John Wiley.

Kollock, Peter, Philip Blumstein, and Pepper Schwartz. 1985. "Sex and Power in Interaction: Conversational Privileges and Duties." *American Sociological Review* 50:34–46.

Lopata, Helen Z. and Barrie Thorne. 1978. "On the Term 'Sex Roles.' " *Signs: Journal of Women in Culture and Society* 3:718–21.

Maccoby, Eleanor E. and Carol Jacklin. 1974. *The Psychology of Sex Differences.* Stanford, CA: Stanford University Press.

Mehan, Hugh M. and Houston W. Wood. 1975. *The Reality of Ethnomethodology.* New York: John Wiley.

Money, J. and Anke Ehrhardt. 1972. *Man and Woman, Boy and Girl.* Baltimore: Johns Hopkins University Press.

Morris, Jan. 1974. *Conundrum.* New York: Harcourt Brace Jovanovich.

Rich, Adrienne. 1980. "Compulsory Heterosexuality and Lesbian Existence." *Signs: Journal of Women in Culture and Society* 5:631–60.

Rosenkrantz, Paul S., Susan R. Vogel, H. Bee, Inge K. Broverman, and Donald M. Broverman. 1968. "Sex-Role Stereotypes and Self Concepts among College Students." *Journal of Consulting and Clinical Psychology* 32:287–95.

Rubin, Lillian. 1976. *Worlds of Pain: Life in the Working Class Family.* New York: Basic Books.

Schwartz, Pepper and Virginia Rutter. Forthcoming. *Gender, Sex, and Society.* Thousand Oaks, CA: Sage.

Thorne, Barrie, Cheris Kramarae, and Nancy Henley. 1983. *Language, Gender, and Society.* Rowley, MA: Newbury House.

Unger, Rhoda and Mary Crawford. 1992. *Women and Gender: A Feminist Psychology.* New York: McGraw-Hill.

Vander Zanden, James W. 1990. *The Social Experience: An Introduction to Sociology.* New York: McGraw-Hill.

Visher, Christy A. 1983. "Gender, Police Arrest Decisions, and Notions of Chivalry." *Criminology* 21(1):5–28.

von Baeyer, Carl L., Debbie L. Sherk, and Mark P. Zanna. 1981. "Impression Management in the Job Interview: When the Female Applicant Meets the Male (Chauvinist) Interviewer." *Personality and Social Psychology Bulletin* 7:45–51.

Weisstein, Naomi. 1970. " 'Kinder, Kuche, Kirche' as Scientific Law: Psychology Constructs the Female." Pp. 205–20 in *Sisterhood Is Powerful,* edited by R. Morgan. New York: Vintage.

Wooley, Helen Thompson. 1910. "Psychological Literature: A Review of the Most Recent Literature on the Psychology of Sex." *Psychological Bulletin* 7:335–42.

29

Gender as Structure

Barbara J. Risman

The gender structure so pervades our lives that we often do not even see it. We fail to recognize that these differential expectations for men and women, for husbands and wives, are how sexual difference is transformed into gender stratification . . . [G]ender structure at the interactional level is at the core of the male privilege still obvious in marriage and the family and that the structure of our interactional encounters recreates gender stratfication even when the people involved are committed to equality.

This is a difficult but a very interesting and critical analysis of the understanding of gender inequality as structure. Too often, Risman argues, we emphasize individualistic explanations of inequality or simply rational choices that are made by individuals. Structure is described here as a property of society, a pattern that is so embedded in society that most of us do not always recognize its importance. It influences us at the individual, interactional, and institutional levels. It is often "the logic of gendered choices" that matter, rather than simple choices that individuals make; it is often cultural expectations and taken-for-granted situations that matter, rather than simple choices that individuals make; it is often distribution of advantage and organizational patterns that matter, rather than simple choices individuals make. Risman tries to take all of us to an understanding of gender at a truly social and sociological level of analysis.

I build on this notion that gender is an entity in and of itself and has consequences at every level of analysis. And I share the concern that the very creation of difference is the foundation on which inequality rests. In my view, it is most useful to conceptualize gender as a structure that has consequences for every aspect of society. And while the language of structure suits my purposes better than any other, it is not ideal. Despite its ubiquity in sociological discourse, no definition of the term "structure" is widely shared (see Smelser 1988 for a review of various structural traditions). So I begin by explaining what I mean by structure and how I have derived my definition. Some consensus exists. All structuralists presume that social structures exist outside individual desires or motives and that the structures can at least partially explain human action. All structural theorists would agree that social structure constrains human action or makes it possible.

Blau's (1977) now classic definition of social structure focused solely on the constraint that collective life imposes on the individual. In their influential work, Blau and his colleagues (e.g., Rytina et al. 1988) have argued that the concept of structure is trivialized if it is located inside an individual's head in the form of internalized norms and values. Structure must be conceptualized, in this view, as a force opposing individual motivation. Structural concepts must be observable, external to the individual, and independent of individual motivation. This definition of structure imposes a clear dualism between structure and action, with structure as constraint and action as choice. I incorporate Blau's analysis of structure as constraint, but I reject the notion that structure constrains action only externally.

In order to analyze human action, we must understand not only how the social structure acts as constraint but also how and why actors choose one alternative over another. Burt (1982) suggests that actors compare themselves and their options to those in structurally similar positions. In this view, actors are purposive, rationally seeking to maximize their self-perceived well-being under social structural constraints.[1] Actions are a function of interests, but interests and ability to choose are patterned by the social structure. Burt suggests that norms develop when actors occupying similar network positions in the social structure evaluate their own options vis-à-vis the alternatives of similarly situated others. From such comparisons evolve both norms and feelings of relative deprivation or advantage. The social structure as the context of daily life creates action indirectly by shaping actors' perceptions of their interests and directly by constraining choice.

Giddens' (1984) theory adds considerable depth to the analysis of social structures as existing in a recursive relationship to individuals. That is, social structures shape individuals even as individuals are shaping their social structure. Giddens rejects a structuralism (e.g., Blau 1977) that ignores the transformative power of human action. He insists that any structural theory must be concerned with reflexivity and actors' interpretations of their own lives. When people act on structure, they do so for their own reasons. We must, therefore, be concerned with why people act as they do. Giddens insists that this concern go beyond the verbal justification easily available from actors because much of social life is so routine that actors will not articulate, or even

consider, why they act. Giddens refers to this reality as practical consciousness. I refer to it as the cultural aspect of the social structure: the taken-for-granted or cognitive image rules that belong to the situational context (not only or necessarily to the actor's personality). Within this framework, we must pay considerable attention to how structure makes action possible as well as constrains it. We must bring individuals back into structural theories.

Connell (1987) applies Giddens' theory of social structure as both constraint and as created by action in his treatise on gender and power (see particularly chap. 5).[2] In his analysis, structure is assumed to specify what constrains action, and yet "since human action involves free invention . . . and is reflexive, practice can be turned against what constrains it; so structure can deliberately be the object of practice" (95). Action may turn against structure, but it can never escape it. An accurate analysis of any hierarchical relationship requires a focus both on how structure shapes interaction and on how human agency creates structure (Blackwelder 1993). A multilevel theory of gender as a social structure must acknowledge causality as recursive—action itself may change the immediate or future context. I build on Connell's analysis of the reflexivity of action and structure, although I return to that argument primarily in the last chapter.

Gender itself must be considered a structural property of society. It is not manifested just in our personalities, our cultural rules, or other institutions. Gender is deeply embedded as a basis for stratification, differentiating opportunities and constraints. This differentiation has consequences on three levels: (1) at the individual level, for the development of gendered selves; (2) at the interactional level, for men and women face different expectations even when they fill the identical structural position; and (3) at the institutional level, for rarely will women and men be given identical positions. Differentiation at the institutional level is based on explicit regulations or laws regarding resource distribution, whether resources be defined as access to opportunities or actual material goods. (See figure 1 for a schematic summary of the argument thus far.)

While the *gender structure* clearly affects selves, cultural rules, and institutions, far too

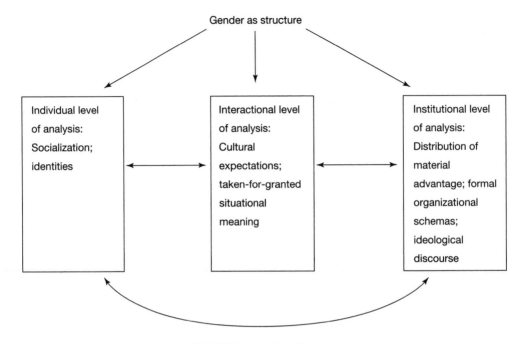

FIGURE 1.   Gender as Structure

much explanatory power is presumed to rest in the motivation of gendered selves. We live in a very individualistic society that teaches us to make our own choices and take responsibility for our own actions. What this has meant for theories about gender is that a tremendous amount of energy is spent on trying to understand why women and men "choose" to devote their life energies to such different enterprises. The distinctly sociological contribution to the explanation hasn't had enough attention: even when individual women and men do *not* desire to live gendered lives or to support male dominance, they often find themselves compelled to do so by the logic of gendered choices. That is, interactional pressures and institutional design create gender and the resultant inequality, even in the absence of individual desires.

My argument and the data presented throughout this book show the strength of our gender structure at the interactional and institutional levels. Choices often assumed to be based on personalities and individual preferences (e.g.,

consequences of the gender structure at the individual level) are better understood as social constructions based on institutionally constrained opportunities and the limited availability of nongendered cognitive images. Eagly and Wood (1991) offer a useful conceptual scheme for understanding both the continued importance of gender at the individual level and how it differs from an understanding of gender at the contextual level.[3] They suggest that we see individual gendered selves and the cultural expectations of interaction as alternative paths by which gendered institutions influence individual behavior.

Even if individuals are capable of change and wish to eradicate male dominance from their personal lives, the influence of gendered institutions and interactional contexts persists. These contexts are organized by gender stratification at the institutional level, which includes the distribution of material resources organized by gender, the ways by which formal organizations and institutions themselves are gendered, and gendered ideological discourse. For example, in a society in which girls are not taught to read, we could never find a young woman who would be considered a potential international leader. Nor would men denied access to jobs with "family wages" be seen by middle-class American women as good catches for husbands.

At this moment in American society, cultural rules and cognitive images that operate at the interactional level are particularly important in the persistence of gender stratification in families. It is not that sex-role socialization or early childhood experience is trivial; gender structure creates gendered selves. But, at this point in history, sex-role socialization itself is ambivalent. In addition, it is clear that even women with feminist worldviews and substantial incomes are constrained by gender structures.

In spite of the removal of some gender discrimination in both law and organizations, gender stratification remains. That is, formal access to opportunities may be gender neutral, yet equality of results may not ensue. Therefore, neither the individual-level explanations nor those based solely on institutional discrimination can explain continued gender stratification in families. Instead, the cognitive images to which we must respond during interaction are the engines that drive continued gender stratification when individuals desire egalitarian relationships and the law allows them (cf. Ridgeway 1997). . . .

The reconceptualization of gender as a social structure at every level helps us to understand stability and change in contemporary American marriage. Gender rules and cognitive expectations operate as interactional constraints that often create gender hierarchy even among heterosexual feminist couples who bring equivalent external material resources to their relationship. We find that the few heterosexual couples who can repudiate internalized gendered selves and overcome many of the barriers to equality in the workplace still often fail to find equality in marriage. Alternatives are so constrained within our gender structure that even those who consciously reject inequality based on gender may be contributing to the re-creation of gender stratified marriages and to a social structure that disadvantages women. The re-creation of a gender-stratified society is an unintended consequence of institutionally constrained actions—even of

those committed to gender equality, and even in a society where laws are at least nominally gender-neutral. Gender structure at the interactional and institutional levels so thoroughly organizes our work, family, and community lives that even those who reject gender inequality in principle sometimes end up being compelled by the "logic" of gendered situations and cognitive images to choose gendered strategies.[4]

I do not mean to suggest that we do not all own gendered selves, or that institutional sexism has disappeared. Rather, I am simply suggesting that even if we overcame our gendered predispositions and were lucky enough to overcome most of the barriers of institutional sexism, the consequences of gender at the interactional level would still constrain our attempts at social change.

FEMINIST MARRIAGE: CONFLICT AMONG IMAGES, INSTITUTIONS, AND NEW SELVES

Traditional marriage is male dominated. The very terminology used to describe the husband— "the head of the household"—says it clearly. Yet it would be hard to isolate how gender structure *constrains* individuals when individual ideologies, cultural cognitive images, and the institutional force of law are all consistent and interdependent. The consequences of gender structure at the interactional and institutional levels are most easily illustrated when the structure operates in opposition to internalized normative desires. It is currently possible to analyze the effects of gender structure at the interactional and institutional levels despite individual-level opposition to stratification. That is, it is possible to imagine and locate couples committed to gender equality and to analyze how contextual and institutional levels of gender structure affect them. I argue that our gender structure pushes even committed feminists toward a gendered division of labor and toward male-dominated relationships.

On the cultural level, the consequences of gender structure clearly exist beyond the individuals involved. The normative expectations attached to gender in marriage (one aspect of the "rules") are very strong. Gender remains a "master status" (e.g., Hughes 1945), an organizing principle of marriage; expectations imputed to actors nearly always differ by sex. For example, men are not expected to assume a reflective identity (e.g., to become a Mr. Her) upon marriage. Because a reflective identity is based on association with someone else, it is a subordinate identity. Similarly, routine marital rituals are gender stratified. Bridal showers are based on the assumption that women will shoulder the responsibility for domestic labor. Fathers give away brides to the bridegrooms. Not all couples follow these rituals, of course. But when they do not, they are seen as making a choice that requires explanation. No choice is perceived, no explanations are needed, if rituals are followed. Most young couples, at least those without strong ideological commitments, follow the routine path without considering the unintended consequences: creating yet another stratified marriage.

Marriage is only one institution in which gender stratification is manifested, and it may not even be the most oppressive institution, softened as it can be by warm feelings. Yet marriage is one of the linchpins of inequality in American society. In what other institution are social roles, rights, and responsibilities based—even ideologically— on ascribed characteristics? When life options are tied to racial categories we call it racism at best and apartheid at worst. When life options are tied to gender categories we call it marriage.

The social structure clearly constrains gendered action even as it makes it possible. Wives, even those who have no motivation to provide domestic service to their husbands, are constrained to do so by social expectations. A husband who has a disheveled appearance reflects poorly on his wife's domestic abilities (in real life as well as "ring around the collar" commercials). A wife will be sanctioned by friends and family for keeping a cluttered and dusty home; a husband will not be. Husbands' behaviors are constrained as well. A husband who is content with a relatively low-wage, low-stress occupation may be pressured (by his wife, among others) to provide more for his family. Few wives, however, are pressured into higher-stress, higher-wage occupations by their families. The expectations we face during ongoing interaction often push us to behave as others want us to (Heiss 1981).

Cultural images within marriage also make gendered action possible. Husbands are not free to work long hours in order to climb the career ladder or increase income unless they are superordinate partners in a system in which wives provide them the "leisure" (i.e., freedom from responsibility for self-care or family care) to do so. Some married women may leave jobs they dislike because the position of domestic wife is open to them. A husband and father unable to keep a job has few other options for gaining self-esteem and identity.

Individuals often act in a structurally patterned fashion, without much thought. Routine is taken for granted even when the action re-creates the inequitable social structure. A woman may choose to change her name upon marriage simply because it seems easier. (Some women may not even know they are making a choice, as name change is so routine in their social circle.) Yet by changing her name a woman implicitly supports and re-creates a reflective definition of wifehood. She does gender. Similarly, when a woman assents to her children carrying her husband's surname (even when she herself has retained her own), she is re-creating a patrilineal system by which family identity is traced primarily through the male line. In both these examples a couple's intention may be to create a nuclear family identity and to avoid the awkwardness of hyphenated names for children. Whatever the intention, the structure has constrained the possible choices available to them. Their purposive actions may provide them with both the desired consequences (one family name) and the unintended consequence of re-creating a gender structure based on reflective female identity and patrilineal family names. . . .

SUMMARY

I have argued that gender is a social structure. It organizes our entire world. At the individual level we learn who we are and want to be within a world where boys and girls are treated almost as though they were different kinds of creatures. At the interactional level our expectations for others' behaviors are filtered through a gender lens (Howard et al. 1996). The cultural rules and cognitive images that give shape and substance to our daily lives—especially those rules and images that surround our most intimate relationships—are profoundly attached to our biological sex. As the twentieth century closes, much of the formal, legalized, institutional sex discrimination has been eliminated, at least in Western societies. But the formal institutions to which we must all adapt—our workplaces, in particular—were built on assumptions both of gender difference and sexual inequality. Industrial capitalism could never have been organized as it now exists unless there was an implicit belief that paid workers were not, or should not be, responsible for the weak, the infirm, the aged, or the young.

The gender structure so pervades our lives that we often do not even see it. We fail to recognize that these differential expectations for men and women, for husbands and wives, are how sexual difference is transformed into gender stratification. I have argued that our gender structure at the interactional level is at the core of the male privilege still obvious in marriage and the family and that the structure of our interactional encounters re-creates gender stratification even when the people involved are committed to equality.

But does this theoretical perspective mean that we are doomed forever to re-create gender inequality? In the next three chapters I hope to convince the reader that gender is a social structure that we can get beyond. Gender need not organize our family systems, even if it always has done so.

NOTES

1. Burt's notion of purposive and rational action differs from that of more atomistic theorists because he does not assume that actors necessarily have enough information to act effectively in their own best interest. Nor does he assume that the consequences of actions are necessarily intended.
2. Connell refers to action as "practice."
3. Eagly and Wood do not use the same language I use. I am confident that our conceptual schemes are parallel, and I prefer not to add still more inconsistent language to the text. They describe the institutional level of analysis as the "division of labor between the sexes in society." They use "gender role expectations" for the contextual/interactional level of analysis, and they refer to the individual level of analysis as sex-typed skills and beliefs. They are concerned with explaining empirically identified sex differences in social behavior as dependent variables in psychological research.
4. Choosing the best of bad alternatives is clearly not a free choice at all. Still, I use the language of choice to remind readers that individual actors wrestle with alternatives and make decisions.

REFERENCES

Blackwelder, Stephen P. 1993. "Duality of Structure in the Reproduction of Race, Class, and Gender Inequality." Paper presented at the Society for the Study of Social Problems Meetings, Miami.

Blau, Peter M. 1977. *Inequality and Heterogeneity.* New York: Free Press.

Burt, Ronald S. 1982. *Toward a Structural Theory of Action.* New York: Academic Press.

Connell, Robert W. 1987. *Gender and Power: Society, the Person, and Sexual Politics.* Stanford, CA: Stanford University Press.

Eagly, Alice H., and Wendy Wood. 1995. "The Origins of Sex Differences in Human Behavior: Evolved Dispositions Versus Social Roles. *American Psychologist* 54:408–423.

Giddens, Anthony. 1979. *Central Problems in Social Theory.* Berkeley: University of California Press.

Heiss, Jerold. 1981. "Social Rules." In *Social Psychology: Sociological Perspectives*, edited by Morris Rosenberg and Ralph H. Turner. New York: Basic Books.

Howard, Judith, Barbara Risman, Mary Romero, and Joey Sprague. 1996.

Hughes, Everett C. 1945. "Dilemmas and Contradictions of Status." *American Journal of Sociology* 50: 353–359.

Ridgeway, Cecilia. 1997. "Interaction and the Conservation of Gender Inequality: Considering Employment." *American Sociological Review* 62:218–235.

Rytina, Steve, Peter Blau, Jenny Blum, and Joseph Schwartz. 1988. "Inequality and Intermarriage: Paradox of Motive and Constraint." *Social Forces* 66:645–675.

Smelser, Neil J. 1988. "Social Structure." In *Handbook of Sociology*, edited by Neil J. Smelser. Beverly Hills, CA: Sage.

30

The Working Wife
as an Urbanized Peasant

Arlie Russell Hochschild with Anne Machung

Today, it is women who are establishing a new basis of power and identity. If
women previously based their power mainly on attractiveness to men or influence
over children and kin, now they base their power more on wages or authority
on the job. . . . Given the wage gap, and given the greater effect of divorce on
women, the modern woman may not have a great deal more power
than before, but what power she has is based differently.

We are witnessing a very important revolution in family, work, and gender. Arlie
Hochschild discusses much of the history and nature of this revolution, but she also
clearly explains why inequality continues, and in analyzing the balance between
the work at home and the work outside the home, she describes many problems that
women face in this revolution. Men and women have a different history and different traditions; these are not simply erased. The patterns embedded in social structure, often unrecognized as important, continue to make it difficult for women to
compete on an equal basis in the world of work outside the home.

Before the industrial revolution in America, most
men and women lived out their lives on the private family farm—where crops were grown and
craft work done mainly for domestic consumption. With industrialization, more crops and
goods were produced and distributed to wider
markets for money. But industrialization did not
affect men and women at the same time or in the
same way. It has affected men and women at different times and in different ways. In a sense,
there is a "his" and a "hers" to the history of industrialization in America.

Painting the picture in broad strokes, the
growth of factories, trades, and businesses in early
American cities first began to draw substantial
numbers of men and women away from farm life
around the 1830s. Many single girls worked in the
early New England textile mills for four and five
years until they married, but mill girls represented
a tiny fraction of all women and less than ten percent of all those who worked for wages.[1] In 1860,
most industrial workers were men. Only 15 percent of women worked for pay, most of them as domestic servants. As men entered factory work, they
gradually changed their basic way of life; they
moved from open spaces to closed-in rooms, from
loose seasonal time to fixed industrial time, from
life among a tight circle of kinsfolk and neighbors
to a life of more varied groupings of kin and

neighbors. At first, we might say, men did something like trying to "have it all." In the early New England rural factories, for example, men would work in these factories during the day and go home in the evenings to work in the fields. Or they moved in and out of factory work depending on the season and the crop ready for harvest. But over time, the farmer became an urban worker.

On the whole, the early effects of industrial employment probably altered the lives of men in a more dramatic and immediate way than it altered the lives of women, most of whom maintained a primary identity at home. To be sure, life changed for women, too. Earlier in the century, a young mother might churn butter and raise chickens and hogs. Later in the century, a young mother was more likely to live in the city, buy her butter and eggs at the grocery store, take in boarders, be active in the church, and subscribe to what the historian Barbara Welter has called a "cult of true womanhood" centered in the home, and based on the special moral sensibility of women. Through this period, most women who married and raised children based their role and identity at home. "Home" changed. But, as the historian Nancy Cott argues in *Bonds of Womanhood*, throughout the nineteenth century, compared to men, women maintained an orientation toward life that was closer to what had been. Thus, if we compare the overall change in the lives of married women to the overall change in the lives of married men, we might conclude that during this period men changed more.

Today, it is women whose lives are changing faster. The expansion of service jobs has opened opportunities for women. Given that women have fewer children now (in 1800 they gave birth to about eight and raised five or six to adulthood; in 1988, they average less than two) and given that their wage has been increasingly needed at home, it has become "the woman's turn" to move into the industrial economy. It is now women who are wrenched out of a former domestic way of life. If earlier it was men who tried to combine an old way of life with a new one, now it is women who are, by trying to combine the duties of the housewife and full-time mother with an eight-hour day at the office.

In the early nineteenth century, it was men who began to replace an older basis of power—

land—with a new one—money. It was men who began to identify their "manhood" with having money in a way they had never done before. Through the great value on a man's purchasing power, the modern worship of goods—or what Karl Marx criticized as a "commodity fetishism"—became associated with "being a man."

Today, it is women who are establishing a new basis of power and identity. If women previously based their power mainly on attractiveness to men or influence over children and kin, now they base their power more on wages or authority on the job. As Anita Judson, the billing clerk married to the forklift driver, commented, "After I started earning money, my husband showed me more respect." Given the wage gap, and given the greater effect of divorce on women, the modern woman may not have a great deal more power than before, but what power she has is *based* differently.

Altering her source of power, earning money also gives some women, like Carol Alston, a new basis of identity. As Carol, the systems analyst whose husband did carpentry around the house and helped a lot in a "male" way, described her reaction to quitting work after the birth of her first child, "I really discovered how important it was to my identity to earn money." While earning money didn't make Carol feel more like a woman in the same sense that earning money made Ray Judson feel more like a man, earning money was more important to her identity than it had been to her mother's. Furthermore, the greater autonomy that often comes with working outside the home has probably changed the identity of women such as Carol to the same extent that it earlier changed that of men.

Housewives who go out to paid work are like the male farmers who, in an earlier era, left the country for the city, farm for factory. They've made an exodus "for the city." If earlier it was men who changed the social patterns of their fathers faster than women changed those of their mothers, today it is women who are changing these faster.

Paid work has come to seem exciting, life at home dull. Although the most acceptable motive for a woman to work is still "because I have to," most of the working mothers I talked to didn't work just for the money. In this way they have begun to participate in a value system once exclusively male and have developed motivations more like those of men. Many women volunteered to me that they would be "bored" or would "go bananas just staying home all day," that they were not, on any permanent basis, the "domestic type." This feeling held true even among women in low-level clerical jobs. A nationwide Harris poll taken in 1980 asked women: "If you had enough money to live as comfortably as you'd like, would you prefer to work full time, work part time, do volunteer-type work, or work at home caring for the family?" Among working women, 28 percent wanted to stay home. Of all the women in the study, including housewives, only 39 percent wanted to stay home—even if they had enough money to live as comfortably as they liked. When asked if each of the following is an important reason for working or not, 87 percent of working women responded "yes" to "providing you with a sense of accomplishment and personal satisfaction," 84 percent to "helping ends meet," and 81 percent to "improving your family's standard of living."[2] Women want paying jobs, part-time jobs, interesting jobs—but they want jobs, I believe, for roughly the same complex set of reasons peasants in modernizing economies move to the cities. (In the United States we speak of farmers, not "peasants." The term *farmer* connotes free ownership of land, and a certain pride, while the term *peasant* suggests the humility of a feudal serf. I draw the analogy between modern American women and the modernizing peasantry because women's inferior social, legal, educational, and economic position had until recently been like that of peasants.)

In many ways, the twentieth-century influx of married women into an industrial economy differs from the earlier influx of men. For one thing, through the latter half of the nineteenth century up until the present, women's tasks at home have been reduced. Store-bought goods gradually replaced homespun cloth, home-made soap and candles, home-cured meats, and home-baked bread. More recently, women have been able to buy an array of preprepared meals, or buy "carry-out," or, if they can afford it, to eat out. Some send out clothes to a "wash and fold" laundry, and pay for mending and alterations. Other tasks women used to do at home have also gradually

come to be done elsewhere for pay. Day care for children, retirement homes for the elderly, homes for delinquent children, mental hospitals, and even psychotherapy are, in a way, commercial substitutes for jobs a mother once did at home.

To some extent, new services and goods have come to be preferred over the older domestic ones. Products and services of the "native" housewife have given way to mass production outside the home. Store-bought clothes, utensils, and foods have come to seem just as good if not better. In the two-job couple this trend moves even faster; working couples do less at home and buy more goods and services instead. A woman's skills at home are then perhaps also less valued. One working mother remarked: "Sometimes when I get upset and want to make a point, I refuse to cook. But it doesn't work. My husband just goes and picks up some Colonel Sanders fried chicken; the kids love it." Another mother said, "When I told my husband I wanted him to share the laundry, he just said, 'Let's take it to a laundry.' " The modern industrial versions of many goods and services come to be preferred over the old-fashioned domestic ones, even as colonial cultures came to prevail over old-fashioned "native ways." Just as the First World has raised its culture over the Third World's indigenous culture, so too the store-bought goods and services have marginalized the "local crafts" of the housewife.

THE TWO CULTURES: THE HOUSEWIFE AND THE WORKING WOMAN

Not only are many of the products and services of the home available and cheap elsewhere, the status of the full-time housewife has been eroded. As the role of housewife has lost its allure, the wives who "just" stay home have developed the defensiveness of the downwardly mobile. Facing the prospect of becoming a housewife after quitting her job, Ann Myerson said, "If you want to know what shunning feels like, go to a cocktail party, and when they ask you what you do, say 'I'm a housewife.' " One illustration in the November 1970 issue of *True* magazine sums up the housewife's predicament: a commuter train is filled with businessmen reading morning newspapers and office memos. A bewildered middle-aged housewife in bathrobe and furry slippers, hair in curlers, searches the aisles for her husband, his forgotten briefcase in hand. Her husband is hiding behind his seat, embarrassed that his wife looks so ridiculous, so out of place. In their suits, holding their memo pads, reading their newspapers, the men of the commuter car determine what is ridiculous. They represent the ways of the city; the housewife represents those of the peasant.

Working mothers often feel poised between the cultures of the housewife and the working man. On one hand, many middle-class women feel severely criticized by relatives or neighbors who stay home, and who, feeling increasingly threatened and militant about their own declining position, inspect working mothers with critical eye. Nina Tanagawa felt the critical eye of the nonworking mothers of her daughter's friends. Jessica Stein felt it from affluent neighbors. Nancy Holt and Adrienne Sherman felt scrutinized by their mothers-in-law. Some of these watchful relatives and neighbors cross over the big divide themselves. When Ann Myerson's mother was a housewife, she criticized Ann for her overzealous careerism, but when her mother got a job herself, she questioned Ann's decision to quit.

At the same time, many working mothers seemed to feel both superior to housewives they know and envious of them. Having struggled hard to achieve her position as a systems analyst, Carol Alston didn't want to be confused with "ordinary" women who had not. Whenever she saw a housewife with a child, Carol recalled thinking, Why isn't she doing something *productive?* But seeing housewives slowly pushing their carts down the aisle at the Safeway at midday, she also questioned her own hectic life. When she dropped out of her "real" job to consult part time and care for her two children—and crossed the deepening rift—she began to sympathize with housewives.

Women who've remained back in the "village" as housewives have been burdened with extra tasks—collecting delivered parcels, letting in repairmen, or keeping afternoon company with the children of neighborhood mothers who work. Their working neighbors seldom have time to stop and chat or, sometimes, to fully return favors.

Their traditional source of honor, like the peasant's, has been threatened. In a preindustrial setting, a woman's claim to honor was based primarily on her relation to her husband, her children, her home. As the cash economy spread, money has become the dominant symbol of honor and worth. Unpaid work, like that of housewives, came to seem like not "real" work. The housewife became "just a housewife," her work became "just housework." In their book *For Her Own Good,* Barbara Ehrenreich and Deirdre English have described how at the turn of the century, the Home Economics Movement struggled against the social decline of the housewife by trying to systematize and upgrade the role into a profession. Women, its leaders claimed, could be dignified "professionals" in their own homes. Ironically, the leaders of the Home Economics Movement thought housework was honorable—not because it was *intrinsically* valuable—but because it was just as real as *paid* work, a concession revealing how much moral ground had been lost already.

CLASS DIFFERENCES

If working wives are the modern-day urbanizing peasant, then there are important differences between some "peasants" and others. In addition to the split between housewives and working women, this social revolution also widens a second split among women—between the women who do jobs that pay enough to pay a baby-sitter and the women who baby-sit or tend to other home needs. Carmen Delacorte, who sat for the children of two other families I talked to; Consuela Sanchez, the Salvadorian woman who babysat for the Livingstons' daughter and whose mother was raising Consuela's child back in El Salvador; the Myersons' Filipino baby-sitter, who had an eight-year-old daughter in the Philippines; the Steins' housekeeper and assistant housekeeper: all these women are part of a growing number of workers forming an ever-broadening lower tier of women doing bits and pieces of the housewife's role for pay. Most likely, three generations back, the grandmothers of all these women—professional women, baby-sitters, housekeepers—were housewives, though perhaps from different social classes. Since class has a remarkable sticking power, it may be that the granddaughters of working-class housewives moved into the economy mainly as maids, daycare workers, laundry and other service workers—doing low-paid "female" work—while the granddaughters of upper-middle and upper-class housewives tended to move in as lawyers, doctors, professors, and executives—doing mainly high-status "male" (and some "female") professional work. The granddaughters of the middle class may have tended to move into the expanding world of clerical jobs "in between." There is an important class difference between Carmen Delacorte and Ann Myerson: both form part of the new "peasantry," but as in the industrial revolution of the nineteenth century, some newcomers to the city found it much tougher going than others, and were more tempted to go home.

PRESERVING A DOMESTIC TRADITION?

But many women of every social class and in every kind of job are faced with a common problem: how shall I preserve the domestic culture of my mother and grandmother in the age of the nine-to-five or eight-to-six job? In some ways, the experience of Chicana women condenses the experience of all working women. Many Chicanas have experienced the strains of three movements—that from rural to urban life, from Mexican to American life, and from domestic work to paid employment. In her research on Chicana working women, the sociologist Beatrice Pesquera discovered that many conceived it to be their job as women to keep alive *la cultura*, to teach their children Spanish songs, stories, religious rituals; to teach their daughters to cook tortillas and chile verde. Their task is to maintain an ethnic culture eroded by television and ignored by schools in America. The Chicana considers herself a cultural bridge between present and past and this poses yet another task in her second shift. When they don't have time to be the bridge themselves, Chicana working mothers often seek a "tortilla grandma" to baby-sit and provide *la cultura*. Many white working mothers have

fought a similar—and often losing—battle to carry forward a domestic culture—a culture of homemade apple pie, home-sewn Halloween costumes, hand-ironed shirts. On weekends and holidays most working woman revert to being housewives.

Many traditional women such as Carmen Delacorte and Nina Tanagawa feel they should carry on *all* of the domestic tradition. To them, the female role isn't simply a female role; it is part of a cultural tradition, like a rural or ethnic tradition. To the traditional, it seems that *only women* can carry on this tradition. Having secured a base in the industrial economy, having forged a male identity through their position in that economy, men have then relied on women to connect them back to a life outside it. In *The Remembered Gate*, Barbara Berg argues that as Americans moved off the land, the values of farm life moved into the home. The woman at home became the urban agrarian, the one who preserved the values of a bygone rural way of life while living in the city. By "staying back" in this sense, she eased the difficult transition for the men who moved ahead. Who is easing the transition for women now?

Although traditional women want to preserve the "domestic heritage" their mothers passed on, most working mothers I talked to felt ambivalent about it. "Do I really *need* to cook an elaborate meal every night?" they ask themselves. Cutting back on tasks at home often means working mothers are not living up to their mothers' standards of care for home or child, nor to the collective female tradition of the recent past. One woman summed up the feelings of many others: "I'm not the type that has to see my face in the kitchen floor. That part of my mother's cleaning routine I can let go, no problem. But I don't give my child as much as my mother gave me. That's why I want my husband involved—to make up for that."

Some men have responded to the declining domestic culture, much as colonizers once responded to the marginalization of traditional peasant life. Secure in their own modern culture, the colonizers could collect peasant rugs, jewelry, or songs, or cultivate a taste for the indigenous cuisine. Today, some successful professional men, secure in their own modern careers, embrace a few tokens of the traditional female culture. They bake bread or pies on Saturdays, or fix a gourmet meal once a month. But very few men go completely "native"; that would take an extra month a year.

UNEQUAL WAGES AND FRAGILE MARRIAGES—THE COUNTERTENDENCY

Women's move into the economy, as a new urban peasantry, is the basic social revolution of our time. On the whole, it has increased the power of women. But at the same time, other realities lower women's power. If women's work outside the home increases their need for male help inside it, two facts—that women earn less and that marriages have become less stable—inhibit many women from pressing men to help more.

Today, women's average earnings are only a bit higher, relative to men's, than they were a hundred years ago; for the last hundred years women have earned 60 percent of what men earn; today it's 70 percent. Given this difference, women still have more of an economic need for marriage than men do.

Meanwhile, what has changed is the extent to which a woman can depend on marriage. The divorce rate has risen steadily through the century and between 1970 and 1980, it actually doubled. Experts estimate that 49 percent of all men and women who marry today are likely to divorce sometime before they die. Whatever causes divorce, as the sociologist Terry Arendell points out in *Divorce: Women and Children Last*, the effect of it is much harder on women. Divorce usually pushes women down the class ladder—sometimes way down. According to Lenore Weitzman's *The Divorce Revolution*, in the first year after divorce women experience a 73 percent loss in standard of living, whereas men experience a 42 percent gain. Most divorced men provide surprisingly little financial support for their children. According to the Bureau of the Census in 1985, 81 percent of divorced fathers and 66 percent of separated fathers have court orders to pay child support. Twenty percent of these fathers fully comply with the court order; 15 percent pay irregularly. (And how much child support a father pays is not related to his capacity to pay.)[3]

Most divorced fathers have distressingly little emotional contact with their children as well. According to the National Children's Survey conducted in 1976 and 1981 and analyzed by sociologist Frank Furstenberg, 23 percent of all divorced fathers had no contact with their children during the past five years. Another 20 percent had no contact with their children in the past one year. Only 26 percent had seen their children for a total of three weeks in the last year. Two-thirds of fathers divorced for over ten years had not had any contact with their children in more than a year. In line with this finding, in her study of divorced women, sociologist Terry Arendell found that over half of the children of divorced women had not received a visit or a call from their father in the last year; 35 percent of these children had not seen their fathers in the last five years. Whatever job they took, these women would also have be to the most important person in their children's lives.

Arendell also found that many middle-class divorced women didn't feel they could turn to their parents or other family members for help. Thus, divorced women are often left in charge of the children, are relatively poorer—often just plain poor—and often lack social and emotional support. The frightening truth is that once pushed down the class ladder, many divorced women and their children get stuck there. This is because they have difficulty finding jobs with adequate pay and because most of them have primary responsibility for the children. Also, fewer divorced women than men remarry, especially older women with children.

While women's entrance into the economy has increased women's power, the growing instability of marriage creates an anonymous, individualistic "modern" form of oppression. In the nineteenth century, before a woman could own property in her own name, get a higher education, enter a profession, or vote, she might have been trapped in a marriage to an overbearing husband and have had nowhere else to go. Now we call that woman "oppressed." Yet today, when a woman can legally own property, vote, get an education, work at a job, and leave an oppressive marriage, she walks out into an apparently "autonomous" and "free" form of inequality.

Divorce is an undoing of an economic arrangement between men and women. Reduced to its economic bare bones, traditional marriage has been what the economist, Heidi Hartmann, calls a "mechanism of redistribution": in a sense, men have "paid" women to rear their children and tend their home. In the late nineteenth and early twentieth centuries, unions fought for and won a higher "family wage" for male workers, on the grounds that men needed the money more than women in order to support wives and children. At that time it seemed reasonable that men should get first crack at the better-paying jobs, and even earn more than women for doing the same work because "women didn't support a family." Since this arrangement put men and women in vastly unequal financial positions, the way most women got a living wage was to marry. In the job market, the relation between men and women was as the upper to the lower class in society. Marriage was the economic equalizer.

But as marriage—this "mechanism of redistribution"—has grown more fragile, most divorced men still earn a "family wage" but no longer "redistribute" it to their children or the ex-wife who cares for them. The media stresses how men and women both have the freedom to choose divorce, and surely this choice is an important advance. But at the same time, the more men and women live outside marriage, the more they divide into separate classes. Three factors— the belief that child care is female work, the failure of ex-husbands to support their children, and higher male wages at work—have taken the economic rug from under that half of married women who divorce.

Formerly, many men dominated women within marriage. Now, despite a much wider acceptance of women as workers, men dominate women anonymously outside of marriage. Patriarchy has not disappeared; it has changed form. In the old form, women were forced to obey an overbearing husband in the privacy of an unjust marriage. In the new form, the working single mother is economically abandoned by her former husband and ignored by a patriarchal society at large. In the old form, women were limited to the home but economically maintained there. In the new form, the divorced woman does the work of the home but isn't paid for it.

The "modern" oppression of women outside of marriage has also reduced the power of women *inside* marriage as well. Married women are becoming more cautious, more like Nina Tanagawa or Nancy Holt who look at their divorcing friends and say to themselves, "Put up with the extra month a year or divorce? I'll put up with it."

The influx of women into paid work and her increased power raise a woman's aspirations and hopes for equal treatment at home. Her lower wage and status at work and the threat of divorce reduce what she presses for and actually expects.

The "new" oppression outside marriage thus creates a tacit threat to women inside marriage. Married women say to themselves, "I don't want what happened to her to happen to me." Among the working parents I talked with in this study, both men and women expressed sympathy for the emotional pain of divorcing friends. But women told these stories with more anxious interest, and more empathy for the plight of the divorced woman. For example, one evening at the dinner table, a mother of two who worked at word processing had this exchange with her husband, a store manager, and her former boss, as they were telling me about the divorce of a friend:

> A good friend of mine worked as a secretary for six years, putting her husband through dental school. She worked like a dog, did all the housework, and they had a child too. She didn't really worry about getting ahead at the job because she figured they would rely on his work and she would stop working as soon as he set up practice. Well, he went and fell in love with another woman and divorced his wife. Now she's still working as a secretary and raising their little boy. Now he's got two other children by the other woman.

Her husband commented: "That's true, but she was hard to get along with, and she had a drinking problem. She complained a lot. I'm not saying it wasn't hard for her, but there's another side to the story."

The wife answered, surprised, "Yeah, but she was had! Don't you think?"

Her husband said, "Oh, I don't know. They both have a case."

Earlier in our century, the most important cautionary tale for women was of a woman who "fell" from chastity before marriage and came to a bad end because no man would have her. Among working mothers of small children, and especially the more traditional of them, the modern version of the "fallen woman" is the divorcée. Of course, not all women fear the prospect of divorce—for example, not Anita Judson. But the cases of Nancy Holt and Nina Tanagawa are also telling because their fear of divorce led them to stop asking for more help in the second shift. When life is made to seem so cold "out there," a woman may try to get warm inside an unequal marriage.

All in all, then, two forces are at work: new economic opportunities and needs, which draw women to paid work and which put pressure on men to share the second shift. These forces lend appeal to an egalitarian gender ideology and to strategies of renegotiating the division of labor at home. But other forces—the wage gap between men and women, and the effect on women of the rising rate of divorce—work in the opposite direction. These forces lend appeal to a traditional gender ideology and to the female strategy of the supermom and to the male strategy of resistance to sharing. All the couples I studied were exposed to both these sets of forces, though they differed in their degree of exposure: some women were more economically dependent than others; some were in more precarious marriages. It is the background of this "modern" oppression that made many women, like Carol Alston or Ann Myerson, feel very grateful for the men they had, even when they didn't share the whole strain of the second shift.

THE HAVES AND HAVE-NOTS OF BACKSTAGE SUPPORT FOR WORK

The trends I have described constitute the stall in the revolution and stack the cards in favor of husbands not sharing the second shift with their working wives. Once all these forces are set in motion, one final pattern keeps men doing less: women's lack of "backstage support" for their paid jobs.

It sets up a cycle that works like this: because men put more of their "male" identity in work, their work time is worth more than female work time—to the man and to the family. The greater worth of male work time makes his leisure more valuable, because it is his leisure that enables him to refuel his energy, strengthen his ambition, and move ahead at work. By doing less at home, he can work longer hours, prove his loyalty to his company, and get promoted faster. His aspirations expand. So does his pay. So does his exemption from the second shift.

The female side of the cycle runs parallel. The woman's identity is less in her job. Since her work comes second, she carries more of the second shift, thus providing backstage support for her husband's work. Because she supports her husband's efforts at work more than he supports hers, her personal ambitions contract and her earnings, already lower, rise more slowly. The extra month a year that she works contributes not only to her husband's success but to the expanding wage gap between them, and keeps the cycle spinning.

More than wages, what affects a man's contribution at home is the value a couple puts on the husband's or wife's job. That judgment depends on the investment in education, the occupational status, and the future expectations each partner has with regard to the other. In general, the more important a man's job, the more backstage support he receives, and the less backstage support for her job a woman receives, the less important her job becomes.

The inequality in backstage support has received little notice because most of it is hidden from view. One cannot tell from sheer workplace appearance who goes home to be served dinner and who goes home to cook, any more than we can tell rich from poor these days just by how people dress. Both male and female workers come to work looking the same. Yet one is "poorer" in backstage support than the other. One irons a spouse's uniform, fixes a lunch, washes clothes, types a résumé, edits an office memo, takes phone calls, or entertains clients. The other has a uniform ironed, a lunch fixed, clothes washed, a résumé typed, an office memo edited, phone calls taken, and clients entertained.

Women (with traditional or transitional ideologies) believe they ought to give more backstage support than they get. Career-centered egalitarian women gunning for promotion feel they deserve to receive as much as they give. But family-oriented egalitarians—men and women alike—aren't eager to clear the decks at home for more time at the office. They consider the home as their front stage. The rise of the two-job family has reduced the supply of housewives, thus increased the demand for backstage support, and finally somewhat redistributed the supply of that support.

There is a curious hierarchy of backstage "wealth." The richest is the high-level executive with an unemployed wife who entertains his clients and runs his household; and a secretary who handles his appointments, makes his travel arrangements, and orders anniversary flowers for his wife. The poorest in backstage support is the single mother who works full time and rears her children with no help from anyone. Between these two extremes lie the two-job couples. Among them, the husbands of working wives enjoy less support than husbands of housewives, and the men whose working wives do all the second shift enjoy more support than men who share. In general, men enjoy more support than women, and the rich enjoy more of it than the poor.

In a study I did of the family life of workers in a large corporation, I discovered that the higher up the corporate ladder, the more home support a worker had. Top executives were likely to be married to housewives. Middle managers were likely to be married to a working spouse who does some or most of the housework and childcare. And the clerical worker, if she is a woman, is likely to be single or a single mother and does the work at home herself.[4] At each of these three levels in this company, men and women fared differently. Among the female top executives, 95 percent were married to men who also worked and 5 percent were single or single parents. Among male top executives, 64 percent were married to housewives, 23 percent were married to working wives, and 5 percent were single or single parents. So compared to men, female top executives worked in a disadvantageous environment of backstage support. As one female manager remarked: "It's all men at my level in the company and most of them are married to housewives. But even the ones whose wives work seem to have more time at the office than I do." As women executives at this company often quipped, "What I really need is a wife."

In the middle ranks, a quarter of the men were married to housewives, nearly half were married to working wives, and about a third were single. Among women in the middle ranks, half were part of two-job couples and carried most of the second shift. The other half were single or single parents. Among lower-level clerical workers, most were single or single mothers.

Being "rich" or "poor" in backstage support probably influences what traits people develop. Men who have risen to the top with great support come to be seen and to actually be "hard driving," ambitious, and "committed" to their careers. Women who have had little support are vulnerable to the charge of being "uncommitted." Sometimes, they do become less committed: Nancy Holt and Nina Tanagawa withdrew their attention to work in order to take care of "everything else." These women did not lack ambition; unlike Ann Myerson, their work felt very real to them. They did not suffer from what the psychologist Matina Horner calls a "fear of success," in her book *Women's Will to Fail.* Rather, their "backstage poverty" raised the emotional price of success impossibly high.

In an earlier economic era, when men entered industrial life, their wives preserved for them—through the home—a link to a life they had known before. By "staying back," such wives eased a difficult transition for the men who were moving into the industrial age. In a sense Nancy Holt is like a peasant new to a factory job in the city; she is part of a larger social trend, doing what others like her are doing. In the nineteenth century, men had women to ease the transition for them but in the twentieth century, no one is easing the transition for women like Nancy Holt.

NOTES

1. Alice Kessler-Harris, *Out to Work* (New York: Oxford University Press, 1982). Also see Julie A. Mattaie Bradby, *An Economic History of Women in America* (New York: Schocken Books, 1982).
2. Louis Harris and Associates, "Families at Work," General Mills American Family Report, 1980–81. Other research also shows that even working-class women who do not have access to rewarding jobs prefer to work. See Myra Ferree, "Sacrifice, Satisfaction and Social Change: Employment and the Family," in Karen Sacks and Dorothy Remy, eds., *My Troubles Are Going to Have Trouble with Me* (New Brunswick, NJ.: Rutgers University Press, 1984), pp. 61–79. Women's paid work leads to their personal satisfaction (Charles Weaver and Sandra Holmes, "A Comparative Study of the Work Satisfaction of Females with Full-Time Employment and Full-Time Housekeeping," *Journal of Applied Psychology* 60 [1975]: 117–28) and—if a woman has the freedom to choose to work or

not—it leads to marital happiness. See Susan Orden and N. Bradburn, "Working Wives and Marriage Happiness." *American Journal of Sociology* 74 (1969): 107–123.

3. See U.S. Bureau of the Census, *Current Population Reports: Households, Families, Marital Status and Living Arrangements*, series P-20, no. 382 (Washington D.C.: U.S. Government Printing Office, 1985). Also see *Statistical Abstracts of the U.S. National Data Book, Guide to Sources* (Washington, D.C.: U.S. Government Printing Office, 1985). Spousal support is awarded in less than 14 percent of all divorces, and in less than 7 percent

of cases do women actually receive it. See Lenore Weitzman, *The Divorce Revolution* (New York: Free Press; London, Collier Macmillan, 1985).

4. These findings are based on questionnaires I passed out to every thirteenth name on the personnel roster of a large manufacturing company. Of those contacted, 53 percent replied. The results show that the typical form of a worker's family life differs at different levels of corporate hierarchy. The traditional family prevails at the top. Dual-work families prevail in the middle, and single-parent families and singles prevail at the bottom, as the chart below shows:

| Level in Company | *Family Type* | | | |
	Traditional Family	Dual Work	Single/Single Parent	*Total*
Top executive	54%	39%	8%	101%*
Middle manager	13%	50%	37%	100%
Clerical worker	—	50%	50%	100%

*This adds up to 101 due to rounding error.

◆ 31 ◆

The Betrayal of the American Man

Susan Faludi

As men struggle to free themselves from their crisis, their task is not, in the end, to figure out how to be masculine—rather, their masculinity lies in figuring out how to be human. . . . [Men must] learn to wage a battle against no enemy, to own a frontier of human liberty, to act in the service of a brotherhood that includes us all.

Susan Faludi began researching her book on the American man believing that he is the source of the inequality between men and women through his need to control. Instead, she came to a more sympathetic view: Men, like women, are faced with a society in which neither "are the masters of their fate." In fact, Faludi describes the reality of men rather than women in society as more of a serious social problem.

[A]s the nation wobbled toward the millennium, its pulse-takers all seemed to agree that a domestic apocalypse was underway: American manhood was under siege. Newspaper editors, legislators, preachers, marketers, no matter where they perched on the political spectrum, had a contribution to make to the chronicles of the "masculinity crisis." Right-wing talk-radio hosts and left-wing men's-movement spokesmen found themselves uncomfortably on common ground. MEN ON TRIAL, the headlines cried, THE TROUBLE WITH BOYS. Journalists—myself included—raced to report on one young-male hot spot after another: Tailhook, the Citadel, the Spur Posse, South Central gangsters, militiamen blowing up federal buildings and abortion clinics, schoolyard shooters across the country.

In the meantime, the media's softer lifestyle outlets happily turned their attention to male-crisis lite: the retreat to cigar clubs and lap-dancing emporiums, the boom in male cosmetic surgery and the abuse of steroids, the brisk sales of Viagra. Social scientists pontificated on "endangered" young black men in the inner cities, Ritalin-addicted white "bad boys" in the suburbs, "deadbeat dads" everywhere and, less frequently, the anguish of downsized male workers. Social psychologists issued reports on a troubling rise in male-distress signals—from depressive disorders to suicides to certain criminal behaviors.

Pollsters investigated the electoral habits of a new voting bloc they called "the Angry White Male." Marketers hastened to turn the crisis into entertainment and profits from TV shows like "The Man Show" to T shirts that proclaimed DESTROY ALL GIRLS or WIFE BEATER. And by the hundreds of thousands, men without portfolio confirmed the male-crisis diagnosis, convening in Washington for both the black Nation of Islam–led Million Man March and a largely white, evangelical-led Promise Keepers rally entitled, hopefully, "Stand in the Gap."

If so many concurred in the existence of a male crisis, consensus collapsed as soon as anyone asked the question Why. Everyone proposed a favorite whipping boy or, more often, whipping girl, and blame-seekers on all sides went after their selected culprits with righteous and bitter relish. Feminist mothers, indulgent liberals, videogame makers or testosterone itself all came under attack.

AT GROUND ZERO OF THE MASCULINITY CRISIS

The search for an answer to that question took me on a six-year odyssey, with stops along the way at a shuttered shipyard in Long Beach, a suburban living room where a Promise Keepers group met, a Cleveland football stadium where fans grieved the loss of their team, a Florida horse farm where a Vietnam vet finally found peace, a grassy field in Waco where militiamen searched for an enemy and a slick magazine office where young male editors contended with a commodified manhood. But I began investigating this crisis where you might expect a feminist journalist to begin: at the weekly meetings of a domestic-violence group. Wednesday evenings in a beige stucco building a few blocks from the freeway in Long Beach, Calif., I attended a gathering of men under court order to repent the commission of an act that stands as the emblematic masculine sin of our age. What did I expect to divine about the broader male condition by monitoring a weekly counseling session for batterers? That men are by nature brutes? Or, more optimistically, that the efforts of such a group might point to methods of "curing" such beastliness?

Either way, I can see now that I was operating from an assumption both underexamined and dubious: that the male crisis in America was caused by something men were doing unrelated to something being done to them. I had my own favorite whipping boy, suspecting that the crisis of masculinity was caused by masculinity on the rampage. If male violence was the quintessential expression of masculinity run amok, then a domestic-violence therapy group must be at the very heart of this particular darkness.

I wasn't alone in such circular reasoning. I was besieged with suggestions along similar lines from journalists, feminists, antifeminists and other willing advisers. Women's rights advocates mailed me news clips about male office stalkers and computer harassers. That I was not ensconced in the courtroom for O. J. Simpson's murder trial struck many of my volunteer helpers as an appalling lapse of judgment. "The perfect case study of an American man who thinks he's entitled to just control everything and everybody," one of them suggested.

But then, I had already been attending the domestic-violence group for several months—the very group O. J. Simpson was, by coincidence, supposed to have attended but avoided with the promise that he would speak by phone to a psychiatrist—and it was already apparent to me that these men's crises did not stem from a preening sense of entitlement and control. Each new member in the group, called Alternatives to Violence, would be asked to describe what he had done to a woman, a request that was met invariably with the disclaimer "I was out of control." The counselors would then expend much energy showing him how he had, in fact, been in control the entire time. He had chosen his fists, not a knife; he had hit her in the stomach, not the face. No doubt the moment of physical contact for these men had grown out of a desire for supreme control fueled by a need to dominate. I cannot conceive of a circumstance that would exonerate such violence. By making the abusive spouse take responsibility for his actions, the counselors were pursuing a worthy goal. But the logic behind the violence still remained elusive.

A serviceman who had turned to nightclub-bouncer jobs and pastry catering after his military base shut down seemed to confirm the counselors' position one evening shortly before his "graduation" from the group. "I denied it before," he said of the night he pummeled his girlfriend. "I thought I'd blacked out. But looking back at that night, I didn't black out. I was feeling good. I was in power, I was strong, I was in control. I felt like a man." But what struck me most strongly was what he said next: that moment of control had been the only one in his recent life. "That feeling of power," he said, "didn't last long. Only until they put the cuffs on. Then I was feeling again like I was no man at all."

He was typical in this regard. The men I got to know in the group had, without exception, lost their compass in the world. They had lost or were losing jobs, homes, cars, families. They had been labeled outlaws but felt like castoffs. There was something almost absurd about these men struggling, week after week, to recognize themselves as dominators when they were so clearly dominated, done in by the world.

Underlying all the disagreement over what is confusing and unnerving to men runs a constant line of thinking that blinds us—whatever our political beliefs—to the nature of the male predicament. Ask feminists to diagnose men's problems and you will often get a very clear explanation: men are in crisis because women are properly challenging male dominance. Ask antifeminists and you will get a diagnosis that is, in one respect, similar. Men are troubled, many conservative pundits say, because women have gone far beyond their demands for equal treatment and now are trying to take power away from men.

Both the feminist and antifeminist views are rooted in a peculiarly modern American perception that to be a man means you are at the controls at all times. The popular feminist joke that men are to blame for everything is the flip side of the "family values" reactionary expectation that men should be in charge of everything.

The man controlling his environment is today the prevailing American image of masculinity. He is to be in the driver's seat, the king of the road, forever charging down the open highway, along that masculine Möbius strip that cycles endlessly through a numbing stream of movies, TV shows, novels, advertisements and pop tunes. He's a man because he won't be stopped. He'll fight attempts to tamp him down; if he has to, he'll use his gun. But we forget that true Daniel Boone frontiersmanship was only incidentally violent, and was based on creating, out of wilderness, a communal context to which a man could moor himself through work and family.

Modern debates about how men are exercising or abusing their control and power neglect to raise whether a lack of mooring, a lack of context, is causing men's anguish. If men are the masters of their fate, what do they do about the unspoken sense that they are being mastered, in the marketplace and at home, by forces that seem to be sweeping away the soil beneath their feet? If men are mythologized as the ones who make things happen, then how can they begin to analyze what is happening to them?

More than a quarter century ago, women began to free themselves from the box in which they were trapped by feeling their way along its contours, figuring out how it was shaped and how it shaped them. Women were able to take action, paradoxically, by understanding how they were acted upon. Men feel the contours of a box, too, but they are told that box is of their own manu-facture, designed to their specifications. Who are they to complain? For men to say they feel boxed in is regarded not as laudable political protest but as childish whining. How dare the kings com-plain about their castles?

What happened to so disturb the sons of the World War II GIs? The prevailing narrative that the sons inherited—fashioned from the battle-fronts of Europe and the Pacific, laid out in countless newspapers, newsreels and movies—was a tale of successful fatherhood and mascu-line transformation: boys whose Depression-era fathers could neither provide for them nor guide them into manhood were placed under the benevolent wing of a vast male-run orphanage called the army and sent into battle. There, firm but kindly senior officers acting as surrogate fa-thers watched over them as they were tempered into men in the heat of a heroic struggle against malevolent enemies. The boys, molded into men, would return to find wives, form their fami-lies and take their places as adults in the commu-nity of a nation taking its place as a grown-up power in the world.

This was the story America told itself in dozens of war movies in which tough but tender-hearted commanding officers prepared their ap-preciative "boys" to assume their responsibilities in male society. It was the theme behind the 1949 film "Sands of Iwo Jima," with John Wayne as Sergeant Stryker, a stern papa molding his wet-behind-the-ears charges into a capable fraternity. "Before I'm through with you, you're gonna move like one man and think like one man," he tells them. "If I can't teach you one way, I'll teach you another, but I'm gonna get the job done." And he gets the job done, fathering a whole squad of youngsters into communal adulthood.

The veterans of World War II were eager to embrace a masculine ideal that revolved around providing rather than dominating. Their most important experiences had centered on the sup-port they had given one another in the war, and it was this that they wished to replicate. As artillery-man Win Stracke told oral historian Studs Terkel in "The Good War," he came home bearing this most cherished memory: "You had 15 guys who for the first time in their lives could help each other without cutting each other's throat or trying

to put down somebody else through a boss or whatever. I had realized it was the absence of competition and all those phony standards that created the thing I loved about the army."

The fathers who would sire the baby-boom generation would try to pass that experience of manhood on intact to their sons. The grunts who went overseas and liberated the world came home to the expectation that they would liberate the country by quiet industry and caretaking. The vets threw themselves into their federally funded edu-cations, and later their defense-funded corporate and production-line jobs, and their domestic lives in Veterans Administration–financed tract homes. They hoped their dedication would be in the serv-ice of a higher national aim.

For their children, the period of soaring ex-pectations that followed the war was truly the era of the boy. It was the culture of "Father Knows Best" and "Leave It to Beaver," of Pop Warner rit-uals and Westinghouse science scholarships, of BB guns and rocket clubs, of football practice and lettered jackets, of magazine ads where "Dad" seemed always to be beaming down at his scampy, cowboy-suited younger son or proudly handing his older son the keys to a brand-new convertible. It was a world where, regardless of the truth that lay behind each garden gate, popu-lar culture led us to believe that fathers were spending every leisure moment in roughhouse play and model-airplane construction with their beloved boys.

In the aspiring middle-class suburb where I came of age, there was no mistaking the belief in the boy's pre-eminence; it was evident in the solic-itous attentions of parents and schoolteachers, in the centrality of Cub Scouts and Little League, in the community life that revolved around boys' championships and boys' scores—as if these outposts of tract-home America had been built mainly as exhibition rings for junior-male achieve-ment, which perhaps they had.

The speech that inaugurated the shiny new era of the 1960s was the youthful John F. Kennedy's address to the Democratic National Convention, a month before the launch of Echo. The words would become, along with his Inaugural oration, a haunting refrain in adoles-cent male consciousness. What Kennedy implic-itly presented was a new rite of passage for an untested male generation. "The New Frontier of which I speak is not a set of promises," he told them. "It is a set of challenges." Kennedy understood that it was not enough for the fathers to win the world for their sons; the sons had to feel they had won it for themselves. If the fathers had their Nazis and "Nips," then Kennedy would see to it that the sons had an enemy, too. He promised as much on Inauguration Day in 1961, when he spoke vaguely but unremittingly of communism's threat, of a country that would be defined by its readiness to "pay any price" and "oppose any foe." The fight was the thing, the only thing, if America was to retain its masculinity.

The drumrolls promised a dawning era of superpower manhood to the boy born on the New Frontier, a masculine honor and pride in exchange for his loyalty. Ultimately, the boy was double-crossed. The fix was in from the start: corporate and cold-war America's promise to continue the World War II GI's wartime experience of belonging, of meaningful engagement in a mission, was never authentic. "The New Frontier" of space turned out to be a void that no man could conquer, let alone colonize. The astronaut was no Daniel Boone; he was just a flattened image for TV viewers to watch—and eventually, to be bored by. Instead of sending its sons to Normandy, the government dispatched them to Vietnam, where the enemy was unclear and the mission remained a tragic mystery. The massive managerial bureaucracies of postwar "white collar" employment, especially the defense contractors fat on government largesse, produced "organization men" who often didn't even know what they were managing—and who suspected they weren't really needed at all. What these corporations offered was a secure job, not a vital role—and not even that secure. The postwar fathers' submission to the national-security state would, after a prosperous period of historically brief duration, be rewarded with pink slips, with massive downsizing, union-breaking and outsourcing. The boy who had been told he was going to be the master of the universe and all that was in it found himself master of nothing.

As early as 1957, the boy's diminished future was foreshadowed in a classic sci-fi film. In "The Incredible Shrinking Man," Scott Carey has a good job, a suburban home, a pleasure boat, a pretty wife. And yet, after he passes through a mist of atomic radiation while on a boating vacation in the Pacific, something happens. As he tells his wife in horror, "I'm getting smaller, Lou, every day."

As Carey quite literally shrinks, the promises made to him are broken one by one. The employer who was to give him lifetime economic security fires him. He is left with only feminine defenses, to hide in a doll house, to fight a giant spider with a sewing pin. And it turns out that the very source of his diminishment is implicitly an atomic test by his own government. His only hope is to turn himself into a celebrated freak and sell his story to the media. "I'm a big man!" Carey says with bitter sarcasm. "I'm famous! One more joke for the world to laugh at."

The more Carey shrinks, the more he strikes out at those around him. "Every day I became more tyrannical," he comments, "more monstrous in my domination of my wife." It's a line that would ring a bell for any visitor to the Alternatives to Violence group and for any observer of the current male scene. As the male role has diminished amid a sea of betrayed promises, many men have been driven to more domineering and some even "monstrous" displays in their frantic quest for a meaningful showdown.

THE ORNAMENTAL CULTURE

If few men would do what Shawn Nelson did one evening in the spring of 1995, many could relate. A former serviceman whose career in an army tank unit had gone nowhere, a plumber who had lost his job, a former husband whose wife had left him, the 35-year-old Nelson broke into the National Guard armory, commandeered an M-60 army tank and drove it through the streets of San Diego, flattening fire hydrants, crushing 40 cars, downing enough utility poles to cut off electricity to 5,000 people. He was at war with the domestic world that he once thought he was meant to build and defend. He was going to drive that tank he had been meant to command if it killed him. And it did. The police shot Shawn Nelson to death through the turret hatch.

If a man could not get the infrastructure to work for him, he could at least tear it down. If the nation would not provide an enemy to fight, he could go to war at home. If there was to be no brotherhood, he would take his stand alone. A handful of men would attempt to gun down enemies they imagined they saw in family court, employee parking lots, McDonald's restaurants, a Colorado schoolhouse and, most notoriously, a federal office building in Oklahoma. A far greater number would move their destruction of the elusive enemy to the fantasy realm to a clear-cut and controllable world of action movies and video combat, televised athletic tournaments and pay-per-view ultimate-fighting bouts.

But none of it would satisfy, because the world and the fight had changed. . . .

Ornamental culture has proved the ultimate expression of the century, sweeping away institutions in which men felt some sense of belonging and replacing them with visual spectacles that they can only watch and that benefit global commercial forces they cannot fathom. Celebrity culture's effects on men go far beyond the obvious showcasing of action heroes and rock musicians. The ordinary man is no fool: he knows he can't be Arnold Schwarzenegger. Nonetheless, the culture reshapes his most basic sense of manhood by telling him that masculinity is something to drape over the body, not draw from inner resources; that it is personal, not societal; that manhood is displayed, not demonstrated. The internal qualities once said to embody manhood—surefootedness, inner strength, confidence of purpose—are merchandised to men to enhance their manliness. What passes for the essence of masculinity is being extracted and bottled and sold back to men. Literally, in the case of Viagra. . . .

In a culture of ornament, manhood is defined by appearance, by youth and attractiveness, by money and aggression, by posture and swagger and "props," by the curled lip and flexed biceps, by the glamour of the cover boy and by the market-bartered "individuality" that sets one astronaut or athlete or gangster above another. These are the same traits that have long been designated as the essence of feminine vanity—the objectification and mirror-gazing that women have denounced as trivializing and humiliating qualities imposed on them by a misogynist culture. No wonder men are in such agony. At the close of the century, men find themselves in an unfamiliar world where male worth is measured only by participation in a celebrity-driven consumer culture and awarded by lady luck.

The more I consider what men have lost—a useful role in public life, a way of earning a decent living, respectful treatment in the culture—the more it seems that men are falling into a status oddly similar to that of women at midcentury. The '50s housewife, stripped of her connections to a wider world and invited to fill the void with shopping and the ornamental display of her ultrafemininity, could be said to have morphed into the '90s man, stripped of his connections to a wider world and invited to fill the void with consumption and a gym-bred display of his ultramasculinity. The empty compensations of a "feminine mystique" are transforming into the empty compensations of a masculine mystique, with a gentlemen's cigar club no more satisfying than a ladies' bake-off.

But women have rebelled against this mystique. Of all the bedeviling questions my travels and research raised, none struck me more than this: why don't contemporary men rise up in protest against their betrayal? If they have experienced so many of the same injuries as women, the same humiliations, why don't they challenge the culture as women did? Why can't men seem to act?

The stock answers don't suffice. Men aren't simply refusing to "give up the reins of power," as some feminists have argued. The reins have already slipped from most of their hands. Nor are men merely chary of expressing pain and neediness, particularly in an era where emoting is the coin of the commercial realm. While the pressures on men to imagine themselves in control of their emotions are impediments to male revolt, a more fundamental obstacle overshadows them. If men have feared to tread where women have rushed in, then maybe women have had it easier in one very simple regard: women could frame their struggle as a battle against men.

For the many women who embraced feminism in one way or another in the 1970s, that consumer culture was not some intangible force; they saw it as a cudgel wielded by men against women. The mass culture's portfolio of sexist images was propaganda to prop up the myth of male superiority, the argument went. Men, not the marketplace, many women believed, were the root problem and so, as one feminist activist put it in 1969, "the task of the women's liberation movement is to collectively combat male domination in the home, in bed, on the job." And indeed, there were virulent, sexist attitudes to confront. But the 1970s model of confrontation could get feminism only halfway to its goal.

The women who engaged in the feminist campaigns of the '70s were able to take advantage of a ready-made model for revolt. Ironically, it was a male strategy. Feminists had a clearly defined oppressive enemy: the "patriarchy." They had a real frontier to conquer: all those patriarchal institutions, both the old ones that still rebuffed women, like the U.S. Congress or U.S. Steel, and the new ones that tried to remold women, like Madison Avenue or the glamour and media-pimp kingdoms of Bert Parks and Hugh Hefner. Feminists also had their own army of "brothers": sisterhood. Each GI Jane who participated in this struggle felt useful. Whether she was working in a women's-health clinic or tossing her bottles of Clairol in a "freedom trash can," she was part of a greater glory, the advancement of her entire sex. Many women whose lives were touched by feminism felt in some way that they had reclaimed an essential usefulness; together, they had charged the barricades that kept each of them from a fruitful, thriving life.

The male paradigm of confrontation, in which an enemy could be identified, contested and defeated, proved useful to activists in the civil-rights movement, the antiwar movement, the gay-rights movement. It was, in fact, the fundamental organizing principle of virtually every concerted countercultural campaign of the last half century. Yet it could launch no "men's movement." Herein lies the critical paradox, and the source of male inaction: the model women have used to revolt is the exact one men not only can't use but are trapped in.

Men have no clearly defined enemy who is oppressing them. How can men be oppressed when the culture has already identified them as the oppressors, and when even they see themselves that way? As one man wrote plaintively to Promise Keepers, "I'm like a kite with a broken string, but I'm also holding the tail." Men have invented

antagonists to make their problems visible, but with the passage of time, these culprits—scheming feminists, affirmative-action proponents, job-grabbing illegal aliens—have come to seem increasingly unconvincing as explanations for their situation. Nor do men have a clear frontier on which to challenge their intangible enemies. What new realms should they be gaining—the media, entertainment and image-making institutions of corporate America? But these are institutions already run by men; how can men invade their own territory? Is technological progress the frontier? Why then does it seem to be pushing men into obsolescence, socially and occupationally? And if the American man crushes the machine, whose machine has he vanquished?

The male paradigm of confrontation has proved worthless to men. Yet maybe that's not so unfortunate. The usefulness of that model has reached a point of exhaustion anyway. The women's movement and the other social movements have discovered its limits. Their most obvious enemies have been sent into retreat, yet the problems persist. While women are still outnumbered in the executive suites, many have risen in the ranks and some have achieved authoritative positions often only to perpetuate the same transgressions as their male predecessors. Women in power in the media, advertising and Hollywood have for the most part continued to generate the same sorts of demeaning images as their male counterparts. Blaming a cabal of men has taken feminism about as far as it can go. That's why women have a great deal at stake in the liberation of the one population uniquely poised to discover and employ a new paradigm—men.

BEYOND THE POLITICS OF CONFRONTATION

. . . As men struggle to free themselves from their crisis, their task is not, in the end, to figure out how to be masculine—rather, their masculinity lies in figuring out how to be human. The men who worked at the Long Beach Naval Shipyard, where I spent many months, didn't go there and learn their crafts as riggers, welders and boilermakers to be masculine; they were seeking something worthwhile to do. Their sense of their own manhood flowed out of their utility in a society, not the other way around.

And so with the mystery of men's nonrebellion comes the glimmer of an opening, a chance for men to forge a rebellion commensurate with women's and, in the course of it, to create a new paradigm for human progress that will open doors for both sexes. That was, and continues to be, feminism's dream, to create a freer, more humane world. It will remain a dream without the strength and courage of men who are today faced with a historic opportunity: to learn to wage a battle against no enemy, to own a frontier of human liberty, to act in the service of a brotherhood that includes us all.

Part VII

CULTURE

As people interact over time, they come to develop a shared reality; a perspective; a working consensus; a common definition of what they believe is true, moral, and worthwhile. This consensus, to most sociologists, is the meaning of culture.

Americans share a culture. The history of our society has developed that culture. We are a people who have brought cultures from other societies, but over time, as we interact with one another, a different culture has arisen, and as immigrants arrive here, they learn our culture and are able to alter our shared culture. The railroad, television, airplanes, telephone, computers allow us to interact with one another like never before; isolated places increasingly learn and understand the larger culture easier than ever before. Yet, each community, each neighborhood, each organization develops its own culture too, often very similar to the larger culture, sometimes very different and even antagonistic to that larger culture.

Culture is dynamic, changing according to new problems that an organization or society must confront. The culture that exists today has changed dramatically because of the wars we have fought, urbanization, new technology, immigration, big business, worldwide trade, and scientific breakthroughs—to name only a few obvious causes.

A common culture is one way society is held together. It facilitates mutual understanding, cooperation, and a shared sense of reality. It is made up of a people's assumptions, truths, rules, and values.

Five selections are included in Part VII. Howard S. Becker introduces the meaning of culture in an excellent, interesting, and clear manner, drawing on his experience as a sociologist and a jazz musician. Elijah Anderson describes the culture of the street, and shows us the power of this culture when it is in conflict with the culture learned in the home. David Karp highlights some of the internal conflicts that exist in American culture as well as conflicts which involve difficult choices that many of us must make. (Specifically, our culture values individualism to a very high degree, yet it also encourages us to commit ourselves to the larger community.) Alan Wolfe asks us to confront the issue of "moral freedom" in modern society. Is moral freedom inconsistent with culture? Finally, Manfred Steger, in an excerpt from his excellent book on globalization, reminds us all that globalization has real consequences for societal culture. Indeed, to what extent is societal culture becoming less and less important as we become a postmodern world?

Culture: A Sociological View

Howard S. Becker

On the one hand, culture persists and antedates the participation of particular people in it. Indeed, culture can be said to shape the outlooks of people who participate in it. But cultural understandings, on the other hand, have to be reviewed and remade continually, and in the remaking, they change.

This article is an attempt to describe the meaning of *culture* and to show its subtleties and importance. The following questions might be a good guide through Becker's analysis:

1. What is culture?
2. How does culture aid collective action?
3. How does culture arise?
4. Why does culture stay the same and why does it change?
5. How does culture guide public behavior?
6. How does culture socialize the individual?
7. Why does culture make it easier for people to plan their lives?

I was for some years what is called a Saturday night musician, making myself available to whoever called and hired me to play for dances and parties in groups of varying sizes, playing everything from polkas through mambos, jazz, and imitations of Wayne King. Whoever called would tell me where the job was, what time it began, and usually would tell me to wear a dark suit and a bow tie, thus ensuring that the collection of strangers he was hiring would at least look like a band because they would all be dressed more or less alike. When we arrived at work, we would introduce ourselves—the chances were, in a city the size of Chicago (where I did much of my

From Howard S. Becker, "Culture: A Sociological View," *Yale Review*, September 2 1982. 71:513–527. Copyright Yale University.

playing), that we were in fact strangers—and see who we knew in common and whether our paths had ever crossed before. The drummer would assemble his drums, the others would put together their instruments and tune up, and when it was time to start, the leader would announce the name of a song and a key—"Exactly Like You" in B flat, for instance—and we would begin to play. We not only began at the same time, but also played background figures that fit the melody someone else was playing and, perhaps most miraculously, ended together. No one in the audience ever guessed that we had never met until twenty minutes earlier. And we kept that up all night, as though we had rehearsed often and played together for years. In a place like Chicago, that scene might be repeated hundreds of times during a weekend.

What I have just described embodies the phenomenon that sociologists have made the core problem of their discipline. The social sciences are such a contentious bunch of disciplines that it makes trouble to say what I think is true, that they all in fact concern themselves with one or another version of this issue—the problem of collective action, of how people manage to act together. I will not attempt a rigorous definition of collective action here, but the story of the Saturday night musicians can serve as an example of it. The example might have concerned a larger group—the employees of a factory who turn out several hundred automobiles in the course of a day, say. Or it might have been about so small a group as a family. It needn't have dealt with a casual collection of strangers, although the ability of strangers to perform together that way makes clear the nature of the problem. How do they do it? How do people act together so as to get anything done without a great deal of trouble, without missteps and conflict?

We can approach the meaning of a concept by seeing how it is used, what work it is called on to do. Sociologists use the concept of *culture* as one of a family of explanations for the phenomenon of concerted activity. . . . Robert Redfield defined culture as "conventional understandings made manifest in act and artifact." The notion is that the people involved have a similar idea of things, understand them in the same way, as having the same character and the same potential, capable of being dealt with in the same way; they also know that this idea is shared, that the people they are dealing with know, just as they do, what these things are and how they can be used. Because all of them have roughly the same idea, they can all act in ways that are roughly the same, and their activities will, as a result, mesh and be coordinated. Thus, because all those musicians understood what a Saturday night job at a country club consisted of and acted accordingly, because they all knew the melody and harmony of "Exactly Like You" and hundreds of similar songs, because they knew that the others knew this as they knew it, they could play that job successfully. The concept of culture, in short, has its use for sociologists as an explanation of those musicians and all the other forms of concerted action for which they stand. . . .

Culture, however, explains how people act in concert when they *do* share understandings. It is thus a consequence (in this kind of sociological thinking) of the existence of a group of acting people. It has its meaning as one of the resources people draw on in order to coordinate their activities. In this it differs from most anthropological thinking in which the order of importance is reversed, culture leading a kind of independent existence as a system of patterns that make the existence of larger groups possible.

Most conceptions of culture include a great deal more than the spare definition I have just offered. But I think, for reasons made clear later, that it is better to begin with a minimal definition and then to add other conditions when that is helpful. . . .

How does culture—shared understanding—help people to act collectively? People have ideas about how a certain kind of activity might be carried on. They believe others share these ideas and will act on them if they understand the situation in the same way. They believe further that the people they are interacting with believe that they share these ideas too, so that everyone thinks that everyone else has the same idea about how to do things. Given such circumstances, if everyone does what seems appropriate, action will be sufficiently coordinated for practical purposes. Whatever was under way will get done—the meal served, the child dealt with, the job finished—well enough that life can proceed.

The cultural process, then, consists of people doing something in line with their understanding of what one might best do under the given circumstances. Others, recognizing what was done as appropriate, will then consult their notions of what might be done and do something that seems right to them, to which others in return will respond similarly, and so on. If everyone has the same general ideas in mind, and does something congruent with that image or collection of ideas, then what people do will fit together. If we all know the melody and harmony of "Exactly Like You," and improvise accordingly, whatever comes out will sound reasonable to the players and listeners, and a group of perfect strangers will sound like they know what they are doing.

Consider another common situation. A man and woman meet and find each other interesting.

At some stage of their relationship, they may consider any of a variety of ways of organizing their joint activities. Early on, one or the other might propose that they "have a date." Later, one or the other might subtly or forthrightly suggest that they spend the night together. Still later, they might try "living together." Finally, they might decide to "get married." They might skip some of these stages and they might not follow that progression, which in contemporary America is a progression of increasingly formal commitment. In other societies and at other times, of course, the stages and the relationships would differ. But, whatever their variety, insofar as there are names for those relationships and stages, and insofar as most or all of the people in a society know those names and have an idea of what they imply as far as continuing patterns of joint activity are concerned, then the man and woman involved will be able to organize what they do by referring to those guideposts. When one or the other suggests one of these possibilities, the partner will know, more or less, what is being suggested without requiring that every item be spelled out in detail, and the pair can then organize their daily lives, more or less, around the patterns suggested by these cultural images.

What they do from day to day will of course not be completely covered by the details of that imagery, although they will be able to decide many details by consulting it together and adapting what it suggests to the problem at hand. None of these images, for example, really establishes who takes the garbage out or what the details of their sexual activity may be, but the images do, in general, suggest the kind of commitments and obligations involved on both sides in a wide range of practical matters.

That is not the end of the matter, however. Consider a likely contemporary complication: The woman, divorced, has small children who live with her. In this case, the couple's freedom of action is constrained, and no cultural model suggests what they ought to do about the resulting difficulties. The models for pairing and for rearing children suggest incompatible solutions, and the partners have to invent something. They have to improvise.

This raises a major problem in the theory of culture I am propounding. Where does culture come from? The typical cultural explanation of behavior takes the culture as given, as preexisting the particular encounter in which it comes into play. That makes sense. Most of the cultural understandings we use to organize our daily behavior are there before we get there and we do not propose to change them or negotiate their details with the people we encounter. We do not propose a new economic system every time we go to the grocery store. But those understandings and ways of doing things have not always been there. Most of us buy our food in supermarkets today, and that requires a different way of shopping from the corner grocery stores of a generation ago. How did the new culture of supermarkets arise?

One answer is that the new culture was imposed by the inventors of the concept, the owners of the new stores that embodied it. They created the conditions under which change was more or less inevitable. People might have decided not to shop in supermarkets and chain stores, but changing conditions of urban life caused so many of them to use the new markets that the corner grocery, the butcher shop, the poultry and fish stores disappeared in all but a few areas. Once that happened, supermarkets became the only practical possibility left, and people had to invent new ways of serving themselves.

So, given new conditions, people invent culture. The way they do it was suggested by William Graham Sumner a century ago in *Folkways*. We can paraphrase him in this way. A group finds itself sharing a common situation and common problems. Various members of the group experiment with possible solutions to those problems and report their experiences to their fellows. In the course of their collective discussion, the members of the group arrive at a definition of the situation, its problems and possibilities, and develop a consensus as to the most appropriate and efficient ways of behaving. This consensus thenceforth constrains the activities of individual members of the group, who will probably act on it, given the opportunity. In other words, new situations provoke new behavior. But people generally find themselves in company when dealing with these new situations, and because they arrive at their solutions collectively, each assumes that the others share them. The beginnings of a new shared understanding thus come into play quickly and easily.

The ease with which new cultural understandings arise and persist varies. It makes a difference, for one thing, how large a group is involved in making the new understandings. At one extreme, as I have noted, every mating couple, every new family, has to devise its own culture to cover the contingencies of daily interaction. At the other, consider what happens during industrialization when hundreds of thousands—perhaps millions—of people are brought from elsewhere to work in the new factories. They have to come from elsewhere because the area could not support that many people before industrialization. As a result, the newcomers differ in culture from the people already there, and they differ as well in the role they play in the new industries, usually coming in at the bottom. When industrialization takes place on a large scale, not only does a new culture of the workplace have to be devised, but also a new culture of the cities in which they all end up living—a new experience for everyone involved.

The range of examples suggests, as I mean it to, that people create culture continuously. Because no two situations are alike, the cultural solutions available to them are only approximate. Even in the simplest societies, no two people learn quite the same cultural material; the chance encounters of daily life provide sufficient variation to ensure that. No set of cultural understandings, then, provides a perfectly applicable solution to any problem people have to solve in the course of their day, and they therefore must remake those solutions, adapt their understandings to the new situation in the light of what is different about it. Even the most conscious and determined effort to keep things as they are would necessarily involve strenuous efforts to remake and reinforce understandings so as to keep them intact in the face of what was changing.

There is an apparent paradox here. On the one hand, culture persists and antedates the participation of particular people in it. Indeed, culture can be said to shape the outlooks of people who participate in it. But cultural understandings, on the other hand, have to be reviewed and remade continually, and in the remaking, they change.

This is not a true paradox, however: The understandings last *because* they change to deal with new situations. People continually refine them, changing some here and some there but never changing all of them at once. The emphasis on basic values and coherence in the definition of culture arises because of this process. In making the new versions of the old understandings, people naturally rely on what they already have available, so that consciously planned innovations and revolutions seem, in historical perspective, only small variations on what came before.

To summarize, how culture works as a guide in organizing collective action and how it comes into being are really the same process. In both cases, people pay attention to what other people are doing and, in an attempt to mesh what they do with those others, refer to what they know (or think they know) in common. So culture is always being made, changing more or less, acting as a point of reference for people engaged in interaction.

What difference does it make that people continually make culture in the way I have described? The most important consequence is that they can, as a result, cooperate easily and efficiently in the daily business of life, without necessarily knowing each other very well.

Most occupations, for example, operate on the premise that the people who work in them all know certain procedures and certain ways of thinking about and responding to typical situations and problems, and that such knowledge will make it possible to assemble them to work on a common project without prior team training. Most professional schools operate on the theory that the education they offer provides a basis for work cooperation among people properly trained anywhere. In fact, people probably learn the culture that makes occupational cooperation possible in the workplace itself. It presents them with problems to solve that are common to people in their line of work, and provides a group of more experienced workers who can suggest solutions. In some occupations, workers change jobs often and move from workplace to workplace often (as do the weekend musicians), and they carry what they have learned elsewhere with them. That makes it easy for them to refine and update their solutions frequently, and thus to develop and maintain an occupational culture. Workers who do not move but spend their work lives in one place may develop a more idiosyncratic work culture, peculiar to that place and its local problems—a culture of IBM or Texas Instruments or (because the process is not limited to large firms) Joe's Diner.

At a different level of cooperative action, Goffman has described cultural understandings that characterize people's behavior in public. For instance, people obey a norm of "civil inattention," allowing each other a privacy that the material circumstances of, say, waiting for a bus, do not provide. Because this kind of privacy is what Americans and many others find necessary before they can feel comfortable and safe in public (Hall has shown how these rules differ in other cultures), these understandings make it possible for urban Americans to occupy crowded public spaces without making each other uneasy. The point is not trivial, because violations of these rules are at least in part responsible for the currently common fear that some public areas are "not safe," quite apart from whatever assaults have taken place in them. Most people have no personal knowledge of the alleged assaults, but they experience violation of what might be called the "Goffman rules" of public order as the prelude to danger and do not go to places that make them feel that way.

Cultural understandings, if they are to be effective in the organization of public behavior, must be very widely held. That means that people of otherwise varying class, ethnic, and regional cultures must learn them routinely and must learn them quite young, because even small children can disrupt public order very effectively. That requires, in turn, substantial agreement among people of all segments of the society on how children should be brought up. If no such agreement exists, or if some of the people who agree in principle do not manage to teach their children the necessary things, public order breaks down, as it often does.

In another direction, cultural understandings affect and "socialize" the internal experiences people have. By applying understandings they know to be widely accepted to their own perhaps inchoate private experiences, people learn to define those internal experiences in ways that allow them to mesh their activities relevant to those topics with those of others with whom they are involved. Consider the familiar example of falling in love. It is remarkable that one of the experiences we usually consider private and unique—falling in love—actually has the same character for most people who experience it. That is not to say that the experience is superficial, but rather that when people try to understand their emotional responses to others, one available explanation of what they feel is the idea, common in Western culture, of romantic love. They learn that idea from a variety of sources, ranging from the mass media to discussion with their peers, and they learn to see their own experiences as embodiments of it. Because most people within a given culture learn to experience love in the same way from the same sources, two people can become acquainted and successfully fall in love with each other—not an easy trick.

Because shared cultural understandings make it easy to do things in certain ways, moreover, their existence favors those ways of doing things and makes other ways of achieving the same end, which might be just as satisfactory to everyone involved, correspondingly less likely. Random events, which might produce innovations desirable to participants, occur infrequently. In fact, even when the familiar line of activity is not exactly to anyone's liking, people continue it simply because it is what everyone knows and knows that everyone else knows, and thus is what offers the greatest likelihood of successful collective action. Everyone knows, for instance, that it would be better to standardize the enormous variety of screw threads in this country, or to convert the United States to the metric system. But the old ways are the ones we know, and, of course, in this instance, they are built into tools and machines that would be difficult and costly to change. Many activities exhibit that inertia, and they pose a problem that sociologists have been interested in for many years: Which elements of a society or culture are most likely to change? William Fielding Ogburn, for instance, proposed sixty years ago that material culture (screw threads) changed more quickly than social organization, and that the resultant "lag" could be problematic for human society.

A final consequence: The existence of culture makes it possible for people to plan their own lives. We can plan most easily for a known future, in which the major organizational features of society turn out to be what we expected them to be and what we made allowances for in our planning. We need, most importantly, to predict the actions of other people and of the organizations that consist of their collective actions. Culture makes those actions, individual and collective, more predictable than they would otherwise be. People in traditional societies may not obey in every detail the complex marriage rules held out to them, but those rules supply a sufficiently clear guide for men and women to envision more or less accurately when they will marry, what resources will be available to them when they do, and how the course of their married life will proceed. . . .

In modern industrial societies, workers can plan their careers better when they know what kinds of work situations they will find themselves in and what their rights and obligations at various ages and career stages will be. Few people can make those predictions successfully in this country any more, which indicates that cultural understandings do not always last the twenty or thirty years necessary for such predictability to be possible. When that happens, people do not know how to prepare themselves for their work lives and do not receive the benefits of their earlier investments in hard work. People who seemed to be goofing off or acting irrationally, for example, sometimes make windfall profits as the work world comes to need just those combinations of skills and experiences that they acquired while not following a "sensible" career path. As technical and organizational innovations make new skills more desirable, new career lines open up that were not and could not have been predicted ten years earlier. The first generation of computer programmers benefited from that kind of good luck, as did the first generation of drug researchers, among others.

✦ 33 ✦

The Code of the Street

Elijah Anderson

The hard reality of the world of the street can be traced to the profound sense of alienation from mainstream society and its institutions felt by many poor inner-city black people, particularly the young. The code of the street is actually a cultural adaptation to a profound lack of faith in the police and the judicial system—and in others who would champion one's personal security.

Elijah Anderson distinguishes between two opposing cultures in the poor black community: the "decent" and the "street." He shows how this conflict pulls at the individual, making individual directions unpredictable to some extent.

From Elijah Anderson, *Code of the Street: Decency, Violence, and the Moral Life of the Inner City.* Copyright © 1999 by Elijah Anderson. Used by permission of W.W. Norton & Company, Inc.

Of all the problems besetting the poor inner-city black community, none is more pressing than that of interpersonal violence and aggression. This phenomenon wreaks havoc daily on the lives of community residents and increasingly spills over into downtown and residential middle-class areas. Muggings, burglaries, carjackings, and drug-related shootings, all of which may leave their victims or innocent bystanders dead, are now common enough to concern all urban and many suburban residents.

The inclination to violence springs from the circumstances of life among the ghetto poor—the lack of jobs that pay a living wage, limited basic public services (police response in emergencies, building maintenance, trash pickup, lighting, and other services that middle-class neighborhoods take for granted), the stigma of race, the fallout from rampant drug use and drug trafficking, and the resulting alienation and absence of hope for the future. Simply living in such an environment places young people at special risk of falling victim to aggressive behavior. Although there are often forces in the community that can counteract the negative influences—by far the most powerful is a strong, loving, "decent" (as inner-city residents put it) family that is committed to middle-class values—the despair is pervasive enough to have spawned an oppositional culture, that of "the street," whose norms are often consciously opposed to those of mainstream society. These two orientations—decent and street—organize the community socially, and the way they coexist and interact has important consequences for its residents, particularly for children growing up in the inner city. Above all, this environment means that even youngsters whose home lives reflect mainstream values—and most of the homes in the community do—must be able to handle themselves in a street-oriented environment.

This is because the street culture has evolved a "code of the street," which amounts to a set of informal rules governing interpersonal public behavior, particularly violence.[1] The rules prescribe both proper comportment and the proper way to respond if challenged. They regulate the use of violence and so supply a rationale allowing those who are inclined to aggression to precipitate violent encounters in an approved way. The

rules have been established and are enforced mainly by the street-oriented; but on the streets the distinction between street and decent is often irrelevant. Everybody knows that if the rules are violated, there are penalties. Knowledge of the code is thus largely defensive, and it is literally necessary for operating in public. Therefore, though families with a decency orientation are usually opposed to the values of the code, they often reluctantly encourage their children's familiarity with it in order to enable them to negotiate the inner-city environment.

At the heart of the code is the issue of respect—loosely defined as being treated "right" or being granted one's "props" (or proper due) or the deference one deserves. However, in the troublesome public environment of the inner city, as people increasingly feel buffeted by forces beyond their control, what one deserves in the way of respect becomes ever more problematic and uncertain. This situation in turn further opens up the issue of respect to sometimes intense interpersonal negotiation, at times resulting in altercations. In the street culture, especially among young people, respect is viewed as almost an external entity, one that is hard-won but easily lost—and so must constantly be guarded. The rules of the code in fact provide a framework for negotiating respect. With the right amount of respect, individuals can avoid being bothered in public. This security is important, for if they are bothered, not only may they face physical danger, but they will have been disgraced or "dissed" (disrespected). Many of the forms dissing can take may seem petty to middle-class people (maintaining eye contact for too long, for example), but to those invested in the street code, these actions, a virtual slap in the face, become serious indications of the other person's intentions. Consequently, such people become very sensitive to advances and slights, which could well serve as a warning of imminent physical attack or confrontation.

The hard reality of the world of the street can be traced to the profound sense of alienation from mainstream society and its institutions felt by many poor inner-city black people, particularly the young. The code of the street is actually a cultural adaptation to a profound lack of faith in the police and the judicial system—and in others who would champion one's personal security. The police, for instance, are most often viewed as representing the dominant white society and as not caring to protect inner-city residents. When called, they may not respond, which is one reason many residents feel they must be prepared to take extraordinary measures to defend themselves and their loved ones against those who are inclined to aggression. Lack of police accountability has in fact been incorporated into the local status system: the person who is believed capable of "taking care of himself" is accorded a certain deference and regard, which translates into a sense of physical and psychological control. The code of the street thus emerges where the influence of the police ends and where personal responsibility for one's safety is felt to begin. Exacerbated by the proliferation of drugs and easy access to guns, this volatile situation results in the ability of the street-oriented minority (or those who effectively "go for bad") to dominate the public spaces.

NOTE

1. For a plausible description tracing the tradition and evolution of this code, with its implications for violence on the streets of urban America, see Fox Butterfield, *All God's Children* (New York: Knopf, 1995).

◆ 34 ◆

American Culture: Individualism and Community

David A. Karp

Although writers are correct to emphasize America's ethic of individualism, it would be wrong to think that cultural ideas about community and strict mandates about obligation to others have disappeared. A more accurate discription is that Americans believe in community and individualism at the same time. . . . It is no wonder that caregivers are confused about boundary lines. They are taught to believe simultaneously in the sanctity of the self and of attachments to others.

How can we be individualistic, pursuing individualistic goals, caring about our own lives, and simultaneously, caring for the welfare of others? This is the question of culture that David Karp asks in his book, *The Burden of Sympathy*, a study of individuals who take on the responsibility of caring for a member of the family who is mentally ill.

As individualistic as we are, there are a number of ways we exhibit commitment to other people in the public arena and in the privacy of our family life. Karp concludes that the family, a place where care and responsibility for others is almost taken for granted, needs even more recognition and support from the larger government and culture. "As strong as they are, the bonds of love, caring and commitment cannot by themselves sustain the family, besieged as it is by inimical cultural ideas and a government indifferent to its needs. . . . The fate of American families must be viewed as a national problem." Families have for a long time been alone in caring for each of its individuals; David Karp believes the family should not be expected to solve the crisis of individual members without greater outside support.

. . . Americans, I shall argue, are deeply conflicted about what they owe themselves and what they owe others. Our culture, far more than most, provides mixed messages and viewpoints about this central life issue. No single script or blueprint guides our judgments about proper feelings, thoughts, behaviors, and relationships. We listen to a pluralism of cultural voices dictating conflicting messages. It is a cacophony of moral relativism that some say defines the condition of postmodern America.[1]

POSTMODERNITY AND INDIVIDUALITY

All of social life involves a tension between freedom and constraint. Living in a society inevitably involves a trade-off between personal liberty and commitment to others. We judge some societies as immoral because they allow virtually no personal freedoms and others because they seem unable to constrain their members. For much of its history, American democracy provided a healthy balance between commitment and freedom. For a long time, the pursuit of personal happiness and individual goals seemed compatible with a set of cultural values that Americans willingly embraced and held them together as a nation. Now a group of sociologists who call themselves communitarians argue that the balance between freedom and constraint, between rights and responsibilities has fallen dangerously out of whack.[2] . . .

As communitarians read American history, traditional morality has been in a particularly

sharp tailspin over the last few decades. Although the "happy days" of the fifties also disenfranchised women and maintained sharp racial divisions, Americans still emphasized an ethic of personal responsibility during those years. Certainly the turmoil of the 1960s and 1970s began to significantly reshape the society as young people questioned virtually all significant American values and the institutions that produced them. The demand for greater "participatory democracy" during those years, [Amitai] Etzioni maintains, went too far and drifted into "rampant moral confusion and social anarchy."[3]

By the 1980s Americans had become deeply imbued with the idea that the society owed them all kinds of "rights" without any corresponding responsibilities. Etzioni shares a piece of data that crystallized for him the kind of damaging imbalance that had been created between rights and responsibilities. It was a finding that the majority of young people in America believed that they had the right to a jury trial while indicating at the same time that they would not want to serve on a jury![4] Indeed, by the Reagan years of the 1980s, Gordon Gekko, the protagonist in the movie *Wall Street* could passionately claim that "greed is good" for America. The country had clearly moved from a "we" to a "me" orientation to such a degree that the historian Christopher Lasch could describe America as a "culture of narcissism."[5] Etzioni comments on these transformations and the ethic of his communitarian philosophy.

> The eighties tried to turn vice into virtue by elevating the unbridled pursuit of self-interest and greed to the level of a social virtue. It turned out that the *economy* could thrive (at least for a while) if people watched out only for themselves. . . . But it has become evident that a *society* cannot function well

given such self-centered, meistic orientations. It requires a set of do's and don'ts, a set of moral values, that guides people toward what is decent and encourages them to avoid that which is not.[6]

Other contemporary theorists sustain the same view, emphasizing the degree to which an ethic of "expressive individualism" minimizes persons' felt obligation to each other. Robert Bellah writes that "individualism lies at the very core of American culture. . . . We believe in the dignity, indeed the sacredness, of the individual."[7] Postmodern writers say that contemporary American society is defined by increasingly short-lived and superficial relationships, geographical mobility that diminishes our commitment to place, and a mass media that confronts us with multiple and contradictory points of view on nearly everything.[8] Zygmunt Bauman has described the "postmodern self" as composed of "momentary identities, identities 'for today', until further notice identities."[9] Such momentary and fluid identities, which are furthermore dedicated to self-enhancement, conspire to minimize our sense of responsibility to each other. Thus, the prevailing opinion of sociologists from the nineteenth century to the present seems to be that we may live in a world *with* others, but an ethic of individualism makes it increasingly difficult to live *for* others.

The kind of individualism decried by Etzioni and others is surely reflected in the cultural values underlying a number of sectors of the society. In the world of work, for example, at least for "white collar" workers, there has been, until recently, a kind of *quid pro quo*. Organizations provided long-term security and received, in turn, worker loyalty, commitment, and responsibility. Loyalty, responsibility, security, commitment. These are the binding features of social systems, the glue that sustains the bond between individuals and social institutions. Unhappily, America's emerging "postindustrial" economy seems to have fundamentally altered the meaning of work for many by eroding loyalty, commitment, and mutual responsibility between organizations and workers.[10] Critics of capitalism, however, would maintain that the negative effects of capitalism on human relationships are far more inclusive than those in the workplace. In a more general way, the values underpinning capitalism are evident in a large variety of face-to-face encounters.

Competition, for example, is one of the cornerstones of capitalism. Advocates of capitalism maintain that competition is a necessary ingredient in both maintaining organizational efficiency and motivating individuals. On the negative side, however, competition pits individuals against each other, diminishes trust, and generally dehumanizes relationships. Capitalism contributes to a culture of inauthenticity. In a society in which everything and everyone is evaluated by their profit potential, individuals are aware that they are constantly being manipulated, seduced, and conned by those who want to sell them or "take them." In a world held together by appearances and a tissue of illusions and deceptions, everyone becomes an enemy of sorts whose motives cannot be accepted at face value. In short, the abstract values of capitalism "trickle down" to everyday consciousness in a way that induces human beings to distrust and withdraw from each other. In contemporary America, characterized by a kind of hyperindividuality, the "choice" to care becomes problematic in a way that would have been unfathomable in simpler societies. Patricia Benner and Suzanne Gordon write that

> Caring thus becomes a free choice made by human beings who are depicted as rational choicemakers. These rational choicemakers can stand back and objectively choose whether or not to care for friends, loved ones, colleagues, or strangers. They are said to care because they "feel like it," and "get something out of it," just as they choose not to care if it "feels" inconvenient or doesn't feel good. This instrumental frame not only turns caring into a choice, it also transforms connectedness, responsiveness, and interdependence into signs of moral lapse or sources of embarrassment or shame.[11]

POSTMODERNITY AND COMMUNALITY

Although writers are correct to emphasize America's ethic of individualism, it would be wrong to think that cultural ideas about community and strict mandates about obligation to others have disappeared. A more accurate description is that Americans believe in community and individualism *at the same time*. We are provided scripts or narratives that stress both. The postmodern paradox is that we are expected to be committed both to ourselves and to others at the same time. This paradox is evident in a wide range of cultural stories, some of which celebrate connection and community and others that applaud individualism. It is no wonder that caregivers are confused about boundary lines. They are taught to believe simultaneously in the sanctity of the self and of attachments to others. The underlying tension of postmodernity is the urge of persons to be involved and uninvolved, connected and disconnected at the same time.

The coexisting tension between versions of individualism and commitment to others is nicely illustrated in Robert Wuthnow's book *Acts of Compassion.*[12] Although there are sharp differences between the requirements of full-time caring for desperately sick family members and the feelings of compassion that lead people to volunteer their time in soup kitchens and the like, Wuthnow's analysis turns on the coexistence of seemingly opposed cultural values. Data from surveys and personal interviews indicate that Americans are deeply involved in a range of charitable efforts. They give huge amounts of time and money to this "third sector" of the economy.[13] Moreover, his interviews indicate that large numbers of Americans express in word and deed a fundamental altruism that seems at odds with images of the United States as a place where people are interested *only* in their personal welfare. At the end of his first chapter, Wuthnow sets out an important research question. He asks, "How is it that we as a people are able to devote billions of hours to volunteer activities, to show care and compassion in so many ways to those around us, and still be a nation of individualists who pride ourselves on personal freedom, individual success, and the pursuit of self-interest?"[14] His answer is that we incorporate both sets of values into our thinking. It's not one or the other.

Other analyses point to countervailing cultural forces that blunt radical individualism, emphasizing as they do our connection to each other. For example, in her book *Misery and Company: Sympathy in Everyday Life* Candace Clark describes, documents, and analyzes the deep cultural roots of compassion and sympathy.[15] Clark's book catalogues the cultural rules that surround the expression and the acceptance of sympathy. She persuasively maintains that sympathy is an integral part of the glue that holds a culture together. Clark shows that sympathy rules are well elaborated and clearly understood in the United States. Properly socialized persons know when and how much sympathy to extend in a wide array of circumstances. Sympathy is to be extended to persons, who through no fault of their own, face "bad luck" situations. In the wide array of such circumstances we know that the expression of too much or too little sympathy will mark us as deviant. Moreover, she argues that there are "sympathy entrepreneurs" who are constantly engaged in an enterprise to expand the circumstances for which sympathy is rightly expressed. The Hallmark card company, for example, has a significant investment in shaping the cultural norms surrounding the expression of sympathy.

Clark's work testifies to the fact that while we elevate the self, we also expect moral persons to maintain certain commitments. Even as postmodernity fosters the ascendancy of the self, we retain strong cultural convictions that we owe others sympathy, commitment, and caring. This is not to say that individuals are disingenuous when they feel compassion for another, when their heart goes out to them. That their feelings of compassion are socially profiled does not make them any less real. The social origin of all feelings does not diminish their reality because, as Russell Jacoby puts it, "the social does not [simply] 'influence' the private, it dwells within it."[16] Even those feelings that we think arise from the deepest preserves of our individual hearts and souls arise from society. Of all such feelings that might engage our attention here, love deserves special mention. Americans' conception of romantic love demonstrates our simultaneous yearnings for connection and separation.

The advice columns of daily newspapers, television programming, and popular fiction all indicate the extent to which the depth and quality of our intimate ties occupy our time and thoughts. Even in the context of the sort of individualism that pushes us away from each other, our attitudes about love reveal how much we want to care for others and to be cared about. We all expect to, "fail" in love and from early adolescence on we wait for that moment when "that old black magic has us in its spell." The "romantic ideal" is celebrated in music, art, cinema, and literature.[17] One particularly thriving industry capitalizes on our love of love, our need for intimacy, and our wish for total, timeless commitment. Although romance novels do not appear on the *New York Times* bestseller lists, their sales easily match those of other bestsellers. In 1988, Harlequin books, one of the largest publishers of romance novels, sold 202 million books, a rate of 550,000 per day.[18] Perhaps, though, such sales figures are evidence that we rarely find the intimacy we seek, that, as another popular song put it a while back, millions or people are desperately "looking for love in all the wrong places."

It may not be an exaggeration to say that love has become a social problem of sorts in America. The difficulties in establishing the connections we dearly wish for are affirmed by a trip to any local bookstore. The shelves in the psychology and "self-help" sections are routinely filled with titles promising formulas for the right ways and places to find love. Thomas McNight's and Robert Phillips's *Love Tactics* provides "effective techniques for winning over or getting back the one you love." Susan Page promises to answer the question *If I'm So Wonderful Why Am I Still Single?* Straight to the point of this chapter, Jordan and Margaret Paul's book speaks about the quintessentially American danger that, in finding love, we might lose ourselves. Their book is entitled *Do I Have to Give Up Me to be Loved by You?* Apparently, the problem of finding and maintaining love is greater for women than for men. On the same shelves you can find Susan Kelly's *Why Men Stray, Why Men Stay.* There are, however, no comparable books explaining to men how to recognize a "commitment-phobic" woman before she breaks your heart.

The cultural imagery of romantic love provides one essential "vocabulary of motives" that emphasizes the goals, albeit hard to realize, of caring and commitment.[19] Religious vocabularies of love and commitment provide another set of caring ideals. A religious ethic teaches us to love our neighbors as we love ourselves. To be kind, giving, altruistic, unselfish, and caring in all our relationships, but especially toward those less fortunate than ourselves, is a bedrock message of all religious groups. In America, a place

with more churches and synagogues per capita than any society on earth, the idea is promoted at least once a week to millions of people that it is surely their duty to care for their families, but also for the "family of man." Although Americans seem to have far more celebrities than moral heroes, we do revere Jesus Christ, Mother Teresa, and Martin Luther King as historical figures whose compassion deserves emulation. The parable of the Good Samaritan remains a religious/cultural story that reminds us of our responsibilities to others and of the redemptive potential of human compassion.

A related language of spirituality also stresses commitment and connection. More than ever, Americans seem to be on a "collective search for identity."[20] Now, at the millennium, those millions of people browsing the psychology and self-help sections of the bookstore are just aisles away from the spirituality section where they find inspiration and instruction in their search for self. Although the search for self has, by definition, an individualistic motif to it—it is, after all, a search for *self*—seekers often find inspiration in Eastern religious texts that preach a communitarian message. It is that we can discover our selves only through connection with others. Millions of Americans are trying to incorporate into their lives the spiritual message that all things and people are part of a seamless web, that independence is an illusion, and that spiritual enlightenment and happiness depend less on self-reliance than on mutual alliances. In a message that contradicts our notion of rugged individualism, we learn that selflessness is the only route to self-realization. It seems safe to conclude that people are drawn to spiritual, religious, and communitarian messages because they have an inchoate feeling that a life committed to self-enhancement has not been a recipe for satisfaction and happiness.

Let me offer one more example that illustrates our longing to embrace a more communal and caring ethic. For over a year, a book entitled *Tuesdays with Morrie* topped the bestseller lists.[21] The book touches me in a very particular way since I knew Morrie Schwartz, whose death the book chronicles. Morrie was special because he was able to turn his dying process from Lou Gehrig's disease into a celebration of love, connection, and community. When he learned of his terminal illness, Morrie did not withdraw from the world, as is the usual case. Rather, he created a community in his home filled with family and many friends, drawn to his bedside by Morrie's extraordinary openness and humanity, ever as his death relentlessly approached.[22] Morrie's death mirrored his life. Both his personal life and public teachings as a sociology professor centered on the importance of community and care. The millions of people who learned of Morrie on Ted Koppel's *Nightline* and subsequently have read about him are moved by his story because of what they already suspect, but often cannot act on—the route to self-discovery and personal fulfillment is through community and commitment.

The cultural languages of religion, love, and spirituality incline; Americans toward relationships of caring and commitment instead of self-absorption. In one realm of our lives, however, these messages are hardly necessary. Whatever influence the ethic of individualism has had in directing the *public* lives of Americans, a modified set of cultural expectations circumscribes the *private* realm of the family. Although ideas about self-expression and a life dedicated to self-enhancement have surely influenced the American family, it is the one institution that has been relatively insulated and exempted from the widely shared belief that one should consider one's own welfare before that of any social group. Moreover, if the bonds of blood are thought to supersede an individual's wishes and needs, this is most especially true for women.

In a culture otherwise dedicated to expressive individualism, women—mothers in particular—often measure their morality through an ethic of care and a willingness to subordinate self-interest to the greater good of the family. The privatizing and "engendering" of care within the family is not a cultural accident. It is the structural analogue of America's *political decision* not to bear responsibility for all the groups and individuals in need of care. In contrast to Scandinavian societies, for example, that have chosen to place the responsibility for the welfare of individuals squarely within the domain of government, the United States is groping for some consistency in the way that the poor, the ill, and the dispossessed should be cared for. As a society, we cannot agree whether individuals ought to care for themselves,

whether it is primarily the family's responsibility, or whether it is ultimately society's duty to care for the less fortunate. Our economy is mixed, our cultural motives are mixed, our social sentiments are mixed, and, consequently, many of us are mixed up.

TAKING CARE: WHOSE PROBLEM IS IT ANYWAY?

The way that the sixty people interviewed for this study tried to answer the question "What do I owe to a mentally ill family member?" cannot be separated from the way American society, as embodied in its social programs, has decided what it owes to its members in all kinds of trouble; whether or not it will care for those who, for whatever reason, cannot care for themselves. The caregiving difficulties faced by individuals on a daily basis are intimately connected with the political decisions about who deserves help and care and what institutions will be set up to provide it. Indeed, the most heated policy debates in the United States are about care. What kinds of government provisions will be made for Americans beneath the poverty line? What kind of welfare support will be provided for our unemployed? What shall we do to help our homeless? What kind of medical benefits will we extend to the elderly? How much aid shall we provide to single mothers with dependent children? And so on.

The social structures we create are a reflection of our cultural values. It is, therefore, not terribly surprising that our society, rooted in the cherished values of rational self-interest and profit maximization, has opted not to care very much for its citizens. It's my personal judgment that, although America's version of capitalism has produced unbelievable wealth for some, we are in a period of unparalleled governmental uncharitability. In the same society that pays certain athletes up to $250,000 a week to hit baseballs, more than 25 percent of the children in America go to bed hungry.[23] Rather than being appalled that less than 1 percent of the population owns between 20 and 25 percent of all wealth in America, such concentration of income, stocks, bonds, and real estate in the hands of so few is often applauded as reflecting the glory of a free-market economy.[24] Al, a custodian and one of the people I interviewed for *Speaking of Sadness*, viscerally understands marginality and its consequences. In explaining his emotional difficulties, he told me

> A big thing about depression in the United States is a lack of a sense of community . . . we aren't a people. We are a collective . . . and nobody feels like they owe anyone. . . . It's like a tough shit society. You know, if you're homeless, tough shit. If you get AIDS, tough shit. They say in England "I'm all right, Jack." You know, "I've got mine, Jack." And to that degree I find the United States a pretty uncivilized society. There is just a dreadful shallowness that promotes sociopathic thinking in even normal people.

To use Al's indelicate, but accurate phrase, we need to ask just how a "tough-shit" society affects the architecture of the American family. The family, like every institution in a society, mirrors broad cultural values and is deeply shaped by them. If a society has made its choice not to step in when a person needs help, the burden placed on family members to pick up the slack is dramatically increased. At this point in our history, we have decided that when a person is troubled and somehow cannot manage life, it is up to family members to struggle with the problem as best they can. We have privatized human problems by expecting families to solve them, largely out of public view. It is an extraordinary burden to place on a few individuals whose culture also provides mixed messages about commitment to self and to others. Reliance on the family creates a kind of cultural double whammy. Family members are expected to carry the moral burden of being primary caregivers in a culture that is, at the least, ambivalent about caring. They need to care enough to avoid the stigma of abandoning injured kin, but cannot care so much that they compromise their own aspirations and identities. . . .

In recent years, we have increasingly heard the traditional values of personal responsibility and self-reliance invoked as the basis for reducing the role of government in caring for needy citizens.[25] Such arguments are more easily made when the family is seen as the primary safety net for people in personal crisis. It's easier to say that individuals who are dispossessed, sick, or otherwise needy should be primarily responsible for themselves when their families will be there to care should their circumstances utterly deteriorate. Thus, whenever politicians and others talk the language of strengthening family values, a goal that seems so completely laudable, a less visible, but pernicious agenda is to push off onto the family certain obligations that arguably belong to the government. . . .

CARING FOR THE FAMILY

Although people across the political spectrum agree that the American family needs strengthening, the discussion is hampered by disagreements on what forms of family life are "normal" and "desirable." Rather than focusing on concrete proposals for supporting the multiple forms of family life that now exist in the United States, the conversation too often bogs down in disputes about the meaning of "family values" and the "appropriate" structure of family life. Whatever one's beliefs about family life, bolstering the family will require far more than lofty rhetoric about values and morality. It is too easy to blame the fragility of American families on the failure of individuals to acquire the "right" values. The bigger problem is that families have been abandoned by society to solve, on their own, the increasingly complex problems of their individual members. In applying a version of rugged individualism to the family, we have increasingly isolated an institution whose health requires the nourishment of public, social, and legislative support.

Societies that emphasize individualism accomplish a kind of social sleight of hand. When personal achievement is extolled above all else, those who fail are encouraged to believe that they have only themselves to blame. Victims of a system of institutionalized inequality are conned into blaming themselves for their state of affairs.[26] They suffer from a kind of false consciousness that prevents them from seeing how their fate is linked to society's failure in living up to the principles of democracy, fairness, and equality of opportunity. A similar blind spot leads us to blame families for their troubles. A few years ago, millions of people read John Bradshaw's claim that 96 percent of American families are "dysfunctional."[27] His message is that families are toxic environments and terribly hazardous to the health of their members. To be sure, many awful things happen within families. The question, though, is how best to understand why families unravel. Shall we chalk it up exclusively to the behaviors of bad people? Is the family somehow intrinsically flawed? Or might there be something wrong with the cultural soil in which families grow, thrive, or increasingly dissemble?

As with most big and pressing questions, no one explanation will do. However, by now, you will not be surprised by my perspective on the matter. The privatization of the family and the corresponding expectation that it deal largely on its own with every member's problem, big and small, is unreasonable.[28] The family, like any system, will simply begin to break down when too much is demanded from it, when its caring capacity is reached. Expecting family members to care for each other in a society that shows so little care and regard for the family is a prescription for pathology. It is specious and wishful thinking that individuals operating within a society dedicated to rationality, free choice, and individual achievement will easily shuck off those values once in the privacy of their homes. No American institution escapes the logic of a market economy and it is far more likely "that considerations of self interest associated with the economy will serve as moral codes within the family than that the family will serve as a moral world capable of influencing behavior in the economy."[29]

In their book, *The War Against Parents*, Sylvia Hewlett and Cornell West argue that government support for families has badly eroded over the last thirty years.[30] Shortly after WWII, as veterans returned home, new mortgage loan programs, the policies of the Federal Housing Administration, and the massive federal funding of an interstate highway program encouraged home ownership in the suburbs. Jobs were plentiful, workers were protected by robust unions, and tax incentives favored the family. Beginning in the 1970s, profamily policies were increasingly replaced with pro-business policies and forms of "corporate welfare" that redirected government largesse away from people in need. My colleague Charles Derber, in a book aptly titled *Corporation Nation*, demolishes the fiction that American corporations are private enterprises. He writes that "as business leaders and politicians rhapsodize about the virtues of privatization, corporations have grown so dependent on public provision that the whole corporate system would collapse without it."[31] Through a range of government subsidies, loan guarantees, tax breaks, and tax loopholes "corporations collect more government handouts than all of the nation's poor combined."[32]

Earlier in this chapter I remarked on the writings of nineteenth-century theorists who were concerned with the weakening of social ties as societies modernized. Among them, a sociologist named Georg Simmel presciently argued that "a money economy and the dominance of the intellect are intrinsically connected."[33] In emerging capitalist economies, Simmel wrote, the individual increasingly "reacts with his head instead of his heart."[34] While Simmel's prediction generally rings true, we should not conclude that rationality thoroughly supersedes emotionality when it comes to caring for an ill family member. A more accurate description, based on the interviews in this book, is that family caregivers struggle to reconcile the conflicting demands of head and heart.

In this last chapter I have tried to understand, in terms of divergent cultural messages, the kind of ambivalence family members feel in drawing caregiving boundaries. Such ambivalence, I maintain, is predictable in a society that offers confusing messages about obligations to self and others, devalues caring work, privatizes family life, and increasingly withdraws structural support from a system already dramatically overloaded with obligations. Some observers are chagrined by the erosion of family life and find remarkable the sort of callousness that too often describes family relationships. What seems far more remarkable to me is the extraordinary reservoir of love, caring, and connection that holds families together, even at a time when family life is so meagerly supported. The data presented throughout this book testify that habits of the heart are exceedingly hard to break. However, as strong as they are, the bonds of love, caring, and commitment cannot by themselves sustain the family, besieged as it is by inimical cultural ideas and a government indifferent to its needs.

The fate of American families must be viewed as a national problem, and, as such, it is the responsibility of federal and state governments to intervene in revitalizing troubled families. Just as government neglect has undermined the infrastructure of the family, it will take substantial federal support to reverse long-term processes that have been contrary to the health of families and, thus, to the well-being of us all. Just as "globalization" increasingly illustrates that we live in a small and organically interconnected world, it is critical to realize that the fates of societies and families are intertwined. A coherent national policy must be constructed with the goal of saving families in trouble rather than standing by idly as they decay. Societies must care for and nourish families in order to ensure that parents, spouses, children, and siblings can extend compassionate care to each other during moments of vulnerability, crisis, and illness.

NOTES

1. Discussions of "postmodernity" dominate thinking in the humanities and social sciences these days. Although the term *postmodern* has been used in a variety of different ways that make precise definition difficult, I find Kenneth Gergen's discussion in his book *The Saturated Self: Dilemmas of Identity in Contemporary Life* (New York: Basic Books, 1991) helpful. Gergen describes the period prior to the rise of scientific thinking as *premodern*. In the premodern period religious ideas provided explanations for life's most basic mysteries. The modern period is associated with the rise of science, the scientific method, and the Newtonian idea that definitive laws about the universe could be discovered. The Newtonian imagery of modernity is that the universe is like a giant machine whose mechanisms could ultimately be understood through rational investigation. Modernity, in other words, is characterized by a belief in the possibility of discovering truth. In our current postmodern period, the notion that there are discoverable and absolute truths has come under attack. One of Gergen's chapters is titled "Truth in Trouble." Postmodernists argue that all claims to truth are really rooted in ideological ideas that, under close examination, can be "deconstructed." In the postmodern world, characterized by an explosion of information technologies, people are confronted with multiple and contradictory messages about virtually everything. In this way, postmodernity replaces faith in science with a radical relativism that undermines any claims to truth. Gergen writes that "under postmodern conditions, persons exist in a state of continuous construction and reconstruction; it is a world where anything goes that can be negotiated. Each reality of self gives way to reflexive questioning, irony, and ultimately the playful probing of yet another reality" (p. 7).

2. The communitarian ethos is spelled out in A. Etzioni, *The Spirit of Community: The Reinvention of American Society* (New York: Simon and Schuster, 1993) and in A. Etzioni (ed.), *The Essential Communitarian Reader* (Lanham, MD: Rowman and Littlefield Publishers, 1998).

3. Etzioni, 1993, ibid., p. 24.

4. Etzioni, 1998, op. cit., p. xvi.

5. C. Lasch, *The Culture of Narcissism* (New York: W. W. Norton, 1978).

6. Etzioni, 1993, op. cit., p. 24.

7. R. Bellah et al., *Habits of the Heart: Individualism and Commitment in American Life* (Berkeley: University of California Press, 1985), p. 142.

8. See, for example, S. Pfohl, *Death at the Parasite Cafe* (New York: St. Martin's, 1992) and S. Gottschalk, "Uncomfortably numb: Countercultural impulses in the postmodern era," *Symbolic Interaction* 16 (1993): 351–78.

9. Z. Bauman, *Mortality, Immortality, and Other Life Strategies* (Stanford, CA: Stanford University Press, 1992), p. 167.

10. Recent critiques of a national and global corporate ascendancy and its impact on the nature of work can be found in C. Derber, *Corporation Nation* (New York: St. Martin's Press, 1998) and R. Sennett, *The Corrosion of Character* (New York: W. W. Norton, 1998).

11. P. Benner and S. Gordon, "Caring practice," in S. Gordon, P. Benner, and N. Noddings (eds.), *Caregiving: Readings in Knowledge, Practice, and Politics* (Philadelphia: University of Pennsylvania Press, 1996), p. 50.

12. R. Wuthnow, *Acts of Compassion: Caring for Others and Helping Ourselves* (Princeton, NJ: Princeton University Press, 1991).

13. See P. Schervish, *Taking Giving Seriously* (Indianapolis: Indiana University Center on Philanthropy, 1993) and P. Schervish, *Care and Community in Modern Society* (San Francisco: Jossey-Bass, 1995).

14. Wuthnow, op. cit., p. 17.

15. C. Clark, *Misery and Company: Sympathy in Everyday Life* (Chicago: University of Chicago Press, 1997).

16. R. Jacoby, *Social Amnesia* (Boston: Beacon Press, 1975); quoted in L. Rubin, *Intimate Strangers: Men and Women Together* (New York: HarperCollins, 1983), p. 4.

17. The romantic love ideal, formulated in France and Germany during the twelfth century, filtered down from the nobility to the lower classes over the centuries. In its pure form the ideal of romantic

love involves the notion that there is only one person in all the world we are meant to love.

18. C. Castano, "When Fairy Tales Grow Up" (Unpublished senior honor's thesis: Boston College, 1990).

19. C. W. Mills, "Situated actions and vocabularies of motive," in J. Manis and B. Meltzer (eds.), *Symbolic Interaction* (Boston: Allyn and Bacon, 1972).

20. See O. Klapp, *The Collective Search for Identity* (New York: Holt, Rinehart, and Winston, 1969).

21. M. Albom. *Tuesdays with Morrie* (New York: Doubleday, 1997).

22. It is interesting to observe that the kind of public, community death that gained Morrie such attention at the end of his life was the norm for the way people died during the Middle Ages. The social historian Phillipe Aries points out that people in the late Middle Ages and the Renaissance period actively participated in their own dying process. Dying was an open, public, and collective community process. See P. Aries, "The reversal of death: Changes in attitudes toward death in western societies," in D. Stannard (ed.), *Death in America* (Philadelphia: University of Pennsylvania Press, 1975). Death has shifted from being a moral, religious, community event to a technological event. In North America, most especially, "death is a technical matter, a failure of technology in rescuing the body." See E. Cassell, "Dying in technological society," in P. Steinfels and R. Veatch (eds.), *Death Inside Out* (New York: Harper and Row, 1975), p. 31.

23. See C. Derber, op. cit., p. 12.

24. See C. Derber, ibid., p. 12.

25. For example, W. Bennett, *The Book of Virtues: A Treasury of Great Moral Stories* (New York: Simon and Schuster, 1993).

26. See W. Ryan, *Blaming the Victim* (New York: Vintage Books, 1976).

27. For example, J. Bradshaw, *Coming Home: Reclaiming and Championing Your Inner Child* (New York: Doubleday, 1992).

28. Years ago the sociologists Talcott Parsons and Rene Fox predicted that the "nuclear family" would not be able to bear the burdens placed on it as societies modernized. See T. Parsons and R. Fox, "Illness, therapy, and the modern urban American family," *Journal of Social Issues* 8 (1952): 31–44.

29. Wolfe, op. cit., p. 54.

30. S. Hewlett and C. West, *The War Against Parents* (New York: Chapters Publications, 1998).

31. Derber, 1998, op. cit., p. 156.

32. This statement comes from Ralph Nader and was quoted in Derber, ibid., p. 156.

33. G. Simmel, "The metropolis and mental life," in K. Wolff (ed.), *The Sociology of Georg Simmel* (Glencoe, IL: The Free Press, 1950), p. 411.

34. G. Simmel, ibid., p. 410.

◆ 35 ◆

Culture and Moral Freedom

Alan Wolfe

. . . moral freedom is as inevitable as it is impossible. Once people are free to choose their cars and their candidates, they will not for long be satisifed with letting others determine for them the best way to live. As correct as critics of America's moral condition are to insist on the need for shared understandings of the moral life, it is better, given moral freedom's inevitability, to think of it as a challenge to be met rather than as a condition to be cured.

Freedom is a word we casually throw around. Often, we do not critically evaluate what it is we are speaking about. Often, we do not examine the consequences of freedom in relation to society and its culture. Political freedom, religious freedom, freedom of speech, freedom of the press—these are freedoms with which we seem to have some familiarity. But what about "moral freedom"? Is this a different level of freedom? Is this even a possibility in society? Or, as Alan Wolfe asks, is it even impossible to prevent in American society?

This selection is from a book that summarizes a study done by Wolfe and his associates concerning the relationship of moral freedom—a consequence of the 1960s—to American culture. It is a very big step for a society to encourage moral freedom—it almost seems contradictory to the existence of society. How much must a culture form society's citizens? How much moral consensus must there be for society to exist? Even our economic system depends on a moral system to a great extent.

Increasingly, this is the issue that is dividing America's politics, religion, education, and family life. Some worry about moral freedom; some see moral freedom as the epitome of what freedom must be. If one of the central values in the American culture becomes moral freedom, then can there even be a working culture?

Most people, throughout most of the world, have lived under conditions in which their morality was defined for them. Now, for the first time in human history, significant numbers of individuals believe that people should play a role in defining their own morality as they contemplate their proper relationship to God, to one another, and to themselves. . . .

The twenty-first century will be the century of moral freedom. Moral freedom has become so ubiquitous in America that we sometimes forget how pathbreaking it is. We simply no longer live in a world in which women are encouraged to stay home and raise their children, government's

Excerpts from *Moral Freedom: The Search for Virtue in a World of Choice* by Alan Wolfe. Copyright © 2001 by Alan Wolfe. Used by permission of W.W. Norton & Company, Inc.

word is to be trusted, teachers can discipline as well as instruct, the police enforce laws against what is considered immoral conduct, and religious leaders are quick to offer—and their parishioners are quick to accept—unambiguous prescriptions for proper Christian conduct. Now women will want for themselves a greater say in how they ought to live, employees will look for jobs that give them some say in the work they do, churchgoers will ask questions and not just receive answers, young people will manage their own sexuality, and political leaders will take moral instruction from the voters rather than the other way around.

Although political freedoms are enormously important, they are restricted to one sphere of human activity: obtaining and exercising political power. The same is true of economic freedom, which, by definition, is limited to such essential (but essentially mundane) matters such as the buying and selling of commodities. Moral freedom involves the sacred as well as the profane; it is freedom over the things that matter most. The ultimate implication of the idea of moral freedom is not that people are created in the image of a higher authority. It is instead that any form of higher authority has to tailor its commandments to the needs of real people.

Moral freedom is so radical an idea, so disturbing in its implications, that it has never had much currency among any but a few of the West's great moral theorists. Even those who made passionate arguments in defense of freedom in general did not extend their argument to moral freedom. Indeed, the common position among most Western thinkers has been to argue the necessity for moral constraint as a precondition for freedom in all other aspects of life.

It has long been recognized that economic freedom assumes a preexisting moral consensus. For if there are no binding moral rules—if individuals are as free to drop or add their moral beliefs with the same alacrity with which they can buy or sell stocks—then all social relations, including those of free exchange, will be threatened. What, in the absence of binding moral rules, would prevent me from deciding, after you had given me possession of the car I agreed to buy from you, that I ought to keep my money after all? As the philosopher David Hume pointed out, exchange premised upon the notion

of a contract requires prior agreement to a moral ideal—in this case, the existence of a promise—that cannot itself be treated contractually.[1] . . .

[T]he late-nineteenth-century sociologist Emile Durkheim argued that society could not exist without morality; indeed, he wrote, society *was* morality. Durkheim called the moral rules that delineate what is deemed permissible and what is considered out-of-bounds the "collective conscience." According to theorists of republican virtue, both order and liberty were possible because humans listened to their conscience instead of following their desires. In the modern world, where social interactions are far more voluminous and impersonal, society becomes possible only to the degree to which the "no" that the conscience speaks to the individual becomes generalized to society as a whole. Ideally, the collective conscience would act in an almost mystical way; we would imbibe its teachings in ways that would never make us quite realize how coercive society can be. But if that failed, there was always the state—an institution sometimes painted by Durkheim in magisterial colors—to back morality up.[2]

If there was anything of a consensus in an area of thought as disputatious as moral theory, it was the notion that moral freedom was an impossible idea. For any one of a number of representative thinkers, a term like "moral freedom" would have seemed an oxymoron. Timeless, transcendental, absolute—morality stood in the sharpest possible contrast to the realm of freedom, which was transient, inconsistent, and dependent upon mere circumstance. Even when Friedrich Nietzsche launched his attack on morality's claims for privileged status, he hardly did so in the name of moral freedom (although many of his twentieth-century disciples would nonetheless interpret him that way). Thinkers might disagree on the extent to which people ought to be free, with conservatives preferring less and liberals advocating more. But almost no one, conservative or liberal, disagreed with the proposition that some ways of life could never be free. At the dawn of the twentieth century, moral freedom remained as strange an idea as it had been since freedom first became an object of modern longing. . . .

There are at least two reasons that it took so long for the idea of moral freedom to become a powerful force in American life. One is that many forms of freedom also took a long time to come to fruition. A significant number of Americans, so long as there was slavery, had no freedom at all, and even after their emancipation, many African-Americans were denied the most elementary forms of freedom until halfway through the twentieth century. The first great statement from the U.S. Supreme Court defending free speech was made in 1925, and that was made in dissent.[3] The first decision protecting the religious freedom of unpopular religious groups like the Jehovah's Witnesses did not come until 1940, a time when the court had in front of it the horrors of societies that denied basic liberties to their citizens.[4] And when the Supreme Court finally spoke about sex—"a great and mysterious force in human life," which was "a subject of absorbing interest" and "one of the vital problems of human interest," as the court put it—it did so in the context of upholding a conviction for violating obscenity laws.[5] A society that for the first century and a half of its existence had barely gotten used to the idea that people ought to be free to express their beliefs, practice their faith, vote, demonstrate for their rights, and read what they wanted was far from ready to accord people the freedom to construct their lives as best as they saw fit.

A second reason that moral freedom came so late is the absence of a political constituency in favor of the idea. Conservatives in American history had spoken on behalf of authority, not freedom, and when the subject was moral authority, their defense of established institutions and practices was even more vehement. More important, the left—which sees itself as in the forefront of social change—has historically been as uncomfortable with the idea of moral freedom as the right. Groups denied freedom by American customs and practices were, like conventional feminists, less interested in challenging what freedom meant than they were in obtaining it in its political form. Movements to free the slaves, and later on movements to secure equality for the descendants of slaves, generally based themselves on the most conservative of moral sources: the dignity of work, faith in God, respect for human dignity, the autonomy guaranteed by property. Leaders of America's labor movement had little sympathy for Marxism, but they shared with Marxism its contempt for

libertinism, which they associated with bourgeois decadence; one could hardly find a morally more respectable rebel than Samuel Gompers, the founder of the American Federation of Labor. To the degree that American progressivism had a moral vision, it had much in common with sterner forms of Protestant restraint.[6] The New Deal may or may not have been economically radical—historians are still debating that question—but there is no doubt that it was morally conventional.[7] When Franklin Roosevelt in 1941 announced the four freedoms—of speech, of worship, from want, from fear—moral freedom was not among them. Moral freedom could not take root in American life because so few significant constituencies were willing to advocate on its behalf.

It was the challenge presented to the United States by nations with no commitments to freedom at all that ironically proved the value of a certain skepticism toward moral freedom. How, one wonders, could the Nazis in Germany—and later the Communists in the Soviet Union—ever have been stopped if we had allowed every individual to decide for himself or herself whether anti-Semitism was truly evil or whether communism was the wave of the future? World War II and the Cold War illustrate the wisdom of Durkheim's emphasis on the importance of coordinating our actions. What greater proof does one need for the proposition that achieving collective moral ends—economic security for citizens at home, respect for all regardless of religion and race, resistance in the face of totalitarian aggression, and the preservation of world peace—can be ensured only by people who are not free to choose their moral ends however they so desire?

When the generation that survived the Depression and fought World War II finally witnessed a more normal world, it puts its faith not in a vision of individuals as free choosers of their own moral beliefs, but in miracles of social cooperation: a national highway system, the continuance of Social Security, modified economic planning, and a large military establishment mobilized in the hopes of preserving the peace. Security, not freedom, was the watchword of this generation. That its conformity became something of a cliché does not detract from the fact that, morally speaking, this was a generation that longed for the tried-and-true: the Pledge of Allegiance, the suburban home, the picket fence, the gray flannel suit, Boy Scouts and Girl Scouts, prayer in school, the stay-at-home mom.

The postwar generation was probably the last generation to act as if moral freedom was an unthinkable idea. These were people who may not have read Kant and Durkheim and may not have known much about the history of republican virtue, but the lessons taught by those thinkers were second nature to them. No one had to instruct them in the fact that liberty and restraint were dependent on each other. The principles that told them the proper way to act stressed the importance of delayed gratification, binding vows, sexual fidelity, faith in God, sobriety, loyalty to country, duty to others. We know, of course, because the novels and social criticism of the 1950s told us so, that not everyone lived up to those ideals. But we .also know that even moral codes honored in the breach are still moral codes. If in eighteenth-and nineteenth-century European philosophy moral freedom was an idea rarely thought, in the first half of twentieth-century America moral freedom was an idea rarely practiced. Had you asked most Americans in 1950 whether they lived in a free country, they would have quickly answered in the positive. And had you asked them whether this meant that they could pretty much live in any manner that best seemed to fit their inclinations—that they could join or quit any church at will, enter into divorce as frequently as they entered into marriage, join or not join the armed forces as they saw fit, and pick the school that, in their opinion, would best educate their children—they would not have understood the question.

ENTER THE 1960s

All this changed in the 1960s and—as the journalist David Frum has recently pointed out—the 1970s.[8] For the first time in American history a number of thinkers began to take the idea of moral freedom seriously, and enough people paid them attention to launch a significant challenge against moral authority. The result was a radical transformation in the moral and theological framework of American society. Reviewing the entire history of religion in America since the first Spanish and French settlements, the historian Sidney Ahlstrom concluded that "only in the 1960s would it become apparent that the Great Puritan Epoch in American history had come to an end."[9] If nothing is so powerful as an idea whose time has come, then the idea of moral freedom, when it finally came, was powerful enough, at least for a time, to sweep all before it.

Sheer, unapologetic, fulsome praise of moral freedom characterized the writings of Norman O. Brown, Wilhelm Reich, Herbert Marcuse, Charles Reich, and other theorists of 1960s cultural liberation. What had once appeared to earlier theorists of freedom as the necessary restraint that made all other freedoms possible appeared to them as repression pure and simple. Marcuse's *Eros and Civilization* (1955) and Brown's *Life Against Death* (1959) were quintessential expressions of this point of view. Freud was for both men a weapon to be aimed against all those thinkers for whom a preexisting moral order was held to be a requirement of human freedom. . . .

The moment moral freedom emerged out of the turmoil of the 1960s, there also developed a sustained reiteration of all those ideas central to the Western tradition that emphasized the absurdity of the idea. "Every culture," wrote Philip Rieff, a University of Pennsylvania sociologist shocked by the 1960s, "is so constituted that there are actions one cannot perform; more precisely, would dread to perform."[10] To attack culture was to attack all those constraints on human instincts that made civilization—and, with it, freedom in any meaningful sense—possible. . . .

So broad is the current complaint against moral freedom in America that it is no longer the sole property of theological and political conservatives. Whether expressed in the data-driven language of social science, through the nostalgic lens of the historian, or in the message of communitarianism, there is a widespread feeling that the legacy of the 1960s is corrosive of the American social fabric.[11] True, the excesses of the 1960s, especially its rampant drug culture and free-floating sexuality, have been somewhat tamed, but the underlying message of putting one's own needs first has survived. Disrespectful of established authority, cut off from tradition, unwilling to focus on the long term, Americans, we have been told by a cacophony of different voices, live with moral freedom and experience, in a lack of close attachments to family and faith, the painful results. . . .

Finding the balance between institutional authority and moral freedom will never be easy. Critics point out that some institutions, such as the United States military, may not be able to carry out their most important functions if they become too sensitive to the demands of women for greater equality and autonomy.[12] One can only wonder whether individuals dedicated to moral freedom can find the resources to stick with the not always pleasurable tasks of raising children and committing oneself to a spouse. Individuals intent on finding a sympathetic physician may ignore the advice of someone who knows best what makes them sick. Like alcohol, too much moral freedom can be a dangerous thing.

Yet in a time of moral freedom, no institution will be able to stick its head in the sand and pretend that the people who approach it for advice and guidance can be treated as supplicants. Morality has long been treated as if it were a fixed star, sitting there far removed from the earthly concerns of real people, meant to guide them to the true and the beautiful. In the contemporary world, however, people experience in their own lives many situations for which traditional conceptions of morality offer little guidance: What do you do when the pursuit of one virtue, say honesty, conflicts with another, such as avoiding cruelty? Does the zealous application of any virtue, by the mere fact of its zealousness, become a vice? How do you apply moral precepts to situations unforeseen by those religious and philosophical traditions developed for another time and place? Can seemingly unambiguous moral principles be capable of multifaceted interpretations? No matter how strong their religious and moral beliefs, nearly all people will encounter situations in which they feel the need to participate in interpreting, applying, and sometimes redefining the rules meant to guide them. Are they somehow less moral if they do? Telling them that they are will cut no ice with a gay couple determined to legalize their union in an era of heterosexual divorce; women

who find that an early marriage stultifies their desire to become more autonomous later in life; or religious believers who find that the best way to express one's faith in God is to reject traditional denominations.

Because we can never know what freedom will bring in its wake, defenders of social order have never, at least at first, been comfortable with any of the forms taken by freedom in the modern world. Economic freedom did not create a hoped-for society of independent yeoman but a regime of mass consumption. Political freedom did not result in active and enlightened civic participation but in voter apathy and disinterest. In a similar way, moral freedom is highly unlikely to produce a nation of individuals exercising their autonomy with the serious and dispassionate judgment of an Immanuel Kant. Yet moral freedom is as inevitable as it is impossible. Once people are free to choose their cars and their candidates, they will not for long be satisfied with letting others determine for them the best way to live. As correct as critics of America's moral condition are to insist on the need for shared understandings of the moral life, it is better, given moral freedom's inevitability, to think of it as a challenge to be met rather than as a condition to be cured.

"I should have loved freedom, I believe, at all times, but in the times in which we live I am ready to worship it," wrote Alexis de Tocqueville at the end of *Democracy in America.* Those times were despotic ones, and Tocqueville's great fear was that the establishment of a government committed to equality under such conditions would "not only oppress men, but would eventually strip each of them of several of their highest qualities of humanity." Despite his misgivings, Tocqueville never became an enemy of democracy, because democracy, he knew, was a force that could not be stopped. "I am persuaded that all those who attempt in the ages upon which we are entering, to base freedom upon aristocratic privilege will fail; that all who attempt to draw and to retain authority within a single class will fail."[13] Like democracy, the arrival of moral freedom is bound to have consequences we will regret. But if we appreciate political and economic freedom, we will have to find a way to appreciate the moral freedom that cannot help but accompany it.

NOTES

1. David Hume, "An Inquiry Concerning Human Understanding," in *Essays: Moral, Political, Literary*, ed. T. H. Greene and T. H. Gorse (London: Longmans Green, 1875), 2:72–73.
2. For a helpful overview of Durkheim's writings in this area, see Robert N. Bellah, ed., *Emile Durkheim on Morality and Society* (Chicago: University of Chicago Press, 1973).
3. *Gitlow v. New York*, 268 U.S. 652 (1925).
4. *Cantwell v. Connecticut*, 310 U.S. 296 (1940).
5. *Roth v. U.S.*, 354 U.S. 476 (1957).
6. Robert Crundun, *Ministers of Reform: The Progressive's Achievement in American Civilization, 1889–1920*. (New York: Basic Books, 1982).
7. For a treatment of the question of how economically radical the New Deal was, see Alan Brinkley, *Liberalism and Its Discontents* (Cambridge, Mass.: Harvard University Press, 1998).
8. David Frum. *How We Got Here: The 70's, The Decade That Brought You Modern Life—for Better or Worse* (New York: Basic Books, 2000).
9. Sidney E. Ahlstrom, *A Religious History of the American People* (New Haven: Yale University Press, 1972), 8.
10. Philip Rieff, *The Feeling Intellect: Selected Writings,* ed. Jonathan Imber (Chicago: University of Chicago Press, 1990), 223.
11. For various examples of nostalgic treatments of this issue, see Ray Oldenburg, *The Great Good Place: Cafés, Coffee Shops, Community Centers, Beauty Parlors, General Stores, Bars, Hangouts, and How They Get You Through the Day* (New York: Paragon House, 1989); James Howard Kunstler, *The Geography of Nowhere: The Rise and Decline of America's Man-Made Landscape* (New York: Simon and Schuster,1993); Stephen L. Carter, *Civility: Manners, Morals, and the Etiquette of Democracy* (New York: Basic Books, 1998); Stephen L. Carter, *Integrity* (New York: Basic Books, 1996); Deborah Tannen, *The Argument Culture: Moving from Debate to Dialogue* (New York: Random House, 1998); Alan Ehrenhalt, *The Lost City: Discovering the Forgotten Virtues of Community in the Chicago of the 1950s* (New York: Basic Books, 1995); and Ray Suarez, *The Old Neighborhood: What We Lost in the Great Suburban Migration, 1966—1999* (New York: Free Press, 1999).
12. Stephanie Gutmann, *The Kinder, Gentler Military: Can America's Gender-Neutral Fighting Force Still Win Wars?* (New York: Scribners, 2000).
13. Alexis de Tocqueville, *Democracy in America*, ed. Phillips Bradley (New York: Knopf, 1966), 2:322.

36

The Cultural Dimension
of Globalization

Manfred B. Steger

As images and ideas can be more easily and rapidly transmitted from one place to another, they profoundly impact the way people experience their everyday lives. Today, cultural practices frequently escape fixed localities such as town and nation, eventually acquiring new meanings in interaction with dominant global themes.

Manfred Steger highlights with clarity and objectivity the trends of both globalization and localization. On the one hand we are creating a world culture; on the other, at the same time, people continue to belong to local and national cultures. Modernization may affect all of us, but modernization will be integrated into individual traditional cultures, and this will mean continued uniqueness.

Steger asks us to examine both the positives and negatives related to cultural globalization. He asks questions about culture that touch many of the issues that face all of us who care about our society's future and the future of the world: imperialism, assimilation, relativism, univerality, worldwide capitalism, nationalism, world peace and war, and ethnocentrism.

Even a very short introduction to globalization would be woefully inadequate without an examination of its cultural dimension. Cultural globalization refers to the intensification and expansion of cultural flows across the globe. Obviously, "culture" is a very broad concept; it is frequently used to describe the whole of human experience. In order to avoid the ensuing problem of overgeneralization, it is important to make analytical distinctions between aspects of social life. For example, we associate the adjective "economic" with the production, exchange, and consumption of commodities. If we are discussing the

From *Globalization: A Very Short Introduction*, by Manfred B. Steger, 2003. Permission by Oxford University Press (United Kingdom).

"political," we mean practices related to the generation and distribution of power in societies. If we are talking about the "cultural," we are concerned with the symbolic construction, articulation, and dissemination of meaning. Given that language, music, and images constitute the major forms of symbolic expression, they assume special significance in the sphere of culture.

The exploding network of cultural interconnections and interdependencies in the last decades has led some commentators to suggest that cultural practices lie at the very heart of contemporary globalization. Yet, cultural globalization did not start with the worldwide dissemination of rock 'n' roll, Coca-Cola, or football. As noted in Chapter 2, expansive civilizational exchanges are much older than modernity. Still, the volume and extent of cultural transmissions in the contemporary period have far exceeded those of earlier eras. Facilitated by the Internet and other new technologies, the dominant symbolic systems of meaning of our age—such as individualism, consumerism, and various religious discourses—circulate more freely and widely than ever before. As images and ideas can be more easily and rapidly transmitted from one place to another, they profoundly impact the way people experience their everyday lives. Today, cultural practices frequently escape fixed localities such as town and nation, eventually acquiring new meanings in interaction with dominant global themes. . . .

GLOBAL CULTURE: SAMENESS OR DIFFERENCE?

Does globalization make people around the world more alike or more different? This is the question most frequently raised in discussions on the subject of cultural globalization. A group of commentators we might call "pessimistic hyperglobalizers" argue in favour of the former. They suggest that we are not moving towards a cultural rainbow that reflects the diversity of the world's existing cultures. Rather, we are witnessing the rise of an increasingly homogenized popular culture underwritten by a Western "culture industry" based in New York, Hollywood, London, and Milan. As evidence for their interpretation, these commentators point to Amazonian Indians wearing Nike training shoes, denizens of the Southern Sahara purchasing Texaco baseball caps, and Palestinian youths proudly displaying their Chicago Bulls sweatshirts in downtown Ramallah. Referring to the diffusion of Anglo-American values and consumer goods as the "Americanization of the world," the proponents of this cultural homogenization thesis argue that Western norms and lifestyles are overwhelming more vulnerable cultures. Although there have been serious attempts by some countries to resist these forces of "cultural imperialism"—for example, a ban on satellite dishes in Iran, and the French imposition of tariffs and quotas on imported film and television—the spread of American popular culture seems to be unstoppable.

But these manifestations of sameness are also evident inside the dominant countries of the global North. American sociologist George Ritzer coined the term "McDonaldization" to describe the wide-ranging sociocultural processes by which the principles of the fast-food restaurant are coming to dominate more and more sectors of American society as well as the rest of the world. On the surface, these principles appear to be rational in their attempts to offer efficient and predictable ways of serving people's needs. However, looking behind the façade of repetitive TV commercials that claim to "love to see you smile," we can identify a number of serious problems. For one, the generally low nutritional value of fast-food meals—and particularly their high fat content—has been implicated in the rise of serious health problems such as heart disease, diabetes, cancer, and juvenile obesity. Moreover, the impersonal, routine operations of "rational" fast-service establishments actually undermine expressions of forms of cultural diversity. In the long run, the McDonaldization of the world amounts to the imposition of uniform standards that eclipse human creativity and dehumanize social relations.

Perhaps the most thoughtful analyst in this group of pessimistic hyperglobalizers is American political theorist Benjamin Barber. In his popular book on the subject, he warns his readers against the cultural imperialism of what he calls "McWorld"—a soulless consumer capitalism that is rapidly transforming the world's diverse populations into a blandly uniform market. For Barber, McWorld is a product of a superficial American popular culture assembled in the 1950s and 1960s, driven by expansionist commercial interests. Music, video, theatre, books, and theme parks are all constructed as American image exports that create common tastes around common logos, advertising slogans, stars, songs, brand names, jingles, and trademarks.

Barber's insightful account of cultural globalization also contains the important recognition that the colonizing tendencies of McWorld provoke cultural and political resistance in the form of "Jihad"—the parochial impulse to reject and repel the homogenizing forces of the West wherever they can be found. As we noted in our deconstruction of Osama bin Laden in Chapter 1,

Jihad draws on the furies of religious fundamentalism and ethnonationalism which constitute the dark side of cultural particularism. Fuelled by opposing universal aspirations, Jihad and McWorld are locked in a bitter cultural struggle for popular allegiance. Barber asserts that both forces ultimately work against a participatory form of democracy, for they are equally prone to undermine civil liberties and thus thwart the possibility of a global democratic future.

Optimistic hyperglobalizers agree with their pessimistic colleagues that cultural globalization generates more sameness, but they consider this outcome to be a good thing. For example, American social theorist Francis Fukuyama explicitly welcomes the global spread of Anglo-American values and lifestyles, equating the Americanization of the world with the expansion of democracy and free markets. But optimistic hyperglobalizers do not just come in the form of American chauvinists who apply the old theme of manifest destiny to the global arena. Some representatives of this camp consider themselves staunch cosmopolitans who celebrate the Internet as the harbinger of a homogenized "techno-culture." Others are free-market enthusiasts who embrace the values of global consumer capitalism.

It is one thing to acknowledge the existence of powerful homogenizing tendencies in the world, but it is quite another to assert that the cultural diversity existing on our planet is destined to vanish. In fact, several influential commentators offer a contrary assessment that links globalization to new forms of cultural expression. Sociologist Roland Robertson, for example, contends that global cultural flows often reinvigorate local cultural niches. Hence, rather than being totally obliterated by the Western consumerist forces of sameness, local difference and particularity still play an important role in creating unique cultural constellations. Arguing that cultural globalization always takes place in local contexts, Robertson rejects the cultural homogenization thesis and speaks instead of "glocalization"—a complex interaction of the global and local characterized by cultural borrowing. The resulting expressions of cultural "hybridity" cannot be reduced to clear-cut manifestations of "sameness" or "difference." As we noted in our previous discussion of Osama bin Laden, such processes of hybridization have become most visible in fashion, music, dance, film, food, and language.

In my view, the respective arguments of hyperglobalizers and sceptics are not necessarily incompatible. The contemporary experience of living and acting across cultural borders means both the loss of traditional meanings and the creation of new symbolic expressions. Reconstructed feelings of belonging coexist in uneasy tension with a sense of placelessness. Cultural globalization has contributed to a remarkable shift in people's consciousness. In fact, it appears that the old structures of modernity are slowly giving way to a new "postmodern" framework characterized by a less stable sense of identity and knowledge.

Given the complexity of global cultural flows, one would actually expect to see uneven and contradictory effects. In certain contexts, these flows might change traditional manifestations of national identity in the direction of a popular culture characterized by sameness; in others they might foster new expressions of cultural particularism; in still others they might encourage forms of cultural hybridity. Those commentators who summarily denounce the homogenizing effects of Americanization must not forget that hardly any society in the world today possesses an "authentic," self-contained culture. Those who despair at the flourishing of cultural hybridity ought to listen to exciting Indian rock songs, admire the intricacy of Hawaiian pidgin, or enjoy the culinary delights of Cuban-Chinese cuisine. Finally, those who applaud the spread of consumerist capitalism need to pay attention to its negative consequences, such as the dramatic decline of communal sentiments as well as the commodification of society and nature.

Part VIII

SOCIAL INSTITUTIONS:
ECONOMIC AND POLITICAL

Social institutions are the accepted, legitimate means by which a society operates. For society to continue, institutions must work. If they do not, sevices will not be adequately provided for people, social problems will become increasingly serious, and problems of social order will arise more regularly. Each society develops its unique set of institutions. Over time institutions come to seem part of the natural order, and it is usually difficult for people to understand or appreciate alternatives.

Peter L. Berger and Thomas Luckmann introduce us to social institutions through defining what they are and showing us how they emerge in social interaction.

The rest of Part VIII focuses on economic and political institutions. Economic institutions are those patterns created in a society for purposes of producing, distributing, and consuming goods and services. Political institutions are patterns that are established to govern society. Both economic and political institutions are critical sources of social power in society, and sociologists often emphasize their interrelationships.

Michael Zweig introduces capitalism as a central institution. Charles Perrow examines the history of business in the nineteenth and twentieth centuries, and he attempts to show us why it was that the large business organization became a dominant institution. Aronowitz and DiFazio look at how the scientific-technological revolution has changed how people work in our society. Carl Boggs highlights the power of the modern corporation, not only as the central economic institution, but increasingly central to political power.

John Kenneth Galbraith ties economics to politics: American government, he claims, is dominated by a large affluent contented class, and increasingly the rest of society is excluded from the important political institutions. Part VIII ends with a very thoughtful analysis of democracy by Larry Diamond, who focuses on the underlying political culture necessary for the development and continuation of democratic political institutions.

37

The Meaning and Origin of Social Institutions

Peter L. Berger and Thomas Luckmann

An institutional world, then, is experienced as an objective reality. It has a history that antedates the individual's birth and is not accessible to his biographical recollection. It was there before he was born, and it will be there after his death.

Social patterns arise in interaction. They come to be objective forces—institutions— that confront and control the individual. How do they arise? What are their qualities? Here, Peter Berger and Thomas Luckmann examine the process of "institutionalization," how social patterns become an integral part of organization, and how they acquire an independent existence from specific actors. It might be useful to keep in mind the following outline:

1. Interaction and habituation
2. Transmission and historicity
3. Objectivity
4. Legitimation
5. Social controls

. . . As *A* and *B* interact, in whatever manner, typifications will be produced quite quickly. *A* watches *B* perform. He attributes motives to *B*'s actions and, seeing the actions recur, typifies the motives as recurrent. As *B* goes on performing, *A* is soon able to say to himself, "Aha! There he goes again." At the same time, *A* may assume that *B* is doing the same thing with regard to him. From the beginning, both *A* and *B* assume this reciprocity of typification. In the course of their interaction, these typifications will be expressed in specific patterns of conduct. That is, *A* and *B* will begin to play roles vis-à-vis each other. This will occur even if each continues to perform actions different from those of the other. The possibility of taking the role of the other will appear with regard to the same actions performed by both. That is, *A* will inwardly appropriate *B*'s reiterated roles and make them the models for his own role-playing. For example, *B*'s role in the activity of preparing food is not only *typified* as such by *A*, but enters as a constitutive element into *A*'s own food-preparation role. Thus a collection of reciprocally typified actions will emerge, *habitualized* for each in roles, some of which will be performed separately and some in common.[1] Although this reciprocal typification is not yet institutionalization (there being only two individuals, there is no possibility of a typology of actors), it is clear that institutionalization is already present *in nucleo.*

At this stage, one may ask what gains accrue to the two individuals from this development. The most important gain is that each will be able to predict the other's actions. Concomitantly, the interaction of both becomes predictable. The "there he goes again" becomes a "there *we* go again." This relieves both individuals of a considerable amount of tension. They save time and effort, not only in whatever external tasks they might be engaged in separately or jointly, but in terms of their respective psychological economies. Their life together is now defined by a widening sphere of taken-for-granted routines. . . .

Let us push our paradigm one step further and imagine that A and B have children. At this point, the situation changes qualitatively. The appearance of a third party changes the character of the ongoing social interaction between A and B, and it will change even further as additional individuals continue to be added.[2] The institutional world, which existed *in statu nascendi* in the original situation of A and B, is now passed on to others. In this process, institutionalization perfects itself. The habitualizations and typifications undertaken in the common life of A and B— formations that until this point still had the quality of *ad hoc* conceptions of two individuals— now become historical institutions. With the acquisition of *historicity*, these formations also acquire another crucial quality, or, more accurately, perfect a quality that was incipient as soon as A and B began the reciprocal typification of their conduct: This quality is *objectivity*. This means that the institutions that have now been crystallized (for instance, the institution of paternity as it is encountered by the children) are experienced as existing over and beyond the individuals who "happen to" embody them at the moment. In other words, the institutions are now experienced as possessing a reality of their own, a reality that confronts the individual as an external and coercive fact.[3]

As long as the nascent institutions are constructed and maintained only in the interaction of A and B, their objectivity remains tenuous, easily changeable, almost playful, even while they attain a measure of objectivity by the mere fact of their formation. . . .

A and B alone are responsible for having constructed this world. A and B remain capable of changing or abolishing it. What is more, because they themselves have shaped this world in the course of a shared biography that they can remember, the world thus shaped appears fully transparent to them. They understand the world that they themselves have made. All this changes in the process of transmission to the new generation. The objectivity of the institutional world "thickens" and "hardens," not only for the children, but (by a mirror effect) for the parents as well. The "there we go again" now becomes "this is how these things are done." A world so regarded attains a firmness in consciousness; it becomes real in an ever more massive way, and it can no longer be changed so readily. For the children, especially in the early phase of their socialization into it, it becomes *the* world. For the parents, it loses its playful quality and becomes "serious." For the children, the parentally transmitted world is not fully transparent. Because they had no part in shaping it, it confronts them as a given reality that, like nature, is opaque in places at least.

Only at this point does it become possible to speak of a social world at all, in the sense of a comprehensive and given reality confronting the individual in a manner analogous to the reality of the natural world. Only in this way, *as* an objective world, can the social formations be transmitted to a new generation. . . .

The process of transmission simply strengthens the parents' sense of reality; . . . to put it crudely, if one says, "this is how these things are done," often enough, one believes it oneself.[4]

An institutional world, then, is experienced as an objective reality. It has a history that antedates the individual's birth and is not accessible to his biographical recollection. It was there before he was born, and it will be there after his death. This history itself, as the tradition of the existing institutions, has the character of objectivity. The individual's biography is apprehended as an episode located within the objective history of the society. The institutions, as historical and objective facticities, confront the individual as undeniable facts. The institutions are *there*, external to him, persistent in their reality, whether he likes it or not.

He cannot wish them away. They resist his attempts to change or evade them. They have coercive power over him, both in themselves, by the sheer force of their facticity, and through the control mechanisms that are usually attached to the most important of them. The objective reality of institutions is not diminished if the individual does not understand their purpose or their mode of operation. He may experience large sectors of the social world as incomprehensible, perhaps oppressive in their opaqueness, but real nonetheless. Because institutions exist as external reality, the individual cannot understand them by introspection. He must "go out" and learn about them, just as he must to learn about nature. This remains true even though the social world, as a humanly produced reality, is potentially understandable in a way not possible in the case of the natural world.[5]

At the same point, the institutional world requires *legitimation*, that is, ways by which it can be "explained" and justified. This is not because it appears less real. As we have seen, the reality of the social world gains in massivity in the course of its transmission. This reality, however, is a historical one that comes to the new generation as a tradition rather than as a biographical memory. In our paradigmatic example, A and B, the original creators of the social world, can always reconstruct the circumstances under which their world and any part of it was established. That is, they can arrive at the meaning of an institution by exercising their powers of recollection. A and B's children are in an altogether different situation. Their knowledge of the institutional history is by way of "hearsay." The original meaning of the institutions is inaccessible to them in terms of memory. Therefore, it becomes necessary to interpret this meaning to them in various legitimating formulas. These will have to be consistent and comprehensible in terms of the institutional order if they are to carry conviction to the new generation. The same story, so to speak, must be told to all the children. It follows that the expanding institutional order develops a corresponding canopy of legitimations, stretching over it a protective cover of both cognitive and normative interpretation. These legitimations are learned by the new generation during the same process that socializes them into the institutional order. . . .

The development of specific mechanisms of social controls also becomes necessary with the historicization and objectivation of institutions. Deviance from the institutionally "programmed" courses of action becomes likely once the institutions have become realities divorced from their original relevance in the concrete social processes from which they arose. To put this more simply, it is more likely that one will deviate from programs set up for one by others than from programs one has helped establish oneself. The new generation posits a problem of compliance, and its socialization into the institutional order requires the establishment of sanctions. The institutions must and do claim authority over the individual, independently of the subjective meanings he may attach to any particular situation. The priority of the institutional definitions of situations must be consistently maintained over individual temptations at redefinition. The children must be "taught to behave" and, once taught, must be "kept in line." So, of course, must the adults. The more conduct is institutionalized, the more predictable and thus the more controlled it becomes. If socialization into the institutions has been effective, outright coercive measures can be applied economically and selectively. Most of the time, conduct will occur "spontaneously" within the institutionally set channels. The more (on the level of meaning) conduct is taken for granted, the more possible alternatives to the institutional "programs" will recede, and the more predictable and controlled conduct will be.

NOTES

1. The term "taking the role of the other" is taken from Mead. Here, we are taking Mead's paradigm of socialization and applying it to the broader problem of institutionalization. The argument combines key features of both Mead's and Gehlen's approaches.
2. Simmel's analysis of the expansion from the dyad to the triad is important in this connection. The following argument combines Simmel's and Durkheim's conceptions of the objectivity of social reality.
3. In Durkheim's terms, this means that, with the expansion of the dyad into a triad and beyond, the original formations become genuine "social facts," that is, they attain *choséité*.
4. For an analysis of this process in the contemporary family, *cf.* Peter L. Berger and Hansfried Kellner,

"Marriage and the Construction of Reality," *Diogenes* 46 (1964), 1 ff.

5. The preceding description closely follows Durkheim's analysis of social reality. This does *not* contradict the Weberian conception of the meaningful character of society. Because social reality always originates in meaningful human actions, it continues to carry meaning even if it is opaque to the individual at a given time. The original may be *reconstructed*, precisely by means of what Weber called *Verstehen*.

◆ 38 ◆

The Institution of Capitalism

Michael Zweig

The moral authority to limit individualism comes from the reality that the individual is also social. The individual has obligations to the social network that helps create, shape, sustain, and also has the power to destroy, individuals. Society can make claims on individuals to be responsible to that social reality, while the individual has a claim to fair and respectful treatment in the social network.

For many of us, capitalism is the key to America's economic success in the world. For Michael Zweig, capitalism as it is practiced sacrifices community and cooperation for individualism and self-interest. Zweig argues that capitalism ignores community responsibility, refuses to recognize the role of luck in economic success, and unfairly assumes the moral superiority of those who become wealthy.

The search for the proper balance between self-interest and service to others suggests the basis of an ethical evaluation of the market economy and capitalism, because capitalism poses the very same problem: What is the connection between self-interest and service to the community? The pursuit of self-interest may be an essential life priority, but when does following self-interest stop being a legitimate priority of business and keep companies from serving the larger community? What happens when self-interest becomes the whole point of economic activity?

It's fine to pursue narrow self-interest, except when it cuts us off from or disrespects the social connections and responsibilities that help to define us as we participate in the larger society. Just as a firefighter pursues self-interest as a priority, but not as an end, self-interested economic activity needs to be understood as a priority, perhaps, but not as an end. The end is playing a constructive part in the larger society, not out of a misty

Reprinted from Michael Zweig, *The Working Class Majority: America's Best Kept Secret.* Copyright © 2000 by Michael Zweig. Used by permission of the publisher, Cornell University Press.

sense of altruism, but to nourish the relationships that give us our character, place, and meaning in the world. . . .

SELF-INTEREST IS NOT ENOUGH

The conservative agenda asserts the superiority of the capitalist market system. In this view, self-interest is the dominant motive for economic activity, and private ownership of business with minimum restrictions is necessary to allow people to capture for themselves the benefits that come from their economic activity.

It is no mystery that this view should appeal to capitalists, who are the core supporters of the conservative cause. But the implications of such a market society for ethics and values are grim indeed. Let's look at three ways the exaggerated assertion of individualism and self-interest breaks away from reality: it disregards the connections among us; it ignores the role of luck; and it denies the social origin of wealth.

Connectedness

Seeing the world in terms solely of the market ignores the complex interconnectedness of human beings. Even Adam Smith, the great original champion of early capitalism, wrote of the conflict between market exchange and morality. Over two hundred years ago Smith described how the capitalist division of labor ended self-sufficiency and the market brought people together to coordinate their activities. He pointed out:

> It is not from the benevolence of the butcher, the brewer, or the baker, that we expect our dinner, but from their regard to their own interest. We address ourselves, not to their humanity but to their self-love, and never talk to them of our own necessities but of their advantages.[1]

Smith, a professor of moral philosophy when he founded the modern study of economics, tells us here that self-love and humanity are in opposition. He tells us that, in a market economy, each of us acts without concern for others, with a concern only for ourselves. Each person appeals to others' self-interest, but actually only as a means to serve his or her own ends.

This approach defeats "humanity," as Smith calls it, or community responsibility, as I have called it, because it undermines and denies true mutual concern. The point of ethics and morality in social conduct is to find ways to guide our responsibility toward others. If the only thing that counts is me, there is no place for ethics of any sort as a guide to my behavior, because social ethics are about relationships between people, the terms of mutual responsibility, a guide to each of us about our obligations to others.

An overriding belief in the market and reliance on self-interest defeat morality. They trivialize ethics by making true concern for others irrelevant or, worse, self-defeating, as in "nice guys finish last." Even the idea of "enlightened self-interest"—in which we appear to behave altruistically now only as a means to a longer-term self-interest that would be undermined by immediate selfishness—doesn't solve the problem. In the world of "enlightened self-interest," we still see ourselves as isolated individuals in a sea of other isolated individuals. This way of thinking about society fails to recognize the ways that individuals are also social, created and sustained in a network of other people. It cannot guide us to a recognition of our interdependence and of the moral emptiness of individualism.

We are social beings. But the usual way we think about the social nature of human beings doesn't fully capture what is going on. Everyone knows that "no man is an island," that we live in groups, that we need one another to survive. As Adam Smith put it: "In civilized society, [a person] stands at all times in need of the cooperation and assistance of great multitudes, while his whole life is scarce sufficient to gain the friendship of a few persons."[2] The strength Adam Smith found in the market was exactly its ability to coordinate the economic connections among us so that, through buying and selling in the market, we could get what we need from one another without knowing one another. Through the market, we can reach beyond the personal connections and personal obligations that were the limits of earlier societies—a positive result of the growth of markets.

But people are social in different and more complicated ways. We are each distinctive beings, but each of us is also a set of relationships. We are created in relationships; our ideas and values and needs arise in our connections with others, not solely out of our minds and bodies fully distinct from others. We are social because we are, in part but literally, the connections we have with others.

Adam Smith was right to point out that in the modern, capitalist world, these connections extend beyond the immediate circle of family, friends, and co-workers we know directly. These are the people who immediately come to mind when we think of the communities that have shaped us. But in the modern world, our very nature as people and the very content of our individuality is also created in an extensive and impersonal network of relationships. Our life chances and experiences are not just our own doing; they are not just the making of our family's influence; they are also the product of the entire structure of society as it bears on each of us.

This is why we cannot protect ourselves individually by referring only to our immediate self-interest. We have to be concerned with the relationships we have to the broader community as well. To protect ourselves, we need to protect and nurture and make healthy and look after the interests of all those in society with whom we jointly make a life on this planet. Their lives literally are our own. . . .

Individuality, privacy, and self-interested behavior are essential ingredients of Western life. No political or ethical system that denies them can be effective. We wouldn't want the stifling eradication of individual initiative that so often characterized collectivist societies in the twentieth century. But neither can the kind of individualism that capitalism fosters play a positive role. By separating the individual from social connections, raw individualism becomes dysfunctional because it is false to the reality of our mutual dependence and mutual responsibilities. . . .

In short, any discussion of values in society has to include the terms on which we limit the activity of private business. Of course, many owners oppose limits on what they can do with their businesses and resist the idea that business has any purpose beyond making money. They are only too happy to welcome the recent emphasis on family values, because it lets them off the hook and puts greedy, predatory business practices beyond the reach of moral review.

Luck

"There but for the grace of God go I." Whether you take life's chances as the work of God, or as the effect of social and natural processes beyond our powers to control, or as the result of random events, it remains a fact that we do not fully control our destiny. Luck of all sorts plays an enormous role. Successful athletes and artists often talk about luck. Successful business leaders also acknowledge it on occasion. As one mutual fund manager put it, "When you're younger, you are more inclined to believe that the profits you make in the market are due to your own wit or talent. When you get older, maybe you get a little wiser and discover that it's exogenous [external] forces that are making you all that money."[3] We saw in Chapter 2 that even Horatio Alger put luck at the heart of many rags-to-riches tales that became icons of the American Dream.

Of course, being in the right place at the right time does not guarantee success. A person has to be able to make something out of a lucky break, and that ability comes from the successful person's own skills and talents. But the central place of luck in our lives cannot be denied. It requires humility from the successful, as well as compassion for those who fail. And it certainly rules out any conclusions about the relative moral worth of those who succeed compared with those who fail.

The place of luck in our lives has other ethical consequences. The Golden Rule, "do unto others as you would have others do unto you," is not a call for tit-for-tat reciprocity, like "an eye for an eye and a tooth for a tooth." It involves a recognition that you might well *become* the other. Social ethics need to reflect the risky reality we all face. Laws and regulations need to be acceptable no matter who you are, no matter who you might become.[4]

A philosophy of individualism that ignores the place of luck and the shaping power of social relationships beyond the individual accentuates the hubris of those who succeed and intensifies the sense of worthlessness of those who fail. The widespread lack of self-esteem among poor and other working class children and young adults is a serious problem, reaching almost epidemic proportions. It holds back their learning and their productivity, as well as causing deep personal suffering. But the successful can also suffer from the effects of extreme individualism. Their often overblown sense of self-importance has its own unreality, which leads to the self-doubts that gnaw at many of the rich and powerful, and to the personal despair that follows the fall from power many of them experience at one time or another.

The Origins of Wealth

A third problem with market individualism that leads it to moral bankruptcy is its failure to acknowledge that private wealth is socially created. Here again it helps to look at the problem through the lens of class. . . .

To see how this is true, it may help to take the discussion away from capitalism for a moment, with all the controversies that a frank discussion of it brings, and look instead at slavery. No one doubts any longer that the wealth of the slave owner originated in the work of the slave. Whatever the slave received in the way of sustenance came from the work of the slaves themselves, given back to the slave only after the owner took it from the slaves who had produced it in the first place. In fact, the slave owner took everything the slaves produced as his own, by right of ownership over the slaves themselves. What the slave owner did not return to the slave, he kept, and this was the basis of his wealth.

Likewise, feudal kings and other nobility drew their wealth from the work of the serfs and other producers who were forced to give up a share of what they made. The specific mechanisms that accomplished this transfer of wealth from those who created it to those who took it as their right were different under feudalism than under slavery. But the two systems shared a common fundamental fact: the wealth of the property owners was the fruit of the labor of others.

Although slave owners and feudal lords developed different arguments to justify their right to take the wealth created by others, their justifications shared a common theme. They routinely asserted the moral weakness and personal and intellectual inferiority of the producer, whether slave or serf, and, by contrast, the moral superiority and natural goodness and intelligence of the owners and rulers themselves.

This is not to say that the slave owner and the feudal aristocrat didn't do a full day's work. They had a lot to do, organizing and enforcing the everyday operations of their societies and dealing with the many levels of intrigue and conflict that challenged their power. But, looking back, the work that occupied them was not like the work of those from whom they took their wealth. The self-righteous claims to moral authority advanced by the slaveholding and aristocratic elites of earlier times look quaint and ignorant by modern, capitalist standards.

Now capitalism dominates the world economy and has established the new standards of political and economic life. Since the end of the Cold War, the capitalist way has been virtually unchallenged. It appears natural, and its standards and justifications are conventional wisdom widely accepted as self-evident. But, if we look more closely, we can see remarkable similarities between capitalism and earlier societies.

Adam Smith, the first person to take a serious look at wealth in capitalist society, had this to say about where wealth comes from when it is capitalist profit:

> The value which the workmen add to the materials, therefore, resolves itself . . . into two parts, of which the one pays their wages, the other the profits of their employer. . . . He would have no interest to employ them unless he expected from the sale of their work something more than what was sufficient to replace his stock. . . .[5]

In other words, profits come from the value workers add when they make new products. Not only do the workers' wages come from what they have produced; all that the capitalist claims as his own as the profit of his enterprise *also* comes from what the workers have produced, and these words of wisdom are from the man whose face decorated neckties proudly worn by the free market economists of the Reagan administration! In fact, Adam Smith tells us, the only reason a capitalist employs anyone at all is the expectation that the employee will generate a profit for the owner through his labor. In short, you are employed to make your employer rich, which comes as no surprise to employers and employees alike, even today.

Most executives of the capitalist class probably put in full days at work, as much or more than the slave owner or the feudal lord. Again, the work of modern executives is different from the work of their employees. It is the work of control, of strategic planning, the work of managing intrigue and challenges to their control, whether from their workforce or from other businesses, or the government, or foreign competition. It is the work necessary to organize and maintain the structures that allow them to become and remain rich through the taking Adam Smith described.

Capitalists work hard at what they do. Theirs is not a life of leisure. But it isn't true, as the popular wisdom so often holds, that workers have an easy life by comparison. We often hear that the lucky worker goes home at five o'clock to an evening of beer and television, while the boss stays back to worry about all the details required to keep the business running. Even when the worker doesn't go off to a second job and the boss does work longer hours, the popular wisdom misses the fact that work stress comes less from the number of hours worked than from lack of control on the job. For all the pressures and tough decisions managers and executives face, workers experience more stress and, as a result, have a much higher incidence of ulcers, high blood pressure, heart disease, and other stress-related disorders compared with the managers, professionals, and executives above them.[6]

Capitalists like to say they are the risk takers in society, and this is why they should be richly rewarded. But workers are at constant risk for their jobs and livelihood. Workers risk their health and safety at work and in their neighborhoods to a far greater extent than their employers do. And in every aspect of life, workers face their risks with far less cushion in case of hard times or bad breaks than do the capitalists. . . .

Here we come back to the reality of individual success and failure. In some important ways, success comes from the work of the individual, of course. But there are limits to what an individual can claim as his or her own accomplishment (or failure). As we saw earlier in this chapter, each of us is not just an individual, isolated from others, making it, or not, on our own. Each of us is also a set of relationships with others, near and far, who help create us and shape what we can and cannot accomplish as individuals, to whom we owe much

that cannot be repaid directly in the market. The capitalist, even more than the rest of us, is a social creation. The capitalists' sense of entitlement is out of touch with reality because it denies the social foundation of their wealth. Poor people's claims to society's help with the provision of basic needs, or to common courtesy and respect, are more in tune with the realities of our mutual responsibilities. But typically the poor are not militantly insistent about these claims. Too often, they are meek. It is the capitalists who adamantly demand respect, power, deference, a right to their wealth untouched. Whatever excessive claims to entitlement some poor people may make, it is a weak echo of the hubristic demands of the wealthy.

THE RISE OF "FAMILY VALUES"

In the 1980s and 1990s, as the living standards of the working class steadily deteriorated, "values" came to increasing prominence as a political issue. But values were separated from economic questions. Instead of considering economic justice and social responsibility, values came to mean what some called "family values." As right-wing political forces came to prominence, they redirected the focus of moral debate by asserting conservative responses to such vital questions as abortion, the rights of women, and homosexuality. The energy of these assertions, backed by grass-roots mobilizations through many right-wing Christian churches, created a climate in which the moral character of political candidates and party platforms seemed to rest on their stands on these "family values" issues—not on policies to deal with poverty, inequality, military budgets, or the rights of workers to organize unions.

Liberal and pro-labor politicians have answered these attacks in policy terms. But these leaders have too often been on the defensive in the moral debate. They have not expressed a coherent moral code of their own to answer the right's claims of moral leadership. They have not articulated an ethical system to justify their policies, integrate their views on family values with workers' needs, and motivate broad political participation by people who seek moral leadership as well as improvements in their everyday lives. . . .

Individualism has a powerful appeal to the American psyche, open as Americans are to the mythic history of struggling immigrants and pioneers surviving by their own wits and growing rich through initiative, hard work, and true grit. The notion resonates with the early history of this country, a time of small farmers, merchants, and individual artisans, before capitalism and its vast, impersonal social networks and institutions came into existence. Appeals to individualism are especially attractive to modern workers, who so often feel fenced in, without power, independence, and apparent future prospects in their daily lives. No one wants to be told they can't do what they want, especially after a long day at work; no one wants to believe that a better future is closed off to them, especially those for whom it is most likely true. . . .

ETHICAL LIMITS ON CAPITALISM

The moral challenge capitalism poses operates in practical ways at every level of society. It is most obvious when the rigors of capitalist life first come to a community, before people come to accept capitalist norms as "human nature." But even in an advanced capitalist country like the United States we can see the moral corrosion capitalism entails, and find it appalling.

We see it when a rural community finds itself assaulted by waves of development radiating out from nearby cities. Small merchants are driven out of business by national retail chains in new malls. Farm land and beautiful vistas are destroyed when building advances with no regard for community character or traditions, when property values dominate community values. The pace of life changes, becomes more intense. Everyone notices. It's a new way of life.

This is what happens when HMOs push doctors to sacrifice patient care to protect the bottom line. It's what happens when university professors must find corporate support for their scholarship in the new, entrepreneurial university. In particular, it's what shocked photographers working for *National Geographic*, when the venerable nonprofit magazine opened for-profit outlets for their photographers' work and demanded to keep all the proceeds from use of the photos, after years of respectful working relations with this vital part of their workforce.[7]

In matters great and small, most people think of these developments as wrong, not just unfortunate. We tend to see the naked workings of capitalism as morally degrading. "Money is the root of all evil" isn't about money; it's about putting money at the forefront. It's about allowing the drive for money to be all-consuming, as it becomes when society puts no restrictions on the drive to maximize profit, and self-interest turns to greed.

Market activity needs institutions and rules to guide it. The social institutions that the Russians and the Chinese must now create to protect themselves from raw market power, we in the United States must also protect *and strengthen* in our own way. The institutions and policies we create to limit capitalist behavior must be based on some ethical values. These values cannot be rooted in individualism, since it is exactly the excesses of individualism that need to be curbed.

The moral authority to limit individualism comes from the reality that the individual is also social. The individual has obligations to the social network that helps create, shape, sustain, and also has the power to destroy, individuals. Society can make claims on individuals to be responsible to that social reality, while the individual has a claim to fair and respectful treatment in the social network.

We cannot outlaw greed, any more than we can outlaw any other feeling or attitude. But we can outlaw some of the practical effects of greed, by requiring that the effects of pursuing self-interest not undermine the rights of others. The debate about values needs to be refocused, to articulate values and morality that can help limit capitalist power. This means product standards, labor standards, environmental standards, standards that have bite, enforced with real consequences for those who violate them. It also means some form of social control on investment and other strategic business decisions. These are not easy things to do, technically or politically; they require concentrated will and careful thought. Looking at the problems with class in mind will help develop the moral compass we need to get it right.

Being against greed is not being against business. Many small, family-run businesses operate in socially responsible ways. Their owners want to make a living, but they also take pride in workmanship, treat their employees well, and respect the community and natural environments in which they do business. The same is true for some big business as well. But, too often, individual good intentions are overwhelmed by market imperatives, driving owners to socially irresponsible action out of the needs of survival. Some of my friends who own small businesses talk about this pressure with the pain and resentment typical of middle class experience. When market imperatives drive business to antisocial action— eat or be eaten, kill or be killed, do what is necessary or go broke—we have a moral problem with far-reaching consequences.

The fact that the capitalists' wealth is social means that the claim working people make on that wealth is not a request for charity. It is a claim for what they themselves have already created. And, if it is true that it is better to teach a person how to fish than to give that person a bucket of fish, it is also true that workers' demand for wealth need not be put in terms of redistributing existing wealth. Rather, workers' need for wealth is better served by a claim for power over the process and machinery of wealth creation itself.

Because capitalists have a hard time accepting limits, they must be imposed by an opposing power. As the majority in society, the working class can have that power. Unlike capitalists, workers have an interest in understanding and acting upon values that challenge individualism. Working class politics can be bound up with these values. And a working class person, so much more attuned to direct mutual aid on the job and in daily survival than the capitalist, has a greater potential for understanding the interdependent nature of social reality.

Looking at "family values" from a class perspective shows us that the values needed to support families are the values of economic justice, values that give their due to mutual obligations, values that put limits on capitalism and create institutions that promote the material and spiritual well-being of working class families, and all people.

Twenty-first century politics, if they are to improve the lives of working class people, will need to challenge the rule of the marketplace. It will take the working class as an organized political force to assert the values of economic justice and muster the power needed to implement policies that flow from those values. From the point of view of working people, the task now is to make class issues the wedge issues of the new century. Economic

justice must become the new moral litmus test, the basic ethical standard against which we measure candidates, public officials, and our social institutions. In the concluding chapters of this book, I turn to the prospects for such a working class politics, already beginning to bubble up in the United States at the start of the twenty-first century.

NOTES

1. Adam Smith, *The Wealth of Nations* [1776] (New York: Modern Library, 1937), 14.
2. Ibid.
3. Leon Levy, interviewed by Jeff Madrick, in "Wall Street Blues," *New York Review of Books*, Vol. XLV, No. 15, October 8, 1998, 10. Levy was partner and is now chairman of the board of trustees of the Oppenheimer Funds.
4. This basic idea has been elaborated by John Rawls, *A Theory of Social Justice* (Cambridge, Mass.: Harvard University Press, 1971). Rawls, however, constructs his ethical principles outside of any particular society, before anyone knows his or her position in what will come. In reality, ethics are forged in the conflicts of interests among classes and other groups in actual societies. What is thought to be "right" and what "wrong" is complicated by the relative power of those who stand to win or lose according to the answer. This is why the debate over values and social ethics is not just a question of logic or the better argument. The debate over values is a contest of power.
5. Smith, *Wealth of Nations*, 48.
6. See, for example, T. Alterman, et al., "Decision Latitude, Psychological Demand, Job Strain, and Coronary Heart Disease in the Western Electric Study," *American Journal of Epidemiology*, No. 139 (1994), 620–627; R. L. Repetti, "The Effects of Workload and the Social Environment at Work on Health," in L. Goldberger and S. Breznitz (eds.), *Handbook of Stress: Theoretical and Clinical Aspects*, 2nd ed. (New York: Free Press, 1993), 368–385; P. L. Schnall, et al., "The Relationship Between Job Strain, Workplace, Diastolic Blood Pressure, and Left Ventricular Mass Index," *Journal of the American Medical Association*, No. 263 (1990), 1929–1935; Cary L. Cooper and Michael J. Smith, *Job Stress and Blue Collar Work* (New York: John Wiley & Sons, 1985); Robert D. Caplan, et al., *Job Demands and Worker Health* (Washington, D.C.: U.S. Department of Health, Education, and Welfare, April 1975). Similar findings were reported in a nontechnical way in Erica Goode, "For Good Health, It Helps To Be Rich and Important," *New York Times*, June 1, 1999, F1.
7. Alex Kuczynski, "National Geographic Angers Its Photographers," *New York Times*, February 1, 1999, C1.

39

The Rise of Big Business in the United States

Charles Perrow

. . . a weak state allowed the private accumulation of wealth and power through the medium of big organizations. Elites developed modern bureaucracy over the century, and it was to be the means for maintaining an inequality of wealth, despite periodic reform efforts. . . . We have become a society of organizations, big ones, and it was not inevitable.

Charles Perrow's book *Organizing America: Wealth, Power and the Origins of Corporate Capitalism,* attempts to carefully and systematically describe the various forces in our history that eventually led us to the institution of the big corporation. This selection is from the last, summary chapter of the book. It leaves out many of the details of his research, but it highlights his conclusions. Perrow focuses on our traditionally weak political institutions, weak reform movements, high wage dependency by workers, mass production, and the development of a national railroad system.

How did it come about that the United States developed an economic system based upon large corporations, privately held, with minimal regulation by the state? Two hundred years ago there were none. Until the 1890s there were only a few large ones, in textiles and railroads and the steel and locomotive industries. Then there was a spurt at the turn of the century; in about five years most of the 200 biggest corporations of the time were formed, and most of these still rule their industries.

Nothing comparable occurred in Europe. Until the 1950s the corporate structure of the United States was unique, and it was dominant in the industrialized world. Some of the reasons for this American "exceptionalism" are familiar: the industrial revolution found fertile ground in a resource-rich land with mass markets and democratic institutions and a culture of individual freedom and entrepreneurship. But two things have not been emphasized enough: in the United States a weak state did not prevent large concentrations of economic power and did not provide strong state regulation, in contrast to Europe's stronger states. Second, concentrated power with large-scale production was also possible for organizational reasons: organizations changed the legal system to give organizations sovereignty, and they had a wage-dependent population that permitted a bureaucratic structure with tight labor control.

From Perrow, Charles, *Organizing America.* © 2002 by Princeton University Press. Reprinted by permission of Princeton University Press.

For large corporations to spring into existence at the end of the century, the legal structure of the commonwealth had to be reworked. It had to favor the accumulation of private capital for large-scale production for national markets, rather then the dispersion of capital into smaller enterprises with regional markets. It appears that the United States centralized private wealth and power a century sooner than Europe did. Our global success then forced our solution upon Europe in the last half of the twentieth century.

The weak state and the organizational arguments are interdependent. Assuming a minimal degree of democracy, we can argue that (a) a weak state will allow private organizations to grow almost without limit and with few requirements to serve the public interest; and (b) private organizations will shape the weak state to its liking (this requires state action, in the form of changing property laws). A strong state, however, would have sufficient legislative independence of private economic organizations, and sufficient executive branch strength and will to check the power of private organizations. Together these could limit their growth and require some attention to the public interest. This happened to a greater degree in Europe than in the United States. . . .

The United States was blessed with a fear and hatred of two gigantic organizations the immigrants had experienced in Europe: the official church and the state. No national church was established, and the federal state was kept small, weak, and divided. With no significant state, there was no nobility. Without a nobility, there was no feudalism and all those immobile peasants. With no strong state, there could not be a strong church; it takes a state to impose one. Without a crown, church, and nobles to be jealous of the rise of private economic power, large organizations were able to flourish, though resistence to them was strong through much of the nineteenth century. Farmers and laborers and some politicians objected to the lack of regulation and the lack of public representation in the new corporations, and objected to their market control, but the strong demand for their goods, and their ability to corrupt politicians, gave these objections only a limited effect. . . .

Regarding labor, the towns along the mid-Atlantic and New England coast soon filled with workers dependent upon a wage for a living. This was new in the early nineteenth century. Many were immigrants, but many were also the younger sons of the farmers who could no longer subdivide the land into viable plots for all sons, or who found their New England soil exhausted and discovered that easy migration to the West was no longer possible as the distances increased and Native Americans blocked movement just east of the Great Lakes. As with England a few decades before, a wage-dependent population became available for manufacturing. Where there was not wage dependency, that is, where workers could choose farming, skilled trades, or a mix of these and some casual day labor, factories could not find workers. As in England, a generation earlier, the first factories were staffed by orphans, paupers, and criminals; no one else would accept "wage slavery" as it was called, so new was it. When the New England textile mills were built in the 1830s, they were in remote areas where waterpower was available and land cheap. But there were no wage-dependent workers there. They had to recruit farmers' daughters, who worked for three or four years until they had a dowry and could marry, and the mills had to treat them well. They were not wage dependent, they could always go back to the farm. But once the famished Irish came over and a railroad could bring them from the Boston port to the inland mill towns, a dependent work force was available. Wages were cut, the New England daughters left, exploitation increased, and the handsome mill towns became slums. Profits soared, the companies were returning 25 percent per year on their investments.

This was one path of development available to the industrializing nation—centralized capital, high wage dependency, mass production of cheap goods, little technological development, and large externalities, or social costs to be born by workers and communities. It did not become the dominant path until late in the century. . . .

Why did we have the surge of giant organizations at the end of the century? Because of the railroads. First, they made mass markets possible. This encouraged economies of scale, but for most industries with late-nineteenth-century technologies, this was achieved with only modest-sized firms of, say, 500 employees. The cheap, dependable, all-weather transportation that the railroads provided would have been quite consistent with a decentralized, regionalized economy with modest-sized firms—the economy we had before the railroads arrived. Goods could be made in a variety of places and inexpensively distributed locally and regionally. One four-state railroad operated this way for several years, with efficient short-haul service and innovative maintenance and shipping practices that the national railroads copied, but it was bought out by a national line. The national lines—there were six major ones by the end of the century—could make the most money by promoting long-haul transport, with low rates, and charging very high rates for short hauls. They were capital intensive and were the biggest organizations in the world, with economic and political resources that allowed them to favor a national, rather than a regional, economy. Major centers for livestock processing, food processing, steel, petroleum, and durable goods manufacturing were established, with huge organizations dominating the national market. A national railroad system needed national production centers, centralizing the economy, and since it was in private hands, centralizing wealth and power. . . .

Eventually the democratic ethos put something of a brake upon the private accumulation of wealth and power. Labor unions did what they could, despite a hostile judiciary, and an increasingly broad electorate sent messages to the federal government about corporations and private wealth during the Progressive era. Though sometimes misguided and full of bucolic idiocy, these messages often slowed centralization. . . .

But it could have been far better. Look at what the United States had going for it: the first and the second industrial revolutions occurring in a nature-rich land that hardly had to be conquered; ample labor supply; no fixed class structure or nobility; no religious wars to fight or religious traditions strong enough to uphold the subjection of women; early enfranchisement; and perhaps most often unnoted, only one war of consequence, our Civil War, in contrast to our competitors. We were under the British umbrella on the high seas and used them to protect our expanding trade.

Being "far better" would have meant less human carnage in the factories and mines, less unrestrained devouring of natural resources and less pollution, and a far less steep rise in the degree of wealth and income inequality, as well as smaller, more flexible and competitive organizations, and stronger social welfare provisions by a strong federal government. (There were still orphan trains running in the 1920s, handing out kids picked up in New York and Boston to Midwestern farmers and factory owners, something really close to "wage slavery.") And, of course, we were far behind England in abolishing slavery. A weak central government waffled and quivered about slavery under the pressure of a fabulously rich Southern aristocracy running huge plantations, and of Northern textile and shipping interests—organizations all.

To sum up, a weak state allowed the private accumulation of wealth and power through the medium of big organizations. Elites developed modern bureaucracy over the century, and it was to be the means for maintaining an inequality of wealth, despite periodic reform efforts. Over the nineteenth century, the organization won the freedom to select its own officers and thus could keep public or governmental representatives off the board, even though it enjoyed public largess, and to choose its own successors, so that it could exist forever. Its owners and stockholders, who collected the profits, could not be sued for its debts or failures or accidents. Until the end of the century an employee or his or her family could not recover damages for any work-connected injury or death. The organization could control the social behavior of its employees (initially the control was crude, and legal, such that one could be fired for voting for the wrong candidate, not attending church, or not attending the right church; later the socialization of employees relied on more subtle pressures). The strongest pressure the large organizations exercised was building an economy that insured wage dependency, initially with blacklisting, then with urban work that cut employees off from a rural or small-town environment that provided other means of survival. It was hard to get people to work in factories; when they lived in large cities they had little choice. It was declared legal for the firm to pollute the environment, flood a farmer's land, and cause other negative externalities. Legally it could discriminate on the basis of gender, race, and ethnicity in hiring. The firm was ruled to be a fictitious person, so it could buy up other firms, increasing its market power, and use its resources to go into any business it wished, expanding its scope as well as scale. This was all new, and often contested since people feared centralized, uncontrolled power. But we take most of these powers for granted today. In 1820, about 20 percent of the population worked for wages and salaries; by 1900 it was 50 percent; today it is well over 90 percent, with over half of that number working for big organizations, often with the power to control the small ones. We have become a society of organizations, big ones, and it was not inevitable.

This is an *organizational* interpretation of our nineteenth-century experience. It might invite some scepticism since throughout most of the nineteenth century we were a rural rather than an industrial nation, and until late in the century there were few large organizations. Indeed, during most of the century, I have argued, production was in the hands of small- and moderate-sized firms with local and regional markets. But the explosion of big firms at the end of the century did not come from nowhere, and certainly not out of our culture, or the play of democratic politics, or the supposed efficiency of the instruments of large-scale production. It began with a mobile labor supply dependent upon wages for existence, and a series of crucial legal decisions that created instruments that could make production independent of public scrutiny and regulation and allow mergers once the railroads made mass markets available. The natural wealth of the continent and the easy removal of its small native population, together with the industrial revolution, converged, at the end of the century, with the steel-rail girdling of the vast land into an *organizational society*. The efficiency of unobtrusive and remote controls that railroad bureaucracy fashioned penetrated all organizations, even public and nonprofit ones, and made combination the order of the day. Belatedly, the Progressive movement of the early twentieth century sought to redress the power imbalances and the costly externalities for workers and communities. But the organizational infrastructure of the nation was not to be seriously disturbed or even ideologically challenged, up to the present. A society with small- and modest-sized firms, regional rather than national markets, and with civic welfare provisions that are a right of citizenship rather than a benefit of employment—a society with wealth and power distributed widely—is now out of the question. Large bureaucratic organizations, public and private, will be our fate for the foreseeable future. It might have been otherwise.

40

Jobs—and Joblessness—in a Technological America

Stanley Aronowitz and William DiFazio

... The shape of things to come—as well as those already in existence—signals the
emerging proletarianization of work at every level below top management
and a relatively few scientific and technical occupations.

There is a revolution going on in society concerning our economic institutions. Specifically, it has to do with work. This selection examines that revolution and ties it to a scientific-technological revolution. Aronowitz and DiFazio show us what is happening and why. Jobs will never be the same as they were; incomes and standard of living for most people will be considerably lower than they are now; mobility will become more difficult, and a greater gap will be created between those at the top of the economic order and everyone else. This selection deserves careful examination and debate. It will probably happen in the classroom more than it will in the political order.

OVERVIEW

In 1992, the long-term shifts in the nature of paid work became painfully visible not only to industrial workers and those with technical, professional, and managerial credentials and job experience but also to the public. During that year, "corporate giants like General Motors and IBM announced plans to shed tens of thousands of workers." General Motors, which at first said it would close twenty-one U.S. plants by 1995, soon disclaimed any definite limit to the number of either plant closings or firings and admitted that

the numbers of jobs lost might climb above the predicted 70,000, even if the recession led to increased car sales. IBM, which initially shaved about 25,000 blue- and white-collar employees, soon increased its estimates to possibly 60,000, in effect reversing the company's historic policy of no layoffs. Citing economic conditions, Boeing, the world's largest airplane producer, and Hughes Aircraft, a major parts manufacturer, were poised for substantial cuts in their well-paid workforces. In 1991 and 1992, major retailers, including Sears, either shut down stores or drastically cut the number of employees; in late January 1993, Sears announced that it was letting about 50,000 employees go. The examples could be multiplied. Millions, worldwide, were losing their jobs in the industrialized West and Asia. Homelessness was and is growing. . . .

From Stanley Aronowitz and William DiFazio, *The Jobless Future: Sci-Tech and the Dogma of Work*. Published by University of Minnesota Press, copyright © 1994 by the Regents of the University of Minnesota. All rights reserved.

. . . The scientific-technological revolution of our time, which is not confined to new electronic processes but also affects organizational changes in the structure of corporations, has fundamentally altered the forms of work, skill, and occupation. The whole notion of tradition and identity of persons with their work has been radically changed.

Scientific and technological innovation is, for the most part, no longer episodic. Technological change has been routinized. Not only has abstract knowledge come to the center of the world's political economy, but there is also a tendency to produce and trade in symbolic significations rather than concrete products. Today, knowledge rather than traditional skill is the main productive force. The revolution has widened the gap between intellectual, technical, and manual labor, between a relatively small number of jobs that, owing to technological complexity, require more knowledge and a much larger number that require less; because the mass of jobs are "de-skilled," there is a resultant redefinition of occupational categories that reflects the changes in the nature of jobs. As these transformations sweep the world, older conceptions of class, gender, and ethnicity are called into question. For example, on the New York waterfront (until 1970, the nation's largest), Italians and blacks dominated the Brooklyn docks and the Irish and Eastern Europeans worked the Manhattan piers. Today, not only are the docks vanishing as sites of shipping, the workers are gone as well. For those who remain, the traditional occupation of long-shoreman—dangerous, but highly skilled—has given way, as a result of containerization of the entire process, to a shrunken workforce that possesses knowledge but not the old skills[1] . . . This is just an example of a generalized shift in the nature and significance of work.

As jobs have changed, so have the significance and duration of joblessness. Partial and permanent unemployment, except during the two great world depressions (1893–1898 and 1929–1939) largely episodic and subject to short-term economic contingencies, has increasingly become a mode of life for larger segments of the populations not only of less industrially developed countries, but for those in "advanced" industrial societies as well. Many who are classified in official

statistics as "employed" actually work at casual and part-time jobs, the number of which has grown dramatically over the past fifteen years. This phenomenon, once confined to freelance writers and artists, laborers and clerical workers, today cuts across all occupations, including the professions. Even the once buoyant "new" profession of computer programmer is already showing signs of age after barely a quarter of a century. We argue that the shape of things to come—as well as those already in existence—signals the emerging proletarianization of work at every level below top management and a relatively few scientific and technical occupations.

At the same time, because of the permanent character of job cuts starting in the 1970s and glaringly visible after 1989, the latest recession has finally and irrevocably vitiated the traditional idea that the unemployed are an "industrial reserve army" awaiting the next phase of economic expansion. Of course, some laid-off workers, especially in union workplaces, will be recalled when the expansion, however sluggish, resumes. Even if one stubbornly clings to the notion of a reserve army, one cannot help but note that its soldiers in the main now occupy the part-time and temporary positions that appear to have replaced the well-paid full-time jobs.

Because of these changes, the "meaning" (in the survival, psychological, and cultural senses) of work—occupations and professions—as forms of life is in crisis. If the tendencies of the economy and the culture point to the conclusion that work is no longer significant in the formation of the self, one of the crucial questions of our time is what, if anything, can replace it. When layers of qualified—to say nothing of mass—labor are made redundant, obsolete, *irrelevant*, what, after five centuries during which work remained a, perhaps *the*, Western cultural ideal, can we mean by the "self"? Have we reached a large historical watershed, a climacteric that will be as devastating as natural climacterics of the past that destroyed whole species?

. . . Science and technology (of which organization is an instance) alter the nature of the labor process, not only the rationalized manual labor but also intellectual labor, especially the professions. Knowledge becomes ineluctably intertwined with, even dependent on, technology.

Even so-called labor-intensive work becomes increasingly mechanized and begins to be replaced by capital- and technology-intensive—*capitech-intensive*—work. Today, the regime of world economic life consists of scratching every itch of everyday life with sci-tech: eye glasses, underarm deodorant, preservatives in food, braces on pets. Technology has become the universal problem solver, the postmodern equivalent of *deus ex machina*, the ineluctable component of education and play as much as of work. No level of schooling is spared: Students interact with computers to learn reading, writing, social studies, math, and science in elementary school through graduate school. Play, once and still the corner of the social world least subject to regimentation, is increasingly incorporated into computer software, especially the products of the Apple corporation. More and more, we, the service and professional classes, are chained to our personal computers; with the help of the modem and the fax, we can communicate, in seconds, to the farthest reaches of the globe. We no longer need to press the flesh: By e-mail, we can attend conferences, gain access to library collections, and write electronic letters to perfect strangers. And, of course, with the assistance of virtual reality, we can engage in electronic sex. The only thing the computer cannot deliver is touch, but who needs it, anyway?[2]

... The new electronic communication technologies have become the stock-in-trade of a relatively few people because newspapers, magazines, and television have simply refused to acknowledge that we live in a complex world. Instead, they have tended to *simplify* news, even for the middle class. Thus, an "unintended" consequence of the dissemination of informatics to personal use is a growing information gap already implied by the personal computer. A relatively small number of people—no more than ten million in the United States—will, before the turn of the century, be fully wired to world sources of information and new knowledge: libraries, electronic newspapers and journals, conferences and forums on specialized topics, and colleagues, irrespective of country or region around the globe. Despite the much-heralded electronic highway, which will be largely devoted to entertainment products, the great mass of the world's population,

already restricted in its knowledge and power by the hierarchical division of the print media into tabloids and newspapers of record, will henceforth be doubly disadvantaged.

Of course, the information gap makes a difference only if one considers the conditions for a democratic—that is, a participatory—society. If popular governance even in the most liberal-democratic societies has been reduced in the last several decades to *plebiscitary* participation, the potential effect of computer-mediated knowledge is to exacerbate exclusion of vast portions of the underlying populations of all countries. ...

New uses of knowledge widen the gap between the present and the future; new knowledge challenges not only our collectively held beliefs but also the common ethical ground of our "civilization." The tendency of science to dominate the labor process, which emerged in the last half of the nineteenth century but attained full flower only in the last two decades, now heralds an entirely new regime of work in which almost no production *skills* are required. Older forms of technical or professional knowledge are transformed, incorporated, superseded, or otherwise eliminated by computer-mediated technologies—by applications of physical sciences intertwined with the production of knowledge: expert systems—leaving new forms of knowledge that are *inherently* labor-saving. But, unlike the mechanizing era of pulleys and electrically powered machinery, which retained the "hands-on" character of labor, computers have transferred most knowledge associated with the crafts and manual labor and, increasingly, intellectual knowledge, to the machine. As a result, although each generation of technological change makes some work more complex and interesting and raises the level of training or qualification required by a (diminishing) fraction of intellectual and manual labor force, for the overwhelming majority of workers, this process simplifies tasks or eliminates them, and thus eliminates the worker. ...

THINGS FALL APART

... Of course, the introduction of computer-mediated technologies in administrative services—especially banks and insurance companies and retail and wholesale trades—preceded that in goods production. From the early days of office computers in the 1950s, there has been a sometimes acrimonious debate about their effects. Perhaps the Spencer Tracy–Katharine Hepburn comedy *Desk Set* best exemplifies the issues: When a mainframe computer is introduced into the library of a large corporation, its professional and technical staff is at first alarmed, precisely because of their fear of losing their jobs. The film reiterates the prevailing view of the period (and ours?) that, far from posing a threat, computers promise to increase work by expanding needs. Significantly, the film asserts that the nearly inexhaustible desire for information inherent in human affairs will provide a fail-safe against professional and clerical redundancy. In contradistinction to these optimistic prognostications, new information technologies have enabled corporations, large law firms, and local governments to reduce the library labor force, including professional librarians. In turn, several library science schools have closed, including the prestigious library school at Columbia University.

By the 1980s, many if not most large and small businesses used electronic telephone devices to replace the live receptionist. A concomitant of these changes has been the virtual extinction of the secretary as an occupational category for all except top executives and department heads, if by that term we mean the individual service provided by a clerical worker to a single manager or a small group of managers. Today, at the levels of line and middle management, the "secretary" is a word-processing clerk; many middle managers have their own answering machines or voice mail and do their own word processing. They may have access to a word-processing pool only for producing extensive reports. Needless to say, after a quarter of a century during which computers displaced nearly all major office machines—especially typewriters, adding machines, and mechanical calculators—and all but eliminated the job category of file clerk, by the 1980s, many major corporations took advantage of the information "revolution" to decentralize their facilities away from cities to suburbs and exurbs. Once concentrated in large urban areas, data processing now can be done not only in small rural communities but also in satellite- and wire-linked, underdeveloped offshore sites. This has revived the once-scorned practice of working at home. Taken together, new forms of corporate organization, aided by the computer, have successfully arrested and finally reversed the steady expansion of the clerical labor force and have transferred many of its functions from the office to the bedroom.

Visiting a retail food supermarket in 1992, President George H. Bush was surprised to learn that the inventory label on each item enabled the checkout clerk to record the price by passing it through an electronic device, a feature of retailing that has been in place for at least fifteen years. This innovation has speeded the checkout process but has also relieved the clerk of punching the price on the register, which, in turn, saves time by adding the total bill automatically. The clerk in retail food and department stores works at a checkout counter and has been reduced to handling the product and observing the process, but intervenes only when it fails to function properly. Supermarket employers require fewer employees and, perhaps equally important, fewer workers in warehouses: An operator sits at a computer and identifies the quantity and location of a particular item rather than having to search for its location and count the numbers visually. The goods are loaded onto a vehicle by remote control and a driver operating a forklift takes them to the trucking dock, where they are mechanically loaded again. Whereas once the warehouse worker required a strong back, most of these functions are now performed mechanically and electronically.

Some of the contraction of clerical and industrial employment is, of course, a result of the general economic decline since the late 1980s. But given the astounding improvements in productivity of the manual industrial and clerical work force attributable to computerization, as we argued earlier, there is no evidence that a general economic recovery would restore most of the lost jobs in office and production sites—which raises the crucial issue of the relationship between measures designed to promote economic growth and job creation in the era of computer-mediated work. . . .

The American cultural ideal is tied not only to consumer society but also to the expectation that, given average abilities, with hard work and a little luck almost anyone can achieve occupational and even social mobility. Professional, technical, and managerial occupations perhaps even more than the older aspiration of entrepreneurial success are identified with faith in American success, and the credentials acquired through post-secondary education have become cultural capital, the necessary precondition of mobility. Put another way, if scientifically based technical knowledge has become the main productive force, schooling becomes the major route to mobility. No longer just places where traditional culture is disseminated to a relatively small elite, universities and colleges have become the key repositories of the cultural and intellectual capital from which professional, technical, and managerial labor is formed.

For the first quarter century after World War II, the expansion of these categories in the labor force was sufficient to absorb almost all of those trained in the professional and technical occupations. In some cases—notably education, the health professions, and engineering—there were chronic shortages of qualified professionals and managers. Now there is growing evidence of permanent redundancy within the new middle class. . . .

In the two decades beginning in the mid-1960s, the United States experienced the largest-scale restructuring and reforming of its industrial base in more than a century. Capital flight, which extended beyond U.S. borders, was abetted by technological change in administration and in production. Millions of workers, clerical and industrial, lost their high-paying jobs and were able to find employment only at lower wages. Well-paid union jobs became more scarce, and many, especially women, could find only part-time employment. But the American cultural ideal, buttressed by ideological—indeed, sometimes mythic—journalism and social theory, was barely affected in the wake of the elimination of millions of blue- and white-collar jobs. As C. Wright Mills once remarked in another context, these public issues were experienced as private troubles.

The persistence, if not so much the real and exponential growth, of poverty amid plenty was publicly acknowledged, even by mainstream politicians, but, like alienated labor, it was bracketed as a discrete "racial problem" that left the mainstream white population unaffected. Job

creation precluded serious consideration of the old Keynesian solutions; these had been massively defeated by the state-backed, yet ideologically antistatist, free-market ideologies. We were told that deregulation would free up the market and ensure economic growth that eventually would employ the jobless, provided they cleaned up their act. Even in the halcyon days of the Great Society programs of the war-inflated Johnson years, the antipoverty crusade offered the long-term unemployed only literacy and job training and, occasionally, the chance to finish high school and enter college or technical school. The Great Society created few permanent jobs and relied on the vitality of the private sector to employ those trained by its programs. . . .

The question now is not only what the consequences of the closing of routes to mobility of a substantial fraction of sons and daughters of manual and clerical workers may be, but also whether the professional and technical middle class can expect to reproduce itself at the same economic and social level under the new, deregulated conditions. For . . . the older and most prestigious professions of medicine, university teaching, law, and engineering are in trouble: Doctors and lawyers and engineers are becoming like assembly-line clerks . . . proletarians. Although thus far there are only scattered instances of long-term unemployment among them, the historical expectation, especially among doctors and lawyers, that they will own their own practices, has for most of them been permanently shattered. More than half of each profession (and a substantially larger proportion of recent graduates) have become salaried employees of larger firms, hospitals, or group practices; with the subsumption of science and technology under large corporations and the state engineers have not, typically, been self-employed for over a century.

Similarly, the attainment of a Ph.D. in the humanities or the social or natural sciences no longer ensures an entry-level academic position or a well-paid research or administrative job. Over the past fifteen years, a fairly substantial number of Ph.D.s have entered the academic proletariat of part-time and adjunct faculty. Most full-time teachers have little time and energy for the research they were trained to perform. Of course, the reversal of fortune for American colleges and universities is overdetermined by the stagnation and, in some sectors, decline of some professions; by the long-term recession; by organizational and technological changes; and by twenty years of conservative hegemony, which often takes the cultural form of anti-intellectualism. Since the 1960s, universities have been sites of intellectual as well as political dissent and even opposition. A powerful element in the long-term budget crises that many private as well as public institutions have suffered is at least partially linked to the perception among executive authorities that good money should not be thrown after bad.

And, with the steep decline in subprofessional and technical jobs, universities and colleges, especially the two-year community colleges, are re-examining their "mission" to educate virtually all who seek postsecondary education. In the past five years, we have seen the reemergence of the discourse of faculty "productivity," the reimposition of academic "standards," and other indicators that powerful forces are arrayed to impose policies of contraction in public education. . . .

In the subprofessions of elementary and secondary school teaching, social work, nursing, and medical technology, to name only the most numerically important, salaries and working conditions have deteriorated over the past decade so that the distinction, both economically and at the workplace, between the living standards of skilled manual workers and these professionals has sharply narrowed. Increasingly, many in these categories have changed their psychological as well as political relationship to the performance of the job. The work of a classroom teacher, line social worker, or nurse is, despite efforts by unions and professional organizations to shore up their professional status, no longer seen as a "vocation" in the older meaning of the term. Put succinctly, many in these occupations regard their work as does any manual worker: They take the money and run. More and more, practicing professionals look toward management positions to obtain work satisfaction as well as improvements in their

living standard because staying "in the trenches" is socially unappreciated and financially appears to be a dead end. Consequently, in addition to a mad race to obtain more credentials in order to qualify for higher positions, we have seen a definite growth in union organization among these groups even as union membership in the private sector, especially as a proportion of the manual labor force, has sharply declined. . . .

The economic and technological revolutions of our time notwithstanding, work is of course not disappearing. Nor should it. Rebuilding the cities, providing adequate education and child care, and saving the environment are all labor-intensive activities. The unpaid labor of housekeeping and child rearing remain among the major social scandals of our culture. The question is whether work as a cultural ideal has not already been displaced by its correlates: status and consumption. Except for a small proportion of those who are affected by technological innovation—those responsible for the innovations, those involved in developing their applications, and those who run the factories and offices—most workers, including professionals, are subjugated by labor-saving, work-simplification, and other rationalizing features of the context within which technology is introduced. For the subjugated, paid work has already lost its intrinsic meaning. It has become, at best, a means of making a living and a site of social conviviality.

NOTES

1. William DiFazio, *Longshoremen: Community and Resistance on the Brooklyn Waterfront* (South Hadley, MA: Bergin and Garvey, 1985).
2. Phillip K. Dick, *The Three Stigmata of Palmer Eldritch* (London: Jonathan Cape and Granada Books, 1978). First published in 1964, Dick's novel foreshadows the development of virtual reality technology, linking it to a future when most people can no longer live on Earth but are afforded the means to simulate a life on this planet from a position somewhere in the galaxy.

◆ 41 ◆

The Dominance of the Corporation

Carl Boggs

The immense growth of corporate power is probably the most fundamental development of the past 20 or 30 years.

This selection comes from a book entitled *The End of Politics: Corporate Power and the Decline of the Public Sphere.* This title represents well the point of this selection. What Boggs is describing is the issue of power in society. For most people the word *power* is associated with government. To Boggs, and to most sociologists, power is much more than government. Boggs's point is that government has been overshadowed by the power of the modern corporation. He describes the "corporate colonization of the public sphere," a "depoliticized society," "corporate hegemony," "economic globalization," and "the twilight of the nation state" as the reality we exist in today.

Despite significant governmental changes, policy shifts, and evolving social patterns over several decades, one element of continuity in American life remains, namely, the persistent expansion of corporate power. Far from being a simple economic fact of life, this process takes on political, social, and cultural meanings that penetrate into the deepest regions of everyday life. In political terms growing corporate power has worked most of all to hollow out the public sphere, as huge industrial, technical, and financial institutions have won more freedom to mobilize enormous resources for the purpose of shaping public dialogue and social existence. Corporations foster a mood of antipolitics by means of their power to commodify virtually every human activity as well as through their ownership and control of the mass media, their capacity to manipulate electoral and legislative politics toward sought goals, and their key role in globalizing the economy.

Since the 1970s big business in the United States has developed well beyond its traditionally hegemonic status, filling large parts of the void left by weakened labor unions, deradicalized social movements, the waning of broad progressive coalitions, and the growing ennui of the Democratic Party. Today's corporate behemoths (IBM, General Motors, AT&T, Microsoft, General Electric, Disney) depart from their predecessors in that they are· generally much larger, more far-flung and diversified, more organizationally streamlined, and far more technologically developed, even as they retain the same profit-driven agendas. At the same time, such giant entities actually begin to constitute a new public sphere of their own by virtue of having taken over many functions of political decision making, including investment and allocation of resources—but in a setting that allows for no internal democratic

From Carl Boggs, "Corporate Expansion and Political Decline," pp. 69–76 in *The End of Politics: Corporate Power and the Decline of the Public Sphere,* New York: Guilford Publications, Inc., 2000.

governance or popular accountability. Corporate networks dominate the state apparatus, own and control the mass media, profoundly shape education and medicine, and penetrate into even the most intimate realms of social life (e.g., the family, sexuality). Societal priorities relating to both domestic and foreign investment, foreign policy, technology, work, and culture are set or overwhelmingly influenced by a narrow stratum of industrial, financial, and technical elites.[1] For the most part, these elites now exercise far more control over the state than the state over the elites. And multinational corporations are relatively unconstrained by the strictures of democratic participation and the open exchange of ideas, being run as disciplined, centralized, and routinized hierarchies in the service of highly instrumental goals such as technical efficiency, material growth, and enhanced market shares. Viewed in this way, corporations function by their very raison d'etre to restrict development of an open, dynamic public sphere in which major issues of the day can be confronted. Much like quasi-feudal institutions, they are set up to guarantee elite domination, rank-and-file obedience, and minimal accountability to outside agencies and constituencies. The post-Fordist corporate system (like the capitalist legacy as a whole) is consciously designed in myriad ways to undercut citizenship, devalue politics, and resist the pull of democratic legitimating principles.[2]

The all-consuming "industrial civility" fostered by multinational corporations and Wall Street financial institutions has manifestly depoliticizing effects: not only are these structures themselves rigidly enclosed, but they exercise enough power to limit political debates and policy choices and also possess enough wealth to influence the entire field of candidates in electoral campaigns. Market principles, shaped and redefined by the modern technocratic apparatus, commodify and instrumentalize virtually all public discourses, practically everything that takes place in the political system. The "public good," insofar as it lives on in liberal discourse as a viable construct, does not exist outside of what elites may regard as contributing to efficient, pragmatic, and marketable outcomes; inevitably, economic discourse winds up conquering the public sphere, crowding out general societal concerns

such as collective consumption, social planning, and ecological sustainability.

The immense growth of corporate power is probably the most fundamental development of the past 20 or 30 years. As economic globalization proceeds, more than 40,000 multinational companies have moved into a position to dominate the international and domestic landscape, controlling vast wealth, resources, and institutional power—and with it a greater capacity than ever to reshape the public sphere. The leading corporations build power plants, mine and distribute natural resources, control the flow of the world's oil, gas, and electricity, manage the circulation of money, manufacture and sell the world's automobiles, electronic goods, ships, planes, weapons, computers, chemicals, and satellite technology, and grow most of the world's agricultural goods. They supply the world's military and police forces with equipment, arms, and munitions. In the process of doing all this they have maintained control over about 90 percent of all technology, including what goes into the mass media, information systems, and popular culture. From this vantage point the largest corporations are able to dominate virtually every phase of economic, political, and cultural life; they set the agenda for nearly every dimension of public policy.

In the United States, huge corporations like Microsoft, AT&T, Time Warner, Disney/ABC, IBM, and General Electric have assumed unprecedented power to delimit, directly and indirectly, what takes place in the realm of public discourse. They can shape the images and exchanges that effectively engage mass audiences, in part by employing sophisticated opinion-polling, telemarketing, and public relations in order to manipulate discourse toward specific (private) ends, resulting in a subversion of the public interest (defined in even the loosest sense). The corporations use a wide array of media influences, lobbies, PAC campaigns, experts, and lawyers to undercut the threat from consumer groups, labor, social movements, and community interests.

Intensified corporate colonization of the public sphere took a dramatic turn with passage in February 1996 of the Telecommunications Act. This legislation was ostensibly designed to enhance market competition among rival communications firms, thus stimulating improved services, greater popular access, and technological innovation. It would unleash a new era of heightened deregulation in keeping with the Reaganesque "free market" ethos of the times; indeed, this epochal rewriting of the 1934 Communications Act occurred at the very crest of the deregulatory ideological tide, as Patricia Aufderheide makes clear in her book on this legislation.[3] The result, of course, was precisely the opposite of what the legislation's partisans had claimed: it served mainly to pave the way toward more complete economic control over communications networks by a relatively small number of corporate giants. With the regulatory power of government now minimized, the private interests could more easily take control and set agendas in the entire information realm, including the Internet. Thus, while the Telecommunications Act promised a more interactive, open, even democratic setting, in practice anything resembling the public interest wound up as mere whispering amidst the established players' loud clamor for increased market share and profits. As Aufderheide writes: "It makes the American public, and public life itself, a derivative of the vigor and appetites of large business."[4] In this case the public domain was even further eviscerated by a decision-making process that unfolded largely outside of the public's purview, in a narrow process that received little media attention and involved no input from community groups, labor, consumers, and others left outside the corporate orbit. In Robert W. McChesney's words, "The analysis of the commercialization of the Internet is predicated on the thorough absence of any political debate concerning how best to employ cyberspace."[5] The all-important Telecommunications Act was the product of a closed system in which political "differences"—for example, those between Newt Gingrich and Al Gore—more or less vanished in the powerful field of privileged interests.

One of the hallmarks of a depoliticized society is the largely taken-for-granted character of deeply entrenched forms of domination. Nowadays, the Washington establishment makes certain that oppositional currents are confined to the most limited corridors of debate and participation, where political choices are ultimately instrumentalized, reduced to matters of technique and efficiency. Critical issues that revolve around the undeniably *public* character of corporations—such matters as the structure of authority, what is produced, the rights of labor, trade policies, and so forth—are rarely posed in the political arena. Tobacco production, sales, and advertising are viewed as the prerogative of "private" companies functioning in a "free" market, answerable only to their "stockholders." Similarly, the U.S. military interventions in Iraq during 1991 and later, costing tens of thousands of lives, were undertaken to defend U.S. "security" interests and protect American markets' easy access to oil, to ensure "the American way of life" (in President George H. Bush's language). And continued large-scale worker layoffs and dislocations resulting from corporate downsizing are justified as necessary to keep capitalist firms internationally competitive—examples of that are legion.

Corporate power is reproduced and reinforced in two ways: through the perpetual rationalization of economic structures and through increased atomization of social life outside the confines of the corporation. The rather extreme individualism that has always infused America's liberal tradition, in effect, helps to reproduce corporate power. What needs to be emphasized here is that the celebrated "unity," cohesion, and purposive development of large corporations feeds on a high degree of mass inertia, much of it derived from popular belief in the fiction (again, rooted in liberalism) of a "private" ownership that confers nearly absolute "rights" and "freedoms" on the owners of capital. In this scheme of things "politics" represents an unwelcome challenge to managerial autonomy and flexibility at a time when intensified global competition seems to demand greater adaptation and fluidity. Elites want maximum "freedom" from state intervention that taxes, regulates, influences markets, and otherwise impedes the open flow of resources, goods, and profits. While corporations do not always succeed in fighting off government supervision in certain areas, the legitimating ethos of private firms maximizing their interests in a presumably self-regulating market economy still holds sway and has even enjoyed a resurgence in the 1990s. To the extent that politics is devalued in favor of such presumed economic rationality, the main possible counterweight to corporate power—a strong, dynamic public sector—is eviscerated, undermined by an appeal to laissez-faire ideology. By the end of the twentieth century the balance between governmental and corporate power had tipped strongly in favor of the latter, despite continued (and generally unconvincing) protests against the tyranny of "big government" by conservatives and neoliberals.

Modern corporations, stronger, more rationalized, more ideologically self-conscious, and increasingly global in scope, have stepped into the political breach, indeed, many nominally "private" firms have for some time performed governing functions normally the purview of the state. Greider describes General Electric as such a company, which not only manufactures light bulbs, jet engines, and nuclear power equipment but also plays a significant role in the mass media (it owns NBC and CNBC), the military, the environment, foreign trade, and of course the larger expanse of the international economy. It devotes huge resources to advertising, controls important segments of media programming, and influences election campaigns along with legislation, not only through its enormous power and wealth but through its ubiquitous institutional presence. Few other entities came close to duplicating such far-reaching activities or exercising such influence in the media. As Greider writes, "Given the failure of the other institutions to adapt and revitalize themselves, corporate politics has become the organizational core of the political process—the main connective tissue linking people to their government."[6] The great impact of corporations like GE, of course, is weighted overwhelmingly on the side of conservatism—in economics if not in social and cultural values. Such quasi-governing institutions hire large teams of lawyers, lobbyists, public relations agents, and advertisers to protect their interests and propagate their values, all the while manufacturing the image of a "responsible corporate citizen" dedicated to human rights, democracy, environmental protection, Mom, and apple pie. The economic health of GE is naturally equated with and might pass for the common good: sustained growth and profits are presented as a necessary link to greater material affluence, proliferation of jobs, a better environment, a more

powerful country. In this schema GE does maintain an extensive work force, much of it well-paid, with nearly 250,000 employees at 280 plants in the United States and overseas.

The political reality is that General Electric has worked aggressively, often ruthlessly, for a strong military, a fiercely nationalistic foreign policy, free trade, reductions in taxes and social programs, and loosened environmental regulations. As a major producer of nuclear power equipment it has, not surprisingly, been in the forefront of a pronuclear agenda. Further, with its multiple internal and external constituencies, GE has taken on the character of an expanded and updated urban political machine—though with far less accountability. GE executives and managers have been found guilty of corruption and criminal fraud, but penalties have rarely been harsh enough to deter repeated violations. Thus, in 1990 GE was convicted of criminal fraud for cheating the Army on a $254 million contract for battlefield computers, for which the corporation paid $16.1 million in criminal and civil fines—including $11.7 million to settle roughly 200 other government charges. At GE, as in the rest of the corporate economy, ethics have all too often been bypassed in favor of more instrumental pursuits; while fervently upheld in theory, in practice ethics have been quietly subordinated to the operational criteria of control, efficiency, and profits. And the influence of workers and consumers on vital areas of decision making at GE has been minimal, especially at a time when downsizing and layoffs further erode popular leverage. Managerial elites want to escape governmental regulations of *any* sort, and—at least since the later 1970s—there has been a major impetus toward the resurgence of laissez-faire ideology in the United States. By means of a sustained mobilization of professional expertise, moreover, these elites have been able to exercise pervasive influence over the flow of political and cultural information, seeking ever to suppress such tame liberal ideas as the free exchange of ideas, government involvement as needed, and active participation by all citizens in political decision making.

Corporate hegemony is further solidified by the workings of economic globalization, the information revolution, mass media, and the culture industry—all of which are interwoven in a matrix of commodified production. Multinational corporations exercise nearly total control over resource allocation, investment decisions, commerce, and world trade, severely reducing the role of specifically national actors (whether governments or firms).[7] "Global cities" like Tokyo, Mexico City, New York, Singapore, Los Angeles, and Sao Paolo, with no particular regional or national allegiances, become magnetic centers of capital and technology flows that resist the force of territorial boundaries. Working through the World Bank, World Trade Organization (WTO), and the International Monetary Fund (IMF), and aided by such trade arrangements as GATT and NAFTA, multinationals use their financial leverage to push for a market-centered capitalism featuring minimal governmental controls, fiscal austerity, and privatization wherever feasible. Any genuine form of political regulation is regarded as a threat to the "free market," which is glibly passed off as representative of a form of economic "democracy." The deep structural impacts of a highly globalized and interconnected market system have yet to be fully comprehended. On the downside, though, economic upheavals emanating from Asia from late 1997 through most of 1998 (the "Asian contagion" scare) may well offer some clues to the future. The first ripples of economic crisis already reveal momentous forces that are exacerbating class (and possibly racial) divisions in many countries. Meanwhile, globalization has led to a decline of national governmental power and local autonomy to such a degree that many basic economic decisions are being usurped by multinational corporations and allied international organizations. In the absence of effective multinational planning or regulation mechanisms, development will surely have little in common with the utopian vision of elites who see — not chaos and polarization — but only unfettered economic growth, a worldwide strengthening of human freedoms and rights, and the increased technological capacity to solve the world's major problems.

We know that corporate power does in fact translate into dynamic economic development, but the penetration of capital into every region of the world brings with it highly uneven forms of growth, sharpened class divisions, social dislocations, and mounting ecological crises. The process reproduces the same emphasis on privatized modes of production and consumption, market priorities over social goods, technological manipulation of resources and information, and material growth for its own (and profits') sake — leading to the same extreme maldistribution of wealth, authoritarian governance, and familiar coupling of urban decay and violence. With global political instrumentalities lacking sufficient leverage, the public sphere — such as it is — inevitably succumbs to the ceaseless pressures of the economic powers that be, leaving no ethical or governing framework for solving urgent problems. (The failure of the U.N.-sponsored Earth Summit to deal decisively with the global ecological crisis at its meeting in Rio de Janeiro in 1992, among many other such failures, reflects this predicament.) The subordination of politics to the all-powerful commodity underpins the strong corporate drive toward a unified world economy where diversity means little more than capitalist rivalries, where genuine cultural and ideological pluralism are submerged by the homogenizing ethic of market relations.

Economic globalization creates a shrinking world even as markets expand, the flow of capital, technology, material resources, transportation, and telecommunications having generally increased at an accelerating pace since the 1970s. Further, goods and services are no longer produced in only one location but rather enter the market through what Robert Reich dubs the "global web" of producers, computers, and satellites that link designers, engineers, contractors, and distributors worldwide. Resources, knowledge, and customized services are more easily than ever exchanged instantaneously across manufacturing and distribution sectors, across national boundaries. Thus, in an evolving complex global and high-value economy, "fewer products have distinct nationalities. Quantities can be produced efficiently in many different locations, to be combined in all sorts of ways to serve customer needs in many places. Intellectual and financial capital can come from anywhere, and be added instantly."[8] This is just as true for cultural products like film and music as it is for such durable goods as autos, electronic goods, and computers. To be sure, there are still remnants of national economic identity in the multinational system—Japan versus the United States, competition among developing Asian powers for markets, conflict among Latin American countries, and so on—but the entire corporate system, while still tied to specific governments, is becoming more and more disconnected from the nation-state. In Reich's words, "The emerging American company knows no national boundaries, feels no geographic constraint."[9] Moreover, as interdependence weakens nationalism, it also renders national and local politics weaker and more vulnerable to the inexorable pressures of the cosmopolitan market.

We have thus reached what Jean-Marie Guehenno describes as "the twilight of the nation-state," a political construct that has ultimately adapted poorly to the web of economic interdependence and the vast power of global corporations. It follows that a politics organized historically around viable nation-states will be far less today a locus of a mass mobilization, legitimacy, and decision making than it has been for the past 200 years. The result is what Guehenno terms a "crisis of the spatial perception of power," in which the connection between the exercise of power (both economic and political) and territoriality is severely weakened.[10] As politics becomes increasingly subordinated to a mosaic of private interests, governing structures tend to simply follow a variety of short-term, instrumental agendas of the moment, bereft of any larger vision or public sense of purpose that might transcend the pull of corporate power. Globalization undermines the strong historical connection between capitalism and nationalism. As Greider argues: "The obsession with nations in competition misses the point of what is happening: The global economy divides every society into new camps of conflicting economic interests. It undermines every nation's ability to maintain social cohesion. It mocks the assumption of shared political values that supposedly unite people in the nation-state."[11] Here globalism extends and deepens the domestic logic of corporate colonization, making a charade of democracy as it transforms the entire landscape. . . .

What the analysis presented in these pages suggests, however, is that even in the event of the corporate hegemony becoming fragile—that is, even once its contradictions begin to explode—any future revival of politics at the level of mass

publics will face tremendous obstacles. The deep, collective sense of empowerment that must catalyze such a political revival runs up against not only the awesome might of global capital but, closer to home, the devastating effects of a hollowed-out public sphere and civic culture. The problem is further complicated once we take into account the disabling limits of those formal liberal-democratic structures that remain from an earlier period; clearly any political rebirth will be forced to reappropriate and transcend that harshly compromised tradition, one that has lately run counter to the creative, empowering psychological energies needed to produce an engaged citizenry.[12] Lacking these energies, even the most ambitious radical-democratic ideals and arrangements, even the most celebrated participatory schemes, will ultimately lose their popular appeal. In an age of corporate colonization, unfortunately, the historical processes at work seem relentless in subverting what is needed for a revival of true participatory politics.

At the end of the twentieth century the corporate order appears more stable and in control than at any other time in the recent past, despite a series of mounting contradictions that might have been expected to undermine the whole edifice. This is so largely because the system, in its globalized incarnation, has been able to maintain an unprecedented degree of ideological and cultural hegemony over both state and civil society; opposition is subverted before it can fully confront the multiple contradictions of the system. Elites can more easily solidify their position since their claim to rule is rarely questioned enough to place their interests and priorities fundamentally into question. Unlike the popular strata involved with daily struggles and grassroots movements, elites typically do not suffer the well-known "postmodern" malaise of sharply fragmented identities and purposes; despite internal divisions, their overall class orientation is far more unified. As capital becomes more fluid, mobile, and global, as material and technological resources become more concentrated, the multinational corporations begin to enjoy new leverage, qualitatively, vis-à-vis virtually everything that stands before them (including even the most powerful nation-states). And where citizen participation and local sovereignty are already devalued in the domestic society, as in the case of the United States, such leverage expands even further. In the absence of strong global or national counterweights, the worldwide market is much freer to pursue its deadly course of expansionism (and ultimately destruction of the planet). A "new world order" built along these lines—that is, featuring the massive concentration of economic and political power—inevitably conflicts with even the most rudimentary requirements of democratic politics, namely, an open public sphere, a thriving civic culture, broad allocation of material resources, and minimal differences between rich and poor. After all, sustained citizen involvement in community life and political decision making hardly fits the corporate demands for hierarchy, profit maximization, cost cutting, and "market flexibility" in a period of heightened global competition. Whether corporate hegemony can be maintained in a world riven with economic crisis, social polarization, and civil strife—a world ultimately faced with ecological catastrophe—is yet another matter.

NOTES

1. Stanley A. Deetz, *Corporate Colonization* (Albany, NY: SUNY Press, 1992).
2. See Bowles and Gintis, *Capitalism and Democracy*, ch. 2, on this historic conflict between two competing forces.
3. Patricia Aufderheide, *Communications Policy and the Public Interest* (New York: Guilford Press, 1999), 22–23.
4. Ibid., 62.
5. Robert W. McChesney, *Corporate Media and the Threat to Democracy* (New York: Seven Stories Press, 1997), 34.
6. William Greider, *Who Will Tell the People?* (New York: Simon & Schuster, 1992), 336.
7. See Robert Reich, *The Work of Nations* (New York: Vintage, 1992), chs. 10, 11.
8. Ibid., 112.
9. Ibid., 124.
10. Jean-Marie Guehenno, *End of the Nation State* (Minneapolis: University of Minnesota Press, 1995), 20.
11. Greider, *One World, Ready or Not* (New York: Simon and Schuster, 1997), 18.
12. For an extended discussion of the requirements for a participatory citizenship, see Paul Barry Clarke, *Deep Citizenship* (London: Pluto, 1996), chs. 4, 7.

◆ 42 ◆

The Politics of the Contented

John Kenneth Galbraith

*[The Contented Majority] rule under the rich cloak of democracy, a democracy
in which the less fortunate do not participate . . . they are [not] silent in their
contentment. They can be . . . very angry and very articulate about
what seems to invade their state of self-satisfaction.*

Americans pride themselves on a set of political institutions they call democracy.
However, can a democracy exist when large numbers of people are excluded from
the process (or exclude themselves from the process), especially if they are the
most discontented and the most disadvantaged in the society? In this critique of
American democracy, Galbraith describes the views of those who are active in and
have come to control our political system. They are not a few rich people, but instead a large diversity of contented people who work together to keep what they have
and protect themselves through action and through a set of principles they claim to
be democratic. Galbraith's book describes these contented people, and this selection is an analysis worth serious attention if we are to understand the working of our
political institutions.

. . . In past times, the economically and socially
fortunate were, as we know, a small minority—
characteristically a dominant and ruling handful.
They are now a majority, though . . . a majority
not of all citizens but of those who actually vote.
A convenient reference is needed for those so situated and who so respond at the polls. They will
be called the *Contented Majority*, the *Contented Electoral Majority*, or more spaciously, the
Culture of Contentment. There will be adequate
reiteration that this does not mean they are a majority of all those eligible to vote. They rule under
the rich cloak of democracy, a democracy in

which the less fortunate do not participate. Nor
does it mean—a most important point—that they
are silent in their contentment. They can be, as
when this book goes to press, very angry and very
articulate about what seems to invade their state
of self-satisfaction.

• • •

Although income broadly defines the contented majority, no one should suppose that that
majority is occupationally or socially homogeneous. It includes the people who manage or otherwise staff the middle and upper reaches of the
great financial and industrial firms, independent
businessmen and women, and those in lesser em-
ployments whose compensation is more or less
guaranteed. Also the large population—lawyers,
doctors, engineers, scientists, accountants and
many others, not excluding journalists and

professors—who make up the modern professional class. Included also are a certain, if diminishing, number who once were called *proletarians*—those with diverse skills whose wages are now, with some frequency, supplemented by those of a diligent wife. They, like others in families with dual paychecks, find life reasonably secure.

Further, although they were once a strongly discontented community, there are the farmers, who, when buttressed by government price supports, are now amply rewarded.[1] Here, too, there is a dominant, if not universal, mood of satisfaction. Finally, there is the rapidly increasing number of the aged who live on pensions or other retirement allowance and for whose remaining years of life there is adequate or, on occasion, ample financial provision.

None of this suggests an absence of continuing personal aspiration or a unanimity of political view. Doing well, many wish to do better. Having enough, many wish for more. Being comfortable, many raise vigorous objection to that which invades comfort. What is important is that there is no self-doubt in their present situation. The future for the contented majority is thought effectively within their personal command. Their anger is evident—and, indeed, can be strongly evident—only when there is a threat or possible threat to present well-being and future prospect—when government and the seemingly less deserving intrude or threaten to intrude their needs or demands. This is especially so if such action suggests higher taxes.

As to political attitude, there is a minority, not small in number, who do look beyond personal contentment to a concern for those who do not share in the comparative well-being. Or they see the more distant dangers that will result from a short-run preoccupation with individual comfort. Idealism and foresight are not dead; on the contrary, their expression is the most reputable form of social discourse. Although self-interest, as we shall see, does frequently operate under a formal cover of social concern, much social concern is genuinely and generously motivated.

Nonetheless, self-regard is, predictably, the dominant—indeed the controlling—mood of the Contented Majority. This becomes wholly evident when public action on behalf of those outside this electoral majority is the issue. If it is to be effective, such action is invariably at public cost. Accordingly, it is regularly resisted as a matter of high, if sometimes rather visibly contrived, principle. Of this, more later.

• • •

In the recent past, much has been held wrong with the performance of the United States government as regards both domestic and foreign policy. This has been widely attributed to the inadequacy, incompetence, or generally perverse performance of individual politicians and political leaders. Mr. Reagan and his now accepted intellectual and administrative detachment, and Mr. Bush, his love of travel and his belief in oratory as the prime instrument of domestic action, have been often cited. Similarly criticized have been leaders and members of the Congress, and, if less stridently, governors and other politicians throughout the Republic.

This criticism, or much of it, is mistaken or, at best, politically superficial. The government of the United States in recent years has been a valid reflection of the economic and social preferences of the majority of those voting—the electoral majority. In defense of Ronald Reagan and George [H.] Bush as Presidents, it must be said and emphasized that both were, or are, faithful representatives of the constituency that elected them. We attribute to politicians what should be attributed to the community they serve.

• • •

The first and most general expression of the Contented Majority is its affirmation that those who compose it are receiving their just deserts. What the individual member aspires to have and enjoy is the product of his or her personal virtue, intelligence, and effort. Good fortune being earned or the reward of merit, there is no equitable justification for any action that impairs it—that subtracts from what is enjoyed or might be enjoyed. The normal response to such action is indignation or, as suggested, anger at anything infringing on what is so clearly deserved.

There will be, as noted, individuals—on frequent occasion in the past, some who have inherited what they have—who will be less certain that they merit their comparative good fortune. And more numerous will be those scholars, journalists, professional dissidents, and other voices who will express sympathy for the excluded and concern for the future, often from positions of relative personal comfort. The result will be political effort and agitation in conflict with the aims and preferences of the contented. The number so motivated is, to repeat, not small, but they are not a serious threat to the electoral majority. On the contrary, by their dissent, they give a gracing aspect of democracy to the ruling position of the fortunate. They show in their articulate way that "democracy is working." Liberals in the United States, Labour politicians and spokesmen in Britain, are, indeed, vital in this regard. Their writing and rhetoric give hope to the excluded and, at a minimum, ensure that they are not both excluded *and* ignored.

Highly convenient social and economic doctrine also emerges in defense of contentment, some of which is modern and some ancient. As will be seen, what once justified the favored position of the few—a handful of aristocrats or capitalists—has now become the favoring defense of the comfortable many.

• • •

The second, less conscious but extremely important characteristic of the Contented Majority, one already noted, is its attitude toward time. In the briefest word, short-run public inaction, even if held to be alarming as to consequence, is always preferred to protective long-run action. The reason is readily evident. The long run may not arrive; that is the frequent and comfortable belief. More decisively important, the cost of today's action falls or could fall on the favored community; taxes could be increased. The benefits in the longer run may well be for others to enjoy. In any case, the quiet theology of laissez faire holds that all will work out for the best in the end.

Here, too, there will be contrary voices. These will be heard, and often with respect, but not to the point of action. For the Contented Majority, the logic of inaction is inescapable. For many years, for example, there has been grave concern in the northeastern United States and extending up to Canada over acid rain caused by sulphurous emissions from the power plants of the Midwest. The long-run effects will, it is known, be extremely adverse—on the environment, the recreational industries, the forest industry, maple sugar producers, and on the general benignity of local life and scene. The cost of corrective measures to the electric power plants and their consumers will be immediate and specific; the longer-term conservation reward will, in contrast, be diffuse, uncertain, and debatable as to specific

incidence. From this comes the policy avowed by the contented. It does not deny the problem, this not being possible; rather, it delays action. Notably, it proposes more research, which very often provides a comforting, intellectually reputable gloss over inaction. At the worst, it suggests impaneling a commission, the purpose of which would be to discuss and recommend action or perhaps postponement thereof. At the very worst, there is limited, perhaps symbolic, action, as in recent times. Other long-run environmental dangers—global warming and the dissipation of the ozone layer—invite a similar response.

Another example of the role of time is seen in attitudes toward what is called, rather formidably, the *economic infrastructure of the United States*—its highways, bridges, airports, mass transportation facilities, and other public structures. These are now widely perceived as falling far below future need and even present standards of safety. Nonetheless, expenditure and new investment in this area are powerfully and effectively resisted. Again the very plausible reason: Present cost and taxation are specific; future advantage is dispersed. Later and different individuals will benefit; why pay for persons unknown? So again the readily understandable insistence on inaction and the resulting freedom from present cost. Contentment is here revealed to be of growing social influence, more decisive than in the past. The interstate highway system, the parkways, the airports, even perhaps the hospitals and schools of an earlier and financially far more astringent time but one when the favored voters were far fewer, could not be built today.

In the 1980s, the preference for short-run advantage was dramatically evident, as will later be noted, in the continued deficits in the budget of the United States and in the related and resulting deficits in the international trade accounts. Here, the potential cost to the favored voting community, the Contented Electoral Majority, was highly specific. To reduce the deficit meant more taxation or a reduction in expenditures, including those important to the comfortable. The distant benefits seemed, predictably, diffuse and uncertain as to impact. Again, no one can doubt that Presidents Reagan and Bush were or are in highly sympathetic response to their constituency on this matter. Although criticism of their action or inaction has been inevitable, their instinct as to what their politically decisive supporters wanted has been impeccable.

• • •

A third commitment of the comfortably situated is to a highly selective view of the role of the state—of government. Broadly and superficially speaking, the state is seen as a burden; no political avowal of modern times has been so often reiterated and so warmly applauded as the need "to get government off the backs of the people." The albatross was not hung more oppressively by his shipmates around the neck of the Mariner. The need to lighten or remove this burden and therewith, agreeably, the supporting taxes is an article of high faith for the comfortable or Contented Majority.

But although government in general has been viewed as a burden, there have been, as will be seen, significant and costly exceptions from this broad condemnation. Excluded from criticism, needless to say, have been Social Security, medical care at higher income levels, farm income supports, and financial guarantees to depositors in ill-fated banks and savings and loan enterprises. These are strong supports to the comfort and security of the Contented Majority. No one would dream of attacking them, even marginally, in any electoral contest.

Specifically favored also have been military expenditures, their scale and fiscally oppressive effect notwithstanding. This has been for three reasons. These expenditures, as they are reflected in the economy in wages, salaries, profits, and assorted subsidies to research and other institutions, serve to sustain or enhance the income of a considerable segment of the Contented Electoral Majority. Weapons expenditure (unlike, for example, spending for the urban poor) rewards a very comfortable constituency.

More important, perhaps, [is that] military expenditures—and those for the associated operations of the CIA and (to a diminishing extent) the Department of State—have been seen in the past as vital protection against the gravest perceived threat to continued comfort and contentment. That threat was from Communism, with its clear and overt, even if remote, endangerment of the economic life and rewards of the comfortable. This fear, in turn, extending on occasion to clinical paranoia, ensured support to the military establishment. And American liberals, no less than conservatives, felt obliged, given their personal commitment to liberty and human rights, to show by their support of defense spending that they were not "soft on Communism."

The natural focus of concern was the Soviet Union and its once seemingly stalwart satellites in Eastern Europe. Fear of the not-inconsiderable competence of the Soviets in military technology and production provided the main pillar of support for American military spending. However, the alarm was geographically comprehensive. It supported expenditure and military action against such improbable threats as those from Angola, Afghanistan, Ethiopia, Grenada, El Salvador, Nicaragua, Laos, Cambodia, and, massively, tragically, and at great cost, from Vietnam. From being considered a source of fear and concern, only Communist China was, from the early 1970s on, exempt. Turning against the Soviet Union and forgiven for its earlier role in Korea and Vietnam, it became an honorary bastion of democracy and free enterprise, which, later repressive actions notwithstanding, it rather substantially remains.

The final reason that military expenditures have continued to be favored is the self-perpetuating power of the military and weapons establishment itself—its control of the weaponry it is to produce, the missions for which it is to be prepared, and in substantial measure the funds that it receives and dispenses.

Until World War II, the fortunately situated in the United States, the Republican Party in particular, resisted military expenditures, as they then resisted all government spending. In the years since, the presumed worldwide Communist menace, as frequently it was designated, brought a major reversal: Those with a comfortable concern for their own economic position became the most powerful advocates of the most prodigal of military outlays. With the collapse of Communism, an interesting question arises as to what the attitude of the contented will now be. That the military establishment, public and private, will continue on its own authority to claim a large share of its past financial support is not, however, seriously in doubt.

• • •

Such are the exceptions that the Contented Majority makes to its general condemnation of government as a burden. Social expenditure favorable to the fortunate, financial rescue, military

spending and, of course, interest payments—
these constitute in the aggregate by far the largest
part of the federal budget and that which in recent times has shown by far the greatest increase.
What remains—expenditures for welfare, low-
cost housing, health care for those otherwise
unprotected, public education, and the diverse
needs of the great urban slums—is what is now
viewed as the burden of government. It is
uniquely that which serves the interests of those
outside the Contented Electoral Majority; it is,
and inescapably, what serves the poor. Here
again, Mr. Reagan and now Mr. Bush showed or
now show a keen sense of their constituency. So
also they do with regard to one further tendency
of the Contented Majority.

• • •

The final characteristic here to be cited and
stressed is the tolerance shown by the contented of
great differences in income. These differences
have already been noted, as has the fact that the disparity is not a matter that occasions serious dispute.
A general and quite plausible convention is here
observed: The price of prevention of any aggression against one's own income is tolerance of the
greater amount for others. Indignation at, and ad-
vocacy of, redistribution of income from the very
rich, inevitably by taxes, opens the door for consideration of higher taxes for the comfortable but less
endowed. This is especially a threat given the position and possible claims of the least favored part of
the population. Any outcry from the fortunate half
could only focus attention on the far inferior position of the lower half. The plush advantage of the
very rich is the price the Contented Electoral Majority pays for being able to retain what is less but
what is still very good. And, it is averred, there
could be solid social advantage in this tolerance of
the very fortunate: "To help the poor and middle
classes, one must cut the taxes on the rich."[2]

Ronald Reagan's single-most celebrated economic action (the acceptance of the related
budget deficit possibly apart) was his tax relief for
the very affluent. Marginal rates on the very rich
were reduced from a partly nominal 70 percent to
50 percent in 1981; then, with tax reform, the rate
on the richest fell to 28 percent in 1986, although
this was partly offset by other tax changes. The result was a generous increase in the after-tax income in the higher income brackets. That part of

Mr. Reagan's motivation was his memory of the
presumptively painful tax demands on his Hollywood pay seems not in doubt. He was also influenced by the economic ideas that had been
adapted to serve tax reduction on the rich—
broadly, the doctrine that if the horse is fed amply
with oats, some will pass through to the road for
the sparrows. But once again there was also the
sense of what served his larger constituency, as
well as that of the concurring Congress. This constituency accepted the favor to the very rich in
return for protection for itself.

• • •

In summary, we see that much that has been
attributed in these past years to ideology, idiosyn-
crasy, or error of political leadership has deep
roots in the American polity. It has been said, and
often, in praise of Ronald Reagan as President
that he gave the American people a good feeling
about themselves. This acclaim is fully justified
as regards the people who voted for him, and
even perhaps as regards that not inconsiderable
number who, voting otherwise, found themselves
in silent approval of the very tangible personal effect of his tax policies.

In past times in the United States, under government by either of the major parties, many experienced a certain sense of unease, of troubled
conscience and associated discomfort when con-
templating those who did not share the good fortune of the fortunate. No such feeling emanated
from Ronald Reagan; Americans were being rewarded as they so richly deserved. If some did not
participate, it was because of their inability or
by their choice. As it was once the privilege of
Frenchmen, both the rich and the poor, to sleep
under bridges, so any American had the un-
doubted right to sleep on street grates. This might
not be the reality, but it was the presidentially
ordained script. And this script was tested by
Ronald Reagan, out of his long and notable the-
atrical training, not for its reality, not for its truth,
but, as if it were a motion picture or a television
commercial: for its appeal. That appeal was widespread; it allowed Americans to escape their consciences and their social concerns and thus to feel
a glow of self-approval.

Not all, of course, could so feel, nor, necessarily, could a majority of all citizens of voting age.
And there was a further and socially rather bitter

circumstance, one that has been conveniently, neglected: the comfort and economic well-being of the Contented Majority was being supported and enhanced by the presence in the modern economy of a large, highly useful, even essential class that does not share in the agreeable existence of the favored community.

NOTES

1. "The average 1988 income of farm operator households was $33,535, compared with $34,017 for all

U.S. households. However, 5 percent of farm operator households had incomes above $100,000, compared to 3.2 percent of all U.S. households." *Agricultural Income and Finance: Situation and Outlook Report* (Washington, D.C.: U.S. Department of Agriculture Economic Research Service, May 1990), p. 26.
2. George Gilder, *Wealth and Poverty* (New York: Basic Books, 1981), p. 188. He is quoted by Kevin Phillips in *The Politics of Rich and Poor: Wealth and the American Electorate in the Reagan Aftermath* (New York: Random House, 1990), p. 62.

✦ 43 ✦

Liberal Democracy and Democratic Culture

Larry Diamond

> *[Political culture is often treated as] a people's predominant beliefs, attitudes, values, ideals, sentiments, and evaluations about the political system of their country and the role of the self in that system. . . . [Various views of political culture] imply several important ingredients of liberal democracy: tolerance for opposing political beliefs and positions and also more generally for social and cultural differences; pragmatism and flexibility . . . ; trust in other political actors and in the social environment; a willingness to compromise . . . ; and civility of political discourse and respect for other views.*

Political culture and political institutions are interdependent. Through describing political culture in this selection, Larry Diamond explains the "correlates of democracy," the essential attitudes, values, and beliefs that are necessary for developing and extending democratic institutions. He focuses on the importance of pragmatism, views of authority, and commitment to democracy itself among both the political elites and the public.

From Diamond, Larry, *Developing Democracy: Toward Consolidation*, pp. 7–19, 161–174. © 1999 by The Johns Hopkins University Press. Reprinted with permission of The Johns Hopkins University Press.

CONCEPTUALIZING DEMOCRACY

. . . Where conceptions of democracy diverge today is on the range and extent of political properties encompassed by democracy. Minimalist definitions of what I call *electoral democracy* descend from Joseph Schumpeter, who defined democracy as a system "for arriving at political decisions in which individuals acquire the power to decide by means of a competitive struggle for the people's vote."[1] . . .

Liberal Democracy

Specifically, *liberal democracy* has the following components:

- Control of the state and its key decisions and allocations lies, in fact as well as in constitutional theory, with elected officials (and not democratically unaccountable actors or foreign powers); in particular, the military is subordinate to the authority of elected civilian officials.
- Executive power is constrained, constitutionally and in fact, by the autonomous power of other government institutions (such as an independent judiciary, parliament, and other mechanisms of horizontal accountability).
- Not only are electoral outcomes uncertain, with a significant opposition vote and the presumption of party alternation in government, but no group that adheres to constitutional principles is denied the right to form a party and contest elections (even if electoral thresholds and other rules exclude small parties from winning representation in parliament).
- Cultural, ethnic, religious, and other minority groups (as well as historically disadvantaged majorities) are not prohibited (legally or in practice) from expressing their interests in the political process or from speaking their language or practicing their culture.
- Beyond parties and elections, citizens have multiple, ongoing channels for expression and representation of their interests and values, including diverse, independent associations and movements, which they have the freedom to form and join.[2]
- There are alternative sources of information (including independent media) to which citizens have (politically) unfettered access.
- Individuals also have substantial freedom of belief, opinion, discussion, speech, publication, assembly, demonstration, and petition.

- Citizens are politically equal under the law (even though they are invariably unequal in their political resources).
- Individual and group liberties are effectively protected by an independent, nondiscriminatory judiciary, whose decisions are enforced and respected by other centers of power.
- The rule of law protects citizens from unjustified detention, exile, terror, torture, and undue interference in their personal lives not only by the state but also by organized nonstate or antistate forces.

These ten conditions imply an eleventh: if political authority is to be constrained and balanced, individual and minority rights protected, and a rule of law assured, democracy requires a constitution that is supreme. Liberal democracies in particular "are and have to be constitutional democracies. The lack of a constitutional spirit, of an understanding of the centrality of constitutional stability, is one of the weaknesses" of many illiberal third-wave democracies in the postcommunist world, as well as in the Third World.[3] A constitutional state is a state of justice, a *Rechtsstaat* in the German, in which the state acts predictably, in accordance with the laws, and the courts enforce restrictions on popularly elected governments when they violate the laws or the constitutional rules.[4] This in turn requires a legal and judicial system and, more broadly, a state with some capacity. Thus Juan Linz's dictum: "no state, no *Rechtsstaat*, no democracy."[5] . . .

There is not now and has never been in the modern world of nation-states a perfect democracy, one in which all citizens have roughly equal political resources and in which government is completely or almost completely responsive to all citizens. . . .

It is important, then, not to take the existence of democracy, even liberal democracy, as cause for self-congratulation. Democracy should be viewed as a developmental phenomenon. Even when a country is above the threshold of electoral (or even liberal) democracy, democratic institutions can be improved and deepened or may need to be consolidated; political competition can be made fairer and more open; participation can become more inclusive and vigorous; citizens' knowledge, resources, and competence can grow; elected (and appointed) officials can be made more responsive and accountable; civil liberties can be better protected; and the rule of law can become more efficient and secure.[6] Viewed in this way, continued democratic development is a challenge for all countries, including the United States; all democracies, new and established, can become more democratic. . . .

Viewed from a developmental perspective, the fate of democracy is open-ended. The elements of liberal democracy emerge in various sequences and degrees, at varying paces in the different countries.[7] . . .

There is no guarantee that democratic development moves in only one direction, and there is much to suggest that all political systems (including democracies, liberal or otherwise) become rigid, corrupt, and unresponsive in the absence of periodic reform and renewal.[8] Democracy not only may lose its quality, it may even effectively disappear, not merely through the breakdown of formal institutions but also through the more insidious processes of decay. . . .

THEORIES OF POLITICAL CULTURE AND DEMOCRACY

Conceptualizing Political Culture

. . . [Political culture is often treated as] *a people's predominant beliefs, attitudes, values, ideals, sentiments, and evaluations about the political system of their country and the role of the self in that system.* These components of political culture (which may be summarized simply as distinctive predispositions, or "orientations to action")[9] have been classified into three types of orientation: a *cognitive* orientation, involving knowledge of and beliefs about the political system; an *affective* orientation, consisting of feelings about the political system; and an *evaluational* orientation, including commitments to political values and judgments (making use of information and feelings) about the performance of the political system relative to those values.[10] Pure evaluations, of course, may change readily with empirical experience, but norms and values represent the most deeply embedded and enduring orientations toward political action and the political system. It is these affective and evaluational orientations to democracy that are the main concern of this chapter. . . .

The Cultural Correlates of Democracy

Theories about the relationship between political culture and democracy date back at least to the classical Greek political thinkers. From Aristotle in particular, political culture theory has inherited concerns for the importance of moderation and tolerance and for the dangers of political extremism and unfettered populism, which continue to resonate in the contemporary literature. The development of a pattern, and ultimately a culture, of *moderation, accommodation, cooperation,* and *bargaining* among political elites has emerged as a major theme of the dynamic, process-oriented theories of democratic transition and consolidation. But well before this generation of work, theorists such as Gabriel Almond, Sidney Verba, Seymour Martin Lipset, Robert Dahl, and Alex Inkeles identified these orientations in political culture as necessary for the development and maintenance of democracy, to cope with one of the central dilemmas of democracy: to balance cleavage and conflict with the need for consensus.[11]

These orientations tend to fit together. They imply several important ingredients of liberal democracy: tolerance for opposing political beliefs and positions and also more generally for social and cultural differences; pragmatism and flexibility, as opposed to a rigid and ideological approach to politics; trust in other political actors and in the social environment; a willingness to compromise, springing from a belief in the necessity and desirability of compromise; and civility of political discourse and respect for other views. To be sure, these orientations may be induced by structural and institutional incentives and constraints, absent underlying norms; that is a key point of the transitions literature. But they will be difficult to sustain unless, for both elites and the mass, they become embedded in a deeper, more coherent and encompassing syndrome of beliefs and values.

The interrelationships among these factors are dense and intricate. Pragmatism, a quality Tocqueville identified as a distinct property of American democracy, facilitates bargaining and compromise by rendering goals negotiable and opinions and beliefs open to engagement and new information. Such intellectual openness promotes tolerance, by accepting "the idea that no one has a monopoly on absolute truth and that there can be no single, correct answer to public policy issues."[12] Thus, pragmatism restrains the role of ideology in politics and, hence, the danger of conflict polarization. Moreover, because the beliefs of democratic pragmatists are implicit and their goals adaptable to circumstances, these beliefs and goals are less likely to be abandoned under challenge or stress (in the way that a communist may suddenly become a fascist or some other "true believer"). From this perspective, the implicit and flexible character of democratic commitments is also their strength.[13]

Because pragmatism generates flexible goals, it is consistent with a commitment to democratic procedural norms that takes precedence over substantive policy objectives. This overriding commitment to democratic proceduralism is a critical political cultural condition for democracy. Democratic proceduralism, policy pragmatism, and political tolerance promote moderate partisanship and are the qualities most likely to limit the politicization of social life and the rancor of political intercourse. Similarly, a diffuse sense of political and social trust—what Harold Lasswell calls "confidence in the benevolent potentialities of man"—not only facilitates bargaining and compromise but encourages political discussion, makes political conflicts less threatening, and thus helps to transform politics into a non-zero-sum game, in which leaders and followers of defeated parties can accept exclusion from state power without fearing for their basic interests. Trust is also a key element of the social capital that, in facilitating cooperation through horizontal networks of civic engagement, leads to a more vibrant (and economically prosperous) democracy.[14]

Dispositions toward Authority

Dispositions toward authority drive to the very heart of what democracy is about. Early in the development of the political culture literature, Inkeles portrayed democratic political culture as the inverse of an authoritarian personality syndrome, which includes faith in powerful leaders, hatred of outsiders and deviates, a sense of powerlessness and ineffectiveness, extreme cynicism, suspicion and distrust of others, and dogmatism. A democratic culture thus encompasses flexibility,

trust, efficacy, openness to new ideas and experiences, tolerance of differences and ambiguities, acceptance of others, and an attitude toward authority that is neither "blindly submissive" nor "hostilely rejecting" but rather "responsible . . . even though always watchful."[15] In the words of Sidney Hook, "A positive requirement of a working democracy is an intelligent distrust of its leadership, a skepticism stubborn but not blind, of all demands for the enlargement of power, and an emphasis upon critical method in every phase of social life."[16] Intimately connected to this is a belief in what Jacques Maritain called the "inalienable rights of the person" and Sidney Hook the "intrinsic worth or dignity" of "every individual."[17]

Because Pye sees Asian political cultures as generally lacking these orientations of individualism and suspicion of authority, he views the prospects for liberal, competitive democracy in Asia as limited. Treating conceptions of power (and authority and legitimacy) as the crucial cultural axis for understanding alternative paths of political development, Pye identifies (within the considerable political cultural variation in Asia) common tendencies to emphasize loyalty to the collectivity over individual freedom and needs; to favor paternalistic authority relations that "answer deep psychological cravings for the security of dependency"; and to therefore personalize political power, shun adversary relations, favor order over conflict, mute criticism of authority, and neglect institutional constraints on the exercise of power.[18]

"Distaste for open criticism of authority," writes Pye, "fear of upsetting the unity of the community, and knowledge that any violation of the community's rules of propriety will lead to ostracism, all combine to limit the appeal of Western democracy. As a result, the development of more open and enlightened politics in Asia is likely to produce a much more contained form of popular participation in public life. At best, it is likely to be a form of democracy which is blended with much that Westerners regard as authoritarian."[19] While Pye may impute more staying power to political culture orientations than is warranted, he offers a particularly lucid theoretical expression of the compatibility between democracy and core elements of political culture and of the way institutional forms like democracy may operate differently in different cultural contexts.

Nevertheless, political culture theorists do not assert that democracy is served by unqualified individualism. Common to all of these theoretical formulations, most notably that of Almond and Verba, is a concern for balance among conflicting values. Authority must be questioned and challenged, but it also must be supported. For J. Roland Pennock, democracy requires that individuals be "conscious of their rights and willing to stand up and struggle for them." Yet individualism must be balanced by a "public spirit" that offers commitment to the welfare of the collectivity and to a "unifying sentiment," such as nationalism.[20] Similarly, for Michael Thompson, Richard Ellis, and Aaron Wildavsky, democracy requires both "the participatory norms that come with the . . . cultures of individualism and egalitarianism" and the culture of "hierarchy to inculcate the norm that the parts should sacrifice for the whole."[21]

Legitimacy, Participation, and the Civic Culture

It is by now a cardinal tenet of empirical democratic theory that stable democracy also requires a *belief in the legitimacy of democracy.* Indeed, the growth of this belief and behavioral commitment is the defining feature of the consolidation process. Ideally, this belief should be held at two levels: as a general principle, that democracy is the best (or at least the least bad) form of government possible; and as an evaluation of one's own country's democratic regime: that in spite of its failures and shortcomings, it is better than any nondemocratic regime that might be established.[22] Both of these assessments, but particularly the latter, are relative judgments, rendered in comparison with known alternatives. Direct and recent experience with regime alternatives can powerfully shape the readiness of publics to embrace the legitimacy of democracy, not necessarily as an ideal form of government but as preferable to any other system that has been tried.[23]

Public opinion surveys have used several types of question to assess levels of democratic legitimacy (or what is sometimes termed "support for democracy"). At the most abstract level, they have explored support for "the idea" of democracy "in principle." Somewhat less abstract (and inevitably eliciting at least somewhat less support in established democracies) is the question of whether "democracy is the best form of government, whatever the circumstance" or whether "sometimes an authoritarian government can be preferable."

Much more concrete, and less stable, is the question of whether citizens are "satisfied with the way democracy is working" in their country. This is frequently taken as a measure of support for the democratic system and is the measure most widely and systematically available across many countries and time points. Yet this is not a measure of legitimacy or system support per se.[24] For one thing, identical responses to this question can have different meanings in different institutional contexts; depending on how democratic the country is (and the respondent as well), dissatisfaction could mean support for democratic reform or preference for a nondemocratic regime.[25] Citizens may be dissatisfied with the way democracy works in their country but still be deeply committed to the principle of democracy and unwilling to countenance any other form of government. This was the case in Italy throughout the 1980s and early 1990s, and this is one reason Italy's political earthquake over revelations of systemic corruption led to political reform and a reorganization of the party system rather than a diminution or suspension of democracy.

Alternatively, a citizen may see democracy as functioning reasonably well at the moment but may nevertheless be prepared to support an authoritarian regime at the first sign of trouble. In this case, the belief in legitimacy is not intrinsic— that is, internalized and deeply rooted, or what José María Maravall calls "autonomous"[26]—but instrumental, or conditional on effective performance. This is not real legitimacy, certainly not the kind that sustains and consolidates democracy. For at some point, democracy is likely to experience problems and public perceptions of decline in its effectiveness. Only when support for democracy has become intrinsic and unconditional can democracy be considered consolidated and secure. As Lipset argues, a long record of effective performance may generate a deep reservoir of intrinsic legitimacy, but the two are different, and legitimacy has many potential sources.[27] Historical survey data from Western

Europe supports Lipset's thesis that once public support for democracy becomes deeply rooted, it does not soften in the face of poor economic performance, even if trust in political leaders or institutions declines.[28]

At the same time, publics may be committed to the idea of democracy in principle but be so disillusioned and disgusted with its failures in their own country that they may judge it an inappropriate form of government *for their country, at the time.* They may thus support and rally behind a temporary suspension of democracy, with the expectation that subsequent structural reforms will enable it to work better. This was close to the sentiment that appeared to prevail among the public in Nigeria when the military overthrew the Second Republic in December 1983, after four years of escalating abuse; and among the public in Peru in April 1992, when Alberto Fujimori staged his *autogolpe* amid terrorism and economic stagnation; and among the public in Thailand in February 1991, when the military overthrew a notoriously corrupt party-based government. In each case, the public supported the suspension of democracy with real and spontaneous enthusiasm, but that support was limited and pragmatic, not a philosophical rejection of democracy itself.

In a consolidated democracy, judgments of legitimacy must therefore refer to the political system as it actually operates, with its real institutions and informal rules, and not merely to its legal form.[29] Legitimacy thus reflects the depth of commitment to the substance of the political system and process (and to the boundaries and identity of the state that democracy governs). All of this suggests that the most revealing measure of democratic legitimacy would probe the extent to which a public views democracy as the best, the most appropriate, or the most suitable system for the country at the current time. Strangely, few surveys have posed the question this way.[30] Neither have they made the notion of democracy very concrete or probed very far to determine whether people's understanding of democracy matches the conception of multiparty electoral competition with constitutional freedoms, which is assumed by the researchers designing the questionnaire.[31]

Democratic legitimacy derives partly from the performance over time of the democratic regime.

It is also influenced (especially in its early life) by how specific democratic institutions articulate with traditionally legitimate forms of authority and, later, by socialization, expanding education, and other types of social and cultural change. Regime performance is assessed in terms of not only economic growth and social reform but also several crucial *political* dimensions: the capacity to maintain order, to govern transparently, to maintain a rule of law, and to otherwise respect and preserve the democratic rules of the game.

One factor that seems to enhance the legitimacy of democracy among citizens is personal experience with it. For this reason, as well as for the quality and authenticity of democracy, participation is another central element of the ideal-typical mass democratic culture. This implies both valuing popular participation as a norm of political life and a disposition to actually participate in politics, based on an informed interest in public affairs.[32] For Almond and Verba, a "participant political culture" involves "an 'activist' role of the self in the polity,"[33] manifested not only through voting but also through political interest, information, knowledge, opinion formation, and organizational membership. Underlying a participant orientation is political efficacy, the self-confidence and sense of competence on the part of the citizenry that their political action may produce a change in policy or a redress of grievances.

Almond and Verba argue that the distinctive property of a civic culture is not its participant orientation but its mixed quality: the participant role is fused with and balanced by the political subject role (which embodies acceptance of political authority and allegiance to it) and the parochial role (which binds the individual to traditional, nonpolitical groups, such as family and church, and absorbs some of the energy and affect that might otherwise be focused on politics). This mixture of roles moderates the intensity of political participation by giving it (for most citizens) an "intermittent and potential character." It provides the system with legitimacy and support and yet preserves institutions outside the state that might check the abuse or excessive accumulation of power by the state. The civic culture also tempers the intensity of politics with social trust and cooperativeness and overarching commitments to the system, the nation, and the community. All of these moderate the conflicts and bridge the cleavages of politics; and trust also facilitates the vertical ties between elites and their constituencies that keep politics functioning within the institutional boundaries and constraints of democracy.[34]. . .

Without question, elite political culture is crucial to democratic consolidation. Unless elites accept, in a regular and predictable way, the rules and limits of the constitutional system and the legitimacy of opposing actors who similarly commit themselves, democracy cannot work. But this is not the whole story. Ultimately, if democracy is to become stable and effective, the bulk of the democratic citizenry must develop a deep and resilient commitment to it. This is why democratic civil society leaders in so many emerging democracies have placed such a high priority on civic education and mobilization efforts that seek to inculcate democratic values, knowledge, and habits at the mass level.

NOTES

1. Joseph Schumpeter, *Capitalism, Socialism, and Democracy*, 2d ed. (New York: Harper, 1947), 269. For Schumpeter, Held explains, "the democratic citizen's lot was, quite straightforwardly, the right periodically to choose and authorize governments to act on their behalf" (*Models of Democracy*, 165). Schumpeter was clearly uneasy with direct political action by citizens, warning that "the electoral mass is incapable of action other than a stampede" (283). Thus, his "case for democracy can support, at best, only minimum political involvement: that involvement which could be considered sufficient to legitimate the right of competing elites to rule" (ibid., 168). This is, indeed, as spare a notion of democracy as one could posit without draining the term of meaning.
2. This is a particular emphasis of Schmitter and Karl, "What Democracy Is," 78–80, but it has long figured prominently in the work and thought of democratic pluralists such as Robert A. Dahl. In addition to his *Polyarchy*, see Dahl, *Who Governs?* (New Haven: Yale University Press, 1961); Dahl, *Dilemmas of Pluralist Democracy: Autonomy versus Control* (New Haven: Yale University Press, 1982).
3. Juan J. Linz, "Democracy Today: An Agenda for Students of Democracy," *Scandinavian Political Studies* 20, no. 2 (1997): 120–21.
4. Richard Rose, William Mishler, and Christian Haerpfer, *Democracy and Its Alternatives: Understanding Post-Communist Societies* (Oxford: Polity Press, 1998).
5. Linz, "Democracy Today," 118.
6. On civic competence and the challenges to improving it in contemporary, large-scale, complex, media-intensive, and information-saturated societies, see Robert A. Dahl, "The Problem of Civic Competence," *Journal of Democracy* 3, no. 4 (1992): 45–59.
7. Richard L. Sklar, "Towards a Theory of Developmental Democracy," in *Democracy and Development: Theory and Practice*, edited by Adrian Leftwich (Cambridge: Polity Press, 1996).
8. Such a developmental perspective may help to inoculate democratic theory against the tendency toward teleological thinking that Guillermo O'Donnell discerns in the literature on democratic consolidation: that is, the underlying assumption that there is a particular natural path and end state of democratic development.
9. Harry Eckstein, "A Culturalist Theory of Political Change," *American Political Science Review* 82, no. 2 (1988): 790. The relatively firm and enduring character of these orientations (for which "early learning conditions later learning") generates "economy of action and predictability in interaction" in Eckstein's "culturalist theory" (792).
10. Almond and Verba, *The Civic Culture*, 15; Gabriel Almond, "The Intellectual History of the Civic Culture Concept," in *The Civic Culture Revisited*, edited by Gabriel A. Almond and Sidney Verba (Boston: Little, Brown, 1980), 27–28; Gabriel A. Almond, *A Discipline Divided: Schools and Sects in Political Science* (Newbury Park, Calif.: Sage, 1990), 153.
11. See Almond and Verba, *The Civic Culture*, 489–93; Sidney Verba, "Comparative Political Culture," in Pye and Verba, *Political Culture and Political Development*, 544–50; Lipset, *Political Man*, 78–79; Dahl, *Polyarchy*; Alex Inkeles, "National Character and Modern Political Systems," in *Psychological Anthropology: Approaches to Culture and Personality*, edited by Francis L. K. Hsu (Homewood, Ill.: Dorsey, 1961), 193–99. Also see Larry Diamond, "Three Paradoxes of Democracy," *Journal of Democracy* 1, no. 3 (1990): 56–58. For an earlier, political and psychological treatment that influenced several of the above approaches, see Harold Lasswell, *The Political Writings of Harold Lasswell* (Glencoe, Ill.: Free Press, 1951), 465–525.
12. Pye, "Political Science and the Crisis of Authoritarianism," 15.
13. Verba, "Comparative Political Culture," 546.
14. Lasswell, *Political Writings*, quotation on 502; Almond and Verba, *The Civic Culture*; Verba, "Comparative Political Culture"; Dahl, *Polyarchy*; Robert D. Putnam with Robert Leonardi and Raffaella Y. Nanetti, *Making Democracy Work: Civic Traditions in Modern Italy* (Princeton: Princeton University Press, 1993). For an analysis emphasizing the implications of trust and social capital for economic scale, efficiency, and flexibility, see Francis Fukuyama, *Trust: The Social Virtues*

and the Creation of Prosperity (New York: Free Press, 1995).

15. Inkeles, "National Character," 195–98.

16. Sidney Hook, *Reason, Social Myth, and Democracy* (New York: Humanities, 1950), cited in Inkeles, "National Character," 196.

17. Jacques Maritain is quoted in Inkeles, "National Character," 195–96; see also J. Roland Pennock, *Democratic Political Theory* (Princeton: Princeton University Press, 1979), 240–41.

18. Pye, *Asian Power and Politics*, vii; see also 18–19, 22–29, 326–41.

19. Ibid., 341.

20. Pennock, *Democratic Political Theory*, 257, 245–46, 258–59. On the importance of public-spiritedness and civic engagement, see also Putnam et al., *Making Democracy Work*.

21. Thompson et al., *Cultural Theory*, 256–57.

22. Linz, *Breakdown of Democratic Regimes*, 16; Lipset, *Political Man*, 64.

23. Although they do not use the term *legitimacy*, this conception of support for democracy as inherently comparative in nature drives the theory and methodology of Richard Rose, William Mishler, and Christian Haerpfer in their analysis of attitudinal trends in the postcommunist states. See their *Democracy and Its Alternatives: Understanding Post-Communist Societies* (Oxford: Polity Press, 1998).

24. A particularly suspect feature of this item as a measure of democracy is that supporters of the governing party evince substantially higher levels of satisfaction with democracy than do supporters of the opposition party, irrespective of whether it is the left or the right that is governing. In some cases, these differences are very large (30–40 percentage points). Dieter Fuchs, Giovanna Guidorossi, and Palle Svensson, "Support for the Democratic System," in *Citizens and the State*, edited by Hans-Dieter Klingemann and Dieter Fuchs (Oxford: Oxford University Press, 1995), 345–46. Typical of the misuse of this item is an otherwise rigorous and widely cited study of "legitimation," which takes satisfaction with the way democracy works as equivalent to other, more appropriate, measures of legitimacy. Frederick D. Weil, "The Sources and Structure of Legitimation in Western Democracies: A Consolidated Model Tested with Time-Series Data in Six Countries since World War II," *American Sociological Review* 54, no. 4 (1989): 682–706.

25. Rose et al., *Democracy and Its Alternatives*, 99–101.

26. José María Maravall, *Regimes, Politics, and Markets: Democratization and Economic Change in Southern and Eastern Europe* (Oxford: Oxford University Press, 1997), 204.

27. Lipset, *Political Man*, 68–70.

28. Weil, "The Sources and Structure of Legitimation."

29. Fuchs et al., "Support for the Democratic System," 328.

30. Two exceptions are a series of Spanish surveys that asked whether "democracy is the best system for a country like ours," and the New Korea, Barometer, which asks Koreans to rate from 1 to 10 how "suitable" democracy was for the country during the authoritarian era and is today. José Ramón Montero, Richard Gunther, and Mariano Torcal, "Democracy in Spain: Legitimacy, Discontent, and Disaffection," Estudio/Working Paper 1997/100, Centro de Estudios Avanzados en Ciencias Sociales, Instituto Juan March de Estudios e Investigaciones, 1997, 5; Doh Chull Shin and Peter McDonough, "The Dynamics of Popular Reaction to Democratization in Korea: A Comparative Perspective," unpublished draft, December 1997, Department of Political Science, University of Illinois at Springfield.

31. This is the principal criticism of the standard research approach advanced in Arthur H. Miller, Vicki L. Hesli, and William M. Reisinger, "Understanding Democracy: A Comparison of Mass and Elite in Post-Soviet Russia and Ukraine," Studies in Public Policy 247, Centre for the Study of Public Policy, University of Strathclyde, 1995. In Russia and Ukraine, elite and mass have different conceptions of democracy, and "beliefs about democracy vary across demographic and political categories rather than reflecting a shared common culture" (16). Rose et al., *Democracy and Its Alternatives*, avoid or diminish potential ambiguity in interpreting a commitment to "democracy" by specifying the system as involving "free elections and many parties" or by specifying concrete types of authoritarian alternatives.

32. Alex Inkeles, "Participant Citizenship in Six Developing Countries," *American Political Science Review* 63, no. 4 (1969): 1120–41.

33. Almond and Verba, *The Civic Culture*, 19.

34. Ibid., 482, 490.

Part IX

SOCIAL INSTITUTIONS: FAMILIAL, RELIGIOUS, EDUCATIONAL

Social institutions are most easily understood by dividing them into the areas of life—"orders" or "spheres"—that they regulate. Part VIII of this Reader examined political and economic institutions, patterns that have developed over time and have become legitimate practices in the political and economic orders. Part IX briefly looks at institutions in the familial, educational, and religious orders.

Three selections introduce the family. Arlene and Jerome Skolnick give us an excellent overview of the changes that have taken place in the American family, asking us always to consider the complexity, causes, and consequences of these changes. Daniel McMurrer and Isabel Sawhill examine the importance of family in placing the individual into social class. Nancy Tatom Ammerman's selection describes family structure in fundamentalist religious communities, underlining the diversity of family life in the United States.

Ammerman's selection also introduces us to the study of religion in society through linking fundamentalist religion to family structure. Emile Durkheim attempts to define religion as an essential part of society, and Phillip Hammond looks at the history of religion in the United States, focusing his attention primarily on the last half of the twentieth century.

Two selections examine educational institutions. Jonathan Kozol reports on New York public schools, educational institutions characterized by "savage inequalities," and Kenneth Ehrensal describes the various ways in which higher education teaches many of us to become the sort of citizens who are accepting of our economic institutions.

✦ 44 ✦

Family in Transition

Arlene S. and Jerome H. Skolnick

> *. . . a knowledge of family history reveals that the solution to contemporary problems*
> *will not be found in some lost golden age. Families have always struggled with*
> *outside circumstances and inner conflict. Our current troubles inside and*
> *outside the family are genuine, but we should never forget that many of*
> *the most vexing issues confronting us derive from benefits of*
> *modernization few of us would be willing to give up.*

To understand the history of the family in society is to become aware of the many ways it has changed. It is the product of change, and it is responsible for change. It adjusts to modern society, and it contributes to what modern society becomes. It is, the Skolnicks warn us, not something that used to be wonderful and no longer is, but something that is no longer what it used to be. For good or bad—and it depends on one's perspective—we have witnessed a very basic transformation. There are many themes that the Skolnicks highlight in this selection that are worth paying attention to: the diversity of family structures, nostalgia for a past that never was, the Victorian model of the family that emerged during the industrial revolution, the companionate model that eventually replaced the Victorian model in the early twentieth century, and a triple revolution in the mid-twentieth century that brought significantly new patterns—including a lot more choices for young people, changing female roles, and more emphasis on the ideals of emotional satisfaction in the family and democratic structure. The family is alive and well as we enter the twenty-first century; it has, however, undergone very important changes that we need to understand.

It was one of the oddest episodes in America's political history—a debate between the vice president of the United States and a fictional television character. During the 1992 election

From Arlene S. Skolnick & Jerome H. Skolnick, *Family in Transition*, 9/e © 1997. Published by Allyn and Bacon, Boston, MA. Copyright © 1997 by Pearson Education. Reprinted/adapted by permission of the publisher.

campaign, former Vice President Dan Quayle set off a firestorm of debate with a remark denouncing a fictional television character for choosing to give birth out of wedlock. The *Murphy Brown* show, according to Quayle, was "mocking the importance of fathers." It reflected the "poverty of values" that was responsible for the nation's ills. From the talk shows to the front pages of newspapers to dinner tables across the nation, arguments broke out about the meaning of the vice president's remarks.

Comedians found Quayle's battle with a TV character good for laughs. But others saw serious issues being raised. Many people saw Quayle's comments as a stab at single mothers and working women. Some saw them as an important statement about the decline of family values and the importance of the two-parent family. In the opening show of the fall season, *Murphy Brown* fought back by poking fun at Quayle and telling the audience that families come in many different shapes and sizes. After the election, the debate seemed to fade away. It flared up again in the spring of 1993, after the *Atlantic Monthly* featured a cover story entitled "Dan Quayle was Right."

Why did a brief remark in a political speech set off such a heated and long-lasting debate? The Dan Quayle-Murphy Brown affair struck a nerve because it touched a central predicament in American society: the gap between the everyday realities of family life and our cultural images of how families ought to be. Contrary to the widespread notion that some flaw in American character or culture is to blame for these trends, comparable shifts are found throughout the industrialized world. All advanced modern countries have experienced shifts in women's roles, rising divorce rates, lower marriage and birth rates, and an increase in single-parent families. In no other country, however, has family change been so traumatic and divisive as ours.

The transformation of family life has been so dramatic that, to many Americans, it has seemed as if "an earthquake had shuddered through the American family" (Preston 1984). Divorce rates first skyrocketed, then stabilized at historically high levels. Women have surged into the workplace. Birth rates have declined. The women's movement has changed the way men and women think and act toward one another, both inside the home and in the world at large. Furthermore, social and sexual rules that once seemed carved in stone have crumbled away: Unmarried couples can live together openly; unmarried mothers can keep their babies. Abortion has become legal. Remaining single and remaining childless, once thought to be highly deviant (although not illegal), have both become acceptable lifestyle options.

Today, most people live in ways that do not conform to the cultural ideal that prevailed in the 1950s. The traditional breadwinner/housewife family with minor children today represents only a small minority of families. The "typical" American family in the last two decades of the twentieth century is likely to be one of four other kinds: the two-wage-earner family, the single-parent family, the "blended" family of remarriage, or the "empty nest" couple whose children have grown up and moved out. Indeed, in 1984, fully half of American families had no children under age 18 (Norton and Glick 1986: 9). Apart from these variations, large numbers of people will spend part of their lives living apart from their families—as single young adults, as divorced singles, as older people who have lost a spouse.

The changes of recent decades have affected more than the forms of family life; they have been psychological changes as well. A major study of American attitudes over two decades revealed a profound shift in how people think about family life, work, and themselves (Veroff, Douvan, and Kulka 1981). In 1957, four-fifths of respondents thought that a man or woman who did not want to marry was sick, immoral, and selfish. By 1976, only one-fourth of respondents thought that choice was bad. Two-thirds were neutral, and one-seventh viewed the choice as good. Summing up many complex findings, the authors conclude that America underwent a "psychological revolution" in the two decades between surveys. Twenty years earlier, people defined their satisfaction and problems—and indeed themselves—in terms of how well they lived up to traditional work and family roles. More recently, people have become more introspective, more attentive to inner experience. Fulfillment has come to mean finding intimacy, meaning, and self-definition, rather than satisfactory performance of traditional roles.

A DYING INSTITUTION?

All these changes, occurring as they did in a relatively short period of time, gave rise to fears about the decline of the family. Since the early 1970s, anyone watching television or reading newspapers and magazines would hear again and again that the family is breaking down, falling apart, disintegrating, and even becoming "an endangered species." There also began a great nostalgia for the "good old days" when Mom was in the kitchen, families were strong and stable, and life was uncomplicated. This mood of nostalgia mixed with anxiety contributed to the rise of the conservative New Right and helped propel Ronald Reagan into the White House.

In the early 1980s, heady with victory, the conservative movement hoped that by dismantling the welfare state and overturning the Supreme Court's abortion decision, the clock could be turned back and the "traditional" family restored. As the 1990s began, it became clear that such hopes had failed. Women had not returned to full-time homemaking; divorce rates had not returned to the levels of the 1950s. The "liberated" sexuality of the 1960s and 1970s had given way to greater restraint, largely because of fear of AIDS, although the norms of the 1950s did not return.

Despite all the changes, however, the family in America is "here to stay" (Bane 1976). The vast majority of Americans—at least 90 percent—marry and have children, and surveys repeatedly show that family is central to the lives of most Americans. They find family ties their deepest source of satisfaction and meaning, as well as the source of their greatest worries (Mellman, Lazarus, and Rivlin 1990). In sum, family life in America is a complex mixture of both continuity and change.

Although the transformations of the past three decades do not mean the end of family life, they have brought a number of new difficulties. For example, most families now depend on the earnings of wives and mothers, but the rest of society has not caught up to the new realities. There is still an earnings gap between men and women. Employed wives and mothers still bear most of the workload in the home. For both men and women, the demands of the job are often at odds with family needs. Debates about whether or not the family is "in decline" do little to solve these dilemmas.

During the same years in which the family was becoming the object of public anxiety and political debate, a torrent of new research on the family was pouring forth. The study of the family had come to excite the interest of scholars in a range of disciplines—history, demography, economics, law, psychology. As a result of this research, we now have much more information available about the family than ever before. Ironically, much of the new scholarship is at odds with the widespread assumption that the family had a long, stable history until hit by the social "earthquake" of the 1960s and 1970s. We have learned from historians that the "lost" golden age of family happiness and stability we yearn for never actually existed. . . .

THE STATE OF THE CONTEMPORARY FAMILY

Part of the confusion surrounding the current status of the family arises from the fact that the family is a surprisingly problematic area of study; there are few if any self-evident facts, even statistical ones. Researchers have found, for example, that when the statistics of family life are plotted for the entire twentieth century, or back into the nineteenth century, a surprising finding emerges: Today's young people—with their low marriage, high divorce, and low fertility rates—appear to be behaving in ways consistent with long-term historical trends (Cherlin 1981; Masnick and Bane 1980). The recent changes in family life appear deviant only when compared to what people were doing in the 1940s and 1950s. But it was the postwar generation that married young, moved to the suburbs, and had three, four, or more children that departed from twentieth-century trends. As one study put it, "Had the 1940s and 1950s not happened, today's young adults, would appear to be behaving normally" (Masnick and Bane 1980: 2).

Thus, the meaning of "change" in a particular indicator of family life depends on the time frame in which it is placed. If we look at trends over too short a period of time—say ten or twenty years—we may think we are seeing a marked change, when, in fact, an older pattern may be reemerging. For some issues, even discerning what the trends are can be a problem. Whether or not we conclude that there is an "epidemic" of teenage pregnancy depends on how we define adolescence and what measure of illegitimacy we use. Contrary to the popular notion of skyrocketing teenage pregnancy, teen-aged childbearing has actually been on the decline during the past two decades (Luker). It is possible for the *ratio* of illegitimate births to all births to go up at the same time as there are declines in the *absolute number* of births and in the likelihood that an individual will bear an illegitimate child. This is not to say that concern about teenage pregnancy is unwarranted; but the reality is much more complex than the simple and scary notion an "epidemic" implies.

Given the complexities of interpreting data on the family, it is little wonder that, as Joseph Featherstone observes (1979: 37), the family is a "great intellectual Rorschach blot." One's conclusions about the current state of the family often derive from deeper values and assumptions one holds in the first place about the definition and role of the family in society. . . .

THE MYTH OF A STABLE, HARMONIOUS PAST

Laments about the current state of decay of the family imply some earlier era in which the family was more stable and harmonious. But unless we can agree what "earlier time" should be chosen as a baseline and what characteristics of the family should be specified, it makes little sense to speak of family decline. Historians have not, in fact, located a golden age of the family.

Recent historical studies of family life also cast doubt on the reality of family tranquillity. Historians have found that premarital sexuality, illegitimacy, generational conflict, and even infanticide can best be studied as a part of family life itself rather than as separate categories of deviation. For example, William Kessen (1965), in his history of the field of child study, observes:

Perhaps the most persistent single note in the history of the child is the reluctance of mothers to suckle their babies. The running war between the mother who does not want to nurse and the philosopher-psychologists who insist she must stretches over two thousand years (pp. 1–2).

The most shocking finding of the recent wave of historical studies is the prevalence of infanticide throughout European history. Infanticide has long been attributed to primitive peoples or assumed to be the desperate act of an unwed mother. It now appears that infanticide provided a major means of population control in all societies lacking reliable contraception, Europe included, and that it was practiced by families on legitimate children. Historians now believe that increases and decreases in recorded birth rates may actually reflect variations in infanticide rates.

Rather than being an instinctive trait, having tender feelings toward infants—regarding a baby as a precious individual—seems to emerge only when infants have a decent chance of surviving and adults experience enough security to avoid feeling that children are competing with them in a struggle for survival. Throughout many centuries of European history, both of these conditions were lacking.

Another myth about the family is that of changelessness—the belief that the family has been essentially the same over the centuries, until recently, when it began to come apart. Family life has always been in flux; when the world around them changes, families change in response. At periods when a whole society undergoes some major transformation, family change may be especially rapid and dislocating.

In many ways, the era we are living through today resembles two earlier periods of family crisis and transformation in American history (Skolnick 1991). The first occurred in the early nineteenth century, when the growth of industry and commerce moved work out of the home. Briefly, the separation of home and work disrupted existing patterns of daily family life, opening a gap between the way people actually lived and the cultural blueprints for proper gender and generational roles (Ryan 1981). In the older pattern, when most people worked on farms, a father was not just the head of the household, but also the boss of the family enterprise. Mother and children and hired hands worked under his supervision. But when work moved out, father—along with older sons and daughters—went with it, leaving behind mother and the younger children. These dislocations in the functions and meaning of family life unleashed an era of personal stress and cultural confusion.

Eventually, a new model of family emerged that not only reflected the new separation of work and family, but glorified it. No longer a workplace, the household now became idealized as "home sweet home," an emotional and spiritual shelter from the heartless world outside. Although father remained the head of the family, mother was now the central figure in the home. The new model celebrated the "true woman's" purity, virtue, and selflessness. Many of our culture's most basic ideas about the family in American culture, such as "women's place is in the home," were formed at this time. In short, the family pattern we now think of as traditional was in fact the first version of the modern family.

Historians label this model of the family "Victorian" because it became influential in England and Western Europe as well as in the United States during the reign of Queen Victoria. It reflected, in idealized form, the nineteenth-century middle-class family. However, the Victorian model became the prevailing cultural definition of family. Few families could live up to the ideal in all its particulars; working-class, black, and ethnic families, for example, could not get by without the economic contributions of wives, mothers, and daughters. And even for middle-class families, the Victorian idea prescribed a standard of perfection that was virtually impossible to fulfill (Demos 1986).

Eventually, however, social change overtook the Victorian model. Beginning around the 1880s, another period of rapid economic, social, and cultural change unsettled Victorian family patterns, especially their gender arrangements. Several generations of so-called "new women" challenged Victorian notions of femininity. They became educated, pursued careers, became involved in political causes—including their own—and created the first wave of feminism. This ferment culminated in the victory of the women's suffrage movement. It was followed by the 1920s' jazz age era of flappers and flaming youth—the first, and probably the major, sexual revolution of the twentieth century.

To many observers at the time, it appeared that the family and morality had broken down. Another cultural crisis ensued, until a new cultural blueprint emerged—the companionate model of marriage and the family. The new model was a revised, more relaxed version of the Victorian family; companionship and sexual intimacy were now defined as central to marriage.

This highly abbreviated history of family and cultural change forms the necessary backdrop for understanding the family upheavals of the late twentieth century. As in earlier times, major changes in the economy and society have destabilized an existing model of family life and the everyday patterns and practices that have sustained it. We have experienced a triple revolution: First, the move toward a postindustrial service and information economy; second, a life course revolution brought about the reductions in mortality and fertility; and third, a psychological transformation rooted mainly in rising educational levels.

Although these shifts have profound implications for everyone in contemporary society, women have been the pacesetters of change. Most women's lives and expectations over the past three decades, inside and outside the family, have departed drastically from those of their own mothers. Men's lives today also are different from their fathers' generation, but to a much lesser extent.

THE TRIPLE REVOLUTION

The Postindustrial Family

The most obvious way the new economy affects the family is in its drawing women, especially married women, into the workplace. A service and information economy produces large numbers of jobs that, unlike factory work, seem suitable for women. Yet as Jessie Bernard (1982) once observed, the transformation of a housewife into a paid worker outside the home sends tremors through every family relationship. It creates a more "symmetrical" family, undoing the sharp contrast between men's and women's roles that marks the breadwinner/housewife pattern. It also reduces women's economic dependence on men, thereby making it easier for women to leave unhappy marriages.

Beyond drawing women into the workplace, shifts in the nature of work and a rapidly changing globalized economy have unsettled the lives of individuals and families at all class levels. The well-paying industrial jobs that once enabled a blue-collar worker to own a home and support a family are no longer available. The once-secure jobs that sustained the "organization men" and their families in the 1950s and 1960s have been made shaky by downsizing, an unstable economy, corporate takeovers, and a rapid pace of technological change.

The new economic climate has also made the transition to adulthood increasingly problematic. The reduction in job opportunities is in part responsible for young adults' lower fertility rates and for women flooding into the workplace. Further, the family formation patterns of the 1950s are out of step with the increased educational demands of today's postindustrial society. In the post-war years, particularly in the United States, young people entered adulthood in one giant step—going to work, marrying young, moving to a separate household from their parents, and having children quickly. Today, few young adults can afford to marry and have children in their late teens or early twenties. In an economy where a college degree is necessary to earn a living wage, early marriage impedes education for both men and women.

Those who do not go on to college have little access to jobs that can sustain a family. Particularly in the inner cities of the United States, growing numbers of young people have come to see no future for themselves at all in the ordinary world of work. In middle-class families, a narrowing opportunity structure has increased anxieties about downward mobility for offspring and parents as well. The "Hamlet syndrome" or the "incompletely launched young adult syndrome" has become common: Young adults deviate from their parents' expectations by failing to launch careers and become successfully independent adults, and may even come home to crowd their parents' empty nest (Schnaiberg and Goldenberg 1989).

The Life Course Revolution

The demographic transformations of the twentieth century are no less significant than the economic ones. We cannot hope to understand current predicaments of family life without understanding how radically the demographic and social circumstances of twentieth-century Americans have changed. In earlier times, mortality rates were highest among infants, and the possibility of death from tuberculosis, pneumonia, or other infectious diseases was an ever-present threat to young and middle-aged adults. Before the turn of this century, only 40 percent of women lived through all the stages of a normal life course—growing up, marrying, having children, and surviving with a spouse to the age of 50 (Uhlenberg 1980).

Demographic and economic change has had a profound effect on women's lives. Women today are living longer and having fewer children. When infant and child mortality rates fall, women no longer have to have five or seven or nine children to make sure that two or three will survive to adulthood. After rearing children, the average woman can look forward to three or four decades without maternal responsibilities. Because traditional assumptions about women are based on the notion that they are constantly involved with pregnancy, child rearing, and related domestic concerns, the current ferment about women's roles may be seen as a way of bringing cultural attitudes in line with existing social realities.

As people live longer, they can stay married longer. Actually, the biggest change in twentieth-century marriage is not the proportion of marriages disrupted through divorce, but the potential length of marriage and the number of years spent without children in the home. By the 1970s, the statistically average couple would spend only 18 percent of their married lives raising young children, compared with 54 percent a century ago (Bane 1976). As a result, marriage is becoming defined less as a union between parents raising a brood of children and more as a personal relationship between two individuals.

A Psychological Revolution

The third major transformation is a set of psycho-cultural changes that might be described as "psychological gentrification" (Skolnick 1991). That is, cultural advantages once enjoyed only by the upper classes—in particular, education—have been extended to those lower down on the socioeconomic scale. Psychological gentrification also involves greater leisure time, travel, and exposure to information, as well as a general rise in the standard of living. Despite the persistence of poverty, unemployment, and economic insecurity in the industrialized world, far less of the population than in the historical past is living at the level of sheer subsistence.

Throughout Western society, rising levels of education and related changes have been linked to a complex set of shifts in personal and political attitudes. One of these is a more psychological approach to life—greater introspectiveness and a yearning for warmth and intimacy in family and other relationships (Veroff, Douvan, and Kulka 1981). There is also evidence of an increasing preference on the part of both men and women for a more companionate ideal of marriage and a more democratic family. More broadly, these changes in attitude have been described as a shift to "postmaterialist values," emphasizing self-expression, tolerance, equality, and a concern for the quality of life (Inglehart 1990).

The multiple social transformations of our era have brought both costs and benefits: Family relations have become both more fragile and more emotionally rich; mass longevity has brought us a host of problems as well as the gift of extended life. Although change has brought greater opportunities for women, persisting gender inequality means women have borne a large share of the costs of these gains. But we cannot turn the clock back to the family models of the past.

Paradoxically, after all the upheavals of recent decades, the emotional and cultural significance of the family persists. Family remains the center of most people's lives and, as numerous surveys show, a cherished value. Although marriage has become more fragile, the parent-child relationship— especially the mother-child relationship— remains a core attachment across the life course (Rossi and Rossi 1990). The family, however, can be both "here to stay" and beset with difficulties. There is widespread recognition that the massive social and economic changes we have lived through call for public and private sector policies in support of families. Most European countries have recognized for some time that governments must play a role in supplying an array of supports to families—health care, children's allowances, housing subsidies, support for working parents and children (such as child care, parental leave, and shorter workdays for parents), as well as an array of services for the elderly.

Each country's response to these changes . . . has been shaped by its own political and cultural

traditions. The United States remains embroiled in a cultural war over the family; many social commentators and political leaders have promised to reverse the recent trends and restore the "traditional" family. In contrast, other Western nations, including Canada and the other English-speaking countries, have responded to family change by establishing policies aimed at mitigating the problems brought about by economic and social changes. As a result of these policies, these countries have been spared much of the poverty and social disintegration that has plagued the United States in the last decade.

LOOKING AHEAD

The world at the end of the twentieth century is vastly different from what it was at the beginning, or even in the middle. Families are struggling to adapt to new realities. The countries that have been at the leading edge of family change still find themselves struggling with yesterday's norms, today's new realities, and an uncertain future. As we have seen, changes in women's lives have been a pivotal factor in recent family trends. In many countries, there is a considerable difference between men's and women's attitudes and expectations of one another. Even where both partners accept a more equal division of labor in the home, there is often a gap between attitudes and behavior. In no country have employers, the government, or men fully caught up to the changes in women's lives.

But a knowledge of family history reveals that the solution to contemporary problems will not be found in some lost golden age. Families have always struggled with outside circumstances and inner conflict. Our current troubles inside and outside the family are genuine, but we should never forget that many of the most vexing issues confronting us derive from benefits of modernization few of us would be willing to give up—for example, longer, healthier lives, and the ability to choose how many children to have and when to have them. There was no problem of the aged in the past, because most people never aged—they died before they got old. Nor was adolescence a difficult stage of the life cycle when children worked, education was a privilege of the rich, and a person's place in society was determined by heredity rather than choice. And when most people were hungry illiterates, only aristocrats could worry about sexual satisfaction and self-fulfillment.

In short, there is no point in giving in to the lure of nostalgia. There is no golden age of the family to long for, nor even some past pattern of behavior and belief that would guarantee us harmony and stability if only we had the will to return to it. Family life is bound up with the social, economic, and ideological circumstances of particular times and places. We are no longer peasants, Puritans, pioneers, or even suburbanites circa 1955. We face conditions unknown to our ancestors, and we must find new ways to cope with them.

REFERENCES

Bane, M. J. 1976. *Here to Stay.* New York: Basic Books.

Bernard, J. 1982. *The Future of Marriage.* New York: Bantam.

Blake, J. 1978. "Structural Differentiation and the Family: A Quiet Revolution." Presented at American Sociology Association, San Francisco.

Cherlin, A. J. 1981. *Marriage, Divorce, Remarriage.* Cambridge, MA: Harvard University Press.

Demos, John. 1986. *Past, Present, and Personal.* New York: Oxford University Press.

Featherstone, J. 1979. "Family Matters." *Harvard Educational Review* 49, no. 1: 20–52.

Gagnon, J. H., and W. Simon. 1970. *The Sexual Scene.* Chicago: Aldine/Transaction.

Inglehart, Ronald. 1990. *Culture Shift.* New Jersey: Princeton University Press.

Keller, S. 1971. "Does the Family Have a Future?" *Journal of Comparative Studies* Spring.

Kessen, E. W. 1965. *The Child.* New York: John Wiley.

Masnick, G., and M. J. Bane. 1980. *The Nation's Families: 1960–1990.* Boston: Auburn House.

Mellman, A., E. Lazarus, and A. Rivlin. 1990. "Family Time, Family Values." In *Rebuilding the Nest,* edited by D. Blankenhorn, S. Bayme, and J. Elshtain. Milwaukee: Family Service America.

Norton, A. J. and P. C. Glick. 1986. "One-Parent Families: A Social and Economic Profile." *Family Relations* 35: 9–17.

Preston, S. H. 1984. "Presidential Address to the Population Association of America." Quoted in *Family and Nation* by D. P. Moynihan (1986). San Diego: Harcourt Brace Jovanovich.

Rossi, A. S. and P. H. Rossi. 1990. *Of Human Bonding: Parent-Child Relations Across the Life Course.* Hawthorne, New York: Aldine de Gruyter.

Ryan, M. 1981. *The Cradle of the Middle Class.* New York: Cambridge University Press.

Schnaiberg, A. and S. Goldenberg. 1989. "From Empty Nest to Crowded Nest: The Dynamics of Incompletely Launched Young Adults." *Social Problems* 36, no. 3 (June) 251–69.

Skolnick, A. 1991. *Embattled Paradise: The American Family in an Age of Uncertainty.* New York: Basic Books.

Uhlenberg, P. 1980. "Death and the Family." *Journal of Family History* 5, no. 3: 313–20.

Veroff, J., E. Douvan, and R. A. Kulka. 1981. *The Inner American: A Self-Portrait from 1957 to 1976.* New York: Basic Books.

◆ 45 ◆

Families and Class Placement

Daniel P. McMurrer and Isabel V. Sawhill

Of the many possible reasons for the importance of family background [in relation to future success], we focus on three: genetic inheritance, material resources, and a good home environment. . . . If genetics are all-important . . . public policy can do little to affect the degree of inequality other than to redistribute income after the fact. If material resources are crucial, it will help to provide the less advantaged with more money. If home environment is critical, greater efforts to ensure responsible childbearing and good parenting are in order.

Here is a selection that tries to summarize why families are important to the class placement of children. It nicely summarizes the issues and the research in this area. It raises questions, takes stands, and acts as a good introduction to a difficult and important topic.

HOW IMPORTANT IS FAMILY BACKGROUND?

As stressed in chapter 6, family background or class is important. (The term "family background" can be defined in different ways. It is more commonly understood to mean the economic and social status of the family in which one grew up, as measured by the income, occupation and/or education of one or both parents. But the definition can be expanded to include parents' marital status, number of siblings, race, residential location, and other descriptors of early environment.)

Although most studies find that family background matters, its effect should not be exaggerated. It cannot explain more than 20 to 30 percent[1] of the variation in an individual's economic status as an adult. This should not be surprising. Children with very similar family backgrounds often have different abilities, receive different amounts of schooling, and make different choices or confront different opportunities as they mature and enter their adult years. Even siblings raised in the same families often turn out quite differently, a fact that has been used by a number of researchers to study the influence of family environment versus factors external to the family in determining who gets ahead.[2] Some of these other factors, such as education, can be measured and

From "Why Families Matter," in *Getting Ahead: Economic and Social Mobility in America*, by Daniel P. McMurrer and Isabel V. Sawhill, The Urban Institute Press, 1998. By permission.

have enabled researchers to explain, at most, 40 to 50 percent of the variation in various measures of adult success.

But this still leaves the glass half empty. Much is not explained by either family background or anything else we can measure. So we are a long way from having a full understanding of why some people succeed and others don't. It could be hard-to-measure qualities such as persistence, social skills, good judgment, or appearance. It could be historical events, such as a war or a depression occurring at a critical juncture in one's life. It could reflect institutional or cultural evaluations that favor some attributes (e.g., having white skin or being a good athlete) over others. Or it could be just plain luck.[3]

Still, family background is at least as important to later success as anything else that can be measured, with the possible exception of education (which is indirectly affected by background in any case).[4] What is it about family background that explains its importance for later success?

Why Is Family Background Important?

Of the many possible reasons for the importance of family background, we focus on three: genetic inheritance, material resources, and a good home environment. In other words, we suspect that higher-income parents may produce more-successful children because they are more able, because they invest more money in their children, and because they are better parents.

A full-scale review of any one of these three topics could fill an entire book. We report some suggestive findings here, as a guide to understanding these extremely important issues. In the absence of such understanding, public policies aimed at improving opportunities for less-advantaged children are likely to produce disappointing results. If genetics are all-important, for example, public policy can do little to affect the degree of inequality other than to redistribute income after the fact. If material resources are crucial, it will help to provide the less advantaged with more money. If home environment is critical, greater efforts to ensure responsible childbearing and good parenting are in order.

GENETIC INHERITANCE

One frequent explanation for the importance of family background is that successful parents pass on good genes to their children. We know that individuals who share the same or similar genes (because they are identical twins or biologically related in some other way) are more similar in terms of their intelligence, sociability, health, and other characteristics than individuals who are not related to each other—even when these individuals have been separated since birth and have experienced quite different environments. For example, children who are adopted end up with educations far more similar to their biological parents' than to those of their adoptive parents. Similarly, identical twins who have been raised apart and may never have known each other share many of the same characteristics.[5]

Of all the characteristics that matter for success, the genetic transmission of cognitive ability—or "intelligence"—has received the most attention. In their controversial and much discussed book, *The Bell Curve*, Richard Herrnstein and Charles Murray suggest that as much as 40 to 80 percent of differences in IQ across individuals are genetically based.[6] Moreover, they suggest that cognitive ability is a critical determinant of economic success and that its importance has increased as society has become more complex and the economy more technologically advanced. They believe we are moving toward a society which is increasingly stratified by intellectual ability, one in which the cognitively elite will receive the greatest rewards and the cognitively disadvantaged the fewest.

Both the substance and the implications of the Herrnstein-Murray argument have been questioned by other researchers. Some researchers argue that they overstate the extent to which ability is inherited, and suggest that a more accurate reading of the evidence on this question may be that 35 to 45 percent of IQ differences across individuals are related in some way to genetic factors.[7] Others cite evidence to support a larger role for genetics.[8] In the end, the importance of genetics in determining individual IQ remains an unresolved and intensely debated topic.

Lower estimates of the genetic component reflect the important interaction between "nature" and "nurture" in determining intelligence. There is evidence that IQ is malleable, with one of the most striking illustrations of this being the so-called "Flynn effect." James R. Flynn found that average IQ scores have been increasing—often dramatically—in every industrialized country for which data are available.[9] Because the gene pool cannot change nearly as quickly as scores have increased throughout this century, the Flynn effect suggests that some significant component of cognitive ability must be shaped by environmental factors.

Whatever the proportion of IQ differences that is in fact genetically based, most research agrees that differences in educational attainment and other environmental factors are more important than IQ or test score differences in determining individual economic outcomes.[10] Recent estimates suggest that no more than 10 to 15 percent of differences in earnings or income is associated with differences in cognitive ability.[11] Still, it seems clear that some significant component of IQ is inherited, that this inherited advantage (or disadvantage) is one of the attributes parents pass on to their children, and that it has some effect on future success. When Thomas Jefferson wrote that "all men are created equal," he was expressing a political statement, not a scientific fact.

MATERIAL RESOURCES

Another possible explanation for the relationship between family background and economic success is that children from low-income families fare poorly because their parents lack the income to provide them with what money can buy—food and clothing, good schools, adequate health care, and housing in a safe neighborhood. In addition, lack of resources may create a stressful environment for the parent, leading to inadequate parenting and poor outcomes for the child.

Many studies find a link between family income during childhood and later measures of success during adolescence or adult life. For example, children from poor families are twice as likely as those from nonpoor families to drop out of high school, to repeat a grade, to be expelled or suspended from school, and to be "economically inactive" in their early 20s (not employed, in school, or taking care of preschool children). As adolescents, they are more likely to bear a child out of wedlock, to commit a crime, and to engage in other risky behaviors.[12] These correlations are frequently used to conclude that low income causes undesirable outcomes among children from poor families. But these correlations do not prove that low income *causes* poor outcomes any more than the World Series occurring in the fall proves that baseball causes cold weather.

To get around the problem of causation, researchers often control for the influence of other factors that may affect adult success but may also be correlated with income. One recent and very ambitious effort of this sort, led by Greg Duncan and Jeanne Brooks-Gunn, involved 13 different research teams, using different data and focusing on different child and adult outcomes but within a consistent analytical framework. Each team looked at the question of how much difference income makes. Their answers varied in size of effect but were consistent in suggesting that—even after controlling for parental education, family structure, and various demographic characteristics—living in poverty, especially persistent poverty, has an effect on later outcomes, especially on children's intellectual achievements when they are young (ages two through eight).[13] Fewer effects were found for older children, for adults, or for behavioral or health outcomes. In a slightly earlier but extremely comprehensive review of the literature, Robert Haveman and Barbara Wolfe noted that a 10 percent increase in parental income typically increases a child's adult earnings by between 1 and 3 percent, even after controlling for other variables.[14]

Even these carefully controlled studies may exaggerate the true effect of material resources on child outcomes, since income often serves as a marker for something else within a family—something that cannot be measured, and thus controlled for, using existing data but which is equally or more important to the welfare of children. Some of the same characteristics that enable adults to achieve success in the labor market and earn more income may also contribute to their being good parents. These difficult-to-measure characteristics could include their own intelligence, attitudes and values, diligence, good health, sense of responsibility, emotional maturity, parenting methods, and so forth.[15]

The general point, that income may be a marker for something else, has been especially well made by Susan Mayer,[16] who has used a variety of creative analytic techniques to ferret out the extent to which income is associated with better outcomes for children, because it is telling us something about their parents' unobserved characteristics rather than because it is having a direct impact on the welfare of children. She concludes that money does matter somewhat in determining child outcomes, but not nearly as much as most researchers have assumed. It has a small effect on each of a wide range of outcomes, but even a significant increase in the incomes of poor families (like a *doubling* of income for those in the bottom 20 percent of the income distribution) would result in only slight improvements in such later outcomes as educational attainment, dropping out of high school, and becoming pregnant as a teen.

Does this mean the nation can safely eliminate welfare and other parts of the safety net with no consequences? The answer is almost certainly no. For one thing, the research is quite clear that increasing the incomes of children in families below the poverty line has a bigger impact than increasing it for those higher up the income scale.[17] In large part, this is probably because parents with very limited incomes lead extremely stressful lives, may be depressed, and may take out some of their frustrations on their children.[18] Further, current safety net programs effectively protect most families from the kind of serious material hardship that might otherwise interfere with healthy child development—most poor children do get the basic necessities most of the time. It is not clear how generous this safety net needs to be to prevent damage to the next generation. One could easily argue, for example, that until a guarantee of adequate health care exists, children from lower-income families will remain at risk of poor health with all its attendant consequences. Mayer does find, however, that despite already wide variation across states in the size of the safety net, there are no clearly detectable effects on the next generation.

In short, whatever its other merits, it is doubtful that any politically feasible increase in the material resources provided to parents would appreciably change the life trajectories of their children. Mayer's research is hardly the last word on this topic, of course, but it should caution us against assuming that the inheritance of social position in our society is primarily a story about what money can buy.

From a policy perspective, the important point here is that providing greater income transfers to poor families without changing their other characteristics will not necessarily break the link between poverty in one generation and poverty in the next. It may be the right thing to do—as a simple matter of fairness—but it is not likely to transform future lives.

PARENTING AND HOME ENVIRONMENT[19]

As a child grows up, parents do much more, of course, than simply provide material resources. Good parents provide an appropriate mix of warmth and discipline. This is often referred to in the literature as "authoritative" parenting and is usually contrasted to two other styles, overly "permissive" and overly strict or "authoritarian" parenting. Good parenting is not just an abstraction. It has been found to produce better-adjusted and more-successful children.[20] In addition to warmth and discipline, good parents also tend to provide their children with intellectual stimulation (such as reading materials in the home), strong values, and a growing network of connections outside the family—all of which may also contribute to their success.

None of this would matter if good parenting and a stimulating home environment were randomly distributed across the population. But they are not. Most studies have shown that good parenting and a positive home environment often go hand in hand with higher levels of parental income and education.[21]

Further, the structure of the family itself has a significant effect on children's outcomes. Children who grow up with only one biological parent are less successful, on average, than children who grow up living with both parents. This is true across a broad range of outcomes, including labor market success as an adult. And these effects can be found even in families with similar levels of income. In fact, the effects of family structure on various outcomes seem to be due partly to the typically lower incomes in such families and partly to the absence of the second parent, with the two effects being roughly comparable in size.[22] Because about 40 percent of all children now live apart from one parent, up from 12 percent in 1960, the effects of this factor have likely increased.

Thus, some significant component of the effect of family background on success can be explained by factors that take place within the home itself. Disadvantaged children are less likely to experience desirable forms of parenting, to have access to learning experiences that are vital to their early cognitive development, and to grow up in a two-parent family. Overall, differences in parenting practices, home learning environment, and family structure across different family income groups may account for something like one-third to one-half of the overall relationship between family income and children's development.[23] Given the difficulty of measuring such intangibles as "good parenting," these and other figures from the literature are probably lower-bound estimates of the importance of home environment.

CONCLUSION

Genetic inheritance, material resources, and home environment are all correlated with family background and help to explain why it is a strong predictor of later success. The existing literature has not adequately sorted out their relative importance and leaves much unexplained. However, the evidence at least suggests that genetic factors and material resources account for a small part of the association between family background and later success. Home environment (including parenting practices, access to learning experiences, and family structure) appears to play a larger role. However, the three cluster in ways that make distinguishing their separate effects difficult. A single parent who is a high school dropout with few resources—and who out of frustration, despair, or ignorance mistreats or neglects her children—is a

case in point. Providing her with additional resources would make her job as a mother easier, but it cannot replace an absent father or guarantee that she will know what to do as a parent to ensure a better future for her children.

NOTES

1. See, e.g., Christopher Jencks et al., *Who Gets Ahead? The Determinants of Economic Success in America* (New York: Basic Books, 1979), 292; Robert Haveman, *Poverty Policy and Poverty Research: The Great Society and the Social Sciences* (Madison, WI.: University of Wisconsin Press, 1987), 114–116; Robert Haveman and Barbara Wolfe, "The Determinants of Children's Attainments: A Review of Methods and Findings," *Journal of Economic Literature* 33:1829–1878 (December 1995); Robert M. Hauser and Megan M. Sweeney, "Does Poverty in Adolescence Affect the Life Chances of High School Graduates," ed. Greg J. Duncan and Jeanne Brooks-Gunn, *Consequences of Growing Up Poor* (New York: Russell Sage Foundation, 1997), 585.
2. Jencks et al. (1979); Gary Solon et al., "A Longitudinal Analysis of Sibling Correlations in Economic Status," *Journal of Human Resources* 26:509–534 (Summer 1991).
3. See, e.g., Christopher Jencks et al., *Inequality: A Reassessment of the Effect of Family and Schooling in America* (New York: Basic Books, 1972).
4. The relative impact of family background versus education depends on how well family background is measured, but when one includes in family background hard-to-measure influences that affect siblings similarly, the role of background looms at least at large as that of education. For further discussion and some evidence, see Jencks et al. (1979), 10, 214. The best recent reviews of the literature can be found in Haveman and Wolfe (1995) and Duncan and Brooks-Gunn (1997).
5. Edward F. Zigler and Matia Finn Stevenson, *Children in a Changing World: Development and Social Issues*, second edition (Pacific Grove, CA: Brooks/Cole Publishing Company, 1993), 105–112.
6. Richard Herrnstein and Charles Murray, *The Bell Curve: Intelligence and Class Structure in American Life* (New York: Free Press, 1994).
7. Bernie Devlin et al., "Galton Redux: Eugenics, Intelligence, Race, and Society: A Review of *The Bell Curve: Intelligence and Class Structure in American Life*," *Journal of the American Statistical Association*, 1483–1488 (1995).
8. Zigler and Stevenson (1993), 105–106.
9. Data for 20 industrialized countries suggest that IQ scores have been rising at a rate of about 15 points (or one standard deviation) per generation.

James R. Flynn, "IQ Trends over Time: Intelligence, Race, and Meritocracy," *Meritocracy and Equality*, ed. Steven Durlauf (Princeton, NJ: Princeton University Press, 2000).

10. Claude S. Fischer et al., *Inequality by Design: Cracking the Bell Curve Myth* (Princeton, NJ: Princeton University Press, 1996), 84–86.

11. William Dickens, Thomas J. Kane, and Charles Schultze, *Does the Bell Curve Ring True? A Reconsideration* (Washington, D.C.: Brookings Institution, 1998); and McKinley L. Blackburn and David Neumark, "Omitted-Ability Bias and the Increase in Return to Schooling," *Journal of Labor Economics* 11:521–544 (1993). Similar results are reported using 1962 data in Jencks et al. (1972).

12. Jeanne Brooks-Gunn and Greg J. Duncan, "The Effects of Poverty on Children," Center for the Future of Children, The David and Lucile Packard Foundation, *The Future of Children* 7:58–59 (summer/fall 1997).

13. Greg J. Duncan and Jeanne Brooks-Gunn, "Income Effects across the Life Span: Integration and Interpretation," *Consequences of Growing Up Poor*, ed. Greg J. Duncan and Jeanne Brooks-Gunn (New York: Russell Sage Foundation, 1997).

14. Haveman and Wolfe (1995), 1864.

15. Duncan and Brooks-Gunn (1997), 601. Duncan and Brooks-Gunn appear to believe that the quality of the home environment—including the quality of mother-child interactions, the physical condition of the home, and opportunities to learn—is responsible for a substantial portion of the effects of income on cognitive outcomes. And although providing such things as educational toys, reading materials, or a safe play area can cost money, they are not necessarily large items in most family budgets.

16. Susan E. Mayer, *What Money Can't Buy: Family Income and Children's Life Chances* (Cambridge, MA: Harvard University Press, 1997).

17. Duncan and Brooks-Gunn (1997), 597. John Shea, "Does Parents' Money Matter?" Working paper 6026 (Cambridge, MA: National Bureau of Economic Research, Inc., May 1997).

18. Rand Conger et al., "A Family Process Model of Economic Hardship and Adjustment of Early Adolescent Boys," *Child Development* 63:526–541 (1992).

19. We are indebted to Deborah Phillips (Board on Children, Youth, and Families; Institute of Medicine; National Research Council) and Edward Zigler (Yale University) for their assistance in guiding us through some of the relevant literature on this topic.

20. This typology was developed by Diana Baumrind, who showed, in a series of studies, that parenting practices are a major influence on child development (Zigler and Stevenson [1993], 373). Also see Eleanor Maccoby, "Socialization in the Context of the Family: Parent-Child Interaction," *Handbook of Child Psychology*, ed. Paul H. Mussen (New York: John Wiley and Son, 1983), 39–51.

21. For further discussion and cites to the literature, see Thomas L. Hanson, Sara McLanahan, and Elizabeth Thomson, "Economic Resources, Parental Practices, and Children's Well-Being," in Duncan and Brooks-Gunn (1997), 190–238. These authors find that household income and debt are only weakly related to effective parenting, but note that "our results differ from those of other studies," which find stronger effects. The differences may relate to the peculiarities of the data used for this one study. Also see endnote 23.

22. Sara McLanahan, "Parent Absence or Poverty: Which Matters More?" in Duncan and Brooks-Gunn (1997), 35–48.

23. Duncan and Brooks-Gunn (1997) find that the home learning environment alone can explain up to one-third of the overall relationship.

Religious Fundamentalism and the Family

Nancy Tatom Ammerman

*All of Southside's husbands and wives must find ways to live with the tension
between Fundamentalist norms for family structure and modern norms
of individuality and equality. While adopting the ideal of priestly
fathers, full-time mothers, and submission to male authority,
each family works out its own compromises.*

The typical family is hard to find in the United States. Change has created a complexity of choices for all of us. Where strict institutional patterns were characteristic in more traditional periods of our history, modern life has made many family patterns increasingly acceptable to us. Many of us fight against family life without formal marriage, gay marriage, the ease of divorce, singlehood, families without children, but these have increasingly become acceptable alternatives.

Nancy Tatom Ammerman examines the family life in a fundamentalist church. She wants to understand the attempt by some people to hold onto strict traditional family imperatives in a modern industrial individualistic society, and discovers that although the "normal" family is clearly laid out, the realities of modern life often create difficulties and compromise in their homes.

Ammerman's description is a good one because she tries to carefully understand people without judging them. She shows us the conflicts that some people face in living in a society that challenges principles they want to live by, and she causes the reader to better understand the wide variety of family structures that exist in modern society, structures that seem to many of us to be "old-fashioned" or even wrong.

The church is not the only safe harbor for believers. It is not the only institution in which Fundamentalist rules can be made to apply. Other social units can earn the name *Christian* and can share with the church in the maintenance of the believer's faith. Foremost among these is the home. It too, is to be structured according to Christian principles, demonstrating to the world that God's way is best. Like the church, homes can reinforce and sustain believers by creating an environment where the Fundamentalist way of life is taken for granted. But in homes, more than in churches, Fundamentalist rules come up

From Ammerman, Nancy Tatom, *Bible Believers: Fundamentalists in the Modern World*, copyright © 1987, by Rutgers, The State University. Reprinted by permission of Rutgers University Press.

against hard realities that sometimes demand compromise. Both the rules and the compromises shape the lives believers live.

The importance of Christian homes is a recurring theme at Southside. Members are often reminded from the pulpit that the world's families are falling apart, that there is a "50 percent divorce rate," and that the problem of juvenile delinquency can be traced to the lack of discipline in today's homes. In contrast, believers point to evidence that Fundamentalist homes are much more successful than others. The fact that their children are polite and honest is an important affirmation of the rightness of living by God's rules. The fact that their marriages are surviving when divorce is so pervasive reassures them that using God's plan for husbands and wives is indeed the only right way to structure a marriage. Having a Christian home is one of the ways believers distinguish themselves from the rest of the world.

When they talk about how a Christian home is different from any other, the theme of discipline is almost always present. Jim Forester explained, "You can see a stark contrast between our home life and our habits and our ideals and the way we run our household compared to some others." They see uncommitted, undisciplined families as the root cause of most social problems and believe they offer a distinct alternative.

It is not accidental that marriage and family are given so much attention at Southside. This is a congregation of young families; and singles and seniors are all the more left out because "Christian homes" (that is, households with two Christian parents and one or more children) are so important to the church's identity. Women married to unsaved men may say they have a "half-Christian" home; and Howard Otto talked as if he would no longer have a Christian family when his divorce was final, even though he would have custody of his children. The culture of the congregation establishes only one family structure as normative, and the dominant life experiences of the group reinforce that norm. This is a group where people learn to be successfully married, and where young children learn about God. Being a "member" requires sharing that group identity.

Because marriage is so important, believers take special care in the selection of a mate. Yet they do not face the task alone. Just as they are sure that God has a plan for their salvation, their church, and their vocation, they are sure that their mate has already been chosen for them by God. There is one perfect partner who is now (or eventually will be) a Christian. One young woman talked about the man she was seriously dating: "I have prayed for a long time that I would meet somebody that was, you know, different, somebody that knew the Lord. And I waited a long time, but it finally happened."

A clear answer, however, is not always so apparent. If she were to marry someone who was not a believer, they would be said to be "unequally yoked" (II Corinthians 6:14). That is most assuredly not God's will, but it does sometimes work out in the end. Jim Forester explained: "We were unequally yoked, but God did not—I'm sure God wasn't happy about it. That was God's permissive will. God let that happen to bring Doris and I together so that I would get saved and so that Liz, Donald, Jonathan, and Billy would have a Christian home." Even though it was not God's will in the beginning, there was still a reason; and the long-term good has outweighed the short-term problems. The norm of a God-chosen mate survives even when practical realities would seem to dictate otherwise. The idea that God has life under control is as important at home as it is at church.

Likewise, the idea of biblical authority pervades the homes of believers no less than it does their church. Their notion of proper family life is built on their reading of scripture. They are sure that the Bible prescribes the only correct way for husbands and wives to relate to each other and for parents to raise their children: "Everything revolves around the Word. What does God have to say about this? Because there is no other authority. That's why I feel so sorry for children in non-Christian homes." Bonnie Towles recalled that even in unhappy times the Bible still had rules that applied: "I remember one time coming home and screaming at my husband, opening the Bible and saying, 'See this? See this? That's why I'm here. Not because I want to be here, but I have to be here. The Bible says I have to be here. God says that I have to be here, and that's why I'm here.'" At home, as in the rest of life, the Bible's rules should not be broken.

The Bible decrees that husbands and wives stay together until death and that they relate to each other as Christ to the church. Southside members come to expect, then, that Christian homes will be headed by a saved man who takes responsibility for the physical, emotional, and spiritual needs of the household. By his side will be a saved woman who accepts her role as wife and mother in reverent submission. Ideally, she should spend full time maintaining their home and caring for their children. The imperative seems so clear to believers that they come to expect anyone who is saved to try to establish a family according to God's rules.

To say that the imperatives are clear, however, does not mean that everyday realities conform to the ideal.[1] Southside members live in the same economic world as do other Americans, and sometimes those economic realities overshadow Fundamentalist ideals. For instance, although the "ideal" Christian home has a full-time mother, not nearly all of Southside's mothers are outside the labor force. Of the mothers who currently have children under twenty-five, only about 15 percent have stayed out of the labor force entirely during their children's growing-up years. About 35 percent have worked at jobs that still allowed them to spend most of their time at home, but nearly half of all the mothers at Southside are employed full-time outside the home.

Despite this rather massive deviation from the norm, Southside's women continue to hold forth the idea of full-time motherhood. Most of those who work have occupations rather than careers; and they still do the bulk of the work that must be done at home. They share with the rest of Southside's mothers the ideal of being the most important influence in their children's lives, of creating a warm and loving environment in which children grow to be happy, healthy, Christian people. Jim Forester described his wife (who does stay at home full-time) in just such glowing terms: "She works twenty hours a day. Today the housewife and mother seem to be looked down upon in many places. Without moms, without the right kind of mothers in this country, we wouldn't be where we are today. . . . I appreciate very much my wife and the tremendous effort that she puts forth just to give us a good, stable home life." Doris agreed that her primary source of fulfillment was

creating a good home: "I never held a job outside the home, but I do work twenty hours a day. But I enjoy it. I don't feel right now like I've missed anything. Now probably when Billy is in school full-time, I'll just go bonkers and go outside the home and do something. But right now I enjoy being home and making a home for everyone."

Those who do not have the luxury of staying at home nevertheless identify themselves first as wives and mothers. Ann Lazzaro works and goes to school, but she says, "My family does come first, and my husband approves of my going to school, so that is what makes a difference." Whatever Southside wives and mothers actually do, husbands must approve. Although most mothers may violate the letter of the rule about working, they by no means violate its spirit.

In the day-to-day lives of families, then, women shoulder the responsibility of maintaining the home. If they are employed, they may persuade their husbands to help with a few chores; but cooking, cleaning, and child rearing are the God-given tasks of women. Major purchases and repairs are delegated to husbands, while the general physical and emotional condition of the home and family is the job of the mother. The father's primary job is to provide the resources, make the right decisions, and preside over the spiritual well-being of the family.

The husband's role as priest in the family is, however, no less ambiguous than the wife's role as full-time homemaker. Among other reasons, wives are often the first in a family to convert. When the husband is not saved, wives usually take over as spiritual leaders in the home. A woman whose husband is not saved described her arrangement this way: "He is head of the house in the sense that he's the head of the house, but not the head of the Christian house." Bonnie added, "I hope to see my husband saved and for us to have family devotions for all of us and not just me and the children." Out of necessity, these women learn to be priests to their families, but most, like Bonnie, long to relinquish that role.

Besides the fact that wives are often the first to convert, they often find themselves the more enthusiastic supporters of the church and of the Fundamentalist way of life. Another woman, who does have a Christian husband, was almost as dissatisfied as she would have been if her husband were unsaved. And she was, therefore, equally involved in leading her family: "I want my husband to be the head of the Christian home, not passive. I don't want to have to do it; I want him to, you know." These three women and dozens of others in the church are in fact the spiritual leaders in their homes. The norm of male authority is strong enough to make them dissatisfied and to shape the goals they hold up for their children; but this too is a norm that is not perfectly followed.

Among the father's responsibilities in the "ideal" Christian home is to lead his family in daily devotions. The church encourages every family to set aside a special time for Bible reading and prayer in which the whole family participates. In the rhetoric of Southside, missing "family altar" is almost as grave as missing Sunday services.

However, although gathering the whole family for father-led devotions is a model to which nearly every family refers, it is by no means the most prevalent actual behavior, even when everyone in the family is saved. Many, like Jim, have simply found it impractical: "Getting everybody together in the same room at the same time—it just didn't work out. So now I get up early in the morning, and I read the Bible and pray. First thing in the morning I have a time of prayer with the Lord. And the kids do the same thing; Liz reads the Bible. But as far as a formal family devotional time, I'm embarrassed to say that 'no, I don't.' It hasn't worked out." The norm is strong enough to make him feel embarrassed but not strong enough to survive the practical difficulties.

More often reading the Bible and praying are a constant but informal part of the everyday lives of Southside's families. The Danners, for instance, tried to have a special time for family devotions but often found themselves too busy. For them, mealtimes became a "family altar."

> So the table was a sharing time. That is one reason I could never sell our kitchen table. So much has happened around it. I have given it to our son. But it seemed like around the table we cried and shared and talked. And because Christ is a way of life with us, it does enter into our daily life. So he [Ray] does come home sharing who he is talking with, and I would come home doing the same thing. Then, of course, you would have to go look up a verse, and you would have to go to the Bible. We were doing a lot about evolution at one time. That seemed to be

our area of sharing because the children were challenged with it in school.

Sharing in everyday life thus included witnessing, taking a stand against evolution, reading the Bible, and praying. This practice may not have precisely fit the recommended model for family devotions, but it even more effectively accomplished the same purpose.

Family altar is not the only ideal that must bend to the realities of everyday family life. In the relationship between Christian wives and husbands, a husband theoretically has all the authority. As one husband described it, "I believed that it was my position, whether I liked it or not, to be the head of the home, that my wife's religion came from me. As it says in Ephesians 5, that Christ is to the church as the husband is to the wife." Christian wives agree. Decision making is the husband's responsibility. When Rebecca Hughes talked about how the family might approach a major decision like moving, she said, "I'd like my husband to be the head of the house. I believe it's a decision that we both have to talk about, but I believe that in the end the husband decides." Although the husband decides, then, the couple should talk it over, presumably arriving at a consensus they believe to be God's will. The "ideal" of male domination is thus subtly accommodated to the reality of modern expectations for equality.

This question of female equality and power is a murky one at Southside. In a variety of ways, Christian wives are both powerful and powerless. Within their households, they have enormous powers of persuasion that are based in part on their intimate involvement with the everyday details of the family's life. They simply have more information, more emotional investment, and often more skill than their husbands. They may be able to run their homes so smoothly that their husbands rarely have any decisions to make, and they may discover ways to influence the decisions their husbands do make. As Janet Slavin put it, "Being submissive, the way I understand it, does leave me an active role and doesn't leave me in a quiet, nowhere role. I mean, I still can offer my opinion, which still leaves it with Joe to make the final decision. . . . If I honor his opinion after I've given him mine, and then if I go along with him, the Lord will make it right, and Joe will come around." Part of the lore that is passed from older wives to younger ones is how to keep a husband from making an unwise decision without appearing to usurp his rightful authority.

This delicate balance of submission and influence is even more difficult to maintain, however, when one party is not a believer. The conversion of one spouse, usually the wife, sets the stage for conflict. Often the other spouse will follow in fairly short time, but equally often a wife must resign herself to living with a man whose priorities and lifestyle she has chosen to reject but to whom she is tied for life. A few "unequally yoked" couples manage to build loving, tolerant and healthy marriages despite the difficulties. But occasionally husbands take unfair advantage of their wives' unquestioning loyalty. Or wives subject their husbands to constant reminders that God is not pleased with their lives. And sometimes husbands cannot take the strain and leave.

A wife with an unsaved husband often finds herself in uncomfortable situations. Even if she has learned to live with his eternal damnation, she still must chafe at the temporal decisions he makes about their money, their friends, and their time. She wants to give substantial amounts of money to the church, but he objects.[2] She wants to go to church, but he would rather go fishing. And when he invites his friends for dinner or insists that she go along to a party, she finds herself in company she would otherwise choose to avoid: "All I've got really is Al's friends, and while I like them they're—they all drink. I'm out with a crowd that drinks, and I don't drink. And they smoke, and I don't smoke. And sometimes they have friends—these three couples that we go with know that they can't tell dirty jokes when I'm there, but we occasionally meet friends of theirs who don't mind spitting all these dirty jokes out. I'd like to get lost." Another woman added, "I would like to be separated from the world. But it is hard to be separated with my husband because I certainly can't let him go off by himself with those people!" Although she may learn to become priest to the family, the Christian wife with an unsaved husband also learns to compromise. She knows she cannot always live by the biblical rules for families she would like to follow.

Unsaved men rarely object to a wife who converts and decides to be submissive. American husbands rarely expect their wives to dominate the marriage anyway. One husband who was saved after his wife remembered noticing that his usually "strong-willed" wife was suddenly letting him make all the decisions. Now he credits that change and his conversion with saving the marriage. If, however, in rare cases, the husband converts and decides unilaterally to assume a role as "head of the household," he is almost guaranteed to meet opposition. An unsaved wife has little incentive to submit. Even though Howard's wife is saved, she found the submissive role of wife less attractive than he did. His insistence on her submission brought an end to the marriage. Fundamentalist men do not have the power to impose their authority on women who do not choose to submit.

Most Southside wives do choose to submit, and, in doing so, they embrace both the rewards and the limitations of their role. Among the rewards is the joy of bearing and raising children. Here Southside women are encouraged to use their full creative powers (cf. DeJong 1965). Yet their role in even this process is limited by their submission to God and to their husbands. Almost every woman I talked to saw conception as something outside her control, despite the fact that birth control (other than abortion) is not openly condemned. Few members limit or plan their families. Neither do they seek help for infertility. Two women who had no children and one who had only one lamented that God had not provided the children they wanted, but none had sought any medical help. Those who had more children than they wanted also saw the situation as out of their hands. One whose third and fourth children were unplanned (and had put a serious strain on the marriage) has since had a fifth. Another who was expecting her fifth while I was there commented that "the Lord always gives you more than you ask for." Having and raising children are sources of status and power for women; but that power is limited by the fact that women do not control whether and when those children arrive.

To outsiders, such dependence on male authority may seem incomprehensible. Fundamentalist norms for structuring marriages are genuinely at odds with the norms in the larger society. The people at Southside argue that their way works, that they do not suffer from divorce and unhappy homes precisely because they abide by rules for a clear division of labor and authority. Each spouse knows what is expected. To support their success claims, Southside couples often point to their own marriages; there is, in fact, little divorce in the congregation. In addition, a remarkable number (20 percent of those currently married) claim that Fundamentalist beliefs have saved their marriages. Janet talked about their situation: "When we first got married, we both liked music and loved dancing and drink, and that was one of our common grounds. We both liked philosophy. But it seemed like a lot of our common ground was a terrible common ground. . . . We would have ended up with a divorce, not because we didn't love each other but because we didn't know how to be married." What she meant by knowing "how to be married" was that she and Joe were failing in their attempt to structure a marriage around two independent personalities, and they did not know any other model. Southside offered them an alternative. Learning to be a submissive wife was worth it to Janet if it meant saving her marriage.

For Joe and Janet, the effort was a joint one and came along rather smoothly. For others, however, the task is much more difficult. Another Southside wife described the years of agony that preceded her full acceptance of her proper role in the family.

> We had both very much been part of the world. I went back to school. I became very caught up in my own life. I had married young and had never really grown up before I had gotten married or really had a chance to be independent. And so I had two babies, and when they started nursery school, I started back to college. And I got very caught up in the modernism movement. I was influenced a lot by most of my professors who were divorced because they were out seeking their own identity. Consequently, I started picking up my own identity. And my husband needed a homebody-type wife for the type of person that he is. And I was becoming more and more independent and growing further and further away. The marriage had been troubled before, but I was doing my best to wreck it, without even trying. . . . It resulted in a split, and there were some really bad years together, until we were saved. And even then, there were years of struggle. Consequently, I used to pray to God to

make him a better husband and father. And finally, it dawned on me, you know, "Lord, change me! Make me the kind of wife that I should be!"

Her story is not unlike Bonnie's.

> I would go to pastor in tears, expecting sympathy because of my miserable marriage and my miserable husband. . . . I'd go to pastor, and he would bring out the Word, and he would say, "Bonnie, read this." And, he would make me read it, and it would be, of course, God's plan for the wife. And I would go out of there so mad I couldn't see to drive home. . . . I used to say over and over again I hated my husband. I was so full of rebellion. But I began to see that it was me that needed to change too, because my prayer for those two years was "Change him, Lord, I can't stand him. Change him." Little by little, I began to see that my prayer needed to be "How can I change so that he will see Christ in me?" . . . The Lord has taught me how important my husband is and how important his feelings are. Until then, nothing was working. Nothing was working right.

In each case, women chose to give up their overt power in the marriage in exchange for avoiding divorce.

The norms against divorce are so strong, in fact, that some Southside marriages are preserved because no other option appears plausible. For believers divorce is never legitimate just because they cannot get along. Only if one partner commits adultery or abandons the family entirely can the remaining partner feel innocent. Even then, they may change churches to avoid facing their old friends.

Therefore, when Southside couples fight, they know that they must find a way to resolve their differences. Some, like Jim and Doris, credit God with keeping them together despite all their disagreements.

> [If we were not Christians,] we wouldn't be married. We would have been divorced a long time ago. . . . I'm very, very thankful for many things, especially that the Lord has seen fit to keep us together. We could have quit. We could have given up. There were times in our marriage when it could have gone either way. It was nip and tuck, touch and go. But ultimately, after we went through all our plans, and the marriage counseling, and all this stuff, we finally went to God and asked him for help, and that's when things started to look up.

Others reflect similar sentiments.

> *Husband:* We did get through our problems, many of them bumpy.
>
> *Wife:* Without Christ we wouldn't be together, would we, Dad?
>
> *Husband:* No, we wouldn't. That's right. We wouldn't have gotten through all those rough places.

> It's by the grace of God. I think everybody has a self-ish nature, and sometimes little things—it's little things Satan works with—and I oftentimes wonder, if it wasn't for the Lord, if we'd be a family today.

Again, part of the pattern couples learn for keeping the peace in their homes is that in the end wives must give in rather than cause too much trouble. As Janet put it, she is learning to "keep my mouth shut when I don't want to." Abiding by Fundamentalist rules for marriage was cited by nearly half the couples in the Southside congregation as the way they keep the peace at home.

In most cases, then, Southside couples eventually find a comfortable accommodation to the biblical mandate for submission. Wives learn to give up the ideal of independence in exchange for the goal of living according to the plan of God and the reality of the influence they are able to have. Occasionally, however, the exchange simply does not work out as planned. The message of the church is that the Bible binds couples together for life, no matter how bad the marriage may seem. Some can live with that. A woman whose marriage is miserable said simply, "I've adjusted to my life, to the way things are between Bill and I."

Others cannot adjust to these demands; and when they fail to live up to the visible standards of the church, they often suffer enormously. When Mary Lou Otto filed for divorce, she also ended her relationship to the church. She knew she would not be accepted there, even if she wanted to participate. Even innocent partners in a divorce can be barred from positions of honor in the church. For some the resulting sense of isolation can have serious psychological consequences. Although Howard was maintaining his relationship with the church, he felt it becoming increasingly tenuous. He also had a tremendous load of anger and fear that was keeping him up at night and sending him to a variety of other sources of solace.

For some, these norms against divorce keep them in marriages long past the time when it is healthy for them to stay. One woman in the congregation had a major emotional breakdown before she finally concluded that divorce was in her best interests. Two other women were continuing to struggle with marriages that kept them in or near a state of depression.

The disjuncture between Fundamentalist norms and family realities is the primary cause of psychological disturbance in the Southside congregation. The number of people I found experiencing difficulties is not unlike what would be expected in a sample of urban people in the Northeast.[3] The content of their problems, however, bears the imprint of the religious community of which they are a part.

Besides divorce, other deviations from the Fundamentalist norm for families can cause problems. For women, child rearing is a special case. Three women in the church who had had major breakdowns dated the beginning of their problems to the birth of their first child.[4] Another woman had suffered the death of her favored child and was left with only the child whose emotional and behavioral problems made her feel totally inadequate as a Christian mother. Worse, this child did not like to go to church with her, while the child who died had been a star Sunday School pupil who had made her proud. Left with only an unsaved husband and a rebellious child, this woman was seeking psychological counseling; but the problem had distinctly religious dimensions.

Even for men, children can pose indirect difficulties. When faced with the injunction to be a provider and priest, some Christian fathers may feel like failures. Finding themselves totally responsible for a young family precipitated trouble for two of the men I interviewed.

Finally, failing to get married was the central problem for two other women. They had each reached an age where a lifetime of singleness was likely. "I'd really like a home of my own and family of my own to take care of. I like to take care of other people. . . . Some people think I want to escape into home, but that's the kind of life I, you know, was brought up with. I was brought up in an old-fashioned way. . . . I think I was born in the wrong century."

This woman indirectly put her finger on the common problem. She was not the only woman to complain that she was born in the wrong century. The values and expectations these women and men have acquired at home and at church have failed to equip them for the reality they must face in this century. Family problems often cause people distress, but they are intensified when a church like Southside defines one and only one family form as the Christian ideal. Those whose family lives are less than ideal are likely to suffer emotional and spiritual consequences. Some believers cannot conform, and others suffer silently rather than deviate. For some the strain is incapacitating, while others eventually find ways to cope.

All of Southside's husbands and wives must find ways to live with the tension between Fundamentalist norms for family structure and modern norms of individuality and equality. While adopting the ideal of priestly fathers, full-time mothers, and submission to male authority, each family works out its own compromises. Many men do not wish to be priests. Many women do not feel able to stay home full-time. Most families miss the ideal of daily devotional times. And most women learn to influence family decision making while still deferring to their husbands' authority. For a few, the model is oppressive and brings adverse psychological consequences. But for most of Southside's families, the ideals and the compromises offer a viable model, a model many claim has saved their marriages.

NOTES

1. Richardson and his associates (1979) and Tipton (1982, chap. 2) offer similar descriptions of Fundamentalist norms of family life. Rose (1985) and McNamara (1985) provide additional strong ethnographic accounts and also describe the subtle ways in which rhetoric and reality do not match.
2. Interestingly, all those whose spouses do not attend reported giving less than 10 percent of their income to the church in stark contrast to the patterns in other kinds of families.
3. A 1969 community survey conducted in New Haven found that 14 percent of the people interviewed reported moderate numbers of depressive symptoms. A 1975 survey provided an estimate of about 7 percent of the population that might be considered clinically depressed, while only one percent had ever been hospitalized (Weissman and Myers 1978). My data do not include a formal measure of depression, but many of the people I interviewed spontaneously reported information about their emotional and functional states. Those who mentioned three or more of the symptoms contained in the Weissman and Myers checklist are those I classified as distressed. As in their study, exactly 14 percent of my sample could be so classified. In addition, 5 percent of those at Southside were seriously enough depressed to have been so diagnosed, and 4 percent had at some point been hospitalized.
4. Rose (1985) documents a similar pattern of breakdowns among women in another Fundamentalist congregation. Women far outnumber men among the troubled people at Southside. This finding is in line with those of most mental-health surveys; see Gove (1978) for a review. That their illness is related to constraints on available roles for women is consistent with the findings of Gove and Tudor (1973) and with the observations of many others, including Bernard (1972).

REFERENCES

Bernard, J. 1972. *The Future of Marriage.* New York: Bantam.

DeJong, G. F. 1965. "Religious Fundamentalism, Socio-economic Status, and Fertility Attitudes in the Southern Appalachians." *Demography* 2:540–548.

Gove, W. R. 1978. "Sex Differences in Mental Illness among Adult Men and Women: An Evluation of Four Questions Raised Regarding the Evidence on the Higher Rates of Women." *Social Science and Medicine* 12B:187–198.

Gove, W. R., and J. F. Tudor. 1973. "Adult Sex Roles and Mental Illness." *American Journal of Sociology* 78:812–835.

McNamara, P. H. 1985. "The New Christian Right's Views of the Family and Its Social Science Critics: A Study in Differing Presuppositions." *Journal of Marriage and the Family* 47:449–458.

Richardson, J. T., M. W. Stewart, and R. B. Simmonds. 1979. *Organized Miracles: A Study of a Contemporary, Youth, Communal, Fundamentalist Organization.* New Brunswick, N.J.: Transaction Books.

Rose, S. 1985. "Women Warriors: Power and Prayer in Family Relations." Paper presented to the Association for the Sociology of Religion, Washington, D.C.

Tipton, S. M. 1982. *Getting Saved from the Sixties.* Berkeley: University of California Press.

Weissman, M. M., and J. K. Myers. 1978. "Rates and Risks of Depressive Symptoms & in a United States Urban Community." *Acta Psychiatrica Scandinavica* 57:219–231.

◆ 47 ◆

The Meaning of Religion

Emile Durkheim

This division of the world into two domains, the one containing all that is sacred,
the other all that is profane, is the distinctive trait of religious thought. . . .

What is religion? Here is a classic statement by an exciting social thinker who
focuses on a single theme that characterizes all religion to him: the creation of a
world apart from the everyday or profane, a world we call a "sacred" world.

The study which we are undertaking is therefore a
way of taking up again, *but under new conditions,*
the old problem of the origin of religion. To be
sure, if by origin we are to understand the very first
beginning, the question has nothing scientific
about it, and should be resolutely discarded.
There was no given moment when religion began
to exist, and there is consequently no need of finding a means of transporting ourselves thither in
thought. Like every human institution, religion
did not commence anywhere. Therefore, all spec-
ulations of this sort are justly discredited; they can
only consist in subjective and arbitrary constructions which are subject to no sort of control. But
the problem which we raise is quite another one.
What we want to do is to find a means of discerning the ever-present causes upon which the most
essential forms of religious thought and practice
depend. . . .

The general conclusion of the book which the
reader has before him is that religion is something

eminently social. Religious representations are
collective representations which express collective realities; the rites are a manner of acting
which take rise in the midst of the assembled
groups and which are destined to excite, maintain
or recreate certain mental states in these groups.
So if the categories [through which we under-
stand] are of religious origin, they ought to participate in this nature common to all religious facts;
they too should be social affairs and the product of
collective thought. . . .

All known religious beliefs, whether simple or
complex, present one common characteristic: they
presuppose a classification of all the things, real
and ideal, of which men think, into two classes or
opposed groups, generally designated by two distinct terms which are translated well enough by the
words *profane* and *sacred (profane, sacré)*. This division of the world into two domains, the one containing all that is sacred, the other all that is profane, is the distinctive trait of religious thought; the
beliefs, myths, dogmas and legends are either representations or systems of representations which
express the nature of sacred things, the virtues and
powers which are attributed to them, or their relations with each other and with profane things. . . .

In all the history of human thought there
exists no other example of two categories of

Reprinted and abridged with the permission of The Free
Press, a Division of Simon & Schuster Adult Publishing
Group, from *The Elementary Forms of Religious Life* by Emile
Durkheim, translated by Joseph Ward Swain. Copyright ©
1915 by George Allen and Unwin. Copyright © 1965 by The
Free Press. All rights reserved.

things so profoundly differentiated or so radically opposed to one another. The traditional opposition of good and bad is nothing beside this; for the good and the bad are only two opposed species of the same class, namely morals, just as sickness and health are two different aspects of the same order of facts, life, while the sacred and the profane have always and everywhere been conceived by the human mind as two distinct classes, as two worlds between which there is nothing in common. The forces which play in one are not simply those which are met with in the other, but a little stronger; they are of a different sort. In different religions, this opposition has been conceived in different ways. Here, to separate these two sorts of things, it has seemed sufficient to localize them in different parts of the physical universe; there, the first have been put into an ideal and transcendental world, while the material world is left in full possession of the others. But howsoever much the forms of the contrast may vary, the fact of the contrast is universal. . . .

The opposition of these two classes manifests itself outwardly with a visible sign by which we can easily recognize this very special classification, wherever it exists. Since the idea of the sacred is always and everywhere separated from the idea of the profane in the thought of men, and since we picture a sort of logical chasm between the two, the mind irresistibly refuses to allow the two corresponding things to be confounded, or even to be merely put in contact with each other; for such a promiscuity, or even too direct a contiguity, would contradict too violently the dissociation of these ideas in the mind. The sacred thing is *par excellence* that which the profane should not touch, and cannot touch with impunity. To be sure, this interdiction cannot go so far as to make all communication between the two worlds impossible; for if the profane could in no way enter into relations with the sacred, this latter could be good for nothing. But, in addition to the fact that this establishment of relations is always a delicate operation in itself, demanding great precautions and a more or less complicated initiation, it is quite impossible, unless the profane is to lose its specific characteristics and become sacred after a fashion and to a certain degree itself. The two classes cannot even approach each other and keep their own nature at the same time.

Thus we arrive at the first criterium of religious beliefs. Undoubtedly there are secondary species within these two fundamental classes which, in their turn, are more or less incompatible with each other. But the real characteristic of religious phenomena is that they always suppose a bipartite division of the whole universe, known and knowable, into two classes which embrace all that exists, but which radically exclude each other. Sacred things are those which the interdictions protect and isolate; profane things, those to which these interdictions are applied and which must remain at a distance from the first. Religious beliefs are the representations which express the nature of sacred things and the relations which they sustain, either with each other or with profane things. Finally, rites are the rules of conduct which prescribe how a man should comport himself in the presence of these sacred objects. . . .

The really religious beliefs are always common to a determined group, which makes profession of adhering to them and of practicing the rites connected with them. They are not merely received individually by all the members of this group; they are something belonging to the group, and they make its unity. The individuals which compose it feel themselves united to each other by the simple fact that they have a common faith. A society whose members are united by the fact that they think in the same way in regard to the sacred world and its relations with the profane world, and by the fact that they translate these common ideas into common practices, is what is called a Church. In all history, we do not find a single religion without a Church. Sometimes the Church is strictly national, sometimes it passes the frontiers; sometimes it embraces an entire people (Rome, Athens, the Hebrews), sometimes it embraces only a part of them (the Christian societies since the advent of Protestantism); sometimes it is directed by a corps of priests, sometimes it is almost completely devoid of any official directing body. But wherever we observe the religious life, we find that it has a definite group as its foundation. Even the so-called private cults, such as the domestic cult or the cult of a corporation, satisfy this condition; for they are always celebrated by a group, the family or the corporation. Moreover, even these particular religions are ordinarily only special forms of a more general religion which embraces all; these restricted Churches are in reality only chapels of a vaster Church which, by reason of this very extent, merits this name still more. . . .

Thus we arrive at the following definition: *A religion is a unified system of beliefs and practices relative to sacred things, that is to say, things set apart and forbidden—beliefs and practices,* which unite into one single moral community called a Church, all those who adhere to them. The second element which thus finds a place in our definition is no less essential than the first; for by showing that the idea of religion is inseparable from that of the Church, it makes it clear that religion should be an eminently collective thing.

❖ 48 ❖

The Third Disestablishment of Religion in the United States

Phillip E. Hammond

Religion since the 1960s, to the degree it is important, is more likely to be individually *important and less likely to be* collectively *important.*

To Emile Durkheim, the importance of religion is tied to community. Its whole existence is traceable to tying the community together and supporting a common morality. The 1960s was a revolution in morality and in religion, according to Phillip Hammond and other sociologists, in that religion became increasingly individualistic, voluntary. The trend since has been the declining importance of established religion in the United States, a "third disestablishment" according to Hammond.

The trends, however, are highly complex, and probably we are all too close to what is taking place in our religious institutions to be objective. In our age of individualism many people seem to cry out for even more community and turn toward more strong religious communities, sometimes established and traditional forms, often new forms. It is clear that religion—individual or collective—still has an important role in American life, but the actual trends seem difficult to unravel.

From Phillip E. Hammond, *Religion and Personal Autonomy: The Third Disestablishment in America,* Columbia, SC: University of South Carolina Press, 1992, p. 1–18.

During a summer weekend every year in Santa Barbara, a Greek Festival is held in one of the city parks.[1] The booths selling souvlaki and dolmas are operated by—and for the benefit of—the Greek Orthodox parish in town. And this sponsorship is prominently displayed by a sign on each booth. In 1986 something interesting could be noted about those signs. Carefully and beautifully printed, they announced the sponsor as "The Greek Church of Santa Barbara." Then inscribed in longhand, between the words "Greek" and "Church," someone had added "Orthodox." Whoever first prepared the signs, in other words, had failed to mention the part of the label that, in substance, is of greatest importance: What church is sponsoring this booth? The Greek *Orthodox* Church!

Of course nobody was misled or in doubt. Perhaps only perverse sociologists of religion would even notice. But something interesting was implied by the original omission: The signmaker, while acknowledging by choice of words that there could be Greek sponsorship which is *not* the church, was also implying that churchgoing Greeks in Santa Barbara go to *one church only.*

Such is one view of the church—that it is more or less dictated by one's primary group allegiances. And not just dictated by, but expressive of, those allegiances. Indeed, in the original formulation by Ernst Troeltsch (1911) the "church," as distinct from the "sect," is something one is born into rather than voluntarily joining. In America, no doubt, this view of the church was strongest in the nineteenth century, when ethnicity, immigrant status, and various aspects of socioeconomic status all overlapped. By now the church decreasingly plays this "collective-expressive" role, even if exceptions may remain, as the Santa Barbara Greek Festival would suggest. After all, fewer and fewer of us are embedded in primary groups, and—what may be more important—the few primary group ties we do have are not overlapping. Instead, as the classic sociological formulation has it, we are chiefly involved in a series of segmented relationships.

For many therefore—especially those not embedded in primary groups—the church is simply one of these segmented relationships. Far from expressing collective ties, the church is one of the ways by which individuals (often joined by other members of their nuclear families) may try to cope with this segmented life. Very much a voluntary association for such people, the religious organization represents for them not an inherited relationship but a relationship that can be entered and left with little or no impact on their other relationships. Church for them is not simultaneously a gathering of kin, neighbors, fellow workers, and leisure-time friends but rather a separate activity, expressing another meaning. For such people it is not a necessary moral compass, an anchorage in a world of conflicting expectations, but rather a safe harbor, one place to sort out life's dilemmas. If such people do get involved in a church, they are therefore more likely to do so for their *own* reasons, even if they have friendly relations there. Their view of the church might therefore be called "individual-expressive." Put another way, whereas others may regard the church as a natural extension of their social worlds, these people regard it as an avenue to some privately chosen goal—for example, to commune with God, educate their children religiously, enjoy music, or get therapy.

Of course, just as persons with an individual-expressive view of the church may have friends in the church, so may private goals be held by those for whom the church is collective-expressive. But whereas the former will likely withdraw their participation if their goals are not met, the latter are likely to maintain their church involvement irrespective of their personal agendas. For them, to put it simply, the church is not an object that they, as individuals, may freely accept or reject.

Of course, this characterization is exaggerated. No population can be divided neatly into two churchgoing groups: one that "must" go and another that "chooses" to go. How much pressure one feels—and the nature of the obligation felt as a result—will differ from one person to another. At the same time, so will the freedom to choose—and the way *it* is felt—differ from person to person. Thus, over and beyond the view of the church carried by persons is the set of circumstances peculiar to each as they live their lives, sensitive now to some people, beholden to others, oblivious to yet others. . . .

RELIGION AND IDENTITY

The distinction we are making—between the church as more collective-expressive or more individual-expressive—has a parallel in what role the church may play in how people think of themselves. The "identities" of both types may be informed by religion, but they will be differently informed, as the two concepts of identity used in the social sciences would suggest (Mol 1978). One way of looking at identity suggest the immutable—or at least the slowly changing—core of personality that shows up in all of a person's encounters, irrespective of differing role partners. The second way suggests the transient and changeable self as persons move from one social encounter to another, offering a somewhat different identity, as it were, in each place. The first notion of identity suggests that it is involuntarily held; the second, that it can be put on and off. The first is nourished in primary groups, probably early in life; the second exists precisely because much of life is lived in arenas outside of primary groups. . . .

We have already noted about the first kind of identity that it is involuntary—that it is thrust upon its possessor by so many others, in so many circumstances, for such a long time, that even if one wanted to escape it, one could not. The phenomenon of "passing" (e.g., of a black as white, a Jew as Gentile)—now no longer much noted—illustrated by its poignancy this essentially involuntary character; one chose to discard an identity of the first sort at great social risk, of course, but also at great psychic cost because this was no facade being peeled away but a pulling out of roots.

Now, it was Durkheim's great insight that religion is born out of the social circumstances providing those involuntary roots (Durkheim 1961). People are led, he said, to represent their sense of unity in the groups of which they are members—to express that unity in ceremony and symbol, in belief and ritual. In the case of the central Australian aborigines he studied, there was no choice in the matter.

Because modern society so little resembles the Australian outback, and because the religions Durkheim described so little resemble religions of our day, we may too easily dismiss this Durkheimian insight as no longer applicable. But that would be a mistake. What can be granted is that, in societies of the sort about which Durkheim wrote, religion was coextensive with social life, and that situation no longer exists anywhere in the modern world. But we must recognize that even in modern society, the church may still be an expression of primary group ties, especially if those ties are to overlapping groups. That is the possible significance of the Greek Festival in Santa Barbara—the maintenance of the first kind of religion-and-identity relationship.

At the same time, however, we must also recognize that for others the church is a secondary association—a voluntary activity that may be switched on and off. Under these circumstances the church may be very important to some people, and thus a source of identity for them; but the identity provided will be an identity of the second sort. . . .

The thesis here is that the social revolution of the 1960s and 1970s accelerated the shifting balance of these two views of the church, doing so by greatly escalating a phenomenon we will call "personal autonomy." Personal autonomy thus has not only led to a decline in parish involvement—by increased individual-over collective-expressiveness and increased secondary over primary identity—but it has also led to an alteration in the meaning of that involvement. The result we are calling the "third disestablishment."

THE PROCESS OF DISESTABLISHMENT

It is true that, in the legal sense, the United States has never had a national established church. Nonetheless, churches, especially Protestant churches, have historically enjoyed a kind of "establishment" status in American culture. Their leaders have been community leaders, for example, and, in the nineteenth century especially, they were prominent in what Donald Mathews called "an organizing process"—the establishment of schools, hospitals, orphanages, colleges, magazines, etc. (1969, 23–24). It might be said, therefore, that churches once played a significant role in the first kind of identity formation of many people, even if that role was being overtaken by the second kind of identity formation. What might be further noted, and as the above discussion on identity formation would suggest, to the degree the individual-expressive view of churches was replacing the collective-expressive view, the effect was a decline in their "establishment" status, that is, a reduction in the public linkage of religion with social collectivities. The change, in brief, was a step toward "disestablishment." The *legal* situation had not changed, of course, since in the eyes of the law no churches were ever established nationally (in 1833 Massachusetts became the final state to dismantle its tax-supported religious activity). But, as we will now review, the disestablishment process has been occurring right along, though churches and the American people have experienced it not smoothly but in jolts—at times when the disestablishment shift has been accelerated.

The first jolt, we may surmise, took place with the adoption of the Bill of Rights. Actually the jolt must have preceded the Constitution because historians agree that no serious effort was made by any denomination at the time of the nation's founding to gain favored status by law. As Sidney Mead writes:

> When the American Revolution was completed, let us say with John Adams by around 1815, not only had the Established Church of England been rejected, but, more important, the very idea of "Establishment" had been discarded in principle by the new Constitution. (1977, 76)

Roger Finke states the case somewhat differently:

> With the new rules of law, upstart sects and new religions were not only given a right to exist (toleration), they were given "equal" rights; and the once privileged religious establishments lost the legislative and financial support of the state. By denying the establishment of any religion, and granting the free exercise of religion to all, they could no longer support regulation that denied privileges to or imposed sanctions on specific religious organizations—or their members. The state was denied the privilege, and freed of the obligation, of regulating religion. (1990, 609)

What followed in the nineteenth century was nevertheless, for all intents and purposes, a continued Protestant "establishment"—kind of "American Christendom," as Eldon Ernst labels it.

> Protestants conceived of an American Christian democracy infused by their church traditions. . . . Protestant-dominated politics, from fugitive slave laws to know-nothing nativist elections to prohibition legislation, was geared to protect white Anglo-Saxon Protestant civilization. The arts, economics, politics, even war, bore the Protestant imprint. (1987, 151)

Of course, this hegemonic position of Protestantism was challenged, not least by the massive immigration of Roman Catholics, whose leaders had their own image of an "American Christendom."

> But no sooner had Catholics come of age in America than they, along with Protestants, would find themselves plunged into a whole new quest for their Christian identity in a post-Christendom environment. . . . Historically, the demise of Protestant America can be traced most precisely to the period of World War I and the changing temper of life in the 1920s. (Ernst 1987, 154, 156)

The consequence thus was a second jolt, appropriately called by Robert Handy "the second disestablishment":

> The hopes for a Christian America as envisioned by nineteenth-century evangelicals were fast fading in the face of the realities of postwar America; the enthusiasm and morale needed to sustain the crusade were undermined. . . . The prestige of Protestantism was further lessened by the bitter controversy between fundamentalists and modernists. (1984, 169, 175–76)

Following the religious downturn of the 1920s, the economic depression of the 1930s, and the disruption of a second World War, churches bounced back, and among those bouncing back were Protestant churches, of course. But the second step toward disestablishment was not reversed. Instead, even with record-setting memberships, attendance, and church construction—taken by some to mean a "revival," the authenticity of which was much debated—churches found themselves popular but less powerful. More precisely, they enjoyed greater popularity than ever before, but they were reduced in their role as carriers of American values to being more custodial than directorial. Needless to say, Protestants felt this loss more keenly because they had once uniquely played that role, but the disestablishment of religious organizations in the sense of a declining public presence was true for all churches. By the 1950s this alteration in the relationship between churches and the sociopolitical culture was becoming clear. As Will Herberg's *Protestant, Catholic, Jew* (1955) helped us see, the vast majority of Americans were committed to a tolerant, bland religion that happened to come in three major flavors. The choice was theirs. The potential for a new blossoming of the individual-expressive church was therefore great.

THE THIRD DISESTABLISHMENT

The third jolt is what Roof and McKinney call "the collapse of the religious and cultural middle" and thus the loss of religion's "integrative force." They even suggest that this collapse represents a possible "third disestablishment" (1987, 33–39). Religion, they say, may be no less visible in American life, but now it is more likely to divide than to integrate. In other words, religion since the 1960s, to the degree it is important, is more likely to be *individually* important and less likely to be *collectively* important. We concur in this assessment and agree, moreover, that it marks such a change from the previous decades as to warrant the label "third disestablishment." Probably, too, it is in the social revolution of the 1960s and '70s where we find the major cause of this third jolt, this further radical shift in the balance of collective-expressive and individual-expressive views of the church. The mechanism of the social revolution by which this radical shift came about will be called here "personal autonomy," a view of life that gained such strength during this time.

PERSONAL AUTONOMY

Nobody doubts that some sort of "revolution" took place in the 1960s and 1970s. Debate may exist over how much took place, the forms it took, and what it should be called, but few would deny that radical changes occurred during this period,

changes that were adopted by many and resisted by others. (In addition to works already cited in the preface, the following offer important views of the 1960s–'70s revolution: Bibby 1987; Cox 1965; Fitzgerald 1986; McLoughlin 1978; Neuhaus 1984.) We suggest that these changes, taken together, can be understood as a significant increase in "personal autonomy," meaning both an enlarged arena of voluntary choice and an enhanced freedom from structural restraint. Many ways of doing and thinking were changed, and the changes were in the direction of greater individual autonomy.[2]

Two areas of change—quite distinct and unrelated but both having considerable impact on people's view of the church and thus on further disestablishment—are found in 1) profoundly contradictory moral codes (especially in the family and sexual sphere) emerging from the revolution, and 2) a significant decrease in community ties. In anticipation of the analysis lying ahead, we wish here simply to identify the linkages between these two areas of change and persons' views of the church.

THE NEW MORALITY

Perhaps of all aspects of the countercultural revolution that began in the 1960s, the most visible (and visibly lasting) is the emergence of an alternative moral outlook on many personal matters (Morris 1984; D'Antonio and Aldous 1983; Hunt 1974), with such diverse dimensions as women's rights, sexual norms, family authority, abortion, and single parenthood. The moral arena referred to as "the family and sexual sphere" cannot adequately be thought of as a single thing, of course. Despite this fact, however, a common theme runs through all of these dimensions (and many more on any moral agenda), and that is the notion of expanded individual *choice*. Decisions that were once the prerogative of males, or of parents, or of government, are now seen as matters of *personal, individual right*—of women to have equal access to the work force, for example, or of adult children to cohabit whether married or not.

This wholesale introduction of a new morality must be seen for what it was and is—an *alternative* definition of what is right and proper in many of life's most sensitive aspects. Behavior that was once widely regarded as deviant (even if relatively common, like divorce) was now being promulgated as a preferred, or at least legitimate, option (Yankelovich 1981). Divorce, for example, not only became more common but oftentimes no longer led to apologies by the divorcing parties; instead it was justified on mental health grounds. The rapid spread of so-called no fault divorce laws reflected exactly this remarkable increase in personal choice.

Such changes carried enormous implications for churches. Why? At the height of religion's popularity in the 1950s, little or no dissent was heard in the realm of family and sexual morality. Churches espoused the prevailing view of the intact nuclear family, and, more important, they were *seen* as upholders of this view. When the 1960s brought forth an alternative morality, therefore, churches—even though many of their leaders took forthright stands in favor of such issues as female ordination, homosexual rights, or abortion—were still regarded as bastions of the traditional values. How people felt about this new morality of radical individualism influenced their views of the church.

This radical individualism extended to religion in the form of what Roof and McKinney call the "new voluntarism." This includes not just the free choice of *how* to be religious but also the free choice of *whether* to be religious. (In Canada this free choice is documented by Bibby [1987] and in Belgium by Dobbelaere and Voyé [1990].) Among the rights being claimed by children against parents or spouse against spouse, in other words, is the right to be religious in one's own way, including the right to join a bizarre cult, meditate privately, or be altogether nonreligious.[3] There is every reason to expect a connection, therefore, between commitment to individual choice applied to religion and commitment to individual choice applied to the various dimensions of the family/sexual sphere. Rejection of the traditional code and adoption of the alternative code has as its religious parallel a shift in the view of the church from collective-expressive to individual-expressive.

LOCAL TIES

There is a second way in which the increased personal autonomy arising out of the 1960s can be said to have jolted churches and thus contributed to a further step in the direction of disestablishment. Reference is to the greater fluidity of the population, perhaps up and down a status ladder, but certainly fluidity in geographic and social territory. The anonymity of social life has been frequently noted since World War II, as has the superficial quality of most interpersonal relationships (Bernikow 1987; Packard 1972; Perin 1988; Wireman 1984). People change residences as well as partners with great frequency, and any "sense of place" is honored more in nostalgia than in reality.[4] Unlike much of what is meant by "moral outlook" and a correlative sense of the right to be moral or religious in one's own way, however, this fluidity is oftentimes not a matter of individual choice—though it may be felt as "freedom" to choose—but is imposed by social circumstances. That is to say, whereas one's moral outlook may be fundamentally a matter of personality and culture, the degree to which people move, make friends, and maintain attachments to places is significantly a function of social structure—one's occupation, for example, or the age of one's children. . . .

This capacity to form and keep local social ties is, like moral outlook, obviously variable. Moreover, also like moral outlook, its influence extends to churches—in this case, in the form of the differential likelihood that persons will translate local ties into parish friendships. Some people have many such friendships, others none, and most are some place in between. Partly this difference reflects individual choice, but significantly it is "built into" the situations persons cannot change but instead must adjust to. The impact is to make churches less collective-expressive and more individual-expressive.

Like an increase in moral choice, then, anything that leads to a decrease in friendship ties in churches is a jolt in the direction of further disestablishment. As Stark and Glock point out:

> A criterion of the ideal church . . . is that it function as a primary group. In turn, a criterion for the ideal church member is that he be related to his church by bonds of friendship and affection. . . . But it has been recognized that these ideals are frequently, and perhaps typically, not fulfilled either by churches or by church members in actual practice. (1968, 164)

Writing in 1967, Stark and Glock could not have known the full impact of the disestablishment jolt only then becoming manifest. They did note how the religious commitment patterns of the young were weaker than those of older persons, however, and they even conclude their volume speculating on whether that signal and others they detect in their data foretell a "post-Christian era." A new step in the direction of disestablishment was clearly a possibility in their thinking.

THE SHIFTING MEANING OF CHURCH

That possibility has now become an obvious reality, although weakened religious commitment or declining church attendance rates alone are not the criterion. For one thing, not all church attendance rates are down; some remain steady while others actually are increasing. Another reason for withholding judgment on implications for church attendance of the third disestablishment, however, has to do with the nature of the disestablishment jolt that has come out of the 1960s. A competing morality and weakened community ties do not *necessarily* discourage involvement in the church. Increased personal autonomy also permits persons to choose to be *more* involved. We shall see presently that for many people personal autonomy does discourage involvement, but for others it does not. In this sense the case of religion again resembles the case of ethnicity, where the changed role played by middle-class, white ethnic identity inhibits one kind of ethnic identity but may actually facilitate another, "voluntary" kind of ethnic identity. But a change in the meaning of ethnicity is obviously involved. Likewise, we would contend, this new adjustment in the relationship between religion and culture must also be understood as a change in the meaning the church has in people's lives, a change from a collective-expressive view to an individual-expressive view. It is thus only a first question to ask whether increased personal autonomy has led to declining parish involvement.

The necessary second question is whether the *meaning* of parish involvement has also changed. Evidence suggests that it has. For example, in 1924 the Lynds found that Middletown's church members named "habit" as their chief reason for going to church (Lynd and Lynd 1929). It was the choice of 44 percent, while 35 percent

claimed "enjoyment," and another 8 percent cited the benefits for their children. Thirteen percent gave other reasons. In 1978, by contrast, Caplow and his associates report that "habit" was selected by only 15 percent of Middletown's church members, whereas "enjoyment" and "children's benefit" reasons had jumped to rates of 65 percent and 13 percent (Caplow, et al. 1983, 80). Even these latter authors, by referring to the modern reasons as "more positive," appear unwittingly to confirm the greater legitimacy accorded individuals' right to determine what the church will mean to them. Certainly it seems clear that Middletowners today feel more freedom than their predecessors of a half-century ago to make choices regarding their churchgoing. Caplow, et al. report no reduction in people's attachment to their own faith, but "they are reluctant to impose it on others or even to assert that it ought to be imposed" (1983, 98).

This shift from collective-expressive to individual-expressive meaning of the church is also suggested by evidence from an entirely different quarter: the decreasing practice of Roman Catholic confession. Once common, confession is now sought "at least monthly" by only 9 percent of the laity and by only 35 percent of clergy. John Dart, the religion writer for the *Los Angeles Times* who reported these findings (*Los Angeles Times*, February 24, 1990), quoted the U.S. bishops' study of confession practices as stating that the "variety of religious philosophies in America had eroded Catholic belief in certain church practices." Catholics, the study concluded, "may withhold assent and commitment to some individual church teaching without . . . feeling that their relationship with the church is affected in any way" (D'Antonio, et al. 1989, confirms this interpretation).[5]

Surely here is another example of the shift in the church's meaning in the individual-expressive direction. That shift, we will be arguing, is great enough to be called the third disestablishment. . . .

NOTES

1. This chapter is a revised version of a presidential address to the Society for the Scientific Study of Religion (Hammond, 1988). In that address I advanced a thesis regarding the changing role of the

church in America since the 1960s. At the time I had hope that the Lilly Endowment would fund the research necessary to test the thesis. It did, and this book is the result. A comparison of the address with this chapter will reveal where modifications in the thesis have occurred.

2. Andrew Greeley (1990, 24–25) introduces the concept of "loyalty" to explain the dogged disposition of some Catholics to remain faithful in the face of acknowledged disagreements with church policies and practices. Insofar as loyalty arises "because it is their birthright," loyalty is the antithesis of what we are calling personal autonomy. But insofar as loyalty leads to making "a choice to stay . . . even in the face of opposition," it is an expression of personal autonomy. Greeley, of course, is trying to understand persistence in religious observance, while we are focused on the changing meaning of that observance.

3. Hammond (1986) shows the major increase—from 6 percent of Protestants born before World War II to 34 percent born after World War II—in the rate at which persons defected altogether from parental religion. This increase is found in all denominations for which sufficient data exist, and the pattern is found too among Catholics and Jews.

4. See, e.g., Bellah, et al. (1985, 204–06; 251, 283) for a discussion of the "yearning for small town ideals."

5. Patrick McNamara's recent (1991) study over time of successive cohorts of Catholic parochial school students uses to good advantage the framework of collective- to individual-expressive meaning to organize and understand the changes he observes.

REFERENCES

Bellah, Robert. 1964. *Habits of the Heart.* Berkeley and Los Angeles: University of California Press.

Bernikow, Louise. 1987. *Alone in America.* London: Faber and Faber.

Bibby, Reginald. 1987. *Fragmented Gods.* Toronto: Irwin Publishing.

Caplow, Theodore, et al. 1983. *All Faithful People.* Minneapolis: University of Minnesota Press.

Cox, Harvey. 1965. *The Secular City.* New York: Macmillan.

D'Antonio, W. V., and J. Aldous, eds. 1983. *Families and Religions: Conflict and Change in Modern Society.* Beverly Hills: Sage Publications.

D'Antonio, W. V., et al. 1989. *American Catholic Laity.* Kansas City, MO: Sheed and Ward.

Dobbelaere, Karel, and Liliane Voye. 1990. "From Pillar to Postmodernity: The Changing Situation of Religion in Belgium." *Sociological Analysis* 51, suppl.: S1–S13.

Durkheim, Emile. 1961. *The Elementary Forms of Religious Life.* Trans. J. W. Swain. New York: Collier.

Ernst, Eldon G. 1987. *Without Help or Hindrance,* 2nd ed. Lanham, MD: University Press of America.

Finke, Roger. 1990. "Religious Deregulation: Origins and Consequences," *Journal of Church and State* 32 (Summer): 609–26.

Fitzgerald, Frances. 1986. *Cities on a Hill* New York: Simon and Schuster.

Greeley, Andrew M. 1990. *The Catholic Myth.* New York: Scribner's.

Hammond, Phillip E. 1986. "The Extravasation of the Sacred and the Crisis in Liberal Protestantism" in Robert Michaelsen and W. Clark Roof, eds. *Liberal Protestantism: Realities and Prospects.* New York: Pilgrim Press.

———. 1988. "Religion and the Persistence of Identity." *Journal for the Scientific Study of Religion* 27 (Mar.): 1–11.

Handy, Robert T. 1984. *A Christian America.* 2nd ed. New York: Oxford University Press.

Herberg, Will. 1955. *Protestant, Catholic, Jew.* Garden City, NY: Doubleday.

Hunt, Morton. 1974. *Sexual Behavior in the 1970s.* Chicago: Playboy Press.

Lynd, Robert S., and Helen M. Lynd. 1929. *Middletown.* New York: Harcourt, Brace.

McLoughlin, William G. 1978. *Revivals, Awakenings, and Reform.* Chicago: University of Chicago Press.

McNamara, Patrick. 1991. *Conscience First, Tradition Second: A Study of Young American Catholics.* Albany: State University of New York Press.

Mathews, Donald G. 1969. "The Second Great Awakening as an Organizing Process, 1780–1830." *American Quarterly* 21: 23–43.

Mead, Sidney E. 1977. *The Old Religion in the Brave New World.* Berkeley and Los Angeles:

Mol, Hans, ed. 1978. *Identity and Religion.* Beverly Hills: Sage Publications.

Morris, C. R. 1984. *A Time of Passion.* Harmondsworth: Penguin.

Neuhaus, Richard John. 1984. *The Naked Public Square.* Grand Rapids: Eerdmans.

Packard, Vance. 1972. *A Nation of Strangers.* New York: McKay.

Perin, Constance. 1988. *Belonging in America.* Madison: University of Wisconsin Press.

Roof, W. Clark, and W. McKinney 1987. *American Mainline Religion.* New Brunswick, NJ: Rutgers University Press.

Troeltsch, Ernst. [1911] 1960. *The Social Teaching of the Christian Churches.* Trans. Olive Wyon. New York: Harper.

Wireman, P. 1984. *Urban Neighborhoods, Networks, and Families.* Lexington, MA: Lexington Books.

Yankelovich, Daniel. 1981. *New Rules.* New York: Random House.

49

American Education:
Savage Inequalities

Jonathan Kozol

*In effect, a circular phenomenon evolves: The richer districts . . . have more revenue,
derived from taxing land and homes, to fund their public schools. The reputation
of the schools, in turn, adds to the value of their homes, and this, in turn, expands
the tax base for their public schools. . . . Few of the children [in the poorer districts]
will, as a result, be likely to compete effectively with kids [in the wealthier districts]
for admissions to the better local colleges and universities of New York state.
Even fewer will compete for more exclusive Ivy League admissions. And few
of the graduates or dropouts of those poorer systems, as a consequence, are
likely ever to earn enough to buy a home in [the wealthier districts]. . . .*

Jonathan Kozol's work, *Savage Inequalities*, is a detailed examination of the public schools in several American cities. The theme was the same wherever he looked: Some districts provide the best opportunities; others barely get by. This selection is an excerpt from his description of schools in New York City. Most of us probably have a hunch that public education is characterized by great inequalities; Kozol's description confirms these suspicions.

"In a country where there is no distinction of class," Lord Acton wrote of the United States 130 years ago, "a child is not born to the station of its parents, but with an indefinite claim to all the prizes that can be won by thought and labor. It is in conformity with the theory of equality . . . to give as near as possible to every youth an equal state in life." Americans, he said, "are unwilling that any should be deprived in childhood of the means of competition."[1]

It is hard to read these words today without a sense of irony and sadness. Denial of "the means of competition" is perhaps the single most consistent outcome of the education offered to poor children in the schools of our large cities; and nowhere is this pattern of denial more explicit or more absolute than in the public schools of New York City.

Average expenditures per pupil in the city of New York in 1987 were some $5,500. In the highest spending suburbs of New York (Great Neck or Manhasset, for example, on Long Island) funding levels rose above $11,000, with the highest districts in the state at $15,000. "Why," asks the city's Board of Education, "should our students receive less" than do "similar students" who live elsewhere? "The inequity is clear. . . ."[2,3]

New York City's public schools are subdivided into 32 school districts. District 10 encompasses a large part of the Bronx but is, effectively, two separate districts. One of these districts, Riverdale, is in the northwest section of the Bronx. Home to many of the city's most sophisticated and well-educated families, its elementary schools have relatively few low-income students. The other section, to the south and east, is poor and heavily nonwhite.

The contrast between public schools in each of these two neighborhoods is obvious to any visitor. At Public School 24 in Riverdale, the principal speaks enthusiastically of his teaching staff. At Public School 79, serving poorer children to the south, the principal says that he is forced to take the "tenth-best" teachers. "I thank God they're still breathing," he remarks of those from whom he must select his teachers. . . .

Sometimes a school principal, whatever his background or his politics, looks into the faces of the children in his school and offers a disarming statement that cuts through official ambiguity. "These are the kids most in need," says Edward Flanery, the principal of one of the low-income schools, "and they get the worst teachers." For children of diverse needs in his overcrowded rooms, he says, "you need an outstanding teacher. And what do you get? You get the worst."

• • •

In order to find Public School 261 in District 10, a visitor is told to look for a mortician's office. The funeral home, which faces Jerome Avenue in the North Bronx, is easy to identify by its green awning. The school is next door, in a former roller-skating rink. No sign identifies the building as a school. A metal awning frame without an awning supports a flagpole, but there is no flag.

In the street in front of the school is an elevated public transit line. Heavy traffic fills the street. The existence of the school is virtually concealed within this crowded city block.

In a vestibule between the outer and inner glass doors of the school is a sign with these words: "All children are capable of learning."

Beyond the inner doors, a guard is seated. The lobby is long and narrow. The ceiling is low. There are no windows. All the teachers I see at first are middle-aged white women. The principal, who is also a white woman, tells me that the school's "capacity" is 900, but that there are 1,300 children here. The size of classes for fifth and sixth grade children in New York, she says, is "capped" at 32, but she says that class size in the school goes "up to 34." (I later see classes, however, as large as 37.) Classes for younger children, she goes on, are "capped at 25," but a school can go above this limit if it puts an extra adult in the room. Lack of space, she says, prevents the school from operating a pre-kindergarten program.

I ask the principal where her children go to school. They are enrolled in private school, she says.

"Lunch time is a challenge for us," she explains. "Limited space obliges us to do it in three shifts, 450 children at a time."

Textbooks are scarce and children have to share their social studies books. The principal says there is one full-time pupil counselor and another who is here two days a week: A ratio of 930 children to one counselor. The carpets are patched and sometimes taped together to conceal an open space. "I could use some new rugs," she observes.

To make up for the building's lack of windows and the crowded feeling that results, the staff puts plants and fish tanks in the corridors. Some of the plants are flourishing. Two boys, released from class, are in a corridor beside a tank, their noses pressed against the glass. A school of pinkish fish inside the tank are darting back and forth. Farther down the corridor a small Hispanic girl is watering the plants.

Two first-grade classes share a single room without a window, divided only by a blackboard. Four kindergartens and a sixth-grade class of Spanish-speaking children have been packed into a single room in which, again, there is no window. A second-grade bilingual class of 37 children has its own room, but again there is no window.

By eleven o'clock, the lunchroom is already packed with appetite and life. The kids line up to get their meals, then eat them in ten minutes. After that, with no place they can go to play, they sit and wait until it's time to line up and go back to class.

On the second floor, I visit four classes taking place within another undivided space. The room has a low ceiling. File cabinets and movable blackboards give a small degree of isolation to each class. Again, there are no windows.

The library is a tiny, windowless, and claustrophobic room. I count approximately 700 books. Seeing no reference books, I ask a teacher if encyclopedias and other reference books are kept in classrooms.

"We don't have encyclopedias in classrooms," she replies. "That is for the suburbs."

The school, I am told, has 26 computers for its 1,300 children. There is one small gym, and children get one period, and sometimes two, each week. Recess, however, is not possible because there is no playground. "Head Start," the principal says, "scarcely exists in District 10. We have no space."

The school, I am told, is 90 percent black and Hispanic; the other 10 percent are Asian, white, or Middle Eastern.

In a sixth-grade social studies class, the walls are bare of words or decorations. There seems to be no ventilation system, or, if one exists, it isn't working.

The class discusses the Nile River and the Fertile Crescent.

The teacher, in a droning voice: "How is it useful that these civilizations developed close to rivers?"

A child, in a good loud voice: "What kind of question is that?"

In my notes, I find these words: "An uncomfortable feeling—being in a building with no windows. There are metal ducts across the room. Do they give air? I feel asphyxiated...."

On the top floor of the school, a sixth grade of 30 children shares a room with 29 bilingual second graders. Because of the high class size, there is an assistant with each teacher. This means that 59 children and four grown-ups—63 in all—must share a room that, in a suburban school, would hold no more than 20 children and one teacher. There are, at least, some outside windows in this room—it is the only room with windows in the school—and the room has a high ceiling. It is a relief to see some daylight.

I return to see the kindergarten classes on the ground floor and feel stifled once again by lack of air and the low ceiling. Nearly 120 children and adults are doing what they can to make the best of things: 80 children in four kindergarten classes,

30 children in the sixth-grade class, and about eight grown-ups who are aides and teachers. The kindergarten children, sitting on the worn rug, which is patched with tape, look up at me and turn their heads to follow me as I walk past them.

As I leave the school, a sixth-grade teacher stops to talk. I ask her, "Is there air conditioning in warmer weather?"

Teachers, while inside the building, are reluctant to give answers to this kind of question. Outside, on the sidewalk, she is less constrained: "I had an awful room last year. In the winter, it was 56 degrees. In the summer, it was up to 90. It was sweltering."

I ask her, "Do the children ever comment on the building?"

"They don't say," she answers, "but they know."

I ask her if they see it as a racial message.

"All these children see TV," she says. "They know what suburban schools are like. Then they look around them at their school. This was a roller-rink, you know.... They don't comment on it, but you see it in their eyes. They understand."

On the following morning, I visit P.S. 79, another elementary school in the same district. "We work under difficult circumstances," says the principal, James Carter, who is black. "The school was built to hold one thousand students. We have 1,550. We are badly overcrowded. We need smaller classes but, to do this, we would need more space. I can't add five teachers. I would have no place to put them."

Some experts, I observe, believe that class size isn't a real issue. He dismisses this abruptly. "It doesn't take a genius to discover that you learn more in a smaller class. I have to bus some 60 kindergarten children elsewhere, since I have no space for them. When they return next year, where do I put them?"

"I can't set up a computer lab. I have no room. I had to put a class into the library. I have no librarian. There are two gymnasiums upstairs, but they cannot be used for sports. We hold more classes there. It's unfair to measure us against the suburbs. They have 17 to 20 children in a class. Average class size in this school is 30."

"The school is 29 percent black, 70 percent Hispanic. Few of these kids get Head Start. There is no space in the district. Of 200 kindergarten children, 50 maybe get some kind of preschool."

I ask him how much difference preschool makes.

"Those who get it do appreciably better. I can't overestimate its impact but, as I have said, we have no space."

The school tracks children by ability, he says. "There are five to seven levels in each grade. The highest level is equivalent to 'gifted,' but it's not a full-scale gifted program. We don't have the funds. We have no science room. The science teachers carry their equipment with them."

We sit and talk in the nurse's room. The window is broken. There are two holes in the ceiling. About a quarter of the ceiling has been patched and covered with a plastic garbage bag.

"Ideal class size for these kids would be 15 to 20. Will these children ever get what white kids in the suburbs take for granted? I don't think so. If you ask me why, I'd have to speak of race and social class. I don't think the powers that be in New York City understand, or want to understand, that if they do not give these children a sufficient education to lead healthy and productive lives, we will be their victims later on. We'll pay the price someday—in violence, in economic costs. I despair of making this appeal in any terms but these. You cannot issue an appeal to conscience in New York today. The fair-play argument won't be accepted. So you speak of violence and hope that it will scare the city into action."

While we talk, three children who look six or seven years old come to the door and ask to see the nurse, who isn't in the school today. One of the children, a Puerto Rican girl, looks haggard. "I have a pain in my tooth," she says. The principal says, "The nurse is out. Why don't you call your mother?" The child says, "My mother doesn't have a phone." The principal sighs. "Then go back to your class." When she leaves, the principal is angry. "It's amazing to me that these children ever make it with the obstacles they face. Many *do* care and *they do* try, but there's a feeling of despair. The parents of these children want the same things for their children that the parents in the suburbs want. Drugs are not the cause of this. They are the symptom. Nonetheless, they're used by people in the suburbs and rich people in

Manhattan as another reason to keep children of poor people at a distance."

I ask him, "Will white children and black children ever go to school together in New York?"

"I don't see it," he replies. "I just don't think it's going to happen. It's a dream. I simply do not see white folks in Riverdale agreeing to cross-bus with kids like these. A few, maybe. Very few. I don't think I'll live to see it happen."

I ask him whether race is the decisive factor. Many experts, I observe, believe that wealth is more important in determining these inequalities.

"This," he says—and sweeps his hand around him at the room, the garbage bag, the ceiling— "would not happen to white children. . . ."

• • •

Two months later, on a day in May, I visit an elementary school in Riverdale. The dogwoods and magnolias on the lawn in front of P.S. 24 are in full blossom on the day I visit. There is a well-tended park across the street, another larger park three blocks away. To the left of the school is a playground for small children, with an innovative jungle gym, a slide, and several climbing toys. Behind the school are two playing fields for older kids. The grass around the school is neatly trimmed.

The neighborhood around the school, by no means the richest part of Riverdale, is nonetheless expensive and quite beautiful. Residences in the area—some of which are large, free-standing houses, others condominiums in solid red-brick buildings—sell for prices in the region of $400,000, but some of the larger Tudor houses on the winding and tree-shaded streets close to the school can cost up to $1 million. The excellence of P.S. 24, according to the principal, adds to the value of these homes. Advertisements in the *New York Times* will frequently inform prospective buyers that a house is "in the neighborhood of P.S. 24."

The school serves 825 children in the kindergarten through sixth grade. This is approximately half the student population crowded into P.S. 79, where 1,550 children fill a space intended for 1,000, and a great deal smaller than the 1,300 children packed into the former skating rink; but the principal of P.S. 24, a capable and energetic man named David Rothstein, still regards it as excessive for an elementary school.

The school is integrated in the strict sense that the middle- and upper-middle-class white children here occupy a building that contains some Asian and Hispanic and black children; but there is little integration in the classrooms because the vast majority of the Hispanic and black children are assigned to "special" classes on the basis of evaluations that have classified them EMR—"educable mentally retarded"—or else, in the worst of cases, TMR—"trainable mentally retarded."

I ask the principal if any of his students qualify for free-lunch programs. "About 130 do," he says. "Perhaps another 35 receive their lunches at reduced price. Most of these kids are in the special classes. They do not come from this neighborhood."

The very few nonwhite children that one sees in mainstream classes tend to be Japanese or of other Asian origins. Riverdale, I learn, has been the residence of choice for many years to members of the diplomatic corps.

The school therefore contains effectively two separate schools: one of about 130 children, most of whom are poor, Hispanic, black, assigned to one of the 12 special classes; the other of some 700 mainstream students, almost all of whom are white or Asian.

There is a third track also—this one for the students who are labeled "talented" or "gifted." This is termed a "pull-out" program because the children who are so identified remain in mainstream classrooms but are taken out for certain periods each week to be provided with intensive and, in my opinion, excellent instruction in some areas of reasoning and logic often known as "higher-order skills" in the contemporary jargon of the public schools. Children identified as "gifted" are admitted to this program in first grade and, in most cases, will remain there for six years. Even here, however, there are two tracks of the gifted. The regular gifted classes are provided with only one semester of this specialized instruction yearly. Those very few children, on the other hand, who are identified as showing the most promise are assigned, beginning in the third grade, to a program that receives a full-year regimen.

In one such class, containing ten intensely verbal and impressive fourth-grade children, nine are white and one is Asian. The "special" class I enter first, by way of contrast, has twelve children of whom only one is white and none is Asian. These racial breakdowns prove to be predictive of the schoolwide pattern.

In a classroom for the gifted on the first floor of the school, I ask a child what the class is doing. "Logic and syllogisms," she replies. The room is fitted with a planetarium. The principal says that all the elementary schools in District 10 were given the same planetariums ten years ago, but that certain schools, because of overcrowding, have been forced to give them up. At P.S. 261, according to my notes, there was a domelike space that had been built to hold a planetarium, but the planetarium had been removed to free up space for the small library collection. P.S. 24, in contrast, has a spacious library that holds almost 8,000 books. The windows are decorated with attractive, brightly colored curtains and look out on flowering trees. The principal says that it's inadequate, but it appears spectacular to me after the cubicle that holds a meager 700 books within the former skating rink.

The district can't afford librarians, the principal says, but P.S. 24, unlike the poorer schools of District 10, can draw on educated parent volunteers who staff the room in shifts three days a week. A parent organization also raises independent funds to buy materials, including books, and will soon be running a fund-raiser to enhance the library's collection.

In a large and sunny first-grade classroom that I enter next, I see 23 children, all of whom are white or Asian. In another first grade, there are 22 white children and two others who are Japanese. There is a computer in each class. Every classroom also has a modern fitted sink.

In a second-grade class of 22 children, there are two black children and three Asian children. Again, there is a sink and a computer. A sixth-grade social studies class has only one black child. The children have an in-class research area that holds some up-to-date resources. A set of encyclopedias (World Book, 1985) is in a rack beside a window. The children are doing a Spanish language lesson when I enter. Foreign languages begin in sixth grade at the school, but Spanish is offered also to the kindergarten children. As in every room at P.S. 24, the window shades are clean and new, the floor is neatly tiled in gray and green, and there is not a single light bulb missing.

Walking next into a special class, I see twelve children. One is white. Eleven are black. There are no Asian children. The room is half the size of mainstream classrooms. "Because of overcrowding," says the principal, "we have had to split these rooms in half." There is no computer and no sink.

I enter another special class. Of seven children, five are black, one is Hispanic, one is white. A little black boy with a large head sits in the far corner and is gazing at the ceiling.

"Placement of these kids," the principal explains, "can usually be traced to neurological damage."

In my notes: "How could so many of these children be brain damaged?"

Next door to the special class is a woodworking shop. "This shop is only for the special classes," says the principal. The children learn to punch in time cards at the door, he says, in order to prepare them for employment.

The fourth-grade gifted class, in which I spend the last part of the day, is humming with excitement. "I start with these children in the first grade," says the teacher. "We pull them out of mainstream classes on the basis of their test results and other factors such as the opinion of their teachers. Out of this group, beginning in third grade, I pull out the ones who show the most potential, and they enter classes such as this one."

The curriculum they follow, she explains, "emphasizes critical thinking, reasoning, and logic." The planetarium, for instance, is employed not simply for the study of the universe as it exists. "Children also are designing their own galaxies," the teacher says.

A little girl sitting around a table with her classmates speaks with perfect poise: "My name is Susan. We are in the fourth-grade gifted program."

I ask them what they're doing, and a child says, "My name is Laurie, and we're doing problem-solving."

A rather tall, good-natured boy who is half-standing at the table tells me that his name is David. "One thing that we do," he says, "is logical thinking. Some problems, we find, have more than one good answer. We need to learn not simply to be logical in our own thinking but to show

respect for someone else's logic even when an answer may be technically incorrect."

When I ask him to explain this, he goes on, "A person who gives an answer that is not 'correct' may nonetheless have done some interesting thinking that we should examine. 'Wrong' answers may be more useful to examine than correct ones."

I ask the children if reasoning and logic are innate or if they're things that you can learn.

"You know some things to start with when you enter school," Susan says. "But we also learn some things that other children don't."

I ask her to explain this.

"We know certain things that other kids don't know because we're *taught* them."

She has braces on her teeth. Her long brown hair falls almost to her waist. Her loose white T-shirt has the word *TRI-LOGIC* on the front. She tells me that Tri-Logic is her father's firm.

Laurie elaborates on the same point: "Some things, you know. Some kinds of logic are inside of you to start with. There are other things that someone needs to teach you."

David expands on what the other two have said: "Everyone can think and speak in logical ways unless they have a mental problem. What this program does is bring us to a higher form of logic."

The class is writing a new "Bill of Rights." The children already know the U.S. Bill of Rights and they explain its first four items to me with precision. What they are examining today, they tell me, is the very *concept* of a "right." Then they will create their own compendium of rights according to their own analysis and definition. Along one wall of the classroom, opposite the planetarium, are seven Apple II computers on which children have developed rather subtle color animations that express the themes—of greed and domination, for example—that they also have described in writing.

"This is an upwardly mobile group," the teacher later says. "They have exposure to whatever New York City has available. Their parents may take them to the theater, to museums. . . ."

In my notes: "Six girls, four boys. Nine white, one Chinese. I am glad they have this class. But what about the others? Aren't there ten black children in the school who could enjoy this also?"

The teacher gives me a newspaper written, edited, and computer-printed by her sixth-grade gifted class. The children, she tells me, are provided with a link to kids in Europe for transmission of news stories.

A science story by one student asks whether scientists have ever falsified their research. "Gregor Mendel," the sixth grader writes, "the Austrian monk who founded the science of genetics, published papers on his work with peas that some experts say were statistically too good to be true. Isaac Newton, who formulated the law of gravitation, relied on unseemly mathematical sleight of hand in his calculations. . . . Galileo Galilei, founder of modern scientific method, wrote about experiments that were so difficult to duplicate that colleagues doubted he had done them."

Another item in the paper, also by a sixth-grade student, is less esoteric: "The Don Cossacks dance company, from Russia, is visiting the United States. The last time it toured America was 1976. . . . The Don Cossacks will be in New York City for two weeks at the Neil Simon Theater. Don't miss it!"

The tone is breezy—and so confident! That phrase—"Don't miss it!"—speaks a volume about life in Riverdale.

"What makes a good school?" asks the principal when we are talking later on. "The building and teachers are part of it, of course. But it isn't just the building and the teachers. Our kids come from good families and the neighborhood is good. In a three-block area, we have a public library, a park, a junior high. . . . Our typical sixth grader reads at eighth-grade level." In a quieter voice he says, "I see how hard my colleagues work in schools like P.S. 79. You have children in those neighborhoods who live in virtual hell. They enter school five years behind. What do they get?" Then, as he spreads his hands out on his desk, he says: "I have to ask myself why there should be an elementary school in District 10 with fifteen hundred children. Why should there be an elementary school within a skating rink? Why should the Board of Ed allow this? This is not the way that things should be. . . ."

The differences *between* school districts and *within* school districts in the city are, however, almost insignificant compared to those between the city and the world of affluence around it—in Westchester County, for example, and in largely prosperous Long Island.

Even in the suburbs, nonetheless, it has been noted that a differential system still exists, and it may not be surprising to discover that the differences are once again determined by the social class, parental wealth, and sometimes race, of the schoolchildren. A study, a few years ago, of 20 of the wealthiest and poorest districts of Long Island, for example, matched by location and size of enrollment, found that the differences in per-pupil spending were not only large but had approximately doubled in a five-year period. Schools, in Great Neck, in 1987, spent $11,265 for each pupil. In affluent Jericho and Manhasset, the figures were, respectively, $11,325 and $11,370. In Oyster Bay, the figure was $9,980. Compare this to Levittown, also on Long Island but a town of mostly working-class white families, where per-pupil spending dropped to $6,900. Then compare these numbers to the spending level in the town of Roosevelt, the poorest district in the county, where the schools are 99 percent nonwhite and where the figure dropped to $6,340. Finally, consider New York City, where, in the same year, $5,590 was invested in each pupil—less than half of what was spent in Great Neck. The pattern is almost identical to that which we have seen outside Chicago.

Again, look at Westchester County, where, in the same year, the same range of discrepancies was found. Affluent Bronxville, an attractive suburb just north of the Bronx, spent $10,000 for each pupil. Chappaqua's yearly spending figure rose above $9,000. Studying the chart again, we locate Yonkers—a blue-collar town that is predominantly white but where over half the student population is nonwhite—and we find the figure drops to $7,400. This is not the lowest figure, though. The lowest-spending schools within Westchester, spending a full thousand dollars less than Yonkers, serve the suburb of Mount Vernon, where three quarters of the children in the public schools are black.[4]

"If you're looking for a home," a realtor notes, "you can look at the charts for school expenditures and use them to determine if your neighbors will be white and wealthy or, conversely, black or white but poor. . . ."

In effect, a circular phenomenon evolves: The richer districts—those in which the property lots and houses are more highly valued—have more revenue, derived from taxing land and homes, to fund their public schools. The reputation of the schools, in turn, adds to the value of their homes, and this, in turn, expands the tax base for their public schools. The fact that they can levy lower taxes than the poorer districts but exact more money, raises values even more; and this, again, means further funds for smaller classes and for higher teacher salaries within their public schools. Few of the children in the schools of Roosevelt or Mount Vernon will, as a result, be likely to compete effectively with kids in Great Neck and Manhasset for admissions to the better local colleges and universities of New York state. Even fewer will compete for more exclusive Ivy League admissions. And few of the graduates or dropouts of those poorer systems, as a consequence, are likely ever to earn enough to buy a home in Great Neck or Manhasset. . . .

The point is often made that, even with a genuine equality of schooling for poor children, other forces still would militate against their school performance. Cultural and economic factors and the flight of middle-income blacks from inner cities still would have their consequences in the heightened concentration of the poorest children in the poorest neighborhoods. Teen-age pregnancy, drug use, and other problems still would render many families in these neighborhoods all but dysfunctional. Nothing I have said . . . should leave the misimpression that I do not think these factors are enormously important. A polarization of this issue, whereby some insist on the primacy of school, others on the primacy of family and neighborhood, obscures the fact that both are elemental forces in the lives of children.

The family, however, differs from the school in the significant respect that government is not responsible, or at least not directly, for the inequalities of family background. It *is* responsible for inequalities in public education. The school is the creature of the state; the family is not. To the degree, moreover, that destructive family situations may be bettered by the future acts of government, no one expects that this could happen in the years immediately ahead. Schools, on the other hand, could make dramatic changes almost overnight if fiscal equity were a reality.

If the New York City schools were funded, for example, at the level of the highest-spending suburbs of Long Island, a fourth-grade class of 36 children such as those I visited in District 10 would have had $200,000 *more* invested in their education during 1987.[5] Although a portion of this extra money would have gone into administrative costs, the remainder would have been enough to hire two extraordinary teachers at enticing salaries of $50,000 each, divide the class into *two classes* of some 18 children each, provide them with computers, carpets, air conditioning, new texts and reference books, and learning games—indeed, with everything available today in the most affluent school districts—and also pay the costs of extra counseling to help those children cope with the dilemmas that they face at home. Even the most skeptical detractor of "the worth of spending further money in the public schools" would hesitate, I think, to face a grade-school principal in the South Bronx and try to tell her that this "wouldn't make much difference."

It is obvious that urban schools have other problems in addition to their insufficient funding. Administrative chaos is endemic in some urban systems. (The fact that this in itself is a reflection of our low regard for children who depend on these systems is a separate matter.) Greater funding, if it were intelligently applied, could partially correct these problems—by making possible, for instance, the employment of some very gifted, high-paid fiscal managers who could ensure that money is well used—but it probably is also true that major structural reforms would still be needed. To polarize these points, however, and to argue, as the White House has been claiming for a decade, that administrative changes are a "better" answer to the problem than equality of funding and real efforts at desegregation is dishonest and simplistic. The suburbs have better administrations (sometimes, but not always), and they also have a lot more money in proportion to their children's needs. To speak of the former and evade the latter is a formula that guarantees that nothing will be done *today* for children who have no responsibility for either problem.

To be in favor of "good families" or of "good administration" does not take much courage or originality. It is hard to think of anyone who is opposed to either. To be in favor of redistribution of resources and of racial integration would require a great deal of courage—and a soaring sense of vision—in a president or any other politician. Whether such courage or such vision will someday become transcendent forces in our nation is by no means clear. . . .

• • •

Until 1983, Mississippi was one of the few states with no kindergarten program and without compulsory attendance laws. Governor William Winter tried that year to get the legislature to approve a $60-million plan to upgrade public education. The plan included early childhood education, higher teacher salaries, a better math and science program for the high schools, and compulsory attendance with provisions for enforcement. The state's powerful oil corporations, facing a modest increase in their taxes to support the plan, lobbied vigorously against it. The Mid-Continent Oil and Gas Association began a television advertising campaign to defeat the bill, according to a *Newsweek* story.[6]

"The vested interests are just too powerful," a state legislator said. Those interests, according to *Newsweek*, are "unlikely" to rush to the aid of public schools that serve poor children.

It is unlikely that the parents or the kids in Rye or Riverdale know much about realities like these; and, if they do, they may well tell themselves that Mississippi is a distant place and that they have work enough to do to face inequities in New York City. But, in reality, the plight of children in the South Bronx of New York is almost as far from them as that of children in the farthest reaches of the South.

All of these children say the Pledge of Allegiance every morning. Whether in the New York suburbs, Mississippi, or the South Bronx, they salute the same flag. They place their hands across their hearts and join their voices in a tribute to "one nation indivisible" which promises liberty and justice to all people. What is the danger that the people in a town like Rye would face if they resolved to make this statement true? How much would it really harm their children to compete in a fair race?

NOTES

1. Lord Acton cited: George Alan Hickrod, "Reply to the 'Forbs' Article," *Journal of School Finance*, vol. 12 (1987).
2. Per-pupil Spending, New York City and Suburbs: Office for Policy Analysis and Program Accountability, New York State Board of Education, "Statistical Profiles of School Districts," (Albany: 1987).
3. Question Asked by New York City Board of Education and Response of Community Service Society: Community Service Society of New York, "Promoting Poverty: The Shift of Resources Away from Low-Income New York City School Districts," (New York: 1987).
4. Per-pupil Spending in Long Island and Westchester County: New York State Department of Education, "Statistical Profiles of School Districts," cited above. Also see *Newsday*, May 18, 1986. According to Sandra Feldman, President of the United Federation of Teachers in New York City, "the average per-pupil expenditure is nearly $2,500 higher" in the suburbs "right outside the city." (*The School Administrator*, March 1991.) According to the *New York Times* (May 4, 1991), New York City now spends $7,000 for each pupil. The wealthiest suburbs spend approximately $15,000.
5. $200,000 More Each Year: In the school year ending in June 1987, per-pupil funding was $5,585 in New York City, about $11,300 in Jericho and Manhasset. For 36 children, the difference was over $200,000.
6. Mississippi Data: *Time*, November 14, 1988; *Newsweek*, December 13, 1982; *Governing Magazine*, January 1990.

50

The Hidden Curriculum in Undergraduate Business Education

Kenneth N. Ehrensal

The various forms of pedagogic action within the business school curriculum can be seen as mechanisms for the inculcation of management habitus within the student population. By the time a student successfully leaves a business school program, he or she is a ready foot soldier for the capitalist enterprise.

Socialization is the process by which society and its institutions shape the individual in order for the individual to accept the social patterns—structure, culture, and institutions. Of course, there is more than socialization that helps assure conformity, but socialization is highly efficient and effective, and if it works, social order is usually assured without too much reliance on social sanctions.

In American society, elementary and high schools, undergraduate and graduate universities are institutions we rely on for proper socialization. Indeed, one of the arguments for a widespread public school system in this country is that it is necessary for teaching the values, attitudes, and practices of democratic citizenship.

Much of the curriculum, however, is hidden. It is not clearly and explicitly stated, and more importantly, people are socialized to accept certain ideas without careful analysis. Often, what really is an option looks to students as a fixed reality.

Specifically, Kenneth Ehrensal is trying to show us that an undergraduate business education offers few choices for the student, but tends to turn out graduates who believe in and support certain ideas and institutions that they never have the chance to critically evaluate in the business college curriculum. It might be all right for the student interested in climbing the corporate ladder, and it certainly is good for many businesses, Ehrensal maintains, but it is not good for educated people in a democratic society. Ehrensal examines both the subject matter and the techniques of teaching in the business school. I believe he is actually asking all students, whatever their major, to become aware of the assumptions made in their own education, and critically evaluate the understandings, attitudes, values, and skills they are too often encouraged to accept.

This chapter is about the education of "white collar" workers. I use this term very loosely to include professionals, technical specialists in and around corporate headquarters, and *managers* — the foot soldiers of corporate power. I find this group particularly interesting because of the way in which they see themselves. In a society where the conventional wisdom states that we do not see ourselves in class terms, these workers, who make up about 15 percent of the labor force, do see themselves as a group separate from and with different interests than blue-collar workers. In many ways, this group's self-image mirrors the traditional Marxist cosmology that the world was divided into the working class (or labor), the managerial class, and the capitalist class. This division of the world is, of course, problematic in that it ignores the fact that managers, like labor, are employees of capital. This leads to the general question that typically interests me. That is, by what processes do white-collar workers come to imagine their interests as linked to the interests of capital, rather than the interests of the broader working-class?

This question is not irrelevant to the study of the capitalist labor process. Clearly, in order to take on their role as organizational agents for capital, a change in their subjective perception of self is required. This chapter will argue that this change in self-perception is a key ingredient to the group of employees' *consent* to the division of labor and the capitalist labor process. . . . That is, consent is first created in people's heads and then reinforced by the playing of the game. Institutions beyond the workplace, such as the media and, as I argue here, schools, function to

> inculcate individuals with the values, beliefs, and codes of behavior that will integrate them into the institutional structures of the larger society. (Herman and Chomsky 1988, 1)

SCHOOLING AND CAPITALISM

What I will argue is that we cannot understand the control of the labor process, and in particular control of white-collar labor processes, without understanding the role of schooling in capitalism. For it is schooling that creates the subjective arena in which consent will take place. . . . It falls

on the public school system to supply capital with the necessary labor to take these positions, and requires the schooling system to ensure that while these white-collar workers have the required technical skills, they also have appropriate attitudes to carry out the tasks that will be asked of them.

Socialization to this role is both subtle and incomplete. It starts early in schooling, with the purposeful skimming of the top 10 percent (or so) of students into what will eventually become the "college track" curriculum in the secondary school. Simultaneously, tracking starts the process of socializing these individuals' perception of a world divided into "us and them." This is further solidified by the secondary school experience, where the isolation of the college-bound is accomplished not only in the academic but also in the extracurricular arena.[1] By the time individuals find themselves in college they have spent a substantial portion of their time isolated from those whom they will later be asked to manage. . . .

In a commentary in the *Journal of Management Education*, Wanda Smith (1994, 238) explicitly posited that it is the role of (undergraduate) management education to "satisfy management's expectation of anticipatory socialization." She explains:

> Business faculty have been given the responsibility of instilling students with the desired technical skills, as well as with anticipatory socialization — exposing them to beliefs and values of organizations of which they aspire to become members. Principally, employers expect business graduates to have developed belief systems and a variety of survival skills . . . prior to joining their organization.

Thus, business professors are imbued with pedagogic authority, and delegated the right *and* responsibility to impose the required ideological training upon their charges so that when graduates join organizations after the completion of their studies, they will accept the system of authority as legitimate.

However, only those who are "designated as fit" may be assigned these roles. This is no trivial point in American business education. Currently there are two non–governmental organizations for the accreditation of business programs and schools—the American Assembly of Collegiate Schools of Business (AACSB) and the Association of Collegiate Business Schools and Programs (ACBSP). While specifics of the criteria for accreditation differ between the two organizations (AACSB accreditation is geared primarily for research-oriented schools, while ACBSP focuses on teaching-oriented programs), each has specific guidelines concerning the credentials of the faculty, the structures of the curriculum, and content of specific courses. . . .

Both the overall curriculum and the content of specific courses are also dictated by the accrediting organizations (Ehrensal 1999). The principal purpose of undergraduate business education is to inculcate in students various forms of habitus that are both adaptive to and desired by the organizations with which they seek to find employment. This habitus serves the organization's interests by making the inculcated individuals "self-controlling" actors within the organization, and by elevating the need for various overt control systems (supervision, technological controls, and bureaucratic controls). The inculcation of this managerial habitus is accomplished through several types of pedagogic action commonly found in business school classrooms.

All undergraduate business students are exposed to the same core of courses during the early stages of their business education (Ehrensal 1999). These courses consist of micro- and macroeconomics, a year of financial accounting, principals of management, principals of marketing, and an introductory course in corporate finance. These courses share the following common features:

- The teaching of these courses is highly textbook dependent, that is, instructors rarely, if ever, use primary sources.
- An examination of the various textbooks in the market for any of these courses reveals that they are highly uniform in content, varying only in such features as the level of writing and the use of color and graphics.
- A significant portion of the textbook is dedicated to introducing the student to new specialized vocabulary.
- Typical mass-market texts come with significant amounts of instructor "resources," including detailed lecture outlines and notes; test banks with both objective and essay questions; plus outlines of

correct answers for the essays; and instructor's case notes, detailing the correct student responses to end-of-the-chapter case studies and problems.

The world portrayed in business textbooks is one of simplified certainty. There are distillations of management practice and knowledge (both folk and expert), which in the world are highly context-bound, contingent, and probabilistic. In contrast, text knowledge appears to be normative, certain, and based on universal precepts. I will return in a moment to the issues of how and what is included (and what is excluded), but first, I will look at the pedagogic authority of the textbook.

Written in third person passive voice, it does not present what the particular author thinks or believes to be true about management, but rather a litany of what the recognized "experts" have found to be "true." Thus, what is included in the text becomes the received knowledge of the sages, and as management professors Stephen Fineman and Yannis Gabriel (1994, 379) noted in their analysis of rhetorical techniques in organizational behavior textbooks, "[a] text's persuasiveness can depend as much on what is excluded as what is included." Strategic exclusions (the null curriculum [Eisner 1985]) can reduce ambiguity and given the authority of the text, banish particular perspectives from the field. Excluded from the textbooks are any perspectives that question the capitalist project, suggest that organizations are or could be dysfunctional, or suggest that any interests beyond those of the stockholders might be seriously taken account of in the decision-making process.

The second form of pedagogic action is the classroom lecture. This in many ways is more complex than the issues raised by textbooks. Here, both the lecturer and the lecture bear their own (somewhat) independent pedagogic authority. The lecturer often brings two forms of authority with her or him. The first is based upon his or her institutional role. As the faculty of record, with the authority to both present material and evaluate student performance (an issue to be discussed later), the faculty assume an identity transcendent of their particular personalities. In this sense, they share pedagogic authority with all other faculty in all other disciplines. Here, however, we are interested in examining their pedagogic authority to inculcate managerial habitus.

In that role, we must examine how business faculty establish pedagogic authority beyond their purely institutional role. It is not uncommon for business faculty to create pedagogic authority by making reference to their connections to the business community. This is done either by reference to the business careers that they had prior to coming to academia or by claims about the business consulting practices that they have. Reference to these is made either when they are talking about their biographies, or as anecdotes in lectures where reference to their experience is meant to illustrate a point being transmitted in the lecture. Thus, in the business school classroom the pedagogic authority of the lecturer is derived through a combination of institutional and personal authority.

The pedagogic authority of the lecture itself is similarly highly complex. In part, the lecture derives authority from its consistency with the textbook. That is, to the degree that it is consistent with the textbook it is deemed acceptable by the student. This is not as problematic as it may seem on its face. All mass-market textbooks in this area come accompanied by extensive supplemental materials for the instructor, including highly detailed lecturer notes that summarize material included in the text as well as "enrichment" materials that reinforce the message in the text, but are not included in it (e.g., blue boxes). Thus, the typical lecture is one that reiterates material from the text, utilizes third party examples—from sources like the lecturer's notes—and often inserts relevant examples from the individual's own experience. To the degree that these are consistent with the messages derived directly from the text, they are seen as having authority.

However, we must recognize that beyond consistency, lectures themselves—consistent or not—bear pedagogic authority. As Bourdieu (1991) pointed out, lectures are a form of the "discourse of authority" and as such are authorized language. They represent the delegation of that authority from higher, yet potentially obscured sources. Thus, the lecturer, in his or her speech act, is not recognized necessarily as speaking for herself or himself, but rather is seen as speaking for the institution itself. Thus, the lecture, like the relationship of the textbook to its author, has the potential to be transcendent of its speaker.

Case Studies

Case study analysis as a form of pedagogic action has its origin in the business school but has, over time, spread to other administrative programs. The case study itself presents the student with a scenario, sometimes based upon reality and sometimes fictional, in which the student is to bring to bear appropriate theoretical and conceptual frameworks for its analysis. In doing so, the student demonstrates that she or he can take the general and universal and apply it correctly to the specific. As Stewart (1991, 121) explained: "The management case study teaches theory by fulfilling two functions: (1) illustration (translating from the abstract to the concrete), and (2) socialization (conveying the paradigm that governs the theory's application)." Stewart (1991, 122) continued:

> The second function of the case study [socialization] is to help bring the neophyte into the community of the discipline. A case study conveys the theoretical paradigm to new members of the theoretical community by telling a story that shows the paradigm in action. Reading a case study, the neophyte sees not only what problems look like, but also what problem-solvers look like. By setting out the problem in such a way as to suggest how to play the role of the problem-solver, the case is in effect socializing the neophyte.

Stewart's statements about case studies in general can also be applied to the case studies that would be included at the ends of chapters of the typical business school textbook. However, these cases vary in one important way from the more general model of case studies in that they always include specific questions that direct the analysis that the (undergraduate) student will do. Thus, in the early stages of socialization, the directive nature of the questions points the student to the specific theory that they need to apply—very little is left to chance.

The case, as part of the textbook, thus carries with it the transcendent voice and therefore the pedagogic authority of the text. In addition, all textbooks come with instructor's resource material, which includes the answers to the questions at the end of the case. Thus, not only does the question direct the student, but also the answers ensure that the lecturer follows the appropriate line of action in her or his discussion of the case.

Within the classroom itself there may be further forms of pedagogic action. One often finds the use of experiential exercises, typically in the form of role-playing and games. In these exercises, students are asked to demonstrate behaviorally their mastery of appropriate management behaviors in the simulated organizational situations in which they are placed. These are often filmed for review, and always critiqued by the instructor and often by fellow classmates. Behavioral errors are highlighted, not only for the individual's learning, but also in order to heighten social learning among all classroom participants.

In addition to behavioral evaluations that occur in experiential exercises, behavioral modeling also takes more subtle forms in business classrooms. Business faculty traditionally come to class wearing "business attire," with haircuts appropriate for the corporate sector, and usually, among male faculty, without facial hair, as would be appropriate in business. Additionally, it is not uncommon for faculty to require students to come to class in "appropriate" business attire on days when the students are scheduled to give in-class presentations.

Films are also heavily used in business school teaching. Often they are commercially produced training films used to reinforce particular points already made in the lecture material. However, faculty in the field of management frequently use popularly released feature films or television shows that can be analyzed in class using the lens of this or that particular theory. The logic of these exercises is that business school theory can be used to analyze anything in life.

There are also a number of forms of pedagogic action in the business school that take place outside the immediate classroom setting. Among these are "outside" speakers from the business community used either on campus or during site visits, where students meet with business "leaders" at their location. In these activities, classroom lessons are validated and extended. Students observe that real live business people actually *act* and *think* in ways consistent with portraits in lectures and texts. Additionally, these activities allow the student to observe particular modeled behavior in the "real world."

Outside speakers and site visits are often orchestrated by student clubs such as Students in Free Enterprise (SIFE), Society for the Advancement of Management (SAM), and the American Marketing Association (AMA). The goals of these clubs are to promote careers in areas under their purview—SIFE for entrepreneurship, SAM for corporate management, and AMA in the areas of marketing and advertising. These clubs also function to bring newer, less experienced students into contact with students more advanced in their program, thus allowing the junior students the opportunity to see what they should be like at the end of their educational process.

Probably the most powerful form of pedagogic action outside of the classroom is the use of internships in the latter part of students' educational experience. During these internships students spend from 120 to 240 hours gaining "practical firsthand experience of business enterprise" by working in a job for which they receive academic credit. Role-playing of the experiential exercise and the other modeling behaviors is transported to the "real" world of the business organization. In this setting the student's adeptness to perform appropriate behavioral responses to particular organizational situations is judged, not by a professor but by a member of the business community. As interns, demonstrating that one has inculcated the appropriate habitus not only leads to a grade, but often to an offer of employment. Thus, internship evaluations are often seen as external validations of the internal pedagogic actions.

The various forms of pedagogic action within the business school curriculum can be seen as mechanisms for the inculcation of management habitus within the student population. By the time a student successfully leaves a business school program, he or she is a ready foot soldier for the capitalist enterprise.

THE HIDDEN CURRICULUM IN THE COLLEGE OF BUSINESS

In the previous section we reviewed the various forms of pedagogic action used in business school classrooms. The purpose of this pedagogic action is to inculcate business school students with certain cultural arbitraries that benefit the organization in the form of managerial habitus. Now we can examine some specific details of the hidden curriculum that socializes business students:

- *Soviet-style centrally planned economies failed; therefore, any economy that is not based upon free market economics will fail.* Mainstream economics and business texts teach about economic systems by contrasting the ideal free market with (evil) Soviet-style centrally planned economies. For example, in one of the best-selling introduction to business textbooks, a photograph from China accompanies the discussion of planned economies, which has the following caption:

  > *"Volunteers" in a planned economy.* These students are among the 100,000 recruited by the Chinese government to spruce up the city of Beijing for the 11th Asian games. Though called "volunteers," the students probably had little choice, and the banners and overseers give the sense that the government is watching (Pride, Hughes, and Kapoor 1993, 22).

  The text gloss over the fact that most economies are really mixed. They never offer a serious discussion of northern European welfare-based socialist economies, nor of successful socialist economic enterprises such as the kibbutz.

- *Decision making in organizations is the outcome of the application of rational (quantitative) techniques.* A substantial portion of the business school curriculum focuses upon the mastery (memorization) of quantitative analysis tools in finance, statistics, economics, and accounting. Throughout the students' training, professors or texts supply all the necessary information so that the student may plug in numbers to get the "right" answer. However, simplifying assumptions, issues of imperfect information, or the epistemological/metaphysical issues of these techniques are never discussed. Thus, students come to believe that the application of these techniques in practice is inherently objective and value-free. Articles from critical journals such as *Accounting, Organizations and Society* are not discussed.

- *Decisions made at the top of the organization use rational and objective procedures.* The prescribed capstone course in the business curriculum is "Strategy and Business Policy." Each of the available texts for this course starts by describing a process known as "comprehensive strategic planning," which has its theoretical roots in decision science. Researchers have shown that few if any firms actually practice comprehensive strategic

planning, and also that it is a less than effective means of doing strategy. Furthermore, none of the mainstream texts discuss the issues of power and politics that exist during strategy-making, even though the research literature stresses their importance. Why is it taught, then? I contend that it is for the "Wizard of Oz" effect. It is not the overt curriculum that is important but the socialization of lower-status individuals in the organization who will be asked to implement organizational strategy. They will be more effective foot solders if they believe that corporate strategy is rational, and "pay no attention to the man behind the curtain."

- *Unions are illegitimate.* The discussion of labor relations in management or human resource management texts starts with discussion of labor history. After a brief discussion of why workers form unions, the texts devote the rest of the time to discussing "union avoidance" strategies. The messages are subtle, but by the end of their training the typical business student will be avidly antiunion, seeing unions as nothing more than corrupt troublemakers, full of lazy and greedy workers.

- *How to commit murder.* In his essay "Eichmann in the Organization," Jerry Harvey (1988) examined the implications of Hannah Arendt's *Eichmann in Jerusalem: A Report on the Banality of Evil* for understanding the dynamics of behavior in organizations. He discussed the idea that organizations progressively ask their members to commit "little murders" on the way to an all-out holocaust. I contend that the pedagogy of the business school allows its students to practice these little murders in simulated situations. Throughout schooling, the students are asked to discipline unruly subordinates through the analyses of case studies, role-playing, and experiential exercises. These exercises are structured to put the students in the role of the manager and ask them to exercise their organizational authority. They quickly inculcate a number of beliefs. Probably most important is that in a dispute between a manager and a worker, the worker is always wrong, and the organization is always right. Cases, role-playing, and "experiential exercises" reinforce students' right to carry out banal acts of evil, and "internships" hold their hands and prepare them for the time that they are asked to do so in the "real world."

- *Managers and professionals are motivated by intrinsic factors in a job (money is not a motivator).* White-collar workers have *careers*, not jobs; therefore, "investing" in their current job will have long-term benefits. Most discussions of motivation in the undergraduate curriculum draw on the models of Herzberg and McClelland, who associated motivation with the fulfillment of higher-order needs and the beneficial traits of individuals who score high in a need for achievement. Particularly in the works of McClelland, being "not motivated" becomes equated with being lazy. Thus, those who do a job for the sheer pleasure of seeing it done well become idealized as the norm; deviations from this norm are stigmatized.

Undergraduate students are urged to invest in their careers. A key feature of most business school curricula is the internship "opportunity." Here the student is assigned to a company in which he or she works at least twenty hours a week under the supervision of both a manager and a faculty member. The student gains "real-world experience" and receives college credit. Most internships are unpaid or low paying and the students pay tuition for the credits they receive. But it "looks good on the resume."

DISCUSSION

Johnson and Gill (1993, 34) argued that for control systems to be effective they must be expressed through the actions and attitudes of individual managers and employees. They must operate as *self-controls*, which is defined as the controls people exert over their own behavior. In order for this to happen the norms embodied in administrative or social controls must be "either directly or indirectly . . . internalized by the members of the enterprise and operate as personal controls over attitudes and behaviour."

A substantial part of the "management" portion of a business student's training (particularly in the area of organizational behavior) has as its goal the inculcation of a self-view and worldview that benefit the organization. As noted earlier, the essential process of learning to see oneself as different from other elements of the working-class begins in the public schools. The social construction of the blue-collar; "other" becomes fully formed at the business school. Students are taught that the difference between them and blue-collar workers (blue-collar work is portrayed as unskilled, assembly-line jobs) is that white-collar work is inherently satisfying because the work itself is interesting and rewarding. It is essential to the inculcation of self-control that

white-collar workers are socialized to identify with their job independent of the financial rewards. They are taught, for instance, that because it will be good for their career, they should always be willing to work more hours than they are actually paid for.

The foregoing analysis illustrated some of the cultural arbitraries that the pedagogic action of management "education" instills. I believe that this analysis makes a strong argument for understanding management education as a form of symbolic violence. If education and in particular management education is a form of symbolic violence, then we can only conclude that consent to the labor process under monopoly capitalism is, in fact, established in advance of "playing the game."

Where does this analysis lead? This is a vexing question for those of us who depend upon appointments in business schools to pay the mortgage. After laying bare the fact that we are the agents in which pedagogic authority has been vested, what can we, as professors and scholars, do to emancipate rather than enslave our students?

Hugh Willmott (1994) suggested transforming the paradigm of management education to one based upon critical action learning. While applauding his approach, I am not optimistic that business schools will, or even could, move in that direction. My analysis indicates that the legitimacy of management education is firmly rooted in serving the interests, as my colleagues often put it, of the business community. In the United States, at least, the common discourse is that business schools have two customers — the students, and the firms that will eventually employ them. To many of my colleagues the second of these is the more important of the two. This being the case, a pedagogy that demystifies the moral and political framework of management practice would lead to a rapid withdrawal of the support that university-based management education currently receives.

As with many other critical pedagogies, the perspective that I offer here will remain marginal to the mainstream of "real" business scholarship. As individuals, we can, of course, act. But doing so will likely be a solitary walk in the wilderness. We can teach our students to "resist well."[2] Teach them of the dark forces at work. So even if they will not be able to avoid playing the game, they will at least know which rules are truly operative. Similarly, we can distinguish between being a professor of management and being a social scientist studying management behavior.[3] This approach will probably not make us many friends among our business school colleagues, but perhaps social isolation is a small price to pay for maintaining integrity.

NOTES

1. For the management ramifications of this dilemma, see Edwards (1979).
2. I take this phrase from my colleague Mike Elmes who talks often of "teaching our students to resist well."
3. I acknowledge my colleague, Christa Walck, for this idea.

REFERENCES

Bourdieu, P. 1991. Authorized Language: The Social Conditions for the Effectiveness of Ritual Discourse. In *Language and Symbolic Power*, edited by J. B. Thompson. Cambridge, Mass.: Harvard University Press.

Edwards, R. 1979. *Contested Terrain: The Transformation of the Workplace in the Twentieth Century.* New York: Basic Books.

Ehrensal, K. 1999. Establishing Pedagogic Authority: Accreditation and Staffing of (US) University Business Schools. In *Pierre Bourdieu: Language, Culture, and Education*, edited by M. Grenfell and M. Kelly. 235–45. Bern and New York: Peter Lang.

Eisner, E. W. 1985. *The Educational Imagination: On the Design and Evaluation of School Programs.* New York: Macmillan Publishing.

Fineman, S., and Y. Gabriel. 1994. Paradigms of Organizations: An Exploration of Textbook Rhetorics. *Organization* 1:375–99.

Harvey, J. B. 1988. *The Abilene Paradox and Other Meditations on Management.* Lexington, Mass.: Lexington Books.

Herman, E. S., and N. Chomsky. 1988. *Manufacturing Consent: The Political Economy of the Mass Media.* New York: Pantheon Books.

Johnson, P., and J. Gill. 1993. *Management Control and Organizational Behaviour.* London: Paul Chapman.

Pride, W. M., R. J. Hughes, and J. R. Kapoor. 1993. *Business.* 4th ed. Boston: Houghton Mifflin.

Smith, W. J. 1994. Comment on Of Dinosaurs and Sacred Cows: The Grading of Classroom Participation. *Journal of Management Education* 18:237–240.

Stewart, A. H. 1991. The Role of Narrative Structure in the Transfer of Ideas: The Case Study and Management Theory. In *Textual Dynamics of the Professions: Historical and Contemporary Studies of Writing in Professional Communities*, edited by C. Bazerman and J. Paradis. Madison: University of Wisconsin Press.

Willmott, H. 1994. Management Education: Provocations to a Debate. *Management Learning* 25:105–36.

Part X

SOCIAL CHANGE

The sociological view is to understand the individual in the context of society. We are located in structure, learn culture, are socialized, and are subject to institutions that direct our lives.

However, human beings also act back on society, and in their actions, they sometimes change society. Society takes on a dynamic character, always changing, less static and predictable, less of a solid social order. Change sits alongside structure, culture, and social institutions as inevitable social patterns.

What exactly causes society to change? Is it the individual, is it collections of people we sometimes call social movements, is it technology, is it huge social trends that are almost impossible to stop? It is all of these—and more—and it is as complex as it is inevitable. In Part X we will examine an assortment of views. All of them have one common quality: social conflict. No matter the cause of change, there is always conflict between people who welcome change and those who do not.

Karl Marx, more than any social thinker, highlights the role of social conflict in social change. It is conflict itself that is the driving force for change, and it is conflict between workers and capitalists—proletariat and bourgeoisie—that creates change in the modern world. The first selection is from a political tract, *The Communist Manifesto*, that well represents his view of social change.

Michel Crozier looks at what we often call intentional change, and warns that the unintentional consequences that we do not foresee are often what create much of the change we face.

Two selections introduce the role of social movements. Lane Crothers introduces the role of social movements in the United States (specifically the militia movement), and Bernard Lewis discusses the role of religious social movements in the Middle East. Both selections focus on conflict between people who have different visions of society, some looking back, some looking to the future. Both examine the role of violence in social change.

Finally, Anthony Giddens introduces us to long-term social trends as the real source of change. The whole world is undergoing a very basic change—globalization—and this trend affects every aspect of our lives, leaving traditional societies in the dust, and bringing truly revolutionary change to how most of us live our lives.

51

Class, Social Conflict, and Social Change

Karl Marx

The history of all hitherto existing society is the history of class struggles. . . .
The bourgoisie, historically, has played a most revolutionary part. . . . [Eventually]
it creates a world after its own image . . . [and] more massive and more colossal
productive forces than have all preceding generations together. . . .
What the bourgeoisie . . . produces, above all, is its own grave-diggers.
Its fall and the victory of the proletariat are equally inevitable.

The *Communist Manifesto*, published in 1848, was meant to be a propoganda tract rather than a scholarly essay. It simplifies Marx's view of social change, but, at the same time, makes his argument clear. Real social change arises because of class conflict. In his world he identified two dominant classes: the bourgeoisie and the proletariat (the capitalists and the workers). Here is a description of the rise of both classes and the inevitable conflict that he foresees.

The history of all hitherto existing society is the history of class struggles.

Freeman and slave, patrician and plebeian, lord and serf, guild-master and journeyman—in a word, oppressor and oppressed, stood in constant opposition to one another, carried on an uninterrupted, now hidden, now open fight, a fight that each time ended either in a revolutionary re-constitution of society at large or in the common ruin of the contending classes.

In the earlier epochs of history, we find almost everywhere a complicated arrangement of society into various orders, a manifold gradation of social rank. In ancient Rome we have patricians, knights, plebeians, slaves; in the Middle Ages, feudal lords, vassals, guild-masters, journeymen, apprentices, serfs; in almost all of these classes, again, subordinate gradations.

The modern bourgeois society that has sprouted from the ruins of feudal society has not done away with class antagonisms. It has but established new classes, new conditions of oppression, new forms of struggle in place of the old ones.

Our epoch, the epoch of the bourgeoisie, possesses, however, this distinctive feature: it has simplified the class antagonisms. Society as a whole is more and more splitting up into two great hostile camps, into two great classes directly facing each other: Bourgeoisie and Proletariat.

From *Manifesto of the Communist Party*, in *Karl Marx and Frederick Engels Collected Works*, Vol IV. Lawrence and Wishart, London, 1976, pp. 477–518.

From the serfs of the Middle Ages sprang the chartered burghers of the earliest towns. From these burgesses the first elements of the bourgeoisie were developed.

The discovery of America, the rounding of the Cape, opened up fresh ground for the rising bourgeoisie. The East Indian and Chinese markets, the colonization of America, trade with the colonies, the increase in the means of exchange and in commodities generally, gave to commerce, to navigation, to industry, an impulse never before known, and thereby, to the revolutionary element in the tottering feudal society, a rapid development.

The feudal system of industry, under which industrial production was monopolized by closed guilds, now no longer sufficed for the growing wants of the new markets. The manufacturing system took its place. The guild-masters were pushed on one side by the manufacturing middle class; division of labour between the different corporate guilds vanished in the face of division of labour in each single workshop.

Meantime the markets kept ever growing, the demand ever rising. Even manufacture no longer sufficed. Thereupon, steam and machinery revolutionized industrial production. The place of manufacture was taken by the giant, Modern Industry, the place of the industrial middle class, by industrial millionaires, the leaders of whole industrial armies, the modern bourgeois.

Modern industry has established the world-market, for which the discovery of America paved the way. This market has given an immense development to commerce, to navigation, to communication by land. This development has, in its turn, reacted on the extension of industry; and in proportion as industry, commerce, navigation, railways extended, in the same proportion the bourgeoisie developed, increased its capital, and pushed into the background every class handed down from the Middle Ages.

We see, therefore, how the modern bourgeoisie is itself the product of a long course of development, of a series of revolutions in the modes of production and of exchange.

Each step in the development of the bourgeoisie was accompanied by a corresponding political advance of that class. An oppressed class under the sway of the feudal nobility, an armed and self-governing association in the medieval commune; here independent urban republic (as in Italy and Germany), there taxable 'third estate' of the monarchy (as in France), afterwards, in the period of manufacture proper, serving either the semi-feudal or the absolute monarchy as a counterpoise against the nobility, and, in fact, cornerstone of the great monarchies in general, the bourgeoisie has at last, since the establishment of Modern Industry and of the world-market, conquered for itself, in the modern representative State, exclusive political sway. The executive of the modern State is but a committee for managing the common affairs of the whole bourgeoisie.

The bourgeoisie, historically, has played a most revolutionary part.

The bourgeoisie, wherever it has got the upper hand, has put an end to all feudal, patriarchal, idyllic relations. It has pitilessly torn asunder the motley feudal ties that bound man to his 'natural superiors,' and has left remaining no other nexus between man and man than naked self-interest, than callous 'cash payment.' It has drowned the most heavenly ecstasies of religious fervour, of chivalrous enthusiasm, of philistine sentimentalism, in the icy water of egotistical calculation. It has resolved personal worth into exchange value, and in place of the numberless indefeasible chartered freedoms, has set up that single, unconscionable freedom—Free Trade. In one word, for exploitation, veiled by religious and political illusions, it has substituted naked, shameless, direct, brutal exploitation.

The bourgeoisie has stripped of its halo every occupation hitherto honoured and looked up to with reverent awe. It has converted the physician, the lawyer, the priest, the poet, the man of science into its paid wage-labourers.

The bourgeoisie has torn away from the family its sentimental veil, and has reduced the family relation to a mere money relation. . . .

The need of a constantly expanding market for its products chases the bourgeoisie over the whole surface of the globe. It must nestle everywhere, settle everywhere, establish connections everywhere. . . .

The bourgeoisie, by the rapid improvement of all instruments of production, by the immensely facilitated means of communication, draws all, even the most barbarian, nations into civilization.

The cheap prices of its commodities are the heavy artillery with which it batters down all Chinese walls, with which it forces the barbarians' intensely obstinate hatred of foreigners to capitulate. It compels all nations, on pain of extinction, to adopt the bourgeois mode of production; it compels them to introduce what it calls civilization into their midst, i.e., to become bourgeois themselves. In one word, it creates a world after its own image.

The bourgeoisie has subjected the country to the rule of the towns. It has created enormous cities, has greatly increased the urban population as compared with the rural, and has thus rescued a considerable part of the population from the idiocy of rural life. Just as it has made the country dependent on the towns, so it has made barbarian and semi-barbarian countries dependent on the civilized ones, nations of peasants on nations of bourgeois, the East on the West.

The bourgeoisie keeps more and more doing away with the scattered state of the population, of the means of production, and of property. It has agglomerated population, centralized means of production, and has concentrated property in a few hands. The necessary consequence of this was political centralization. Independent or but loosely connected provinces, with separate interests, laws, governments, and systems of taxation, became lumped together into one nation, with one government, one code of laws, one national class-interest, one frontier, and one customs-tariff.

The bourgeoisie, during its rule of scarcely one hundred years, has created more massive and more colossal productive forces than have all preceding generations together. Subjection of Nature's forces to man, machinery, application of chemistry to industry and agriculture, steam-navigation, railways, electric telegraphs, clearing of whole continents for cultivation, canalization of rivers, whole populations conjured out of the ground—what earlier century had even a presentiment that such productive forces slumbered in the lap of social labour? . . .

We see then that the means of production and of exchange, on whose foundation the bourgeoisie built itself up, were generated in feudal society. At a certain stage in the development of these means of production and of exchange, the conditions under which feudal society produced and exchanged, the feudal organization of agriculture and manufacturing industry, in one word, the feudal relations of property become no longer compatible with the already developed productive forces; they became so many fetters. They had to be burst asunder; they were burst asunder.

Into their place stepped free competition, accompanied by a social and political constitution adapted to it, and by the economical and political sway of the bourgeois class. . . .

In proportion as the bourgeoisie, i.e., capital, is developed, in the same proportion is the proletariat, the modern working class, developed—a class of labourers, who live only so long as they find work, and who find work only so long as their labour increases capital. These labourers, who must sell themselves piecemeal, are a commodity, like every other article of commerce, and are consequently exposed to all the vicissitudes of competition, to all the fluctuations of the market.

Owing to the extensive use of machinery and to division of labour, the work of the proletarians has lost all individual character, and, consequently, all charm for the workman. He becomes an appendage of the machine, and it is only the most simple, most monotonous, and most easily acquired knack, that is required of him. Hence, the cost of production of a workman is restricted, almost entirely, to the means of subsistence that he requires for his maintenance, and for the propagation of his race. But the price of a commodity, and therefore also of labour, is equal to its cost of production. In proportion, therefore, as the repulsiveness of the work increases, the wage decreases. Nay more, in proportion as the use of machinery and division of labour increases, in the same proportion the burden of toil also increases, whether by prolongation of the working hours, by increase of the work exacted in a given time or by increased speed of the machinery, etc.

Modern industry has converted the little workshop of the patriarchal master into the great factory of the industrial capitalist. Masses of labourers, crowded into the factory, are organized like soldiers. As privates of the industrial army they are placed under the command of a perfect hierarchy of officers and sergeants. Not only are they slaves of the bourgeois class, and of the bourgeois State; they are daily and hourly enslaved by the machine, by the overlooker, and, above all, by the individual bourgeois manufacturer himself. The more openly this despotism proclaims gain to be its end and aim, the more petty, the more hateful, and the more embittering it is. . . .

The lower strata of the middle class—the small tradespeople, shopkeepers, and retired tradesmen generally, the handicraftsmen and peasants—all these sink gradually into the proletariat, partly because their diminutive capital does not suffice for the scale on which Modern Industry is carried on, and is swamped in the competition with the large capitalists, partly because their specialized skill is rendered worthless by new methods of production. Thus the proletariat is recruited from all classes of the population.

The proletariat goes through various stages of development. With its birth begins its struggle with the bourgeoisie. At first the contest is carried on by individual labourers, then by the workpeople of a factory, then by the operatives of one trade, in one locality, against the individual bourgeois who directly exploits them. They direct their attacks not against the bourgeois conditions of production, but against the instruments of production themselves; they destroy imported wares that compete with their labour, they smash to pieces machinery, they set factories ablaze, they seek to restore by force the vanished status of the workman of the Middle Ages.

At this stage the labourers still form an incoherent mass scattered over the whole country, and broken up by their mutual competition. If anywhere they unite to form more compact bodies, this is not yet the consequence of their own active union, but of the union of the bourgeoisie, which class, in order to attain its own political ends, is compelled to set the whole proletariat in motion, and is moreover yet, for a time, able to do so. At this stage, therefore, the proletarians do not fight their enemies, but the enemies of their enemies, the remnants of absolute monarchy, the landowners, the non-industrial bourgeois, the petty bourgeoisie. Thus the whole historical movement is concentrated in the hands of the bourgeoisie; every victory so obtained is a victory for the bourgeoisie.

But with the development of industry the proletariat not only increases in number; it becomes concentrated in greater masses, its strength grows, and it feels that strength more. The various interests and conditions of life within the ranks of the proletariat are more and more equalized, in proportion as machinery obliterates all distinctions of labour, and nearly everywhere reduces wages to the same low level. The growing competition among the bourgeois, and the resulting commercial crises, make the wages of the workers ever more fluctuating. The unceasing improvement of machinery, ever more rapidly developing, makes their livelihood more and more precarious; the collisions between individual workmen and individual bourgeois take more and more the character of collisions between two classes. Thereupon the workers begin to form combinations (Trades' Unions) against the bourgeois; they club together in order to keep up the rate of wages; they found permanent associations in order to make provision beforehand for these occasional revolts. Here and there the contest breaks out into riots.

Now and then the workers are victorious, but only for a time. The real fruit of their battles lies, not in the immediate result, but in the ever-expanding union of the workers. This union is helped on by the improved means of communication that are created by modern industry and that place the workers of different localities in contact with one another. It was just this contact that was needed to centralize the numerous local struggles, all of the same character, into one national struggle between classes.

Of all the classes that stand face to face with the bourgeoisie today, the proletariat alone is a really revolutionary class. The other classes decay and finally disappear in the face of Modern Industry; the proletariat is its special and essential product.

The lower middle class, the small manufacturer, the shopkeeper, the artisan, the peasant, all these fight against the bourgeoisie, to save from extinction their existence as fractions of the middle class. They are therefore not revolutionary, but conservative. Nay more, they are reactionary, for they try to roll back the wheel of history. If by chance they are revolutionary, they are so only in view of their impending transfer into the proletariat; they thus defend not their present, but their future interests, they desert their own standpoint to place themselves at that of the proletariat.

The 'dangerous class,' the social scum, that passively rotting mass thrown off by the lowest layers of old society, may, here and there, be swept into the movement by a proletarian revolution; its conditions of life, however, prepare it far more for the part of a bribed tool of reactionary intrigue. . . .

All previous historical movements were movements of minorities, or in the interests of minorities. The proletarian movement is the self-conscious, independent movement of the immense majority, in the interests of the immense majority. The proletariat, the lowest stratum of our present society, cannot stir, cannot raise itself up, without the whole superincumbent strata of official society being sprung into the air.

Though not in substance, yet in form, the struggle of the proletariat with the bourgeoisie is at first a national struggle. The proletariat of each country must, of course, first of all settle matters with its own bourgeoisie.

In depicting the most general phases of the development of the proletariat, we traced the more or less veiled civil war, raging within existing society, up to the point where that war breaks out into open revolution, and where the violent overthrow of the bourgeoisie lays the foundation for the sway of the proletariat. . . .

The essential condition for the existence, and for the sway of the bourgeois class, is the formation and augmentation of capital; the condition for capital is wage-labour. Wage-labour rests exclusively on competition between the labourers. The advance of industry, whose involuntary promoter is the bourgeoisie, replaces the isolation of the labourers, due to competition, by their revolutionary combination, due to association. The development of Modern Industry, therefore, cuts from under its feet the very foundation on which the bourgeoisie produces and appropriates products. What the bourgeoisie, therefore, produces, above all, is its own grave-diggers. Its fall and the victory of the proletariat are equally inevitable.

◆ 52 ◆

Society and Change

Michel Crozier

We will never succeed in changing society the way we want. . . . Every society is a complex system, and this is why it cannot be changed or renewed simply by a decision, even one arrived at democratically by majority rule.

Michel Crozier, a French sociologist, regards social change as very complex. Although we may think that society changes because someone is successful in changing it, it rarely changes because of the will of the individual. Our efforts may bring unintended consequences and even have the opposite effect of what we intended. Yet it is still important to try to make change because retreat from attempting change will bring even worse problems.

From "The Future of French Society," by Michel Crozier, in *Strategies for Change*, MIT Press, Trans. William R. Beer, 1982. English translation copyright © 1982 by the Massachusetts Institute of Technology.

We will never succeed in changing society the way we want. Even if we were to persuade the majority of our fellow citizens to follow our lead, we would not succeed in enacting a plan for society because society, human relations, and social systems are too complex. We would have succeeded in mobilizing nothing but an abstract and unsubstantial agreement, the awakened dreams of our fellow men. This desire, this fantasy, never determines how people really act.

It is possible to work within a system only by understanding its characteristics. This assertion is not as self-evident as it may appear because all too often we are not willing to understand society as it is. Instead, we spend our time making social blueprints that do not have the slightest chance of success because they do not take into account the complex working of human relationships and everyday social interaction.

Every society is a complex system, and this is why it cannot be changed or renewed simply by a decision, even one arrived at democratically by majority rule. This is not to say that there are fixed laws of society, imposed on humanity like a sort of divine will. This all-too-human construction is the product of human history, and so it can be shaped, reworked, and changed. But at the same time, it is a system, an interdependent framework of relations that is beyond the conscious will of individual people.

Of course, neither these relations nor the whole system are unalterable. They do change as a result of human action, but the overall result of this action is different from the wishes of individual people. It is possible to bring about change more consciously and effectively, but it is not possible to impose a specific program simply through the agreement of individual people. This may seem contradictory, particularly if the profound difference that exists between people's individual preferences and their real behavior toward others is not appreciated.

Behavior in social relationships is like a game in which each person depends on the other. To win, or simply not to lose, you have to take the possible reactions of others into account. The games of social life make us obey rules that are independent of us. These games are regulated, commanded, corrected, and maintained by mechanisms to which we do not have direct access.

These games are the building blocks of systems that organize every one of our activities, including the biggest and most complex, society itself.

When a warehouse worker sets aside a special supply of goods to meet unexpected requests of production workers, while at the same time politely refusing to provide for the maintenance workers, he is neither obeying his boss nor hoping for the final victory of the working class. It is not because of some personal character trait that he is easy-going with his old assistant and strict with his new one. This is the only way he can succeed in keeping the wheels turning in the department that is his world of work, while at the same time keeping the respect of his peers and influencing events that affect him. This is as true at the level of society as it is at the level of a business.

Games, systems, and society are the necessary mediators of all human action, but they are structured in such a way that this mediation can have an effect opposite to what most participants want or think they want. The road to hell, as everyone knows, is paved with good intentions. To set up the rule of virtue, hypocrisy and eavesdropping are brought in, and have been from the time of Savonarola to Mao; the control of excess profits strengthens the black market. And very often in the attempt to free people, new chains are forged for them. Every organized human action, every collective effort, and even ideological movements lead to what can be called the *perverse effect*, effects that are the opposite of what the participants wanted. These perverse effects cannot be blamed on some force of evil—neither on the powerful at the top of the social scale nor on agitators at the bottom. They are the necessary consequence of interdependent relationships among people.

This will come as a surprise to those who still believe in the myth of the social contract, who believe that the collective will of people, the sum of their individual wishes, naturally produces rational decisions. The use of opinion polls has given new respectability and weight to this idealistic view of democracy. In fact, we are prisoners of our social situation, of our relationships, of our need to exist for, with, and against other people. Outside of this situation and these interactions, we cannot decide what we want because we literally do not know. This is why abstract opinion, cut off from the real context of social relations, only partially indicates what our real behavior is. In the spring of 1968, opinion polls registered satisfaction in France, and the pollsters said that the students had never been so happy.

It would be tempting to conclude that it is better not to try to intervene at all because every social action leads to a series of effects that can be the exact opposite of what was intended. This is the temptation of pessimism that has recently reappeared among the "new philosophers." It must be resisted, not simply because it leads people to give up but also because it leads to an even worse state of affairs. Every situation in which we do not intervene tends to deteriorate. Every analysis of businesses or institutions that are not working reveals that the same rules and principles that were successful twenty or thirty years ago are the cause of disorder and failure today.

So it is not a question of choosing between action and retreat but of finding the means and direction of the action that cannot be avoided. In everyday life, we continually make choices on the basis of tested rules based on our experience. Unfortunately, we cannot transpose this principle to a broader area because individually we are helpless against large-scale organizations, nationwide societies, and the world order. The inescapable recognition of our limitations leads us to examine two principles of action.

The first principle is that of giving priority to the understanding of real systems, not to the discussion of aims and ideals. We can find out what we want only if we know what we are doing. As long as we are not aware of what is really going on, our ideals and goals are nothing but projections of our inadequacies and inabilities. We can progress only by bringing the ideal back to earth, by putting the system of relations on its feet: reality first, ideals later.

The second principle, a consequence of understanding the perverse effect, is that we have to get away from the guesswork of everyday activity. We have to spend as much energy on the ongoing operation of the system as we do on utopian projects for changing the whole system radically and idealistically. We cannot do our job as responsible people and citizens unless we go beyond the sort of blind empiricism that led an English minister of foreign affairs to declare shortly before the war in 1914, "You know, nothing really ever happens."

Social Movements and Social Change: The Case of the Militia Movement

Lane Crothers

Social movements involve challenges to established political and social institutions and practices. Groups form to oppose the "normal" way society works. In addition, movements often use tactics that fall outside the political mainstream in order to achieve their goals.

This selection is about the meaning and importance of social movements. Social movements have been a central part of the history of the United States, and still are an important force for social change. The labor movement, the civil rights movement, the anti-Vietnam War movement, the feminist movement, and the environmental movement made a great difference in the twentieth century. Crothers, however, introduces us to another social movement—the Militia Movement—having roots in our nation's history, critical of many modern trends it perceives to be undermining traditional values and institutions, attractive to those facing financial difficulties, and willing to use violent means to achieve its ends. Crothers sees this movement as a threat to American democratic institutions because of its commitment to achieving its ends through violent—and often highly destructive—means. Where, we might ask, is the line between terrorism and legitimate social movements?

Rage is a powerful, angry emotion. It is a passionate, intense expression of frustration and aggression. It is almost always triggered by some event that may or may not be related to the root causes of the explosion and so is an unfocused, frighteningly irrational experience—both for the person feeling rage and for those who suffer its effects.

"Rage" is also a very powerful word. To say that someone is in a rage is to imply that he is feeling and expressing an emotion that is exceptional, out of control. It is to say that his actions are in a unique category; that however justified the person in the rage state feels in his behavior, to an outside observer it is clear that he is in fact behaving inappropriately, even dangerously. Accordingly, the word rage should not be used lightly.

As will be explored throughout this book, rage is a central principle of the modern American militia movement. This movement, which is also sometimes known as the Patriot movement, swept across the rural areas of western, midwestern, and southern states in the 1990s. It became

From Lane Crothers, *Rage on the Right: The American Militia Movement from Ruby Ridge to Homeland Security*, New York: Rowman & Littlefield Publishers, Inc., 2003, pp. 1–8.

an important dimension of American political life. Indeed, at its most extreme, members of the movement engaged in acts of intimidation and terrorism across the country, most notably epitomized in Timothy McVeigh's destruction of the Alfred P. Murrah Federal Building in Oklahoma City, Oklahoma, on April 19, 1995.

Motivated by values core to American democracy, the movement's members hold a set of beliefs that encourage violence and other extreme forms of political behavior. While the rest of this work addresses the cultural, ideological, and behavioral dimensions of the American militia movement in detail, a brief introduction to the argument that follows will set the stage for the analysis to follow.

In short, the character of American political culture informs militia ideology, activities, and potential influence in American political life. The contemporary militia is not "alien" or "exceptional." Instead, militia members invoke core principles that are commonly recognized as central to American political life. They then interpret these values in a way that ultimately justifies their actions and attitudes. Members believe they are struggling to protect America as they think it ought to be, and no price, including violence, is too high. In particular, militiamen and -women argue that the federal government has been corrupted. Its activities, controlled by some conspiracy of bankers, international agencies like the United Nations and the International Monetary Fund, American political elites that members of the militia movement refer to as the "Shadow Government" or the "New World Order," and others, are aimed at the destruction of American liberties and freedoms. Members claim that the federal government has passed a series of laws that improperly limit the rights of Americans to, for example, own guns, associate with (and discriminate against) anyone they wish, or use their land as they please. Resistance, including violent resistance, against these corrupt laws is believed to be appropriate and moral.

As the rest of this book makes clear, the ideas and values that shape militia activity tend to encourage and legitimate the use of violence for political ends. Moreover, these ideas, while informed by principles, myths, and historical events that are common in the United States, are

actually well outside the political mainstream. By closely examining the contemporary militia movement, this book seeks to understand the threat the militia poses in both the near and the long term. It also explores the ideas and attitudes that shape the militia movement and link it to broader traditions in American political history.

SOCIAL MOVEMENTS AND THE MILITIA

This book takes the position that the modern militia movement can best be understood as a culturally embedded social movement. In order to clarify this point, some attention to the nature and content of social movement theory is necessary. However, since this is a book not about social movement theory but about a particular social movement, and since the literature in this field is so extensive, the following brief discussion of the field will serve to frame this work.

Social movements involve challenges to established political and social institutions and practices. Groups form to oppose the "normal" way society works. In addition, movements often use tactics that fall outside the political mainstream in order to achieve their goals.[1] For example, the civil rights movement used mass rallies, economic boycotts, and civil disobedience, rather than voting, to challenge established patterns of racial discrimination in the United States. Such tactics were necessary because the racism that was central to U.S. society guaranteed that activities like voting would not lead to the changes the civil rights movement sought. Movements, then, link individuals into groups that work to change society through nontraditional means.

So why do social movements form? Why do some people break established patterns and norms of behavior in order to challenge the status quo? First, as might be expected, it is generally the case that those who form and participate in social movements are motivated by ideas and values. In particular, as della Porta and Diani put it, "social action is driven largely by the fundamental principles with which the actor identifies. Values influence the ways in which the actor defines specific goals and identifies behavioral strategies which are both efficient and morally acceptable."[2] In times of social stability, then, individual values correspond, at least in general, with the individual's perception of the general goals of the broader community. But when social and individual goals begin to diverge, the individual may be motivated to try to change society so that its actions correspond with the individual's beliefs.[3] This is particularly likely to occur when individuals perceive injustices, suffered either by themselves or by others with whom the actor is sympathetic.[4] In other words, individuals who perceive that injustices have been committed against the values and ideals through which they define the purpose of their lives, the nature of right and wrong, and the purposes and ends of the community's shared life are likely to react and push for social change.

Second, the literature on social movements often emphasizes the role(s) the mobilization of resources plays in group formation, action, and outcomes. For example, external forces, sometimes known as structural conditions, can also shape movement formation.[5] A social crisis like economic chaos, losing a war, or the mass migration of populations into or out of a particular country can make it difficult for the government or other groups to provide services to a people. Under such conditions, individuals may rise up to demand changes intended to fix the problems they believe society is facing. Thus, when structural conditions are tense, when established patterns of social norms and behaviors are under stress, social movements rise to remake the social order in light of new—or resurrected—ideas about what rules, behaviors, and values ought to organize society.

Similarly, changes in the existing political system can serve as resources that can be mobilized by emerging social movements. New leaders capable of mobilizing previously latent groups can arrive on the scene. The wealth embedded in societies or groups experiencing significant levels of economic growth may provide previously inactive groups with the means to organize and struggle for change. Shifts in patterns of support for the dominant regime may provide formerly weak groups with potential alliances that may advantage their group's interests, thereby encouraging group formation and activity. Thus, when examining a social movement, it is important to consider

the resources that were available to it and how group members and leaders used these resources to attempt to achieve their goals.

From a resource mobilization perspective, the late 1980s and early 1990s were a time of remarkable economic and social transition in the United States. Globalization and economies of scale increasingly led to the transformation of the American farming industry from family- to corporate-owned enterprises. This, in turn, caused many family farmers to search for explanations of their loss; militias and similar groups provided answers.[6] Similarly, a shift in political power to the suburbs, with the attendant values-shift to postmodern attitudes regarding appropriate lifestyles,[7] led to the assertion of new rules for land use, restrictions on hunting, and other examples of nonrural people shaping policies for rural land usage that undermined the traditional patterns of local life.[8] Thus, at the same moment the social-political order was remaking itself (the power shift to the suburbs combined with the rise of the globalist economy), it stimulated policies that caused feelings of injustice to rise among many who saw their way of life undermined and attacked.

In addition, as is developed in chapter 3, the existence of previous movements played a crucial role in militia formation. Long-standing right-wing groups like the Ku Klux Klan and the John Birch Society established a pattern of antigovernment activity and rhetoric. Groups like the Order, the Aryan Nations, and other hate groups that emerged in the 1970s and 1980s but were substantially eliminated prior to the militias' rise in the 1990s nonetheless provided a template of paranoia and anger from which the militias drew their ideas and organizational structure.[9] And, of course, the original militias of the Revolutionary War stood as a model for militia formation and action: whatever the reality of the Revolutionary militia, the modern militias constructed an idealized image of citizen-farmers arming themselves, leaving their homes, and defeating the occupying British Army. These historical foundations, when linked to the events described in detail in chapters 4, 5, and 6, provided significant resources for the development of the militia movement.

Another important consideration when engaging in social movement analysis is why movements take the organizational forms they do. Two

factors, previous movements and the response of
the political system, can be seen as particularly
important in the construction of particular movement organizations.

Like individuals, movements are embedded
in cultural, historical, and ideological contexts.
New movements inevitably are inspired by, draw
on the language of, and develop the successes of
earlier movements and social challenges through
mechanisms like cultural frames and long-
standing activist subcultures.[10] Thus, rather than
forming entirely new modes of organization and
operation, movements develop systems of action
and goals that mimic previous movements.

In addition to previous movements, newer
movements are also shaped by the reaction of the
established authorities to the group's challenge.
Thus, if the state responds to social challenges
with violence—arrests, coercion, or other means
of isolating the deviant actors—there is a tendency for the movement to react with violence
or to go underground, hiding its operations. If the
state fails to respond in any way, the movement's
members may be emboldened, pressing their
challenges publicly and actively. Or if the state
acts to co-opt the movement, addressing some of
its concerns while ignoring others, the result may
encourage group members to use established
means of political participation, such as voting,
lobbying, and the like.[11]

In the case of militias, organizational forms
have varied over time. In their formative period,
the "typical" militia group consisted of a central
leader, often referred to as a colonel regardless
of former rank, if any, in the armed forces of the
United States. Such a group purchased or used
the land of a member as a training compound
in which its members practiced guerrilla warfare tactics against agents of the federal government. Members came to the site at some predetermined period to train. In addition to
weapons training, the group also engaged in education of members and sympathizers. Finally,
all groups maintained an active Internet presence—some more sophisticated than others—
to recruit new members and raise funds for
their operations. These organizations formed
the nucleus of an armed resistance to the evil
intrusions of the corrupted government—the
Shadow Government.

In its early days, there were few, if any, connections among different parts of the militia movement. It was less a unified movement than clus-
ters of individuals who shared values and
attitudes. Two groups, the Militia of Montana
(MOM) and the Michigan Militia, were the early
progenitors of the militia model: isolation, guns,
and ideology. These groups then provided a template that hundreds of other groups and individuals followed.[12] However, these groups did share a
common reliance on the Internet to advance
their ideology: its existence has provided members and leaders the opportunity to spread their
messages quickly, easily, and cheaply around the
world. This common ideological front tended to
give a greater appearance of movement unity
than was really the case; there were limited, if any,
institutional structures linking different groups.

In recent years, particularly after the
Oklahoma City bombing, the shape of the movement has changed in two significant ways. First, as
the number of groups and overt members has declined, group activities have gone underground.
(These events are described in detail in chapter 7.)
Indeed, like the French Resistance in World
War II, some groups have moved to the model of
leaderless resistance, with cell members knowing
the names and personal information of only a few
others in the movement. Thus, in theory, if one is
captured (a real fear in terms of their ideology),
that person cannot betray more than a few other
members of the group. Second, many militia
groups and sympathizers have reopened an ideological and political dialogue with the reemergent
components of the racist right. Thus, the militia
movement is transforming itself into a more explicitly racist movement that is organized, omi-
nously, for violent resistance to the operations of
the federal government.

Finally, some sense of how and why movements succeed—and how and why they fail—is
important if the way(s) the modern militia movement is likely to affect the United States is to be
understood. Several key factors, like the breadth
of the movement's goals and the relations between the movement and the dominant culture,
are relevant here. For example, specific social
movements can lead to the development of
"master protest frames."[13] These are ideologies of
legitimate protest activity that come to be shared

by a variety of social movements. These frames can promote movement success over time as new modes of life are recognized as legitimate and appropriate by large segments of the community. Alternatively, social movements can lead to the foundation of new identities within a community. Thus, as more and more people identify themselves with the movement's ideals, the movement becomes embedded in a given society. Successful social movements can also serve as examples of techniques that future social movements can use to advance their own protests and political activities. Thus, while a specific movement may or may not achieve its goals, the legacy of ideas and strategies it leaves behind can inform other, potentially more successful, movements. Finally, when a group has broad goals it is more likely to be a powerful influence in society; such goals provide a platform on which large segments of society can stand for shared political action, thus enhancing the movement's chances of success.[14] The successes and failures of the militia movement are discussed in chapter 7.

Social movements, then, involve collective action by individuals and groups dissatisfied with current conditions to reshape the political and/or social order. This transformative enterprise is inevitably shaped and informed by the institutional, political, and cultural contexts in which it operates. The broader environment similarly contextualizes its successes and failures. In order to understand any social movement, then, it is necessary to engage the goals it pursues (and why these goals are chosen), the organizational form it takes (and why this is the case), and the cultural and political context in which it exists. . . .

NOTES

1. William Gamson and William Meyer, *Comparative Perspectives on Social Movements: Political Opportunities, Mobilizing Structures, and Cultural Framings* (New York: Cambridge University Press, 1996), 283.

2. Donatella della Porta and Mario Diani, *Social Movements: An Introduction* (Malden, Mass.: Blackwell Publishers, 1999), 66.

3. C. Mueller, "Building Social Movement Theory," in *Frontiers in Social Movement Theory*, ed. A. Morris and C. Mueller (New Haven: Yale University Press, 1992), 7.

4. Doug McAdam, *Political Process and the Development of Black Insurgency, 1930–1970* (Chicago: University of Chicago Press, 1982); R. Turner and L. Killian, "The Field of Collective Behavior," in *Collective Behavior and Social Movement*, ed. R. Curtis Jr. and E. Aguirre (Boston: Allyn & Bacon, 1993).

5. M. Zald and R. Ash, "Social Movement Organizations: Growth, Decay and Change," *Social Forces* 44 (March 1966): 3–4.

6. Joel Dyer, *Harvest of Rage: Why Oklahoma City Is Only the Beginning* (Boulder, Colo.: Westview, 1998).

7. As discussed in Ronald Inglehart, *Modernization and Postmodernization: Cultural, Economic, and Political Change in Forty-three Societies* (Princeton, N.J.: Princeton University Press, 1997).

8. Dyer, *Harvest*.

9. For a fuller discussion of these points, see Richard Abanes, *American Militias: Rebellion, Racism, and Religion* (Downer's Grove, Ill.: Intervarsity Press, 1996); Morris Dees, *Gathering Storm: America's Militia Threat* (New York: HarperCollins, 1996); Neil Hamilton, *Militias in America* (Denver: ABC-CLIO, 1996); David Niewert, *In God's Country: The Patriot Movement and the Pacific Northwest* (Pullman: Washington State University Press, 1999); Robert Snow, *The Militia Threat: Terrorists Among Us* (New York: Plenum Trade, 1999); and Kenneth Stern, *A Force upon the Plain: The American Militia Movement and the Politics of Hate* (New York: Simon & Schuster, 1996).

10. Doug McAdam, "Culture and Social Movements," in *New Social Movements: From Ideology to Identity*, ed. Enrique Laraña, Hank Johnston, and Joseph Gusfield (Philadelphia: Temple University Press, 1994).

11. della Porta and Diani, *Social Movements*.

12. Abanes, *American Militias*; Dees, *Gathering Storm*; Hamilton, *Militias in America*; Niewert, *God's Country*; Snow, *Militia Threat*; Stern, *Force upon the Plain*.

13. D. Snow et al., "Frame Alignment Processes, Micromobilization, and Movement Participation," *American Sociological Review* 51 (1986): 464–81.

14. McAdam, "Culture and Social Movements."

◆ 54 ◆

Islamic Fundamentalism and Social Change

Bernard Lewis

Broadly speaking, Muslim fundamentalists are those who feel that the troubles of the Muslim world at the present time are the result not of insufficient modernization but of excessive modernization, which they see as a betrayal of authentic Islamic values. For them the remedy is a return to true Islam.

Bernard Lewis is professor of Near Eastern Studies, and much of his work is an attempt to understand the historical, social, religious, and political forces that have shaped Islamic nations in the Middle East. This selection introduces us to recent history, the development of the Saudia Arabian nation, the Western intervention because of oil, and the rising tensions that often turn to terrorism and war between the West and Islamic peoples. Lewis turns our attention to religion, nationbuilding, nationalism, politics, sudden wealth, and culture as forces for social conflict and social change.

The conflict that divides Islam is between those who try to modernize and those who fear that modernization means westernization and threats to traditional Islamic society. The recent rise of militant Islamic fundamentalism is traced back to the same anti-Western reactions that helped form the present Saudi monarchy.

Change versus anti-change. Tradition versus modernization. Christianity versus Islam. Democracy versus monarchy. Peace versus terrorism. Wealth versus poverty. Such conflicts bring even more change.

The rejection of modernity in favor of a return to the sacred past has a varied and ramified history in the region and has given rise to a number of movements. The most important of these was undoubtedly that known, after its founder, as Wahhabism. Muhammad ibn 'Abd al-Wahhab (1703–1792) was a theologian from the Najd area

From Bernard Lewis, *The Crisis of Islam: Holy War and Unholy Terror*, New York: Random House, Inc., 2003, pp. 120–136.

of Arabia, ruled by local sheikhs of the House of Saud. In 1744 he launched a campaign of purification and renewal. His declared aim was to return to the pure and authentic Islam of the Founder, removing and where necessary destroying all the later accretions and distortions.

The Wahhabi cause was embraced by the Saudi rulers of Najd, who promoted it, for a while successfully, by force of arms....

The rise of Wahhabism in eighteenth-century Arabia was in significant measure a response to the changing circumstances of the time. One of these was of course the retreat of Islam and the corresponding advance of Christendom....

The ire of the Wahhabis was directed not primarily against outsiders but against those whom they saw as betraying and degrading Islam from within: on the one hand those who attempted any kind of modernizing reform; on the other—and this was the more immediate target—those whom the Wahhabis saw as corrupting and debasing the true Islamic heritage of the Prophet and his Companions....

Two developments in the early twentieth century transformed Wahhabism into a major force in the Islamic world and beyond. The first of these was the expansion and consolidation of the Saudi kingdom [notably the conquest of the Hijaz].... Their forces first captured Mecca; then, on December 5, 1925, after a siege of ten months, Medina surrendered peacefully. Two weeks later King 'Ali, who had succeeded his father, Hussein, asked the British vice consul in Jedda to inform Ibn Saud of his withdrawal from the Hijaz with his personal effects. This was taken as an abdication, and on the following day the Saudi forces entered Jedda. The way was now open for Ibn Saud to proclaim himself King of the Hijaz and Sultan of Najd and its Dependencies on January 8, 1926. The new regime was immediately recognized by the European powers, notably by the Soviet Union in a diplomatic note of February 16 to Ibn Saud, "on the basis of the principle of the people's right to self-determination and out of respect for the Hijazi people's will as expressed in their choice of you as their king."[1] A formal treaty between Ibn Saud and Great Britain, recognizing the full independence of the kingdom, was signed on May 20, 1927. Some other European states followed suit....

Ibn Saud proceeded rapidly with the reorganization and restructuring of his far-flung kingdom and in September 1932 proclaimed a new unitary state, to be called the Saudi Arabian Kingdom. In the following year he appointed his eldest son, Saud, as heir to the throne.

The same year saw the other major development affecting the region, with the signature, on May 19, 1933, of an agreement between the Saudi minister of finance and a representative of Standard Oil of California. Saudi politics and Wahhabi doctrines now rested on a solid economic foundation.

Western interest in Middle Eastern oil dated from the early twentieth century and was mainly operated by British, Dutch, and French companies. American interest began in the early 1920s, with growing concern about the depletion of domestic oil resources and the fear of a European monopoly of Middle Eastern oil. American companies initially entered the Middle Eastern oil market as junior partners in European combines. Standard Oil of California was the first American company to undertake serious oil exploration. After some inconclusive efforts in the Gulf states, Standard Oil finally turned to the Saudis and in 1930 requested permission for a geological exploration of the eastern province: King Ibn Saud at first refused this request but then agreed to negotiations, which culminated in the agreement of 1933. One of the factors which induced the king to change his mind was no doubt the depression that began in 1929 and brought a serious and growing deterioration in the finances of the kingdom.

Less than four months after the signature of the agreement, the first American geologists arrived in eastern Arabia. By the end of the year, the exploratory mission was well established, and in the following year American teams began the extraction and export of oil. The process of development was interrupted by the Second World War but was resumed when the war ended. Some indication of the scale of development may be seen in the figures for oil extracted in Arabia, in millions of barrels: 1945, 21.3; 1955, 356.6; 1965, 804.8; 1975, 2,582.5.

The outward flow of oil and the corresponding inward flow of money brought immense changes to the Saudi kingdom, its internal structure and way of life, and its external role and influence, both in the oil-consuming countries and, more powerfully, in the world of Islam. The most significant change was in the impact of Wahhabism and the role of its protagonists. Wahhabism was now the official, state-enforced doctrine of one of the most influential governments in all Islam—the custodian of the two holiest places of Islam, the host of the annual pilgrimage, which brings millions of Muslims from every part of the world to share in its rites and rituals. At the same time, the teachers and preachers of Wahhabism had at their disposal immense financial resources, which they used to promote and spread their version of Islam. Even in Western countries in Europe and America, where the public educational systems are good, Wahhabi indoctrination centers may be the only form of Islamic education available to new converts and to Muslim parents who wish to give their children some grounding in their own inherited religious and cultural tradition. This indoctrination is provided in private schools, religious seminars, mosque schools, holiday camps and, increasingly, prisons.

In traditional Islamic usage the term *madrasa* denoted a center of higher education, of scholarship, teaching, and research. The classical Islamic madrasa was the predecessor of and in many ways the model for the great medieval European universities. In modern usage the word madrasa has acquired a negative meaning; it has come to denote a center for indoctrination in bigotry and violence. A revealing example may be seen in the backgrounds of a number of Turks arrested on suspicion of complicity in terrorist activities. Every single one of them was born and educated in Germany, not one in Turkey. The German government does not supervise the religious education of minority groups. The Turkish government keeps a watchful eye on these matters. In Europe and America, because of the reluctance of the state to involve itself in religious matters, the teaching of Islam in schools and elsewhere has in general been totally unsupervised by authority. This situation clearly favors those with the fewest scruples, the strongest convictions, and the most money.

The result can perhaps be depicted through an imaginary parallel. Imagine that the Ku Klux Klan or some similar group obtains total control of the state of Texas, of its oil and therefore of its oil revenues, and having done so, uses this money to establish a network of well-endowed schools and colleges all over Christendom, peddling their peculiar brand of Christianity. This parallel is somewhat less dire than the reality, since most Christian countries have functioning public school systems of their own. In some Muslim countries this is not so, and the Wahhabi-sponsored schools and colleges represent for many young Muslims the only education available. By these

means the Wahhabis have carried their message all over the Islamic world and, increasingly, to Islamic minority communities in other countries, notably in Europe and North America. Organized Muslim public life, education, and even worship are, to an alarming extent, funded and therefore directed by Wahhabis, and the version of Islam that they practice and preach is dominated by Wahhabi principles and attitudes. The custodianship of the holy places and the revenues of oil have given worldwide impact to what would otherwise have been an extremist fringe in a marginal country.

• • •

The exploitation of oil brought vast new wealth and with it new and increasingly bitter social tensions. In the old society inequalities of wealth had been limited, and their effects were restrained — on the one hand, by the traditional social bonds and obligations that linked rich and poor and, on the other hand, by the privacy of Muslim home life. Modernization has all too often widened the gap, destroyed those social bonds, and through the universality of the modern media, made the resulting inequalities painfully visible. All this has created new and receptive audiences for Wahhabi teachings and those of like-minded groups, among them the Muslim Brothers in Egypt and Syria and the Taliban in Afghanistan.

Oil wealth also had negative political effects, by inhibiting the development of representative institutions. "No taxation without representation" marks a crucial step in the development of Western democracy. Unfortunately, the converse is also true — no representation without taxation. Governments with oil wealth have no need for popular assemblies to impose and collect taxes, and can afford, for some time at least, to disregard public opinion. Even that term has little meaning in such societies. Lacking any other outlet, new and growing discontents also find expression in religious extremist movements.

It has now become normal to describe these movements as fundamentalist. The term is unfortunate for a number of reasons. It was originally an American Protestant term, used to designate certain Protestant churches that differed in some respects from the mainstream churches. The two main differences were liberal theology and biblical criticism, both seen as objectionable. Liberal theology has been an issue among Muslims in the past and may be again in the future. It is not at the present time. The literal divinity and inerrancy of the Qur'an is a basic dogma of Islam, and although some may doubt it, none challenge it. These differences bear no resemblance to those that divide Muslim fundamentalists from the Islamic mainstream, and the term can therefore be misleading. It is however now common usage, and has even been translated literally into Arabic, Persian, and Turkish.

The eclipse of pan-Arabism left Islamic fundamentalism as the most attractive alternative to all those who felt that there has to be something better, truer, and more hopeful than the inept tyrannies of their rulers and the bankrupt ideologies foisted on them from outside. These movements feed on privation and humiliation and on the frustration and resentments to which they give rise, after the failure of all the political and economic nostrums, both the foreign imports and the local imitations. As seen by many in the Middle East and north Africa, both capitalism and socialism were tried and have failed; both Western and Eastern models produced only poverty and tyranny. It may seem unjust that in post-independence Algeria, for example, the West should be blamed for the pseudo-Stalinist policies of an anti-Western government, for the failure of the one and the ineptitude of the other. But popular sentiment is not entirely wrong in seeing the Western world and Western ideas as the ultimate source of the major changes that have transformed the Islamic world in the last century or more. As a consequence, much of the anger in the Islamic world is directed against the Westerner, seen as the ancient and immemorial enemy of Islam since the first clashes between the Muslim caliphs and the Christian emperors, and against the Westernizer, seen as a tool or accomplice of the West and as a traitor to his own faith and people.

Religious fundamentalism enjoys several advantages against competing ideologies. It is readily intelligible to both educated and uneducated Muslims. It offers a set of themes, slogans, and symbols that are profoundly familiar and therefore effective in mobilizing support and in formulating both a critique of what is wrong and a program for putting it right. Religious movements enjoy another practical advantage in societies like those of the Middle East and north Africa that are under more or less autocratic rule: dictators can forbid parties, they can forbid meetings—they cannot forbid public worship, and they can to only a limited extent control sermons.

As a result the religious opposition groups are the only ones that have regular meeting places where they can assemble and have at their disposal a network outside the control of the state or at least not fully subject to it. The more oppressive the regime, the more it helps the fundamentalists by giving them a virtual monopoly of opposition.

Militant Islamic radicalism is not new. Several times since the beginnings of the Western impact in the eighteenth century, there have been religiously expressed militant opposition movements. So far they have all failed. Sometimes they have failed in an easy and relatively painless way by being defeated and suppressed, in which case the crown of martyrdom brought them a kind of success. Sometimes they have failed the hard way, by gaining power, and then having to confront great economic and social problems for which they had no real answers. What has usually happened is that they have become, in time, as oppressive and as cynical as their ousted predecessors. It is in this phase that they can become really dangerous, when, to use a European typology, the revolution enters the Napoleonic or, perhaps one should say, the Stalinist phase. In a program of aggression and expansion these movements would enjoy, like their Jacobin and Bolshevik predecessors, the advantage of fifth columns in every country and community with which they share a common universe of discourse.

Broadly speaking, Muslim fundamentalists are those who feel that the troubles of the Muslim world at the present time are the result not of insufficient modernization but of excessive modernization, which they see as a betrayal of authentic Islamic values. For them the remedy is a return to true Islam, including the abolition of all the laws and other social borrowings from the West and the restoration of the Islamic Holy Law, the shari'a, as the effective law of the land. From their point of view, the ultimate struggle is not against the Western intruder but against the Westernizing traitor at home. Their most dangerous enemies, as they see it, are the false and renegade Muslims who rule the countries of the Islamic world and who have imported and imposed infidel ways on Muslim peoples.

The point is clearly made in a tract by 'Abd al-Salam Faraj, an Egyptian who was executed along with others in April 1982 on the charge of having plotted and instigated the assassination of President Sadat. His remarks throw some light on the motivation of that act:

> The basis of the existence of imperialism in the lands of Islam is these self-same rulers. To begin with the struggle against imperialism is a work which is neither glorious nor useful, and it is only a waste of time. It is our duty to concentrate on our Islamic cause, and that is the establishment first of all of God's law in our own country and causing the word of God to prevail. There is no doubt that the first battlefield of the jihad is the extirpation of these infidel leaderships and their replacement by a perfect Islamic order, and from this will come the release of our energies.[2]

In the few moments that passed between the murder of President Sadat and the arrest of his murderers, their leader exclaimed triumphantly: "I have killed Pharaoh! I am not afraid to die." If, as was widely assumed in the Western world at the time, Sadat's offense in the eyes of the murderers was making peace with Israel, Pharaoh would seem a singularly inappropriate choice of epithet. Clearly, they were not referring to the Pharaoh of modern Egyptian schoolbooks, the embodiment of the greatness and glory of ancient Egypt. It is the Pharaoh of the Exodus, who, in the Qur'an as in the Bible, is the pagan tyrant who oppresses God's people. It is no doubt in this sense that Usama bin Ladin spoke of President Bush as the Pharaoh of our day. At the time of the Exodus, the Children of Israel were God's people. Present-day Muslims for the most part do not recognize the modern State of Israel as the legitimate heir of the ancient Children of Israel—in the Qur'an *Banu Isra'il*—and the assassins of Sadat certainly did not approve of his deal with that state. But as the subsequent interrogation of the murderers and their accomplices made clear, the peace with Israel was, in their eyes, a relatively minor phenomenon—a symptom rather than a cause of the greater offense of abandoning God's faith, oppressing God's people, and aping the ways of the infidel.

NOTES

1. Cited in Alexei Vassiliev, *The History of Saudi Arabia* (London, 1988), p. 265.
2. 'Abd al-Salam Faraj, *Al-Jihād: al-Farīda al-Ghā'iba* (Amman, 1982): English translation in Johannes J. G. Jansen, *The Neglected Duty: The Creed of Sadat's Assassins and Islamic Resurgence in the Middle East* (New York, 1986), pp. 159ff.

55

Globalization

Anthony Giddens

We are the first generation to live in this [global cosmopolitan] society, whose contours we can as yet only dimly see. It is shaking up our existing ways of life, no matter where we happen to be. This is not—at least at the moment—a global order driven by collective human will. Instead, it is emerging in an anarchic, haphazard, fashion, carried along by a mixture of influences.

Globalization is more than an economic revolution. It changes every aspect of people's lives. This is the central point of Gidden's selection.

A friend of mine studies village life in central Africa. A few years ago, she paid her first visit to a remote area where she was to carry out her fieldwork. The day she arrived, she was invited to a local home for an evening's entertainment. She expected to find out about the traditional pastimes of this isolated community. Instead, the occasion turned out to be a viewing of *Basic Instinct* on video. The film at that point hadn't even reached the cinemas in London.

Such vignettes reveal something about our world. And what they reveal isn't trivial. It isn't just a matter of people adding modern paraphernalia— videos, television sets, personal computers and so forth—to their existing ways of life. We live in a world of transformations, affecting almost every aspect of what we do. For better or worse, we are being propelled into a global order that no one

fully understands, but which is making its effects felt upon all of us.

Globalisation may not be a particularly attractive or elegant word. But absolutely no one who wants to understand our prospects at century's end can ignore it. I travel a lot to speak abroad. I haven't been to a single country recently where globalisation isn't being intensively discussed. In France, the word is *mondialisation*. In Spain and Latin America, it is *globalización*. The Germans say *Globalisierung*.

The global spread of the term is evidence of the very developments to which it refers. Every business guru talks about it. No political speech is complete without reference to it. Yet even in the late 1980s the term was hardly used, either in the academic literature or in everyday language. It has come from nowhere to be almost everywhere.

Given its sudden popularity, we shouldn't be surprised that the meaning of the notion isn't always clear, or that an intellectual reaction has set in against it. Globalisation has something to do with the thesis that we now all live in one world—but in what ways exactly, and is the idea really valid? Different thinkers have taken almost completely opposite views about globalisation in debates that have sprung up over the past few years. Some dispute the whole thing. I'll call them the sceptics.

According to the sceptics, all the talk about globalisation is only that—just talk. Whatever its benefits, its trials and tribulations, the global economy isn't especially different from that which existed at previous periods. The world carries on much the same as it has done for many years.

Most countries, the sceptics argue, gain only a small amount of their income from external trade. Moreover, a good deal of economic exchange is between regions, rather than being truly world-wide. The countries of the European Union, for example, mostly trade among themselves. The same is true of the other main trading blocs, such as those of Asia-Pacific or North America.

Others take a very different position. I'll label them the radicals. The radicals argue that not only is globalisation very real, but that its consequences can be felt everywhere. The global market-place, they say, is much more developed than even in the 1960s and 1970s and is indifferent to national borders. Nations have lost most of the sovereignty they once had, and politicians have lost most of their capability to influence events. It isn't surprising that no one respects political leaders any more, or has much interest in what they have to say. The era of the nation-state is over. Nations, as the Japanese business writer Kenichi Ohmae puts it, have become mere "fictions." Authors such as Ohmae see the economic difficulties of the 1998 Asian crisis as demonstrating the reality of globalisation, albeit seen from its disruptive side.

The sceptics tend to be on the political left, especially the old left. For if all of this is essentially a myth, governments can still control economic life and the welfare state remain intact. The notion of globalisation, according to the sceptics, is an ideology put about by free-marketeers who wish to dismantle welfare systems and cut back on state expenditures. What has happened is at most a reversion to how the world was a century ago. In the late nineteenth century there was already an open global economy, with a great deal of trade, including trade in currencies.

Well, who is right in this debate? I think it is the radicals. The level of world trade today is much higher than it ever was before, and involves a much wider range of goods and services. But the biggest difference is in the level of finance and capital flows. Geared as it is to electronic money—money that exists only as digits in computers—the current world economy has no parallels in earlier times.

In the new global electronic economy, fund managers, banks, corporations, as well as millions of individual investors, can transfer vast amounts of capital from one side of the world to another at the click of a mouse. As they do so, they can destabilise what might have seemed rock-solid economies—as happened in the events in Asia.

The volume of world financial transactions is usually measured in US dollars. A million dollars is a lot of money for most people. Measured as a stack of hundred-dollar notes, it would be eight inches high. A billion dollars—in other words, a thousand million—would stand higher than St. Paul's Cathedral. A trillion dollars—a million million—would be over 120 miles high, 20 times higher than Mount Everest.

Yet far more than a trillion dollars is now turned over *each day* on global currency markets. This is a massive increase from only the late 1980s, let alone the more distant past. The value of whatever money we may have in our pockets, or our bank accounts, shifts from moment to moment according to fluctuations in such markets.

I would have no hesitation, therefore, in saying that globalisation, as we are experiencing it, is in many respects not only new, but also revolutionary. Yet I don't believe that either the sceptics or the radicals have properly understood either what it is or its implications for us. Both groups see the phenomenon almost solely in economic terms. This is a mistake. Globalisation is political, technological and cultural, as well as economic. It has been influenced above all by developments in systems of communication, dating back only to the late 1960s.

In the mid-nineteenth century, a Massachusetts portrait painter, Samuel Morse, transmitted the first message, 'What hath God wrought?', by electric telegraph. In so doing, he initiated a new phase in world history. Never before could a message be sent without someone going somewhere to carry it. Yet the advent of satellite communications marks every bit as dramatic a break with the past. The first commercial satellite was launched only in 1969. Now there are more than 200 such satellites above the earth, each carrying a vast range of information. For the first time ever, instantaneous communication is possible from one side of the world to the other. Other types of electronic communication, more and more integrated with satellite transmission, have also accelerated over the past few years. No dedicated transatlantic or transpacific cables existed at all until the late 1950s. The first held fewer than 100 voice paths. Those of today carry more than a million.

On 1 February 1999, about 150 years after Morse invented his system of dots and dashes, Morse Code finally disappeared from the world stage. It was discontinued as a means of communication for the sea. In its place has come a system using satellite technology, whereby any ship in distress can be pinpointed immediately. Most countries prepared for the transition some while before. The French, for example, stopped using Morse Code in their local waters in 1997, signing off with a Gallic flourish: "Calling all. This is our last cry before our eternal silence."

Instantaneous electronic communication isn't just a way in which news or information is conveyed more quickly. Its existence alters the very texture of our lives, rich and poor alike. When the image of Nelson Mandela may be more familiar to us than the face of our next-door neighbour, something has changed in the nature of our everyday experience.

Nelson Mandela is a global celebrity, and celebrity itself is largely a product of new communications technology. The reach of media technologies is growing with each wave of innovation. It took 40 years for radio in the United States to gain an audience of 50 million. The same number was using personal computers only 15 years after the personal computer was introduced. It needed a mere 4 years, after it was made available, for 50 million Americans to be regularly using the Internet.

It is wrong to think of globalisation as just concerning the big systems, like the world financial order. Globalisation isn't only about what is "out there," remote and far away from the individual. It is an "in here" phenomenon too, influencing intimate and personal aspects of our lives. The debate about family values, for example, that is going on in many countries might seem far removed from globalising influences. It isn't. Traditional family systems are becoming transformed, or are under strain, in many parts of the world, particularly as women stake claim to greater equality. There has never before been a society, so far as we know from the historical record, in which women have been even approximately equal to men. This is a truly global revolution in everyday life, whose consequences are being felt around the world in spheres from work to politics.

Globalisation thus is a complex set of processes, not a single one. And these operate in a contradictory or oppositional fashion. Most people think of globalisation as simply "pulling away" power or influence from local communities and nations into the global arena. And indeed this is one of its consequences. Nations do lose some of the economic power they once had. Yet it also has an opposite effect. Globalisation not only pulls upwards, but also pushes downwards, creating new pressures for local autonomy. The American sociologist Daniel Bell describes this very well when he says that the nation becomes not only too small to solve the big problems, but also too large to solve the small ones.

Globalisation is the reason for the revival of local cultural identities in different parts of the world. If one asks, for example, why the Scots want more independence in the UK, or why there is a strong separatist movement in Quebec, the answer is not to be found only in their cultural history. Local nationalisms spring up as a response to globalising tendencies, as the hold of older nation-states weakens.

Globalisation also squeezes sideways. It creates new economic and cultural zones within and across nations. Examples are the Hong Kong region, northern Italy, and Silicon Valley in California. Or consider the Barcelona region. The area around Barcelona in northern Spain extends into France. Catalonia, where Barcelona is located, is closely integrated into the European Union. It is part of Spain, yet also looks outwards.

These changes are being propelled by a range of factors, some structural, others more specific and historical. Economic influences are certainly among the driving forces—especially the global financial system. Yet they aren't like forces of nature. They have been shaped by technology, and cultural diffusion, as well as by the decisions of governments to liberalise and deregulate their national economies.

The collapse of Soviet communism has added further weight to such developments, since no significant group of countries any longer stands outside. That collapse wasn't just something that just happened to occur. Globalisation explains both why and how Soviet communism met its end. The former Soviet Union and the East European countries were comparable to the West in terms of growth rates until somewhere around the early 1970s. After that point, they fell rapidly behind. Soviet communism, with its emphasis upon state-run enterprise and heavy industry, could not compete in the global electronic economy. The ideological and cultural control upon which communist political authority was based similarly could not survive in an era of global media.

The Soviet and the East European regimes were unable to prevent the reception of Western radio and television broadcasts. Television played a direct role in the 1989 revolutions, which have rightly been called the first "television revolutions." Street protests taking place in one country were watched by television audiences in others, large numbers of whom then took to the streets themselves.

Globalisation, of course, isn't developing in an even-handed way, and is by no means wholly benign in its consequences. To many living outside Europe and North America, it looks uncomfortably like Westernisation—or, perhaps, Americanisation, since the US is now the sole superpower, with a dominant economic, cultural and military position in the global order. Many of the most visible cultural expressions of globalisation are American—Coca-Cola, McDonald's, CNN.

Most of the giant multinational companies are based in the US too. Those that aren't all come from the rich countries, not the poorer areas of the world. A pessimistic view of globalisation would consider it largely an affair of the industrial North, in which the developing societies of the South play little or no active part. It would see it as destroying local cultures, widening world inequalities and worsening the lot of the impoverished. Globalisation, some argue, creates a world of winners and losers, a few on the fast track to prosperity, the majority condemned to a life of misery and despair.

Indeed, the statistics are daunting. The share of the poorest fifth of the world's population in global income has dropped, from 2.3 per cent to 1.4 per cent between 1989 and 1998. The proportion taken by the richest fifth, on the other hand, has risen. In sub-Saharan Africa, 20 countries have lower incomes per head in real terms than they had in the late 1970s. In many less developed countries, safety and environmental regulations are low or virtually non-existent. Some transnational companies sell goods there that are controlled or banned in the industrial countries—poor-quality medical drugs, destructive pesticides or high tar and nicotine content cigarettes. Rather than a global village, one might say, this is more like global pillage.

Along with ecological risk, to which it is related, expanding inequality is the most serious problem facing world society. It will not do, however, merely to blame it on the wealthy. It is fundamental to my argument that globalisation today is only partly Westernisation. Of course the Western nations, and more generally the industrial countries, still have far more influence over world affairs than do the poorer states. But globalisation is becoming increasingly decentred— not under the control of any group of nations, and still less of the large corporations. Its effects are felt as much in Western countries as elsewhere.

This is true of the global financial system, and of changes affecting the nature of government itself. What one could call "reverse colonisation" is becoming more and more common. Reverse colonisation means that non-Western countries influence developments in the West. Examples abound—such as the latinising of Los Angeles, the emergence of a globally oriented high-tech sector in India, or the selling of Brazilian television programmes to Portugal.

Is globalisation a force promoting the general good? The question can't be answered in a simple way, given the complexity of the phenomenon. People who ask it, and who blame globalisation for deepening world inequalities, usually have in mind economic globalisation and, within that, free trade. Now, it is surely obvious that free trade is not an unalloyed benefit. This is especially so as concerns the less developed countries. Opening up a country, or regions within it, to free trade can undermine a local subsistence economy. An area that becomes dependent upon a few products sold on world markets is very vulnerable to shifts in prices as well as to technological change.

Trade always needs a framework of institutions, as do other forms of economic development. Markets cannot be created by purely economic means, and how far a given economy should be exposed to the world market-place must depend upon a range of criteria. Yet to oppose economic globalisation, and to opt for economic protectionism, would be a misplaced tactic for rich and poor nations alike. Protectionism may be a necessary strategy at some times and in some countries. In my view, for example, Malaysia was correct to introduce controls in 1998, to stem the flood of capital from the country. But more permanent forms of protectionism will not help the development of the poor countries, and among the rich would lead to warring trade blocs.

The debates about globalisation I mentioned at the beginning have concentrated mainly upon its implications for the nation-state. Are nation-states, and hence national political leaders, still powerful, or are they becoming largely irrelevant to the forces shaping the world? Nation-states are indeed still powerful and political leaders have a large role to play in the world. Yet at the same time the nation-state is being reshaped before our eyes. National economic policy can't be as effective as it once was. More importantly, nations have to re-think their identities now the older forms of geopolitics are becoming obsolete. Although this is a contentious point, I would say that, following the dissolving of the Cold War, most nations no longer have enemies. Who are the enemies of Britain, or France, or Brazil? The war in Kosovo didn't pit nation against nation. It was a conflict between old-style territorial nationalism and a new, ethically driven interventionalism.

Nations today face risks and dangers rather than enemies, a massive shift in their very nature. It isn't only of the nation that such comments could be made. Everywhere we look, we see institutions that appear the same as they used to be from the outside, and carry the same names, but inside have become quite different. We continue to talk of the nation, the family, work, tradition, nature, as if they were all the same as in the past. They are not. The outer shell remains, but inside they have changed—and this is happening not only in the US, Britain, or France, but almost everywhere. They are what I call "shell institutions." They are institutions that have become inadequate to the tasks they are called upon to perform.

As the changes I have described in this chapter gather weight, they are creating something that has never existed before, a global cosmopolitan society. We are the first generation to live in this society, whose contours we can as yet only dimly see. It is shaking up our existing ways of life, no matter where we happen to be. This is not—at least at the moment—a global order driven by collective human will. Instead, it is emerging in an anarchic, haphazard, fashion, carried along by a mixture of influences.

It is not settled or secure, but fraught with anxieties, as well as scarred by deep divisions. Many of us feel in the grip of forces over which we have no power. Can we reimpose our will upon them? I believe we can. The powerlessness we experience is not a sign of personal failings, but reflects the incapacities of our institutions. We need to reconstruct those we have, or create new ones. For globalisation is not incidental to our lives today. It is a shift in our very life circumstances. It is the way we now live.